Children at Risk:
Poverty, Minority Status,
and Other Issues in
Educational Equity

Children at Risk:
Poverty, Minority Status, and Other Issues in Educational Equity

Edited by

Andrés Barona
Arizona State University

Eugene E. Garcia
University of California, Santa Cruz

National Association of School Psychologists
Washington, DC

First Printing, 1990

Published by the National Association of School Psychologists
808 17th Street, NW #200
Washington, DC 20006

ISBN 0-932955-16-9

Printed in the United States of America

0 9 8 7 6 5 4 3 2 1

Acknowledgments

We gratefully acknowledge the assistance and expertise of several individuals in helping with this book: Lawrence Moran (copyediting); Judy Fulwider (typesetting); and Martha H. Gutierrez (proofreading). Thanks also are extended to Alex Thomas, Cathy Telzrow, and Thomas Fagan for their patience, persistence, trust, and technical assistance in producing the book.

We extend our deepest gratitude to chapter authors, who dedicated their time and expertise to the project. Their contributions to this book are immeasurable. Also, we thank those individuals who reviewed chapters and provided practical suggestions for the review process. We also express our appreciation to Maryann Santos de Barona for her technical and editorial assistance throughout this project. Without the contributions of all these outstanding individuals, this project could not have been completed.

From NASP Publications Policy Handbook

The content of this document reflects the ideas and positions of the authors. The responsibility lies solely with the authors and does not necessarily reflect the position or ideas of the National Association of School Psychologists.

List of Contributors

Bob Algozzine
Professor
University of North Carolina, Charlotte
Department of Teaching Specialties
College of Education
Charlotte, NC 28223

Keith Baker
Director
Research on English Acquisition
   and Development
9521 Seminole Street
Silver Spring, MD 20901

Andrés Barona
Associate Professor and Coordinator,
   School Psychology Program
Arizona State University
Division of Psychology in Education
Tempe, AZ 85287-0611

Doris Benson
Assistant Professor and Coordinator,
   School Psychology Program
California State University, Northridge
Education in Psychology & Counseling
Northridge, CA 91330

Carlos Cardona-Morales
Research Scientist
Northwest Regional Educational
   Laboratory
101 S.W. Main Street
Portland, OR 97204

Olga Carranza
Doctoral Candidate
University of California, Santa Barbara
Counseling Psychology Program
Graduate School of Education
Santa Barbara, CA 93106

Ursula Casanova
Assistant Professor
Arizona State University
Division of Educational Leadership
   and Policy Studies
College of Education
Tempe, AZ 85287-2411

J. Manuel Casas
Associate Professor
University of California, Santa Barbara
Counseling Psychology Program
Santa Barbara, CA 93106

Linda C. Caterino
Certified Psychologist
Diplomate, American Board of
   Professional Psychology
Western Behavioral Professionals
2058 S. Dobson, Suite 7
Mesa, AZ 85202

Vivian I. Correa
Associate Professor
University of Florida, Gainesville
Department of Special Education
College of Education
Gainesville, FL 32611

Steven T. DeMers
Associate Professor
University of Kentucky
Educational & Counseling Psychology
School Psychology Clinic
641 Maxwelton Ct.
Lexington, KY 40506-0034

Rafael M. Diaz
Associate Professor
Stanford University
Area of Child & Adolescent Development
School of Education
Stanford, CA 94305

Patricia A. Edwards
Associate Professor
Michigan State University
Teacher Education Department
330 Erickson Hall
East Lansing, MI 48824-1034

Todd V. Fletcher
Assistant Professor
The University of Arizona
Division of Special Education and
   Rehabilitation
Tucson, AZ 85721

Arthur A. Flores
Doctoral Candidate
Texas A&M University
Program of School Psychology
College of Education
College Station, TX

Sandra H. Fradd
Associate Research Scientist
University of Florida, Gainesville
Institute for Advanced Studies in
  Communication Processes
Gainesville, FL 32611

Michael J. Furlong
School Psychologist
Santa Barbara School District
Lecturer
University of California, Santa Barbara
Graduate College of Education
Santa Barbara, CA 93106

Eugene E. Garcia
Professor & Chair
Board of Studies in Education
University of California, Santa Cruz
Santa Cruz, CA 95064

Martha H. Gutierrez
Research Associate
Arizona State University
Division of Psychology in Education
College of Education
Tempe, AZ 85287-0611

Janice Hale-Benson
Associate Professor
Cleveland State University
Visions Program
Rhodes Tower, 1329
Euclid at East 24th Street
Cleveland, OH 44115

Antoinette Halsell Miranda
Assistant Professor
The Ohio State University
Educational Services & Research
School Psychology Program
Columbus, OH 43210

Arthur E. Hernandez
Assistant Professor
University of Texas at San Antonio
Division of Social & Behavioral Sciences
College of Education
San Antonio, TX 78285

Kathryn J. Lindholm
Assostant Professor
San Jose State University
Child Development Program
School of Education
San Jose, CA 95192

Barry McLaughlin
Professor
University of California, Santa Cruz
Psychology Board
Clark Kerr Hall
Santa Cruz, CA 95064

Cheryll A. Pearson
School Psychologist
Scott County School District
P.O. Box 156
Midway, KY 40347

Robert C. Pianta
Assistant Professor
University of Virginia
Curry School of Education
Charlottesville, VA 22903

Arnulfo G. Ramirez
Professor
State University of New York at Albany
1400 Washington Avenue
Albany, NY 12222

Ronald E. Reeve
Associate Professor
University of Virginia
Curry Program in Clinical & School
  Psychology
Curry School of Education
Charlottesville, VA 22903

Maryann Santos de Barona
Assistant Professor
Arizona State University
School Psychology Program
Division of Psychology in Education
College of Education
Tempe, AZ 85287-0611

V. Scott Solberg
Doctoral Candidate
University of California, Santa Barbara
Counseling Psychology Program
Graduate College of Education
Santa Barbara, CA 93106

Daniel M. Ulibarri
Supervisor
Human Resources & Development
Pacific Gas & Electric Company
245 Market Street, Room 832
San Francisco, CA 94106

Jeanne Weismantel
Consultant
University of Florida, Gainesville
The Center for Community Redevelopment
Department of Urban & Regional Planning
College of Architecture
Gainesville, FL 32611

List of Reviewers

Bruce A. Bracken
Professor
Memphis State University
Department of Psychology
Memphis, TN 38152

James L. Carroll
Associate Dean
Wichita State University
College of Education
Wichita, KS 67208-1595

Jerry Harris
Professor
Arizona State University
School Psychology Program
Division of Psychology in Education
College of Education
Tempe, AZ 85287-0611

Gene V. Glass
Professor
Arizona State University
Division of Educational Leadership
  and Policy Studies
College of Education
Tempe, AZ 85287-0611

Thomas R. Kratochwill
Professor and Director, School
  Psychology Program
University of Wisconsin, Madison
Educational Psychology Department
1025 Johnson Street
Madison, WI 53706

Luis M. Laosa
Principal Research Scientist
Educational Testing Service
Princeton, NJ 08541-0001

Thomas Oakland
Professor
University of Texas at Austin
School Psychology Training Program
Austin, TX 78712

Beeman Phillips
Professor and Director,
  School Psychology Program
Department of Educational Psychology
University of Texas at Austin
Austin, TX 78712

Jonathan Sandoval
Professor
Division of Education
University of California, Davis
Davis, CA 95616

Mary Lee Smith
Professor
Arizona State University
Division of Educational Leadership
  and Policy Studies
College of Education
Tempe, AZ 85287-2411

Joseph E. Zins
Professor
University of Cincinnati
Department of School Psychology and
  Counseling
522 Teachers College
Cincinnati, OH 45221-0002

Preface

Education 2000 and Beyond: The Challenge of Education's "At Risk" Students

National attention continues to focus on American education. More than 50 recent national reports have discussed the many variables that influence our educational institutions and inevitably affect the direction that future "schooling" takes. Two presuppositions appear to underline this renewed attention to the education of our children:

- Societies past, present, and future rest on the fundamental educational capabilities of their members.

- Our society, with its dramatic demographic, employment, and value shifts, must rethink its present educational practices.

As educators and practitioners, we must recognize that more education occurs outside of the kindergarten to college "schooling" than within such a context. As an example, consider the large number of seminars, symposia, conferences, computer literacy classes, and organized educational experiences you have participated in since the termination of your formal education. Most would agree that such learning experiences significantly augment formal coursework and add to the skills or knowledge necessary for progress in a work setting. Today, only one third of all educational endeavors in the United States occur during the primary, secondary, and post-secondary college periods! Education provided outside these periods is specifically designed to fill the needs of the workplace and will continue to outstrip, in both time and resources, the efforts of the kindergarten to college educational system. Schools must determine their role vis-a-vis the work place and the specialized training individuals will receive in these settings. This role determination is particularly important when individuals are likely to undergo two to three career changes and undergo an average of seven to ten job shifts during their working lifetime.

Under such circumstances, schools are unlikely to be able to provide adequate job skill training. Currently, technological innovations are resulting in job markets that are too broad and volatile. Recognizing the need for specific work-related learning, schooling in the United States must take on new responsibilities, some similar to and some significantly different from those in the past. First, it is imperative that schools serve students by providing a curriculum and environment that will enable them to develop a strong foundation of basic generic academic skills. These skills, not surprisingly, are the same three Rs of Reading, 'Riting, and 'Rithmetic that have been taught since the beginning of formal schooling in the United States. Such skills provide the critical stepping stone upon which additional learning can occur. Second, in addition to emphasizing the development of these vital skills for all students, schools must emphasize the development of those dynamic processes which will enhance human relationships, problem solving, and civic responsibility.

At first glance, the challenges of providing these skills, one set being largely rote or mechanical in nature while the other emphasizes creativity and social values, appear disparate. Students in the 21st century, however, will face social, economic, and technological change at an even greater pace than that presently being experienced. To be prepared for the challenges created by these circumstances, students must be able to react to rapidly changing situations with reflection and analysis regardless of the context, be it employment, civic, or culturally related. Thus, it is critical that education for the year 2000 and beyond consist of a curriculum that is collaborative, highly socializing in nature, and process-oriented while at the same time ensuring the development of basic skills.

It is especially important to provide such skills to America's "at-risk" students who historically have not succeeded in this country's educational institutions. These "at-risk" students have been largely relegated to learning from basic skill work sheets; this is a method of teaching often criticized as a repetitive low-level process which does not permit the development of critical thinking skills. It is these students who, because of their increasing representation in tomorrow's population, will be required to shoulder the burden of supporting the large baby-boom generation which will soon reach retirement age and begin to draw social service benefits. The ability of the American system to adequately provide for its greying population will depend upon the productivity of a group that is both vulnerable to institutional and societal influences and itself likely to need such services if not provided adequate "schooling."

The situation can be more clearly described by considering the 1986 cohort of 3.5 million U.S. four-year-olds. As this cohort moves slowly through our society's institutions, family, school, and the work place, a number of trends become apparent:

- Twenty-four percent of these four-year-olds currently live below the poverty line. That adds up to nearly 11 million children under the age of 15 living in poverty (one in five children currently lives in poverty).

- One-third (33%) of these four-year-olds are nonwhite. By the turn of the century, 40% of all children in the U.S. under six years of age will be nonwhite, with half of them speaking a language other than English when they first enter school. Moreover, increasingly these children will live in racial isolation: 56% in 1966 versus 75% in 1986.

- Eighteen percent of today's four-year-olds were born out of wedlock. It is estimated that twenty-one percent of today's four-year-old girls will become pregnant during their teens.

- It is expected that children from this cohort will spend more time watching television than participating in classrooms; television will consume valuable time that ordinarily would be spent in important socialization activities.

- More than forty-five percent of the 1986 four-year-olds will be raised by a single parent before they reach the age of 18; half will experience one or more "family" break-ups.

- Fifty-five percent of these four-year-olds currently have mothers that work outside the home. By 1995, seventy percent of their mothers will work outside the home, most in a full-time capacity.

The future of the United States may depend on understanding how a diverse population, placed in contexts of vulnerability, can achieve social, educational, and employment competence and then taking the steps necessary to ensure that such competence is attained by *all* students. It is in the very best interest of our society that our children, and, in particular, that our children "at risk" obtain these necessary competencies.

Recognizing the situation, our American educational system must undergo a serious self-examination with the objective of planning for the unavoidable future. Self-examination alone, however, will not be enough. If new curriculum, responsibilities, and approaches are to become a reality, this change must be fueled by social energy that propels us forward with vigorous and consistent resolve. As in the eras of Sputnik, the New Frontier, and the War on Poverty, the importance of new educational challenges must be understood and acted upon. Such challenges must be universally adopted if today's children are to be supplied with the necessary competencies for survival in a changing society.

How can "we," the privileged, the well-educated, the well-employed, understand the needs of those made vulnerable if the institutions that have served us well are not likely to serve adequately those on whom we will soon be highly dependent? What can be done to realize our own "self-interest correctly served?" The answer is not one that is readily available. New knowledge, methodology, or curriculum implemented in isolation will not equip students for the future. It will be necessary that those served as well as those who serve take ownership of the educational process. Recent reports have labeled such ownership a university–school–community partnership. This notion calls for informed and collaborative analysis and decision-making with trust between disparate constituency groups. The concept calls for all players to be intricately involved in setting and achieving educational goals. All involved must take a proactive role in ensuring that vulnerability is minimized. As a nation, "we" must accept the responsibility, the risks, and the challenge together. As professional educators, we must personally accept the challenge and provide leadership. It is within this context of need and collaboration that this volume was written. It is imperative for "all" of us that we reduce the next generation's vulnerability and enhance their competencies.

NASP Position Statement On Minority Recruitment

As the purpose of the National Association of School Psychologists is to serve the mental health and educational interests of all youth, and

As the proportion of ethnic minority children is increasing in the total school population, and

As there are disproportionately few ethnic minority school psychologists to serve both regular and special education students, and

As NASP is committed to the recruitment of ethnic minority group members,

Therefore, it is resolved that the National Association of School Psychologists will work actively to increase the numbers of ethnic minority school psychologists working with children and as trainers in school psychology programs;

And will advocate the use of recruitment procedures that are known to be successful, such as flexible admission standards, financial support, and active outreach efforts;

And will encourage its membership to assist school psychology training programs in recruiting ethnic minority group members into the profession;

And will encourage school psychology training programs to conduct research and develop the most appropriate strategies to recruit, train, and graduate greater numbers of ethnic minority individuals from their programs.

NASP Position Statement on Advocacy for Appropriate Educational Services for All Children

PL 94-142 (The Education of All Handicapped Children Act) has achieved major goals in serving handicapped children, many of whom had been previously excluded from appropriate educational programs. Since its enactment in 1975, all handicapped children have been guaranteed a free and appropriate education, the right to due process, and individualization of program according to need. We strongly support the continuation of legislation which has mandated these guarantees.

We also recognize that serious problems have been encountered as school districts strive to meet these mandates and that quality education is still an elusive goal. Some of these problems reflect difficulties within special education; others appear to be special education issues but have their origins in the regular education system.

One major set of problems involves reverse sides of the issue of access to appropriate education: (1) On the one hand, access to special education must be assured for all significantly handicapped children who need and can benefit from it. (2) Conversely, children are being inappropriately diagnosed as handicapped and placed in special education because of: (a) a lack of regular education options designed to meet the needs of children with diverse learning styles, (b) a lack of understanding, at times, of diverse cultural and linguistic backgrounds, and (c) inadequate measurement technologies which focus on labels for placement rather than providing information for program development.

It is not a benign action to label as "handicapped" children who are low achievers but are not, in fact, handicapped, even when this is done in order to provide them with services unavailable in general education. School personnel often resort to labeling because it seems the only way to obtain needed services for children. This is an unfortunate result of categorical models which attach funding to classifications. Other problems originating in the classification system include:

- Labels that are often irrelevant to instructional needs.
- Categories, based on deficit labels, that are rather arbitrarily defined, particularly for mildly handicapped and low achieving students, but which come to be accepted as "real" and may prevent more meaningful understanding of the child's psychoeducational needs. The intent of this statement is not necessarily to endorse mixing children with different moderate to severe handicaps in a single special education classroom.
- Reduced expectations for children who are placed in special needs programs.
- Assessment processes aimed at determining eligibility which often deflects limited resources from the determination of functional educational needs and the development of effective psychoeducational programs.
- A decreased willingness on the part of regular education, at times bordering on abdication of responsibility to modify curricula and programs in order to better meet the diverse needs of all children.

As increasing numbers of children are classified as handicapped and removed from regular classrooms for special instruction, there has been a dramatic reduction in the range of abilities among children who remain within the general education system. Concurrently, as national standards for excellence are being raised, the number of children at risk for school failure is growing dramatically. Without provisions to prepare students for higher expectations through effective instructional programs, many of these children may also be identified as handicapped and placed in special education. This climate, in which children are tested and labeled as failures or as handicapped in increasing numbers, creates an urgent need for reexamination and change in the system which provides access to services.

In view of these problems, and based upon the commitment to see that all children receive effective and appropriate education irrespective of race, cultural background, linguistic background, socioeconomic status, or educational need, we believe:

- All children can learn. Schools have a responsibility to teach them, and school personnel and parents should work together to assure every child a free and appropriate education in a positive social environment.

- Instructional options, based on the individual psychoeducational needs of each child, must be maximized within the general education system. Necessary support services should be provided within general education, eliminating the need to classify children as handicapped in order to receive these services.

- Psychoeducational needs of children should be determined through a multi-dimensional, non-biased assessment process. This must evaluate the match between the learner and his or her educational environment, assessing the compatibility of curriculum and system as they interact with the child, rather than relying on the deficit based model which places the blame for failure within the child. Referral to the assessment and placement process must always relate directly to services designed to meet psychoeducational needs.

- In addition to maintaining current protection for handicapped children, protections and safeguards must be developed to assure the rights of children who are at risk for school failure and require services while remaining in general education without classification as handicapped.

We propose a new national initiative to meet the educational needs of all children:

We propose the development and piloting of alternatives to the current categorical system. This requires reevaluation of funding mechanisms, and advocacy for policy and funding waivers needed for the piloting of alternative service delivery models. It also requires the development of increased support systems and extensive retraining of all school personnel to enable them to work effectively with a broad range of children with special needs within the regular education system.

This initiative will encourage greater independence for children by enabling them to function within the broadest possible environment, and independence for school personnel by providing them with training and support so they can help a wide range of children.

The types and extent of change we are suggesting should be made cautiously. Targeted funds intended for children with moderate and severe handicapping conditions must be protected. Similarly, resources for children who are not handicapped, but who experience learning difficulties, must be protected even though these children are served within general education. We need to assure that no child is put at risk for loss of services while the change process is occurring.

Our task is to reduce the rigidities of the current system without taking away the protections offered by PL 94-142. All experimentation and research must take place within a framework of maximum protection for children. It is highly likely that this may require the development of temporary parallel systems — the traditional system of classification and placement under PL 94-142, and a system of experimental programs, primarily within general education — until satisfactory models can be developed which meet the requirements of accountability, due process, and protection of students' and parents' rights, and provide funding for students in need of services. In addition, while these recommended modifications might reduce the risk of misclassification due to cultural or linguistic differences, we caution that these issues must continue to be monitored and discussed during the transition period and beyond.

Because of the complexity of these issues, the generation of effective solutions will require a national effort of interested persons and organizations which we hope to generate through this task force. We will actively work toward the collaboration of a wide variety of individuals and organi-zations, joining together to develop a strong base of knowledge, research, and experi-ence in order to establish new frameworks and conceptualizations on which to base decisions, design feasible service delivery options, advocate for policy and funding changes needed to implement these alter-natives, and coordinate efforts and share information for positive change. We invite you to join with us.

Table of Contents

Part I:
Issues in Educational Equity

Part IV:
Assessment

Part I:
Issues in Educational Equity

Bilingual Education's 20-Year Failure to Provide Civil Rights Protection for Language-Minority Students

Keith Baker
Research on English Acquisition and Development
——————————————— Silver Spring, Maryland

There seem to be few studies providing information on how schools, in actual practice, go about identifying students for participantion in bilingual programs.[1] Mace-Matluck (1982) described current selection procedures as characterized by (a) home language surveys, (b) oral language proficiency tests, and (3) some use of tests of English reading and writing, usually from grade 2 and up. Cardoza (1984) found that 90% of the districts surveyed used an English oral proficiency test, 72% measured English reading, 56% measured English writing skills, and 6% assessed student native language skills.

The best available data seem to be those of Young et al. (1984), which were derived from a nationally representative sample of 229 school districts serving LM-LEP (language-minority/limited-English-proficiency) students. Table 1 is taken from Young et al. (1984) and describes the procedures used for selecting students for entry into the program.

There are several notable findings illustrated in Table 1. First, teacher and staff judgment appear to play a major role in school selection procedures. About two-thirds of all LM-LEP students were screened by procedures that include staff judgment. Moreover, both Mace-Matluck (1982) and Cardoza (1984) found widespread use of teachers' recommendations in the procedures for exiting from the bilingual program.

This is a significant variance from what is often legally prescribed. There is an intent in the laws, regulations, and many court decisions to eliminate teachers' judgment.

It is also noteworthy that fewer than 2% of all school districts, serving less than 5% of all LEP students, make use of measures of native language proficiency (this would have been absolutely necessary for the assessment of relative language proficiency called for in the proposed Lau regulations.

The *Lau* regulations refers to the 1974 Supreme Court decision on language minority students. The Supreme Court held that language minority students were denied their civil rights if instruction was provided in a language they did not understand. Although the Court mandated that special and appropriate instruction be provided, it did not specify any particular program for students who did not speak English. In 1980 the Department of Education proposed federal regulations for implementing the Lau decision, however, the proposed regulations were never put into effect.

To date, the selection procedures used by most school districts seem to include three steps: First, a home language survey is conducted to identify the potential pool of LEP students; second, the students identified in the home language survey are tested on some measure of academic performance, and classified accordingly; third, the decision is then tempered by staff judgment. Except for the role of staff judgment, these procedures pretty well correspond to what the federal government and the courts have required.

TABLE 1
Classification Procedures in State Laws

State	Home Language Survey	Standardized Test	Language Proficiency Test	Teacher Judgment	Other
Alaska	X				X
Arizona	X	X	X	X	
California	X	X	X	X	X
Colorado	X	X	X		
Connecticut	X	X	X		
Illinois	X	X	X		
Massachusetts	X		X		
Michigan	X	X	X		
New Jersey	X	X	X	X	
New Mexico		X	X	X	
New York			X		
Ohio	X	X	X	X	X
Rhode Island	X	X	X	X	X
Texas	X	X	X	X	X

Conceptually, we can think of the student who needs bilingual education in the abstract — that is, of a student whose dependence on a language other than English places her or him at a disadvantage when taught in the typical classroom setting for monolingual English-speaking children. Having an abstract notion of who the target child is, bilingual programs must somehow turn the abstract into the concrete. In consequence, a variety of methods have been developed to select for bilingual programs. The focus of the discussion that follows is on whether the concrete methods the schools use have succeeded in capturing this abstract idea. Consequently, it is necessary that we have some shorthand expressions to signify when we are referring to the abstract and when to the concrete. In keeping with general practice, those students who have actually been identified for placement in a bilingual program will be called LEP. The abstract concept behind LEP will be called CDONEL (children dependent on a non-English language). Obviously, if the procedures used to identify LEPs work, then LEP and CDONEL become identical. However, if the methods used to identify LEPs are flawed, then some LEPs will not be CDONEL. In this case, some children will not be properly educated; either English-speaking children will be taught in some other language or some children who should be taught in a language other than English will be taught in English.

The issue can easily be described by set theory. If bilingual education programs are perfectly successful in selecting all students who can benefit from bilingual education, then LEP is a set that includes all the elements of CDONEL and no other elements. If the procedures used to select students for bilingual instruction are flawed, then LEP is a set that includes only some of the elements of CDONEL or includes elements from both the sets CDONEL and $\overline{\text{CDONEL}}$ (all students who are not CDONEL).

It is important to note that not all bilingual educators view this issue as a problem. Many bilingual educators believe that it would be good if everyone were bilingual. In their view, there is no such thing as an erroneous placement of a student in a bilingual program; the only possible error is failure to put everybody (CDONEL + $\overline{\text{CDONEL}}$) in the program. The present argument takes a different stand — the position outlined by the courts and in the law that views bilingual education as a compensatory education program for a specific subset of students. *Where "bilingual education" is used in this chapter it refers only to this compensatory type of program.*

THE VALIDITY OF SELECTION PROCEDURES

This section will review research on the validity of the procedures used to identify which students need bilingual education.

Home Language Survey

Home language surveys frequently ask if *someone,* not just the target child, in the home speaks a language other than English. Since there are large intergenerational differences in language use in immigrant groups, knowing that a child's parents or grandparents speak Spanish, for example, provides no information as to what language the child speaks. A monolingual English-speaking child could answer Yes to the question whether someone in the home speaks a language other than English. If an English-proficient or monolingual English-speaking child is identified as potentially in need of instruction in a language he does not speak so that he can improve his English, the remaining procedures commonly used will not necessarily correct the mistake. Similarly, under Title VII of the 1968 Elementary and Secondary Education Act the specific criteria outlined on which to base a student's eligibility for enrollment in a bilingual program may also be misleading. Specifically, Title VII specifies that a student is considered to have a primary language other than English if any of three conditions hold: (a) the first language the student spoke was not English; (b) the language most often spoken in the student's home was other than English; or (c) the language most often spoken by the student was other than English. With all of these criteria, but especially for the first two, a child who was fully proficient in English could be classified as having a primary language other than English.

Standardized Achievement Tests

Reliance on standardized achievement tests and on the assumption that they are a superior means of identifying students in need of bilingual education is evident in several court decisions such as *Aspira v. N.Y.* (1975), *U.S. v. Texas* (1981), and *Keyes v. School District No. 1* (1984)[2]. For example, in the *Keyes* agreement with the Denver school district, after a home language survey identifies whether *anyone* in the home speaks a language other than English, the student takes an oral English language proficiency test. Students falling below the cut-off score on the English proficiency test are placed in the bilingual program. If the student passes, he or she takes the CTBS (California Test of Basic Skills) and is placed in the transitional bilingual program if the score is below the 30th percentile in elementary school or below the 40th percentile in secondary school. Therefore 30% (in elementary) and 40% (in secondary) of a normally distributed monolingual English-speaking population identified by a home language survey to be tested would be misclassified as in need of bilingual education by the standardized test. To the extent that these students come from socioeconomically disadvantaged backgrounds, an even higher proportion will be misclassified because disadvantaged students score lower on standardized tests than does the general population.

The author participated in extensive discussions with the Office for Civil Rights (OCR) staff during the development of the proposed *Lau* regulations. When asked for the justification for the percentile cutoffs used, OCR staff responded that they had picked a score that people seemed to agree would identify a student who was not doing well in school. While that may very well be true, such a score does not tell us whether this student needs special language instruction, because a single score alone cannot differentiate among the several possible causes of a low score.

A second problem with standardized tests is that inappropriate norms are used for judging the performance of bilingual students. Standardized tests are *not* designed to measure whether a student has a sufficient command of English to succeed in school or in society. Standardized tests are designed to differentiate a monolingual population into 100 different, ordered categories. Because the essential language skills that all must possess to get along in society do not serve to differentiate the population, they are not included in the test.

A third problem with using standardized tests to identify students needing bilingual education is that, in test theory terms, the entry-decision test score is extremely unreliable, since it has an enormous error-score component and almost no true-score component. Test scores are based almost entirely on guessing. They do not tell us much about what students know, what their true percentile score is, nor how best to teach them.

A fourth problem with using standardized tests is that a single test in one language (English) is not enough information to determine if a student will be successful in a regular English-speaking classroom. Consider, for example, a 10-year-old girl, a Vietnamese refugee, who enrolls in a school where the 30th percentile is the cutoff score for bilingual education, and who is tested and found to score at the 45th percentile. No special help for her. Somehow, her family managed to bring along her school records from Vietnam and they show that, when tested in French, she has performed at the 85th percentile. This is a student who might be able to benefit from a special language program because she has a lot of English to learn before she can realize her potential in the regular English-speaking classroom.

Now imagine another refugee in a similar situation who tests at the 20th percentile in English. He is put into the bilingual program. His L1 test records, however, show he has previously performed at the 20th percentile in L1. This student seems to have learned English to the full level of his potential and does not belong in a special language program.

The wrong decision is made in both of these hypothetical situations by the simple-minded use of standardized test scores. Rather than correcting the misclassification errors made in the home language

survey, the standardized tests can add misclassification errors of their own.

Before completely dismissing standardized tests, however, we should note that some of the evaluation models described by Baker and Pelavin (1984) and by Ramirez, Wollson, Tallmadge, and Merino (1984), which incorporate standardized tests, may be useful in identifying students who can benefit from special language instruction. It is the way in which standardized tests are currently used to select students that renders them worthless.

Language Proficiency Tests.

Some selection methods use language proficiency tests, or use them in conjunction with standardized tests. Rather than solving the problem, these procedures merely exchange one improperly used test for another. Following the passage of state bilingual legislation requiring language competency tests, both California and Texas, which combined have about 53% of the language-minority population in the United States, set up blue ribbon commissions to identify and recommend satisfactory language competency tests for use throughout the two states. Both commissions concluded there were *no* psychometrically acceptable language competency tests in existence (Texas Education Agency, 1977, 1979; Ramirez, Merino, Bye, & Gold, 1981). Most recently the State of Massachusetts conducted a search for written and oral tests to assess the accomplishments of the students enrolled in bilingual programs in the state. The review team concluded that "no single efficient test is commercially available to meet the need" and recommended that the State Board of Education undertake the development of such a test (State Advisory Council on Bilingual Education, 1987). Other analyses of the language proficiency tests have confirmed their lack of reliability and validity (Northwest Regional Educational Laboratory, 1976; Dissemination and Assessment Center for Bilingual Education, 1976; Bye, 1977; Law, 1978; Northwest Regional Educational Laboratory, 1978; Pletcher, Locks, Reynolds, & Sisson, 1978; Curtis, Lignon, & Weibly, 1979; Horst, Douglas, et al.,

1980a, 1980b; Horst, Johnson, et al., 1980). Nevertheless, both Texas and California produced lists of "approved" tests for their schools to use. Thus, decisions about enrolling the majority of the language-minority students in this country in bilingual education are made with tests that are known to be unreliable or invalid.

Among the most important problems with oral language proficiency tests is their lack of predictive validity for academic achievement (Cummins, 1981, 1983; Canale, 1983; Oller, 1979; Ulibarri, Spencer, & Rivas, 1981). This means the tests cannot differentiate students who will do well in school from those who will do poorly. But this is precisely what any selection method intended to identify students needing special help should be able to do. If a test cannot identify those students who will have trouble in school because they lack English language proficiency, assigning students to programs to improve their proficiency on the basis of the results of such tests is unsound educational practice.

The language proficiency tests share a problem with standardized achievement tests — arbitrary cutoff scores. Language proficiency forms a continuum ranging from no proficiency to fully proficient. How far along this continuum does a student need special language help? There is no agreement in the literature. Indeed, given the current state of knowledge, it appears that there may be no scientific answer to the question.

The *Lau* regulations proposed in 1980 attempted to overcome some of the problems found in other methods of identifying students needing bilingual education by requiring the assessment of relative language proficiency. This was intended to correct the problems inherent in the first two steps of the typical identification process — the home language survey and the test of poor school performance — by adding a third step to determine whether the student was himself primarily an English-speaker or a speaker of a non-English language. The National Institute of Education (1981) analyzed relative language assessment for the U.S. Department of Education, and found no agreement as to what language proficiency is. They cited Spolsky (1978, p. 115):

> While it may be true that the layman's idea of learning a language is learning words, his criterion for knowing a language is usually expressed quite differently. When he judges his own or anyone else's control of a language, he is more likely to make a functional statement: "I know enough French to read a newspaper," "He can't speak enough English to ask the time of day." Such statements refer to language use and not to grammar or phonology (or vocabulary). The questions then arise, how does one go about deciding when someone knows "enough" to carry out a specified function? (NIE, 1981, p. 38)

They also found general agreement that language proficiency tests are unreliable and invalid:

> In addition to such problems as low reliability and questionable validity and variation in theoretical underpinnings, differences in quality and quantity of items selected, and the plain fact of the incredible complexity of language, associated with existing language proficiency assessment instruments, there are serious practical problems associated with assessing language proficiency on the basis of these instruments. Recent empirical studies indicate that the placement of children varies (often significantly) depending on which test is used. Not only is there a significant disagreement among tests (a kind of concurrent validity problem), but evidence has also emerged regarding the lack of comparability (1) between teacher judgments and placement based on tests alone; (2) between test score placements and analyses of language proficiency from taped conversations of natural speech in (a) the classroom, (b) the playground, and (c) the home; and (3) between language proficiency test score placement and achievement test scores (also teacher ratings of achievement). (NIE, 1981, pp. 38–39)

Illustrative of the problems with relative language proficiency tests is a study of relative language proficiency among Hispanic students by Duncan and De Avilla (1979). Their data show that a majority (31) of the 60 students classified as not proficient in Spanish in their sample were also classified as not proficient in English. Of 39 students found not to be proficient in English, fewer than half (15) were found to be proficient Spanish speakers. It is hard to see how sound educational judgments can be made with tests that produce such results.

Causes of Poor Performance in School

The heart of the problem is to determine whether the methods used to identify students for bilingual programs can distinguish students who do poorly in school because of the language barrier (CDONEL) from those who do poorly in school for other reasons. Rosenthal, Baker, and Ginsburg (1983) showed how unsuccessful these identification methods are in sorting out the various causes of poor school performance.

Using standardized test scores and home language data from parent interviews in a nationally representative sample of 15,000 students in Grades 1–6, the authors were able to construct procedures analogous to those in the proposed *Lau* regulations and then use them to identify students in need of bilingual education. Once these students were identified, their performance was analyzed to see to what extent their low achievement was a result of their non-English language background or the result of other home background factors. Although the analysis found there was a home language background effect on achievement, other family characteristics such as parental education, occupation, and income were much more important causes of poor performance in school. In short, the procedures of the proposed *Lau* regulations, which are the most detailed of any of the legal prescriptions, failed to distinguish students who have problems in school because of the language barrier from students who have problems in school for other reasons. In other words, the legally prescribed selection procedures cannot tell the difference between students who need special language services and those who need traditional monolingual English compensatory education.

Mayeske, Okada, Cohen, Beaton, and Wisler (1973) found that among Hispanic students, the use of Spanish at home had no relationship to achievement at school once socioeconomic status was controlled. In other words, Hispanic students have problems in school because they come from impoverished backgrounds. Speaking Spanish has very little or nothing to do with their poor school performance.[3] Although several other studies have found both language background and other home background factors are related to the educational attainment of Hispanics (So & Chan, 1982; Veltman, 1981; De Avila, 1980; Baratz-Snowden & Duran, 1987), the literature in general suggests that nonlanguage factors are more powerful determinants of poor school performance in language-minority students than are language factors.

All of these studies, which used very elaborate procedures to try to identify LEP students, suggest how difficult it is to isolate the educational effects of a non-English home language background. As Roos (1978), a bilingual education advocate, has noted, "The art of language assessment is not sufficiently sophisticated to identify those children who are bilingual and to trace their underachievement to their linguistic background. Indeed, given the multiple variables that affect academic success, it seems unlikely that there will ever be a single test which relates the degree of underachievement to the student's linguistic background."

Turning again to set theory terms, starting with the set of all students, we can identify two subsets, language-minority students (LM) and low achievers. CDONEL is a proper subset of language-minority children, that is, all CDONEL are also language-minority but there are also some language-minority children who are not CDONEL. Both CDONEL and LM share elements with the subset of low-achieving students but there are also some CDONEL and LM who are not low-achievers and vise versa. As noted above, ideally all LEP are CDONEL, but in actuality some LEP are not CDONEL. Likewise, all LEP are low-achieving but some non-LEP CDONEL are not low-

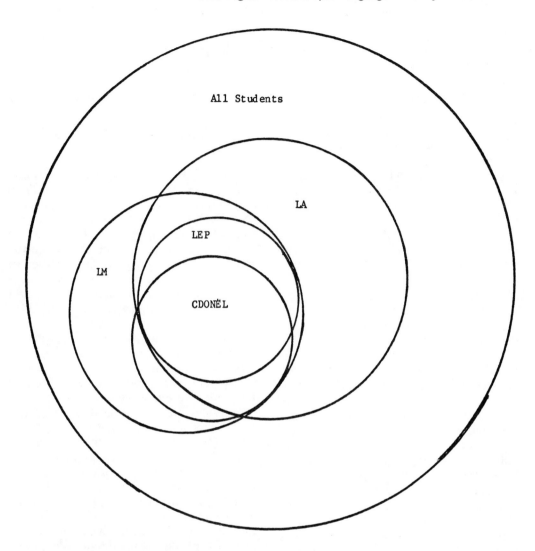

LA = Low Achieving Students
LM = Language Minority Students
LEP = Limited English Proficient Students
CDONEL = Children Dependent on a Non-English Language

FIGURE 1. Venn diagram of the problem of selecting students for special language services.

achieving. Figure 1 is a Venn diagram that describes the problem.

In theory, LEP should be the shaded portion of the Venn diagram. LEP and CDONEL were defined earlier as isotonic, identifying students who do poorly in school because of the language barrier. Therefore the inclusion of a low achievement restriction in the operationalization of LEP is a policy decision. The law and court decisions make the equivalency of LEP & CDONEL impossible, even if there were no other problems with identifying LEP students. In reality, LEP omits some of the shaded portion and includes some elements who are not CDONEL, not LM, not low-achieving, nor any possible combination thereof.

INCIDENCE OF
MISCLASSIFICATION

It is obviously unsound educational practice to teach reading in Spanish to English-speaking students on the grounds that it will help them learn English. Yet the logical flaws in the selection methods make it possible for just such a thing to happen. The next question is: How often does it happen? Here we run into another area that has been little researched. For the most part, we will have to answer the question with indirect evidence.

The American Institutes for Research national evaluation of Title VII programs, which found that Title VII students were performing worse in English and about the same in math as were non-Title VII students, also found that less than a third of the students in Title VII classrooms were there because of their need for English instruction (limited proficiency in English) as judged by their classroom teacher. Only 16% were Spanish monolingual. When asked what happens to Spanish-dominant children after they are able to function in English, 86% of the project directors reported that the children remained in the bilingual project (Danoff, Coles, McLaughlin, & Reynolds, 1978, pp. 10–14).

The Office of the Inspector General of the U.S. Department of Education (IG) (Inspector General, 1982) found widespread misclassification of students as LEP in Title VII projects in Texas when the identification procedures contained in the Bilingual Education Act were used. They found the following:

> Most districts, however, automatically categorized students as LEP even if the home language surveys showed that the child spoke only English and their parents only occasionally spoke Spanish. . . . For example, 812 (53 percent) of the 1,524 LEP-classified students participating in Edgewood's three Title VII projects were categorized as LEP because they had been designated as underachievers by the district (scoring below the 40th percentile on the Comprehensive Tests of Basic Skills total battery score). . . .
> English was the dominant language of most Title VII project participants,

including at least 1,378 or 33 percent of the participating LEP students.

> Most LEP-classified preschool students participating in Austin's demonstration spoke only English, based on the results of oral language proficiency tests. . . . They were classified as LEP mostly because home language surveys showed that Spanish was sometimes used at home. (p. 120)

Title VII requires by law a minimum of 60% LEP enrollment. In the six projects audited, the IG found LEP enrollments of 9%, 40%, 49%, 50%, 58%, and 58%. Thus, the Inspector General's audits document the occurrence of just what the selection procedures make possible: the inclusion of large numbers of English-speaking language-minority students in programs taught in a non-English language and intended for non-English-speaking students.

An evaluation by the State Department of Education in Massachusetts of the bilingual education program in Boston identified two problems: First, many Hispanic students were being kept in transitional bilingual education programs for 6 years or more without ever obtaining an English language score high enough to allow them to exit; and second, Greek and Italian students were in transitional bilingual education programs despite the fact that they were classified as fluent in English. The evaluation found that one-third of the middle school bilingual education students and 45% of the Hispanic middle school bilingual education students had been in the program since kindergarten or first grade; and from 26% to 84% of the students in high school bilingual education programs had been there for 6 years or more. Only 2% of the elementary bilingual education students had scored high enough in English to begin the process of mainstreaming into regular English-speaking classroom (Commonwealth of Massachusetts, Board of Education, 1985).

A problem similar to identifying which students need bilingual education is the problem of estimating how many students in the nation need bilingual education. To do this, the National Institute of Education developed the Language Measurement and Assessment Instrument (LM & AI). This test was administered to a stratified sample of students. Statistical estimating procedures were used to determine that there were 3.6 million LEP students in the nation. Barnes (1983) reanalyzed these data and found that two-thirds, or 2.4 million, of these students spoke English as their dominant language.

Similarly, Berdan, So, & Sanchez (1982) administered the LM & AI to Cherokee students at the request of the Cherokee Nation, which wanted to know the extent of need for Cherokee bilingual education. Through home interviews, Berdan and Sanchez found that 82% of the Cherokee students were English monolinguals. The LM & AI classified 48% of these monolingual English-speaking children as LEPs, presumably in need of instruction in Cherokee so they could improve their English.

The U.S. Department of Education had the LM & AI administered to a nationally representative sample of monolingual English-speaking school-age children. The test classified 42% of them as LEP.

Dulay and Burt (1980) found that only one-third of the Hispanic students identified as LEP in a sample of California school districts were more fluent in Spanish than they were in English. In one school district, almost 40% of the Hispanic LEP children spoke no Spanish at all.

TEACHER JUDGMENT

The procedures we have been discussing were intended as an improvement on teacher judgment. Therefore, it is worth exploring how they compare. Ulibarri et al. (1981) analyzed teacher rating and language proficiency test data from five school districts in a sample of 900 first-, third-, and fifth-grade students. The children were administered standardized achievement tests and oral language proficiency tests: The Language Assessment Scales (LAS); The Bilingual Syntax Measure (BSM); and The Basic Inventory of Natural Language (BINL). Three teacher ratings were gathered: (a) English language proficiency as non-English speaking (NS), limited English speaking (LES), fluent English speaking (FES); (b) competency in reading and math as below, above, or at

grade level; and (c) chance for achievement if instructed in English.

Across grades, teacher variables provided the best predictors of reading and math achievement, explaining 41% of the variance. The BINL showed poor correlations and in general added nothing to the prediction of actual achievement scores. The BSM added only about 1% to the achievement prediction, and the LAS about 4%. Moreover, the authors noted that their findings were consistent with other studies by De Avilla and Ulibarri, which also found teacher variables to be the best predictors of academic achievement in several different Spanish-language groups.

A 7-year longitudinal study by the Southwest Educational Development Laboratory (SEDL) of the reading progress of 800 children in Grades K–4 used a different methodology but came to similar conclusions. Language assessment data were collected with three types of measures: (a) the LAS oral language proficiency instrument, (b) teacher ratings of students' language proficiency; and (c) an "ethnographic verification" of the children's language abilities from half-hour monthly audiotaped samples of free speech from three settings — the classroom, playground, and family (Mace-Matluck, 1980). Teacher ratings of proficiency were highly related to the linguistic analyses of taped free speech of the same children. Most importantly, the LAS rated the children's proficiency in both Spanish and English as significantly lower than did either the teacher ratings or linguistic analysis, categorizing children in the nonspeaker to limited speaker range in both languages when native teacher judgment indicated native or near-native proficiency (Jackson, 1980).

These studies indicate that teacher judgments are better predictors of both language proficiency and academic achievement than are the language proficiency tests. What is the point of prescribing elaborate surveys and testing programs to replace teacher judgment when the empirical literature indicates that teacher judgment is more accurate?

Returning to the discussion in set theory terms, we must conclude that it cannot be assumed that LEP and CDONEL are equivalent sets. It appears certain that LEP includes some students who are not CDONEL, and CDONEL includes students not classified as LEP. Although the extent of the failure of LEP to match CDONEL is not precisely known, the preceding discussion demonstrates it is a major problem.

The failure of LEP procedures to identify CDONEL suggests the next issue to be explored. Bilingual programs are designed to meet the special educational needs of CDONEL students, but it is LEPs who are placed in the programs. Where LEPs are not CDONEL, students will be miseducated. Likewise, where CDONEL are not also LEPs, students will be miseducated. Given that the degree of mismatch between CDONEL and LEP seems to be large enough to worry about, we would expect to find that bilingual education has a poor record of effectiveness. If, for example, we designed a program for Spanish-speaking CDONEL and then populated the program with low-achieving monolingual English-speakers, the consequences of teaching them math in Spanish are not likely to be promising.

PROGRAM EFFECTIVENESS

If CDONEL are to be assured their *Lau*-guaranteed right to an equal education, then the special services provided to them must be effective. As we shall see, this fundamental proposition is not as simple or obvious as it first seems. Special services for CDONEL must accomplish two purposes. First, English must be mastered. Second, their progress in nonlanguage subjects, such as arithmetic, science, social studies, and so forth must be comparable to that of otherwise similar English-speaking children. With respect to mastering English, three broad strategies have emerged: transitional bilingual education (TBE), immersion, and English as a second language (ESL). Two strategies have evolved for teaching nonlanguage subjects: bilingual education and immersion.

It is hypothesized that TBE works something like this: The non-English language is used to teach nonlanguage courses while English is being learned. By teaching the students in the language they already know and understand (L1), appropriate progress in nonlanguage subjects will be made. As English is learned, instruction in L1 is gradually phased out. English is taught through either immersion or ESL methods. In addition, literacy in L1 is taught as part of the development of English. It is argued that (a) it is easier to learn to read in the language already known (L1), and (b) a number of literacy skills transfer from L1 to the process of learning L2, thereby speeding up the process of learning L2. Thus, advocates of TBE claim that mastery of English will occur sooner if the CDONEL is first taught how to read and write in another language (L1) than if instructed only in English from the start of school (this hypothesized phenomenon is often called the facilitation effect).

Immersion by hypothesis works something like this: All instruction is in English, but the English used is pitched at the level of understanding of the learner. Thus, an all-English immersion second-grade teacher would speak very differently to her CDONEL class than would a second-grade teacher of native English-speaking students. Language and subject area instruction are not separated; English is taught through the teaching of the other subjects. Thus, where TBE seeks to make lessons understandable by using the language already spoken (L1), immersion seeks to make lessons understandable by teaching them at the level of understanding of the language learner.

ESL is in flux. ESL instruction used to emphasize formal teaching of grammatical rules and memorization of vocabulary lists. In recent years, ESL philosophy has been redefined to emphasize learning language in a context of natural communication. For all intents and purposes, this makes immersion and ESL the same thing.

Philosophically, then, TBE incorporates either ESL or immersion for part of the school day, and immersion and ESL seem to be the same thing. But there is one other dimension that differentiates the philosophies when they are implemented as instructional programs. Since the school day is of fixed length, a smaller proportion of the school day will be devoted to the use of English under TBE than under immersion or ESL. Moreover, when the older idea of ESL — formal instruction in the rules and learning vocabulary lists — is considered, only part of the school day is taught in ESL.

Questions about the effectiveness of alternative programs then reduce to a comparison of the TBE and immersion strategies. There are three critical dimensions that must be considered:

- The proportion of the school day taught in English;

- Teaching L1 literacy *before* teaching English; and

- Teaching nonlanguage subjects in L1, at least in part.

Obviously, the question is not simply one of whether immersion or TBE is more effective, but rather what mix of these three factors is most effective (zero on either of the last two factors can be part of the mix of factors). Program evaluations rarely specify what combination of factors was studied, which makes interpreting their results problematic. Not knowing how programs are organized along the critical variables makes it difficult or impossible to interpret the results of studies.

Another problem in assessing the impact of programs for CDONEL is the determination of the time interval over which the study should extend. Many bilingual experts argue that 5–7 years are required before the superior benefits of TBE will emerge. A similar argument can be made for immersion as well. Malherbe (1946) collected data from all the white students in elementary school in South Africa. Some students came to a given school speaking Afrikaans and some English, either of which might have been the language of the school. Thus, some students were taught in L1 whereas others were taught in L2. Students taught in L2 showed, in comparison to students taught in L1, a deficit in performance in nonlanguage subjects (math and geography) during the early years of elementary school, but by the end of elementary school the deficit had vanished. Similarly, Lambert and Tucker (1972) found a deficit in verbal IQ measures during the early years of a French immersion program for English-speaking Canadian children, but this deficit also disappeared over time.

Research on the Effectiveness of TBE

I am not going to attempt a comprehensive review of the evaluation literature, as I and others have done that elsewhere (Baker & de Kanter, 1981, 1983a; Rossell & Ross, 1986; Rotberg, 1982). Rather, I intend to show in this section that virtually every claim made for TBE is subject to disproof by counterexample. The purpose of this exercise is not to argue that TBE is necessarily an ineffective program, but rather to argue that there is something wrong with the theoretical model that has been constructed to both explain and guide the design of programs for CDONEL. We begin this exercise by examining three studies in some detail.

Willig (1985) conducted a meta-analysis of a small subset of the evaluation literature. Meta-analysis is a statistical process that attempts to combine the results of different studies by converting study results to a common metric. For each study, the observed differences between the treatment and control groups are computed as a standard deviation difference and the standard deviation differences are then summed over studies. Meta-analysis is not easy to produce (Light & Pillemer, 1984; Hedges & Olin, 1985; Hedges, 1986), and serious questions as to the validity of Willig's meta-analysis have been raised (Baker, 1987). Nevertheless, when kept in proper perspective, Willig's findings are instructive.

Willig combined nine different types of outcome measures including tests in reading, math, attitudes, and motivation. Such a combination of tests can be made procedurally with meta-analysis as long as the study results can be expressed in standard deviations, but such combinations of apples and oranges produce a generally meaningless result. Overall, Willig found a positive effect for TBE. However, this finding, given the mixture of outcomes that went into it, tells us only that something happened; it sheds no light on the details of what happened nor does it necessarily support TBE theory.

By examining some additional analyses that Willig conducted, we can begin to get an idea of what happened in the TBE programs. Willig differentiated the effects measured when students were tested in English from those measured when students were tested in the non-English language. When tested in English, TBE produced a small negative effect ($\underline{ES}$ = -.03). That is, putting LEP children in a program whose primary purpose was to help them master English slightly *retarded* their development of English in contrast to similar children who were not exposed to the supposed benefits of TBE. When tested in the non-English language, a large positive effect was found ($\underline{ES}$ = .33). Thus, Willig's observed overall net positive effect for TBE is a result of the burial of the small negative effect on English development by the large positive improvement in the non-English language.

Thus, Willig's findings clearly contradict the proposition that TBE improves performance in L2 (English). Moreover, Willig's results are also consistent with the following interpretation: TBE programs teach English-speaking children some other language (this thought will be elaborated later). It is assumed that the LEP children placed in TBE programs are CDONEL, but, as we have seen above, such an assumption is not warranted.

The Dade County schools (Rothfarb, Ariza, & McKay, 1985) recently completed a 3-year study of the effects of providing bilingual instruction in math, social studies, and science. Schools were randomly selected to teach these subjects either all in English or half in English and half in Spanish (the previous program had been bilingual instruction, so there was some bias against all-English instruction, since it was a new program, unfamiliar to the formerly bilingual teachers, and the teachers preferred bilingual instruction). There was no difference in performance in math, science, or social studies for testing in either Spanish or English. Thus, the Dade county failed to confirm the second basic tenet of TBE, that LEP students will make greater

progress in nonlanguage subjects when they are taught in L1.

One of fundamental assumptions underlying bilingual education is the hypothesis that students will ultimately come out ahead in developing literacy in their second language (English) if they first master literacy in their native language. The most extensive examination of the research bearing on this hypothesis is the review of Engle (1975), who concluded that it makes no difference in learning a second language whether the student first becomes literate in his native language or plunges right into second language literacy when he first starts school.

However, Engle's review was published a year before the most widely cited study in support of the claim appeared. Skutnabb-Kangas and Toukomaa (1976) looked at students who had immigrated from Finland to Sweden. Two groups of immigrants were compared on their performance in Swedish; those who immigrated before reaching Grade 3 in school and those who immigrated during the third grade or later. It is generally said that the study found that the students who immigrated later on — that is, those students who had been in school in Finland long enough to have first learned literacy in their native language (Finish) — performed better in Swedish than did the children who had moved to Sweden at a younger age and who presumably began learning Swedish at a young age. This study of 150 Finnish students in Sweden seems to be the principal empirical proof of the effectiveness of bilingual education put forward by its advocates.

There are major problems with the Skutnabb-Kangas and Toukomaa study and with the inference that its results support bilingual education for CDONEL students in this country. A detailed discussion of the methodological problems found in the study is to be found in Baker and de Kanter (1981), and Baker (1984), only two which I will mention here. First, Skutnabb-Kangas and Toukomaa reported no statistical analysis of their test data. My colleague, Adriana de Kanter, and I conducted an extensive statistical analysis of the Skutnabb-Kangas and Toukomaa data (Baker

& de Kanter, 1981) and found there was no relationship between length of schooling in the native land and later performance in the second language. Moreover, at the time of the Skutnabb-Kangas study, Swedish, which is the second official language of Finland, was a required field of study in Finnish schools *from the third grade onward*. Thus, if the Skutnabb-Kangas and Toukomaa data show anything, all they show is that students who have a chance to study a second language before immigrating perform better in that language than do students who had no formal instruction in the language before they immigrated. In short, there seems to be little, if any, empirical support here for one of the basic assumptions underlying bilingual education.

Oddly enough, there seems to be some empirical support for the assumption when it is turned upside down. That is, learning a second language improves performance in the first language (Mace-Matluck, 1980, 1982; Eddy, 1981). Later on I will show how this finding relates to studies of cognitive abilities in bilinguals.

The need to first learn the native language is also argued from studies that show that older learners make faster gains in the second language (see Hakuta & Gould, 1987, for an example of this argument). One study often cited in support of this argument is Genesee (1981), who found that 1 year of second-language instruction in Grade 7 is worth 3 years of second-language instruction starting in Grade 1. But this finding has some implications that need to be thought through before any policy conclusions are made. After 3 years of instruction in the second language the student who started second-language instruction in Grade 1 will be in Grade 4. That gives him 4 more years of second-language gain before he reaches the age of the student who first began instruction in Grade 7. Therefore, at any comparable age, the early learner will be well ahead of the late learner. This logical inference is confirmed by research. Reviews of the research (Krashen, Long, & Scarcella, 1979; Eddy, 1981; Hakuta, 1986) concluded that while older learners do indeed make faster initial gains, younger

learners end up with a greater mastery of the second language.[4] Now we can point to some policy implications.

A number of studies (McManus, 1985; McManus, Gould, & Welch, 1983; Batis, 1988; Chiswick, 1987) show that most of the variance explaining the relatively poor job market performance of Hispanics can be accounted for by two factors: (a) low educational attainment and (b) poor English ability. Hispanic students who fail to master English will quite literally pay for it for the rest of their lives. The younger the learner is, the higher a level of performance he will attain in English. Therefore, the future economic success of Hispanic students depends on their learning English as early as possible and not on delaying the study of English until they have first learned how to read and write in Spanish.

The critical issue is not whether younger or older learners make the greatest gain against the norm during a school year. The critical issue is whether, as adults, will younger or older learners have a better command of English? The research evidence favors younger learners and so too should school programs, because the students' future depends on how well they ultimately do in English.

Other counterexamples providing disproof of TBE's two most fundamental claims — that instruction in L1 facilitates learning of L2 and that bilingual instruction in nonlanguage subjects is superior to all-L2 instruction — can be found in Engle (1975), Baker and de Kanter (1983a), and Rossell and Ross (1986).

Recently bilingual educators have been publicizing claims that bilingual education produces a variety of cognitive benefits (Hakuta & Gould, 1987; Hakuta, 1986; Diaz, 1983). To oversimplify a bit, the claim is that bilingualism somehow alters and *improves* the minds. While I have not reviewed this literature in depth, consideration of the quality of research in other areas of bilingual education suggests that claims for benefit from bilingual education should be accepted only with the utmost caution until careful research of the issue has been conducted by nonpartisans (Baker & de Kanter, 1981, 1983a, 1983b, 1986; Baker, 1984; Rossell & Ross, 1986; Baker

& Rossell, 1987; Rossier & Wooster, n.d.). Consideration of a few of the studies of cognitive benefits of bilingualism suggests that there are indeed major methodological problems with this literature.

Peal and Lambert's (1962) is the landmark study in the literature addressing the cognitive benefits of bilingualism. Peal and Lambert administered a collection of test and attitude measures to both bilinguals and monolinguals. Separate factor analyses were carried out on the two populations. Peal and Lambert found that more factors were needed to account for roughly the same proportion of the variance shared among the tests for the bilinguals than for the monolinguals. Peal and Lambert suggested that this factor pattern was evidence of the mental superiority of bilinguals, since the greater number of factors implied they were cognitively more complex. There are two problems with interpreting Peal and Lambert's results as evidence of the cognitive superiority of bilinguals. First (a consideration that was recognized by Peal and Lambert but was overlooked by later advocates of the superiority of bilingualism), Peal and Lambert's results are equally interpretable by the hypothesis that it is easier for more intelligent students to learn a second language. Therefore, the causal ordering that explains the correlation between bilingualism and other cognitive measures could be just the reverse of that posited by the advocates. That is, it well may be that more intelligent people make better bilinguals, not that bilingualism makes people more intelligent.

The second problem with Peal and Lambert's conclusion is that the greater number of factors found in bilinguals can be interpreted as evidence of cognitive confusion equally as well as evidence of cognitive complexity. If it is the latter, the results are to be evaluated as positive for bilingualism; if the former, the effects of bilingualism are negative. I do not see that enough is yet known about the cognitive aspects of bilingualism to enlighten us as to which way the Peal and Lambert results point. In short, Peal and Lambert's results cannot be taken as evidence that bilingualism has positive effects.

Hakuta (1984) reported two other studies that he interprets as showing that bilingualism leads to greater mental flexibility, which he assumes is a good thing. This research looked into how monolingual and bilingual young children reacted to questions like these:

- Let's say "I" is "spaghetti." How do you say "I am hot"?

- Let's call a dog *cow*. Can cows bark?

The "correct" answers, i.e., the answers denoting "mental flexibility," are "spaghetti am hot" and "yes, cows can bark." It is not at all clear that a bilingual child's greater readiness to reply this way should be considered a desirable trait. One could very well claim that the study results merely confirm the point that students learning a second language are prone to making more errors than are native speakers of the language (or, if the bilingual students' native language was English, that bilingualism retards development of English).

Even if Hakuta is right and bilinguals do have greater "mental flexibility" as measured by such an exercise, we must ask, so what? Unless it is shown that such mental flexibility helps students master English, these findings are irrelevant for programs whose goal is to facilitate the assimilation of language-minority children into the mainstream culture.

The final study looking at the cognitive effects of bilingualism I want to mention is the extensive literature review of Darcy (1953), who found a couple of studies in which bilinguals had higher nonverbal IQ scores than did monolinguals. Since the studies Darcy reviewed were generally poorly controlled for sociodemographic factors, these findings must be considered as tentative at best. But if further research should confirm this findings, then we begin to get into some cognitive effects of bilingualism that have relevance for education.

Darcy's major finding is also worth noting: When tested for verbal English performance, bilinguals do not match the performance level of monolingual English speakers. This finding has important implications for the design of bilingual education programs, especially with respect to the setting of the criteria for determining when the student no longer needs special language services. A program that takes as its goal raising the English performance level of CDONEL to that of the native English-speaking population has set an unrealistically high standard. The average CDONEL student will not attain the average level of performance of the monolingual population. The goal of a special language program should not be linguistic equivalence with the monolingual population, but rather a sufficiently high level of English to permit successful performance in the English language classroom (as discussed above, we don't have any idea as to what that level of performance is or how to measure it, but we do know it is something less than full equivalence to the monolingual English-speaking population).

Readers who believe such a policy is "unfair" to LEP students should keep in mind Malherbe (1946), who also showed that bilinguals fell well short of monolingual speakers of a language but who also found that when knowledge of *both* languages was considered, bilinguals far outperformed monolinguals in total language ability (also see Balasubramonian, Seelye, & DeWeffer, 1973).

Evaluation of the Effectiveness of Bilingual Education Programs

There have been a number of reviews and discussions of the effectiveness of bilingual programs on performance in English and other academic subjects (Troike, 1978; Baker & de Kanter, 1981, 1983a, 1983b; Rossell & Ross, 1986; Rotberg, 1982; Willig, 1982, 1985; Yates & Ortiz, 1983; Peterson, Berry, et al., 1976; Holland, 1986; Dulay & Burt, 1978) and there is little point in rehashing the details of this literature here. I find the following conclusions can be drawn from this literature:

1. Poor study design and sloppy methodology abound.

2. Advocates of bilingual education programs reach far more positive conclusions when reviewing the literature than do reviewers from outside the bilingual education field. Reviewers from outside the bilingual education field (Baker & de Kanter, Rossell & Ross, Rotberg, Peterson, Ravitch, & Holland) are quite pessimistic about the effectiveness of bilingual education. The most positive thing that can be said about bilingual education from these reviews is that its effectiveness in meeting the special needs of CDONEL remains to be proven.

3. Most bilingual programs have no effect on raising performance levels of English and other academic subjects. Some programs have a positive effect; some programs have a negative effect.

I want to focus on this last conclusion for a moment because it strikes me as very unusual. It is commonplace in educational research on the effectiveness of just about anything to find a mixture of positive and neutral results. That is, educational programs, innovations, and alternatives sometimes work better than business as usual but often don't seem to make much difference. Very few programs are supported by a large body of evidence consistently showing they are superior to the alternative. In this respect, bilingual programs are not usual. Bilingual programs are usual in the frequency of reported negative results. We found in our literature review (Baker & de Kanter, 1981, 1983a, 1983b) that the probability that a bilingual program would produce significant negative results was almost as high as the probability of its producing positive results. That is, a program's chances of making a student's performance in English *worse* than if no special program had been implemented was about the same as its chances of helping him. The same was found to be true for math.

It is this peculiar pattern of program effectiveness that links this discussion of program effects and the earlier discussion of the shortcomings of the methods used to select students into and out of bilingual education programs. One explanation for the peculiar pattern of program outcomes found in the evaluation literature is that we don't know how to select students for bilingual programs. If selection methods err toward placing low-achieving monolingual English-speakers into bilingual programs, we should not be surprised to find that teaching math in Spanish doesn't work. For a school that got lucky and used selection methods that properly matched its program with the students (or where the Barrio is so concentrated that mistakes cannot be made), we would expect to find positive results. In between these two extremes, it's a muddle and programs make no difference.

Again in set theory terms, the greater the percentage of CDONEL elements included in LEP, the greater the likelihood of negative results from a program that would have been effective with CDONEL.

Thus, the lack of support for program effectiveness found in the evaluation literature may be nothing more than a manifestation of the failure of the selection methods. We don't know whether bilingual education works because we can't figure out who needs it. Moreover, until we can figure out who needs it, we will never know if it works or not.

CONCLUSIONS

We have reviewed the procedures prescribed by the legal system by identifying students in need of bilingual education and the empirical research on the validity of those procedures. The conclusion is straightforward: The procedures required by law do not do the job (in fact, the legally prescribed procedures may be worse than what they are intended to replace — teacher judgment).

For those who may think this is an unimportant issue, Baker and Rossell (1987) offered four reasons why misclassification is not only important, but also dangerous. First, it wastes scarce resources. Spending money on a special program for students who cannot benefit from that program means that other needy students elsewhere in the school system will be denied the extra help they need. Second, students who do not need special language instruction will not benefit from it. Third, providing special language instruction to students who do not need it deprives them of the chance of receiving the kind of special help, such as compensatory education, that they do need. Fourth, providing transitional bilingual education to students who do not need it is worse than ineffective; it can be harmful. To teach a low-achieving English-speaking student math in Spanish, for example, not only denies him a meaningful math lesson, it also denies him the opportunity to learn other subjects. Classroom time is fixed in the normal school day and the addition of a math lesson in Spanish to the curriculum means that something else has to be dropped from the school day.

Rhett (1985), in a reanalysis of nationally representative data from Young et al. (1984), found that when the curriculum of Hispanic background LEPs was compared with that of non-Hispanic LEP students in the first grade, the Hispanic students averaged 92% more instructional time in native language reading, 86% more time in native language oral development, and 63% more time in ethnic heritage instruction. Unfortunately, the Hispanic LEP students also received 24% less instructional time in oral English development, 96% less time in English reading, and 14% less instructional time in mathematics. Hence, the introduction of ethnic heritage studies and instruction in the non-English language in a school day of fixed length leads to a loss of instructional time in the basic skills and, in particular, in the development of English.

Theoretically speaking, children from language-minority homes who do poorly in school are the class of children defined as eligible for help, and transitional bilingual instruction is prescribed as the instructional method to be used to help them. In actual practice the procedures used for identifying students eligible for help do not do a very good job of identifying students who will benefit from bilingual instruction. When English-speaking students are placed in classrooms where they are taught in a non-English language solely because of their ancestry, they are denied equal educational opportunity. Similarly, when English-speaking students who have problems in school because of nonlanguage home background factors, such as poverty are given bilingual instruction as the remedy, they also are denied equal educational opportunity.

In examining the English development of a group of comparable non-English-speakers, Saville-Troike (1984) found great variation in how much English the students learned over a school year. Few, if any, of the variables bilingual educators generally view as important were related to the students' development of English. Obviously, more research must be conducted in order to adequately understand these issues. The present system not only denies equal educational opportunity to some unknown number of language-minority students; it also harms their educational development. It is essential to correct these problems if the effective participation in schooling promised by the *Lau* decision for language-minority students is to be realized.

The author contends that in order to carry out the legal mandate to guarantee the civil rights of children who are so dependent on a language other than English that they cannot successfully learn in a typical all-English-language classroom, the schools must do three things. First, they must determine which children need a special language program. Second, they must determine when the children no longer need it. Finally, the program must be effective in raising the students' level of achievement. That is, the students in the special language program must make more rapid progress in learning English and other subjects than they would have made in the regular English-speaking classroom.

The schools must successfully accomplish *all* three tasks, but we have seen that after 20 years of effort, sometimes heroic, sometimes pathetic, we have not succeeded in any of them. By these standards, which appear to underlie the *Lau* decision, we must conclude that bilingual education has failed to provide the civil rights protections called for by *Lau*.

Moreover, there are other ways in which bilingual education has produced civil rights failures. As the report of the civil rights division of the State of Massachusetts (1985) points out in reviewing Boston's schools, keeping LEP students in a bilingual program too long and/or failing to teach them English produces a segregated school.

Hispanic students who are grouped together in bilingual Spanish classrooms are denied interaction with majority students. Furthermore, some bilingual classrooms for students from European language backgrounds were found by the civil rights division to be a means by which white students were circumventing desegregation with the black students in the school.

Bilingual programs must be more than effective; they must be fast so as to minimize the segregation of the LEP students from the majority school program. Many bilingual advocates argue that bilingual programs should last for 5–7 years (Troike, 1983). From a civil rights perspective, the most serious reservations must be raised about such ideas if they lead to segregating LEP students from majority students for what amounts to the entirety of the student's elementary school career.

FUTURE DIRECTIONS

If the above analysis is even remotely correct, we have a mess on our hands. After nearly 20 years of concerted effort at trying to meet the special language needs of CDONEL, there have been few, if any, gains. The Supreme Court's decision that the schools must take steps to protect the civil rights of CDONEL students in order to ensure that they receive an effective education remains a promise unfulfilled. In the usual course of an analysis such as this, the writer concludes with recommendations as to how to fix the problem elucidated in the analysis. I'm not sure I can do that. There seems to be a major problem here but I don't see anything in the above analysis that points the way to a solution. Obviously, one begins by pointing out that there is a pressing need for better methods of deciding who needs what kind of special language services. But having said that, what then? Where do we find the answer to this question, and more importantly, what are the schools to do to improve the teaching of LEP children until the researchers come up with a valid selection tool?

I am going to take a shot at answering these questions but space constraints prohibit fully spelling out why I recommend the following steps. First, to begin with the more pressing issue, what kind of programs should schools establish for LEP students given that we have little reason to think any particular special language program will work in any particular place? The problem can be stated like this: We know that LEP students, regardless of how they have been identified, have some kind of learning problem. The schools' problem is that they don't know what that problem is, and in consequence, they can't prescribe a program. I think the immediate way out is to put LEP students in *very* small classes, classes of 8–12 students and preferably classes having 8 students per teacher. It would be nice if the teacher knew some of the students' native language, but at this class size I do not think it is critical.

The principal should give the teacher the following instructions at the start of the school year: "Make sure these students master the required curriculum for this grade." The principal, consultants, special teachers, lawyers, and policymakers should then get the hell out of the teacher's way and let her or him have at it. With classes this small, the teacher can individualize a program that fits the needs of each student. The teacher can discover which children need to work on vocabulary lists, who benefits from a quick explanation in Spanish, who needs glasses in order to see the blackboard, and so on. Most importantly, small classes will maximize the opportunity and probability of the student communicating with the teacher in English. The research shows that communicating in a second language is the key to learning it. But communicating is not sitting and listening to the teacher lecture. Communication is a verbal exchange between the teacher and the student and *such exchanges simply cannot occur often enough in large classes for effective language learning to take place.*

Unfortunately, teachers are experienced only in the mass marketing of knowledge to large classes so some preservice work will have to be done with the teachers to teach them how to take advantage of the learning opportunities found in small classes.

Turning now to the problem of improving selection methods, given the way LEP is now conceptualized, a successful test for LEPs would have to be able to discriminate between LEP and Chapter 1 students. I think that it is nearly impossible to ask that of a test (but at least one new test claims to be able to do this; see Gross, 1984). The way out of this dilemma lies in reconceptualizing LEP. There are three directions this could go (these three ideas grew out of an analysis of the problems encountered in evaluating bilingual programs; see Baker and Pelavin, 1984).

First, in spite of the measurement difficulties reviewed above, relative language proficiency seems a reasonable approach to defining LEPs. The principal objection to relative language proficiency tests seems to be that for any individual test, the rank order of superiority of one language to another may not be invariant across various dimensions of language proficiency. But that is a relatively straightforward psychometric problem compared to the alternatives. Moreover, if it turns out that this hypothesis is false (that is, that the rank order of language dominance is invariant across the various dimensions of language), then it doesn't matter what skills are tested.

Although I would favor special help for any student who is dominant in L1, a case can be made for also requiring some minimum level of English proficiency as well.

Second, tests that are "trial lessons" show promise. In the final analysis we want to know if a particular language-minority student can survive in the all-English classroom. The most direct way to answer this question is to put the student in such a class and see what happens. That would be prohibitively expensive, but a test that simulated the classroom experience might work. We are exploring the approach (Pelavin & Baker, 1987; Baker, Pelavin, Celebuski, & Fink, 1988) with an evaluation tool devised by Wong-Filmore and McLaughlin (1985).

Finally, another way to conceptualize the problem is that a LEP student is one who cannot perform up to potential when taught in English. Such a student can be identified when there is a gap between the performance levels measured by a verbal test and by a nonverbal test. The nonverbal test predicts the student's performance potential. Failure to reach that level on an English verbal test means extra help with English is needed. This method has the advantage over the other methods discussed that it is the only approach where it is clear from face validity that the language effect has been separated from other causes of poor performance.

In the same vein, a student is ready for transition from a special language program to the mainstream classroom when there is no longer a gap between verbal and nonverbal scores.

REFERENCES

Aspira of New York, Inc. v. Board of Education of the City of New York, 394 F. Supp. 116 (1975).

Baker, K. (1984, April). *Ideological bias in bilingual education research*. Paper presented at the annual meeting of the American Educational Research Association, New Orleans.

Baker, K. (1986). Selecting students for bilingual education under the *Keys* agreement. *La Raza Law Review, 1*(3), 330–341.

Baker, K. (1987). Comment on Willig's "A meta-analysis of selected studies on the effectiveness of bilingual education." *Review of Educational Research, 57*(3), 351–362.

Baker, K., & de Kanter, A. (1981). *Effectiveness of bilingual education: A review of the literature. Final Draft Report*. Washington, DC: U.S. Department of Education, Office of Technical and Analytic Systems.

Baker, K., & de Kanter, A. (1983a). Federal policy and the effectiveness of bilingual education. In K. Baker & A. de Kanter (Eds.), *Bilingual education: A reappraisal of federal policy* (pp. 33–86). Lexington, MA: Lexington Books.

Baker, K., & de Kanter, A. (1983b). An answer from research on bilingual education. *American Education, 56*, 157–169.

Baker, K., & de Kanter, A. (1986). Assessing the legal profession's contribution to the education of bilingual students. *La Raza Law Review, 1*, 295–329.

Baker, K., & Pelavin, S. (1984, April). *Problems in bilingual education evaluation*. Paper presented at the annual meeting of the American Education Association, New Orleans.

Baker, K., Pelavin, S., Celebuski, C., & Fink, L. (1988, April). *Determining which non-English background students need special language services*. Paper presented at the annual meeting of the American Educational Research Association, San Francisco, CA.

Baker, K., & Rossell, C. (1987). An implementation problem: Specifying the target group for bilingual education. *Educational Policy, 1*(2), 249–270.

Balasubramonian, K., Seelye, H. N., & De Weffer, R. E. (1973, May). *Do bilingual education programs inhibit English language achievement? A report on an Illinois experiment*. Paper presented at the Seventh Convention of Teachers of English to Speakers of Other Languages, San Juan, Puerto Rico.

Baratz-Snowden, J., & Duran, R. (1987). *The Educational Progress of Language Minority Students*. Princeton, NJ: ETC.

Barnes, R. (1983). The size of the eligible language minority population. In K. Baker & A. de Kanter (Eds.), *Bilingual education: A reappraisal of federal policy* (pp. 3–32). Lexington, MA: Lexington Books.

Batiz, F. L. R. (1988, October). *English Language Proficiency and the Economic Progress of Immigrants in the U.S.* Report of the U.S. Department of Labor, Washington, DC.

Berdan, R., So, A., & Sanchez, A. (1982). *Language Among the Cherokee, Patterns of Language Use in Northeastern Oklahoma*. Part 1. Preliminary Report. Los Alamitos, CA: National Center for Bilingual Research.

Bye, T. T. (1977). *Tests that measure language ability: A descriptive compilation*. Berkeley, CA: BABEL/LAU Center.

Canale, M. (1983). On some dimensions of language proficiency. In J. W. Oller, Jr. (Ed.), *Issues in language testing research* (pp. 333–343). Rowley, MA: Newbury House.

Cardoza, D. (1984). *The reclassification survey: A study of entry and exit classification procedures*. Los Alamitos, CA: National Center for Bilingual Research.

Chiswick, B. (1987). Labor market status of Hispanic men. *Journal of American Ethnic History, 7*(1), 30–58.

Commonwealth of Massachusetts Board of Education. (1985). *District of Massachusetts on Boston school desegration* (Report No. 5). Boston, MA: Board of Education.

Cummins, J. (1981). The role of primary language development in promoting educational success for language minority students. In California State Department of Education, *Schooling and Language Minority Students: A Theoretical Framework*. Los Angeles: Evaluation, Dissemination and Assessment Center.

Cummins, J. (1983). *Policy report: Language and literacy learning in bilingual instruction* (NIE Contract No. 400-80-0043). Austin, TX: Southwest Educational Development Laboratory.

Curtis, J., Lignon, G., & Weibly, G. (1979, April). *When is a LEP no longer LEP?* Paper presented at the Annual Meeting of the American Educational Research Association, San Francisco.

Danoff, M. N., Coles, G. J., McLaughlin, D. H., & Reynolds, D. J. (1978). *Evaluation of the impact of ESEA Title VII, Spanish/English Bilingual Education Program: Overview of study and findings.* Palo Alto, CA: American Institutes of Research.

Darcy, N. T. (1953). A review of the literature of effects of bilingualism upon the measurement of intelligence. *Journal of Genetic Psychology, 82,* 21–57.

De Avilla, E. A. (1980). *Relative Language Proficiency Types: A Comparison of Prevalence, Achievement Level and Socio-Economic Status.* Report submitted to the Rand Corporation.

Diaz, R. (1983). Thought and two languages: The impact of bilingualism on cognitive development. *Review of Research in Education, 10,* 23–54.

Dissemination and Assessment Center for Bilingual Education. (1976). *Evaluation instruments for bilingual education: An annotated bibliography.* Austin, TX: Author.

Dulay, H., & Burt, M. (1978). From research to method in bilingual education. In J. E. Alatis (Ed.), *Georgetown University Roundtable on Language and Linguistics* (pp. 1–35). Washington, DC: Georgetown University Press.

Dulay, H., & Burt, M. (1980). The relative proficiency of limited English proficient students. In J. E. Alatis (Ed.), *Georgetown University Roundtable on Language and Linguistics* (pp. 181–200). Washington, DC: Georgetown University Press.

Duncan, S., & De Avilla, E. (1979). *Relative language proficiency and field dependence/independence.* Paper presented at the annual meeting of TESOL, Boston.

Eddy, P. A. (1981). *The Effect of Foreign Language Study in High School on Verbal Ability.* Washington, DC: Center for Applied Linguistics.

Engle, P. L. (1975). The use of vernacular languages in education: Language medium in early school years for minority language groups. *Bilingual education series No. 2.* Arlington, VA: Center for Applied Linguistics.

Genesee, F. (1981). A comparison of early and late second language learning. *Canadian Journal of Behavioral Sciences, 13*(2), 115–128.

Gross, S. (1984). *Executive Summary: Follow-up Evaluation of Mark Twain Students* (Report No. TM 830-415). Rockville, MD: Department of Educational Accountability. (ERIC Document Reproduction Service No. ED 236 158)

Hakuta, K. (1984). *The Causal Relationship Between the Development of Bilingualism, Cognitive Flexibility, and Social Skills in Hispanic Elementary School Children: Final Report* (Report No. NE-G-81-0123). Washington, DC: Department of Education.

Hakuta, K. (1986). *Mirror of Language.* New York: Basic Books.

Hakuta, K., & Gould, L. J. (1987). Synthesis of research on bilingual Education. *Educational Leadership, 44*(6), 38–45.

Hedges, L. (1986). Issues in meta-analysis. In E. Rothkopf (Ed.), *Review of research in education, 13,* 353–398. Washington, DC: American Educational Research Association.

Hedges, L., & Olkin, I. (1985). *Statistical methods for meta-analysis.* New York: Academic Press.

Holland, R. (1986). *Bilingual education: Recent evaluations of local school district programs and related research on second-language learning* (Report No. 86-611). Washington, DC: Congressional Research Service, Library of Congress.

Horst, D. P., Douglas, D. E., Friendly, L. D., Johnson, D. M., Luber, L. M., McKay, J., Nava, H. G., Piestrup, A. M., Roberts, A. O., & Valdez, A. (1980a). *An Evaluation of Project Information Packages (PIPs) as Used for the Diffusion of Bilingual Projects: A Summary Report* (Vol. 1) (Report No. RMC UR 460). Mountain View, CA: RMC Research Corporation. (ERIC Document Reproduction Services No. ED 193 953)

Horst, D. P., Douglas, D. E., Friendly, L. D., Johnson, D. M., Luber, L. M., McKay, J., Nava, H. G., Piestrup, A. M., Roberts, A. O., & Valdez, A. (1980b). *An Evaluation of Project Information Packages (PIPs) as Used for the Diffusion of Bilingual Projects: Technical Discussion and Appendices* (Vol. 2) (Report No. RMC UR 460). Mountain View, CA: RMC Research Corporation. (ERIC Document Reproduction Services No. ED 193 954)

Horst, D. P., Johnson, D. M., Nava, H. G., Douglas, D. E., Friendly, L. D., & Roberts, A. O. H. (1980). *An Evaluation of Project Information Packages (PIPs) as Used for the Diffusion of Bilingual Projects: A Prototype Guide to Measuring Achievement Level and Program Impact on Achievement in Bilingual Projects* (Vol. 3) (Report No. RMC UR 460). Mountain View, CA: RMC Research Corporation. (ERIC Document Reproduction Services No. ED 193 955)

Inspector General. (1982). *Review of federal bilingual education programs in Texas.* Washington, DC: U.S. Department of Education.

Jackson, S. (1980, March). *Analysis procedures and summary statistics of the language data of a longitudinal study of the oral language development of Texas bilingual children.* Paper presented at the National Conference on the Language Arts in the Elementary School, San Antonio.

Keyes v. School District No. 1 (576 F. Supp. 1503, 1983; Consent judgment August 1984).

Krashen, S., Long, M., & Scarcella, R. (1979). Age, rate, & eventual attainment in second language acquisition. *TESOL Quarterly, 13,* 573–582.

Lambert, W. E., & Tucker, G. R. (1972). *Bilingual Education of Children: The St. Lambert Experience.* Rowley, MA: Newbury House.

Lau v. Nichols, 483 F.2d 791 (1973); 414 U.S. 563 (1974).

Law, A. (1978, September 28). *Proceedings of the Bilingual Instrument Review Committee* (AB 3470). Sacramento, CA: California State Department of Education, Office of Program Evaluation and Research.

Light, R. J., & Pillemer, D. B. (1984). *Summing up: The science of reviewing research.* Cambridge, MA: Harvard University Press.

Mace-Matluck, B. J. (1982). *Teaching reading in the bilingual program with emphasis on transferability of Spanish reading skills to English reading.* Paper presented at San Diego State University BESC Multidistrict Preservice Workshop.

Mace-Matluck, B. J. (1980, March). *A longitudinal study of the oral language development of Texas bilingual children.* Paper presented at the National Conference on the Language Arts in the Elementary School, San Antonio.

Malherbe, E. C. (1946). *The bilingual school.* London: Longmans Green.

Mayeske, G. W., Okada, J., Cohen, W., Beaton, A., Jr., & Wisler, C. (1973). *A study of the achievement of our nation's students.* Washington, DC: U.S. Government Printing Office.

McLaughlin, B., & Wong-Filmore, L. (1985, April). *A functional approach to language assessment: The shell and the rock games.* Paper presented at the annual meeting of the National Association for Bilingual Education, San Francisco.

McManus, W. S. (1985). Labor market costs of language disparity: An interpretation of Hispanic earning differences. *The American Economic Review, 75,* 818–827.

McManus, W. S., Gould, W., & Welch, F. (1983). Earnings of Hispanic men: The role of English language proficiency. *Journal of Labor Economics, 1*(2), 101–130.

National Institute of Education. (1981). *Report on the testing and assessment implications of the Title VI language minority proposed rules.* Washington, DC: National Institute of Education.

Northwest Regional Educational Laboratory, Center for Bilingual Education. (1978). *Assessment instruments in bilingual education: A descriptive catalogue of 342 oral and written tests.* Los Angeles: California State University, National Evaluation, Dissemination, and Assessment Center.

Northwest Regional Educational Laboratory. (1976). *Oral language tests for bilingual students: An evaluation of language dominance and proficiency instruments.* Portland, OR: Author.

Oller, Jr., J. W. (1979). *Language testing and schools.* London: Longmans.

Peal, E., & Lambert, W. (1962). The relation of bilingualism to intelligence. *Psychological Monographs, 76,* 1–23.

Pelavin, S., & Baker, K. (1987, March). *Improved methods of identifying who needs bilingual education.* Paper presented at annual meeting of American Educational Association Meeting, Washington, DC.

Peterson, M., Berry, D., Abbott, S., Kruvant, C., Sundusky, N., Chow, C., & Ortega, G. (1976). *Assessment of the Status of Bilingual Vocational Training for Adults: Review of the Literature* (Vol. 3) (Contract No. 300-75-0333). Washington, DC: Department of Health, Education, & Welfare. (ERIC Document Reproduction Services No. ED 131 683)

Pletcher, B. P., Locks, N. A., Reynolds, D. F., & Sisson, B. C. (1978). *A guide to assessment instruments for limited English speaking students.* New York: Santillana.

Ramirez, J. D., Merino, B., Bye, T., & Gold, N. (1981). *Assessment of oral English proficiency: A status report.* Unpublished manuscript.

Ramirez, J. D., Wolfson, R., Tallmadge, G. K., & Merino, B. (1984). Study design of the longitudinal study of immersion programs for language-minority children. Mountain View, CA: SRA Technologies.

Rhett, N. (1985). Personal communication. U.S. Department of Education.

Roos, P. (1978). Bilingual education: The Hispanic response to unequal educational opportunity. *Law and Contemporary Problems, 42*(4), 111–140.

Rosenthal, A. S., Baker, K., & Ginsburg, A. (1983). The effect of language background on achievement level and learning among elementary school students. *Sociology of Education, 56*(4), 157–169.

Rossell, C., & Ross, J. M. (1986). The social science evidence on bilingual education. *Journal of Law and Education, 15,* 385–419.

Rossier, R., & Wooster, M. (n.d.). *Hysteria with Footnotes: The Politics of Bilingual Education Research.* Washington, DC: Learn, Inc.

Rotberg, I. C. (1982). Some legal and research considerations in establishing federal policy in bilingual education. *Harvard Educational Review, 52,* 149–168.

Rothfarb, S., Ariza, M., & McKay, A. (1985). *Evaluation of the bilingual curriculum content (BCC) pilot project: A three-year study, first interim report.* Miami, FL: Dade County Public Schools, Office of Educational Accountability. (ERIC Document Reproduction Service No. ED 283 845)

Saville-Troike, M. (1984). What *really* matters in second language learning for academic achievement? *TESOL Quarterly, 18*(2), 199–219.

Skutnabb-Kangus, T., & Toukomaa, P. (1976). *Teaching migrant children's mother tongue and learning the language of the host country in the context of the social-cultural situation on the migrant family.* Helsinki: The Finnish National Commission for UNESCO.

So, A. Y., & Chan, K. S. (1982). *What matters? A study of the relative impact of language background and socioeconomic status on reading achievement.* Mimeo. Los Alamitos, CA: National Center for Bilingual Research.

Spolsky, B. (1978). *Educational linguistics.* Rowley, MA: Newbury House.

State Advisory Council on Bilingual Education, Commonwealth of Massachusetts. (1987). *General Framework and Criteria for the Development of Statewide English and Language Proficiency Tests for Limited English Proficiency Students, K–12.* Boston, MA: Bureau of Transitional Bilingual Education.

Texas Education Agency. (1977). *Report of the Committee for the Evaluation of Language Assessment Instruments.* Austin, TX: TEA.

Texas Education Agency. (1979). *Report of the Committee for the Evaluation of Language Assessment Instruments* (Winter/Spring 1979 meeting). Austin, TX: TEA.

Troike, R. C. (1978). Research evidence for the effectiveness of bilingual education. *National Association of Bilingual Education Journal, 3*(1), 13–24.

Troike, R. C. (1983). Bilingual Si! *Principal, January Issue,* 8.

Ulibarri, D., Spencer, M., & Rivas, G. (1981). Language proficiency and academic achievement: A study of language proficiency tests and their relationship to school ratings as predictors of academic achievement. *The Journal for the National Association for Bilingual Education, 5*(3), 47–80.

U.S. Department of Education. (1987). *What works.* Second Edition. Washington, DC: Department of Education.

U.S. v. Texas, 506 F.Supp. 405 (1981); 680 F.2d 356 (1982).

Veltman, C. J. (1981). Relative educational attainments of Hispanic-American Children, 1976. *Metas, 2,* 36–51.

Willig, A. C. (1982). The effectiveness of bilingual education: Review of a report. *The Journal for the National Association for Bilingual Education, 6,* 1–19.

Willig, A. C. (1985). A meta-analysis of selected studies on the effectiveness of bilingual education. *Review of Educational Research, 55,* 269–317.

Yates, J., & Ortiz, A. (1983). Baker & de Kanter Review: Inappropriate conclusions of the efficacy of bilingual education. *The Journal for the National Association for Bilingual Education, 7*(3), 75–84.

Young, M., Hopstock, P., Rudes, B., Fleischman, H., Zehler, A., Shaycoft, M., Goldsamt, M., Bauman, J., Burkheimer, G., & Rattner, M. (1984). *The descriptive phase report of the National longitudinal evaluation of the effectiveness of services for language minority/limited English proficient students.* Arlington, VA: Development Associates.

FOOTNOTES

[1]It must be kept in mind that we are considering a compensatory program that argues that teaching LEP students in a language other than English is the best way to make these students capable of successful performance in an English-speaking classroom. The problems we have identified with compensatory bilingual education would not necessarily apply to a bilingual program whose goal was to teach a foreign language. Although we would argue that there should be more such programs in our schools, given the desirability of increasing the foreign language skills of the English-speaking population, we would also argue that this is an entirely different issue from teaching English to LEP students. What may work for one purpose may be totally unacceptable for the other.

[2]The *Keys* case included an out of court settlement on Denver's bilingual education program.

[3]These results apply to Hispanics as a class, not to individual Hispanic students who may not speak English. Mayeske's results are undoubtedly a function of the fact that there are so few students of Hispanic background who do not speak English that their effect on the class as a whole cannot be detected.

[4]Although not directly addressing the issue of bilingual education, the U.S. Department of Education's *What Works,* a compendium of known effective educational practices concludes, in discussing learning a second language, that "Students are most likely to become fluent in a foreign language if they begin studying it in elementary school and continue studying it for six to eight years" (U.S. Department of Education, 1987, p. 73).

CHAPTER 2

Language-Minority Education Litigation Policy: "The Law of the Land"

Eugene E. Garcia
University of California, Santa Cruz

FOUNDATIONS FOR U.S. EDUCATIONAL LITIGATION

The United States draws its system of law and justice from the common law that grew up in England under William the Conqueror following the Normandy invasion in 1066. Apart from the fact that it started some 1,500 years after the Roman law traditions (traditions that serve as a foundation for much of European and Latin American law), the common law is known as "customary" or "unwritten" law, since its rules are founded in judicial decisions of controversies brought before judges by individual litigants. Unlike the Roman tradition, which eschews reliance on the judicial branch, the common law tradition turns on a basic confidence in its judges to decide cases correctly with no or little legislative guidance. The Roman law traditions, usually considered to have begun around 450 B.C., shaped the Napoleonic codes of France in the early nineteenth century and the codes of other European nations that were promulgated thereafter. These traditions regarding the sources of legal rules adhere strictly to the written norms passed by the legislative branch of government, most notably the codes that treat an entire field of law exhaustively and logically to create a comprehensive framework of general rules within which all controversies are contemplated. The same tradition distrusts judges and the judicial branch: The conventional doctrine is that judges simply *apply* the law, but may never *interpret* the legislative rule.

A fundamental disparity between Roman law and common law traditions resides in the fact that legal acts under the Roman tradition most often are accompanied by painstaking formalities and fail to achieve any enforceable judicial effect, whereas in the common law tradition there exists no highly evolved doctrine of special formal requirements before an agreement or other activity by private parties creates rights and obligations recognized by the law.

Functions and Qualities of the U.S. Legal System: The Common Law Tradition

The above description of the derivative traditions does not specifically address the question of the law's *function* in society.

There are many viewpoints from which the function of a legal system can be analyzed, but I will use a synthesis derived from the writings of legal historian and philosopher Hurst (Brooks, 1966). Hurst suggested five basic functions of the legal system (Brooks, 1966):

1. It mediates between interest groups and the interests for the common good.
2. It forces articulation of policy and avoids inertia and drift.
3. It provides leverage both for support of established institutions and for action in new directions.
4. It allocates resources.
5. It protects and promotes release of energy in a way that affords broad access to opportunity.

Hurst emphasizes that a "good law" is one that meets the needs of the present society without placing at risk the future society. Perhaps this is an echo of Kozolchyk's (1971) view that the main function of a proper legal system is to instill trust in its institutions. A system that fails to fulfill the five basic functions of the law will fail almost certainly to instill trust in its institutions; that is, to function as the basis for satisfactorily ordering the society it serves. Hurst argued that there are distinctive qualities of U.S. law that explain the successful fulfillment of its function: (a) power dispersal among governmental powers and among citizens; (b) a middle-class orientation that is manifested in individualism, skeptical moderation, and secular controls; (c) a constitutionalism that provides institutional guarantees that public authorities will wield power in the interests of the public; and (d) regular procedures by which issues are fully ventilated, either within the judicial branch or within the legislative or executive (Brooks, 1966, p. 240).

In addition to the above characteristics regarding the functional aspects of law within a society, there are other features that relate to issues in education:

1. *Pragmatics,* which judges law as a practical system and permits individuals to bring litigation of "any sort" to the bar even if it is only remotely related to legislative mandates;

2. *Individualism* (perhaps well expressed in the saying "See you in court"), which allows the courts to place social responsibilities on almost any individual or institution;

3. *Litigationism,* which emphasizes that a large number of social relations should be covered by specific litigation and trusts judges to serve as interpreters;

4. *Penetration,* in the sense that the legal system directly or indirectly (as individuals maneuver to avoid litigation) reaches many of the citizens within its jurisdiction.

FOUNDATIONS OF LANGUAGE-MINORITY STUDENT "RIGHTS"

In view of the preceding discussion of the function of law in U.S. society, it should not be surprising to learn of the role of the courts in resolution of educational equity issues. The legal issues surrounding language-minority education are a direct consequence of the litigation that accompanied school desegregation during the 1950s, 1960s, and early 1970s. In addition to the parties in desegregation suits, other litigants (the handicapped, women, etc.) sought assistance from courts, in pursuit of correcting perceived educational inequities. Courts began hearing cases involving issues as variable as hair or clothing codes, classroom methodologies, and employment practices. During all these intrusions into school operations, the courts accepted as fundamental the local school board's control over educational systems while occasionally intervening in matters if they deemed it important.

In most educational matters, courts have attempted to define and apply basic principles but refrain from prescribing or formulating educational policy. The clear benchmark of the educational litigation was that citizens should not be denied equal access to valuable governmental services (particularly education) on account of such irrational or discriminatory bases as race, gender, or ethnicity. The simple message of *Brown v. Board of Education* (1954), precluding segregation of public school students by race, was easily adaptable to other identifiable student populations, such as the handicapped, students with limited English proficiency, and female students. The applicable principle was accessible and compelling: equal treatment before the institutions of society.

But the plaintiffs did not rest content with gaining access. Once admitted to the system "equally," they wanted the schools to acknowledge them, to accommodate and satisfy special needs. Most of all, they wanted schools to succeed in transforming disadvantaged or simply different children into adults with comparable life prospects as the masses of middle-class, usually white, children whom the schools prepared for the available managerial, professional, and entrepreneurial slots. The principle of equal opportunity and/or treatment had to be adapted to these complex aspirations and became a demand for educational programs and practices that would accomplish the appropriate goals.

The courts were confronted with a distasteful task. The level of plaintiff demand was clear: Find that the status quo is inappropriate ("the present educational treatment is wrong") and fix it ("this type of program will do it"). Courts were asked to designate specific curricula or methodologies, as well as minimally satisfactory educational results. Courts had traditionally avoided educational policy disputes and had refused to select among pedagogic or curricular choices (Anson and Rist, 1977). That reluctance must have seemed all the more warranted as plaintiffs and defendants produced a procession of experts emphatically described alternatives as irreconcilable theoretical realities and discounted opposing viewpoints. Hence, conclusive answers to rather basic questions remained quite elusive (e.g., Does integration positively affect academic achievement? Do increased expenditures on education influence student achievement?).

Consequently, courts became educational reformers but did so reluctantly and cautiously, attempting to avoid involvement in professional debates regarding the appropriateness of curricula. Judges began to attend meticulously to the proper demarcation between principle and policy, being determined to take action only when the occasional flagrant exclusion or discrimination case arose. Otherwise, courts generally displayed a certain judicial modesty. However, policy has arisen from several decades of adjudication. The following discussion highlights five major federal cases that have defined that judicial policy in specific respect to language-minority education: *Lau v. Nichols*, 1974; *Aspira of New York v. New York Board of Education*, 1975; *U.S. v. Texas*, 1981; *Castaneda v. Pickard*, 1981; and *Keyes v. Denver Public School District No. 1*, 1983. Consideration of these cases along with corollary decisions, requires examination of their extensive legislative and administrative foundations.

The 1964 Civil Rights Act

Title VII of the 1964 Civil Rights Act (Leibowitz, 1982) banned discrimination on the grounds of race, color, or national origin in any program receiving federal financial assistance. A federal regulation following from this act banned recipients of federal funds from restricting an individual in any way in the enjoyment of any advantage or privilege enjoyed by others receiving any service, financial aid, or benefit under the (federally funded) program. An accompanying provision of this regulation indicated that a recipient of federal funds may not utilize criteria or methods that have the effect of impairing accomplishment of the objectives of the federally funded program with respect to individuals of a particular race, color or national origin. Significantly, under the Civil Rights Act, failure of an institution to comply with pursuant regulations raises the possibility of a private cause of action (a lawsuit) to rectify the situation. Therefore, students need not wait for the government to enforce the law; instead they may be able to sue for an implementation of an appropriate program. Because almost all public schools receive federal money, and the mandate is incumbent on the recipient of *any* federal funding, the mandate affects almost all schools.

The May 25, 1970 Memorandum

A May 25, 1970 Department of Health, Education and Welfare memorandum provided the following clarification to previous regulations regarding the 1964 Civil Rights Act that highlights the issue of language-minority students: "Where inability to speak and understand the English language excludes national origin minority group children from effective participation in the educational program offered by a school district, the district must take affirmative steps to rectify the language deficiency in order to open instructional programs to these students." This was the first "quasilegal" mandate that required provision of special services to language-minority students.

The 1974 Equal Educational Opportunities and Transportation of Students Act

This act, together with related regulations, makes "the failure by an educational agency to take appropriate action to overcome language barriers that impede equal participation by its students in its instructional programs" an unlawful denial of equal educational opportunity. This act suggests that any child, irrespective of language, is entitled to language assistance programs if the student can show that participation in school is impeded by a language-related condition.

These particular legislation-related foundations have served to guide the actions of litigants and the courts. Of course, other pertinent legislative sources, including the U.S. constitution, have been used to coax the courts' intervention on behalf of language-minority students. However, court decisions that have formulated litigation policy have returned consistently to the above foundations.

CASE LAW

Lau v. Nichols (1974)

There is a clear starting point for the development of court-related policy regarding language-minority students: the 1974 United States Supreme Court decision *Lau v. Nichols*. This case originated in San Francisco, and involved a claim by a class of non-English-speaking Chinese students that they were being denied equal educational opportunity. The court suit was filed on March 25, 1970, and involved 12 American-born and foreign-born Chinese students. The parents of these students requested that the San Francisco school district meet the recognized needs of non-English-speaking Chinese students in its schools. Prior to the suit, in 1966, at the request of parents, an ESL pullout program was initiated by the district, and in a 1967 school census, the district identified 2,456 limited-English-speaking Chinese students. By 1970, the district had identified 2,856

such students. Of this number more than half (1,790) received no special instruction. In addition over 2,600 of these students were taught by teachers who could not themselves speak Chinese. It is important to note that (a) the district was not unaware of the number of students in need of special language services; and (b) the district had made initial, although admittedly meager, attempts to serve this population.

Therefore, the district was both formally conscious of the problem and had attempted to address it. On May 26, 1970, the Federal District Court found that the school district had no legal obligation to provide the special services, but encouraged the district as an educational policy to attempt to address the problem as an educational (as opposed to legal) obligation to these students. On January 8, 1972, the Ninth Circuit District Court of Appeals upheld this lower court ruling. The plaintiffs appealed to the U.S. Supreme Court.

The Supreme Court's majority opinion overruled the appeals court and favored the pupils and parents. The opinion relied on statutory (legislative) grounds in granting relief, and avoided any reference to constitutional determination, although plaintiffs had argued that the equal protection clause (of the Fourteenth Amendment) of the U.S. Constitution was relevant to the case. Pupils' right to special education services flowed from the district's obligations under Title VII of the 1964 Civil Rights Act and the HEW qualifying regulation articulated in its May 25, 1970 memorandum. The plaintiffs did not request an explicit remedy, such as a bilingual or ESL program, nor did the Court address this issue. Thus, *Lau* does not stand for the proposition that children must receive a particular educational service (such as bilingual/bicultural instruction or ESL) but instead that some form of effective educational programming must be available to "open the instruction" to language-minority students.

Thus, *Lau* was a distinct starting point for taking into consideration, on the basis of Title VI of the 1964 Civil Rights Act, language-minority student status. Furthermore, the opinion quoted from HEW guidelines (the May 25 memorandum) that were quite firm in requiring extra services from the districts to assist language-minority students. The pattern set in *Lau* was to be repeated for other groups of children, such as the handicapped, who arrive at the school's "starting line" bearing special disadvantages; schools would be compelled to adjust the schooling "race" in deference to these students.

After *Lau*, the domain of language-minority education lawsuits belonged almost exclusively to Hispanic litigants. Although some cases were litigated to ensure compliance with the *Lau* requirement of some special assistance, most subsequent cases were about the issues left unanswered in *Lau:* Who are these students? and What form of additional educational services must be provided.

Aspira of New York, Inc. v. Board of Education (1975)

As Roos (1978) indicated, the issue of who "requires" special language assistance has not been clearly delineated by the courts. In *Aspira of New York, Inc. v. Board of Education* (1975), a suit was brought by a community action group on behalf of all Hispanic children in the New York School District whose English language deficiency prevented effective participation in an English schooling context and who could effectively participate in a Spanish language curriculum (Roos, 1984). The district court hearing this case adopted a language dominance procedure to identify those students eligible for non-English, Spanish-language instructional programs. The procedure called for parallel examinations to obtain language proficiency estimates on Spanish and English standardized achievement tests. All students scoring below the 20th percentile on an English language test were given the same (or a parallel) achievement test in Spanish. Students who scored higher on the Spanish achievement test and Spanish language proficiency test were to be placed in a Spanish-language program. These procedures assumed adequate reliability and validity for the language and achievement tests administered. Such an assumption was and still is highly questionable. However, the court argued that it

acted in a "reasonable manner," admitting that in the absence of better assessment procedures it was forced to follow previous (*Lau*) precedents.

A subsequent case, *Otero v. Mesa County School District No. 51* (1977), concluded that a clear relationship between low academic achievement and the English language deficiency of students must be clearly demonstrated before a court could mandate special language services for language-minority students. This court suggested that in the absence of this clear relationship low academic achievement could be attributed to other variables (e.g., socioeconomic background). Therefore, merely showing that Spanish is the home language was insufficient to require a school district to provide special language assistance. Instead, a link between non-English proficiency and low school achievement required to be established. Recall that in *Lau*, the district had conducted its own census and had begun a special language program for some of the students identified as in need. Therefore, the legal obligation related to providing special educational program for language-minority students is based on the link between lack of English proficiency and the lack of school achievement under English-language instruction.

Castaneda v. Pickard (1981)

After the population of students requiring special language services are identified, what types of services must districts provide to language-minority students? In Arizona, a suit was filed against a local school district by a nonprofit corporation, suing on behalf of the children of a community of 5,000 persons, most of whom were of Mexican-American or Yaqui ancestry (*Guadalupe v. Tempe School District No. 3*, 1978). Plaintiffs organized their lawsuit around the claim that the district was acting discriminatorily in failing to provide these children with appropriate educational programs in as much as the district curriculum failed to recognize their special educational needs. The curriculum did not reflect the historical contributions of people of appellants' descent to the State of Arizona and to the United States. The plaintiffs requested a maintenance bilingual program that would ensure competence at graduation in the children's native language and English, with biculturalism reflected throughout the curriculum.

The district court entered judgment in favor of the school district, and the plaintiffs appealed to the Ninth Circuit, which put the dispute to rest by affirming the lower court's order. In their opinion, it is noted that "in answer to interrogatories of the appellees and in argument before the district court, [plaintiffs] admitted they did not complain of the school district's efforts to cure existing language deficiencies." The court concluded, in its constitutional holding, "that the Constitution neither requires nor prohibits the bilingual and bicultural education sought by appellants. Such matters are for the people to decide." In assessing the choices made by Congress in the Civil Rights Act of 1964 and the Equal Educational Opportunity Act of 1974, the court concluded that in previous litigation, courts also have not required districts to provide what the plaintiffs sought, even as a condition to receipt of federal funds. As long as the district responds appropriately to the needs of limited-English-proficiency (LEP) children, effectively remediating their English language deficiency, no federal statute has been violated. Essentially, the court failed to find any statutory or constitutional violation committed by the district.

However, in a key Fifth Circuit decision of *Castaneda v. Pickard* (1981), the court interpreted Section 1703(f) of the Equal Education Opportunity Act of 1974 as substantiating the holding of *Lau* that schools cannot ignore the special language needs of students. Moreover, this court then pondered whether the statutory requirement that districts take "appropriate action" suggested a more precise obligation than the Civil Rights Act requirement that districts do something. The plaintiffs predictably urged on the court a construction of "appropriate action" that would necessitate at least bilingual transitional programs. The court concluded, however, that Section 1703(f) did not embody a congressional mandate that any particular form of remedy be uniformly adopted. If

Congress wished to intrude so extraordinarily on the local districts' traditional curricular discretion, it must speak more explicitly. This conclusion, the court argued, was buttressed by the congressional use of "appropriate action" in the statute, instead of "bilingual education" or any other educational terminology.

However, the court concluded that the Congress did require districts to adopt an appropriate program, and that, by creating a cause of action in federal court to enforce Section 1703(f), it left to federal judges the task of determining whether a given program is appropriate. The court noted that Congress had not provided guidance in the statute or its brief legislative history on what it intended by selecting "appropriateness" as the operative standard. Continuing with clear reluctance and hesitancy, the court described a mode of analysis for a Section 1703(f) case:

1. The court will determine whether a district's program is "informed by an educational theory recognized as sound by some experts in the field or, at least, deemed a legitimate experimental strategy." The court explicitly declined to be an arbiter among competing theorists. The appropriate question is whether some justification exists, not the relative merits of competing alternatives.

2. The court will determine whether the district is implementing its program in a reasonably effective manner (e.g., adequate funding, qualified staffing).

3. The court will determine whether the program, after operating long enough to be a legitimate trial, produces results that indicate that language barriers are being overcome. A plan that is initially appropriate may have to be revised if expectations are not met or if the district's circumstances significantly change in such a way that the original plan is no longer sufficient.

After *Castaneda* it became legally possible to substantiate a violation of Section 1703(f), following from *Lau*, on three grounds: (a) The program providing special language services to eligible language-minority students is not based on sound educational theory; (b) the program is not being implemented in an effective manner; and (c) the program, after a period of "reasonable implementation," does not produce results that substantiate that language barriers are being overcome.

It is obvious that these criteria allow a local school district to continue to implement a program with some educational theoretical support for a "reasonable" time before it will make judgments upon its "positive" or "negative" effects. However, the *Castaneda* court, again reluctantly but firmly, spoke to the issue of program implementation. Particularly, the court indicated that the district must provide adequate resources, including trained instructional personnel, materials, and other relevant support that would insure effective program implementation. Therefore, a district that chooses a particular program model for addressing the needs of its language-minority students must demonstrate that its staffing and materials are adequate for such a program. Implicit in these standards is the requirement that districts staff their programs with language-minority education specialists, typically defined by state-approved credentials or professional course work (similar to devices utilized to judge professional expertise in other areas of professional education).

U.S. v. Texas (1981)

U.S. v. Texas is a case parallel to *Castaneda v. Pickard*. The case was initiated against the Texas Education Agency — a state, as opposed to a local, educational agency. As first filed on March 6, 1970, the U.S. Department of Justice, which served as plaintiff in this action, claimed that the state agency had failed to oversee local school districts' actions related to the desegregation of Texas schools. The Federal District Court (5th U.S. Circuit Court of Appeals) in 1971 found the state agency delinquent in its duty, and after subsequent unsuccessful appeals by the state agency, the agency was ordered to develop a state plan for implementing statewide desegregation. A component of that order (Section G) addressed the issue of eliminating the vestiges of discrimination against students who sustained the discrim-

inatory impact of language barriers (Leibowitz, 1982). Following this order, the state agency prepared an 86-page report (and plan), in which was included a 17-page section entitled "Alternative Programs to Improve Curriculum for Minority Students." Therefore, the state agency met the requirements of the mandated order and in doing so indicated the need for alternative educational programs that addressed the needs of language-minority students in the alternative programs section.

Significantly, on July 10, 1972, a motion to intervene, filed by the GI Forum and the League of United Latin American Citizens (both community groups with a history of desegregation litigation regarding Hispanics in Texas), allowed these parties to participate in the action as representatives of persons of Latino ancestry. Subsequently, on June 3, 1975, these organizations filed an action seeking enforcement of Section G of the 1971 order, and requested supplemental relief (action by the state agency), for Mexican-American students in Texas schools who were limited in their English proficiency. They requested that the state agency require bilingual instruction and compensatory programs. The United States Department of Justice (the original plaintiff) joined in a similar request for enforcement of Section G.

In the *U.S. v. Texas* (1981) decision, the district court spoke to the responsibility of the state agency and to the type of program that should be implemented particularly in reference to the English Educational Opportunity Act of 1974:

> The state's compensatory education program has not succeeded in eradicating the disabling effects of pervasive historical discrimination suffered by Mexican-Americans in the field of education. Bilingual instruction is uniquely suited to remedying the special learning problems of these children and preparing them to enjoy equal educational opportunity in the Texas public schools. The state's existing bilingual program, while an improvement over past practices, is wholly inadequate.
> Serious flaws permeate every aspect of the state's effort. Required program content, described in detail by state law and regulation, is frequently ignored by

local school districts. The scanty coverage of the state's bilingual program leaves tens of thousands of Mexican-American children without the compensatory help they require to function effectively as students. Identification of limited English proficiency students by local school districts is unreliable and unverified. Criteria for transferring students out of bilingual programs and into all-English classrooms are fixed far too low to ensure that all vestiges of discrimination have been removed before relief is cut off. Finally, the state has failed to monitor local bilingual programs in a thorough and diligent manner or to enforce applicable laws and regulation through the imposition of sanctions in appropriate circumstances. Since the defendants have not remedied these serious deficiencies, meaningful relief for the victims of unlawful discrimination must be instituted by court decree.

It is true that bilingual instruction per se is not required by Section 1703(f) or any other provision of law. If the defendants here had implemented another type of program which effectively overcame the language barriers of Mexican-American students and enabled them to participate equally in the school curriculum, without using bilingual instruction of any kind, such a course would constitute "appropriate action" and preclude statutory relief. But the evidence in this case, discussed above, showed that the defendants have failed to remedy this serious educational problem as it exists throughout the State of Texas. A violation of Section 1703(f) has thus occurred. The evidence also demonstrated that bilingual instruction is uniquely suited to meet the needs of the state's Spanish-speaking students. Therefore, the defendants will be required to take further steps, including additional bilingual instruction, if needed, to satisfy their affirmative obligation under the statute and enforce the right of these linguistically deprived children to equal educational opportunity (U.S. v. Texas, 1981, p. 17–18).

Almost immediately, the Texas legislature passed sweeping new language-minority education legislation that addressed many of the issues identified by the court in *U.S. v. Texas.* On July 13, 1982, the Fifth U.S. Circuit Court of Appeals reversed the decision. It did so on several grounds; however, the most compelling was that the 1981 Texas law, which requires bilingual education in elementary school districts, made the previous case moot. The case was remanded to the district court for reconsideration and with the concern that the state law (and the programs generated by that law) be given a "reasonable" time to display its effects (in accordance with the *Castaneda* standard).

Keyes v. School District No. 1, Denver (1983)

This Keyes court decision was originally initiated in 1969 by a class of minority parents on behalf of their minor children attending the Denver public schools, to desegregate the public schools and to provide equal educational opportunities for all children. In granting the preliminary injunction the trial court found that during the previous decade the school board had willfully undertaken to maintain and intensify racial segregation (*Keyes v. School District No. 1, Denver, Colorado*, 1969). The court ordered boundary changes to desegregate the Denver public schools. Years of litigation ensued with multiple appeals to the Court of Appeals and the Supreme Court. In 1973, the district court concluded that the Denver public school system was an unlawful dual system in violation of the United States Constitution and ordered the dismantling of the dual system (*Keyes v. School District No. 1, Denver, Colorado*, 1973).

In 1974, during the development of a desegregation plan, intervention was sought by the Congress of Hispanic Educators (CHE) on behalf of themselves as educators and on behalf of their own minor children who attended the Denver schools. CHE was interested in ensuring that the desegregation plan ordered by the court included the educational treatment of language-minority students to overcome the deficits created by numerous years of attendance in segregated and inferior schools. A sequence of additional proceedings and negotiations followed with final comprehensive court hearings commencing in May 1982.

In December 1983, Judge Richard Matsch issued a 31-page opinion, which is the most lengthy and complete language-programming discussion to date in a judicial decision. Judge Matsch, applying the *Castaneda* standards, found that Denver had failed to direct adequate resources to its language program, the question of teacher skills being a major concern.

Following this decision, a landmark remedial plan was negotiated. As a result of the plan, the Denver public schools have (a) hired a staff of 75 trained ESL teachers; (b) expanded bilingual programs from 11 to 32 schools; (c) set standards for bilingual teachers; (d) revamped the curriculum for limited-English-proficiency students, so that it is consistent with the curriculum provided other students; (e) established an accountability program for assessing student progress; and (f) established special programs for Asian students including ESL, a low ratio of students to native-speaking aides, mandatory hiring of special guidance counselors, and the creation of an Asian parents advocacy committee with a full-time coordinator.

CONCLUSIONS: RIGHTS OF LANGUAGE-MINORITY STUDENTS

The previous discussion has highlighted the increasing number of court opinions related to language-minority pupils over the last two decades. These opinions have in turn generated some understanding of a language-minority pupil's legal standing as it relates to the educational treatment received. At a national level, this legal standing stems from court opinions specifically interpreting Section 1703(f) of the 1974 U.S. Equal Educational Opportunity Act. The courts have consistently refused to invoke a corollary to the Fourteenth Amendment to the U.S. Constitution in respect to educational treatment. Even so it is evident that litigation has increased (and is likely to continue) and has been an avenue of educational program reform that has produced significant changes in educational programs for language-minority students. However, like almost all litigation, it has been a long (range of 4–13 years in court prior to an operational decision) and often highly complicated and resource-consuming enterprise.

Nevertheless, several important conclusions regarding the responsibilities of educational agencies have been established. The following, in a question-and-answer format, sets out some of these responsibilities. These are adapted from Roos (1984) and carry with them a caution that the legal authority both of the federal and of state governments which led to these guidelines, is always subject to legislative change and modifications in court interpretation. However, these conclusions do represent a practical guide for understanding the legal status of the language-minority student and the legal liability of the educational agencies that serve them.

Question: Is there a legally acceptable procedure for identifying language-minority students in need of special instructional treatment?

Answer: Yes. The legal obligation is to identify all students who have problems speaking, understanding, reading, or writing English owing to a home language background other than English. In order to do this, a two-phase approach is common and acceptable. First, the parents are asked, through a home language survey or on a registration form, whether a language other than English is utilized in the child's home. If the answer is affirmative, the second phase is triggered. In the second phase, students identified through the home language survey are given an oral language proficiency test and an assessment of their reading and writing skills.

Question: Once these students are identified, are they any minimal standards for the educational program provided to them?

Answer: Yes. First, a number of courts have recognized that special training is necessary to equip a teacher to provide meaningful assistance to limited-English-proficiency students. The teacher (and it is clear that it must be a teacher, not an aide) must have training in second-language acquisition techniques in order to teach English as a second language.

Second, the time spent on assisting these students must be sufficient to assure that they acquire English skills quickly enough to assure that their disadvantage in the English language classroom does not harden into a permanent educational disadvantage.

Question: Must students be provided with instruction in the student's native language as well as English?

Answer: At the present time, the federal obligation has not been construed to compel such a program. As a practical matter, however, the federal mandate is such that a district would be well advised to offer such a program whenever it is possible.

The federal mandate is not fully satisfied by an ESL program. The mandate requires English language help *plus* programs to assure that students not be substantively handicapped by any delay in learning English. To do this requires either (a) a bilingual program that keeps the students up in their course work while learning English or (b) a specially designed compensatory program to address the educational loss suffered by any delay in providing understandable substantive instruction. Given these alternatives, the legally "safe" posture is to offer native language instruction whenever it can be done. Finally, it is legally necessary to provide the material resources necessary for the instructional components. The program must be reasonably designed to succeed. Without adequate resources, this requirement cannot be met.

Question: What minimal standards must be met if a bilingual program is to be offered?

Answer: The heart of a basic bilingual program is a teacher who can speak the language of the students as well as address the students' limited English proficiency. Thus, a district offering a bilingual program must take affirmative steps to match teachers with these characteristics. These might include allocating teachers with language skills to bilingual classrooms, and affirmative recruitment of bilingual teachers. Additionally, it requires the district to establish a formal system to assess teachers to insure that they have the prerequisite skills. Finally, where there are insufficient teachers, there must be a system to insure that teachers with most (but not all) of the skills are in bilingual classrooms,

that those teachers are on a track to obtain the necessary skills and that bilingual aides are hired whenever the teacher lacks the necessary language skills.

Question: Must there be standards for removal of a student from a program? What might these be?

Answer: There must be definite standards. These generally mirror the standards for determining whether a student is in need of special language services in the first place. Thus, objective evidence that the student can compete with English-speaking peers without a lingering language disability is necessary.

Several common practices are unlawful. First, the establishment of an arbitrary cap on the amount of time a student can remain in a program fails to meet the requirement that all language-minority students be assisted. Second, it is common to have programs terminate at a certain grade level, for example, sixth grade. While programs may change to accommodate different realities, it is unlawful to deny a student access to a program merely because of grade level.

Question: Must a district develop a design to monitor the success of its program?

Answer: Yes. The district is obligated to monitor the program and to make reasonable adjustments when the evidence would suggest that the program is not successful.

Monitoring is necessarily a two-part process. First, it is necessary to monitor the progress of students in the program to assure (a) that they are making reasonable progress toward learning English and (b) that the program is providing the students with substantive instruction comparable to that given to English-proficient pupils. Second, any assessment of the program must include a system to monitor the progress of students after they leave the program. The primary purpose of the program is to assure that the LEP students ultimately are able to compete on an equal footing with their English-speaking peers. This cannot be determined in the absence of such a postreclassification monitoring system.

Question: May a district deny services to a student because there are few students in the district who speak her or his language?

Answer: No. The 1974 Equal Educational Opportunity Act and subsequent court decisions make it clear that every student is entitled to a program that is reasonably designed to overcome any handicaps occasioned by a language deficit. Numbers may, obviously, be considered to determine how to address the student's needs. They are not a proper consideration in determining whether a program should be provided.

Although reluctant, U.S. courts have layed a significant role in shaping language-minority education policy. They have spoken to issues of student identification, program implementation, resource allocation, professional staffing, and program effectiveness. Moreover, they have obligated both local and state educational agencies to language-minority education responsibilities. Most significantly, they have offered to language-minority students and their families a forum in which minority status is not disadvantageous. It has been a highly ritualized forum, extremely time- and resource-consuming, and always reluctant. But it has been a responsive institution and will likely continue to be utilized as a mechanism to air and resolve the challenges of educating language minority students.

REFERENCES

Anson R., & Rist, B. (1977). *Education, social science, and the judicial process.* New York: Teachers College Press.

Aspira of New York, Inc. v. Board of Education, 394 F. Supp. 1161 (S.D. N.Y. 1975).

Brooks, R. (1966). The jurisprudence of Willard Hurst. *Journal of Legal Education, 18,* 257–264.

Brown v. Board of Education, 347 U.S. 483 (1954).

Castaneda v. Pickard, 648 F.2d 989, 1007 (1981).

Department of Health Education and Welfare Memorandum Regarding 1964 Civil Rights Act. May 25, 1970.

Equal Educational Opportunities and Transportation of Students Act of 1974, 294(f) .20 U.S.L.

Guadalupe Organization, Inc. v. Tempe Elementary School District, No. 3, 587 F.2d 1022 (1978).

Keyes v. School District No. 1, Denver Colorado, 423 U.S. 1066 (1983).

Keyes v. School District No. 1, 413 U.S. 189.198 (1973).

Keyes v. School District No. 1, Denver, Colorado, 380 F. Supp. 673 (1969).

Kozolchyk, D. (1971). *Legal foundations of U.S. law.* New York: Allyn & Bacon.

Lau v. Nichols, 414 U.S. 563 (1974).

Leibowitz, A. H. (1982). *Federal recognition of the rights of minority language groups.* Roslyn, VA: National Clearinghouse for Bilingual Education.

Otero v. Mesa County School District #51, 568 F.2d 1312 (1977).

Roos, P. (1984, July). *Legal guidelines for bilingual administrators.* Invited address, Society for Research in Child Development, Austin, Texas.

U.S. v. Texas, 680 F.2d 356 (1981).

CHAPTER 3

Development of Bilingualism: Myth and Reality

Barry McLaughlin
University of California, Santa Cruz

When my wife and I decided to raise our children bilingually, I began to study the literature on the effects of a bilingual experience. This process initially made me question the wisdom of my decision. At least one review article (Jensen, 1962) reported an abundance of negative findings regarding the effects of raising children bilingually. The article indicated that research had shown that bilingual children become mentally uncertain and confused because they must often think in one language and speak in another. They do more poorly on tests of intelligence than do monolingual children. Their language development is impaired because they have a smaller vocabulary in a language than do monolingual children. The bilingual child, the article went on, tends to use fewer different words and develops a confused, mixed vocabulary because of lexical borrowings. Syntactic development is also confused, with unusual word orders and errors in agreement and dependency. Bilingual children misuse idiomatic expressions, err in their choice of synonyms, frequently fail to inflect words, and use the negative incorrectly.

Problems in language, however, were only a small part of the problems to be faced. Bilingual children, I read, may become deficient in reading and study skills as well as in specific subjects such as spelling, history, and geography. Interest, initiative, and responsiveness may decline in class, and the child may develop an inadequate adjustment to school and education. These occurrences could result in dropout from school and consequently severely impair the bilingual person's opportunities for employment.

Bilingualism was also thought to have a detrimental effect on emotional adjustment and character formation. It has been argued, for example, that bilinguals may be morally depraved because they have not received effective religious instruction in their mother tongue (Gali, cited in Weinrich, 1953). Similarly, bilinguals have been labeled "mercenary relativists" who switch principles according to the exigencies of the situation, just as they switch languages (Sanders, cited in Weinrich, 1953). Finally, bilingualism was seen as the cause of tension and emotional lability, as well as such psychological disorders as stuttering.

It should be noted, however, that the Jensen article also reviewed research with very different conclusions from the above findings. Indeed, as I studied the literature in more depth, it became obvious that serious flaws marred the earlier studies that cited negative outcomes attributable to bilingualism. My research and reading in this area have convinced me that the previous statements about bilingualism are incorrect. Nonetheless, there remains a great deal of confusion and controversy regarding bilingualism, its effects on the child, and appropriate schooling techniques.

This chapter will discuss several issues that involve serious misconceptions about child bilingualism. These issues include the effects of learning a second language on the proficiency of the first language, semilingualism, language mixing, the length of time involved in learning a second language, and the question whether there is a critical period for language acquisition. Five portraits of bilingual children that exemplify these classic issues and problems in bilingualism and bilingual development will be presented.

EFFECTS OF A SECOND LANGUAGE ON FIRST-LANGUAGE PROFICIENCY

The first portrait is that of one of my own children:

> Christopher, aged 5½ years, had recently returned from nearly 4 years in Germany. He had heard English spoken by his father, but otherwise had been in a mostly German-speaking environment. Christopher's father asked a student to meet with the boy every week at school to record his acquisition of English. After the first session the puzzled student reported that Christopher's English was fine. This report surprised his father, who had never heard him speak English. When asked about his English-speaking ability, Christopher replied (in German), "At school I can speak English, but when I come home I forget."

This example is interesting for a number of reasons. First, it exemplifies the obvious way in which languages can be situationally defined for children. Second, this example also indicates that second-language acquisition can be quite rapid when a child is "passively" bilingual (McLaughlin, 1984), that is, when there has been extensive exposure to a second language before there has been a need to use it actively. The child's ability to understand the language may be better developed than the ability to produce the language. In such cases, acquiring bilingual skills may be a more passive than active process.

This occurrence is not an isolated phenomenon. For example, many Spanish-speaking children in the United States experience English as the language of the larger social environment but have little opportunity to use English before entering school. For these children, a great deal of English has been passively acquired before they entered school; emphasis shifts from use of Spanish as the dominant language prior to their attendance at school to use of English afterwards. Children who acquire a second language passively by exposure and not through active use have

a different bilingual experience than those children who grow up speaking two languages. Passive bilingualism also is a different process than learning a second language after a first language has been established. A child does not learn two languages equally, since there is a strong imbalance in favor of the language in active use. However, the child is not a complete novice in learning the second language, since there already has been considerable exposure to that language.

Children who experience these language shifts upon entering school may appear to be making fairly rapid progress in the second language. Such "progress," however, may be an example of a "linguistic facade" (Cummins, 1979; Skutnabb-Kangas, 1978), where it appears that a child is a rapid language learner because of surface fluency, when in fact there has been insufficient mastery for its effective use in school-related tasks. This issue will be discussed later.

One final point will be made regarding Christopher. It turned out that Chris's English was not as good as our puzzled student thought. Here are some examples of how he spoke at that stage:

> Look this picture what I made.
> My brother goes in school.
> I don't can see him.
> I'm making a house yet.
> Here the back have this but the front not.
> The dragon spit on my face fire.

I was concerned that Christopher's language was in some ways deficient and that he would not develop the verbal range, agility, and fluency that frequently characterize the monolingual speaker. I became anxious when my son at 5½ years said things such as "That don't looks pretty" and wondered if my child would be able to speak any language fluently. I wondered if the "single space" theory, which posits that an individual has room in the brain only for a single language, was correct. I should add that these concerns were not unlike those of such ancient Romans as Quintilian and Cicero, who both expressed the view that learning Greek interfered with young

Romans' development in the Latin language.

Fortunately, my concerns were unfounded and I am now reasonably confident that these types of deficiencies should be the least of parents' worries. Christopher very quickly was indistinguishable from native, monolingual speakers and there is no indication that bilingualism has interfered with his English language skills. Although his German has deteriorated, I am confident that he is passively bilingual and that his German would quickly return if he spent some time in a German-speaking context. It now is my opinion that the venerable Quintilian and Cicero, as well as many parents throughout the ages, vastly underestimate the language-learning abilities of young children.

The experience of many Europeans as well as individuals throughout the world outside of the United States offers additional evidence against the "single space" theory. In particular, the ability of primitive tribes to master a number of different languages of great complexity (Hakuta, 1986) bears eloquent witness to the human's capacity to learn many languages.

THE ISSUE OF SEMILINGUALISM

The next portrait is a more problematic one. It comes from the work of a Scandinavian linguist, Tove Skutnabb-Kangas (1978), with a 5-year-old Finnish child in a Swedish daycare center:

> He couldn't count to more than three in any language, after that he said: many. He didn't know the names of any colors in any language. He didn't know the names of most of the things around him, either at the day care center or outside (I often took him out and downtown for walks) in any language. In Finnish he used only present tense, in Swedish present and past. Instead of the person inflection in Finnish he often used the infinitive form. Finnish has fifteen cases, and usually children master the 11 most common of them, around the age of three. He used only 6 of them, which meant that he for instance was unable to say that something was on something, or that somebody was going to a place or coming from a place. (p. 224)

Skutnabb-Kangas reported that this child's situation was not unique and that there were many similar immigrant children in Swedish-speaking schools, preschool, and daycare centers. She additionally argued that many of the approximately 5 million immigrant children in industrialized Western European countries did "not know any language properly, at the same level as monolingual children. The language tests and estimates show that they often lag up to four years behind their monolingual peers in language tests in both languages" (Skutnabb-Kangas, 1978, p. 229).

According to Skutnabb-Kangas, this child, as well as many others, was "semilingual," that is, he had "a linguistic handicap which prevents the individual from acquiring the linguistic skill appropriate to his original linguistic capacity in any language" (Toukomaa & Skutnabb-Kangas, 1977, p. 20). Certain aspects of linguistic competence are affected by semilingualism and these include the ability to understand the meaning of abstract concepts and synonyms, and the ability to deal with highly decontextualized language (Toukomaa & Skutnabb-Kangas, 1977). Thus, semilingualism is conceptualized as a low level of linguistic competence that impedes continued development in the first language, interferes with development in the second, and promotes cognitive deficiency and low levels of school achievement.

This bilingual experience obviously resulted in a very different outcome from that experienced by my son Christopher. The children Skutnabb-Kangas spoke of were not from middle-class families but generally hovered around the poverty line. Their bilingual experience was not "additive" or enhancing but rather "subtractive" or detrimental (Lambert, 1979). For many immigrant children of lower socioeconomic status (SES), experience with a second language does more harm than good, according to this view; the child becomes semilingual.

This use of the semilingualism concept has been criticized by a number of authors on various grounds. It has been argued that the notion de-emphasizes social factors and expresses a middle-class bias that is insensitive to the sociolinguistic realities of lower-

SES minority-language children (Brent-Palmer, 1979). It implies conformity to norms implicit in standard language use, namely, the language of the school and of academic and social advancement (Stroud, 1978). Additionally, the empirical validity of the research used to ground the term semilingualism has been questioned, and it has been argued that the concept has become a term of opprobrium that has led to discriminatory thinking and behavior towards immigrant children (Ekstrand, 1983).

Actually the notion of semilingualism has existed for some time in various forms. The famous linguist of bilingualism in America, Einar Haugen, wrote in 1969 about Norwegian-Americans:

> Reports are sometimes heard of individuals who "speak no language whatever" and confuse the two to such an extent that it is impossible to tell which language they speak. No such cases have occurred in the writer's experience, in spite of many years of listening to American-Norwegian speech. (Haugen, p. 70)

Many linguists agree with this assessment and would restrict the use of the term *semilingualism* to those cases in which extreme social deprivation causes bilingual children not to function well in either language. Although instances of extreme linguistic and communicative deprivation may lead to the language pathology observed by Skutnabb-Kangas, usually what appears to be semilingualism is only a temporary phase in language development. Thus there may be a developmental period when lack of use of the first language results in a decline in proficiency at the same time that knowledge of the second language has not yet reached an age-appropriate level. This phenomenon was empirically demonstrated by using reaction time measures in a group of German-speaking children learning Swedish (Maegiste, 1979). It was found that as performance on these measures improved in the second language they declined in the first. These results suggest that language balance — in the sense of equivalent native-like proficiency in two languages — may be impossible to obtain in practice, and there may be times during language acquisition when neither language is at native-like levels.

The concept of semilingualism is not a useful way to refer to this development phase, because even though a bilingual child's performance in either language may lag behind that of monolingual speakers of the language at some point in development, the child may actually possess a total vocabulary and total linguistic repertoire quite similar to that of monolingual speakers (Baetens Beardsmore, 1982). Rather, this occurrence may be more appropriately described as a *language imbalance,* where at certain points in the development of their languages bilingual children do not perform as well as native speakers in either language. Although language use and exposure may result in shifts in proficiency between languages, most children acquire age-level proficiency when provided with increased exposure and opportunities for use of the weaker language.

Even in cases in which children appear to be "semilingual," closer examination usually reveals one language to be well developed. Support for this position was provided by a study of first-grade Corpus Christi (Texas) Spanish–English bilingual children (Gonzalez, 1975) that found that children whose language initially appeared to be an unintelligible mixture of English and Spanish were able to perform all syntactic tasks in Spanish ranging from the most elementary to the most complex. Their syntactic patterns resembled those of normal adult Spanish speakers. Gonzalez concluded:

> This information should serve to effectively dispel the educationally dangerous myth that Mexican American children have no grammar and speak a supposedly corrupt mixture of Spanish and English called "Tex Mex." Our study provides emphatic proof that the Mexican American child follows a quite consistent upward growth in his acquisition of Spanish grammar, and that the grammar he acquires is probably as purely Spanish as that found anywhere in the Spanish-speaking world. (p. 236)

In a study of 6-year-old first-grade Spanish-speaking children living in poverty on the west side of San Antonio (Pena,

1967), children's Spanish was found to be better developed than at first thought. When presented with an object or situation with which they were familiar, these children were able to respond spontaneously in complete and grammatical constructions. Interestingly, although "the children possessed complete grammatical construction in their language, the noun and verb slots were often filled with words borrowed from English or English words they had Hispanicized" (Pena, 1967, p. 158).

Thus, the evidence suggests that "semilingualism" is the product of extreme language deprivation and is relatively rare. Language imbalance is much more common, even in children who appear to be equally fluent in both languages. One reflection of this state of imbalance is language mixing.

THE ISSUE OF LANGUAGE MIXING

One of the arguments against bilingualism is based on the notion that bilingual children confuse their two languages. The child's speech appears to be a hodgepodge of constructions and vocabulary items, some drawn from one language and some from the other. The next portrait samples the speech of some Hispanic children:

> Stay here, Roli. Te quedas aqui.
> Este Ernesto, he's cheating.
> I'm going to el wedding.
> Es muy friendly.
> We were chopeando.

This speech pattern has been somewhat facetiously described as "an unpredictable scattering of Spanish words and phrases used throughout an English conversation" (Chacon, 1969, p. 34). It has parallels in the literature on bilingual children. Here are some examples from the speech of the famous Hildegard, the daughter of Werner Leopold, whose four-volume work on his child's bilingualism (1939, 1947, 1949a, 1949b) remains one of the most important sources in the field. Hildegard spoke English with her mother and German with her father.

> Die Milch pouren (Pour the milk).

> Musik practicen (Practice music).
> Ich habe geyawnt (I yawned).
> For two monthe (For two months).

It has been argued that language mixing is an inevitable consequence of bilingual development. Estimates of the degree to which bilingual children mix language vary: Whereas rates as high as 20% and 34% were reported by Vihman (1982) and Redlinger and Park (1980), much lower rates (2–4%) have also been reported (Lindholm & Padilla, 1978; Swain, 1974).

Reported rates of mixing are difficult to interpret because of several factors (Genesee, 1987). Primary is the fact that bilingual children are differentially exposed to language qualitatively and quantitatively. Even though it is possible that one child may experience two languages in almost equal amounts and quality, it is more likely that most children's language exposure will be highly variant in terms of grammatical constructions as well as in enrichment and elaboration experiences. Some children may engage in language mixing more naturally because adult bilinguals in their environment also mix languages regularly.

Additional problems involved in interpreting rates of language mixing are technical problems in research methodology. For example, adequately sampling a child's use of language is problematic (Genesee, 1987); these issues, which rarely are treated uniformly across research studies, are related to the length of time that language is sampled as well as the conditions under which sampling occurs. Similarly, studies have varied in their operational definitions of language mixing. Finally, there is no acceptable metric of language development with which to compare children's language skills.

Thus, it has not been established definitively whether language mixing occurs naturally at certain ages, if it is a phase of language development, or if it exists to create a social bond. Some evidence suggests that all of these factors may occur to some extent. For example, in a study of the language development of Mexican-American children (McClure, 1977), young bilinguals were found to *code-*

mix more than older bilinguals, that is, to insert single items from one language into the sentence structure of another:

I put the *tenedores* on the table.
I want a motorcycle *verde*.

Such instances of mixes usually involve nouns and, to a lesser degree, adjectives, and — (in contrast to the above examples) they generally involve inserting an English word into a Spanish utterance. In the McClure study, children over the age of 9 used a different strategy; they tended to *code-switch*, or change languages for a phrase or a sentence, as much as they code-mixed. Age differences were also noted in the purpose of switching languages: Whereas younger children switched languages to resolve ambiguities and clarify statements, older children switched to convey social meanings. For older speakers, code switching appears to be a rhetorical strategy used in communicative tasks such as persuading, explaining, requesting, and controlling. It is preferred to other rhetorical devices because it has greater semantic power, which is derived from metaphorical allusion to shared values and to the bilinguals' common problems vis-à-vis the society at large (Penalosa, 1980).

It has been observed (Ervin-Tripp, 1967) that bilinguals who interact primarily with other bilinguals have as their language model not the monolingual version of those languages but rather the languages spoken by the bilinguals themselves. In these situations, the mixed speech becomes a code of its own, or a "contact language" (Haugen, 1969), and it is used in a bilingual setting whenever speakers wish to express in-group behavior or emphasize informality or rapport.

Such mixing has occurred in most languages and cultures. The mixing of Spanish expressions in English and English expressions in Spanish is a speech style common in many Hispanic communities, especially in the Southwest. Similarly, it is not unusual for U.S. Jews to use Yiddish expressions and Italian-Americans certain Italian expressions to mark in-group identity.

Educators must be aware that such code switching is not a sign of linguistic confusion but rather of linguistic vitality. Studies of code switching in adults show it to be a sophisticated, rule-governed communicative device used by linguistically competent bilinguals to achieve a variety of communicative goals, such as conveying emphasis, role-playing, or establishing sociocultural identity (Genesee, 1987; Grosjean, 1982).

In sum, there is little evidence of negative effects from a bilingual experience on children's language development. There may be periods of imbalance due to lack of exposure, and children may adopt a strategy of mixing languages as a way of emphasizing social identity. But the notion that bilingualism interferes with normal language development is a myth.

HOW LONG DOES IT TAKE TO LEARN A SECOND LANGUAGE?

The next portrait describes a Mexican child who learns English in a U.S. classroom:

Ruben is 11 years old. His family moved to the United States from Mexico when he was 7. He knew no English when he entered his first U.S. classroom. He was put in a bilingual class where part of the instruction he received was in Spanish. In 2 years he became fluent in English and is almost indistinguishable from his native English-speaking classmates. But school is difficult for him. He does poorly in reading and writing. The other students laugh at his spelling. Ruben does not enjoy school and plans to drop out as soon as he is old enough to get a job.

Research indicates that it takes about a year for the preschool child to acquire a second language in a naturalistic context. Older children have more to learn since, for example, a 9-year-old child has a considerably larger vocabulary than a 5-year-old, and so fluency is harder to achieve. There is general agreement that approximately 2 years is required for school-age children to communicate fluently in a second language with their peers (McLaughlin, 1985).

This fluency, however, involves person-to-person communication, and is referred to as context-embedded communicative skill (Cummins, 1981). In a school environment, such fluency is not sufficient. The skills that are needed for literacy are known as context-reduced communicative skills and it is important that the child be proficient in these aspects of language to succeed in school.

English proficiency is a confusing concept for many educators, who often use performance on a language assessment instrument to decide if children are ready to leave bilingual programs for English-only classes. Unfortunately, many of these language assessment measures tap only context-embedded skills, or the ability to communicate fluently on a one-to-one basis. Such ability does not mean that the child who is able to communicate effectively in such a situation is ready for the all-English classroom, which demands linguistic proficiency in more abstract and context-disembedded communication. Indeed, the results of a study of 1,210 immigrant children in Canada (Cummins, 1981) indicated that approximately 5–7 years is required to master the context-reduced cognitive skills needed for the regular English curriculum, compared to only 2 years for mastery of the context-embedded, or person-to-person, aspects of English proficiency.

Several other studies have examined the time involved for school-age children to learn a second language. The first study compared Navajo children exposed to monolingual English instruction with an ESL component with Navajo children in a bilingual program that first taught reading in the native language and later transferred to English (Rosier, 1977). Although children in the bilingual program initially performed more poorly on tests of English language ability, this group eventually surpassed the children in the ESL condition. It should be noted that these effects were gradual and were not apparent until 3–4 years of bilingual instruction had taken place.

Similar conclusions were reached by Wong-Fillmore (1982, 1985), who found that although minority-language children generally acquired oral communication skills in the second language within 2–3 years, much more time was needed to attain the proficiency needed to understand the language for instructional use. Typical learners were reported to take as many as 4–6 years to acquire the language skills critical for school success.

Finally, Collier (1987) analyzed the length of time required for proficiency to develop in cognitive-academic English for a sample of 1,548 minority-language children who had received part-time ESL instruction. The results of this study indicated that, as measured by standardized tests, at least 4 years and possibly as many as 8 years or more were needed for the most advantaged students with limited English proficiency (LEP) to acquire full learning proficiency in English at the level of native speakers. Collier argued that all children who are non-native-English-speakers would profit from a minimum of 2 years of continuing cognitive-academic development in their native languages.

One reason for the need for continuing support in the first language relates to reading. There is general agreement that three developmentally sequenced tasks must be mastered to become a fluent reader. The child must first master the rules governing symbol–sound correspondence in English. Second, the child has to use those rules in learning words and progressively refine and automate word-decoding operations. Finally the child must build on the automated decoding skills to acquire and perfect a complex set of processing skills that allows for rapid processing of incoming material and the extraction of meaning.

Extracting meaning from the printed page assumes that words are decoded quickly enough to allow space in working memory to retain their meanings (LaBerge & Samuels, 1974; Perfetti & Hogaboam, 1975). Hence, poor readers may be hampered in the third task if they are unable to automatically decode words or match symbols to sounds.

Children who learn to read in a second language may have more problems than monolingual children because they lack familiarity with the semantic and syntactic characteristics of the target language. If children cannot spontaneously identify and use syntactic relations and are not flexible in their use of semantic context as a guide to prediction, their reading comprehension and speed decline (Carr, 1981). This is a special problem for older learners, who generally have had less time to learn the second language yet have more content to learn. As a result, it is likely that even if their person-to-person language skills are adequate, these older students will be frustrated in reading, writing, and in academic content areas because they do not have sufficient grasp of the language.

IS THERE A CRITICAL PERIOD FOR SECOND-LANGUAGE ACQUISITION?

The final issue to be discussed in this chapter can be exemplified by comparing two rather typical bilingual learners.

> Mario is 12. His family is Italian, but they have lived in Sweden since before Mario's birth. Mario speaks both Italian and Swedish fluently and does well in school. He is the best soccer player in his class and is very popular. Mario plans to go to the university and study architecture.
>
> Georgio is 19. He came to Germany on his own from Italy 2 years ago and works in a large automobile factory. He lives in a factory dormitory with other Italian workers. His German has "fossilized" at a very rudimentary stage of development. Linguistically, his second language could be characterized as a pidginized version of German, with few inflections and simplified syntax and vocabulary.

There is no question that many children raised bilingually are able, like Mario, to achieve linguistic competence in both languages. There is also no question that many late second-language learners, like Georgio, fossilize in their development and do not achieve native-like competence in the second language. For a long time, it was commonly believed that young children were superior to older children and adults in second-language learning. The notion was that there was a "critical period" for second-language learning, and that older children and adults, having passed the critical period, were not able to learn second languages as easily or as quickly as younger children. However, direct comparisons made between adult and adolescent second-language learners and child second-

language learners indicate that adult and adolescent learners performed better on measures of morphology and syntax than did child learners (McLaughlin, 1984). Children, on the other hand, typically — but not always — showed superiority in learning phonology.

Although adults acquire the morphology and syntax of a second language faster than young children, some researchers believe that child learners will ultimately attain higher proficiency levels (Krashen, Long, & Scarella, 1979). This younger-is-better position holds that as a general rule child second-language learners will be superior to adolescents and adults in their ultimate achievement. It should be noted, however, that much of the research cited in support of this position indicates that ultimate language proficiency in morphology and syntax is highest among learners who have begun acquisition during early adolescence — the ages of 12–15.

Furthermore, additional research with school children learning second languages contradicts the younger-is-better hypothesis. In the largest single study of children learning a second language in school, 17,000 British children learning French were compared on the basis of when their second language instruction began (Stern, Burstall, & Harley, 1975). After 5 years of exposure, children who had begun instruction at 11 years were found to be more successful language learners than children who had begun at 9 years. This study suggests that, given equivalent exposure to a second language, older children will learn that language better than younger ones. Similar findings have resulted from a number of other studies in Europe; these studies appear to validate the practice in Europe of delaying second-language instruction until the fourth or fifth grade (cf. McLaughlin, 1985).

One possible reason for these findings is the type of instructional techniques used in language instruction. In much European second-language instruction, heavy emphasis is placed on formal grammatical analysis, and it may be that older children are more skilled in dealing with such an instructional approach. This argument is contradicted, however, by the findings from Canadian immersion programs, which place little emphasis on the formal aspects of grammar. Canadian studies indicate that children in late-immersion programs (in which the second language is introduced in Grades 7 or 8) perform just as well on tests of second-language proficiency as children who begin their immersion experience at kindergarten or grade one (Genesee, 1987).

Although not all research indicates that late-immersion students do as well as early-immersion students (McLaughlin, 1985), differences in performance are by no means as great as the relative amount of classroom exposure would lead one to expect. It appears that older children, because of better-developed cognitive strategies, may do better than younger children at the task of learning a second language in school (Wong-Fillmore, 1982).

The question of the optimal age to begin second-language instruction remains a topic of considerable debate. It is important to note that research on this issue involves the comparison of age groups in which other variables (such as amount of exposure and opportunities for use) are controlled. In practice, however, it is most important to maximize exposure and opportunities for use. This implies that a child should start learning a second language as early as possible. Younger children have more time at their disposal and no variable is as important as time on task.

CONCLUSION

Empirical evidence has shown that, among other common misconceptions of bilingualism and bilingual language development, the belief that introducing a second language hurts the child's development in the first language is mistaken, as are other versions of the "single space" theory. In addition, two related notions also have been found to be without support: the notion that bilingual children will end up either semilingual or confused in their language development. Although there may be developmental periods of language imbalance, bilingual children are able to master two languages when there is adequate exposure and opportunities for use. Instances of language mixing generally are short-

lived. When language mixing persists, it typically takes the form of code-switching a deliberate language style.

Studies have also demonstrated that because of the distinction between language that is embedded in context and language that is decontextualized, mastering a second language in the classroom takes longer than most people realize. Children who appear to have learned the second language quickly in school may be skilled in interpersonal, embedded language use but may experience frustration and failure when they must deal with decontextualized language. Contrary to popular belief, young children do not acquire languages especially easily. Evidence suggests that older children learn syntactic and semantic aspects of a new language faster than younger children. It should be noted, however, that these aspects reflect language embedded in context. Decontextualized language (the language of school) may present difficulties even for older children and adolescents, and bilingual children may require the support of their first language for a longer period of time than is usually afforded them.

Given the changing demographics of our country, bilingualism will continue to be a topic of national interest. It is critical for educators and the general public to be correctly informed abut the nature of bilingualism and bilingual language development and for popular myths to be dispelled.

In the United States there has been much discussion regarding the importance of foreign language education in our schools. In 1980, for example, the Report of the President's Commission on Foreign Languages and International Studies emphasized the need for teaching foreign language in the nation's elementary schools. The Commission argued that as a signatory of the Helsinki Accords, the United States has the obligation "to encourage the study of foreign language and civilization as an important means of expanding communication among peoples."

This position is reminiscent of the enthusiasm for modern languages that occurred during the Sputnik era along with the sense at that time that U.S. education was inferior to that of the Soviet Union. In the 1960s, through the National Defense Education Act of 1958, over a million children received foreign-language instruction in the United States. The present emphasis on second-language learning is largely based on economic considerations: In order for this country to compete for world markets there is a great need for persons who can speak the languages of our trade partners. Like the earlier movement, current emphasis is focused on foreign language instruction for native English speakers. However, the Commission noted another rich source of bilingual speakers:

> The United States is blessed with a largely untapped resource of talent in the form of racial and ethnic minorities who, by being brought into the mainstream of educational and employment opportunities in the areas of foreign language and international studies, can be expected to make rapid, new, and valuable contributions to America's capacity to deal persuasively and effectively with the world outside its borders. (1980, p. 24)

Educational programs that do not attempt to maintain the child's first language deprive many children of economic opportunities they would otherwise have as bilinguals. This is especially true of children who speak world languages used for international communication such as Spanish, Japanese, Chinese, and the like. If these children's first languages are not maintained, one of this country's most valuable natural resources will be wasted.

REFERENCES

Baetens Beardsmore, H. (1982). *Bilingualism: Basic principles.* Clevedon, England: Tieto.

Brent-Palmer, C. (1979). A sociolinguistic assessment of the notion of "immigrant semilingualism"; from a social conflict perspective. *Working Papers in Bilingualism, 17,* 135–180.

Carr, T. (1981). Building theories of reading ability: On the relation between individual differences in cognitive skills and reading. *Cognition, 9,* 73–114.

Chacon, E. (1969). Pochismos. *El Grito, 3,* 34–35.

Collier, V. (1987). Age and rate of acquisition of second language for academic purposes. *TESOL Quarterly, 21,* 617–641.

Cummins, J. (1979). Linguistic interdependence and the educational development of bilingual children. *Review of Educational Research, 49,* 222–251.

Cummins, J. (1981). *Bilingualism and minority language children.* Toronto: The Ontario Institute for Studies in Education.

Ekstrand, H. (1983). Maintenance or transition — or both? A review of Swedish ideologies and empirical research. In T. Husen & S. Opper (Eds.), *Multicultural and multilingual education in immigrant countries* (pp. 141–159). London: Pergamon.

Ervin-Tripp, S. (1967). An Issei learns English. *Journal of Social Issues, 23,* 78–90.

Genesee, F. (1987). *Bilingual development: A critical review.* Unpublished manuscript, McGill University.

Gonzalez, G. (1975). The acquisition of grammatical structures by Mexican American children. In E. Hernandez-Chavez, A. D. Cohen, & A. F. Beltramo (Eds.), *El lenguaje de los chicanos: Regional and social characteristics of language used by Mexican-Americans* (pp. 220–237). Arlington, VA: Center for Applied Linguistics.

Grosjean, F. (1982). *Life with two languages: An introduction to bilingualism.* Cambridge, MA: Harvard University Press.

Hakuta, K. (1986). *The mirror of language: The debate on bilingualism.* New York: Basic Books.

Haugen, E. (1969). *The Norwegian language in America: The bilingual community* (Vol. 2). Philadelphia: University of Pennsylvania Press.

Jensen, J. V. (1962). The effects of childhood bilingualism. *Elementary English, 39,* 132–143, 358–366.

Krashen, S., Long, M., & Scarella, R. (1979). Age, rate, and eventual attainment in second language acquisition. *TESOL Quarterly, 3,* 573–582.

LaBerge, D., & Samuels, S. J. (1974). Towards a theory of automatic information processing in reading. *Cognitive Psychology, 6,* 293–323.

Lambert, W. E. (1979). *A Canadian experiment in the development of bilingual competence: The home-to-school language switch program.* Mimeo, McGill University, Psychology Department.

Leopold, W. F. (1939, 1947, 1949a, 1949b). *Speech development of a bilingual child: A linguist's record. Vocabulary growth in the first two years* (Vol. 1); *Sound learning in the first two years* (Vol. 2); *Grammer and general problems in the first two years* (Vol. 3); *Diary from age two* (Vol. 4). Evanston, IL: Northwestern University Press.

Lindholm, K. J., & Padilla, A. M. (1978). Language mixing in bilingual children. *Journal of Child Language, 5,* 327–335.

Maegiste, E. (1979). The competing language systems of the multilingual: A developmental study of decoding and encoding processes. *Journal of Verbal Learning and Verbal Behavior, 18,* 79–89.

McClure, E. F. (1977). *Aspects of code-switching in the discourse of bilingual Mexican American children* (Technical Report No. 44). Cambridge, MA: Berancek and Newman.

McLaughlin, B. (1984). *Second-language acquisition in childhood. Vol. 1: Preschool Children.* Hillsdale, NJ: Erlbaum.

McLaughlin, B. (1985). *Second-language acquisition in childhood. Vol. 2: School-age Children.* Hillsdale, NJ: Erlbaum.

Pena, A. A. (1967). *A comparative study of selected syntactic structures of the oral language status in Spanish and English of disadvantaged first grade Spanish-speaking children.* Doctoral Dissertation, University of Texas at Austin.

Penalosa, F. (1980). *Chicano sociolinguistics: A brief introduction.* Rowley, MA: Newbury House.

Perfetti, C. A., & Hogaboam, T. W. (1975). The relationship between single word decoding and reading comprehension skill. *Journal of Educational Psychology, 67,* 461–469.

President's Commission on Foreign Languages and International Studies. (1980). *Strength through wisdom: A critique of U.S. capability.* Washington, DC: U.S. Government Printing Office.

Redlinger, W. E., & Park, T. (1980). Language mixing in young bilinguals. *Journal of Child Language, 7,* 337–352.

Rosier, P. (1977). *A comparative study of two approaches of introducing initial reading to Navajo children: The direct method and the native language method.* Doctoral Dissertation, Northern Arizona University.

Skutnabb-Kangas, T. (1978). Semilingualism and the education of migrant children as a means of reproducing the caste of assemble line workers. In N. Ditmar, H. Haberland, T. Skutnabb-Kangas, & U. Teleman (Eds.), *Papers from the First Scandinavian–German symposium on the language of immigrant workers and their children.* Roskilde, Denmark: Roskilde University Rolig.

Stern, H. H., Burstall, C., & Harley, B. (1975). *French from age eight or eleven?* Toronto: Ontario Institute for Studies in Education.

Stroud, C. (1978). The concept of semilingualism. *Working Papers, 6,* 153-172.

Swain, M. (1974). Child bilingual language learning and linguistic interdependence. In S. Carey (Ed.), *Bilingualism, biculturalism and education: Proceedings from the Conference of College Universitaire St. Jean, the University of Alberta.* Edmonton: University of Alberta Press.

Toukomaa, P., & Skutnabb-Kangas, T. (1977). *The intensive teaching of the mother tongue to migrant children at preschool age.* University of Tampere. UNESCO. Uutkimusia Research Reports, Sweden.

Vihman, M. (1982). The acquisition of morphology by a bilingual child: The whole-word approach. *Applied Psycholinguistics, 3,* 141–160.

Vihman, M., & McLaughlin, B. (1982). Bilingualism and second-language acquisition in preschool children. In C. J. Brainerd & M. Pressley (Eds.), *Progress of cognitive development research: Verbal processes in children* (pp. 35–58). Berlin: Springer.

Weinrich, W. (1953). *Languages in contact.* The Hague: Mouton.

Wong-Fillmore, L. (1982). *The development of second-language literacy skills.* Statement to the National Commission on Excellence in Education, Houston, Texas.

Wong-Fillmore, L. (1985). Second language learning in children: A proposed model. In R. Eshch & J. Provinzano (Eds.), *Issues in English language development.* Rosslyn, VA: National Clearinghouse for Bilingual Education.

CHAPTER 4

Bilingual Immersion Education: Educational Equity for Language Minority Students

Kathryn J. Lindholm
San José State University

The dynamics of population change indicate that the United States is becoming an increasingly multiethnic and multilingual society, rather than an ethnically and linguistically more homogeneous one. The major factors contributing to this change include sizable immigration and the fact that the average age of ethnic minorities is about 5 years less than the national average. This means that a larger percentage of ethnic minorities are in or entering the most active childbearing years (Cortes, 1986). According to data from the Census Bureau, between 1970 and 1980, the United States population increased by 11.6%. However, the black population grew by 17.8%, Hispanics by 61%, Native Americans by 71%, and Asian Americans by 233%, and remaining Americans by only 7 to 8%. Schools have, and will have, therefore, a major challenge in dealing with the large number of students of limited English proficiency who are in need of special services. It has been estimated that currently at least 3.4 million children are limited in the English language skills needed to succeed in school programs designed for native English speakers.

Nationally, the academic performance of minority students is considerably below majority norms, and the gap grows wider with each school year (Kagan & Zahn, 1975). Reading is critical to student achievement in all subjects, yet the achievement gap is greatest in reading. By the eighth grade 39.9% of Mexican American children are two or more years behind in reading compared to 12.8% of Anglos (Carter & Segura, 1979). As society moves further into the technological age of computers, with jobs requiring literacy- and computer-based skills, low educational attainment will be even more detrimental. Further, Alatorre Alva and Padilla (1988) point out that children with early delays in their academic attainment are at a higher risk of never completing high school. For example, 77% of whites, 76% of Asians, 69% of blacks, 66% of Native Americans, and only 44% of Hispanics graduated from high school in 1980. In addition, although Asian Americans have succeeded in education, they have, paradoxically, over four times the proportion of persons failing to have any education whatsoever, compared to whites (Sue & Padilla, 1986). These findings show that "the United States public school system is failing with regard to the achievement of minority children" (Kagan, 1986, p. 223).

The public education system in general is not meeting the educational needs of many language-majority students either: About 20% of all U.S. 17-year-olds are functionally illiterate, unable to comprehend simple written instructions (Lerner, 1981); nearly half of our graduating high school students do not know the basics of how our government works (Johnson, Johnson, & Tiffany, 1984); and "Americans' incompetence in foreign language is nothing short of scandalous and is becoming worse" (President's Commission on Foreign Language and International Studies, 1979). At the same time, the great national language resource represented by immigrant and native non-English-background groups is being rapidly eroded, as second and third generations are not learning their natal languages (Campbell & Lindholm, 1987).

Special educational programs to promote educational equity for language-minority students have caused tremendous controversy among educators, lawmakers, and the general public. Bilingual education programs grew out of the civil rights movement of the 1960s, which raised a call for a system of education in which the language-minority student would receive a better and more relevant education. Bilingual education was to provide a situation in which the student's native language and culture would be valued; students would be able to develop a positive self-image, opportunities for academic success would be enhanced, and solidarity with the community would be strengthened (Hernandez-Chavez, 1984). After a decade and a half of bilingual education, the controversy has grown rather than diminished. Research studies have been inadequately designed to provide educators and policy makers with information about the effectiveness of bilingual education, and thus they have fueled rather than cooled the fires of controversy. A carefully conducted analysis of the bilingual education research (Willig, 1985) demonstrated that bilingual education programs can be successful in improving the academic performance in students of limited English proficiency. Unfortunately, bilingual education has not been as effective in its implementation as it could have been if there had been policies defining the implementation of bilingual education, teacher training, and qualified bilingual teachers that were designed to promote educational achievement rather than merely the learning of English. The tragedy of many Native American groups who have lost their native language without gaining any educational advantage is stark evidence that learning English is neither a necessary nor a sufficient condition for enhanced educational achievement.

For a variety of sociopolitical, economic, and pedagogical reasons, many educators have supported short-term "quick fix" solutions that move students with limited English proficiency into mainstream English-only (EO) classes as quickly as possible. Monolingual English immersion education is being increasingly cited as a possible alternative to bilingual education. Immersion programs originally designed to teach language-majority students a second language, use the second language as the medium of instruction for subject matter classes. However, the term *immersion* is often used, incorrectly, with reference to language-minority students. Although the model seems successful for language-majority children, its appropriateness for language-minority children has been strongly called into question by most knowledgeable researchers. A submersion program applies to a curriculum designed for and populated by native English speakers, but is inappropriate to use with non-English-speaking students. A considerable amount of research evidence documents the failure of submersion approaches to meet the educational needs of minority-language students (California State Department of Education, 1982; National Assessment for Educational Progress, 1982). Many educators who are aware of this research readily reject submersion as an appropriate educational treatment for language-minority students. Most educators agree that an educational program designed for students limited in English proficiency must foster dual language development, and assure educational equity as a means to academic achievement and psychosocial development.

This chapter will briefly present issues of educational equity for language-minority students and will present and discuss an education model that can meet the educational equity needs of language minority children.

WHAT GOES INTO EDUCATIONAL EQUITY FOR LANGUAGE-MINORITY STUDENTS?

There are four major school achievement goals that are necessary to enhance the educational opportunities of language-minority students. These goals require promotion of (a) high levels of academic achievement, (b) acquisition of English for both communicative and academic purposes, (c) development of the native language for academic purposes, and (d) positive psychosocial development (e.g., high self-esteem, ethnic identity). A critical educational issue is to determine how to best promote these goals. For years, research on school achievement-related issues among ethnic minority populations has been concerned with examining the level of achievement and school retention among ethnic minority students, and with examining univariate relationships between their school achievement and variables such as language use, family practices and values, generation and acculturation levels, cognitive styles, and socioeconomic factors (Alatorre Alva & Padilla, 1988).

Cortes (1986) and Alatorre Alva and Padilla (1988) have clearly articulated the need for multivariate frameworks that assume that several factors interact to produce school achievement. According to this perspective, "in order to better understand and improve the schooling experience of Mexican American and other linguistic minority children, one must take into account the interactive relationship that exists between the child's sociocultural background and the educational structure and climate of the schooling process" (Alatorre Alva & Padilla, 1988, pp. 16–17). Figure 1 illustrates a multivariate contextual interaction model depicting the relationship between home background characteristics, educational input, instructional elements, and student characteristics in explaining school achievement. As Figure 1 shows, home background characteristics, such as socioeconomic status, parental educational level, and parental sociocultural values and attitudes influence the school context factors of educational input, instructional elements, and student characteristics. Educational input includes the theoretical rationale underlying the education program, as well as the staff and administrative knowledge and support of the program. Instructional elements include the specific goals of the education program, the curriculum design, staff development, the type of teacher–student interactions, classroom composition, ratio of the use of English to that of the non-English language, the characteristics of the language the teacher uses with the students, and the types of grouping arrangements in the classroom. Finally, student characteristics involve language proficiency, academic/readiness skills, and psychosocial development involving perceived competence, motivation, and attitudes. Educational input and instructional characteristics interact with each other and instructional characteristics and student characteristics interact with each other to produce the school achievement outcomes.

The important point of this complicated multivariate model is that it is not enough to say that educational equity involves promoting student achievement. Educational equity necessitates incorporating into the educational model many important factors that influence achievement. As Cortes (1986) noted with respect to the contextual interaction model:

> [this model] illustrates the complex and dynamic nature of the . . . interaction between schools and society, as well as the multiplicity of factors that influence students, including their school achievement. Moreover, it demonstrates the need to examine both societal and school context in analyzing students' achievement and in suggesting educational change to increase that achievement. In short, the Contextual Interaction Model provides a means of visualizing the total educational process for purposes of analysis. (p. 21)

Thus, education equity involves promoting education programs that can meet the academic and language needs of language-minority children by actively attending to the home background, educational input, instructional elements, and student characteristic factors that influence school achievement.

BILINGUAL IMMERSION EDUCATION

The educational model to be presented here, which meets the criteria discussed above for promoting school achievement through an incorporation of the various home and school factors that influence academic achievement, has various names, the most common being *bilingual immersion* or *two-way bilingual education*. The

FIGURE 1

Contextual interaction model for explaining school performance

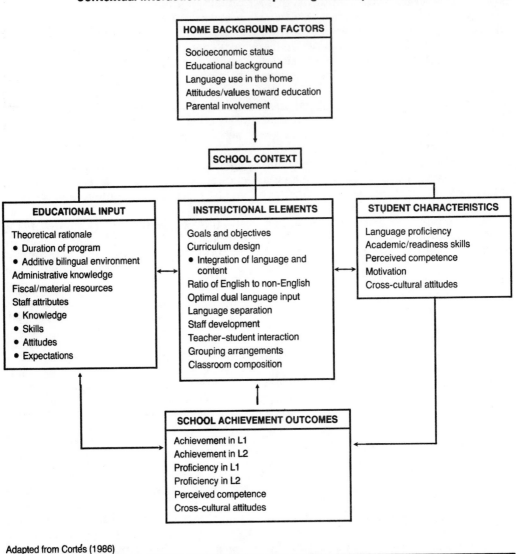

Adapted from Cortés (1986)

bilingual immersion model will be defined and then discussed with respect to the criteria upon which it is based.

Definition of Bilingual Immersion Education

Bilingual immersion education combines the most significant features of bilingual education for language-minority students and immersion education for language-majority students. Academic and language arts instruction is provided to students who are native speakers of two different languages, during which both languages are used; one of the languages is a second language for each group of students. Thus, for language-minority (i.e., non-English-speaking) students, most academic instruction is presented through their first language, but they receive English language arts and, depending on the particular program, portions of their academic instruction in English. For language-majority (i.e., English-speaking) students, most academic instruction is through their second language, but they receive English language arts and, depending on the program design, some portion of their academic instruction in English. The definition encompasses four criterial features: (a) The program essentially involves some form of dual language immersion, which entails use of the non-English language for at least 50% of the students' instructional day; (b) the program involves periods of instruction during which only one language is used; (c) both English-speakers and non-English-speakers (preferably in balanced numbers) are participants; and (d) the students are integrated for all content instruction. Although program designs may vary, most have as part of their goals the development of true bilingual academic competence in English and another language on the part of both groups of participating students.

Critical Features of Successful Language Education Programs

Over the last several years, a number of comprehensive reviews have been conducted of research and evaluation studies concerning bilingual and immersion education (Baker & de Kanter, 1981; Cummins, 1979, 1983; Diaz, 1983; Dolson, 1985; Fisher & Guthrie, 1983; Swain & Lapkin, 1985; Troike, 1978, 1986; Willig, 1985). An examination of these educational investigations points to certain sociolinguistic and instructional factors that tend to contribute to successful dual language programs. The importance of these factors is evident from the frequency and consistency with which they are found in programs that promote high levels of first- and second-language competencies, academic achievement in both languages, and high self-esteem and positive cross-cultural attitudes. Thus, these factors form the core criteria for successful bilingual immersion education.

The first 10 criteria discussed below are essential for successful language education programs. In contrast, the last three criteria apply to educational programs in general; they are mentioned here because they are important elements in an effective program, yet their presence cannot be assumed, but rather must be carefully considered in designing and implementing a successful bilingual immersion program.

Duration of instructional treatment. The instructional treatment is provided to the participating students for a period of *at least* 4–6 years. This is the amount of time required, on average, to reach second-language, or bilingual, proficiency, but not necessarily native-like proficiency, as confirmed by a number of evaluation studies on immersion and bilingual programs (Cummins, 1981; Swain, 1984; Troike, 1978). In its review of foreign language programs, the National Commission on Excellence in Education (1983) also concluded that achieving proficiency ordinarily demands from 4–6 years of study.

Exposure to optimal dual language input. Optimal input has four characteristics: (a) It is adjusted to the comprehension level of the learner, (b) it is interesting and relevant, (c) there is sufficient quantity, and (d) it is challenging. This is accomplished through communicatively sensitive language instruction and subject matter presentation. In the early stages of second language acquisition, input is made more comprehensible through the use of slower, more expanded, simplified, and repetitive speech that is oriented to the "here and now" (Krashen, 1981; Long, 1980); highly contextualized language and gestures (Long, 1980; Saville-Troike, 1987); comprehension and confirmation checks (Long, 1980); and structuring of communication so that it provides scaffolding for the negotiation of meaning by second-language students by constraining possible interpretations of sequence, role, and intent (Saville-Troike, 1987). Balanced with the need to make the second language more comprehensible is the necessity for providing stimulating language input (Swain, 1987), particularly for the native speakers of each language. There are two reasons why students need stimulating language input. First, it will facilitate continued development of language structures and skills. Second, when students are instructed in their first language, the content of their lessons becomes more comprehensible when they are then presented with similar content in the second language.

Focus on academic curriculum. The programs are designed to focus on subject matter as well as language development. Students are exposed to the same academic core curriculum as students in regular programs. For native English-speakers, academic achievement is attained primarily through second-language content instruction and interactions in the second language at home and in the community. Academic achievement is further bolstered by content taught through English. For language-minority students, instruction in and through the native language forms the basis for initial academic advancement. Academic achievement and English language proficiency are further developed through English language arts and content instruction in English.

Integration of language arts with curriculum. Related to Criteria 2 and 3 is the need to provide language arts instruction in both English and the non-English language and to design the instruction so that it is integrated with the academic curriculum. There has been controversy in the area of second-language education about the importance of language arts instruction in the second language (e.g., Krashen, 1981; Long, 1983; Swain, 1987). Many immersion programs, in fact, neglect language arts in the immersion language, assuming that the students will learn the language through the subject matter instruction and will achieve more native-like proficiency if they receive the kind of language exposure that is similar to first-language learning (Swain, 1987). However, as some immersion researchers have discovered (e.g., Harley, 1984; Swain, 1985; Swain & Lapkin, 1985), the fluency and grammar ability of most immersion students is not native-like, and there is a need for formal instruction in the second language. However, formalized language instruction should not follow the route of traditional translation and memorization of grammar and phrases. It is important to utilize a language arts curriculum that specifies which linguistic structures should be mastered (e.g., conditional verb forms) and how these linguistic structures should be incorporated into the academic content (e.g., including the preterit and imperfect verb forms of the verb *ser* [to be] in history subject matter and the conditional, future, and subjunctive tenses of *ser* in mathematics and science content). The language arts class can then focus on the specific linguistic skills, incorporating the content that was used to introduce the linguistic skill. This integrative and content-based approach reinforces both the content taught during subject matter presentation and the linguistic skill.

Separation of languages for instruction. Monolingual lesson designs (in which different time periods are devoted to instruction in and through each of the two languages separately) seem to be superior to designs that rely on language mixing during a single lesson or time frame (Baker & de Kanter, 1981; Dulay & Burt, 1978; Legaretta, 1979, 1981; Swain, 1983). This is not to say that language mixing itself is harmful; rather, it appears that sustained periods of monolingual instruction in each language help to promote adequate language development.

Additive bilingual environment. All students are provided the opportunity to acquire a second language at no cost to their home language and culture. This enrichment bilingualism results in high levels of proficiency in the two languages (Hernandez-Chavez, 1984; Skuttnabb-Kangas, 1981), with no loss to self esteem and with improved crosscultural attitudes. Conversely, subtractive bilingual contexts, in which the native language is replaced by a second language, seem to have negative effects on the school performance of many minority-language students. Native language loss is often associated with lower levels of second-language attainment, with scholastic underachievmenet, and with psychosocial disorders (Lambert, 1984). Successful language development programs seem not only to prevent the negative consequences of subtractive bilingualism, but also to effectively promote the beneficial aspects of additive bilingualism.

Classroom composition. Little research has been conducted to determine the best classroom composition for bilingual education programs, although the federal government has mandated a ratio of at least one-third English-speakers to two-thirds non- or limited-English-speakers. To maintain an environment of educational and linguistic equity in the classroom and to promote interaction among native and non-native English-speakers, the most desirable ratio is 50% English-speakers to 50% non-native English-speakers. However, the ratio of native to non-native English-speakers should never exceed 33:67 or 67:33, to insure that there are enough language models of each language to promote interaction among the two groups of students.

Ratio of English to the non-English language. Immersion education was designed to promote high levels of second-language proficiency while maintaining first-language proficiency. Although there are several program variations, many immersion programs utilize the non-English language for 100% of the instructional day; English is not used at all for at least the initial stages of the program. Other, partial immersion programs involve equal amounts of English and the non-English language. No research has yet determined the best ratio of English to non-English instruction for both language-minority and -majority students. However, research on programs utilizing different amounts of instruction in the non-English language shows that native English-speaking students with greater exposure to the second language have higher levels of second-language proficiency (Campbell, Gray, Rhodes, & Snow, 1985) and that these students also maintain their English and perform at or above grade level in tests of English achievement (Campbell, 1984; Genessee, 1985). Furthermore, research in bilingual education shows that non-native English-speaking students with greater amounts of instruction in their native language achieve at higher levels than students with lesser amounts of instruction in their native language, at least in the early years of schooling (Willig, 1985). From studies of non-native English-speakers in bilingual programs and native

English-speakers in immersion programs then, it appears that a minimum of 50% non-English-language instruction is necessary to promote high levels of the non-English-language proficiency among language-majority students and to promote academic achievement among language-minority students. Furthermore, although studies have not addressed the minimal level of English necessary, a minimum of 10% English instruction initially is important to promote English language development for the non-native speakers of English. Additionally, to develop a high level of academic English language skills among the language-minority students, the amount of content instruction in English should be about 50% for the late elementary school years (grades 4–6).

Promotion of and opportunities for language output and expression. As noted earlier, immersion students, and foreign language students in general, have difficulty in producing native-like speech in the second language. Part of this difficulty stems from an absence of the opportunity to talk with fluent speakers in the language they are learning. According to Swain (1985, 1987), immersion students get few opportunities to produce extended discourse, where they are forced to make their language coherent, accurate, and sociolinguistically appropriate. Thus, promoting highly proficient oral language skills necessitates providing both structured tasks and unstructured opportunities involving oral skills for students to engage in.

A positive school environment. Research has shown that the success of bilingual education programs is dependent on the level of support the program receives from the school administration (Cortes, 1986; Troike, 1978). Drawing on this research, then, a successful bilingual immersion program must have the support of the principal, other administrators, and nonbilingual immersion staff. This support must be based on a knowledge of the program and be demonstrated, through a desire for the program to succeed by an expenditure of resources that is comparable to that of other educational programs in the school, by devoting attention to promoting acceptance of the program among the community and other school staff, and by closely integrating the structure and function of the bilingual immersion program with the total school program.

Positive and reciprocal instructional climate. Promotion of positive interactions between teachers and students and between language-minority and –majority student peers is an important instructional objective. When teachers use positive social and instructional interactions in equal amounts with both minority and majority students, both groups perform better academically (California State Department of Education, 1982; Kerman, 1979). In addition, teachers should adopt a reciprocal interaction model instead of adhering to the traditional transmission model of teaching (Cummins, 1986). The basic premise of the transmission model is that the teacher's task is to impart knowledge or skills to students who do not yet have these abilities. In the reciprocal interaction approach, teachers participate in genuine dialogue with pupils and facilitate rather than control student learning. This model encourages the development of higher-level cognitive skills rather than just factual recall (Cummins, 1986).

The achievement of language-minority pupils is affected not only by the status perceptions of teachers, but also by the status perceptions of majority peers. Allowing only unplanned or incidental contact between majority and minority students may only reinforce negative expectations. Kagan (1986) and others have proposed ways in which contacts between minority and majority students can be organized so that the achievement of both groups can be maximized. These studies suggest that when minority and majority students work interdependently on school tasks with common objectives, students' expectations and attitudes toward each other become more positive and their academic achievement improves. A number of strategies under the rubric of cooperative learning have been developed that utilize these principles. Furthermore, language development is facilitated by extensive interactions among native and nonnative speakers (Long & Porter, 1985).

High-quality instructional personnel. Students receive their instruction from certified teachers. Over the course of the program, students are exposed to a number of teachers who have native or native-like ability in either or both of the language(s) in which they are instructing. The teachers, although bilingual, may assume monolingual roles when interacting with students. It is important that the teachers be able to understand their students' mother tongue in the initial stages of language learning. Teachers who do not understand the native language cannot respond appropriately in the second language to the children's utterances in their native language. In this case, comprehensible input may be severely impaired (Swain, 1985). Furthermore, teachers should be knowledgeable with regard to the curriculum level and how to teach it.

Home/school collaboration. Another important feature of bilingual immersion education is parental involvement and collaboration with the school. When this occurs, parents often develop a sense of efficacy that communicates itself to children, with positive academic consequences, especially in the case of language-minority children (Met, 1987; Tizard, Schofield, & Hewison, 1982). In fact, most parents of minority students have high aspirations for their children and want to be involved in promoting their academic success (Lindholm, 1987b; Wong Fillmore, 1983). Dramatic changes occur in children's academic progress when parents interact with their children at home in certain ways. Activities such as reading and listening to children read are both feasible and practical and contribute to improved scholastic achievement (Cummins, 1986). Effective programs tend to incorporate a variety of home/school collaboration activities. The general outcome on the part of students is an increased interest in schoolwork and improved achievement and behavior.

In summary, the instructional features and sociolinguistic structures that seem to be strongly associated with the success of immersion programs correspond to the same psycholinguistic and sociopedagogical principles that underlie successful bilingual education and regular education programs in the United States. These elements are (a) duration of instructional treatment of at least 4–6 years; (b) exposure to optimal language input; (c) focus on academic curriculum; (d) integration of language arts with academic curriculum; (e) separation of languages for instruction; (f) additive bilingual environment; (g) classroom composition; (h) appropriate ratio of English to the non-English language; (i) promotion of and opportunities for language output (i.e., oral expression); (j) a positive school environment; (k) positive and reciprocal instructional climate; (l) high-quality instructional personnel; and (m) parental involvement in the educational process.

BILINGUAL IMMERSION EDUCATION AS AN EDUCATIONAL EQUITY MODEL

The contextual interaction model predicts that school achievement is influenced by the interaction of home background and school context factors. The effectiveness of an educational model that incorporates these influential home and school factors can be evaluated within the contextual interaction framework; specifically, the bilingual immersion education model can be evaluated within the contextual interaction framework to determine how it meets the educational equity needs of language-minority students.

School Achievement Outcomes

A major criterion for judging whether bilingual immersion programs advance educational equity is whether they actually promote this goal. To answer this question requires turning to evaluation studies of bilingual immersion programs. As Lindholm (1987a) pointed out, most bilingual immersion programs are very new, having been implemented in only the past few years. Evaluation reports from schools that have implemented bilingual immersion programs for a number of years show that the objectives of high levels of language proficiency in both languages and normal to superior academic achievement are being met. For example, evaluation data from the bilingual immersion program of the City of San Diego schools (Lindholm, 1987a) demonstrated that, overall, the Limited English Proficient (LEP) and English Only (EO) students in bilingual immersion programs outperformed their nonprogram peers in math and reading. LEP students gained higher levels of English language proficiency and achievement than their nonprogram LEP peers while maintaining their Spanish language proficiency and achievement. EO students also outperformed their nonprogram EO peers while maintaining their English language proficiency and gaining Spanish language proficiency. More specifically, the evaluation data revealed the following:

- *Spanish oral language proficiency.* LEP students outperformed their comparison group in all but Grade 1. EO students gained functional Spanish proficiency by Grade 4, exceeding the national norm; their comparison group displayed no significant acquisition of Spanish.

- *English oral language proficiency.* LEP students led their comparison group in all grades except Grade 1, after which the bilingual immersion LEP students achieved higher rankings and attained national norms 1 year prior to the comparison group. EO students outperformed their comparison group at all levels, achieving higher rankings in all grades and making greater gains in Grades 3 and 4.

- *Spanish reading achievement.* The bilingual immersion students performed significantly better, on the average, than comparison students in Spanish reading.

- *English reading achievement.* Program LEP students outperformed nonprogram comparison students at all grade levels, and the LEP students achieved reclassification status 1 year earlier than comparison LEP students. EO students scored higher than comparison EOs, achieving higher rankings at all grade levels.

- *Spanish mathematics.* Program students performed significantly better, on the average, than comparison students in Spanish math. LEP students performed well in mathematics from the beginning and EO students also achieved above-average scores.

- *English mathematics.* LEP students outperformed their LEP peers in non-program classes. EO students also obtained higher scores than their non-program EO cohorts.

These findings were replicated in a second group of fourth-, fifth-, and sixth-grade bilingual immersion program students.

Similarly, results from a bilingual immersion program in Washington, DC, have shown that the students consistently performed two to three standard deviations above the district norms on the achievement tests (Lindholm, 1987a). With respect to psychosocial adjustment, Lindholm (1987b) found that 112 kindergarten and first-grade children in a Spanish/English bilingual immersion program in Southern California scored as high as or higher than the mean scores reported by Harter and Pike's (1984) sample of middle-class Anglo kindergarten and first-grade children in Denver. Perceived competence has not been measured in children in other bilingual immersion programs, nor have crosscultural attitudes.

Thus, these studies point to the bilingual immersion model as successfully promoting school achievement in language-minority children while simultaneously meeting the schooling and foreign language needs of language-majority children.

School Context Factors

Educational input factors. As Figure 1 shows, educational input factors are defined here as the theoretical rationale underlying the education program, and the staff and administrative knowledge and support of the program. Troike (1978), among others, has been instrumental in showing the importance of administrative and staff support in a successful bilingual education program. In the bilingual immersion model, the program is supported by the principal, other administrators, and non-bilingual-immersion staff through a knowledge of the program and an expenditure of resources comparable to other educational programs in the school and by integrating the structure and function of the bilingual immersion program with the total school program.

In addition, the theoretical rationales are based on successful bilingual education for language-minority children and immersion education for language-majority children, both of which have been demonstrated to be successful for the populations they were designed to serve. These rationales include continuing the program for at least 6 years to enable children to master the two languages, and promoting an additive bilingual environment which is associated with high levels of proficiency and self-esteem.

Instructional elements. Instructional elements include the specific goals of the education program, the curriculum design, the type of teacher–student interactions, and the types of grouping arrangements in the class. The bilingual immersion model serves to provide optimal instructional elements that promote high achievement outcomes with (a) goals that specify high levels of academic achievement and bilingual/biliterate proficiency; (b) focus on the normal academic curriculum so that the children do not fall behind in their academic studies; (c) integration of language arts with the academic curriculum to further develop both languages for academic purposes; (d) separation of the two languages for instruction; (e) a classroom composition balanced as to ratio of native English-speakers and non-native English-speakers; (f) a high enough ratio of the use of the non-English language to that of English to support the development of the non-English language in the native and second-language learners of that language while also including enough English to support its development among both groups of speakers; (g) exposure to optimal language input for both language-minority and language-majority children; (h) promotion of and opportunities for oral expression; (i) positive and reciprocal instructional climate; and (j) heterogeneous classroom groupings that enable students to work interdependently in such a way that the achievement of all students is maximized.

Student characteristics. Student characteristics are incorporated into the bilingual immersion model in several different ways. First, there is concern for the psychosocial development of the students through promotion of positive perceived competence and self-esteem and positive attitudes toward the two languages and two (or more) cultures of the classroom. Second, students are motivated to achieve through cooperative learning arrangements that have been demonstrated to be related to high academic achievement.

Home background factors. Home background factors are included in the bilingual immersion model by promoting parental involvement in the educational process. In many bilingual immersion programs, parents are invited to attend workshops to help them learn how to help their children with homework or seminars focusing on language instruction (e.g., Spanish for native English-speaking parents; English for native Spanish-speaking parents).

CONCLUSIONS

Bilingual immersion education is a model that has the potential for promoting educational equity for language-minority children. There is a threefold justification for the optimism of this model in promoting educational equity. First, it is based on the theoretical rationale and pedagogical principals that have sustained and promoted successful models of bilingual education for language-minority students and immersion education for language-majority students. Thus, it is not an alternative to successful bilingual education programs, but a variation of bilingual education. Second, the model is based on, and can be evaluated within a multivariate contextual interaction framework that considers home, school, and student factors in enhancing school performance. Third, and perhaps most importantly, bilingual immersion provides an atmosphere of true

integration and equality in the classroom. That is, both languages and cultures are highly valued; students are grouped heterogeneously, following cooperative learning principles to promote interactions among students, equality in peer groups, and motivation among all students working together on a task; and language-majority students are exposed to language-minority students in an atmosphere in which the language-minority students and their language are held in esteem to promote more positive intergroup relations and attitudes and second-language development. In sum, the bilingual immersion model meets the academic and dual language needs of both language-minority and language-majority students and provides an environment conducive to true integration and educational equity.

REFERENCES

Alatorre Alva, S., & Padilla, A. M. (1988). Factors influencing the academic performance of Mexican American students. Stanford University (unpublished manuscript).

Baker, A. K., & de Kanter, A. (1981). *Effectiveness of bilingual education: A review of the literature.* Washington, DC: U.S. Department of Education, Office of Planning, Budget and Evaluation.

California State Department of Education. (1982). *Basic principles for the education of language minority students, an overview.* Sacramento: Office of Bilingual Bicultural Education.

Campbell, R. N. (1984). The immersion education approach to foreign language teaching. In *Studies on immersion education: A collection for U.S. educators* (pp. 114–143). Sacramento: California State Department of Education.

Campbell, R. N., Gray, T. C., Rhodes, N. C., & Snow, M. A. (1985). Foreign language learning in the elementary schools: A comparison of three language programs. *Modern Language Journal, 69,* 44–54.

Campbell, R. N., & Lindholm, K. J. (1987). *Conservation of language resources* (Educational Report No. 6). Los Angeles: University of California, Center for Language Education and Research.

Carter, T. P., & Segura, R. D. (1979). *Mexican Americans in school.* New York: College Entrance Examination Board.

Cortes, C. E. (1986). The education of language minority students: A contextual interaction model. In Bilingual Education Office (Eds.), *Beyond language: Social and cultural factors in schooling language minority students* (pp. 3–33). Los Angeles,

CA: California State University, Evaluation, Dissemination and Assessment Center.

Cummins, J. (1979). Linguistic interdependence and the educational development of children. *Review of Educational Research, 49,* 222-251.

Cummins, J. (1981). The role of primary language development in promoting educational success for language minority students. In *Schooling and language minority students: A theoretical framework* (pp. 1-50). Los Angeles: California State University, Evaluation, Dissemination, and Assessment Center.

Cummins, J. (1983). *Heritage language education: A literature review.* Toronto: Minister of Education.

Cummins, J. (1986). Empowering minority students: A framework for intervention. *Harvard Educational Review, 50,* 18-36.

Diaz, R. M. (1983). Thought and two languages: The impact of bilingualism on cognitive development. In E. Norbeck, D. Price-Williams, & W. McCord (Eds.), *Review of research in education* (pp. 23-54). Washington, DC: American Educational Research Association.

Dolson, D. (1985). Bilingualism and scholastic performance: The literature revisited. *NABE Journal, 10,* 1-35.

Dulay, H., & Burt, M. (1978). From research to method in bilingual education. In J. Alatis (Ed.), *International dimensions of bilingual education.* Washington, DC: Georgetown University Press.

Fisher, C. W., & Guthrie, L. F. (1983). *Executive summary: Significant bilingual instructional features study.* (Document SBIF-83-R.14). San Francisco: Far West Laboratory for Educational Research and Development.

Genessee, F. (1985). Second language learning through immersion: A review of U.S. programs. *Review of Educational Research, 55,* 541-561.

Harley, B. (1984). How good is their French? *Language and Society, 10,* 55-60.

Harter, S., & Pike R. (1984). The pictorial scale of perceived competence and social acceptance for young children. *Child Development, 55,* 1969-1982.

Hernandez-Chavez, E. (1984). The inadequacy of English immersion as an educational approach for language minority students. In California State Department of Education, (Ed.), *Studies on immersion education: A collection for U.S. educators* (pp. 144-183.) Sacramento.

Johnson, D. W., Johnson, R., & Tiffany, M. (1984). Structuring academic conflicts between majority and minority students: Hindrance or help to integration? *Contemporary Educational Psychology, 9,* 61-73.

Kagan, S. (1986). Cooperative learning and sociocultural factors in schooling. *Beyond language: Social and cultural factors in schooling language minority students* (pp. 231-298).Los Angeles: California State University, Evaluation, Dissemination, and Assessment Center.

Kagan, S., & Zahn, G. L. (1975). Field dependence and the school achievement gap between Anglo and Mexican-American children. *Journal of Educational Psychology, 67,* 643-650.

Kerman, S. (1979). *Teacher expectations and student achievement.* Phi Delta Kappan, (June) 1-6.

Krashen, S. (1981). Bilingual education and second language acquisition. In California State Department of Education, Office of Bilingual Bicultural Education (Eds.), *Schooling and language minority students: A theoretical framework* (pp. 51-70). Los Angeles: California State University, Evaluation, Dissemination, and Assessment Center.

Lambert, W. E. (1984). An overview of issues in immersion education. In California State Department of Education (Ed.), *Studies in immersion education: A collection for U.S. educators* (pp. 8-30). Sacramento.

Legaretta, D. (1979). The effects of program models on language acquisition by Spanish-speaking children. *TESOL Quarterly, 8,* 521-534.

Legaretta, D. (1981). Effective use of the primary language in the classroom. In California State Department of Education, Office of Bilingual Bicultural Education (Eds.), *Schooling and language minority students: A theoretical framework* (pp. 83-116). Los Angeles: California State University, Evaluation, Dissemination, and Assessment Center.

Lerner, B. (1981). The minimum competence testing movement: Social, scientific, and legal implications. *American Psychologist, 27,* 1057-1066.

Lindholm, K. J. (1987a). *Directory of bilingual immersion programs* (Educational Report No. 8). Los Angeles: University of California, Center for Language Education and Research.

Lindholm, K. J. (1987b). *Edison Elementary School bilingual immersion program: Student progress after one year of implementation.* (Technical Report No. 9). Los Angeles: University of California, Center for Language Education and Research.

Long, M. H. (1980). *Input, interaction, and second language acquisition.* Unpublished doctoral dissertation. Los Angeles: University of California.

Long, M. H. (1983). Native speaker/non-native speaker conversation in the second language classroom. In M. Clarke & J. Handscombe (Eds.), *On TESOL 82: Pacific perspectives on language, learning and teaching* (pp. 207-225). Washington, DC: TESOL.

Long, M. H., & Porter, P. A. (1985). Group work, interlanguage talk, and second language acquisition. *TESOL Quarterly, 13,* 207–228. Washington, DC: TESOL.

Met, M. (1987). *Parent involvement in foreign language learning.* Unpublished manuscript. Rockville, MD: Montgomery County Public Schools.

National Assessment for Educational Progress. (1982). *Students from homes in which English is not the dominant language: Who are they and how well do they read?* Denver: Education Commission of the States.

National Commission on Excellence in Education. (1983). *A nation at risk: The imperative for educational reform.* Washington, DC: U.S. Department of Education.

President's Commission on Foreign Language and International Studies. (1979). *Strength through wisdom: A critique of U.S. Capability.* Washington, DC: U.S. Government Printing Office.

Saville-Troike, M. (1987). Bilingual discourse: The negotiation of meaning without a common code. *Linguistics, 25,* 81–106.

Skutnabb-Kangas, T. (1982). *Bilingualism or not: The education of minorities* (Vol. 7). Avon, England: Multilingual Matters.

Sue, S., & Padilla, A. M. (1986). Ethnic minority issues in the United States: Challenges for the educational system. In Bilingual Education Office (Eds.), *Beyond language: Social and cultural factors in schooling language minority students* (pp. 35–72). Los Angeles: California State University, Evaluation, Dissemination, and Assessment Center.

Swain, M. (1983). Bilingualism without tears. In M. A. Clarke & J. Handscombe (Eds.), *On TESOL '82: Pacific perspectives on language learning and teaching* (pp. 35–46). Washington, DC: TESOL.

Swain, M. (1984). A review of immersion education in Canada: Research and evaluation studies. In *Studies on Immersion Education: A Collection for United States Educators* (pp. 87–112). Sacramento: California State Department of Education.

Swain, M. (1985). Communicative competence: Some roles of comprehensible input and comprehensible output in its development. In S. M. Gass and C. G. Madden (Eds.), *Input in second language acquisition* (pp. 235–253). Rowley, MA: Newbury House.

Swain, M. (1987). *The case for focused input: Contrived but authentic — Or, how content teaching needs to be manipulated and complemented to maximize second language learning.* Plenary paper presented at TESOL '87 Conference, Vancouver, BC.

Swain, M., & Lapkin, S. (1985). *Evaluating bilingual education: A Canadian case study.* Avon, England: Multilingual Matters, Ltd.

Tizard, J., Schofield, W. N., & Hewison, J. (1982). Collaboration between teachers and parents in assisting children's reading. *British Journal of Educational Psychology, 52,* 1–15.

Troike, R. C. (1978). Research evidence for the effectiveness of bilingual education. *NABE Journal, 3,* 13–24.

Troike, R. C. (1986). *Improving conditions for success in bilingual education programs.* Prepared for Committee on Education and Labor, U.S. House of Representatives.

Willig, A. (1985). A meta-analysis of selected studies on the effectiveness of bilingual education. *Review of Educational Research, 55,* 269–317.

Wong Fillmore, L. (1983). The language learner as an individual: Implications of research on individual differences for the ESL teacher. In M. A. Clarke and J. Handscombe (Eds.), *On TESOL '82: Pacific perspectives on language learning and teaching* (pp. 157–171). Washington, DC: TESOL.

CHAPTER 5

Bilingualism and Cognitive Ability: Theory, Research, and Controversy

Rafael M. Diaz
Stanford University

Research on the relation between bilingualism and intelligence has a long and fascinating history. For almost a hundred years, linguists, psychologists, and educators have investigated, with varying degrees of sophistication, whether proficiency in more than one language affects the way we perceive the world, the way we reason, and the way we solve problems. In present research, the question of bilingualism and intelligence has two distinct and poorly integrated forms. One group of researchers, studying mostly bilingual adults, is interested in how the two languages of a bilingual person are stored and processed. This group works usually within an information-processing paradigm, sorting out the relative dependence–independence of the two languages in the system. A second group of researchers, developmental psychologists and educators for the most part, is interested in how the experience of growing up with two languages or bilingual with education affects the course of cognitive development.

The findings of information-processing studies with adults have been well documented and reviewed elsewhere (see, e.g., Grosjean, 1982, Chapter 5; Hakuta, 1986, Chapter 4). The present chapter, therefore, will concentrate on the findings for the second set of questions regarding bilingual cognitive development. As discussed below, research in this field of inquiry has been at times confusing, considering the methodological flaws of early studies and the abuse of research findings in support of racist sociopolitical ideologies (Hakuta, 1986). In fact, the first four decades of empirical research yielded contradictory findings between linguists and psycholo-gists, which resulted in a very negative climate regarding the potential advantages of childhood bilingualism and bilingual education.

Even though public attitudes towards bilingualism in upbringing and education are still somewhat mixed and controversial, researchers' current view of childhood bilingualism is indeed very positive and optimistic. This view has emerged from consistent findings showing a number of cognitive and linguistic advantages for children who are bilingually educated. Above all, present researchers have learned important methodological lessons from their predecessors and have made finer distinctions among different types of bilingual situations that might mediate the effects of bilingualism on cognitive development. The present chapter will review the cognitive advantages associated with childhood bilingualism as well as the current search for an adequate explanation of the observed positive effects. But first, a bit of history.

EARLY STUDIES ON BILINGUALISM AND INTELLIGENCE

Systematic studies on the relation between bilingualism and intelligence began in the early 1920s and were closely related to the extensive use and popularization of psychometric tests of intelligence. Since performance on IQ tests such as the Stanford-Binet is heavily influenced by a subject's verbal ability, educators and psychologists were concerned about the validity of such tests for bilingual children. The main concern was that bilinguals' relatively low proficiency in the language of the tests could affect or bias the assessment of their intellectual potential. Therefore, earliest studies in the field were concerned with demonstrating bilinguals' (so-called) "language handicap" with respect to IQ test performance. The rationales for the studies were more complex, however, since these studies, as Hakuta (1986) has noted, were at the center of an intense and heated debate regarding the heritability of intelligence.

Nonetheless, the majority of studies done during the first half of the century reported findings consistent with the language handicap hypothesis. When compared with monolinguals, bilingual children scored lower on a wide range of measures of linguistic ability. Among other things, bilinguals were shown to have a poorer vocabulary, deficient articulation, lower standards on written composition, and more grammatical errors (see Darcy, 1953 and 1963, for a detailed review of early studies).

Interestingly enough, evidence of a language handicap did not lead to a serious questioning of the validity of IQ tests for this population. Instead, both researchers and their audiences reasoned that if bilingualism has a negative effect on language abilities, as witnessed by the language handicap, then bilingualism must have a negative effect on intellectual development, as witnessed by the poor performance of bilingual children on IQ tests! The reasoning saved the reputation of the tests, but unjustifiably condemned bilingualism as a source of linguistic confusion and intellectual retardation.

Needless to say, the first 40 years of research on the relation between bilingualism and intelligence created a very negative mood regarding childhood bilingualism and bilingual education. Childhood bilingualism was seen as a handicap to language growth (Thompson, 1952), a hardship devoid of apparent advantage, and even a social plague (Darcy, 1953). Even though the majority of negative statements resulted from poor research or gross misinterpretations of research findings, public attitudes toward bilingual education were greatly affected. For example, Tucker and D'Anglejan (1971)

reported the following commonly held beliefs regarding bilingual education:

1. Children who are instructed bilingually from an early age will suffer cognitive or intellectual retardation in comparison with their monolingually instructed counterparts.
2. They will not achieve the same level of content mastery as their monolingually instructed counterparts.
3. They will not achieve acceptable native language or target language skills.
4. The majority will become anomic individuals without affiliation to either ethnolinguistic group.

Even though the above are just public beliefs based on gross misinterpretation of research data, it is appropriate to stop and reflect for a moment on the reported "language handicap" and its possible impact on the development of bilingual children. The best way to approach this problem is to realize that early studies suffered from serious methodological problems, and their findings do not provide reliable information about the effects of bilingualism on language and cognitive development.

Many early studies, for example, failed to control for group differences in socioeconomic status (SES) between bilingual and monolingual samples. As early as 1930, McCarthy pointed out that bilingualism in the United States was seriously confounded with low socioeconomic status. Specifically, Fukuda (1925) had alerted researchers that high-scoring, English-speaking subjects were mostly in the occupational and executive classes, whereas the opposite was true for bilingual samples. Even though the correlation between IQ tests and socioeconomic variables was well known at the time, most studies investigating the effects of bilingualism on children's intelligence did not account for group differences in socioeconomic status.

A second methodological flaw of early studies is that investigators consistently ignored children's actual degree of bilingualism. Children were considered bilingual if they had a foreign family name or lived in certain geographical areas where recent immigrants lived, or they were simply judged "bilingual" through their parents' nationality (see Brunner, 1929, as an example). There were no attempts to assess children's actual proficiency in the two languages and, therefore, it is possible that many of the children included in the (so-called) bilingual sample were not bilingual at all but rather monolinguals of a minority language group.

Because of the above methodological problems it is difficult to interpret the significance of the reported language handicap. The lower scores of bilingual children on language and intelligence measures most likely represent the performance of poor minority children who do not yet master the language of the tests, rather than the actual effects of bilingualism.

A TURNING POINT

In the early 1960s, the field took a most fortunate turn. Aware of the potential advantages of bilingualism for children's cognitive development, Peal and Lambert (1962) attributed the negative findings of early studies to the failure of researchers to differentiate "pseudobilinguals" from truly bilingual children. "The pseudobilingual knows one language much better than the other, and does not use his second language in communication. The true bilingual masters both at an early age and has facility with both as means of communication" (p. 6). Peal and Lambert believed that even though pseudobilingualism might be a serious problem that could result in intellectual retardation, genuine bilingualism may be a real asset to children's intellectual development. They proposed that because early studies had been lax in their definition of bilingualism and in the assessment of their sample subjects' degree of bilingualism, the negative findings could be attributed to a situation of pseudobilingualism.

To test their hypothesis, Peal and Lambert (1962) administered several measures of degree of bilingualism to 364 10-year-old children in Canada. Three tests were used to determine whether children were "balanced" bilinguals, that is, had age-appropriate abilities in both French and English, or whether they were monolingual. The final sample was composed of 164 children: 75 monolinguals and 89 (genuine or balanced) French–English bilinguals. Children in the sample were administered a modified version of the Lavoie–Larendau Group Test of General Intelligence, the Raven's Progressive Matrices, and a French version of selected subtests of the Thurstone Primary Mental Abilities Test.

Contrary to the findings of earlier studies, the results of the Peal and Lambert study showed that bilingual children performed significantly better than monolinguals in most of the cognitive tests and subtests, even when group differences in sex, age, and socioeconomic status were appropriately controlled. Bilingual children performed significantly higher than monolinguals on tests of both verbal and nonverbal abilities: The superiority of bilingual children on the nonverbal tests was more clearly evident in those subtests that required mental manipulation and reorganization of visual symbols, rather than mere perceptual abilities. A factor analysis of test scores indicated that bilinguals were superior to monolinguals in concept formation and in tasks that required a certain mental or symbolic flexibility. Overall, bilinguals were found to have a more diversified pattern of cognitive abilities than their monolingual peers.

In 1962, for the first time in the educational and psychological literature, childhood bilingualism was portrayed as a potential asset for children's cognitive development. Even though Peal and Lambert's (1962) study has been criticized on account of several methodological shortcomings, their findings have been replicated time and time again in the last 20 years of research. Indeed, when balanced bilingual children are compared with monolinguals on language and cognitive variables, bilinguals tend to outperform monolinguals on a wide range of measures. Above all, Peal and Lambert's study provided a few methodological lessons to the field and encouraged researchers to refine their research methodologies.

At present there are two research paradigms that provide reliable findings on the effects of bilingualism. The first acceptable paradigm is modeled after Peal and Lambert's study. This paradigm involves a comparison between monolingual and balanced bilingual children. Two major requirements are involved: (a) Children in the bilingual sample must demonstrate some degree of "balance" or comparable proficiency in the two languages. Even though there is no general consensus of what constitutes "balanced bilingualism" in absolute terms, a safe working definition is that balanced bilingual children demonstrate age-appropriate abilities in both languages. (b) The researcher using this paradigm should attempt to make the two groups comparable on relevant variables such as socioeconomic status, parental education, years of schooling, and any other possible confounding variables that could make the two groups different for reasons other than bilingualism.

A second acceptable paradigm has been labeled the "within-bilingual" design (see, e.g., Hakuta & Diaz, 1985). The aim of this paradigm is to study the effects of bilingualism by studying children who vary in their second-language proficiency. In these studies, children's relative proficiency in the second language or their "degree of bilingualism" constitutes the independent variable; different cognitive measures constitute the dependent variable. An example of this kind of study is to assess the cognitive abilities of three different groups of children: (a) proficient bilinguals, (b) partial bilinguals, and (c) limited bilinguals; in this categorization children in all three groups are equivalent in their first-language ability but widely different in their second-language proficiency. Another example of this type of study is to use a multiple regression approach, in which cognitive ability is the criterion variable and children's proficiency in their first and second language are the predictor variables. The effects of degree of bilingualism can be assessed by examining the relation between second-language proficiency and cognitive ability, once the effects of first-language ability have been partialed out from the equation (see Hakuta & Diaz, 1985).

THE COGNITIVE ADVANTAGES OF BILINGUAL CHILDREN

In the past 20 years, research has consistently shown that learning a second language in childhood, either by simultaneous acquisition or in the context of bilingual education, is associated with positive cognitive gains. Both in bilingual–monolingual comparisons and in studies using within-bilingual designs, the degree of a child's bilingual mastery is positively related to concept formation, classification, creativity, analogical reasoning, and visuospatial skills, to name a few (see Diaz, 1983, and Hakuta, Ferdman, & Diaz, 1987, for reviews). In addition, bilingual children have demonstrated a particularly refined awareness of the objective properties of language, commonly labeled "metalinguistic awareness." Let us now review some of these findings in more detail.

Several studies have explored the relationship between children's bilingualism and cognitive processes involved in concept formation. In one study of French–English balanced bilingual children in Canada, Bain (1974) examined the effects of bilingualism on "discovery learning" tasks. The study assessed children's discovery of rules that lead to the solution of linear numerical problems such as: 1, 3, 7, 15, (31) or 1, 3, 6, 10 (15). Children were presented with two sets of items on two different days. On the second day of testing, children were told to "use the rules that you learned on the last day to help you solve the problems" (p. 123). The test was chosen because it involved the ability to discover a rule and then use the rule to deduce a certain outcome. In Piagetian terms, the task involved concept formation abilities such as abstraction and generalization of rules. Throughout the study, bilingual children showed superior performance on several concept formation abilities. For example, on the average, bilingual children were able to discover the additive rules 8 minutes earlier than the monolingual children.

Based on tasks similar to those used by Piaget, Inhelder, and Szeminska (1960), Liedtke and Nelson (1968) constructed a test on concepts of linear measurement. The test measured six different aspects of linear measurement: (a) reconstructing relations of distance, (b) conservation of length, (c) conservation of length with change of position, (d) conservation of length with distortion of shape, (e) measurement of length, and (f) subdividing a straight line. The test was administered to English–French bilingual and English monolingual first-grade children in Canada. The bilingual sample consisted of children who were exposed to the two languages at home, that is, simultaneous learners of the language. The monolingual subjects came from monolingual homes and had no functional knowledge of a second language. Subjects' IQ and socioeconomic status, as well as a measure of their kindergarten attendance, were carefully controlled for.

Subtests a–d yielded a measure of children's ability to conserve length, and subtests e and f yielded a measure of children's ability to measure length. On both measures, bilinguals performed significantly better than their monolingual counterparts. After such strict experimental controls, the results were clearly in favor of the bilingual children. The authors concluded enthusiastically: "If bilingualism increases intellectual potential and is beneficial to concept formation [as the study shows], then a second language should be introduced during the early years when experience and environment are most effective in contributing to the development of intelligence" (p. 231). More recently, using a within-bilingual design, Duncan and De Avila (1979) have replicated bilinguals' advantage on a measure of Piagetian conservation concepts.

Since most theorists of intelligence (e.g., Guilford, Spearman, & Piaget) have stressed the central role of analogical reasoning in human cognition, it is important to point out the positive relation between childhood bilingualism and the capacity to reason by analogy. In a longitudinal study of 100 children attending kindergarten and first-grade Spanish–English bilingual education classes, the present author investigated the effects of learning a second language on analogical reasoning ability. Children were asked to complete sentences such as "The princess is beautiful, the monster is (ugly)" or "Snow is ice, rain is (water)." The results indicated that children with greater bilingual proficiency scored significantly higher on the analogy test. Furthermore, progress in the second language during the course of one academic year produced significant increases in children's analogical reasoning abilities as measured at the end of the one-year study.

Interestingly enough, several researchers have found bilingual advantage on measures of visual–spatial abilities. Balkan (1970) reported bilingual–monolingual group differences in a task similar to the Embedded Figures Test that assessed children's ability to reorganize elements in the perceptual field. Even though group differences did not achieve statistical significance, bilinguals showed advantages in the reorganization and reconstruction of the perceptual arrays. In another study with Hebrew–English bilingual children, Ben-Zeev (1977) tested children's abilities in a matrix transposition task. Bilingual children were better than monolinguals at isolating and specifying the underlying dimensions of the matrix. More recently, Hakuta (1987) reported substantial positive correlations between children's degree of bilingualism and their performance on Raven's Progressive Matrices and on the spatial subtest of Thurstone's Primary Mental Abilities Test.

METALINGUISTIC ADVANTAGES OF BILINGUAL CHILDREN

In a detailed account of his daughter Hildegard's bilingual upbringing, Leopold (1949) not only reported adequate language development and minimal confusion between her two languages, but also suggested that bilingualism seemed to be an advantage to his daughter's mental development. Leopold noted Hildegard's special objective awareness of language, proposing that bilingual children, forced to an early separation of word and referent, would develop an early awareness of the abstract and symbolic nature of language. According to Leopold, such awareness would free the child's thinking from the concreteness and "tyranny" of words. At present, such objective awareness of language is commonly referred to as "metalinguistic awareness."

Leopold's observations were tested by Ianco-Worrall (1972) in a study of English–Afrikaans bilingual children in South Africa. The bilingual sample consisted of nursery school children who had been raised in a one-person, one-language environment similar to the situation of Leopold's daughter Hildegard. Two comparable monolingual samples, one English and one Afrikaans, were also selected for the study. In a first experiment, children were administered a semantic–phonetic preferences test. Children were asked questions such as: Which word is more like "cap," *can* or *hat?* Choosing the word *can* or *hat* indicates the child's phonetic or semantic preference, respectively, in analyzing word similarities. As predicted, bilinguals outranked monolinguals in choosing words along a semantic rather than a phonetic dimension. Moreover, the findings suggested that simultaneous learners of two languages reach a stage of semantic development 2–3 years earlier than children raised monolingually.

In a second experiment, Ianco-Worrall (1972) investigated children's understanding of the arbitrariness of language and the conventional nature of linguistic symbols. For example, she asked children whether names of things could be arbitrarily interchanged (e.g., can we call a cow *moon?*). The findings showed that bilinguals more often replied that the names of objects could in principle be changed, whereas the opposite was true for the monolingual sample.

Similar flexibility with respect to the objective use and understanding of language was found in Ben-Zeev's (1977) study with Hebrew–English bilinguals. The investigator gave children a "symbol substitution" task, which measures children's ability to substitute words in a sentence according to the experimenter's instructions. For example, children were asked to substitute the word *I* for the word *spaghetti*. Children were given correct scores when they were able to say sentences like "Spaghetti am cold" rather than "Spaghetti is cold" or a similar sentence that, although grammatically correct, violated the rules of the game. Basically, in the symbol substitution task, children are asked to violate the rules of grammar; in so doing, they demonstrate their control over the somewhat automatic production of correct sentences. Needless to say, this task requires an unusual awareness and attention to linguistic features and detail. Through their performance in this and other related tasks, the bilingual children showed a greater objective awareness of language than their monolingual peers.

In several other studies, bilingual children have shown definite advantages in measures of metalinguistic awareness. Cummins (1978) found that Irish–English and Ukrainian–English bilingual children outperformed monolinguals in the capacity to evaluate tautological and contradictory sentences. Bialystok (1986) has argued that bilingualism increases children's ability to control their linguistic processing. Testing children on grammatically correct items with anomalous meanings, she found a clear bilingual advantage in the capacity to overlook meaning and focus on grammatical form. Similarly, in a study of Spanish–English bilingual children in El Salvador, Galambos (1982) found that bilinguals had a stronger "syntactic orientation" than both English and Spanish monolingual children when judging grammatical and ungrammatical sentences in both languages. Syntactic orientation was defined as the ability "to note errors in constructions, to use syntactic strategies in the correction of these constructions, and to offer syntactically rather than semantically oriented explanations for the ungrammaticality noted" (p. 2).

A REVIEW OF EXPLANATORY HYPOTHESES

The positive relation between bilingualism and children's cognitive and metalinguistic abilities is, by now, a well-documented fact. A major gap in our knowledge, however, is how to explain such positive relation. That is, if bilingualism affects children's intelligence, *how* does it happen? The following hypotheses have been formulated to explain the positive results.

The Code-Switching Hypothesis

Code switching is the capacity of bilinguals to move from one language to the other with relative ease. As an explanatory hypothesis, code switching was proposed first by Peal and Lambert (1962) in explaining their pioneer findings. The investigators believed that the possibility to switch linguistic codes while performing cognitive tasks gave bilingual children an added flexibility that monolingual children did not enjoy. In their own words:

> The [code switching] hypothesis is that bilinguals may have developed more flexibility in thinking. . . . bilinguals typically acquire experience in switching from one language to another, possibly trying to solve a problem while thinking in one language and then, when blocked, switching to the other. This habit, if it were developed, could help them in their performance on tests requiring symbolic reorganization since they demand a readiness to drop one hypothesis or concept and try another. (p. 14)

More often than not, errors in cognitive and academic tasks are caused by children's perseveration on the wrong hypothesis. Bilingual code switching might, indeed, facilitate the development of a more flexible "mental set" to approach cognitive tasks (DeAvila & Duncan, 1979). Furthermore, when a bilingual child is frustratated or blocked when performing a task verbally, he or she has the possibility of switching to the second language, starting the problem once again with a fresh and different perspective.

The Objectification Hypothesis

In a large number of studies, bilingual children have shown a special objective awareness of language. The second hypothesis claims that bilinguals' objectification of language is conducive to higher levels of abstract and symbolic thinking.

As suggested by Leopold (1949), bilingual children have two words for each referent and are forced to realize the conventional nature of language early on in development. The separation of word from referent is seen as one of the major milestones in the development of symbolic thinking. Furthermore, as Vygotsky (1962) suggested, since bilinguals can express the same thought in different languages, a bilingual child will tend to "see his language as one particular system among many, to view its phenomena under more general categories, and this leads to an awareness of his linguistic operations" (p. 110). In other words, learning more than one language leads not only to knowledge of a second language, but to a knowledge of *Language*. Through this objectification process, the hypothesis suggests, children are able to bring their concepts to a higher level of symbolism and abstraction.

The Verbal Mediation Hypothesis

As Soviet developmental theory (Luria, 1961; Vygotsky, 1962) proposes, cognitive development in the preschool years is heavily influenced by children's increasing reliance on language as a tool of thought. The use of language for self-regulatory functions, commonly referred to as "private speech," appears shortly after the onset of social speech and gradually becomes subvocal to constitute inner speech or verbal thinking. The internalization of private speech sets the base for the capacity to use covert verbal mediation. The origins, development, and internalization of private speech have been documented elsewhere (see, e.g., Frauenglass & Diaz, 1985; Zivin, 1979).

Several investigators (Bain & Yu, 1980; Diaz, 1983; Diaz & Padilla, 1985) have suggested that the unique linguistic experience of bilingualism and the accompanying awareness of language might lead to an increasing reliance on verbal mediation in cognitive tasks. In fact, bilingual advantage on some nonverbal measures (such as Raven's Test) has been explained in terms of bilinguals' increasing reliance on covert verbal or linguistic strategies when solving the tasks (Hakuta & Diaz, 1985). It is possible, as the hypothesis suggests, that the bilingual experience and the resulting metalinguistic awareness foster a more efficient and precocious use of language as a tool of thought. Bilinguals' improved performance on so many different tasks could be explained by this efficient reliance on self-regulatory language.

In a study of the self-regulatory private speech of bilingual preschoolers, Diaz and Padilla (1985) reported a relation between degree of bilingualism and a higher production of task-relevant private speech utterances. Children of relatively higher degree of bilingualism in this sample not only made more self-regulatory utterances, but also used a higher number of task-relevant language functions such as labeling and description of materials, transitional utterances, and guiding, planning statements. This finding gives some support to the hypothesis that bilingualism fosters an increased and more efficient reliance on language in cognitive tasks.

Further research is needed, however, in order to validate the above explanatory hypotheses, or to formulate new hypotheses that take into account the findings to date. A descriptive understanding of *how* bilingualism interacts with cognitive and language development could prove very beneficial for both theoretical and practical reasons. Theoretically, such description would substantially improve our understanding of the relation between thought and language in development. In addition, with such knowledge our bilingual education efforts could be tailored to maximize the potential cognitive and linguistic advantages involved in a bilingual experience.

CONCLUSIONS

An overview of recent research and theories in the field of bilingual cognitive development underscores the potential benefits of bilingualism for children's cognitive and linguistic development. It is important to note, however, that the observed advantages occur in "additive" rather than "subtractive" bilingual situation is (Hakuta, Ferdman, & Diaz, 1987). In other words, bilingualism promotes the development of cognitive abilities when the child's two languages are developing and functioning in a parallel manner (additive) rather than when mastery of a second language is achieved at the expense of

competence in the first language (subtractive).

Subtractive bilingual situations tend to produce *semilinguals* rather than *bilinguals*, that is, children who for a good number of years cannot function adequately in either language. Not surprisingly, as Scandinavian studies suggest (Skutnabb-Kangas & Toukomaa, 1976), children in subtractive situations are at high risk for serious academic and intellectual difficulties. There is an urgent need in this country to analyze the nature of many bilingual situations in terms of the additive–subtractive dimension, and thoroughly explore the cognitive, linguistic, and academic consequences for children in nonadditive situations. Above all, it is important for researchers and educators to realize the enormous potential of additive bilingualism as a tool to promote and develop our children's cognitive and linguistic abilities.

REFERENCES

Bain, B. (1974). Bilingualism and cognition: A general theory. In S. T. Carey (Ed.), *Bilingualism, biculturalism and education: Proceedings of the Conference at College Universitaire Saint Jean.* Edmonton: The University of Alberta.

Bain, B., & Yu, R. (1980). Cognitive consequences of raising children bilingually: "One parent, one language." *Canadian Journal of Psychology, 34,* 304–313.

Balkan, L. (1970). *Les effects du bilinguisme francais-anglais sur les aptitudes intellectuelles.* Brussels: Aimav.

Ben-Zeev, S. (1977). The influence of bilingualism on cognitive strategy and cognitive development. *Child Development, 48,* 1009–1018.

Brunner, E. D. (1929). *Immigrant farmers and their children.* New York: Doubleday, Doran.

Bialystok, E. (1986). Factors in the growth of linguistic awareness. *Child Development, 57,* 498–510.

Cummins, J. (1978). Metalinguistic development of children in bilingual education programs: Data from Irish and Canadian Ukranian-English programs. In M. Paradis (Ed.), *The Fourth Locus Forum 1977.* Columbia, SC: Hornbeam.

Darcy, N. T. (1953). A review of the literature on the effects of bilingualism upon the measurement of intelligence. *Journal of Genetic Psychology, 82,* 21–57.

Darcy, N. T. (1963). Bilingualism and the measurement of intelligence: Review of a decade of research. *Journal of Genetic Psychology, 103,* 259–282.

DeAvila, E., & Duncan, S. (1979). Bilingualism and the metaset. *NABE Journal, 3,* 2.

Diaz, R. M. (1983). Thought and two languages: The impact of bilingualism on cognitive development. In E. W. Gordon (Ed.), *Review of research in education* (Vol. 10). Washington, DC: American Educational Research Association.

Diaz, R. M., & Padilla, K. (1985, April). *The self-regulatory speech of bilingual preschoolers.* Paper presented at the 1985 Meeting of the Society for Research in Child Development, Toronto, Canada.

Duncan, S., & DeAvila, E. (1979). Bilingualism and cognition: Some recent findings. *NABE Journal, 4,* 15–50.

Frauenglass, M., & Diaz, R. M. (1985). Self-regulatory functions of children's private speech: A critical analysis of recent challenges to Vygotsky's theory. *Developmental Psychology, 21,* 357–364.

Fukuda, T. (1925). A survey of the intelligence and environment of school children. *American Journal of Psychology, 36,* 124–139.

Galambos, S. (1982, October). *The development of metalinguistic awareness in bilingual and monolingual children.* Paper presented at the Seventh Annual Boston University Conference on Language Development, Boston.

Grosjean, F. (1982). *Life with two languages.* Cambridge, MA: Harvard University Press.

Hakuta, K. (1986). *The mirror of language: The debate on bilingualism.* New York: Basic Books.

Hakuta, K. (1987). Degree of bilingualism and cognitive ability in mainland Puerto Rican children. *Child Development, 58,* 1377–1388.

Hakuta, K., & Diaz, R. M. (1985). The relationship between degree of bilingualism and cognitive ability: A critical discussion and some new longitudinal data. In K. E. Nelson (Ed.), *Children's language* (Vol. 5, pp. 319–344). Hillsdale, NJ: Erlbaum.

Hakuta, K., Ferdman, B. M., & Diaz, R. M. (1987). Bilingualism and cognitive development: Three perspectives. In S. Rosenberg (Ed.), *Advances in applied psycholinguistics* (Vol. 2, pp. 284–319). New York: Cambridge University Press.

Ianco-Worrall, A. D. (1972). Bilingualism and cognitive development. *Child Development, 43,* 1390–1400.

Leopold, W. F. (1949). *Speech development of a bilingual child: A linguist's record.* Evanston, IL: Northwestern University Press.

Liedtke, W. W., & Nelson, L. D. (1968). Concept formation and bilingualism. *Alberta Journal of Educational Research, 14,* 225–232.

Luria, A. (1961). *The role of speech in the regulation of normal and abnormal behavior.* Oxford: Pergamon.

McCarthy, D. R. (1930). *The language development of the preschool child.* Minneapolis: University of Minnesota Press.

Peal, E., & Lambert, W. (1962). The relation of bilingualism to intelligence. *Psychological Monographs, 76,* 1–23.

Piaget, J., Inhelder, B., & Szeminska, A. (1960). *The child's conception of geometry.* New York: Basic Books.

Skutnabb-Kangas, T., & Toukomaa, T. (1976). *Teaching migrant children's mother tongue and learning the language of the host country.* Helsinki: Finnish National Commission for UNESCO.

Thompson, G. G. (1952). *Child psychology.* Boston: Houghton Mifflin.

Tucker, G. R., & D'Anglejan, A. (1971). Some thoughts concerning bilingual education programs. *Modern Language Journal, 55,* 491–493.

Vygotsky, L. S. (1962). *Thought and language.* Cambridge, MA; MIT Press.

Zivin, G. (1979). *The development of self-regulation through private speech.* New York: Wiley.

Part II:

Delivery of Educational Services and Interventions with Low SES and Minority Children

An Examination of Individual Factors Associated with the Academic Success and Failure of Mexican-Americans and Anglo Students

J. Manuel Casas
Mike Furlong
V. Scott Solberg
Olga Carranza
Graduate School of Education
University of California, Santa Barbara

INTRODUCTION

In the United States today the dropout problem is receiving a great deal of attention as a local, state, and national concern. This is not a great surprise, given the fact that every year 700,000 U.S. youngsters leave school for good without graduating (Cordtz, 1989). Although these statistics document the general severity of the dropout problem, the dropout rate is a more serious concern for certain socio-economic and racial/ethnic groups.

Educators have an interest in students maintaining high attendance rates and subsequently graduating from high school. This interest in the dropout problem is also shared across a broad spectrum of U.S. society. Local school boards, working with community agencies and institutions of higher education, have taken action to address the dropout problem. Granting agencies have increased funding to combat the dropout problem. Public interest groups have launched a number of dropout-prevention initiatives. As examples, Mickey and Minnie Mouse encourage students to "Be Cool, Stay in School," and Bill Cosby admonishes us that "if you think keeping kids in school isn't your problem, think again." He warns us that nationwide the equivalent of 80 busloads of students leave school each day and never return. At the governmental level, meetings have been convened, conferences held, committees appointed, studies commissioned, and programs proposed. Politicians are even proposing a variety of programs to combat the dropout problem. For example, the Chair of the California State Senate Education Committee, Senator Gary K. Hart, has proposed a bill that would require students to provide proof of regular school attendance and to maintain a C average before being able to apply for a driver's license.

At first glance, it appears somewhat incongruous that this national concern about dropouts occurs at a time when the proportion of students graduating from high school is near an all-time high (U.S. Department of Education, 1984). This concern, however, is well founded, since the social and economic consequences of dropping out of high school are now more significant than ever. Those who do not attain a high school diploma can be expected to earn approximately $200,000 less over their lifetimes than high school graduates (U.S. Department of Commerce, 1979). Thus, even more than in the past, the high school diploma is the passport to social and economic participation in U.S. society.

This social reality is particularly true for those who are already socioeconomically disadvantaged. According to the High School and Beyond study (Office of Educational Research and Improvement, 1984), about 14% of the sophomores who had been surveyed in 1980 did not complete high school by their expected graduation date in 1982. This study collected data that included parental hardship indicators such as low income and limited educational background; it is notable that the disadvantaged respondents (17%) were three times more likely to drop out than the advantaged (5%). Similarly, the results of a recent survey (Hahn, Danzberger, & Lefkowitz, 1987) indicated that dropout rates tended to increase with the proportion of the student body classified as poor. For instance, city schools in which less than 20% of the student body were poor reported dropout rates of approximately 13%. In contrast, schools in which 50% of the students lived in poverty reported a dropout rate of 30%. According to Hahn et al. (1987), a number of other studies have concluded that dropout rates are highest in schools with a large proportion of racial/ethnic minority students who come from low-income families.

THE MEXICAN-AMERICAN DROPOUT PROBLEM

Mexican-Americans are one of the fastest-growing and youngest ethnic groups in the United States: 43% are under the age of 18 (U.S. Department of Commerce, 1980). Mexican-American children now represent a significant proportion of the elementary school population in a number of urban school districts; in the near future, the proportion in these districts will increase to a majority representation (Pifer, 1984).

Though highly represented at the elementary school level, Mexican-American children are severely underrepresented at the secondary and higher educational levels (Casas & Ponterotto, 1984). According to Casas and Furlong (1986), one of the reasons for this underrepresentation is that Mexican-Americans are plagued with a significant dropout rate, which is as high as 40% in certain urban areas. Unfortunately, this high dropout rate may be an underestimate, owing to the lack of a uniform and accurate system for calculating the

dropout rate at local school systems (Barber & McClellan, 1987), as well as the fact that statistics for Mexican-Americans are often combined with those of other Hispanic groups. The dropout rate for all Hispanics reflects alarming figures, which include 80% in New York, 70% in Chicago, and 50% in Los Angeles (National Commission on Secondary Schooling for Hispanics, 1984). The existence of a high dropout rate among Mexican-Americans may be extrapolated from statistics showing that the states in the Southwest, which have the highest concentration of Mexican-Americans, also suffer the highest dropout rates when compared with other regions of the country (Hahn et al., 1987). Indeed, a study conducted by the National Commission on Secondary Schooling for Hispanics (1984), which focused specifically on Mexican-Americans at the secondary level, found that 45% of Mexican-American students who enter high school never graduate, compared to only 17% of Anglo students.

Dropping out of school before high school graduation is only one part of the educational problems that plague the Mexican-American. At a recent conference sponsored by the University of California (Aldaco, 1988), it was noted that the university's graduating class of the year 2000 is currently in the fourth grade, where Hispanics represent more than 32% of all students. If current trends remain unchanged, the following educational patterns can be expected for these fourth graders:

- Number who will enter the ninth grade   144,000

- Number who will graduate from high school   70,000

- Number who will be qualified to enter the University of California   3,500

- Number who will actually enroll in the University of California   1,700

- Number who will graduate or still be enrolled in the year 2000   1,100

- Number who will earn a doctorate from the University of California   19

Although the precision of these dropout rates have been questioned by several researchers (Hahn et al., 1987; Rumberger, 1986) because of methodological reasons, even these researchers concede that regardless of the precision of dropout statistics, dropout rates are higher for members of racial, ethnic, and language minorities (Rumberger, 1986).

IMPACT OF MEXICAN-AMERICAN DROPOUT PROBLEM

The underrepresentation of Mexican-Americans in high school and college will continue to have a detrimental impact on their socioeconomic development. It is widely accepted that education is an important means to economic progress (Carter & Segura, 1979; Ford Foundation, 1984). As noted earlier, a majority of Mexican-Americans have not received a highschool diploma and consequently it is not surprising to find this group at the lowest levels of professional status, income, and net worth, as well as the highest levels of unemployment and poverty (Crutsinger, 1986; Ford Foundation, 1984).

Nowhere is the severity of the problem and the urgency to address it better stated than by Henry Levin, Professor of Economics at Stanford University's School of Education. He warns that unless action is taken quickly to increase the educational and social opportunities for students from poor and uneducated families, who make up a significant proportion of the Mexican-American population, the consequences will be disastrous. A major consequence will be the deterioration of the labor force, resulting in a decline of U.S. economic competitiveness and a loss in sales and profits (Levin, 1985). It is currently estimated that the chronic unemployment and underemployment of the dropouts from the 1986–1987 class will cost our country $240 billion over their lifetimes (McEvoy, 1988). Furthermore, unless the dropout problem is recognized, the nation's tax base will shrink while costs to the public will expand. It has been suggested that public schools should be held accountable to increase the number of graduates, and when they fail, sanctions should be considered, including replacement of teachers and principals (Levin, 1985).

DROPOUT PERSPECTIVES

It is important to consider that dropping out of school is not an isolated act but rather the culmination of many years of academic frustrations and failures, as well as a souring of a student's attitude toward school. A student drops out of school when the strong traditional value given to education is eroded; the student believes the potential benefits of a high school diploma are not worth the perceived effort required to attain this goal. The reasons why students are "pushed" out of school, such as poor academic performance, poor attendance, pregnancy, disciplinary actions, or the attractiveness of the work force are "end-result" rationalizations (Bloom, 1964; Rumberger, 1986; Wehlage & Rotter, 1986). They do not describe why students become at risk for dropping out, but are rationales given to explain why an otherwise socially desirable outcome was not attained. The appropriate perspective places the emphasis on the *process* of dropping out of school rather than on the rationalizations individuals give after they have actually dropped out.

Thus, the real issue is not just one of how to prevent students from dropping out of school, but rather how students can experience more success in school and realize their potential. This distinction is important, because successful students rarely drop out of school. Conversely, it is assumed that students who experience academic difficulties are at risk for later dropping out of school. Therefore, it is important to have a greater understanding of the academic performance of students prior to their dropping out. Similarly, it is widely accepted that a number of factors affect school success: students' perceptions of themselves, their attitudes towards education, and their experience of personal and emotional stressors can negatively impact on performance. Knowledge of students' academic attitudes and aspirations as well as the occurrence and types of stressful events might provide direction in structuring more beneficial educational experiences. For this reason, the following study sought to identify those characteristics that could differentiate successful from unsuccessful students. Specifically, the profiles of Anglo and Mexican-American junior high school students with successful academic performance were compared to Anglo and Mexican-American students with unsuccessful academic performance. The academic profiles of four groups of students enrolled in the seventh and eighth grades in the Santa Barbara High School District were examined: Anglo–Successful (AS), Mexican-American–Successful (MAS), Anglo–At-Risk (AAR), and Mexican-American–At-Risk (MAAR).

The present investigation was part of a larger study designed to identify factors associated with academic success and failure among Anglo and Mexican-American junior high school students (Casas, Furlong, Carranza, & Solberg, 1986). Data for the larger study were collected by using a model, developed by Barr (1985) and extended by Casas and Furlong (1986), that includes such information on the student, the family, the school, and the community that can affect educational progress. This chapter focuses only on the individual student factors found among successful and at-risk students and addresses the following research questions:

1. What are the academic patterns associated with becoming at risk for school failure for Mexican-American and Anglo students?
2. What are the academic attitudes, expectations, and aspirations of successful and at-risk students?
3. By the seventh and eighth grades, have emotional factors such as self-esteem and the experience of life stress diverged for successful and at-risk students?

METHODS

Sample Pool

The sampling objective was to have equal representation of Anglo and Mexican-American[1] students as well as successful[2] and at-risk[3] students from each of the four junior high schools in the Santa Barbara School District. Given the scope of the study, this meant identifying 20 students at each school, for a total sample size of 80 students. The students who participated in the study were randomly selected[4] from the larger pool of students in each of the four groups; students' parents were contacted to secure informed consent until the requisite number of students was obtained. This screening process and subsequent attrition during the study resulted in a final sample of 74 students with the following number of students in each group: Anglo–Successful (20), Anglo–At-Risk (17), Mexican-American–Successful (16), and Mexican-American–At-Risk (21).

The final sample of 45 males and 29 females had an average age of 14.1 years at the time of the study. Both seventh and eighth grades were equally represented. Grade point averages, described on a 4.0 scale, indicated that the Anglo–Successful (3.4) and Mexican-American–Successful (3.3) students received higher grade point averages than either the Anglo–At-Risk (1.8) or Mexican-American–At-Risk (1.6) students.

Parents' occupation information provided by the students indicated that the majority of the fathers of the Anglo–Successful group held semiprofessional[5] or professional jobs. In comparison, the fathers of the Mexican-American–Successful group were more often employed in blue collar and semiprofessional jobs. The mothers in these two groups held predominantly semiprofessional jobs, or were unemployed. The at-risk groups showed a distinct difference in career backgrounds. The majority of fathers of the Anglo–At-Risk students possessed semiprofessional and blue collar jobs, whereas most of the fathers of the Mexican-American–At-Risk group were blue collar workers. Unlike the mothers of the successful sample, who were often unemployed, almost all the mothers of the Anglo–At-Risk group were employed in semiprofessional and blue collar positions. Similarly, mothers of the Mexican-American–At-Risk group held semiprofessional or blue collar service positions (e.g., janitor, housekeeper), or were unemployed.

A final pertinent sample characteristic is the language use pattern of the Mexican-American students. When asked to identify the language they and their parents preferred to speak, a majority of the Mexican-American–Successful and Mexican-American–At-Risk students (75% and 81%, respectively) reported English as their preferred language. However, there were differences in the reported language preference of their parents. The Mexican-American–At-Risk students were nearly twice as likely to indicate that their parents preferred speaking Spanish only (61.9%) than the Mexican-American–Successful students (37.5%).

Procedure

The data collected consisted of both historical and current information. Students' cumulative records were reviewed and information concerning their academic history was obtained. Such information included the results of group achievement tests, academic marks, and classroom behavior and study habits.

To determine students' current status in a variety of areas, several types of information were obtained. The Matrix Analogies Test (Naglieri, 1985), a nonverbal cognitive ability test, was administered to determine if there were any differences in the groups' academic potential. In addition, several student attitude questionnaires developed specifically for this study were administered in a group format, with the successful and at-risk students grouped separately so that the questionnaires could be read aloud to the at-risk students.

RESULTS AND DISCUSSION

Nonverbal Cognitive Functioning

The results from the Matrix Analogies Test revealed that although all groups obtained scores within the average range, the Anglo–Successful students scored significantly higher (97.6) than the Anglo–At-Risk (87.7) and the Mexican-American–At-Risk (86.5) students. The mean score obtained by the Mexican-American–Successful students (92.8) was not significantly different from the other groups.

Scholastic History of Successful and At-Risk Students

School performance indicators were gleaned from cumulative records to eval-uate similarities of and differences between successful and at-risk students' prior school experience. Data were collected and summarized across Grades 3–6, the years immediately preceding matriculation to junior high school. Information pertaining to the results of academic marks (expressed on a 4.0 scale), group achievement tests, and classroom behavior and study habits (expressed on a 4.0 scale) were averaged across Grades 3–6 and are presented in Table 1.

Academic marks from Grades 3–6. As a general rule, both the Anglo–Successful and Mexican-American–Successful group earned higher grades in specific subject areas than the two at-risk groups. The Anglo–Successful group obtained higher marks than either the Anglo–At-Risk or Mexican-American–At-Risk groups in both Reading Skills and Reading Comprehension. The Mexican-American–Successful group also received higher marks than either of the at-risk groups in Reading Skills, but scores in Reading Comprehension were significantly lower than the Anglo--Successful group's. In Math Computation, Math Comprehension, and Science, the Anglo–Successful and Mexican-American–Successful students earned significantly higher marks than either the Anglo--At-Risk or Mexican-American–At-Risk students. In Social Studies the Anglo–Successful group scored higher than either the Anglo–At-Risk or Mexican-American–At-Risk groups. Although the Mexican-American–Successful group performed at a higher level than the Anglo–At-Risk or Mexican-American–At-Risk groups in this subject area, this difference was not significant.

Achievement test record from Grades 3–6. The results of standardized group achievement testing (Comprehensive Test of Basic Skills or Metropolitan Achievement Test) in Grades 3–6 indicated that the Anglo–Successful group obtained a higher average score in the areas of reading, math, and language skills than the other three groups. There were no differences between the Anglo–At-Risk and the Mexican-American–Successful groups. The Mexican-American–At-Risk students had the lowest average scores (40th to 42nd percentiles)

TABLE 1
Scholastic History of Students Averaged Across Grades 3-6

| | N | Anglo | | Mexican-American | | Significant Differences |
		Successful (1)	At-Risk (2)	Successful (3)	At-Risk (4)	
Academic marks (4.0 scale)						
Reading skills	66	3.1	2.3	2.9	2.3	1, 3 > 2, 4
Reading comprehension	65	3.2	2.3	2.6	2.4	1 > 2, 3, 4
Math computation	66	3.1	2.2	3.1	2.2	1. 3 > 2, 4
Math comprehension	63	3.1	2.3	2.8	2.2	1, 3 > 2, 4
Social studies	68	3.0	2.4	2.9	2.4	1 > 2, 4
Science	67	3.2	2.5	3.1	2.5	1, 3 > 2, 4
Achievement tests (percentiles)						
Reading	67	77	55	55	40	1 > 2, 3, 4
Math	67	83	58	67	41	1 > 2, 3, 4 2, 3 > 4
Language skills	67	82	57	54	42	1 > 2, 3, 4
Behavior ratings (4.0 scale)						
Follow rules	66	2.9	2.2	2.9	2.4	1, 3 > 2, 4
Social skills	66	2.9	2.3	3.0	2.6	1, 3 > 2
Self-confidence	65	2.8	2.3	3.1	2.3	1, 3 > 2. 4
Self-discipline	65	2.8	2.1	2.9	2.3	1, 3 > 2, 4

Note: Group differences were determined by post hoc tests after a one-way analysis of variance confirmed significant differences between the groups. Scores were averaged for each student across Grades 3-6 when two or more marks were available ($p < .05$).

in all three achievement domains, this suggests that as a group the Mexican-American–At-Risk students generally have more severe academic deficits than other students.

The achievement test histories of these students are somewhat surprising in that they indicate that, even though the Mexican-American–Successful group earned grades comparable to those of the Anglo–Successful group and consistently higher grades than the at-risk groups, the Mexican-American–Successful students performed at a level similar to the Anglo–At-Risk levels on nationally standardized group examinations. This finding is extremely important, as it suggests that even when Mexican-American students perform well on a day-to-day basis in school, their level of preparation may not be sufficient for successful competition in postsecondary education. While it presently cannot be determined if this finding is related to differences in test-taking or academic skills, it is most important to further examine the profiles of these groups.

Behavior ratings from Grades 3–6. Behavior ratings in the areas of following rules, social skills, self-confidence, and self-discipline were examined. The Anglo–Successful and Mexican-American–Successful students consistently were rated higher than either the Anglo–At-Risk or Mexican-American–At-Risk groups in the areas that involve following rules, self-confidence, and self-discipline. The Mexican-American–At-Risk group were rated as having social skills comparable to those of the Anglo–Successful or Mexican-American–Successful groups.

Current Student Information

Educational aspirations. To determine if at-risk and successful students held diverging attitudes about school and dropping out, students rated the importance of specific educational goals. There were no significant differences among the four groups on any items (Table 2). All students strongly felt that traditional academic attainment was very important.

TABLE 2
Students' Mean Ratings of the Importance of Educational Goals

How important are each of the following:	Overall mean	Anglo		Mexican-American		Group difference
		Successful	At-Risk	Successful	At-Risk	
1. That you graduate from high school	4.8	4.9	4.4	4.8	5.0	None
2. To your family that you graduate	4.6	4.7	4.4	4.8	4.6	None
3. That you do well in your classes	4.4	4.5	4.0	4.7	4.4	None
4. That you attend college	4.3	4.4	4.1	4.8	3.9	None

Note: The response scale was 1 = not very important; 2 = not important; 3 = neutral; 4 = important; and 5 = very important. None of the average group ratings were significantly different.

The two highest average ratings were given to the traditional values of "graduating from high school," and to the "importance to your family that you graduate from high school." It is particularly interesting that all students in the Mexican-American–At-Risk group gave the highest rating possible to the importance of graduating from high school.

Contrary to stereotypic opinions, this finding indicates that the Mexican-American–At-Risk students have a very strong, positive attitude toward traditional academic attainment. This suggests that dropout prevention programs do not need to invest many resources to convince Mexican-American–At-Risk students to stay in school, or of the positive benefits of academic success. These students appear to value and desire an education; what is needed is to learn to use their resources to overcome any barriers encountered in seeking an education.

Importance of selected behaviors for getting a high school diploma. In rating the importance of behaviors related to getting a high school diploma, there were no differences among the four groups (Table 3) with respect to the top four behaviors: "spend more time studying," "go to classes regularly," "take school more seriously," and "get some help with my homework."

This finding suggests that both the Mexican-American–At-Risk and Anglo–At-Risk students value education and are aware of the generic behaviors necessary for school success.

Acceptability of 25 reasons for dropping out of high school. Students rated the acceptability of 25 reasons for dropping out of high school on a 5-point Likert scale. Mean ratings for each group were computed and the reasons for dropping out of school were then rank-ordered by overall mean. As can be seen from Table 4, the two Anglo groups rated the same five items as most acceptable reasons for leaving school. That is, both Anglo groups indicated that having a major illness, getting a job to help the family with money, becoming pregnant, being kicked out of the home by one's parents, and having a personal or emotional problem were permissible reasons to leave school. The Mexican-American–Successful group rated the above items very highly in acceptability but indicated that a drug or alcohol problem was a more acceptable reason to leave school than having a personal or emotional problem. The Mexican-American–At-Risk group, however, showed some striking contrasts in the reasons found to be acceptable for dropping out of school: Although this group did agree that having a major illness and getting a job to help the family were appropriate reasons for leaving school, they differed from the other groups by indicating that dropping out was acceptable for reasons related to helping out with chores around the home, falling far behind in schoolwork, or getting married.

TABLE 3
Students' Mean Ratings of the Importance of
Specific Behaviors for High School Graduation

| Specific behavior | Overall mean | Anglo | | Mexican-American | | Group difference |
		Successful (1)	At-Risk (2)	Successful (3)	At-Risk (4)	
1. Spend more time studying	4.3	4.2 (2)	4.3 (1)	4.5 (2)	4.4 (1)	None
2. Go to my classes regularly	4.2	4.2 (1)	4.1 (2)	4.6 (1)	4.1 (3)	None
3. Take school more seriously	4.0	3.8 (3)	3.8 (3)	3.9 (3)	4.4 (2)	None
4. Get some heap with my homework	3.6	3.1 (4)	3.8 (4)	3.8 (4)	3.7 (4)	None

Note: The response scale was: 1 = not very important; 2 = not important; 3 = neutral; 4 = important; 5 = very important. Values in parentheses are the rankings of the items for each group. None of these average group ratings were significantly different.

Several significant differences between the groups were found.

1. The Mexican-American–At-Risk student generally felt that becoming pregnant was a less acceptable reason to leave school than the Anglo–At-Risk and the Mexican-American–Successful students. This same group, however, indicated that dropping out to help with home chores or to hang out with friends were more acceptable reasons than did the other three comparison groups.

2. The Anglo–Successful group, in contrast to the other three groups, rated "falling far behind in their units," "getting a job to buy the things they want," and "not being promoted to the next grade," as less acceptable reasons to drop out.

These data suggest that both at-risk and successful students share largely similar and positive educational values regarding education. The students in this survey rated few life experiences as clearly reasonable excuses for dropping out. It was of particular interest that the Mexican-American–At-Risk students, contrary to stereotypic beliefs, do not consider pregnancy as a sufficient reason for dropping out. However, this group appears to be more sensitive to familial, peer-related, and other social concerns by its greater acceptance of such notions as leaving school to assist the family with household chores or to spend time with friends; this finding should

be considered when planning dropout prevention activities. Finally, the Anglo–Successful students were less likely to consider financial problems or school achievement problems such as grade retention and falling behind on units as reasonable barriers to a high school diploma. These results may reflect the fact that this group historically has had more positive school experiences; as a result, they may have more confidence in their ability to overcome educational problems when they occur.

Attitudes toward homework. Students' completion of homework activities on a day-to-day basis can indicate the degree of their involvement and commitment to school. To determine this commitment, students were asked to indicate what they thought they would do if invited to a movie on a school night when they had homework to complete. The most frequently given response for each Mexican-American group was to finish the assignment immediately, whereas most Anglo–Successful students would hope to have time to complete the work at a later time (Table 5). A large percentage of the Anglo–At-Risk group (42%) indicated they would not do the homework and would be unconcerned that it was uncompleted, suggesting that the Anglo–At-Risk group had a more negative attitude toward completing homework assignments than the other three groups.

TABLE 4
Student Mean Ratings of the Acceptability of
Specific Reasons for Dropping Out of High School

Reasons for dropping out of school	Overall mean	Anglo		Mexican-American		Group difference
		Successful (1)	At-Risk (2)	Successful (3)	At-Risk (4)	
1. Having a major illness	3.6	4.1 (1)	3.5 (2)	3.3 (3)	3.5 (1)	None
2. Getting a job to help the family with money	3.5	3.7 (2)	3.3 (3)	3.6 (2)	3.3 (2)	None
3. Becoming pregnant	3.2	3.1 (4)	3.8 (1)	3.8 (1)	2.5	4 < 2, 3*
4. Parents kicking them out of the house	3.0	3.1 (3)	3.3 (4)	3.0 (5)	2.7	None
5. Having a personal/emotional problem	2.8	2.7 (5)	2.8 (5)	2.8	2.8	None
6. School is irrelevant to future goals	2.7	2.5	2.5	3.0	2.8	None
7. Having a drug/alcohol problem	2.7	2.6	2.4	3.1 (4)	2.6	None
8. Problem at home (arguments, financial problems)	2.6	2.5	2.4	2.8	2.7	None
9. Family crisis (divorce, death in the family	2.5	2.5	2.5	2.7	2.6	None
10. Moving to another city and going to a new school	2.5	2.3	2.4	2.6	2.6	None
11. To help out with chores around the home	2.5	2.1	2.1	2.4 (3)	3.2	4 > 1, 2, 3*
12. Getting married	2.5	2.1	2.6	2.3	2.8 (5)	None
13. Feel like a failure at school	2.4	2.1	2.4	2.5	2.7	None
14. Can't find any reason to continue in school	2.4	2.2	2.0	2.7	2.7	None
15. Feeling rejected by other students	2.4	2.3	2.4	2.3	2.7	None
16. Teachers not caring about students	2.4	2.4	2.3	2.6	2.2	None
17. Falling far behind in their units	2.4	1.8	2.1	2.7	2.9 (4)	1 < 2, 3, 4*
18. No friends at school/ Not fitting in	2.3	2.2	2.3	2.5	2.3	None
19. Getting a job to buy the things they want	2.3	1.5	2.7	2.4	2.7	1 < 2, 3, 4*
20. Not being promoted to the next grade	2.3	1.8	2.1	2.4	2.8	1 < 2, 3, 4*
21. School work being too difficult	2.2	1.8	2.1	2.2	2.5	None
22. Unable to keep up with the reading assignments	2.0	1.7	2.1	1.9	2.4	None
23. Being bored with school	1.9	1.2	1.8	2.0	2.6	None
24. To hang out with friends	1.8	1.1	1.7	1.8	2.7	4 > 1, 2, 3*
25. Best friends drop out of school	1.6	1.2	1.7	1.5	1.9	None

Note: The response scale was: 1 = very unacceptable; 2 = unacceptable; 3 = in-between unacceptable/acceptable; 4 = acceptable; 5 = very acceptable. Values in parentheses are the ranks of the top five acceptable reasons for each group.

* These average group scores were statistically different ($p < .05$).

TABLE 5
Percentage of Students Indicating What They Would Do About Homework
if Asked by a Friend to Go to a Movie on a School Night

Would you finish your homework?	Mean percentage	Anglo		Mexican-American	
		Successful	At-Risk	Successful	At-Risk
Yes, finish it	42%	35%	35%	44% (1)	52% (1)
Hope have time to do it later	32%	50% (1)	24%	38%	19%
Forget homework, don't care	22%	10%	42% (1)	19%	19%
Forget homework, feel guilty	3%	5%	0%	0%	5%
Stay home, do nothing	1%	0%	0%	0%	1%

Note: Values in parentheses show the first ranked response for each group.

The students' responses to this motivation-related item are particularly revealing. The findings of this study have shown that the Anglo–At-Risk students do not do well in school although according to their percentile ranking on achievement tests they possess adequate academic skills and an awareness of the behavior necessary for school success. Their poorer behavioral ratings as well as their indication that they would be unconcerned about the consequences of their decision to neglect schoolwork suggests that the low achievement of this group may be due to insufficient motivation and/or a poor attitude towards school. In contrast, the Mexican-American–At-Risk students indicated to a much greater degree than the other groups that they would complete their assignment rather than go to a movie. This finding is particularly interesting in light of the findings discussed earlier in this chapter, which suggest that this group may be more sensitive to social pressures. Although there is strong evidence that the Mexican-American–At-Risk group has strong educational values and is both aware of and wanting to demonstrate appropriate school-related behavior, this sensitivity to the social milieu may make it difficult for them to actually follow through on their intent.

Student self-concept. Students' feelings about their abilities and accomplishments can affect their effort and motivation to succeed in school. To determine how students felt about themselves, they were asked to compare themselves on 25 personal traits with other pupils at their junior high school (the method used was based on work by Marsh, 1986). This intraschool comparison was used to create a meaningful yardstick with which to express their self-perceptions.

Although no significant differences in the total self-concept score were found between the four groups, the Anglo–At-Risk group rated themselves lower than the other groups. The Mexican-American–Successful group rated themselves more favorably than did the Anglo–Successful or the Mexican-American–At-Risk groups.

The Anglo–At-Risk group indicated that eight problematic areas differentiate them from their junior high school peers. These areas included having less desire for good grades, less desire to learn, and less self-control and feeling less able to get along with teachers. They additionally indicated that they did homework less often, performed more poorly in math class, were less excited about school, and were less likely to receive a diploma than other students at their school.

Differences were also noted between the Mexican-American–Successful and Mexican-American–At-Risk groups on four individual items. Specifically, the Mexican-American–At-Risk group was more likely than the Mexican-American–Successful group to indicate that they had less self-control, were less able to get along with their teachers, did their homework less often, and were doing poorly in math class.

Again, this finding reinforces the hypothesis that Mexican-American–At-Risk students may have difficulty following through on behaviors necessary for school success.

It is of interest that six of the eight differences for the Anglo–At-Risk and two of the four differences for the Mexican-American–At-Risk students involved personal attributes related to motivation. In general, the Mexican-American–Successful group indicated they were highly motivated to do well in school, whereas the Anglo–At-Risk group had less positive feelings about school and, for that matter, about the likelihood that they would even graduate from high school. They also had a tendency to feel teachers did not like them as much as other students. Thus, the somewhat lower self-concept ratings appeared to be tied more to the personal or motivational component of school than to the academic component. A final note is that once again the Mexican-American–At-Risk students expressed strong feelings about wanting to do well in school. In fact, they had a very high average rating (2.5 out of 3.0) on the item "How much I worry about grades."

Personal stressors. To identify the kinds of stressful events students experience and in turn to determine the impact such events might have in students' academic progress, the students were asked to indicate if they had experienced any of 50 stressful life events (Herzfeld & Powell, 1986) within the past year. Across all students, at least 30% expressed concern about peer relations at school, relationships with teachers, the world situation and possible war, not having power to get things done, and being in a new school. However, there was also a significant difference in the total number of stressors experienced by each group. As shown in Figure 1, both Mexican-American groups reported experiencing a greater number of stressful events than either Anglo group, the Mexican-American–At-Risk group reporting more than twice the number of stressors as the Anglo–Successful group.

The types of concerns expressed by at least 30% of each group are listed in Table 6 in decreasing order of frequency. The Anglo groups reported experiencing concerns of a more generalized nature, such as the broad issues of peer and teacher relationships, the world situation, and the lack of money. Although the Mexican-American groups also indicated that these events had caused them concern, additional and more specific problems were mentioned. As examples, both of the Mexican-American groups reported that they became embarrassed easily and wanted to work but were unable to find a job. The Mexican-American–Successful group indicated difficulty in public speaking while the Mexican-American–At-Risk group, which reported more numerous as well as more severe stressors than the other three groups, indicated concerns related to being in new classes, having friends move away, feeling peer pressures, lacking privacy at home, fearing for their physical safety, and worrying about changes in their family's composition.

Figure 2 highlights some of the more meaningful group differences among the stressors. As can be seen, both at-risk groups expressed a fear of dying; this concern was particularly pervasive for the Mexican-American–At-Risk group, with 67% identifying fear of dying as a recently experienced event. In contrast, only 5% of the Anglo–Successful students reported experiencing this stressor. Similarly, almost a quarter of the Mexican-American–At-Risk students indicated that a parent had died within the past year, whereas no individuals in the Anglo–Successful group reported experiencing this life event. Another large group difference involved the fear of being in a new class: 67% of the Mexican-American–At-Risk group admitted this concern compared to 31%, 12%, and 10% in the Mexican-American–Successful, Anglo–At-Risk, and Anglo–Successful groups, respectively. These findings suggest that, compared to the other three groups, the Mexican-American–At-Risk group experienced more instability in their lives that was due to personal tragedies, relocation, or other environmental factors.

Finally, while most students indicated that the timely completion of school assignments had been of concern, none of the Anglo–At-Risk students reported that they felt rushed to get reports or homework

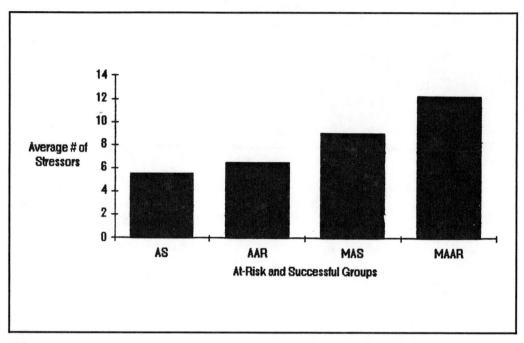

Figure 1. Average number of stressors reported by the students in each of the four groups: Anglo–Successful (AS); Anglo–At–Risk (AAR); Mexican–American–Successful (MAS); Mexican–American–At–Risk (MAAR).

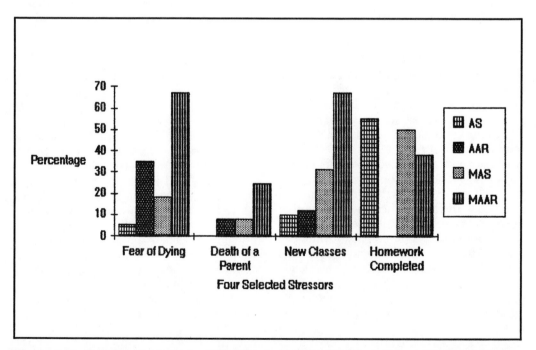

Figure 2. Percentage of students indicating being worried about four selected stressors. Anglo–Successful (AS); Anglo–At–Risk (AAR); Mexican–American–Successful (MAS); Mexican–American–At–Risk (MAAR).

TABLE 6
Percentage Endorsement of Student Concerns Most Commonly Expressed
(≥ 30% of Students)

Anglo		Mexican-American	
Successful	At-Risk	Successful	At-Risk
Peer relationships (65)	Teacher relationships (53)	Not having enough money (63)	Peer relationships (76)
Teacher relationships (55)	The world situation/war (41)	Peer relationships (50)	The world situation/war (67)
Not getting homework done on time (55)	Not having enough money (41)	The world situation/war (50)	Fear of dying (67)
The world situation/war (30)	Feeling as if not accomplishing anything (41)	Not enough personal power (50)	Being in a new school (62)
Not enough personal power (30)	Peer relationships (35)	Being in a new school (50)	New classes (62)
Not having enough money (30)	Not enough personal power (35)	Not getting homework done on time (50)	Teacher relationships (57)
Not enough time to study (30)	Fear of dying (35)	Getting embarrassed easily (38)	Not enough personal power (52)
		Not enough time to study (38)	Getting embarrassed easily (52)
		Wanting to work, but dan't find a job (38)	A friend has moved away (48)
		Feeling as if not accomplishing anything (31)	New crowd I hang around with (48)
		Can't speak in class or in front of a group (31)	Getting homework done on time (38)
			No privacy at home (38)
			Wanting to work, but can't find a job (38)
			Not enough time to study for tests (33)
			Feeling as if not accomplishing anything (33)
			Having a new step-parent (33)
			Being impatient, can't wait (33)
			Not having enough money (30)
			Feeling pressured to do things by friends (30)
			Worry about being beat-up (30)
			Having a new child in the family (30)

done on time. Again, this is felt to reflect lower levels of motivation and lack of concern for the timely completion of school assignments.

SUMMARY RECOMMENDATIONS AND CONCLUSION

A basic assumption of this study is that the dropout problem must be understood and addressed from a prevention perspective. Educators must not merely deter students from leaving school, but must help students experience greater success in school through greater awareness of the factors that influence their school performance. To this end, this study examined the profiles of Anglo and Mexican-American junior high school students with successful and unsuccessful performance. The profiles that emerged were quite interesting.

The academic profiles of the Anglo and Mexican-American successful students were quite similar on most academic variables. The exception occurred with achievement test scores: The Anglo–Successful group obtained consistently higher scores than the Mexican-American–Successful group in the areas of reading, math, and language. This finding is similar to previous studies that show that Hispanics perform poorly at all levels of national standardized tests. Furthermore, this finding suggests that Mexican-American students who earn satisfactory grades may still need assistance to be competitive on national examinations.

In contrast to the similarities noted for both groups of successful students, the academic profiles of the Anglo and Mexican-American–At-Risk students indicated some differences. The Mexican-American–At-Risk students obtained low scores on achievement tests compared to above average scores for the Anglo–At-Risk students. The Mexican-American–At-Risk students appeared highly motivated to complete school work, but the Anglo–At-Risk students indicated general indifference to this task. The Mexican-American–At-Risk group reported experiencing more numerous and qualitatively severe stressful events than the other groups Both the

Anglo–At-Risk and Mexican-American–At-Risk students, however, were perceived by their teachers to have less well developed personal and study skills. Although both groups of students do poorly with respect to grades, the fact that their profiles are strikingly different suggests that the reasons for receiving poor grades are different for the two groups. The poor grades received by the Anglo–At-Risk students may reflect an indifferent or negative attitude towards education, whereas the low performance of the Mexican-American students may reflect weak academic skills and a reaction to significant stress in their personal lives.

Dropout prevention and intervention programs directed at these disparate groups would necessitate different strategies. It is apparent from the data presented in this study that programs that focus only on academic tutoring for all students are too restrictive. For example, programs directed at students demonstrating profiles similar to the Anglo–At-Risk group might be rendered more effective through the provision of early and consistent counseling and guidance interventions. On the other hand, programs directed at students with profiles more similar to the Mexican-American–At-Risk group should employ strategies that provide intensive academic assistance, low student–teacher ratios, and social skills training as well as outreach services when appropriate.

The low-achieving students in this study consistently were rated as having poor social skills, self-discipline, and study habits. These skills deficits likely are the result of unremediated problems from the early school grades and may be a major contributing factor to a student's decision to drop out of school. It is most important that a concerted effort be made in the primary grades to train students in effective social skills, and study habits, as well as in cooperative and individual learning strategies to minimize the negative effect of these variables at the secondary level.

It is interesting that students in all four groups felt that graduating from high school was very important and that they were aware of the behaviors necessary for school success. All students appeared to value educational goals and attainment. However, such values and knowledge may be insufficient to prevent future dropouts: Although Anglo–At-Risk students have satisfactory academic skills, general values, and awareness of the appropriate behavior for success in school, they are unmotivated to perform the tasks that will facilitate academic achievement, particularly when a more attractive behavioral option is available. Similarly, the personal turmoil experienced by many of the Mexican-American–At-Risk students combined with weak academic skills may hinder their goal of a high school diploma.

The presence of significant stress can have a detrimental effect on a person's life and the finding that Mexican-Americans report more numerous and severe stressful events has tremendous programmatic implications. This study's findings indicated that stress is a major socioeducational problem confronting at-risk Mexican-American students. Therefore, there is a need to develop school and community programs to help Mexican-American students and their families to more effectively deal with and prevent the extensive and potentially debilitating stressors affecting them.

Although this study solely focused on students, it is critical that family, school, and community variables be closely examined in seeking greater understanding for the dropout problem, both in a general community and in the Hispanic community. Theories that address the interactive relationship between the individual, the family, the school, and the community must be developed and refined. Some recent work has addressed this issue and has begun to explore the ways in which each of these variables impact on each other (Casas & Furlong, 1986; Casas, Furlong, & Solberg, 1988).

Educators must reconceptualize the dropout problems and begin to seek dynamic, manageable solutions. If the dropout problem is to be successfully addressed for all racial and ethnic groups, and in particular the Mexican-American, it will be necessary to take an action-oriented direction that empowers students, parents, and educators to develop a set of relevant educational goals and objectives for which

they can assume responsibility and identify appropriate strategies. These should include (a) emphasis on excellence and equity in academic instruction for all students; (b) providing early intervention for identified high-risk students; (c) providing a range of alternative and flexible educational approaches and settings specific to the needs of high-risk students; (d) improving outreach and developing working relationships with all parents; (e) improving the coordination and use of community resources; and (f) coordinating, supporting, monitoring, and evaluating efforts to combat the problem.

To attain such objectives will require that the problem be addressed from a multifaceted perspective that considers individual, family, school, and community variables. While programs in line with the above recommendations have significant fiscal implications, failure to take action can have significant and negative economic consequences for the United States. It is therefore imperative that legislators, businesspeople, community agencies, administrators, teachers, parents, and students accept responsibility for solving the significant dropout problem for this country's at-risk students.

ACKNOWLEDGMENTS

A grant for this study was provided by the Santa Barbara School Districts' Dropout Committee. The cooperation and support of principals Rudy Aguilera, Dr. Robert Bowen, and Linton Roberts is gratefully acknowledged. Additional support was provided by school counselors Vee McNeil, Don Skipworth, Irene Stone, and Hal Visser. Herb Petersen and McDonald's restaurants of Santa Barbara also provided support for this study.

REFERENCES

Aldaco, M. (1988). *Update of persistence and graduation rates at the University of California.* Berkeley: University of California, Admission and Outreach Services, Office of the President.

Barber, L., & McClellan, M. (1987). Looking at America's dropouts: Who are they? *Phi Delta Kappan, 68*(4) (December), 264–267.

Barr, R. (1985). *An essay on school dropout for the San Diego Unified School District.* San Diego, CA: San Diego Unified School District, Planning, Research, and Evaluation Division.

Bloom, B. S. (1964). *Stability and change in human characteristics.* New York: Wiley.

Carter, T., & Segura, R. (1979). *Mexican Americans in school: A decade of change.* New York: College Entrance Examination Board.

Casas, J., & Furlong, M. (1986). In search of an understanding and responsible resolution to the Mexican-American educational dropout problem. *California Public School Forum, 1,* 45–63.

Casas, J., Furlong, M., Carranza, O., & Solberg, S. (1986). *Santa Barbara student success study.* Unpublished manuscript. University of California, Santa Barbara.

Casas, J., Furlong, M., & Solberg, S. (1988). *Parent Empowerment Program (PEP-Si): Padres En Poder-Si.* Unpublished manuscript, University of California, Santa Barbara.

Casas, J., & Ponterotto, J. (1984). Profiling an invisible minority in high education: The Chicana. *Personnel and Guidance Journal, 62,* 349–353.

Cordtz, D. (1989). Dropouts: Retrieving America's labor lost. *Financial World, 158*(7), 36–46.

Crutsinger, M. (1986). Typical American family's net worth – $32,667. *Santa Barbara News-Press,* July 20, A–12.

Ford Foundation. (1984). *Hispanics: Challenges and opportunities.* New York: Author.

Hahn, A., Danzberger, J., & Lefkowitz, B. (1987). *Dropouts in America. Enough is known for action.* Washington, DC: Institute for Educational Leadership.

Herzfeld, G., & Powell, R. (1986). *Coping for kids.* West Nyack, NY: Center for Applied Research in Education.

Levin, H. (1985). *The state youth initiatives project* (Working paper #6). Philadelphia: Public/Private Ventures.

Marsh, H. (1986). Self-serving effect (bias?) in academic attributions: Its relation to academic achievement and self-concept. *Journal of Educational Psychology, 78,* 190–200.

McEvoy, A. (1988). Student development and exclusion. *School Intervention Report, 1,* February, entire issue.

Naglieri, J. (1985). *Matrix Analogies Test.* New York: Merrill.

National Commission on Secondary Schooling for Hispanics. (1984). *Make something happen: Hispanics and urban high school reform. Vol. 1.* Washington, DC: Hispanic Policy Development Project.

Office of Educational Research and Improvement. (1984). *Two years in high school: The status of 1980 sophomores in 1982.* Washington, DC: U.S. Department of Education, National Center for Education Statistics.

Pifer, A. (1984). *Speech at Investiture of Tomas Arciniega as President of California State College, Bakersfield.* Bakersfield, May 11th.

Rumberger, R. W. (Fall, 1986). High school dropouts: A problem for research, policy, and practice. *California Public Schools Forum, 1,* 1–19.

U.S. Department of Commerce, Bureau of the Census. (1979). *Lifetime earnings estimates for men and women in the United States.* Washington, DC: U.S. Government Printing Office.

U.S. Department of Commerce, Bureau of the Census. (1980). *Persons of Spanish origin in the United States* (Series P-20, 354). Washington, DC: U.S. Government Printing Office.

U.S. Department of Education, National Center for Educational Statistics. (1984). *Digest of education statistics and the condition of education.* Washington, DC: Author

Wehlage, G., & Rotter, R. (1986). Dropping out: How much do schools contribute to the problem? *Teachers College Record, 87*(3), 374–392.

FOOTNOTES

[1]Ethnicity was determined from the family ethnicity survey required of all students in California.

[2]To generate a sample of successful students, the fall 1985 semester GPAs of all junior high school students in the school district were rank-ordered. Successful Mexican-American students were matched with successful Anglo students to equate GPA levels for each group. All successful students had a GPA of 3.0 or higher. The successful students were then matched with at-risk students on the basis of sex, ethnicity, grade level, and school of enrollment.

[3]Since there is a strong relationship between reading, language skills, and school success, performance in English class was felt to be a reliable at-risk indicator. Therefore, students who had failed or received a D in their Fall semester English class were categorized as at-risk.

[4]A complete description of sample selection and data collection procedures is provided in Casas, Furlong, Carranza, and Solberg (1986).

[5]Semiprofessional work is defined as a job that requires some training or some schooling (e.g., junior college).

CHAPTER 7

A Model for Interventions with Low Achieving Minority Students

Antoinette Halsell Miranda
The Ohio State University

Maryann Santos de Barona
Arizona State University

It has been estimated that as many as 30% of our nation's children face a high risk of educational failure. School failure can be attributed to a variety of reasons: (a) developmental immaturity or a lack of preparation for formal learning; (b) undiagnosed learning disabilities, emotional problems, or physical handicaps; (c) language problems or a non-English speaking background; (d) racial or ethnic prejudice; (e) parents who are indifferent to, or illequipped to handle, their children's emotional and/or educational needs; and (f) schools or instruction of substandard quality (Committee for Economic Development, 1987).

Demographic statistics indicate that the at-risk child tends to be poor and of an ethnic minority: 43% of Black and 40% of Hispanic children currently live in families whose incomes fall below the poverty line. Additionally, the proportion of poor, ethnic minority children in the United States is expected to continue its steady increase: It is anticipated that by the year 2000 at least 38% of all children under the age of 18 years will belong to an ethnic minority group and that a large proportion of this group will be from disadvantaged homes (Committee for Economic Development, 1987; Miller, 1986).

Additional statistics emphasize the problem: "Poverty is most highly pronounced for those children living in single-parent households headed by women" (Committee for Economic Development, 1987, p. 9). Children in one-parent families perform more poorly in school and their dropout rate is nearly twice as high as the overall average. In 1985, 66% of Black children and over 70% of Hispanic children living in female-headed households lived in poverty. "This trend seems to be continuing unabated. Last year, 74.5% of all Black infants were born to unwed mothers, half of them teenagers" (Committee for Economic Development, 1987, p. 9). It appears evident that a great many of these children will lack the family support that is essential to school success.

"Children from poor and single-parent households are more likely than others to be children of teenage parents and to become teenage parents themselves. By age five, the children of teen parents already run a high risk of later unemployability. Not only do teen parents often lack employability skills; they also lack the necessary resources to begin developing their children's future parenting and employability skills." (Committee for Economic Development, 1987, p. 9)

Over the past two decades, a great deal of education literature has reported on the minority child at risk in the educational system. Much of this research has focused on the failure of these minority children to succeed academically. A number of theories have evolved over the years to explain this phenomenon: Whereas early literature attributed failure to the child and the family environment and at times included genetic explanations, later literature has recognized the role of the educational system in inhibiting the academic progress of minority children, particularly in large urban schools.

Today, the problems of the educationally disadvantaged are at unparalleled levels and may in fact jeopardize the ability of the United States to maintain its world leadership role. Researchers and educators have recognized that factors external to the child contribute significantly to educational risk. These external factors can be grouped into categories to include the classroom, school, home, and community (Natriello, Pallas, & McDill, 1987). Subsumed within these groupings are problems related to poverty, teenage pregnancy, high dropout rates from school, poor parenting, and lack of access to adequate educational services; each has seen a steady increase in recent years and together they seriously hinder the academic progress of many of our nation's youth. Problems related to these occurrences threaten to create a long-term and widespread deterioration of the nation's resources and limit our ability to compete successfully. Our youth are the nation's future, and it is important that they be prepared to take the reins of leadership. Therefore, it is imperative that all members of our society recognize this critical situation and endorse a multi-faceted approach to improving the educational achievement of our students.

More recent educational theories and strategies have emphasized the role of economic status, home environment, and cultural characteristics (Murphy, 1986). They generally follow the premise that since the educational system reflects the values of the white middle class culture, minority children are at a disadvantage because their cultural patterns are incongruent with those of the dominant culture.

The concept of cultural differences is widely accepted and is often useful for understanding variation among children. Based on a set of values, goals, and beliefs that are unique to the group experience, a culture reinforces specific patterns of behavior to help the group adapt and survive in their environment while at the same time maintaining the salient characteristics of the group. For minority children, to the extent that such behavior patterns differ from those of a middle class majority culture, the variable of culture may be both important and significant in their educational problems. As an example, when entering the school environment, typified by the norms and expectations of the U.S. middle class, minority children experience a new set of demands for which they have not learned behaviors acceptable to the school. To succeed at school, it is minority children who must change; rarely does the educational setting attempt to alter its structure or accommodate these children's unique style.

Problems exist, of course, in attempts to alter the educational setting. Schools serving the educationally disadvantaged frequently have fewer rather than more resources to deal with the greater needs of their students. They often lack money, equipment, appropriate curriculum, well-trained and supportive teachers, and adequate facilities. "Teachers sometimes have low aspirations for students from poor families and don't expect as much from them as they do from students from higher income homes" (Wagner, 1984, p. 187). Additionally, teachers often perceive minority students as having less academic interest and ability than their white counterparts (Felice, 1981). A disproportionate number of minority students tend to be placed in vocational, special education, and other nonacademic courses or to be taught a diluted version of the standard curriculum (Horn, 1987; Sleeter & Grant, 1986):

> Thinking of at-risk children in terms of failures and grievances can mislead us into lowering our expectations — for them and for ourselves. Such thinking can result in schools that place so much emphasis on remediation, drill, and discipline that they miss the higher purposes of education — and in so doing reflect a profound disrespect for the students. (Glenn, 1986, p. 134)

The consequences of low educational attainment are far-reaching. Research on stratification and occupational mobility has consistently shown that the number of years of education completed is the primary determinant of occupational success (Felice, 1981). Conversely "low educational attainment is the strongest predictor of poverty in later life" and is a major determinant of "the level and nature of occupational achievement; it also significantly influences a wide range of other attributes of individuals over their entire life span" (Blau, 1981, p. 8), among them the ability to begin to develop future parenting and employability skills for their own children (Committee for Economic Development, 1987). Thus, education appears to be a primary mechanism for economic and social mobility.

Although progress has been made, the educational attainment of minority children in the United States has been uneven at best and can be viewed as a series of advances and setbacks. Modest gains have been made on scholastic achievement tests although a significant number of minority children continue to score below their white peers (Hodgkinson, 1986). Increases in the number of Blacks and Hispanics graduating from high school have been noted. Unfortunately, these increased numbers have not resulted in increased college entry. As reported in a special edition of Education Week (Hodgkinson, 1986), although 30% more Blacks graduated from high school in 1982 than in 1975, Black enrollment in college dropped 11% during that same period. The number of Hispanic high school graduates increased by 38%, but their college enrollment declined by 16%. Furthermore, the number of minority students who actually complete their college education is diminishing.

In a similar vein, the school dropout rate is reaching critical levels and may reach 40% of all students by the year 2000 (Horn, 1987). Minorities continue to be more likely to drop out of school than whites, particularly in large urban cities. In 1983, for instance, 75% of all white 18 and 19 year olds graduated from high school, compared to less than 60% of Blacks and slightly more than 50% of Hispanics of the same age group (Hodgkinson, 1986). "A child who is poor, Black, or Hispanic is far more likely to be physically disciplined, suspended, expelled, or made to repeat a grade — all practices shown to increase the likelihood that a child will drop out of school" (Horn, 1987, p. 66).

Thus, the many factors that contribute to educational failure appear to be on the rise and likely are increasing the numbers of children at risk for school failure. Schools faced with the task of educating these children must organize their resources so that educational failure is minimized and learning is optimized. Strategies must be developed to facilitate these efforts with the goal of increasing achievement levels and decreasing failure and subsequent dropout.

The role of the home, school, and community are vital influences for school success. They interact to create an environment that can either facilitate or hinder development. For example, in a school environment that lacks positive role models, motivated and energetic teachers, appropriate materials and resources, and a supportive administration, students may become discouraged with the learning process. And, because many may be from homes that do not foster conditions that facilitate and reinforce learning, they may be unaware of acceptable behaviors for school. Faced with a set of demands and expectations for which, in their opinion, there appears to be little purpose, they may lack confidence in the school setting, and see little reason to achieve.

Indeed, it has been reported that the "typical affective characteristics of the drop-out include low self-esteem, little desire for self-growth, and limited commitment to accepted social values" (Beck & Muia, 1981, p. 16). Potential dropouts, faced with a seemingly unresponsive environment, may perceive their very lives as being beyond their individual control (Conrath, 1987). Although they well may have the ability to succeed in school and may be generally of average intelligence (Beck & Muia, 1981; Felice, 1981), these students fall further and further behind as they become increasingly disenchanted with school.

Such school failure has significant monetary consequences for society as well as the individual. It is estimated that, for the dropouts from only one school year, lost earnings and taxes exceed $240 billion over the lifespan of these individuals (Catterall, 1985). This figure is exclusive of additional billions for legal, medical, and other social services that will be impacted by this group. When these figures are considered, investments in early prevention and other education, health, and welfare programs designed to improve the lives of disadvantaged children appear to be less costly and more effective measures.

STRATEGIES FOR COMBATTING LOW ACHIEVEMENT AND DROPOUT

It is apparent that there is a great need for effective strategies to minimize the effects of factors that negatively influence the school achievement of the minority child at risk. The problems of the at-risk child are not unidimensional but are pervasive and affected by all aspects of our society. Problems of such magnitude rarely have simple solutions: Rather, it is important that programs and policies be developed through a multifaceted approach that targets the whole child. Indeed, the Research and Policy Committee of the Committee for Economic Development (1987) recommended that strategies be implemented in the context of school, family, and community and address "fundamental, structural weaknesses in local and national policies toward children and youth and in our public schools" (p. 4). In order that children at risk be provided with a better start and improved chances for learning, this committee strongly encouraged the development and implementation of efforts emphasizing three investment strategies: prevention through early intervention, restructuring the foundations of education, and retention and reentry. These strategies are notable in that they are broad-based and generally require the cooperation and coordination of several layers of government as well as community and school involvement. The basic thrust of the three strategies are presented along with examples of how such strategies can be implemented. Selected specific programs that utilize these strategies are presented in Table 1 (beginning on page 123), which also provides a brief description of salient program components

Prevention Through Early Intervention

This broad-based strategy aimed at helping disadvantaged children improve their educational status emerged from the Great Society programs of the 1960s. Recognizing that the educational problems of disadvantaged children are obvious long before formal schooling begins, this approach attempted to prevent school failure through programs directed at parents and children. Thus, services such as prenatal care, supplementary food programs, Medicaid, childhood immunizations, and preschool education all represent attempts to intervene at early stages of child development. These programs are notable in that they result in cost benefits by reducing the long-range expenditures of society. For example, every dollar spent on prenatal care can save $3–20 in later medical and social costs (Aleshire, 1989b) and every dollar spent on childhood immunizations saves about $10 in later medical costs (Committee for Economic Development, 1987). Similarly, a dollar investment in quality preschool education returns $4.75 because of the lower costs of special education, public assistance, and crime (Committee for Economic Development, 1987). Included in the early intervention approach are the Head Start program and parent and infant training programs, all of which focus on promoting cognitive development through early stimulation. Most, if not all, of these programs target populations of low socioeconomic status (SES), who are often minorities. Despite the fact that many of these programs positively impact on the social, medical, and educational aspects of at-risk children's lives, resources for these programs continue to be limited. The availability of low-cost prenatal care in some states is declining (Aleshire, 1989a), and preschool programs for the disadvantaged reach fewer than one of every five children eligible for such services.

Also included as an early intervention approach is compensatory education. Compensatory education involves programs designed to improve the academic performance of low-achieving students (Murphy, 1986) and to maintain their reading and math achievement gains

TABLE 1
Programs Utilizing Investment Strategies

Programs	Program Goals	Program Components
Children's Aid Society/Hunter College Team Pregnancy Program 130 E. 101 St. New York, NY 10029	Emphasizes personal development as surest prevention for teenage pregnancy	Family life and sex education; Career and job readiness, self-esteem enrichment through the performing arts, health and medical services, sports and recreation, homework help programs, guaranteed access to college
New Futures School Albuquerque Public Schools 2120 Louisiana Boulevard, N.E. Albuquerque, NM 87110	Help school-age parents make responsible, informed decisions, complete their education, have healthy babies, and become well-adjusted and self-sufficient	Comprehensive educational, health, counseling, vocational, and child-care services for pregnant teens and adolescent parents
Ysleta Pre-Kinder Center Program 7909 Ranchland Drive El Paso, TX 79915	Half-day preschool program for non-English-speaking or low-income four-year-olds; Learning laboratory for teachers and instructional aides	Awareness of language as a means of communication; Use of the five senses to observe the environment; Development of motor skills; Expression of creativity; Social-emotional development; Parent-education program; Parenting classes
Comer Process James P. Comer, Maurice Falk Professor of Child Psychiatry, Yale Child Study Center Yale University 230 Frontage St. New Haven, CT 06510	School-based management approach that focuses on changing the attitudes and working relationships of principals, teachers, counselors, healthcare professionals, and parents	Team decision making; Active parent participation in dealing with school issues and student problems
Miami–Dade County School-Based Management Project Dade County Schools 1450 N.E. Second Avenue Miami, FL 33132	School-based management and shared decision making	Budget decentralization, curriculum planning, program planning, collegial decision making, comprehensive planning as a vehicle for improving school-centered programs and establishing priorities
D.C. Management Institute Washington, DC Public Schools 415 12th Street, N.W. Washington, DC 20004	Local businesses train school administrators to improve managerial planning and decision making in noneducation, noncurricular activities	Participants are trained by instructors from private sector; They then provide training to other school personnel
The Door: Services for Adolescents International Center for Integrative Studies 618 Avenue of the Americas New York, NY 10011	Whole-child approach to development; provides social services to address physical, emotional, intellectual and interpersonal problems for youths 12–20 years	Educational and prevocational preparation; Creative and physical arts; Health center; Mental health and social services; Social and legal services
Middle College High School Long Island City, NY 11101	Alternative school on campus of community college for at-risk students	Small class size; Individualized and self-paced educational program; Regular counseing
Summer Training and Education Program Public/Private Ventures 399 Market Street Philadelphia, PA 19106	Increases high school graduation rates by addressing poor academic performance and adolescent parenthood	Remedial reading and math instruction; Life skills; School-year support activities; Work experience

Beethoven Project The Ounce of Prevention Fund 188 W. Randolph St., Suite 2200 Chicago, IL 60601	Prevention-oriented, provide intensive and comprehensive care to at-risk mothers and their children	Prenatal care; Parenting classes; Developmental programs for infants and toddlers; Preschool education; Provides information related to available healthcare, family counseling, and other services
Atlanta Partnership of Business & Education University Plaza Urban Life Suite 736–739 Atlanta, GA 30303	Business–school partnership promotes higher-quality public school education	Adopt-A-School; Affirmative Action/Adopt-a-Student; Distinguished Scholars–Humanities; Institutionalization; Volunteers/Tutorial
Forward in the Fifth 210 Center Street Berea, KY 40403	Business, education, and community join to combat low achievement and high dropout rates through technical and financial assistance	Enriched education for pupils; Increased involvement by parents and businesses; Greater innovation by teachers and principals; Greater communication between schools and the community; Increased confidence in and commitment to the schools
The Boston Compact 26 Court Street Boston, MA 02108	Collaborative effort from government, business, labor, higher education, and community to improve education and reduce dropout	Emphasis on teacher involvement, student support teams, alternative education, parent outreach
Cities in School Cities in Schools, Inc. 1023 15th Street, N.W. Washington, DC 20005	Public–private partnership establishes dropout prevention programs nationwide for at-risk students and their families	Assess community needs; Establish prototype social services in schools; Replicate services communitywide
Coca-Cola Valued Youth Partnership Intercultural Development Research Association 5835 Callaghan, Suite 350/111 San Antonio, TX 78228	Keep potential dropouts from middle and high school students in school and improve their academic achievement	High-risk students tutor younger children
U.S. Navy and America's Schools: A Shared Commitment Pride, Professionalism, and Personal Excellence Naval Military Personnel Command Washington, DC 20370-5000	Navy participates in educational partnerships at elementary, junior high, and high school levels through three programs	Adopt-A-School; Math/Science Initiative; Saturday Scholars
Ogilvy and Mather: Mentoring in the Graphic Arts Ogilvy and Mather Advertising 876 North St. Clair Chicago, IL 60611	Train students for entry-level positions in graphics	After-school work program; Graphic arts skills; Employment upon graduation; Graduate mentoring for new apprentices

(Committee for Economic Development, 1987). Generally provided under the auspices of federal funding such as Chapter I reading and math programs, these programs have played a significant role in narrowing the achievement gap between disadvantaged and nondisadvantaged students. The cost-benefit ratio of compensatory education is great: It is anticipated that a $500 investment for one year of compensatory education can save $3,000 in the cost of repeating a grade. Unfortunately, because of inadequate funding, only 40–50% of children eligible for such services have actually received them.

Restructuring the Foundations of Education

Central to this investment strategy is the belief that the public school system in the United States has not provided youngsters with the skills needed for success in adult life, especially where ethnic minorities and the disadvantaged are concerned. As they are currently structured, many schools in high-risk areas are unable to provide the environment necessary for active participation in learning. Constraints include organizational, personnel, political, and financial considerations. It is increasingly necessary to consider the many ways schools impact on all aspects of the community and society. For example, it appears that factors related to power and status between minority and majority groups play a significant role in the academic progress of minority students:

> "Students are either empowered or disabled as a direct result of their interactions with educators in the school context. Students who are empowered by their schooling experiences develop the ability, confidence, and motivation to succeed academically. They participate competently in instruction as a result of having developed a confident cultural identity as well as appropriate school-based knowledge and interactional structures (Tikunoff, 1983). Students who are disempowered or disabled by their school experiences do not develop this type of cognitive/academic and social/emotional foundation" (Cummins & McNeeley, 1987, p. 86).

Similarly, the complex and often conflicting interaction of student needs and system resources may create in school personnel a sense of powerlessness or disablement and result in inadequate instruction. Therefore, a restructuring of schools is necessary that will permit active involvement and management by local school personnel, parents, and students in decision making and accountability. While state and local authorities would provide direction by establishing goals and standards for excellence, the schools would have the flexibility to decide on the methods and curriculum best able to enhance the academic achievement of their particular student population (Committee for Economic Development, 1987).

This approach places great emphasis on developing the school as an active part of the community, which requires that the school become responsive to the specific needs of the community. Thus, emphasis is placed on a number of critical educational variables in education (Committee for Economic Development, 1987):

- Selecting, training, supporting, and compensating appropriate and motivated teachers for the community;

- Analyzing the instructional process so that the variables that contribute to success for the community's children are identified and optimized;

- Incorporating recent educational technology into the curriculum, where appropriate;

- Providing opportunities for individual, positive instructional interactions through lower student–teacher ratios;

- Supporting and coordinating community and extracurricular activities that can increase students' school involvement (preschool, childcare, sports, tutoring, life-skills training).

Although such an undertaking appears formidable, several approaches for basic school restructuring have been reported. These approaches do not constitute a definitive set of strategies, but rather describe some ways in which school restructuring has been implemented.

The Comer Process (Committee for Economic Development, 1987) is a school-based management approach that focuses on changing the attitudes and working relationships of principals, teachers, counselors, health-care professionals, and parents. This process utilizes team decision making and encourages active parent participation in dealing with school issues and student problems.

The Miami–Dade County School-Based Management Project also incorporates the principles of shared decision making and school-based management (Committee for Economic Development, 1987). The critical elements in this project's goal to improve school functioning include budget decentralization, prioritization, and comprehensive curriculum and program planning.

Finally, local businesses have become involved in training school administrators at the D.C. Management Institute (Committee for Economic Development, 1987).

School personnel first are trained by personnel from the private sector to improve management and other noneducational skills. Subsequently, they use their expertise as teachers to train other school personnel in the newly acquired skills.

Retention and Reentry

The retention and reentry approach targets students who are either dropouts or dropout risks by combining work experiences with basic skills education and personal attention. Frequently, services are provided in an alternative setting that facilitates the acquisition of important social and self-help skills and reduces students' alienation from school and/or society (Committee for Economic Development, 1987; Hodgkinson, 1985).

Although there are many possible retention and reentry strategies, most occur at the high school level. *Mentor programs* are designed to provide the at-risk student with supportive adult contact as well as an appropriate adult role model. In such programs, an adult volunteer has frequent individual contact with the student to discuss problems and successes; the adult assists in problem solving and facilitates interactions between the student and teachers.

Alternative schools are another method for dropout prevention and for school reentry. Although the concept of alternative schools has been implemented in a variety of ways, all have as a common element the delivery of educational services in a nontraditional manner or setting. As an example, the schools-within-schools approach locates the alternative school within a larger school, usually with a totally different structure and organization. Classes are small and teachers know their students on an individual basis; they thus become aware of students' strengths and weaknesses and plan instruction accordingly. Such programs are able to use more individualized instructional strategies, teach problem-solving skills, and monitor progress closely. While such schools are typically small, their placement in the larger host school provides numerous advantages through access to resources such as the library, gym, and counselors.

Other schools-within-schools that are highly effective comingle at-risk students with more successful students in small classes in the host school rather than separating them in remedial classes (Conrath, 1987). This strategy promotes positive social and school-related interactions.

The school-within-school concept has been implemented successfully in a somewhat different form at New York City's Middle College High School. In this alternative high school, at-risk students attend school on the campus of a local community college. In addition to daily exposure to a college environment, students are provided with an individualized and flexible curriculum that considers the students' personal needs. The effectiveness of the Middle College High program is evident from its 85% graduation rate (Committee for Economic Development, 1987).

Still another effective approach with potential dropouts is to schedule at-risk students into a special class that meets at the beginning of each school day. Students earn high school credit in the class, which covers topics such as assertiveness training, problem-solving strategies, basic math and writing skills, group discussions, and goal setting.

Another component of the retention and reentry approach involves strategies that target actual dropouts. Initially, subsidized work programs were the predominant form of assistance to this group. Because the long-term results of such programs were not encouraging, these programs were modified to include opportunities for improving basic academic and job skills as well as for completing high school. Students participating in programs that included these elements, such as those sponsored through Job Corps, Manpower Demonstration and Research Corporation, and the California Conservation Corps, have demonstrated gains in income and employment and have reported positive feelings about themselves and their communities (Committee for Economic Development, 1987).

Regardless of the specific strategies aimed at preventing students from leaving school before graduation, successful dropout prevention programs share a number of characteristics (Conrath, 1987; Hodgkinson, 1985):

1. Program personnel recognize that students' home environment often hinders educational advancement through the lack of a quiet study area or someone to assist with schoolwork. Such facilities and support staff are provided to students either at the program site or in an alternative setting.

2. The learning environment is viewed as personal and intellectually nonthreatening. Low student–teacher ratios enable teaching staff to know students individually and to encourage them to interact in the school on a personal as well as academic level.

3. Emphasis is on students' developing a sense of internal responsibility and increasing self-esteem. To aid this development, student achievement is consistently rewarded in ways that are reinforcing.

4. Staff first ensure that students have the necessary skills to complete tasks before assigning them. Materials and teaching formats are practical and stress the acquisition of basic academic skills.

5. Program personnel recognizes that students' expressions of disinterest often are a defense against admitting their inability to do a task.

6. Although violence is not tolerated, misconduct does not meet with overreaction, but rather is viewed as a sign of student frustration.

7. Program goals and objectives are clearly delineated and implemented by motivated and compassionate staff.

As previously stated, dropout prevention programs are usually targeted at the high school level. However, it is increasingly recognized that by high school age, potential dropouts have already established a pattern of high absenteeism, low academic achievement, low self-esteem, and lack of self-confidence. Problems frequently are too severe and complex for these programs to make a significant positive impact without personal, long-term, and costly investments.

The need for such investments at an earlier point of development was recognized by Eugene Lang, founder of the "I Have a Dream" Foundation. In a 1981 commencement speech to sixth-grade graduates from his East Harlem alma mater, Mr. Lang guaranteed a college scholarship to each student who completed high school. Unwilling to leave full responsibility for this task to the students who might be faced with a multitude of obstacles, Mr. Lang also provided academic and individual support in the form of tutorial and counseling services as well as his personal involvement to advance the goal of high school graduation. This program has served as a model nationwide; business and other philanthropic organizations in over 15 major U.S. cities have joined together to sponsor similar programs involving more than 4,000 students.

This three-pronged approach of directing efforts in the area of early prevention and intervention, restructuring the foundations of education, and retention and reentry offers a comprehensive means of effecting broad changes to major societal problems as well as improving the educational achievement of at-risk students. Although at first glance these efforts may appear to exclude school psychologists from significant involvement, in actuality the professional school psychologist can and should actively encourage many of the programs and strategies discussed. As an integral part of the school environment with involvement in a variety of multidisciplinary activities, the school psychologist is in a unique position to facilitate student development. It is necessary, however, to depart from the often circumscribed role of referral and assessment specialist and actively participate in a variety of proactive educational activities whose goal is to ensure that at-risk children develop the necessary skills for success.

The training and experiences of more and more school psychologists are uniquely suited to such participation. Increasingly, school psychologists are sophisticated change agents. They understand the school environment to be a complex social organization. They are familiar with the resources of the school organization and its community. They are aware of the dynamics and impact of interpersonal interactions on the organization and can use their skills as both consultants and psychoeducational interventionists to assist the school organization in meeting its goals. A number of specific activities in which school psychologists can participate merits detailed description. A model intervention program that highlights numerous ways in which school psychologists can actively promote students' academic and personal growth is then presented.

INTERVENTION ACTIVITIES FOR THE SCHOOL PSYCHOLOGIST

Prevention Through Early Intervention

Within this investment strategy, it is most important to increase children's access to services and to strengthen the network, resources, and skills of those involved in raising and working with children. To accomplish this, the school psychologist might take the following measures:

1. Assist with screening activities to identify children at risk for school failure because of developmental, physical, social, or medical problems. Such involvement can include working with school personnel to develop criteria to determine when children are at risk, selecting or developing an appropriate screening instrument based on those criteria, providing training activities related to its use, organizing the screening program and providing information to the community, assisting with the actual screening procedures, and working with parents on gaining access to appropriate programs.

2. Consult with preschool programs regarding curriculum, management, and developmentally appropriate activities. The goal in this activity would be to help increase staff's skill in identifying children's abilities and needs and to match them to appropriate program content.

3. Conduct or assist with culturally sensitive parenting classes with emphasis on the single parent or stepparent family As

part of this activity, parents should be provided with up-to-date information regarding available community resources that include health care, educational, and recreational opportunities. The school psychologist may also assist parents in learning how to access these resources.

4. Provide staff with opportunities to increase their knowledge and skills. The school psychologist can be instrumental in conducting needs assessments in the school to identify global needs, in organizing and participating in staff development activities based on those needs, in providing materials to staff for independent study and assisting individual staff as they pursue independent study, and in informing staff of opportunities for continuing education.

5. Create a support network for young children and staff by recruiting and training volunteers to work in school and community settings.

Restructuring the Foundations of Education

This approach requires that both technological and human processes in the school organization be reconsidered and modified in relation to the community served. As part of the attempt to provide education and skills for its children, the school organization may require new resources, skills, and perspectives. To facilitate these efforts, the school psychologist might engage in any of the following.

1. Participate in team decision making and planning. The school psychologist brings to these activities knowledge and skill in the area of child development, behavior management, and evaluation as well as in psychological, educational, and organizational theory. Additionally, expertise in communication and consultation can greatly enhance the group's restructuring activities.

2. Assist school management's efforts to obtain needed resources by writing proposals and grants, participating in lobbying and other legislative efforts, and serving as liaison between school and external funding agencies when appropriate.

3. Help the organization determine the effectiveness of its restructuring efforts by designing and implementing evaluation and monitoring strategies.

Retention and Reentry

The retention and reentry investment strategy requires that efforts be intensive, aggressive, and individualized. The activities of the school psychologist, therefore, are likely to be more direct in orientation and might include the following:

1. Counseling with students and staff in alternative settings. Such counseling may involve individual, group, or family counseling and may emphasize areas such as vocational guidance and the development of social skills.
2. Using observational, counseling, and consultative skills to assist staff of alternative programs on individualizing instruction. The school psychologist may provide assistance in developing the academic program, suggest materials to use in instruction, mediate between student and staff, suggest behavioral interventions, and provide numerous other support activities.
3. Facilitating the personal and educational growth of students and staff by providing relevant referrals as well as by conducting staff development and other training activities.

A MODEL INTERVENTION PROGRAM

As noted earlier, early intervention efforts can have a tremendous impact on the lives of children. It is important that children receive early school encouragement and direction so that their talents and strengths will flourish. Children must experience success both academically and socially and develop a sense of themselves as confident and able individuals who are capable of independent learning. Therefore, intervention programs are needed at the elementary level before the student experiences repeated failure.

Although there are many arenas for school psychologists' involvement, the area of study skills development is provided here because of its potential impact on the social as well as academic development of at-risk minority students, and as a *general* model of the many ways in which school psychologists can intervene in the school organization at a relatively early stage of education. Therefore, readers are encouraged to modify as appropriate for their specific school population.

A Study Skills Development Program

Although students' ability to study often is not addressed as an issue in learning, it has been found that the lack of sufficient study skills in a student's repertoire often leads to failure and frustration in school (Gettinger & Knopik, 1987). Conversely, effective study skills facilitate independent learning (Saleebey, 1984) and more active participation in the educational process: "Effective study skills offer students a means of increasing their sense of personal direction or control. Students who have developed a repertoire of study skills often experience feelings of increased competence and confidence as they learn" (Gettinger & Knopik, 1987, p. 594). Thus, unpreparedness, frustration, and poor grades may not be due to lack of ability, but rather to a lack of effective study skills.

Students, particularly those already at risk for school failure and dropout, need to be provided opportunities to learn study skills and effective learning strategies to improve their chances for success. Unfortunately, it has been found that study skills in most schools are taught in a rather haphazard and unplanned manner; this finding prompted the authors of *A Nation at Risk* (National Commission on Excellence in Education, 1983) to recommend that study skills training be introduced in the early school years and continue through children's education.

With the regular education population, several researchers have found that study skills programs in the elementary school have been successful in improving the academic achievement of low achievers (Crittenden, Kaplan, & Heim, 1984; Wood, 1985). Not only did academic achievement improve but it also was indicated that the student's self-concept, self-confidence, and motivation improved. Self-concept is related to achievement when it involves the perception of ability in a particular subject (Beane, 1982; Jordan, 1981). It may be influenced by teachers' expectations, by the class climate, and by previous achievement. Students must experience some measure of success to feel they can succeed; they must see that their efforts do in fact result in a desired outcome. Indeed, achievers have been found to believe that their efforts can lead to desired outcomes to a much greater degree than do underachievers (Kanoy, Johnson, & Kanoy, 1980). Therefore, a study skills development program targeted at low achievers and potential dropouts should incorporate components designed to improve students' self-concept in school-related tasks as well as increasing their belief in their ability to produce desired results.

Many techniques have demonstrated effectiveness in study skills development. Among them are self-management techniques, such as self-monitoring of study time (Tichenor, 1977) and self-reinforcement contingent on studying for set intervals (Greiner & Karoly, 1976), and anxiety management techniques, as well as specific skills such as underlining and notetaking (McAndrew, 1983) and test-taking skills (McPhail, 1981; Millman, Bishop, & Ebel, 1965). "The key to effective studying is in building good habits, such as organization and time management" (Gettinger & Knopik, 1987, p. 594) and therefore the selection of a particular study skills program should be based on the documented needs of the target population as well as knowledge of available resources. A process for such selection and implementation has been proposed (Wise, Genshaft, & Byrley, 1987) that includes a five-phase process of student needs assessment, program planning and staff training, program implementation, remediation, and program evaluation. This basic process is used to describe school psychologists' involvement throughout the development and implementation of the study skills program.

Student needs assessment. Prior to the development of a program, it was important to identify areas of need regarding study skills. The school psychologist played a major organizational and information-gathering role in this activity. Although a number of instruments were available for assessing learning style preferences and study skills, only a few actually focused on elementary-school-age populations. It was necessary for the school psychologist to provide input regarding the appropriateness of the available instruments for use with the school's population and for surveying how the students approached the task of learning and studying. Additionally, cognizant of the many tasks of teachers and administrators, the school psychologist assumed major responsibility for data collection; information regarding students' strengths and deficits was gathered through contact with teachers and through a sampling of students' use of a variety of study skills and learning strategies. As an assessment specialist, the school psychologist was instrumental in interpreting the findings of this phase.

Program planning and staff training. Using information obtained during the student needs assessment, the team of school personnel decided that the greatest need for an intervention program was at the fourth- and fifth-grade level. The school psychologist worked as part of this program development team to develop the program's components. This consisted of first developing a set of goals for the program, specifying the types of study techniques needed for the group, and finally determining how the techniques would be taught to the students. This process resulted in the following program goals: (a) to teach students a variety of study skills/learning strategies; (b) to provide students the opportunity to use their skills on a regular basis; (c) to provide students with ongoing support in their use of study skills so that they could experience success in their use; and (d) to facilitate students' independent use of a variety of techniques.

The team decided that a program with four major components would facilitate goal attainment.

Microclasses. Small groups of no more than eight students were to be set up in which individualized instruction on techniques by the school psychologist would occur. The microclass format would provide the opportunity to discuss appropriate behaviors, practice study skills, and receive feedback on progress. In addition, the microclass was to serve as a forum where discussion on school-related issues occurred.

Integration with school curriculum. Teachers would support the microclass instruction by providing opportunities to use the study skill techniques throughout the school day.

After-school program. This program would provide students a quiet, supportive environment in which they could practice skills and receive assistance when needed on actual material.

Parent component. Parents would be informed about the program and would be encouraged to provide assistance in a number of ways.

Program implementation. *Microclasses.* The microclass met twice a week for 45 minutes for 10 weeks. After the 10-week program, each microclass had a monthly follow-up "refresher" meeting. During the meetings, students were presented with numerous study skill techniques in a relaxed and nonthreatening atmosphere. Discussions, learning activities, and group projects also were a significant part of these sessions.

As part of this process, the group became aware that behaviors such as punctuality, regular attendance, putting forth one's best effort, and respecting others provided important structure and organization for learning and success in school.

Group discussions focused on the relevance of school, career goals, and motivation. During these discussions, students had the opportunity to discuss academic problems and other concerns regarding themselves and school. All students were encouraged to participate in group discussions and to share ideas; to facilitate participation, discussion activities were developed that attempted to include everybody in the conversation. Activities in the program were designed primarily to help students become more successful and productive as well as to improve a sense of their own ability. Some suggested group activities are listed in Table 2.

One session each week was devoted to developing and practicing study skill techniques. The team-selected techniques that were introduced in the microclass are presented in Table 3. Although the study techniques involved general strategies rather than actual content so that generalization across subjects could occur, students were encouraged to practice the various techniques in group using actual schoolwork. During this time, the program facilitator provided feedback to students on their efforts and was available to answer questions and resolve problems associated with the use of these techniques. Students were encouraged to use the skills and determine those they found most effective for themselves.

Integration with school curriculum. The school psychologist regularly informed teachers of the various techniques that were being introduced and practiced in the microclasses. Teachers were encouraged to integrate the techniques wherever possible into their content classes. The school psychologist was available to work with teachers on the use of these techniques in daily classes.

After-school program. The school psychologist trained and supervised community volunteers and peer tutors for this thrice-weekly program. Emphasis was on creating a friendly and inviting atmosphere in which students felt comfortable requesting and obtaining help. To achieve this, the school psychologist worked with student and community volunteers on appropriate ways to interact helpfully with others. During the after-school program, students were able to work individually or in small groups on content material; they also could receive additional assistance in the use of their study techniques.

Parent component. The school psychologist disseminated information about the program through parent organization and community meetings. During these meetings, ways in which parents could support their child's activities at home were

TABLE 2
Suggested Activities for Microclasses

1. *Student goal setting.* Students set a goal each week for a grade they hope to achieve on a weekly test in their content classes. They are required to write and sign a contract specifying their goal. Students report on their progress towards goal attainment each week. The purpose of this activity is to increase students' ability to take responsibility for their behavior and realize positive effects for their actions.

2. *Journal writing.* Students are encouraged to keep a daily journal of their activities. The purpose of this activity is to strengthen writing skills and enable students to see how they use time in their daily lives.

3. *Examining periodical literature.* Students bring newspapers and other periodicals to the microclass. This activity is designed to improve students' reading skills and broaden their knowledge of the outside world. In addition, students become familiar with the types of information that can be obtained from such literature (i.e., current events, sports, television, entertainment, real estate, want ads, editorials, etc.).

4. *Cultural awareness.* To increase children's insight into their cultural heritage, students work in pairs or alone to develop a project dealing with an aspect of their cultural history or a famous person from their culture. A minimum of 4 weeks should be provided to work on this project; presentations are made to the microclass and, when developed, visual materials may be displayed throughout the school.

5. *Career development.* Students research careers of their choosing and share their information with the group. Issues involved in choosing a career are discussed and these include prerequisites, academic preparation, and financial rewards.

6. *Group challenge.* The purpose of this activity is to foster group cooperation and provide students with the opportunity to use their new skills in an area that interests them. Some suggested activities are: (a) write a school newspaper; (b) conduct a history of their school; (c) write a book about the history of their school; (d) learn more about the community they live in.

7. *Library visitation.* Students visit the local library and become acquainted with its facilities. Students who do not have library privileges should acquire a library card.

TABLE 3
Study Skill Topics to be Taught in Microclasses

I. Time management
    a. Importance of a regular plan
    b. Setting up weekly timetables

II. Organization skills
    a. Keeping track of homework that is due
    b. Focusing on exams and long-term assignments
    c. Having required materials to complete an assignment
    d. Being prepared for class
    e. setting goals

III. Test taking
    a. Different test formats
    b. Know what the test will cover
    c. Break material into small sections when studying
    d. Review at least twice before test
    e. Set a realistic goal for test

IV. Problem solving
    a. Helping students develop effective problem-solving strategies

V. Specific skills
    a. Listening
    b. Notetaking
    c. Underlining
    d. Outlining

suggested; in addition, the school psychologist was available to provide more personalized consultation for parents and parent-groups as requested.

Remediation. The remediation phase occurred concurrently with program implementation. The school psychologist was involved in all four aspects of program implementation and this integrated characteristic facilitated the centralization and exchange of information. Thus, there was an early awareness of students who were experiencing difficulty. These students received additional help through the after-school program, and their parents were enlisted for other support activities. Finally, the teachers of students having difficulty were able to provide additional assistance and clarification through their integration activities.

Program evaluation. The school psychologist helped design evaluation strategies for the four program components and facilitated the collection and interpretation of data. This information was then used to determine further needs regarding study skills and to assist in additional planning efforts.

SUMMARY

The high school dropout rate of minority youth is increasing and their low academic achievement continues to be a concern for educators. It has been recognized that school failure and dropout will have significant repercussions for the economic, social, and political future of the United States. It is necessary for new and comprehensive methods to be developed to combat the problems of the educationally disadvantaged. In particular, the present authors believe that broad-based social and educational interventions are necessary, particularly at the elementary level, since the earlier these students can be reached the more likely they may be motivated and able to continue their education. School psychologists have the opportunity to take the initiative and become involved in motivating and facilitating the progress of disadvantaged students in the education system. This chapter suggested a number of ways in which this could occur and additionally presented a schoolwide model intervention program which highlighted the important role of the school psychologist.

REFERENCES

Aleshire, P. (1989a, February 12). Malpractice costing practices. *The Arizona Republic*, p. 2.

Aleshire, P. (1989b, February 22). Drop in rural "baby doctors" hits crisis level in Arizona. *The Arizona Republic*, pp. 1, 10.

Beane, J. A. (1982). Self-concept and self-esteem as curriculum issues. *Educational Leadership, 39*, 504–506.

Beck, L., & Muia, J. A. (1981). Potential high school dropouts. *Education Digest, 46*, 16–19.

Blau, Z. S. (1981). *Black children/white children: Competence, socialization, and social structure.* New York: Free Press.

Catterall, J. S. (December, 1985). On the social costs of dropping out of school. Stanford University, Stanford Education Policy Institute, School of Education.

Committee for Economic Development. (1987). *Children in need: Investment strategies for the educationally disadvantaged.* New York: Committee for Economic Development.

Conrath, J. (1987). Harvesting what we know: Thinking through programs for at risk youth. *Thrust, 16*, 33–35.

Crittenden, M. R., Kaplan, M. H., & Heim, J. K. (1984). Developing effective study skills and self-confidence in academically able adolescents. *Gifted Child Quarterly, 28*, 25–30.

Cummins, J., & McNeeley, S. N. (1987). Language development, academic learning, and empowering minority students. In S. Fradd & W. Tikunoff (Eds.), *Bilingual and bilingual special education: A guide for administrators* (pp. 75–97). San Diego, CA: College-Hill Press.

Felice, L. G. (1981). Black student drop-out behavior: Disengagement from school rejection and racial discrimination. *Journal of Negro Education, 50*, 415–424.

Gettinger, M., & Knopik, S. N. (1987). Study skills. In A. Thomas & J. Grimes (Eds.), *Children's needs: Psychological perspectives* (pp. 594–602). Washington, DC: The National Association of School Psychologists.

Glenn, C. L. (October, 1986). Rich learning for all our children. *Phi Delta Kappan, 68*, 133–134.

Greiner, J. M., & Karoly, P. (1976). Effects of self control training on study activity and academic performance: An analysis of self-monitoring, self-reward, and systematic planning components. *Journal of Counseling Psychology, 23,* 495–502.

Hodgkinson, H. L. (1985). *All one system.* Washington, DC: The Institute for Educational Leadership.

Hodgkinson, H. L. (1986, May 14). At risk: Pupils and their teachers. *Education Week,* p. 28.

Horn, M. (1987, May 18). The burgeoning educational underclass. *U.S. News and World Report, 102,* 66–67.

Jordan, T. J. (1981). Self-concepts, motivation, and academic achievement of Black adolescents. *Journal of Educational Psychology, 73,* 509–517.

Kanoy, R. C., Johnson, B. W., & Kanoy, K. W. (1980). Locus of control and self-concept in achieving and underachieving bright elementary students. *Psychology in the Schools, 17,* 395–399.

McAndrew, D. (1983). Underlining and notetaking: Some suggestions from research. *Journal of Reading, 27,* 103–108.

McPhail, I. (1981). Why teach test-wiseness? *Journal of Reading, 25,* 32–38.

Miller, L. S. (October, 1986). Nation building and education. *Education Digest, 13,* 13–15.

Millman, J., Bishop, C. H., & Ebel, R. (1965). An analysis of test-wiseness. *Educational and Psychological Measurement, 25,* 707–726.

Murphy, D. C. (1986). Educational disadvantagement: Associated factors, current interventions, and implications. *Journal of Negro Education, 55,* 495–507.

National Commission on Excellence in Education. (1983). *A nation at risk: The imperative for educational reform.* Washington, DC: U.S. Government Printing Office.

Natriello, G., Pallas, A., & McDill, E. (1987). *In our lifetime: The educationally disadvantaged and the future of schooling and society.* Washington, DC: Committee for Economic Development, Subcommittee on the Educationally Disadvantaged.

Saleebey, W. (1984). Study skills are basic skills. *Thrust, 13,* 44–45.

Sleeter, C. E., & Grant, C. A. (1986, December). Success for all students. *Phi Delta Kappan, 68,* 297–299.

Tichenor, J. L. (1977). Self-monitoring and self-reinforcement of studying by college students. *Psychological Reports, 40,* 103–108.

Wagner, H. (1984). Why poor kids quit attending school. *Education, 105,* 85–88.

Wise, P. S., Genshaft, J. L., & Byrley, M. B. (1987). Study-skills training: A comprehensive approach. In C. A. Maher & J. E. Zins (Eds.), *Psychoeducational interventions in the schools* (pp. 66–80). New York: Pergamon.

Wood, J. K. (1985). Teaching students how to study. *Principal, 64,* 52–53.

CHAPTER 8

Rashomon in the Classroom: Multiple Perspectives of Teachers, Parents, and Students

Ursula Casanova
Arizona State University

INTRODUCTION

Children in school are a captive and often unwilling audience. As such, they are particularly vulnerable to the opinions of school personnel. Those adult opinions are especially important at certain points of interaction between educators and students that lead to decisions generating different educational opportunities (Mehan, Herweck, & Miehls, 1986). A teacher's decision to classify a student as *at-risk* constitutes such a decision because it represents a preliminary step in the acknowledgment of classroom difficulties. This acknowledgment is often followed by the more formal process of referral, testing, labeling, and placement in special classes. Learning about the school experiences of at-risk students helps us to understand the meaning of that term as used in the schools and the immediate instructional consequences that such a designation may have for the child.

The Japanese film *Rashomon* relates the story of a crime from the perspective of first the criminal, then the victim, and finally a bystander. By using this strategy the filmmaker depicted how reality is mediated by individual perceptions. The study from which this chapter is derived attempted to describe the school experiences of children considered to be at risk by using a similar strategy. (For a complete study see Richardson, Casanova, Placier, & Guilfoyle, 1989). It was recognized that the school experiences of these children were likely to be viewed differently by the many persons involved, namely, the parents, teachers, school specialists, and the students themselves. Therefore, to be faithful to this guiding concept, the case study method was used for this research (Yin, 1984). Six case studies of second graders and six case studies of third graders at two separate schools were constructed through the use of classroom observations, examination of school records, and interviews with the students' teachers, other school specialists, the students' mothers, and the students themselves.

The resulting data are well deserving of the *Rashomon* appelation. Although overlaps could be discerned among the many descriptions collected for each child, it was evident that each of the participants perceived a different child. As in *Rashomon*, reality was elusive. A set of contrasting views about two of these children are presented here. These two case studies were selected for presentation because they appeared to be the most relevant for discussion in a school psychology/children-at-risk context (see Richardson et al., 1989). To the data collected from these different perspectives are added research observations; these views are then compared and analyzed. By way of conclusion, policy implications that might be derived from this study are proposed.

METHODS

The case study method was selected for this study because it was felt that close observation and interviews with those most closely involved would provide a better understanding of the school experiences of children perceived by their teachers to be

135

at-risk. Using a methodology suggested by Smith (1983), the school life of each of 12 children was studied first hand and at length without intervention in the natural flow of events. As part of the process, the researchers attempted to become close enough to those affecting and affected by these children's experiences to understand them from different points of view.

School Records

School personnel, including the nurse and the speech therapist, saw both of the children under consideration on a regular basis. The school psychologist also met with, tested, and subsequently diagnosed them as learning-disabled. Although these school personnel were all interviewed formally, their perceptions were also available through the school records. The cumulative records permitted an examination of changes over time in attendance, student achievement, and perceptions of school personnel, as well as diagnostic and standardized test data.

Teachers

Three teachers — the homeroom teacher, the learning disabilities teacher, and the English-as-a-second language (ESL) teacher — were in almost daily contact with the students discussed. The children were observed in all of their classes and each teacher was interviewed.

The homeroom teachers were formally interviewed twice, once at the beginning of the study and again at the end. During the first interview, these teachers were asked to provide examples of at-risk children in their classrooms. During the second interview, they were asked to explain what the term *at-risk* meant to them and to match their perceptions to the children named earlier. In keeping with Erickson's notion of socially constructed labels (Erickson, 1987), this process allowed the identification of the teachers' personal construction of "at-riskness" and its manifestation. Twelve students, six from each of two schools, were selected through this process. Among these children were Gilberto and Carmin (pseudonyms have been

used to protect participants' privacy) whose case studies are the focus of this study.

Parents

The data from the parents were collected during two interviews. The first interview was informal and designed to obtain the mothers' permission for the children's participation in the study. Preliminary information as well as an impressionistic view of each child's home situation was also obtained.

The bulk of the data from the parents were obtained during the second interview, based on a semistructured instrument. It was conducted towards the end of the study and lasted over an hour. Questions during this second interview were asked of the mothers about their children's history at home and school, their relationships with the children and with the schools, and their expectations for their children. The interviews were conducted in the parents' language of choice.

The Children

Twelve children were selected for the original study on the basis of a teacher's identification. All twelve children were interviewed. The length of the interview varied, depending on instructional constraints and the children's willingness to participate. Although no child rejected the interview, some were more talkative than others. The two children described in this report were among the most talkative and expressive.

Carmin and Gilberto were in the same third grade classroom. Both were Mexican-American, native speakers of Spanish, and were considered by their teachers to be at-risk. That is, these children did not perform in school according to the expectations of the adults charged with their care.

GILBERTO

The School Records

According to school records, Gilberto attended four different schools between kindergarten and the end of the first grade.

Although a kindergarten record form indicated that Gilberto was not experiencing learning problems, his first withdrawal form indicated that he was an "ESL student below grade level due to language barrier." The form further suggested that the language of instruction at the time of withdrawal was English.

By the first grade, Gilberto's teacher had documented that Gilberto "needed to improve in all areas of learning and that he should be observed the following year." The following year Gilberto was referred to the Child Study Team by his second-grade teacher. The referral was based on "difficulty working independently, especially in tasks in reading, writing, and spelling." The teacher added that Gilberto reversed letters and had trouble "remembering visual cues" and "focusing on written work."

Pursuant to testing, the school psychologist diagnosed Gilberto as learning-disabled on the basis of severe auditory and visual deficits. Remediation in Spanish four times a week was recommended, and it included intensive work in the development of visual processing, memory, attention, and perceptual motor skills.

Gilberto was also evaluated by the speech and language teacher, who decided that he suffered "verbal developmental dyspraxia." On the basis of additional information, Gilberto began receiving language therapy twice a week to improve his "coarticulation skills" for "maximally intelligible speech." In addition, Gilberto was assigned to ESL classes.

The Teachers' View

According to his teachers, Gilberto was a "sweetheart" who had a "sparkling" personality and "tries very hard." They reported Gilberto to be a foster child and one of 10 siblings from more than one father. The teachers further reported he was not well cared for at home and that his love of school treats suggested to them that he lacked such things at home.

Gilberto's reading was reported to be "labored" and at the "sound level." Although he "tried hard and was enthusiastic about school," Gilberto was not learning well and was considered by his homeroom teacher to be at-risk. This was possibly due to his dyspraxia, diagnosed by the speech and language therapist. One teacher stated that dyspraxia meant that Gilberto was unable to fully express his thoughts in language.

The Mother's View

The mother, Ms. G., with whom Gilberto lives, indicated that Gilberto is the middle child in a family of seven and is the youngest child of her first husband. Ms. G. stated that Gilberto had been a healthy baby who walked and talked early, climbed everywhere, and was "tremendo" (*a handful*). She recalled that he was able to communicate effectively very early, but failed for a long time to let her know when he needed a bathroom until after the fact. His grandmother covered up for him.

Ms. G. reported that Gilberto was clever, friendly, daring, and enterprising. He always seemed sure of himself and would engage in conversation with anyone, whether rich or poor. His penchant for pursuing whatever interests him, however, has caused Ms. G. many difficulties. She reported an incident in Mexico in which Gilberto simply took off one day to show a man a hole through which he could cross the Mexico/U.S. border. Ms. G. expressed concern that perhaps Gilberto would meet up with "crazy people who like to hurt children."

Ms. G. also reported that at home Gilberto liked to watch TV and play with his younger brother, who is his favorite family member. She remarked that he often brought him little trinkets and treats from school and protected this young sibling from punishment.

Ms. G. indicated that she did not understand why Gilberto had problems at school since he was so quick and clever at home. Although teachers had reported that Gilberto had trouble remembering things, Ms. G. did not agree because at home Gilberto always repeated the jokes, jingles, and stories he heard on the radio or TV. She stated that although last year Gilberto had struggled to decode words, he had made great improvement during the present year, was currently able to read all kinds of books and was preparing for his First Communion.

Ms. G. has always wanted her children to do well in school; both she and her male companion, the father of the two youngest children, insisted on rules for bedtime and homework. Mrs. G. thought that Gilberto might become distracted at school or that his current teacher might be too easy on him. She claimed that he needed a "short rein." However, the teachers reported he was well-behaved and respectful. Ms. G. was confident that Gilberto loved school.

Gilberto's View

"I start with Spanish language, later come back and go to recess, then . . . I go to music, then I go to this class to talk . . . English, and then to lunch. After lunch I go to play and then I go to another class, Ms. _____'s class (learning disabilities), and then go back to another class, a little one (language therapy), and then go back to the classroom to do some work and then go home."

When asked what he did in his various classes, Gilberto reported that in English "we play games"; in music "(we learn) a bunch of stuff"; in learning disability class we learn "how to read but I already know how to read"; and in math I'm "already doing those that have the two little sticks together, like this" (as he draws an X on the ground). He was learning in school so he "can pass grade." However, he thought he was the "worst in the class" because he only got "B or C . . . never . . . 100."

Gilberto became excited when he described a science lesson on magnets. He was fascinated with the way they attracted and repelled each other: "If you stick it to north it won't stick, if you stick it to south it will . . . you couldn't take them off . . . looked like they were married, they didn't want to let go."

Gilberto chose Spanish for the interview, but he frequently and unconsciously shifted from Spanish to English and back again during the conversation. The interweaving of language during the interview suggests he was equally comfortable in either language. Sometimes he would stop in midsentence and point out that he was now speaking English while the researcher was speaking Spanish, or vice versa. The situation always elicited a big smile from him, as though a private joke was shared.

The Observer's View

The first day the observer visited the classroom, Gilberto greeted her with a smile and wanted to know what she was doing and if she would "tell" if she saw someone hitting another person. Another day, when two observers were present, the class lined up for recess and Gilberto called out: "Aren't you guys coming?" This type of familiar bantering and ease with adults was characteristic of Gilberto throughout the study. Gilberto's poverty, greater than that of any other child in the room, was evident in the condition of his winter jacket and shabby clothes, but he was always clean and did not seem self-conscious about his appearance. On the contrary, he appeared to be a happy, self-confident child.

Gilberto appeared to be equally at ease in either Spanish or English. He often chose Spanish for the more formal communication with his teachers and lapsed into English during informal conversation. One day he answered a teacher's question about beehives correctly in Spanish, and then immediately asked the same teacher in English, "How do they live there?" His understanding of concepts seemed to cross languages. As an example, one day he helped a teacher translate the concept of "horseplay" into Spanish for the other children.

Group size seemed to have considerable influence on Gilberto's behavior. In small groups he was almost always an active and eager participant, but in large groups he often appeared to ignore the teacher. Independent work seemed particularly difficult for him. He sometimes seemed tired, and on one occasion he fell asleep while completing a math worksheet.

Gilberto lagged behind his classmates in reading. He read haltingly in a sing-song style that seemed unrelated to the meaning of the passage. He confused some of the letters and was often accused by his teacher of making "careless errors." However, he demonstrated good comprehension of his schoolwork; for example, he could accurately explain the concept of subtraction even though he applied it carelessly. His practical knowledge and abilities were aptly demonstrated in his conversations about money with his classmates. Gilberto was often heard to comment, "I already know that" and pointed out repetition among the lessons presented by his many teachers.

Fortunately, given his complicated schedule, Gilberto seemed to have an adult's grasp of school routines and rules. He knew how many children in his class went to ESL, when each of his special classes began and ended, how the reward system worked in every classroom, and the likes and dislikes of his teachers.

CARMIN

The School Records

Attendance at two different kindergartens, one in Arkansas and the other in a neighboring district, were recorded for Carmin. All instruction in preschool, kindergarten, and first grade was provided in English. At the end of first grade, a note in her records recommended that Carmin be transferred to a bilingual classroom in the second grade in lieu of retention, since she had not yet received instruction in her vernacular language. However, subsequent records indicated that English continued to be the language of instruction at the beginning of the second grade. In the spring of second grade, Carmin was referred to the Child Study Team and retention was recommended. Her mother refused the recommendation and asked for Carmin to be transferred to a bilingual classroom. This request was denied and Mrs. C. was told that a bilingual class would only serve to confuse Carmin. Subsequently, Carmin's mother transferred her to Escalante (a pseudonym) School.

At Escalante School, Carmin was promoted to a bilingual third grade in spite of her low reading level. She did not participate in ESL because she had received the top grade on an instrument designed to assess her English language competence.

However, Carmin had not made much academic progress and was again referred to the school's Child Study Team. Following evaluation, she was declared Spanish-dominant and was diagnosed as learning-disabled. Her difficulties, according to the school psychologist, were in "information processing" and she was judged to be "especially weak" in perceptual motor skills; visual sequencing, tracking, and organization; and auditory skills. Placement in a learning disabilities class for 30–60 minutes three times a week was recommended.

The Teacher's View

According to her homeroom teacher, Carmin was small for her age but had a "lot of love in her heart." Carmin reportedly was unable to distinguish between Spanish and English and had a great deal of difficulty in reading and math. Furthermore, Carmin could not concentrate for long periods and often became frustrated with school. The teacher wondered if Carmin's problems might be due to immaturity, since she was so small for her age. Her teacher also speculated that Carmin might be performing poorly because of all the changes in schools and programs, in which Carmin sometimes was instructed in English and at other times instructed in Spanish. At any rate, the teacher reported, Carmin had much difficulty retaining what she learned, and would often "drift away" during lessons. Carmin was also described as a foster child who lived with her aunt.

The Mother's View

Mrs. C. appeared to be delighted to talk about Carmin. Although Carmin had been born after her mother's separation from her father, Carmin had been a very desired child. Her mother described her as having been a healthy, active, sociable baby who had walked and talked early and entertained the family by mimicking her relatives and dancing. Her comments were supported by a thick family album replete with pictures of Carmin: Carmin dressed up in costume, Carmin caught in mischief,

Carmin surrounded by relatives, and so forth.

Although Carmin's mother had always been the primary caretaker, an aunt and grandmother also helped to care for Carmin and her younger sister while Mrs. C. worked. Carmin was taken to her aunt's house every morning before school and after school she returned there, where she worked on her homework. Mrs. C. called every afternoon to inquire about Carmin's schoolwork and to remind her to complete everything before going out to play. After a day's work as a bank cashier, Mrs. C. picked up her daughters (the younger child from a daycare center) and returned home to a series of homemaking duties. Mrs. C. reported concern about the long work days and the limited time she had to help Carmin with her schoolwork.

Mrs. C. also reported that her fiancee had assumed the role of father figure in the household. She stated that he was very interested in Carmin's progress in school and had promised her a new bicycle if she was promoted to the fourth grade. He took Carmin to sandlot baseball games, where, because of her enthusiasm, she had become the team's unofficial cheerleader.

Mrs. C. was concerned about Carmin's schoolwork. She could not understand the contrast between Carmin's cleverness at home and her reported failure at school. Carmin was a capable helper who cooked breakfast and attended to her younger sister on weekends and holidays so that her mother could rest. Carmin's social skills and understanding seemed to make her wise beyond her years. Mrs. C. related many stories to substantiate her perception. For example, she related how Carmin's natural father had called one day after months of neglect when Carmin was about 3 years old to offer to take her daughter shopping. Mrs. C. acceded only on condition that she could accompany the girl. They agreed and went on a shopping trip. He was carrying Carmin on his shoulders as they left the store when she thanked him: "Gracias, Chino" (*Thank you, Chino*), she said, addressing him by his nickname. Her father reacted: "What did you call me?" Carmin immediately responded: "Gracias, papa" (*Thank you, daddy*), as she winked from her father's

shoulders at her mother, who could barely contain her laughter.

Mrs. C. had been actively involved in her daughter's education. She had sent her to Arkansas with her aunt during her kindergarten year and was proud of Carmin's ability to learn English quickly. However, the separation was difficult for both mother and daughter and Carmin returned home before the end of the school year. When the first grade teacher recommended retention, Carmin's mother had intervened and, she reported, Carmin instead was placed in a bilingual second grade. (This report conflicts with school records, which indicated placement in an English-only classroom.) Carmin's school problems were not resolved, however, and Mrs. C. returned to the school, prodded by her daughter's complaints that the teacher did not pay any attention to her. Mrs. C. discovered that indeed Carmin's reports were correct: Since Carmin was not up to class level in Spanish, the teacher had her completing worksheets independently in a corner, which, Mrs. C. indicated, was the extent of Carmin's bilingual experience. Subsequently, when the teacher and the principal again had insisted on retention, Mrs. C. moved Carmin to Escalante School.

Mrs. C. stated that she herself was "demoralized" by Carmin's school difficulties, although she still had high hopes for Carmin's future. Escalante School personnel recommended that Carmin be rewarded with the dancing or gymnastic lessons that she wanted. This recommendation was rejected by Mrs. C. because she felt the rewards were inappropriate as "Carmin was not working hard enough at her schoolwork." She reasoned that if Carmin only would stop playing and start paying attention, she would do well and then Mrs. C. would reward her.

Carmin's View

Carmin elected to be interviewed in Spanish. She stated she spoke both languages, but preferred Spanish. Carmin's responses were, for the most part, evasive or an attempt at mimicking adult responses. For example: "What is school like?" "Está bonita" (*It's pretty*). "What do you do in school?" "Muchas cosas" (*Many things*). The latter response was her favorite and she used it repeatedly. Her descriptions of school activities focused, as did Gilberto's, on her movements from one setting to another: "Primero voy con Ms. S. y le traigo todas las tareas y hago 'cursive.' Luego me voy con la otra maestra. Luego vengo pá atrás a jugar. Luego comemos lunche y escribimos y me quedo con Ms. S." (*First I go with Ms. S. and I bring her all the homework and then I do 'cursive.' Then I go with the other teacher. Then I come back to play. Then we eat lunch, we write, and I stay with Ms. S.*)

Carmin described the learning disabilities classes in the following way: "Ella nos enseña palabras de 'che,' 'cha'; leemos, tenemos una prueba y la pasé, me dio una A, la hice bien . . ." (*She teaches us words like "che," "cha"; We read, we have a test and I passed it, she gave me an A. I did it right . . .*).

During the lesson preceding an interview, Carmin had become frustrated and cried. I asked her why: "Si, porque tenia miedo no iba a pasar. Mi mami quiere buenos grados . . ." (*Yes, because I was afraid I would not pass. My mother wants good grades . . .*). To questions about her behavior in school, Carmin responded: "A veces poquito mala. . . . Porque lloro . . . (*Sometimes a little bad. . . . Because I cry.*) (Why?) Porque no lo puedo hacer. . . . Porque no estudio" (*Because I can't do it. . . . Because I don't study*).

Carmin's favorite topic was "cursive," which she said she liked because it is "bonito" (*pretty*). She liked to show off her work in the practice book. However, although Carmin was able to accurately copy lengthy sentences in handwriting, she was unable to read them. She admitted she had difficulty in reading and the showed the interviewer how she could help by covering up portions of words so that only one syllable was exposed at a time.

The Observers' View

To the observers, Carmin appeared younger than most of her classmates, though in fact she was one of the oldest children in the room. Although of slight build, she appeared healthy and energetic. There seemed to be a tension about Carmin and her emotions always appeared to be on the edge. She almost never seemed relaxed or content.

Informally, Carmin spoke both English and Spanish with her classmates, but seemed more comfortable with Spanish. Her English seemed immature, like the language of a much younger native speaker. In contrast, her Spanish was adult-like and formal.

Carmin was very talkative and an eager participant during whole-group lessons. She would almost rise out of her seat in her eagerness to answer and openly expressed her pleasure when her answer was correct. Her eagerness remained unabated in spite of the fact that her answers were wrong about half the time.

Being "in charge" of tasks in the classroom was important to Carmin. When performing these duties, she became serious and officious, sometimes causing complaints from the other children. However, in the cafeteria and on the playground, Carmin was playful and did not lack for companions.

Carmin seemed very dependent on the teachers' attention for both motivation and assistance. When the teacher was not nearby, she would often leave her seat to socialize. On the other hand, she almost always complied with classroom rules and routines and reminded other students of the rules when they forgot. This talent for "studenting" behavior appeared to help mask Carmin's great academic deficiencies. She seemed to have mastered the form but not the substance of student life. When her weaknesses were revealed during the course of a lesson, Carmin appeared to become very anxious and often resorted to tears.

In the classroom, Carmin's favorite activity was handwriting. The neatness and clarity of her writing was often praised by the teacher. However, Carmin could not read what she copied, and her reading competence was below the accomplished preprimer level. She had difficulty decoding words of more than one syllable and appeared to have difficulties with comprehension: After listening to a brief passage from a story in Spanish, Carmin was unable to summarize it or make inferences with any degree of accuracy in either English or Spanish. However, she demonstrated how quickly she could learn the routine followed by the interviewer by predicting her next question: "Ahora an inglés?" (*Now in English?*).

DISCUSSION AND ANALYSIS

After considering the various perceptions of these two children, one is tempted to say, "Will the real Gilberto or Carmin please stand up?" It is of course much easier to analyze these children's situations from the privileged position of an outside observer who is privy to all data and has the luxury of time for analysis. The following discussion attempts to clarify the different perceptions and derive from them an integrated view of each child. This integrated view, however, cannot simply be assumed to be the *real* one, since reality, in a certain sense, can be seen to vary according to each individual's perception. This interpretation, derived from careful analysis of the information obtained, seems logical.

Gilberto

Even though every person interviewed commented on Gilberto's social competence, each, including his mother, agreed that Gilberto had not performed well in school. School specialists, through their statements in the cumulative records, indicated that Gilberto's lack of achievement gains was due to language problems and to serious perceptual problems that impaired his ability to communicate, to see, and to hear. According to these specialists Gilberto was considered learning-disabled. These comments and observations, for the most part, ignored the social and communicative skills that were so highly praised by Gilberto's mother and his teachers and were confirmed by independent observations.

In spite of Gilberto's problems, his mother clearly admired his social competence and cleverness. It was difficult for her to understand shy he would experience

problems in school. She readily acknowledged that he was slow in learning to read but added that he is now a much more competent reader. Although Ms. G. acquiesced to the specialist's diagnosis of Gilberto's memory problem (dyspraxia), she remained unconvinced. Gilberto's behavior at home was not suggestive of any memory problems and Ms. G. described the problem as a matter of selective attention. She acquiesced to the school's wishes because she believed the school staff was trying to help her son.

Gilberto described his school experience as though it were a commuting trip. He had mastered the process and seemed to enjoy it. His opinion of himself as a student, however, was not as self-confident as his handling of his schedule. Gilberto's marks were not the lowest in his class, yet he considered himself to be the "worst in the class." Although some of Gilberto's comments indicated that he was beginning to question the reasons for his special classes and the repetitiveness of his programs, he had apparently internalized adult injunctions that his problems are due to his lack of application.

Gilberto was perceived by the researchers as an articulate student, a competent commuter, and a socially adept young man. His deficiencies in reading were obvious, but his contributions to class discussions, his command of both languages, and his practical knowledge did not indicate cognitive or perceptual deficiencies. Gilberto often appeared to be tired during the school day, a tendency often displayed when he was part of a large group, particularly when doing independent work.

How then can these different perceptions be reconciled? A clue can be found in the school records, which indicated four school changes between kindergarten and first grade. Although early comments about Gilberto were not suggestive of learning difficulties, by the end of the first grade he was identified as one who needed to be "observed." Subsequently he was referred to the Child Study Team in the second grade.

Interestingly, the possible impact of repeated school changes on Gilberto's academic performance was not mentioned by any of the teachers or school specialists. While details of Gilberto's school experiences during those 2 years are not available, recent research makes it reasonable to assume that each of these changes required major social and academic adjustments on Gilberto's part (Ingersoll, Scamman, & Eckerling, 1988). Such adjustments would make it difficult for Gilberto to sustain steady academic progress. In addition, it is not known what the language of instruction was in these different schools. It is possible that Gilberto might have faced additional obstacles if each school change was accompanied by comparable changes in the language of instruction.

The diagnosis of Gilberto as perceptually impaired and having language difficulties and "dyspraxia" might be questioned under the circumstances. Gilberto's behavior did not indicate problems with language. On the contrary, his ability to communicate in both languages was one of his strengths. At no time during the three formal interviews or during many informal exchanges with Gilberto were difficulties noted in his ability to express himself. His conversation was adult-like and witty rather than impaired. Nothing in his behavior, with the exception of an occasional letter reversal, suggested visual impairment. Observations corroborated his mother's comments and suggested that memory lapses were more likely due to selective attention than to cognitive deficiencies.

Gilberto's fatigue also was not mentioned in the school records or by his teachers. We were puzzled about this behavior and considered three alternative explanations: lack of enough sleep, possible nutritional deficiencies, or simply boredom. Each of these alternatives can be partially supported. Although there were strict rules at home regarding bedtime, both Ms. G. and Gilberto commented on his early rising. Gilberto reported that he got up very early to come to school and would then get tired by midday. His mother also commented on his eagerness to go to school and his early rising, even on holidays. Gilberto's home, although clean and orderly, was crowded and it is possible that because he lived in crowded home conditions, he was not getting enough sleep, even though he was required to be in bed by a certain time. It is also possible that these very conditions motivated him to get up and get out of the house very early.

As previously noted, Gilberto's family appeared to be very poor. Although the home was neat and clean, it is likely that family resources were limited. It is therefore possible that Gilberto's diet was inadequate for a developing and active child. Interestingly, this possibility also was not explored or questioned by school personnel.

Finally, observations of Gilberto in different classes, as well as comments made during his interviews, suggest that boredom was implicated in his tiredness. Gilberto was never inattentive in small-group lessons, and he was also active in the schoolyard and at lunchtime. His main problem seemed to be in maintaining attention in large-group settings, and particularly in working independently. Working "independently" in this third-grade classroom meant filling out worksheets. It was during these activities that Gilberto's tiredness was most often observed.

From our perspective, then, Gilberto was a bright boy who might have been experiencing the consequences of repeated changes early in his school career. His academic progress, while slow, appeared to be reasonable, given the likely impact of these changes. Specialists' diagnoses of Gilberto's problems appear to have overlooked the contribution of these changes to his progress. In addition, school staff comments on Gilberto's home appeared to focus on the "problem" of size and supposed neglect of the boy. The present inquiry discovered poverty but not neglect, crowdedness but not disorder. It was felt that the physical consequences of Gilberto's home environment were probably of more importance. Was his diet adequate? Was he getting enough rest? The search for an explanation for Gilberto's school problems might have been better served by attention to these rather pedestrian needs, rather than by the scientific-sounding but dubious labels of perceptual and cognitive deficiencies.

Carmin

In reviewing the data in Carmin's case study, we again find conflicting views of the same child. School records suggest that Carmin's progress in school was noticeably slow from the first grade on and that "language," both English and Spanish, was considered by her teachers as a "contributing factor to her low achievement." According to the school psychologist, Carmin was learning-disabled. She had difficulties in "information processing" and weaknesses in all perceptual–motor skills.

Carmin's homeroom teacher asserted that Carmin could not distinguish between Spanish and English. She gave Carmin credit for the effort she expended on her schoolwork and wondered if immaturity kept Carmin from making progress. She also wondered if all the changes in schools and language of instruction might have contributed to Carmin's problems. Other school specialists saw Carmin as typical of a learning-disabled child. They also considered the problems created by Carmin's "role-confusion" as a member of an extended family.

Carmin's mother could not understand what had happened to her bright, competent child. She had taken strong stands in her behalf when necessary, but in the end saw the problem as one created by Carmin's lack of application to her schoolwork. How else could she explain the huge discrepancy between the child she knows and the one they told her about in school?

Carmin seemed to agree with her mother. She believed she was not a good student because she did not work enough. She desperately tried to mask her problems and fell apart when she was unable to do so. She worked hard, almost too hard, to overcome her deficits. Ironically, given the psychologist's diagnosis of impaired visual tracking, her only rewards so far were in handwriting, which she seemed to approach as an exercise in aesthetics.

Carmin appeared to be a tense little girl who seemed more adept at playing the student role than at learning a student's tasks. The researchers saw no indication of language confusion in Carmin. She was aware of which language she was speaking and when, and she was able to switch from one to the other without difficulty. Although she did on occasion confuse the vowel sounds in the two languages, for example, the sounds of *a* and *e*, and of *e* and *i*, this confusion is not uncommon in transfers from Spanish to English or vice versa. Carmin's development in English conversation seemed less mature than in Spanish. Her Spanish clearly reflected her early upbringing among Spanish-speaking adults and had a formal and almost prim quality about it.

Carmin seemed highly dependent on her teacher, and yet she also loved responsibility. She was popular in the playground and quick to learn the appropriate rules and procedures.

Again, large discrepancies exist between the perceptions of the adults who knew, or presumed to know, Carmin. Most people agreed that Carmin worked hard and was bright enough, and that her progress in school was too slow. The disagreement lay in the reasons for her slow progress. Once again, the school records can provide clues. Carmin began her school career in a kindergarten in Arkansas; by the third grade she had been placed in seven different classrooms at three different schools. Once promoted to the third grade, Carmin was referred to the Child Study Team and diagnosed as learning-disabled because of severe perceptual deficiencies.

Carmin's problems appeared to be exacerbated by several factors. First of all, since her classroom included students who ranged from Spanish monolinguals to English monolinguals and every stage in between, the teacher instructed her class bilingually. This meant continuous phrase-by-phrase translation on the part of the teacher. While this might be helpful to many children, the continuous phrase-by-phrase translation may have contributed to Carmin's difficulties, since there was little opportunity for elaboration in either language.

The instructional activities in the class for learning-disabled students further fragmented Carmin's instruction. Adherence to a district-mandated curriculum by objectives resulted in lessons in which letters, vowels, and words were taught in isolation from context. Carmin did not seem to understand the purpose of reading and was completely befuddled by print, including her own handwriting. Unlike other children who will mask their incompetence by making up stories, Carmin strung syllables together without concern for their meaning.

Finally, Carmin was not helped by the perceptions school personnel held about her home situation. In spite of her mother's interest, intervention, and assertiveness, as well as her consent for testing, she was not included in the Child Study Team meeting. Only later was she asked to permit Carmin to be provided with additional reading instruction (and Carmin's assignment to learning disabilities classes was not mentioned). Mrs. C., eager to see her daughter succeed, promptly agreed.

This case study yielded the conclusion that Carmin was a bright little girl who had suffered extremely from the mistakes of educators and that Carmin would benefit from academic instruction in only one language, probably Spanish. She also seemed to need a holistic approach to reading that would draw on her high level of articulation and social competence and emphasize comprehension, rather than the simple decoding of written words.

Policy Implications

What can be learned about policy from such close scrutiny of these two children's school lives? Although there are numerous implications, three areas of most direct relevance to the two cases described will be discussed: language, special education, and parental involvement.

Language policy. The most pervasive issue affecting these children's school life is language. The lack of a clear and unambiguous language policy to guide the schools, combined with the lack of appropriate assessment techniques, placed these children and others like them at a disadvantage from the time they entered school (Cummins, 1984). Both Gilberto and Carmin began their school careers in English-speaking classrooms. It is not known who made the decision or on what basis, since

neither of those processes has been standardized. In Carmin's case, it is likely that Arkansas had no English/Spanish bilingual education program. In the case of Gilberto, initial instruction in English is more difficult to justify, since he had only recently arrived from Mexico and he had entered a district offering a bilingual education program.

Both children's problems were exacerbated by their frequent moves. However, in Carmin's case those moves were likely made by her mother in response to her desire to improve Carmin's school performance. Gilberto's moves were more clearly due to family instability. Nonetheless, each move, whether between schools or between classrooms, entails numerous adjustments for any young child; these include becoming accustomed to a new social system, school, teacher, and curriculum (Ingersoll, Scamman, & Erickson, 1988). In the case of Gilberto and Carmin, an additional adjustment was necessary for language.

Carmin's situation is particularly poignant. It is likely that her mother's decision to send Carmin to Arkansas was based on her desire that her daughter learn English well so she would succeed in school. Unfortunately, the classroom English Carmin learned during those few months probably contributed to her being classified as English-dominant, thus making it less likely for her to be placed in a bilingual classroom. Ironically, her mother's later request for a change to a bilingual classroom was denied by school officials on the basis that Carmin might get "confused." The consequences of those early choices continue to have a major impact on Carmin's academic progress.

These examples provide powerful evidence for the need to clarify language policies in the schools. It is necessary to provide a less ambiguous policy, clearer guidance for teachers, and a more reliable process to facilitate the assessment of language competence.

Special education. The tendency to classify Speakers of Other Languages (SOLs) as learning-disabled is a common theme in the literature (Willig & Greenberg, 1986). The overrepresentation of Hispanics in this category of special education has also been well documented. In Texas, for example, the overrepresentation of Hispanics in this classification amounts to 300% (Ortiz & Yates, 1983). Several researchers have argued that one of the reasons for the misidentification of SOLs as learning-disabled is the lack of understanding, on the part of educators, of the process of language learning (Cummins, 1985; Ortiz & Maldonado-Colón, 1986; Willig & Greenberg, 1986). This confusion seemed evident in the comments made about these two students. For example, code switching, an accepted strategy among competent adult bilinguals (Genishi, 1979), was characterized as language confusion in the case of Gilberto and Carmin. Thus, normal processes become characterized as permanent deficiencies, such as dyspraxia in Gilberto's case.

Parent involvement. The most extreme differences in perception emerged between the perceptions of the parents and the school support specialists. The potential for these differences is recognized in the legal requirement that parents participate in any decisions leading to assigning their children to any special education program. However, neither mother was present at what is commonly called the "staffing" conference for these two children. Both of them were notified after the fact (an action that is illegal in most states). In Carmin's case, the mother was not informed that her daughter was identified as learning-disabled, but only that she would be receiving additional help in reading.

The importance of attendance by a parent at a staffing at times can be overestimated. It is unlikely that even a relatively well-schooled parent like Carmin's mother (high school graduate, fully bilingual, bank cashier) would be able to sustain any serious objections to the arguments of school specialists (Mehan et al., 1986). Both of these mothers (and all the Mexican-American mothers we interviewed) tended to trust the school staff. Carmin's mother was driven to action only after repeated attempts at influencing her daughter's school experience. Gilberto's mother, while expressing her doubts, was willing to go along and trust the "experts."

Various researchers in recent years have commented on the importance of parent involvement (Clark, 1983; Epstein, 1986; McLaughlin & Shields, 1986). However, even these enlightened observers continue to see the need from the school's perspective and often do not lend credibility to information provided by parents about their children. Although the school in good conscience must communicate with the parents and involve the parents in decisions involving their child, the importance and uniqueness of the parent's contribution must also be acknowledged (Atkin, Bastiani, & Goode, 1988). Acceptance of the value of parental knowledge about the child requires a shift in the educator's view of parents.

In the cases of Gilberto and Carmin, it is interesting how little information had been elicited from the parents by the school. It was also interesting to note how many false or at least not entirely correct assumptions were held by school personnel abut these children; for example, both children were incorrectly assumed to be foster children. Had their parents been requested to contribute to the schools' knowledge about their children, they would have provided accurate information about their child's status in the family as well as their child's behavior outside the school.

Institutional Press

Official policies for language and parent involvement do not emerge in a vacuum. They are embedded in sets of assumptions and expectations that define both appropriate and deviant behavior. Becker (1952) found that teachers' actions were guided by their definitions of the "ideal pupil," which included being interested in lessons, working hard in school, and receiving proper preparation for school at home. Similarly, Douglas (1964) indicated that a student's assignment to instructional tracks was influenced by the child's home situation. Children from well-kept homes who were clean and well-dressed stood a better chance of being assigned to the more advanced tracks. Thus, the notion of an "ideal home" also appears to affect teachers' expectations.

These unstated institutional expectations exert collective pressure on the lives of children in schools and as such may be called an "institutional press."

In the case of language policy the institutional press demands English language fluency. According to Kjolseth (1982), the traditional policy of "speak only English" has been amended to "We will speak only English just as soon as possible and even sooner . . . if we begin with . . . [the] vernacular." That is, the vernacular, or home language, is only important insofar as it accelerates the acquisition of English; beyond that purpose, the vernacular is an obstruction with no intrinsic value. The importance for children of learning English as quickly as possible seems to overshadow any consideration of alternative optimal instructional strategies. Children who do not learn English as quickly as expected often are considered to be deficient even if they are competent Spanish-speakers. This was the opinion even of the Mexican-American teachers participating in this study who were themselves competent bilinguals. As successful products of a system that exercises that institutional press towards English, these teachers assumed a compatible stance. They did this while simultaneously assuming an advocacy role on behalf of their Mexican-American students and of bilingual education.

In the case of special education, specifically of learning disabilities, the institutional press is toward describing a child's learning problems in quasi-scientific terms and labels. Contrary evidence notwithstanding, problems in learning were viewed as inherently within the child, rather than as outcomes of complex interactions between child, adults, and materials in a historical context. Smith (1983) found a similar tendency in a study of learning disability decisions. She argues that this phenomenon is likely an outcome of the increased professionalization of schools. The quasi-scientific language used to report test scores is a vehicle for achieving a higher status within the system. More mundane though logical causes, such as frequent moves and changes in the language of instruction, are often set aside in the search for more esoteric and professional-sounding labels.

Finally, in regard to parent involvement, the press seems to be towards approval and acceptance of the traditional family as "normal," that is, nuclear families with both parents present and perhaps the traditionally acceptable 2.3 children. By these standards the children described in this study did not come from "normal" families. Gilberto's family was too large; Carmin's family was too complex, with extended family members actively involved in childrearing. In both cases, the child's natural father was absent and another man was present in the home, a fact that was viewed as cause for concern. The lack of a "normal" family was assumed to contribute to the child's problems even when there was no indication of unhappiness on the child's part. Again, the participating Mexican-American teachers seemed to substitute the dominant core culture values for their own experience in extended families.

Finally, the institutional press seems to decree that "school knows best." School personnel prefer that parents be involved in the *support* of school policies and not as intelligent informants regarding their children's home lives. This view of parents is an instrumental one that allows for the flow of information and decision making in one direction only, from the school to the parent, but not vice versa.

CONCLUSION

This study was perceived as informative because it assumed a perspective that moved outward from the child. Rather than looking at the reasons why the children were considered to be failures, an attempt was made to get a multidimensional view of each child. These multiple viewpoints allowed for a clearer perspective on the disjointedness between the child at home and the child at school; the child in the classroom and the child described in the records. Through these multiple perspectives, it was possible to see how social constructions of failure had resulted in the labeling of these children and how already they had began to internalize the perceptions of those charged with their care.

One of the most disturbing findings of these case studies was that they were conducted in a school with a reputation for caring and a dedicated and hard-working staff. The school principal, as well as all the teachers involved, were Mexican-American, bilingual and were themselves the products of a bicultural experience. In addition, all were strong advocates of the educational needs of Mexican-American children. These teachers, and their principal, all worked extremely hard at creating a positive school environment for their students. The apparent misguidedness of their actions appears to be the result of district- and state-imposed requirements as well as their own unconscious acceptance of hegemonic practices. As Erickson (1987) has pointed out, the ubiquitousness of the dominant culture, and of the institutional arrangements that are consonant with it, leads dominant and subordinate alike to act routinely in concert with the cultural assumptions and interests of the dominant culture. In their promotion of the benefits of a nuclear family, or of English as opposed to Spanish, or in their acceptance of a quasi-scientific basis for learning difficulties, these teachers were acting on a set of unexamined assumptions subliminally promoted by the dominant culture.

These case studies support McDermott's point of view (1987) that failure is a fabrication. Making believe that failure is something that kids do, rather than something that is done to them, leads us to look for explanations and therefore contribute to the maintenance of school failure. To avoid this syndrome, it is necessary to look at children as competent learners. Educators must become sensitized to the perspectives they bring to the task of observing and teaching children and they must accept responsibility for contributing to an environment in which only some can succeed while others must fail.

While these case studies illustrate the multiple perspectives affecting children in classrooms, their presentation as Rashomon-like may be faulty. Although, as in Rashomon, different perceptions were expressed by a number of adults involved in various capacities with the children, the varied perceptions cannot be excused as merely equally valid points of view. The weight of the school's official perception clearly was more likely to determine not only each child's current academic opportunities but also future ones and eventually his or her life chances. The parents' and the children's personal perceptions were not considered by the school, yet observations suggest they might have been more useful in designing appropriate instruction for each of these children. This study argues for incorporating input from many sources when making these important decisions about children. Public Law 94-142 and various federal, state, and local regulations that require that many sources of information be used when evaluating and diagnosing children; these case histories are first-hand examples of flagrant violations of both the spirit and the letter of the law. It is hoped that, as school psychologists and other support personnel read this chapter, they do not simply consider these case studies to be isolated incidents but rather that they examine their own practices and attitudes as well as the attitudes of school personnel towards information provided from sources external to the school.

REFERENCES

Atkin, J., Bastiani, J., & Goode, J. (1988). *Listening to parents: An approach to the improvement of home/school relations.* London: Croom Helm.

Becker, H. (1952). Social class variations in the teacher–pupil relationship. *Journal of Educational Sociology, 25,* 451–465.

Clark, R. (1983). *Family life and school achievement: Why poor Black children succeed or fail.* Chicago: University of Chicago Press.

Cummins, J. (1984). Wanted: A theoretical framework for relating language proficiency to academic achievement among bilingual students. In C. Rivera (Ed.), *Language proficiency and academic achievement* (pp. 71–76). Avon, England: Multilingual Matters.

Cummins, J. (1985). *Bilingualism and special education: Issues in assessment and pedagogy.* San Diego: College Hill.

Douglas, J. W. B. (1964). *The home and the school.* St. Albans, U.K.: Parether.

Epstein, J. (1986). Parent's reactions to teacher's practices of parent involvement. *Elementary School Journal, 86*(3), 277–294.

Erickson, F. (1987). Transformation and school success: The politics and culture of educational achievement. *Anthropology and Education Quarterly, 18,* 335–356.

Genishi, C. (1979). *Code-switching: A review of the literature and comments on future research* (Report to the National Institute of Education, U.S. Department of Education). Austin, TX: The University of Texas.

Ingersoll, G. M., Scamman, J. P., & Eckerling, W. D. (1988, April). *Impact of student mobility on student achievement in an urban setting.* Paper presented at the Annual Meeting of the American Educational Research Association, New Orleans.

Kjolseth, R. (1982). Bilingual education programs in the United States: For assimilation or pluralism? In P. R. Turner (Ed.), *Bilingualism in the Southwest* (2nd ed., rev.) (pp. 3–28). Tucson, AZ: University of Arizona Press.

McDermott, R. P. (1987). The explanation of minority school failure, again. *Anthropology and Education Quarterly, 18,* 361–364.

Mehan, H., Herweck, A., & Miehls, J. L. (1986). *Handicapping the handicapped: Decision making in student's educational career.* Stanford, CA: Stanford University Press.

CHAPTER 9

Implementing Effective Instructional Interventions for Minority Students

Todd V. Fletcher
The University of Arizona

Carlos Cardona-Morales
Northwest Regional Educational Laboratory, Portland, OR

There is little doubt that the special education reform movement, known as the Regular Education Initiative (Will, 1986), is already beginning to have a significant impact on the job roles and responsibilities of school psychologists and special educators. Unfortunately, most educational personnel, including administrators, classroom teachers, school psychologists, and special educators, are not equipped or prepared to deal effectively with this most recent reform that is sweeping education (Kauffman, 1988).

In the case of school psychology preparation programs, Reschly (1988) has pointed out that the traditional orientation of training has been one of preparing professionals for "eligibility determination, not for design, monitoring, and evaluation of interventions" (p. 464). Reschly called for new dimensions in the breadth of training provided to school psychologists and suggested that there be a "focus on interventions in order to contribute important, essential services in the new delivery system that is developing" (p. 464).

Will (1986) has pointed out that in special education the predominant intervention provided for students with learning difficulties has been placement in a "pullout" program in which students receive services outside the regular classroom. Gartner and Lipsky (1987) suggested that in past practice a "deal" has been made between regular education and special education that has created a dual system of educational services. In this scenario, a regular educator, because of the lack of specialized "skills, resources or prejudice, is often happy to hand over these students to a welcoming special education system" (p. 383). A primary concern in this situation is the lack of communication and coordination between special education support personnel and the regular education teacher, and the negative outcomes for students that can result. Will (1988) further suggested that the new partnership between regular and special education necessitates a shift for special educators and psychologists that "will require greater emphasis on instructional variables that include the curriculum, task features, teaching functions and instructionally based assessment procedures" (p. 478).

Traditionally, both disciplines have perceived students' inability to learn as an "inherent deficiency" in the child and there has been little examination of the teaching or learning ecology (Shapiro, 1987). Part of the rationale for this new direction in educational practice is based on the results of a study to determine the reasons for the disproportionate representation of minority students in special education (Heller, Holtzman, & Messick, 1982). This study, which was performed by a panel appointed by the National Academy of Science in 1979, led to the important recommendation that all available regular and special program personnel must be used to "identify and implement promising alternative instructional strategies in an attempt to reverse the pattern of failure" (Heller et al., 1982, p. 95). This strongly endorses, and has resulted in, the use of an informal delivery system that has come to be known as prereferral intervention. The major intent of this practice is "to enhance communication between special and general education teachers and to prevent the need for lengthy and costly student evaluations and placement in special education by remediating students difficulties in a timely, efficient manner within the general education environment" (Pugach & Johnson, 1988, p. 1).

To effectively implement new strategies and approaches within the general education environment, school support personnel will need refined skills. Within the school setting, West and Idol (1987) have suggested that resource teachers and school psychologists are not likely to find success in using a traditional, top-down, expert-based concept of consultation, since this approach erroneously assumes that only professionals such as school psychologists and special educators are able to provide expertise (Pugach & Johnson, 1988). Rather, consultation based upon a collaborative relationship is recommended. Collaborative consultation has been described as

> an interactive process that enables teams of people with diverse expertise to generate creative solutions to mutually defined problems. The outcome is enhanced, altered and produces solutions that are different from those that the individual team member would produce independently. The major outcome of collaborative consultation is to provide comprehensive and effective programs for students with special needs within the most appropriate context, thereby enabling them to achieve maximum constructive interaction with other nonhandicapped peers. (Idol, Paolucci-Whitcomb, & Nexin, 1986, p. 1)

This reconceptualization of job roles for school psychologists and special educators will require specific training in a collaborative consultation model. The concept of joint deliberation on the triad of curricular, teacher, and learner variables is critical to insure that the teaching–learning ecology is critically examined prior to reaching a conclusion on the educational status of the student.

In response to these concerns, the major thrust of this chapter is to briefly examine the conditions that have led to minority failure in schools and to describe some promising instructional practices and techniques that should be considered by educational personnel such as school psychologists or special educators when collaborating with regular classroom teachers.

STUDENT DIVERSITY AND THE NEED FOR POLICY AND PROGRAM SHIFTS

By examining the past and present academic performance of language-minority students, children from families of low socioeconomic status (SES), and children of poverty in our public schools, patterns emerge that signal a "progressive academic retardation" of these students in our public schools. It is well documented that many of these children have been inappropriately placed and "deported" into remedial, compensatory, and special education classrooms (Dunn, 1968) and ultimately dropout from school. This is substantiated by William Bennett (1988), former Secretary of Education, in a recent published report entitled "American Education: Making It Work." In that report on the state of U.S. education, it is reported that the high school graduation rate of U.S. blacks is 10%, and that of Hispanic school-age students is 20%, below the national average of 75%. It was also noted in that same report that one-fifth of the total school-age population currently live below the poverty level as determined by the Census Bureau.

In addition to the concerns cited above, the current school-age population is undergoing a dramatic shift that is changing the face of the United States. Current statistics indicate that minority enrollment levels in the nation's 15 largest school districts range from 70% to 90%. Presently, in the state of California, one of every four public school students comes from a non-English-speaking home and the white non-Hispanic school-aged population has dropped below 50% (Olsen, 1988). Our current demographic makeup is so ethnically diverse that many of our present school districts around the United States are being overwhelmed with the responsibility of educating a student populace that is becoming increasingly more diverse with regard to language, learning styles, and cultural differences. Projections into the next century suggest that the proportion of majority culture students (i.e., Anglo-Saxon, Northern European) to minority culture students (i.e., Hispanics, African-Americans, Asian-Americans, Native Americans, and other ethnic groups) in the United States will drop to about 60%. The need for our public school system to accommodate this diverse student population and educate them effectively is one of the most challenging issues facing this country.

At present our educational system is poorly equipped to deal with our current and future student population. Olivia Martinez, an elementary school principal in San Francisco, pinpointed the dilemma of the growing student diversity in our school districts throughout the United States:

> Our schools have been designed for one kind of student and in fact we're educating another kind. We've known this for some time. But being able to have the wherewithal to catch up to it is a tremendous task. (Olsen, 1988, p. 77)

What is the cause of the poor academic achievement, the high dropout rate, and the disproportionate representation in special education of students from ethnic and culturally diverse backgrounds? What can be done to reverse the trend of failure for this segment of our society? In a review of the literature on the differential success of minority students in our schools (Arreaga-Mayer, & Greenwood, 1986), it was noted that one line of research has argued that the differences in academic performance could be best explained by variables "in language, values, customs, attitudes, and norms which are characteristically associated with certain ethnic, racial, national origin, gender, and socioeconomic groups" (p. 114). This position is further supported by research involving students from various cultural backgrounds that indicates that less than 50% of the variance in school achievement can be attributed to the childrens' intelligence (Lavin, 1965). These findings appear to call for a closer examination of

school-related factors external to the child that can be altered and modified in the instructional environment. Indeed, it has been pointed out (Ryan, 1971) that the "task to be accomplished is not to revise, and amend, and repair deficient children but to alter and transform the atmosphere and operations of the schools to which we commit these children. Only by changing the nature of the educational experience can we change its product" (p. 2).

Over the past 20 years, costly programmatic changes have been attempted in an effort to change the pattern of minority student academic failure. Special intervention programs have been developed and implemented to reduce the incidence of the patterns of "historical deficiencies" in the instructional treatment of these children. Unfortunately, the outcomes of these programs have done little to change the status of the academic achievement of these students (Cummins, 1986).

In spite of their stated goals, and their costs in the investments of time and energy, these traditional pullout programs have failed to address the unique educational needs of minority-language students. In the process of implementation, traditional pullout programs have denied these students the instructional agenda common to public schools and as a result have not allowed equal access to the core curriculum and active participation in both the school culture and learning (Allington & Shake, 1986). Historically, the academic deficiencies of these students have occurred in those schools in which the education of minority youths is viewed as the sole responsibility of the special and categorical programs. School districts and school personnel who rely on the special categorical funding for the continuation of intervention programs, and consider this funding to be the only source of revenue for educating minority youth, perpetuate these historical deficiencies by preventing the integration of minority students into the school culture. Although these schools may have many programs to address the specific "needs" of minority students, they nonetheless fail to provide them with access to a quality and equal educational program of study.

The inability of our educational system

to deal with the diverse and unique learning characteristics of these students demands a rethinking of traditional approaches in educational programming and instructional practice so that this trend can be reversed. What the current reality demands is not only a reconceptualization of past educational practice, but a reorientation and restructuring of schools and the retraining of school personnel. For any given school system, this will entail a comprehensive effort with high levels of professional and programmatic collaboration. Such a collaboration will necessitate that instructional program units and personnel involved in the delivery and coordination of instruction work together to articulate, adopt, and implement educational philosophies and policies that are congruent with the student's educational needs and to provide the professional flexibility to address those needs. Thus, educational systems must learn to address at-risk students more as learners and active participants in the instructional process and less as tokens in fiscal funding games.

On a programmatic level, it has been generally agreed "that the key to excellence in schools rests with the quality both of the professional personnel and of instruction at the individual school level" (Tikunoff, 1987, p. 231). Although the latest report on the National Assessment of Educational Progress (NAEP) (Applebee, Langer, & Mullins, 1989) indicated that test scores in the academic basic skills had improved, it noted that fundamental changes are necessary to help U.S. schoolchildren gain content knowledge and the ability to reason effectively. It was recommended that such changes deviate from "relatively traditional" classroom teaching practices that rely on textbooks, worksheet exercises, and teacher presentations. The findings from this report appear to echo previous concerns that there may be a need to "reconsider the assumption that if students have the basics, more complex reasoning and problem-solving skills will automatically follow" (NAEP Newsletter, 1983). The 1989 report also recommended a shift in the modes of instruction and suggested that "discussion teams, cooperative work groups, individual learning logs, computer networking and other activities will need

to be added and may even predominate" (Applebee, Langer & Mullins, 1989, p. 41). This corroborates the position that new approaches in classroom structuring and instructional interventions are needed.

The push for a shift in instructional emphasis is not an isolated concern but is related to other academic and scientific endeavors that indicate a more holistic orientation in our society. In general, there is a shift away form dealing with behaviors or events in isolation to examining them in the much broader context of naturalistic and holistic settings. In an educational context, an "interactive/experiential" model of pedagogy has been proposed (Cummins, 1989) as an alternative to the traditional transmission model used in most regular, bilingual, ESL, and special education classrooms. In particular, current pedagogical practice based upon instruction that does not effectively and actively engage the student's background knowledge and concepts are targeted. Pedagogically induced learning problems may arise when there is little congruence in instruction between current teaching approaches and the unique learning characteristics that students bring to the learning environment. Such learning characteristics may include motivational style, cognitive style, social organization, and sociolinguistic factors; in addition, such factors as differing participant structures, unique questioning styles, physical features of the classroom, and the lack of instructional materials that are contextually appropriate may also be involved (Deyhle, 1986). These possible incompatabilities often are not considered at the onset of instruction and it is frequently assumed that students' failure to learn in the current instructional environment is due to an "inherent deficiency," rather than to a set of external conditions that significantly affect students' academic performance.

One of the essential first steps to ameliorate this problem is a redefinition of the roles of teachers and other educational personnel (Cummins, 1986). In this process, the view that differences are deficits is rejected and replaced by an advocacy role that both seeks to empower students and views the child as a treasure of information, experiences, and knowledge. Effective instructional practices are designed and implemented that activate and validate those experiences. In this process, the teacher's essential task is to arrange the learning environment to optimize the learning process (Gagne, 1976). Unfortunately, it is often the amount of material that must be covered in a school year and not the actual curriculum that drives the teacher's approach to instruction; the teacher often does not have the opportunity to consider learner characteristics or alternative instructional interventions that may be more appropriate to the unique needs of individual students.

The challenge of implementing appropriate intervention strategies for these children is made complex by the diverse variables that are brought to the learning environment. Instructional interventions should be broad-based and provide flexibility and continuity in patterns of learning from the home and community to the school; this may be achieved by incorporating children's experiential knowledge into the school culture and curriculum. This holistic paradigm fosters greater congruency between school tasks and the experiential base of knowledge students bring to school and should allow for greater immediate success in children's acculturation to the school setting and lead to familiarity with school tasks and eventually to increased academic achievement. However, although instructional inadequacies may account for many minority students' achievement problems and apparent lack of enthusiasm for learning, this factor is often not seriously considered; rather, the attribute often thought to be responsible for problems in learning is lack of motivation (Brown, 1986). This erroneous assumption lowers teachers' expectations for these students and produces a cycle of teacher-student interaction that, over time, may result in low achievement, retention in grade, placement in special education classrooms for the learning-disabled, and high dropout rates. This cycle of the interaction of teachers' expectations and student achievement is depicted in Figure 1 (Good, 1981).

The redefinition of educators' roles must include a strong acknowledgment that the gender, ethnic, racial, linguistic and socioeconomic factors that create children's unique cultural makeup do not reduce the intellectual prowess of children but rather enhance and enrich it. However, the changes required to implement new roles of teachers vis-a-vis students are often the most difficult to accomplish; therefore it is expected that significant attitudinal changes as well as sustained support for personnel will be needed (Fullan & Pomfert, 1977).

NEW DIMENSIONS OF INSTRUCTION BASED ON HOLISTIC APPROACHES

Most of the current thought about teaching low-SES, disadvantaged, "at risk," language-minority, LEP (limited-English-proficiency), bilingual, and handicapped students centers on the conceptualization of a new holistic paradigm. The traditional approach to instruction in many public schools has fragmented learning into subject areas and has had many negative results, among them undermining children's natural desire to learn, controlling naturally active children's movement for hours in assembly-line classrooms, and ignoring individual and cultural differences (Hart, 1983). In addition, although basic skills generally are acquired, there has been little generalization to other academic areas.

Holistic interventions, on the other hand, have the potential to present "a functional, integrated, and generalized model of education which focuses on the whole teaching/learning situation and varies the teaching/learning strategy to meet the needs of the learner, the teacher and the situation, in an effort to attain educational outcomes which are greater than the sum of the parts" (Rinke, 1982, p. 13). Holistic approaches recognize both teacher and learner needs, abilities, and characteristics, and emphasize the teachers' ability to assess and modify the learning environment. Effective and appropriate instruction in this approach is dependent on curriculum goals and objectives that are relevant, meaningful, and valued by the student; in addition, "individualization" is fostered to encourage students' abilities, talents, and motivation to learn and to

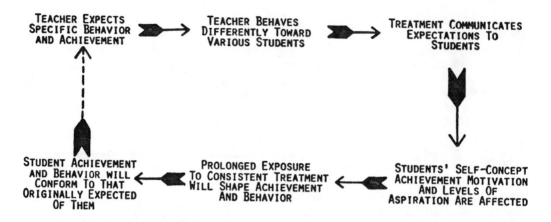

FIGURE 1. Teacher expectations/student achievement cycle (as described by Good, 1981).

provide "contextualization" of instruction. Finally, the educational contexts that are created within the holistic paradigm value, accept, and integrate diversity, and provide a positive environment in which students feel safe to learn.

The social organization of the classroom is one of the key psychocultural features to be considered when working with minority school populations (Tharpe, 1989). The degree to which our educational environment, contexts, and mode of organizing and implementing instructional goals match the cognitive, emotional, and behavioral styles of the learners, the greater the likelihood of increased student participation and success. It has been suggested that many low-income and minority students have a cooperative social orientation; interaction of this style with the frequently competitive and individualistic classroom structures found in U.S. public schools yields negative academic and social schooling results (Kagan, 1986).

Restructuring the classroom in socioculturally congruent ways can address three problems faced by educational systems (Kagan, 1986). First, there will be more equitable educational opportunities, which will raise academic achievement and keep minority and low-income students in schools. Second, positive race relationships and harmony in our schools will be fostered. Finally, students will be provided experiences in socialization that promote the development of the social skills, positive attitudes, and behaviors that are necessary to participate in the workplace.

Cooperative and discovery learning are two instructional strategies for organizing effective classroom learning. Both strategies have a student-centered focus and involve modification of the classroom structure and teaming of students. Cooperative learning, which is based on the premise that restructuring classrooms and teaching students in small heterogeneous groups can significantly improve educational outcomes, should include five basic elements in each cooperative learning lesson (Johnson & Johnson, 1989):

1. Positive interdependence. The intrinsic satisfaction of learning for each individual and the importance of helping other members of the group to learn are emphasized.

2. Face-to-face promotive interaction. Discussion between students regarding what they are learning is encouraged to ensure that all students understand and complete assignments.

3. Individual accountability. All students must be able to demonstrate mastery of the subject matter being covered.

4. Social skills development. Opportunities are provided to help students learn the interpersonal skills necessary to develop leadership abilities and positive working relationships with other group members, and learn how to resolve group differences.

5. Group processing. Students determine how effective the group has been in working together and completing assigned.

Cooperative learning has produced positive outcomes in a number of areas: Improvements in ethnic relations and prosocial development have been found among participating students (Slavin, 1983) and ethnic minority students have demonstrated increased academic achievement (Aronson, Blaney, Stephan, Sikes, & Snapp, 1978; Slavin, 1977; Slavin & Oickle, 1981).

Discovery learning facilitates student interactions through heterogeneous groupings based on language ability and gender as well as reading and math achievement levels. Activities are open-ended and allow each child to work at her or his particular developmental level. As an example, Finding Out/Descubrimiento (Cohen, DeAvila, & Inititi, 1981), a math/science curriculum for Grades 2–5 originally designed for bilingual education classrooms, features multiple learning centers operating simultaneously. Over 170 different math/science activities may be implemented over a 14-week period. The content for each week revolves around a central theme and activities are used to develop higher-order thinking skills such as developing hypotheses, comparing, contrasting, designing, constructing, and drawing inferences and conclusions. The teacher acts as a facilitator and encourages the children to use each other as resources instead of relying solely on the teacher's instructions. Discovery learning also encourages the development of cooperative norms. Appropriate consultation approaches can be taught to participants to increase team participation and productivity. One of the most important constructs of discovery learning is the expectation that different students will contribute to the group in different ways and that students are not expected to excel in all areas (Cohen, 1980). Equal status is bestowed on all participants and all contributions are viewed as valid and meaningful ways to aid the group process. The acceptance of student input into problem-solving situations is one way in which the previously

described cycle of expectations affecting achievement can be modified.

Both cooperative and discovery learning produce changes in the socio–psychological dimensions of the classroom by transforming traditional teacher and learner roles as well as instructional approaches. The traditional teacher-centered approach of direct instruction is de-emphasized and educational strategies are utilized that require a more cooperative/collaborative format. These approaches not only necessitate role redefinitions on the part of both teacher and student but also the development and maintenance of an accompanying organizational support system to ensure program success over time.

Characteristics of LEP Students

LEP students are a more diverse group than ever before. The public schools in the United States currently receive students from numerous countries with varying language and cultural backgrounds and as a result ESL (English as a second language) classrooms may contain LEP students from as many as five or ten different languages and cultures during the same instructional period. In addition to the linguistic and cultural differences of these students, there is also tremendous variability in the types of school-related experiences that these students bring to the U.S. classrooms. Specifically, the LEP population may consist of (a) literate students from literate societies with prior schooling; (b) literate students from literate societies with little prior schooling; (c) nonliterate and nonschooled students from literate societies; and (d) students from preliterate societies (societies without transcribed language systems and without literacy traditions).

Thus, while all LEP students have a common need for English language development through English as a second language and/or other programs, their needs regarding school readiness skills and specific academic content areas may vary widely. Therefore, when working with LEP students, it is important that educators assess their cultural and prior schooling backgrounds to determine the types and extent of instructional interventions required to allow them to achieve school success. Such interventions should address specific students' strengths and weaknesses in learning in linguistically and culturally appropriate ways. For example, the children of career diplomats from major-power countries may only need intensive English instruction in order to succeed in mainstream coursework, whereas some children from Third World or preliterate countries may require that content material be presented in their native language and that their proficiency in the native language be further developed prior to their either learning English or receiving content instruction in English.

The Inventory of Learner Characteristics of Language Minority Students as shown in Figure 2 (Cardona-Morales, 1986) was designed to help educators evaluate a number of variables that should be considered when designing intervention for students. The inventory attempts to identify students' level of preparation for the regular education curriculum. On each of 20 items, the student is rated as either high (1) or low (5) on the basis of prior knowledge, experiences, and linguistic maturity. Students with higher scores on the inventory generally will require more extensive and comprehensive intervention programs. For example, a student who scores within the 90–100 range may not only need bilingual or English as a second language instruction, but also may need to be considered for special education services. In contrast, a student who scores within the 20–35 range will not need the same intensity of services; it is possible that such a student can be successfully mainstreamed in English-only classes, although some specific intervention may be needed as indicated by an item analysis of the inventory.

INSTRUCTIONAL INTERVENTIONS

The following instructional interventions for specific curricula are presented under the distinct categories of oral language, reading, writing, and the language experience approach to learning. This distinction between areas is artificial, and in all cases interventions should be blended whenever possible to integrate the language arts (listening, speaking, reading, and writing instruction) across the curriculum. Critical variables dealing with the affective domain are most closely reflected in the experiential knowledge children bring to the learning task. Experiential knowledge is vital to insure success and continuity in learning regardless of the methodology and must constantly be monitored.

Oral Language

Oral language is fundamental in almost all academic and scholastic tasks in our public schools. For students to learn effectively in the schools, it is necessary that they be able to use language for social purposes and in a variety of settings and that their language skills be sufficiently sophisticated to permit the learning of abstractions and concepts related to the academic disciplines. Vocabulary develops as a function of the students' prior experiences as well as the level of interest in the subject matter being presented. Developing oral language skills through instruction requires that information be presented in a manner that can be understood and that appropriate language be modeled. Cooperative/collaborative learning strategies that incorporate peer tutoring and discovery learning provide opportunities for students to obtain academic and social information through the language of their peers and adults. Since many children enjoy and learn from voluntary, play-like activities, this approach can be used to promote oral language learning and facilitate the sharing of meaningful and authentic communication which should include various forms of literature. As examples, puppets can contextualize interactions, will often facilitate a very reserved child's participation in classroom activities, and can help such children initiate effective communication. Similarly, skits and plays written by the students provide good opportunities to acquire and improve oral and written language skills such as organizing and sequencing.

The development of language (listening, speaking, reading, and writing) occurs through meaningful interaction in natural

INVENTORY OF LEARNING CHARACTERISTICS OF LANGUAGE MINORITY STUDENTS

Student Name _____

For each item, circle the descriptor which most appropriately defines and/or describes the above language minority student. After rating the student on each item, add the number of descriptors circled in each column and multiply by the specified column weight. The total score is obtained by adding the scores of each column.

1. Rate the student usage of the native language, according to age	Excellent	Articulate	Good	Awkward	Poor
2. Rate the student usage of the second language, according to age and to length of time and instruction	Excellent	Articulate	Good	Awkward	Poor
3. The student communicates effectively with peers in L1.	Always	Frequently	Sometimes	Rarely	Never
4. The student associates with and recognizes experiences, values, and items in C1.	Always	Frequently	Sometimes	Rarely	Never
5. The student communicates effectively with peers in L2.	Always	Frequently	Sometimes	Rarely	Never
6. The student relates effectively to experiences, values, and items in C2.	Always	Frequently	Sometimes	Rarely	Never
7. The student's understanding of the purpose of reading can be expressed as:	Conscious/ aware	Interested	Wants/read	Knows print	Not aware
8. Rate student's familiarity and experience with text and language in L1.	Independent	Learn/read	Begin/reader	Nonreader	Pre-literate
9. The student recognizes and understands differences in appropriate patterns of interaction in L1 and L2.	High accuracy	Accuracy	50–50	Low accuracy	Poor accuracy
10. The student can read and write in L2.	Independent	Learn/read	Begin/read	Nonreader	Pre-literate
11. The student's home language when compared with school English is:	Same	Very alike	Alike	Different	Extremely different
12. The student's cultural tradition (C1) when compared to the dominant cultural tradition found in the schools (Western European), is:	Same	Very alike	Alike	Different	Extremely different

(Inventory, continued)

13. The student's cultural background (C1) when compared to the dominant cultural background found in the schools (Anglo-Saxon culture), is:	Same	Very alike	Alike	Different	Extremely different
14. When compared to U.S. public school expectations, the student's familiarity with geographic setting and natural phenomena is:	Same	Very alike	Alike	Different	Extremely different
15. How do schooling requirements in the student's home/community differ with U.S. schooling requirements?	Same	Very alike	Alike	Different	Extremely different
16. The home country (society and economy) of the student may be classified as:	High-tech	Industrial	Market/ agricultural	Developing	Third World
17. The ethnolinguistic community normally resided in:	Industrial/ urban	Developing industrial	Commercial/ agricultural	Semirural agrarian	Rural–remote agrarian
18. The student's socioeconomic status may be represented as:	Wealthy	Affluent	Low Middle class	Working class	Impoverished
19. The student's maturity compared with that of majority culture peers is:	Very alike	Consistent	Compatible	Different	Very different
20. Societal norms and values of the student's community are identical with those of the dominant culture.	Very true	Frequently	Sometimes	Rarely true	Never true
	(x1)	(x2)	(x3)	(x4)	(x5)

TOTAL = _____
(Sum of columns 1, 2, 3, 4, 5)

Unpublished inventory developed by C. Cardona-Morales, Center for National Origin Equity: Northwest Regional Educational Laboratory, Portland, OR 1986.

communicative settings. To assure that instruction is developed that can provide such interaction, Lynn Rhodes (1989) outlined six language learning principles to be incorporated into oral language instruction. Specifically, she suggested that students learn oral (listening and speaking) and written (reading and writing) language by

1. listening, speaking, reading, and writing;

2. using language to learn about or explore personally important and interesting aspects of the world;

3. focusing on meaning and social function as they use language;

4. observing others demonstrate the social functions, processes, and conventions of language;

5. constructing and experimenting with pragmatic, semantic, syntactic, and graphophonic (phonological) rules; and

6. trying to make sense of the world (including language), taking risks and learning from mistakes, utilizing feedback from others on communicative competence, requesting assistance, and monitoring sense-making.

Reading

It has been suggested (Walker, 1978) that the language of newspapers and periodicals mirrors more closely the oral language of primary-school-age children than the basal readers written for children of the same age. It is important that teachers focus on the highly developed and functional oral language repertoire that children bring to the formal learning environment. Traditional reading approaches that use basal texts to develop word attack or phonetic skills lack interest for many mainstream and minority children and can be ineffective in raising their achievement levels (Esquivel & Yoshida, 1985; Walker, 1978); in addition, it has been suggested (Smith, 1978) that breaking skills down into their component parts may make reading more difficult because it makes nonsense out of what should make sense.

To learn to read, a child needs to read, have available interesting materials that make sense, and have an understanding facilitator as a guide (Smith, 1978). The knowledge and background of the reader are important factors in the development of reading skills (Goodman & Goodman, 1981). Reading development is affected by nonvisual information that the subject brings to the reading task, such as familiarity with the content (Smith, 1978). Reading is not simply decoding a number of words in a sentence and recognizing the syntax but rather a process of seeking meaning. Readers construct this meaning during reading while "engaged in the long-distance conversation between themselves and the author" (Goodman & Goodman,

1981). In short, reading involves bringing knowledge and background experiences to the reading material and implementing a "psycholinguistic guessing game" to determine the meaning that is being conveyed. Using this holistic approach, students respond to material when it is related to their community and background experiences. As a result, an instructional method must have the capacity to intrinsically motivate the children so they will become actively involved in the reading task.

The following instructional interventions in reading are approaches designed to enhance the academic achievement of minority students. In many cases, the approaches presented can be used to facilitate the integration of listening, speaking, reading, and writing skills.

Semantic mapping. Semantic mapping has been successfully used to engage, motivate, and actively involve students in the process of concept and vocabulary development, reading, writing, and content area study skills.

This instructional approach is based on research that indicates a high correlation between knowledge of vocabulary and reading comprehension levels (Mezynski, 1983). A graphic representation of semantic organizers provides a way to emphasize the relationships among ideas and concepts. Semantic mapping teaches concepts as they relate to specific contexts or content areas. This is accomplished by incorporating student interests, background knowledge, and language that are related to the specific topics selected. This strategy can be implemented as an alternative to traditional instructional approaches prior to, during, or after reading a passage or story.

Semantic mapping facilitates learning in several ways. First, students' memories are probed for experiences associated with the theme or topic under study. Second, concept tags (words) are associated with the main idea. Finally, accommodating new or dissonant information to students' existing knowledge is accomplished through refinement and elaboration.

The following steps are based on the model suggested by Johnson and Pearson (1984).

1. Choose a word (concept tag) that is central to a topic the class will be studying. This concept tag will be the trigger word around which brainstorming, associations, categorizations, and discussion will occur.

2. Write the selected concept tag on a chart, chalkboard, or transparency.

3. Have students work individually to think of and write down as many words as they can generate that are related to the selected word. They also should categorize these words on paper.

4. Then have the students share words form their lists in an oral class activity. These words are grouped in categories around the concept tag. As the categories around the trigger word are elaborated, the input becomes a map of the students' semantic interpretations to the concept tag.

5. Students then suggest labels for the different categories of associations on the map. For students initially unfamiliar with the semantic mapping process, assistance in labeling may be provided by the teacher.

6. Initiate discussion based on the different entries.

During the discussion students become aware of new words, develop cooperative knowledge by sharing and interacting, see relationships among concepts, and enhance and confirm their understanding of vocabulary.

Semantic mapping has also been successfully used as a prewriting strategy to help develop writing skills (Johnson, Pittleman, & Heimlich, 1986). By the same steps as outlined above, the lesson is expanded by focusing on the development of a main idea and supporting detail, which are written into paragraph form. Color coding each major category and supporting information have been found to be particularly useful to facilitate organization for paragraph and story writing. In addition, this procedure is also an effective study technique in the development of an outline for other content areas such as social studies and science.

Patterned language approach to reading. The patterned language approach is a way of controlling text for a beginning reader. It uses predictions and repetition as a way of providing opportunities for the student and teacher to read together. A sight word approach with heavy reliance on background knowledge and information to facilitate comprehension, patterned language materials alter the text to obtain different outcomes in comprehension. Reading therefore involves interaction with the text. As an example, children's first interaction with books often is by listening to and repeating rhymes, verses and eventually entire books; this natural process is utilized in helping the student to learn to read.

The procedure is based on the principle that patterned language assists students to make connections between spoken language and printed text. A key element for ensuring success is to provide Big Books, patterned language books, and other relevant and interesting materials compatible with the sociocultural and experiential background of the students.

An essential preliminary step in the patterned language approach involves discussing the topic of the book, events, and possible outcomes before the book is ever opened. This allows the students to relate their knowledge and experiences to the book topic. As students (provided with pictures and other clues) discuss and anticipate the book's content and plot, their ability to organize, accommodate, and assimilate new knowledge is enhanced.

A step-by-step patterned language approach was developed by Bridge, Winograd, and Haley (1983) with low-performing first-grade students and includes the following:

1. Start with preliminary discussion of the text as described above.

2. Read the book aloud to the students. Reread the book, inviting the students to join in when they can predict what will come next. Have the students take turns reading the book.

3. Put the text of the book on a large paper without the book's picture cues. Read and choral read the story from the chart. Give the students sentence strips with

sentences from the story. Have them match the strips to the chart and then read the sentences.

4. Give the students individual word cards from the story, in order of first appearance. Have the children place each card under the matching word in the chart.

5. Read and choral read the story from the chart. Place individual word cards from sections of the story in random order at the bottom of the chart. Have the students match the word cards to the words in the story.

This approach is expected to have several positive outcomes. Discussing books prior to reading them both reinforces meaning and provides repeated exposure to content; this increases students' probability of successfully completing associated tasks and consequently maintaining their status in group interactions. Acquiring an extensive vocabulary in specific interest areas that are associated with their experiences facilitates a significant increase in the language power of the children and eases the move from patterned texts to literature-based readers or other basals required in schools, since the student not only can read from text but now also can anticipate what will come next in the text. This success builds students' self-esteem and confidence in their language abilities.

This approach has a number of variations. One variation that greatly enhances students' language experience is an activity known as authoring books: The students in fact generate their own books. The results of this approach are quite powerful because students expand their vocabulary, develop increased skill in prediction, and begin to develop a sense of validation in expressing themselves through writing. This process enables students to learn much more than mere "sight vocabulary" or isolated facts; they also learn that their experiences, background, and language are valued and that they can use these tools to continue learning as well as to contribute to the learning of others around them. This process motivates students to learn and helps them perceive themselves as capable learners.

Language Experience Approach

The basic premise of the language experience approach is that language is a pragmatic system, and that "contextualization" or lack of it contributes to the success or failure of students in reading and in writing. Thus, the language experience approach integrates aspects of oral language, reading, and writing (Van Allen & Allen, 1976) and provides opportunities for the validation of students' linguistic, cognitive, social, and background knowledge.

Research has shown that the language experience approach has resulted in positive gains for diverse groups, among them students from lower-SES groups (Kendrick & Bennett, 1967) and unmotivated older children, as well as black students, bilingual and bicultural students, and language-learning-disabled children.

The language experience approach encompasses a variety of strategies and can include both direct and indirect teaching interventions. Thus, the individual needs of a particular instructional setting can easily be accommodated. Teacher–pupil interactions may occur on an individual, small-group, or large-group basis. In addition, learning centers can be structured to incorporate language experience strategies. Finally, planned instructional programming may also use the language experience orientation to increase students' ability to relate to the content being taught. Key elements of this approach include:

1. Discussion of a story or an experience shared by the group or important to an individual. For a story starter, a picture stimulus may need to be used to elicit oral responses from the students. Open-ended and nonthreatening questions should be asked to encourage students' participation.

Students should be prepared to summarize the main ideas of the story or experience and should include information related to who, what, where, when, why, and how events occurred. The story highlights should be reviewed with the students and additional explanations obtained to ensure comprehension.

2. The story should be recorded as the

class or students dictate it. To ensure a logical sequence of events, work with the group by questioning the narrative order until there is continuity and sequence in the story.

3. The whole group should reread the story after it is written. At that time the story can be embellished by adding adjectives, adverbs, and other figurative language. A title should also be assigned to the story by the students.

4. The story should then be typed and a copy should be distributed to all students. The students could read the story the following day as a whole group. Other alternatives would have students reading different sentences from the story. Throughout this process new words could be filed alphabetically in a "word bank" and these words could be reviewed periodically and used in new stories that are written.

5. A long-term plan of instruction (1–2 weeks) can be developed based upon the story. Students can read the story as a group (Daily Echo and Choral Reading) or individually in sentence groups, or work on basic sight words, phonetic analysis, sequencing sills, close techniques, or other related activities.

6. Keep all stories in a book designated "class authors" for frequent rereading.

Shared-book experiences. Holdaway (1979) developed this approach by adapting favorite children's stories into "big books" for children to view and read together. To maximize the benefits of reading aloud to children, favorite stories are produced in a very large book with print that can be seen by the students from their desks. In this way, the children participate at an early age in all aspects of reading, especially when nursery rhymes or predictable materials are used. The original versions of favorite stories can be changed by the children in some way and reproduced with their own illustrations. Self-created books or the original versions of the stories can be taken home and shared with parents; this strategy has been very effective in increasing reading proficiency while promoting parent satisfaction and interest.

Generating questions for better comprehension. This intervention is designed for older language-minority students with limited English proficiency and reading skills who participate in the regular education curriculum with limited support services. This intervention helps students focus on the learning task and use previously learned skills and knowledge as a bridge to the new concepts and tasks.

1. Have the students scan the assigned material, read the paragraph headings, and generate questions based on these headings. Although assigned material should have a number of official work questions at the end, these questions should not be reviewed at this time.

2. After the students have written their own questions, brainstorm with the class as to what they think the material is about.

3. From the brainstorming and the ensuing discussion, have the students write answers to the questions they have written.

4. Have the students scan the assigned material for possible answers to their remaining questions. Students should write the answers as they find them.

5. Let the students know that their encounter with the material has been successful. They have been able to read quickly and with comprehension.

6. Ask the students to read the questions at the end of the assigned material (Repeat steps 2 and 3).

7. Have the students read a summary of the assigned material and try to answer the questions.

8. Ask the students to read the assigned material and answer any remaining questions. Students should be directed to note the page number where each answer is found.

When students generate their own questions before reading assigned materials and additionally discuss and brainstorm possible answers to these questions, they begin to organize personal knowledge that may be related to the topics encountered. By asking questions and discussing possibilities, those students who may not have extensive background in the subject area can both expand their information base and actively anticipate needed information. Finally, the sequential process of review, question, review, and question allows students to check and modify their predictions of text information.

Writing

In studies in which children's writing and thinking in classrooms was both challenged and nurtured, great growth in writing and thinking skills have been found. However, there is general agreement that unfortunately too little time is spent with students in the writing process and that students are given few choices in topic selection (Bos & Vaughn, 1988). For writing skills to develop, children need guidance; direction must be given in establishing the purposes for writing and in evaluating their writing, as well as assisting them to revise, edit, confer, and publish. The following approach is adapted from Bos & Vaughn (1988) and incorporates these basic elements of writing. This instructional approach combines elements of both direct instruction and cooperative learning.

A process approach to writing. When children are asked to explain what good writing is, they often focus on such mechanics of writing as correct spelling, handwriting, and punctuation. Very seldom do they mention that good writing involves the clear communication of ideas. A process approach to writing emphasizes content and the expression of ideas over mechanics; the mechanics of writing develops as a natural outgrowth of writing every day.

A process approach to writing is student-directed, the students choosing their writing topics. The teacher serves as a resource person rather than a director. Although this approach initially may be frustrating for some students and teachers who are accustomed to teacher-directed instruction, students' increasing interest and willingness to write, as well as their developing independence in writing, soon

overcome any resistance encountered.

There are numerous benefits to using a process approach to writing, the major advantages being the following:

1. The student becomes less resistant to writing. This is generalized into other areas by integrating writing across the curriculum.

2. The student's writing is developed, both in terms of content and mechanics, because of extended daily practice.

3. Independence and self-directed behavior is encouraged.

4. Cooperative behavior with other students is encouraged.

5. The student's background knowledge and experience are validated through "contextualization" of instruction.

6. Self-esteem is developed through the sharing of feelings and thoughts with others in their written samples.

7. During the revising and editing stages, students naturally expand their vocabulary, speech patterns, and understanding of the conventions of written language

Writing programs using a process approach should have three main goals.

1. Create a working atmosphere similar to that of a studio (Graves, 1983). This atmosphere can be created in a number of ways: (a) The teacher can serve as a model for students by writing as the students enter the room. (b) Writing material and supplies should be readily available so that students can begin writing immediately. (c) Each student should have an individual writing folder that contains work in progress, and lists of possible writing topics, of pieces completed, of writing skills mastered, and of topics the students have expertise in, as well as a list of words the students are currently learning to spell. (d) All students should have a permanent book that contains their finished pieces. (e) Students should have an extended amount of time to write daily, preferably a minimum of 30 minutes each day.

2. Create an atmosphere in which students can interact easily. The teacher needs

to set the tone by communicating interest in the children's thoughts and words both verbally and nonverbally. Additionally, the teacher should interact with the students about their writing and help them share their work and thoughts with others. Students should be allowed to work together or individually, and the classroom should be structured to facilitate a variety of work stations.

3. Create an atmosphere that encourages independence. In this setting, the students choose both their writing topic and the style in which they want to write. Students who are undecided about their topic should be encouraged to consult with other students. Student experts in different areas of the writing process can be identified who can assist them with problems. Student–teacher conferences should be conducted frequently, but should be brief, lasting from 30 seconds to a maximum of 10 minutes.

The following sections describe the basic elements that should receive attention with a process approach to writing and suggests some ways in which students can gain greater proficiency in the specific areas. Teachers will need to provide mini-lessons, based on observed student needs, that focus on specific basic skill areas. Students can be cycled into these instructional modules designed from an evaluation of weekly writing samples.

Prewriting. "The most important thing children can learn is what they know and how they know it. (Graves, 1985, p. 39).

In the prewriting stage, students make lists of possible topics that they can write about. Topics are decided on by each student and involve subjects they know about, either through observation, experience, reading, or interview. The students are informed that they will not be required to write about all topics on their list. Each day, they identify three items that they are most interested in writing about that day and return the remaining topics to the folder for later use.

Students who have problems in topic selection can brainstorm with or be interviewed by another student. Students should be reminded to write down new topics whenever they are thought of so that they can be used in later writing sessions. In addition, having students share stories or personal experiences may provide additional ideas for writing. Often, students will copy ideas from other students and this can lead to better-developed stories. Repetition of a topic should not be discouraged, since ideas and stories may become further refined with continued effort; a student should be encouraged to switch topics only if progress is not noted.

Composing. Students often have difficulty planning their writing; consequently they may need to be taught prewriting skills. Techniques for teaching prewriting skills include brainstorming and modeling with a "think aloud" approach. In addition, providing students with the opportunity to read up on their topic and to discuss their pieces with other students can greatly enhance planning. Having classmates listen to their stories may be especially helpful as their audience can indicate the parts where they either have difficulty following the sequence or understanding the story.

Revising. Revising work is a difficult task for most people. When working with beginning writers, it is most important to focus on what is being said rather than on how well it is said. Therefore, to prevent discouragement, first allow the child's writing to proceed to the editing stage without much revision. As time goes on and skills increase, more mechanical accuracy should be required from the students, spelling being emphasized after the composition is completed. Students should be reminded that their main goal is to produce an interesting and meaningful message.

Editing. The editorial process should begin only when the student is satisfied with the content. To ensure that students understand why the mechanics of language are so important in the writing process, students can be provided with an explanation and an example of the importance of the editorial process in a real-life situation. Students should review their work several times, each time looking for a different problem area such as spelling, punctuation and capitalization, and verb/

noun agreement. Following this review, they should have a classmate go over their manuscripts, which then can be subjected to final manuscript proofing by a class editor or teacher.

Publishing. Publishing provides an opportunity for students to share and communicate their ideas and thoughts about a particular topic. In the process, they become encouraged by the acknowledgment and validation of their ideas and hard work. Because of these positive outcomes, all students should at some time be given the opportunity to publish one of their works. Published pieces can be read during "reader's theater" or shared from the "author's chair," and then placed in a permanent book to be displayed and made available for other students to read.

The writing conference. "Conferring, which occurs throughout the writing process, is the heart of the writing procedure" (Bos & Vaughn, 1988, p. 167). In this step, the individual student comes to a conference prepared to read her or his work, describe the problem areas, and answer questions about the work. During these conferences, students should be permitted both to choose a topic of personal interest and to understand that the story can be written in the way they want. Questions about a student's writing should be easily answerable and designed to facilitate reflection on the writing process. The amount of time for conferring will vary but should probably last between two to three minutes.

Dialogue journals. The main purpose of dialogue journals is to increase personal communication and mutual understanding between each student and the teacher. In this approach, the teacher reads a student's entry and responds by writing in the journal. The teacher's entry may take a number of forms; he or she may share, comment on, or react to something the student has written or may take the opportunity either to answer a question or to ask one. Most important of all, the teacher provides a model to the student by writing and encourages students to express themselves in writing. Both teacher and student have equal turns and both respond as an inter-

ested audience, asking questions, offering elaborative comments, or giving opinions. Although the primary focus of dialogue journals is on the functional use of language and interactive content development, there is indirect development of mechanical writing skills: punctuation, capitalization, spelling, and other elements such as syntax and composition. Increased competence in using written language, either a first or second language, is a byproduct of achieving this process. Reading and writing are integrated as each influences the other, and both develop as a natural extension of a child's desire to communicate (Gambrell, 1985). The desire to communicate motivates the student to read the teacher's entry and write a corresponding answer.

Interactive writing develops through modeling. Several techniques can be used and these include asking questions (open-ended, or for clarification) expanding on the student's entry, commenting on the student's entry, changing or introducing a new topic, and providing direct instruction (mini-lessons) on specific areas of need (determined by children's mistakes in journals).

The teacher's strategy of commenting by adding new information and introducing more general principles or meaning provides students with a model for more elaborated, rational thinking in written discourse. As a result, the student uses more critical thinking skills.

Children of all ages and functioning levels can benefit from dialogue journals. These include prereaders and learning-disabled, gifted, LEP, and bilingual students. However, there are some suggestions for responding to children's writing that are of primary importance.

- Since dialogue journal writing is designed to encourage written expression, the focus is upon communication. Student's entries should not be corrected in any way. Rather, if a word is misspelled or an incorrect verb form is used, the correct form can be modeled in the response.

- Keep in mind that your response will affect the student's interest in writing and therefore it should encourage written expression. The length, detail, and content of a student's writing can be dramatically increased with requests for more information such as "Tell me more about . . . ," "Describe . . . ," and "I'd like to know more about . . . ".

• Dialogue journals are private communications. Students should be aware that the journal belongs to both student and teacher, but that it may be shared if the student chooses to.

Benefits of dialogue journals.

1. They provide functional opportunities to use newly acquired abilities in written language expression and comprehension.

2. Research on the use of dialogue journals has shown that reluctant and less proficient writers are motivated to write in them, and this motivation can transfer to other tasks (Hayes & Bahruth, 1985, as quoted in Staton & Tyler, 1987).

3. Substantial improvements in spelling have been observed in younger writers (Staton & Tyler, 1987).

4. Less proficient writers increase in production, become more fluent, and show greater competence in focusing on a topic and elaborating on it over time (Shuy, 1987).

5. The teacher's responses provide clear, comprehensible language input for students to absorb subconsciously as a model for language acquisition.

6. Dialogue journals represent a concrete application of Vygotsky's theory that learning functional human activities initially occurs through the learner's cooperative participation in accomplishing tasks with a more experienced partner.

7. The hard of hearing and the second-language student, and other students with limitations involving comprehension and expression, become very competent at writing to an optimally challenging level for each student, varying their language to insure comprehension.

8. Dialogue journals allow for individualized instruction as well as the chance to build on and enhance each student's abilities.

9. The journals reduce the stress of producing understandable text. Students have time to reread previous entries as well to reflect before responding.

10. Journals provide a means for teachers to become more aware of each student's interests and concerns.

SUMMARY

In conclusion, new patterns of instructional interventions are emerging that suggest a shift in the roles of school support personnel such as school psychologists and special educators toward a more collaborative partnership with regular classroom teachers. In addition, new dimensions of instructional design and practice were discussed; these strategies embrace a more holistic philosophy of teaching to accommodate greater learner variation and diversity. These shifts in job roles and instructional interventions are specifically designed to reverse the trend of "progressive academic retardation" among minority and high-risk students in our schools by viewing schooling in a new way. According to Cummins (1989), this process must "involve the individual classroom teacher and other professional educators actively challenging the educational structure within which they operate" (p. 36).

REFERENCES

Applebee, A. N., Langer, J. A., & Mullins, I. V. S. (1989). *Crossroads in American Education: A Summary of Findings (The National Report Card)*. Princeton, NJ: Educational Testing Services.

Allington, R. L., & Shake, M. C. (1986). Remedial reading: Achieving curricular congruence in classroom and clinic. *Reading Teacher, 39*(7), 648–654.

Aronson, E., Blaney, N., Stephan, C., Sikes, J., & Snapp, M. (1978). *The jigsaw classroom*. Beverly Hills, CA: Sage.

Arreaga-Mayer, C., & Greenwood, C. R. (1986). Environmental variables affecting culturally and linguistically different learners. *NABE Journal, 10*(2), 113–134.

Bennett, W. (1988). American education: Making it work. *Chronicle of Higher Education, 34*(34), A29–41.

Bos, C., & Vaughn, S. (1988). *Strategies for teaching students with learning and behavior problems.* Boston, MA: Allyn and Bacon.

Bridge, C. A., Winograd, P. N., & Haley, D. (1983). Using predictable materials vs. preprimers to teach beginning sight words. *Reading Teacher, 36*(9), 884–891.

Brown, T. (1986). *Teaching minorities more effectively.* Lanham, MD: University Press of America.

Cardona-Morales, C. (1986). *The Inventory of Learner Characteristics of Language Minority Students.* Unpublished manuscript.

Cohen, E. G. (1980). *A multi-ability approach to integrated classrooms.* Paper presented at the American Psychological Association, Montreal.

Cohen, E. G., DeAvila, E., & Inititi, J. A. (1981). *Multicultural improvement of cognitive ability.* Unpublished manuscript. Palo Alto, CA: Stanford University.

Cummins, J. (1986). Empowering minority students: A framework for intervention. *Harvard Educational Review, 56*(1), 18–36.

Cummins, J. (1989). The sanitized curriculum: Educational disempowerment in a nation at risk. In D. Johnson & D. Roen (Eds.), *Richness in writing: Empowering ESL students* (pp.19–38). New York: Longman.

Deyhle, D. (1986). Success and failure: A microethnographic comparison of Navajo and anglo students' perceptions of testing. *Curriculum Inquiry, 16*(4), 365–389.

Dunn, L. M. (1968). Special education for the mildly retarded — Is much of it justifiable? *Exceptional Children, 35,* 5–22.

Esquivel, G., & Yoshida, R. (1985). Special education for language minority students. *Focus on Exceptional Children, 18*(3), 1–6.

Fullan, M., & Pomfert, A. (1977). Research on curriculum and instruction implementation. *Review of Educational Research, 47*(1), 335–397.

Gagne, R. (1976). *The learning basis of teaching methods.* In N. L. Gage (Ed.), The Psychology of Teaching Methods (Seventy-fifth Yearbook of the National Study for the Study of Education, pp. 21–43). Chicago: University of Chicago Press.

Gambrell, L. B. (1985). Dialogue journals: Reading-writing interaction. *Reading Teacher 38*(6), 512–515.

Gartner, A., & Lipskey, D. (1987). Beyond special education: Toward a quality education for all students. *Harvard Educational Review, 57*(4), 367–394.

Good, T. L. (1981). Teacher expectations and student perceptions: A decade of research. *Educational Leadership, 38*(5), 415–422.

Goodman, Y., & Goodman, K. (1981). Twenty questions about teaching language. *Educational Leadership, 38*(6), 437–432.

Graves, D. H. (1983). *Writing: Teachers and children at word.* Portsmouth, NH: Heinemann Educational Books.

Graves, D. H. (1985). All children can write. *Learning Disability Focus, 1*(1), 36–43.

Hart, L. (1983). *Human brain and human learning.* New York: Longman.

Heller, K., Holtzman, W., & Messick, S. (Eds.). (1982). *Placing children in special education: Strategy for equity.* Washington, DC: National Academy Press.

Holdaway, D. (1979). *The foundations of literacy.* Sydney: Ashton Scholastic.

Idol, L., Paolucci-Whitcomb, P., & Nexin, A. (1986). *Collaborative consultation.* Rockville, MD: Aspen Systems.

Johnson, D. D., & Pearson, D. P. (1984). *Teaching reading vocabulary* (2nd ed.). New York: Holt, Rinehart, and Winston.

Johnson, D., Pittleman, S. & Heimlich, J. (1986). Semantic mapping. *Reading Teacher, 39*(8), 778–783.

Johnson, D. W., & Johnson, R. T. (1989). Toward a cooperative effort: A response to Slavin. *Educational Leadership, 46*(7), 80–81.

Kagan, S. (1986). Cooperative learning and sociocultural factors in schooling. In Bilingual Education Office (Ed.). *Beyond language: social and cultural factors in schooling language minority students* (pp. 231–298). Los Angeles, CA: California State University.

Kauffman, J. M. (1988). A revolution can also mean returning to the starting point: Will school psychology help special education complete the circuit? *School Psychology Review, 17*(3), 490–494.

Kendrick, W. M., & Bennett, C. L. (1967). A comparative study of two first grade language arts programs — extended into second grade. *Reading Teacher,* 747–755.

Lavin, D. E. (1965). *The prediction of academic performance: A theoretical analysis and review of research.* New York: Vintage Books.

Mezynski, K. (1983). Issues concerning the acquisition of knowledge: Effects of vocabulary training on reading comprehension. *Review of Educational Research, 53*(2), 253–279.

National Assessment of Educational Progress (1983a). *Reading, Science, & Mathematics Trends: A Closer Look.* Denver, CO: Education Commission of the States.

National Assessment of educational Progress (1983b, Winter). Newsletter, 15, No. 1 (p. 2).

Olsen, L. (1988). *Crossing the schoolhouse border: Immigrant students and the California public schools.* San Francisco: California Tomorrow.

Pugach, M., & Johnson, L. (1988). Rethinking the relationship between consultation and collaborative problem-solving. *Focus on Exceptional Children, 21*(4), 1–14.

Reschly, D. J. (1988). Special education reform: School psychology revolution. *School Psychology Review, 17*(3), 459–475.

Rhodes, L. (1989, Jan.). *Whole Language and Special Education.* (Available from Merle Bradford, Director of Special Education, Blanchard Education Service Center, 501 N. Dixon St., Portland, OR, 97227-1871).

Rinke, W. J. (1982). Holistic education: Toward a functional approach to adult education. *Lifelong Learning, 5*(8), 12–25.

Ryan, W. (1971). *Blaming the victim.* New York: Pantheon.

Shapiro, E. S. (1987). *Behavioral assessment in school psychology.* Hillsdale, NJ: Erlbaum.

Shuy, R. W. (1987). Research currents: Dialogue as the heart of learning. *Language Arts, 64*(8), 890–897.

Slavin, R. E. (1977). How student learning teams can integrate the desegregated classroom. *Integrated Education, 15,* 56–58.

Slavin, R. E. (1983). *Cooperative learning.* New York: Longman.

Slavin, R. E., & Oickle, E. (1981). Effects of learning teams on student achievement and race relations. *Sociology of Education, 54,* 174–180.

Smith, F. (1978). *Reading without nonsense.* New York: Teachers College Press.

Staton, J., & Tyler, D. (1987). Dialogue journal use with learning disabled students. *The Pointer, 32*(1), 4–8.

Tharpe, R. G. (1989). Psychocultural variables and constants: Effects on teaching and learning in schools. *American Psychologist, 44*(2), 349–359.

Tikunoff, W. J. (1987). Providing instructional leadership: The key to effectiveness. In H. Fradd & W. J. Tikunoff (Eds.), *Bilingual education and bilingual special education* (pp. 231–263). Boston, MA: College Hill Publication, Little, Brown and Company.

Van Allen, R. & Allen, C. (1976). *Language Experience Activities.* Boston, MA: Houghton Mifflin.

Walker, R. F. (1978, May). *Developing a research-based language/reading program.* Paper presented at the Annual Meeting of the International Reading Association, Houston.

West, J. F., & Idol, L. (1987). School consultation (Part 1): An interdisciplinary perspective on theory, models, and research. *Journal of Learning Disabilities, 20*(7), 388–402.

Will, M. (1986). *Educating students with learning problems: A shared responsibility.* Washington, DC: U.S. Department of Education.

Will, M. (1988). Educating students with learning problems and the changing role of the school psychologist. *School Psychology Review, 17*(3), 476–478.

Part III:

Educational Support Services

CHAPTER 10

Recruitment and Retention of Minority School Psychologists

Doris Benson
California State University, Northridge

In its *Blueprint for Training and Practice* the National Association of School Psychologists (Ysseldyke, 1984) set forth its commitment to alter the profession so that it will serve all children. The realization of this goal will not only require the Association to transform its service delivery system, but its training practices as well. A critical component in this transformation is the diversification of its membership to include an adequate proportion of minority school psychologists. The term *minorities* for the purposes of this chapter will mean (persons who are members of) those ethnic groups that have been historically underrepresented in higher education and related professions. Included are Blacks, Hispanics, Asian-Americans, and Native Americans. Strategies toward this objective necessarily begin with a focus on attracting and maintaining more minorities at the university level.

That the profession is sensitive to the need to enhance its effectiveness and grow in this direction is indicated by the development and publication of surveys (Zins & Halsell, 1986; Novick, 1978) that reflect the woefully inadequate representation of minorities in professional training programs and by recommendations to reverse this trend.

According to Zins and Halsell (1986), only 11.5% of currently enrolled students in school psychology training programs are minorities. One-half of this amount were concentrated in 15 schools; and the majority of this group were pursuing masters as opposed to terminal degrees. Furthermore, 22% of the training programs had no minority students enrolled at the time of the survey. Though a variety of efforts were

being utilized to recruit minorities, respondents for 14 of the programs in the Zins and Halsell survey expressed a great amount of frustration that none of their strategies were successful. The researchers advocated a more aggressive recruitment approach and offered several recommendations based on those used by the more successful programs among those surveyed. The suggestions included recruitment speaking engagements, program brochures, personal contacts, flexible admissions, and postadmissions support systems. The recommendations were insightful, as was the contention that recruitment of minorities is a professional and not solely a training program issue.

Valuable though these surveys and recommendations may be, they fail to consider the larger perspective within which the underrepresentation of minorities in school psychology training programs occurs. The profession has a major responsibility for the inclusion and status of its minority members; however, external factors exert a powerful influence as well. Some of the more prominent are institutional characteristics, geographical location, political and economic climate, and student characteristics. If the profession fails to consider some of the less salient though crucial elements that affect the issue, it may at best dilute its efforts to increase minority representation. It may, at worst, relegate the profession 10 years hence to be the recipient of yet another survey reflecting a more severe underrepresentation along with recommendations similar to those contained in the Zins and Halsell report, which are almost an exact replica of recommendations that were made almost

8 years earlier (Novick, 1978) but were apparently unheeded or were ineffective.

Efforts to influence the profession's conceptualization of and strategies towards training minority school psychologists will require an attempt to identify the societal, institutional, student, and professional elements that influence the recruitment and retention of minorities and to recommend strategies for intervention.

MINORITIES IN HIGHER EDUCATION — A SOCIETAL QUESTION

Although the United States is becoming increasingly multicultural, this reality is not reflected in our institutions of higher learning. In fact, there is evidence that the past decade has witnessed a decrease in the attendance of most minority groups at predominantly white colleges (Blackwell, 1983; Fleming, 1984). The 1960s, which witnessed a period of changing societal values and advocacy for minority rights, brought an increase in the number of minorities (members of minority groups) in higher education. Though never reaching population proportions, this increase was maintained through the mid-1970s, when it began to decline. Undoubtedly, economic conditions were and remain potent contributors to this reality. Minority enrollment in graduate and professional education is especially disproportionate. The distribution of ethnic minority groups in 1978 was as follows: Blacks, 6.2%; Hispanic groups, 2.5%; Asians/Pacific Islanders, 2.1%; and Native Americans, 0.4%. These percentages are contrasted with the 88.9% white student enrollment at that time. Though some individual ethnic groups increased their total graduate student enrollment by 1980, other groups, specifically the Black student population, decreased their representation in graduate and in professional schools (Blackwell, 1983).

Each year the pool of eligible minority students decreases. All professions are affected to some extent by this diminished pool of minority applicants in graduate and professional schools from which to choose. Yet for some, the magnitude of the effect is greater owing to the differential selection of occupations by various ethnic groups.

Many factors influence an individual person's career choice, including social, political, and economic motivation. However, ethnic group membership is as strong an influence (Axelson, 1985). Individuals from specific ethnic groups tend to cluster in selected professions in predictable rates. Blacks tend to select education, business management, and the social sciences, in order of frequency, whereas Hispanics choose education, foreign languages and the social sciences. Asian-Americans tend to gravitate first towards biological sciences, then business management, and finally engineering. And Native Americans have shown a preference for education and then social sciences. All but the Asian-American group tend to choose education first, and the social sciences last. (Education in this instance refers to teaching, guidance, and administration and not school psychology.)

This revelation represents a significant opportunity to develop a strategy for recruiting, from colleges of education, such professional teachers and guidance counselors as may seek a career change. This is especially plausible because of the close association between school psychology and teacher education training programs. Recognizing the existing ethnic selection factors, training programs may need to adopt specific strategies geared to targeted ethnic groups and designed to challenge their more preferential occupational choices. The tendency of institutions to use a broad-based recruitment approach, individualized solely by personal contacts with various departmental faculty (often including minorities) or administrators, may not adequately alter the more potent ethnic selection patterns.

In addition to the foregoing, the profession of school psychology is also at a disadvantage in competing for minority students because the majority of its training programs are located at predominantly white institutions. Many minority students — particularly Blacks, who make up one of the largest ethnic minority groups represented at the graduate school level – elect to attend an institution where they perceive the social climate will be more palatable to them. This phenomenon may account for the fact that while enrollment in predominantly white institutions has decreased since the late 1970s for Black students, it has increased at majority Black institutions (Fleming, 1984). This allocation of the total pool of minority applicants at the graduate and professional level is illustrated by the circumstance that the three or four Black medical colleges together enroll more Black students than all the 74 predominantly white medical institutions (Blackwell, 1983). As well as working to improve institutional climate, institutions with school psychology programs may need to establish cooperative or joint degree programs with predominantly minority schools where this is geographically feasible. Recruitment and teacher exchange with the colleges could be pursued as well. Such efforts could be spearheaded by the professional organizations, which could provide financial assistance and leadership in this regard to the universities.

CRITICAL INSTITUTIONAL COMPONENTS IN RECRUITMENT

Though often perceived as discrete phenomena, recruitment and retention are interdependent. Many institutions expend an enormous amount of energy and resources on recruitment of minority students, and then virtually abandon them. Many of these students must then try single-handedly to bridge the gap between the preparation derived from a disadvantaged and/or different cultural background and the demands of higher education (Smith, Simpson-Kirkland, Zimmern, Goldenstein, & Prichard, 1986). Retention of minority students requires an institutional atmosphere that is as supportive to currently enrolled students as it is to those who are being recruited.

Climate

There is convincing evidence that one of the most important factors in successful recruitment and retention of minority students is a visible institution-wide commitment to succeed, without which programmatic or department efforts will be thwarted (Arner & Yates, 1979). A very broad and pervasive factor, climate is often elusive and difficult to analyze. Though tangible manifestations can be evaluated positively or negatively, less concrete aspects may defy explanation. Nonetheless, they are often perceived by minorities (particularly by those persons of color or those whose ethnic group membership is obvious) and convey in their perception a sense of acceptance or rejection.

One noted element of social climate is the total minority population on a campus. Apparently the greater the amount, the more involvement minorities have in campus life, and they begin to feel more like part of the campus family, rather than like guests (and perhaps unwelcome ones). One study suggested 20% minority enrollment establishes a "comfortability" factor. Where the enrollment is closer to 10% or below, special efforts on the part of the institution, for example, networking and special events (personal, cultural, social events), will be required to ensure "hospitable" perceptions by minorities (Richardson, Simmons, & de los Santos, 1987).

In addition to the number of minorities enrolled, the climate of an institution is a function of its history and mission. The character of an institution is in part a reflection of who founded the institution and why. This element, and the institution's historical involvement in and relationships to minority affairs, are all factors that training programs seeking to recruit minorities must consider (Olson, 1988). Past weaknesses in this area may need to be addressed directly, and remedial effort may need to be overtly conveyed to students during recruitment. Individual program and departmental efforts can be impeded by negative institutional reputations.

Obviously, school psychology training programs cannot be maximally effective when carried out in isolation. This point was stressed by the Task Force on Minorities in Graduate Education in their report to the Council of Graduate Schools Board in which the need to involve "all campus constituencies in the recruiting effort" was addressed (Olson, 1988, p. 34).

The nature and type of course offerings as well as faculty flexibility, attitudes, academic pressure, and competition among peers have also been related to favorable and unfavorable perceptions of a university's climate by both minority and nonminority students. However, negative perceptions have more dire consequences for minorities. They may withdraw psychologically and ultimately fail academically, or they may manage to graduate, but with internalized insecurities and feelings of vulnerability that are carried over into professional life. The lasting impressions of these students will be transmitted to others through student communication channels, the "grapevine" (a very powerful informal network of communication especially among minority populations), and consequently have a cumulative negative impact on future recruitment efforts.

Students from minority groups have singled out certain particularly detrimental factors that undermine their sense of well-being: patronizing attitudes by faculty, a sense of stigmatization by those who might consider that they owe their very attendance solely to affirmative action quotas, the onus of assuming the role of spokesperson for their ethnic group, and the experience of having their uniqueness obscured.

Most institutions have established formal mechanisms to redress the more overt incidents of discrimination against minorities. But the more covert episodes escape detection and/or resolution through the formal channels. Ultimately, the atmospheric conditions of a campus are a result of the extent to which the top administration explicitly establishes and disseminates throughout the institution a no-nonsense policy of equity, nondiscrimination, and support for all of its students and faculty (Pruitt, 1983; Isaac, 1986; Keeter, 1987).

School psychology programs can be more effective at recruitment by joining forces with institutional efforts and advocating for more active involvement in evaluating the school climate and supporting innovations to improve the climate. Strategies might include incorporating mandated courses on minority cultures, promoting exchanges between cultural groups and interracial dialogue surrounding issues, receiving distinguished minority guest lecturers, and initiating other related

activities that tend to transform attitudes of intolerance into acceptance. The nature of the school psychology profession will lend a great amount of perceived legitimacy to its leadership role in this regard.

Size and Geographical Location

Size and geographical location play important roles in an institution's ability to continuously attract and retain minority students. Older, large departments in urban universities tend to produce more minority doctorates in psychology (Flores, 1985). However, there are many large, urban institutions that are less successful than their nonurban and smaller counterparts. Size and location, obvious advantages, do not compensate for the more important components of success — such special considerations for example as application fee waivers, tutorial and financial support, strong departmental connections to influential national organizations like the American Psychological Association, and systematic and comprehensive institutional commitment (Richardson et al., 1987; Flores, 1985; Olson, 1988).

State Policy of Relationship to University Recruitment and Retention of Minority Students

Positive institutional climate and commitment to affirmative action notwithstanding, the most progress occurs in universities that are located in states where there is visible commitment at the highest governmental level to educating increasing numbers of minorities in higher education, and where these efforts are maintained and monitored through coordinating and governing boards (Richardson et al., 1987). Though institutions in such states may suffer some loss of autonomy, they gain several compensatory benefits. Institutions become the recipients of an expanded information base that enables them to magnify their resources. They benefit from the direction and financial support tied to state priorities, and attain greater clarity and comprehensiveness of purpose as a result of state specifications and monitoring. State-backed efforts toward recruitment and retention can encourage cooperative ventures between universities, such as joint programming and faculty exchange, especially in locations where there are predominantly minority student universities.

A political climate favorable to service to minorities at the state level can energize, direct, and support institutional efforts. In states such as Texas, California, New York, and Pennsylvania, which are highly populated and have many urban centers with large minority populations, there are universities that have taken advantage of the encouraging political atmosphere and have consequently developed model programs that have been very effective in recruiting and maintaining minority students at both undergraduate and graduate levels. According to Richardson et al (1987), in other states (Michigan and New Mexico, for example), there is diminished support and incentive at the state level. Though not an impenetrable deterrent, as evidenced by the highly successful minority enrollment efforts at the University of New Mexico, limited state initiatives do pose special challenges to institutions within those localities to develop more creative and aggressive solutions.

The profession of school psychology can impact upon state policy through lobbying efforts and the introduction and monitoring of relevant legislation. Though several state associations have been active in the legislative arena with regard to licensure, few have pursued legislation as a vehicle to influence policy towards greater enrollment of minority students in higher education. Were the profession to undertake such advocacy, it would no doubt discover new and lasting allies among related professions that face a common dilemma. The publicizing of such advocacy would send a powerful message to ethnic minority groups that school psychology is a profession worth considering as a career option.

At the institutional level, school psychology training programs can, at the very least, endeavor to make their universities aware of the importance of institution–state alliances in conquering the minority underrepresentation in higher education, a problem that transcends professional and institutional parameters.

STUDENT FACTORS THAT MEDIATE SUCCESS OR FAILURE OF MINORITY ENROLLMENT PATTERNS

Minority students bring to their universities certain attributes that differ from those brought by their white peers. The inability of prediction models of educational attainment to be as effective with minorities as with whites underscores these differences (Smith & Allen, 1984), which are broad and related to academic as well as social and personal characteristics. This circumstance does not negate the many similarities found between minority and majority students (Lunneborg & Lunneborg, 1985). The similarities, however, are overshadowed by the nature and extent of the differences, which tend to inordinately regulate the patterns of minority students' success and failure in higher education.

Universities have attempted to meet minority student needs by a potpourri of remedial course offerings and tailored counseling services. Yet remedies tend to be nonsystematic, more intuitive or more theoretically than empirically based, and globally conceptualized and applied. Consequently, individual needs, particularly those less salient, tend to become subordinated to perceived group needs. A review of several studies highlighted below reveals the need for strategies incorporating individualized, differentiated, and more systematic approaches.

Characteristics of Highly At-Risk but Successful Minority Students

Universities have recognized that because of social or economic inequities a disproportionate number of minority students will enter and even graduate from college with less than adequate academic preparation. Some students, by virtue of their entrance examination scores and grade point averages, will be regarded as highly at risk for failure to attain a degree. Yet for many of these students, and more so for minority students, nonacademic criteria will exert the most powerful influence on grades, achievement, and ultimate success in higher education.

Schwartz and DeSimone (1985) were able to identify certain characteristics of undergraduate highly at-risk students who excelled in graduate school. The investigators retroactively used transcripts and interview ratings to compare two groups of students who had attained the masters degree and who had had undergraduate grade point averages below 3.0. Though the cumulative grade point average for both groups of students was below 3.0, the highly successful subgroup had achieved significantly better grades after 2 years in college and a higher percentage of A grades, and they had succeeded in maintaining a B grade level by the end of their undergraduate work. In contrast, the moderately successful subgroup had received less adequate grades and also less favorable admission interview ratings overall, and they had attained significantly less adequate ratings in the areas of clearly stated goals and objectives and in intellectual ability. The moderately successful subgroup performed adequately in graduate school; the highly successful subgroup excelled. And 44% of the highly successful subgroup went on to complete the doctorate, a better record, interestingly, than that of a low-risk group who had undergraduate and graduate grade point averages of 3.26 and 3.38, respectively. Another most significant finding was that almost one-third of the moderately successful subgroup went on to complete the doctorate.

These results can be instructive in efforts to recruit an expanded pool of qualified minority graduate school applicants to school psychology programs. Though screening procedures might target among a high-risk group those with undergraduate GPAs of 2.75 or above, several "A" grades, higher second- than first-half college achievement, clearly conceptualized goals and objectives, and manifest intellectual ability, students with less adequate records may be viable candidates as well. This is underscored in the above study (Schwartz & DeSimone, 1985), by a finding, though not statistically significant, of the tendency for the highly successful

subgroup to be older and to have longer intervals between undergraduate and graduate school. It may be incumbent upon school psychology programs to focus on identifying growth potential and achievement motivation in otherwise high-risk undergraduate students and cultivating in them the ability to clarify and formulate goals and objectives as a means of facilitating maturity, intellectual growth, and higher professional achievement.

Ethnically Specific Learning Styles of Minority Students

Just as important to academic achievement in higher education as ability, motivation, and maturity is a student's *learning style*. This construct, which designates a preferred method of processing information, is most commonly operationalized by positing dichotomous categories referred to as field independence and field dependence. It has been used to explain a portion of the achievement variance between minority and majority children (Witkin & Goodenough, 1981). Although minority students across ethnic groups tend towards a field-dependent style, U.S. schools predominantly employ a field-independence mode of instruction. Through research, attempts to accommodate the styles of field-dependent students have been made that have resulted in specific directives for elementary and secondary education. However, the utility of the directives has been limited in higher education (Scarpaci & Fradd, 1985).

Though not a measure of intelligence, learning style reflects an acquired preference for using and organizing information. Most people exhibit attributes of both field dependence and field independence, yet individuals tend to prefer one over another. Field independence is associated with an analytical, sequential, and linear orientation, whereas field dependence encompasses a relational, holistic, and global perspective. Thus, field-dependent learners tend to prefer cooperative group work as well as question-and-answer sessions for problem solving and projects more than the independent, impersonal, and direct types of instruction preferred by field-independent learners. Greater achievement has been demonstrated by matching instructional and learning styles (Scarpaci & Fradd, 1985).

Though teaching styles vary among higher education faculty, institutions and educational pedagogy favor the field-independent style. This puts the already disadvantaged minorities at greater risk. The research of Scarpaci and Fradd (1985), who found that Anglo and Hispanic students differed significantly in their preferences for studying and interacting in the university setting, corroborated this. The noted ethnic division was similar for graduate and undergraduate students. More specifically, 72% of the Hispanic students preferred to receive help from professors in their offices at least monthly. This is in contrast to the 47% of Anglo students who preferred not to meet with the professors. A more striking difference between the two groups with regard to expectations of meeting socially at home or in a restaurant with a professor was the finding that 74% of Anglo students had no such expectations, whereas 75% of the Hispanic students expected to meet professors either very often (21%) or occasionally (54%).

Hispanic students preferred to work on home assignments with a group of friends or classmates of average or higher ability (71%), but Anglo students preferred to work alone (74%). When visiting a professor's office, Hispanic students preferred to come with a friend or in a small group, or they had no particular preference regarding who accompanied them. In contrast, 78% of the Anglo students preferred to come alone (versus 22% of the Hispanic group). Though Hispanic students found professors to be more formal in class, they found them more lenient than did the Anglo students.

In addition to reaffirming a field-dependence preference among Latino students, the above findings further suggest that minority students may expect a demanding formal class atmosphere yet prefer to have more participation in class and more assistance and informal relationships, particularly cooperative ones, outside of the classroom.

Though the scope of the Scarpaci and Fradd study limits the generality of its findings, it heralds the need for more research with other minority groups to determine how specific ethnic learning styles are manifested, particularly at the college level. Nonetheless, diverse learning styles would be accommodated by more flexible means of relating to students both in and outside of the classroom. For minority students who may feel a sense of isolation on white campuses, cooperative learning groups and more informal faculty-student interactions could be an important first step towards bringing them into the fold.

Role of Self-Perceptions in the Retention of Minority Students

Self-perception plays an important role in success, both in and outside of school. Although they are important to majority as well as minority students, self-perceptions (self-concepts) in higher education are more precariously balanced and have different origins for students from minority group backgrounds. The influence of several variables on the self-concepts of minority students have been examined. The existence of student affirmative action programs was one factor analyzed with a view towards determining its impact on minority students' self-efficacy (a component of self-concept).

Though many professionals view affirmative action to be essential to the recruitment and retention of minority students and to yield positive results, others have suggested that it is detrimental to the academic self-confidence of minority students. Ponterotto, Martinez, and Hayden (1986) reported the results of a survey to determine the self perceptions of minority graduate students relative to affirmative action at a large public university on the West coast. The 65 students surveyed ranged in age from 22 to 52, with an average age of 30 years. This ethnically diverse self-identified sample included 5 American Indians, 5 Blacks, 4 Puerto Ricans, 10 Mexican Americans, 17 Chicanos, 4 Mexicans, 12 Hispanics, 4 Latin Americans, 2 South Americans, 1 Pacific Islander, and 2 (did not identify their ethnic group). The results indicated that minority students perceived themselves as more capable academically than their peers. Furthermore, the students expressed strong positive views towards student affirmative action despite feelings that it was not a factor in their own admission and was only marginally effective in helping minorities. Interestingly, they believed others (students and faculty members) viewed their abilities positively. Researchers contrasted these findings with earlier ones that uncovered feelings of alienation and isolation among students from minority cultures. In this regard they emphasized the fact that statistical results tend to obscure diversity within a group, and in this sample served to camouflage the small though strong adverse impressions of some of the students. The tone and essence of these dissident perceptions are characterized by the following responses to some of the open ended questions within the survey:

" . . . A good number of people I meet have preconceived notions of my abilities as being subpar. Therefore, I have to prove them wrong . . ."

"I hope that with the responses received from this questionnaire you will fully realize the little effect that Student Affirmative Action has on a campus where prejudice is spread more than anything at the administrative level . . ." (p. 344).

Many factors may contribute to the present findings including the particular climate at the setting of the study, or the ethnic composition of this sample. In addition, the relatively advanced age and the graduate status of this population may reflect the attrition of less capable, more isolated, and alienated undergraduates who were unable to negotiate the system and consequently discontinued their studies. Despite minority status and affirmative action quotas, these findings support the fact that some minority status students have positive views of educational equity programs and positive self-perceptions relative to them.

Ethnic consciousness and pride, enmeshed in the fiber of a minority individual's self-perceptions, have served to empower minority individuals and groups and to counterbalance the pernicious effects of discriminatory practices and the concomitant devaluation of minority individuals. The student activists of the 1960s exerted pressures on white campuses that, along with external events unfolding at the time, resulted ultimately in greater minority enrollments and retention in higher education (Hall & Allen, 1982). In light of the decline in recent years of minority enrollment in higher education overall, and especially on predominantly white campuses, it would aid recruitment and retention efforts to assess the relationships of ethnic pride and consciousness of currently enrolled minority students to academic achievement and success in higher education. Although there is a paucity of data for several ethnic groups, there are revealing findings regarding Blacks. Hall and Allen (1982) sampled a national group of Black graduate/professional students on predominantly white campuses to assess the issue of race consciousness and its relationship to outcome variables. Though not directly related to grades, race consciousness did exert a powerful inverse relationship on a vital component of success in graduate school: Black students' perceptions of the possibilities for mentor relationships. Students who had lower race consciousness had favorable perceptions toward the availability of mentor relationships. Interestingly, this variable was the most accurate predictor of achievement. This is understandable in view of the crucial role mentors play in graduate school success and in later professional development. Students who held these positive views presented a specific profile: They were generally males from northern geographical regions, who had attended predominantly white undergraduate schools. On the other hand, lower grades were related to heavy participation in "Black-sponsored organized activities."

Considering the important role that ethnic consciousness has played in the positive self-perceptions and empowerment of minority groups, these findings are alarming, especially in light of the limited numbers of minority faculty, particularly in school psychology, and the importance of the mentor relationship in role-modeling and in shaping professional and personal attitudes and values. Hall and Allen (1982) held that for Blacks, and perhaps for other minorities as well, insofar as the future leadership of the ethnic community is drawn from the 75% of graduate professional students who study on predominantly white campuses, "our results are potentially ominous in their implications." They questioned whether "Black professionals who are graduates of largely white advanced degree programs will prove less willing and/or able to assume effective leadership roles in [their] community (p. 61). The relevance of this concern is underscored by the finding that Black females and Black southern students who are constrained in mentor opportunities because of cross-sex and cross-racial caste system bias have higher ethnic consciousness but lower grades. These findings suggest that for some minorities success in graduate school is obtained at the expense of ethnic consciousness and pride, and ultimately, group empowerment.

Role Perceptions and Role Models as Factors in Recruitment and Retention

In a national survey of over 100 academic programs and 119 Native American communities regarding their needs in higher education, the respondents cited cultural pressures, particularly at the doctoral level, and the lack of role models as major institutional barriers to their achievement and retention (Guyette & Heth, 1983).

The plight of minorities on majority campuses was poignantly illustrated in the Harvard Educational Review by Jacquelyn Mitchell, who proclaimed:

We were reminded of our minority status in a number of ways. Because it was the school's policy to support affirmative action enrollment we were the visible evidence of our university's reparations for society's past injustices. At the same time, we heard comments about how our minority admissions . . . Puerto Ricans, Native Americans, Chicanos . . . were lowering the academic standards of the University. Professors said the intellectual caliber of students was declining; white students were afraid that their degrees would be devalued, just like those homes in suburbia when neighborhoods become integrated and homeowners fear declining property values. We had to deal with the reality that often the institutional forces promoting reparations were the same as those worrying about declining quality. Not only did the institutions transmit mixed messages to us, but individual statements could be seen as double edged: "You're okay, but some of the others . . ." or "Well, you're an exception." We were representatives, different from some of the others and the "unexceptional" mass of minority status people, but representing them just the same. . . . My minority student colleagues and I tried to support each other as we dealt with the terrible bind: If I fail, the minority students fail; if I succeed, I only highlight a general minority student failure by being an exception and thus jeopardize my membership in minority culture. We had to be tricultural, make up for lack of preparation, be both representative and exceptional, and find some way neither to succeed nor fail. These jeopardies are not totally new; they are simply exaggerated in graduate school. (Mitchell, 1982, p. 35)

Thrust into such an ambiguous and precarious atmosphere, minorities have a crucial need for role models. Successful models can reinforce a student's sense of efficacy, increase motivation to succeed in the face of overwhelming obstacles, and thereby legitimize minority students' persistence within majority institutions. However, for many minority students, role models who can relate to their tenuous status can mean the difference between success and failure. Many such students are first-generation college attendees and thus lack models in the home to assist them in learning to successfully negotiate the higher education system. Much more to their detriment, however, is a family that is overtly or covertly discouraging or nonsupportive for a variety of reasons. Often there is a sense that the college student is deflecting needed funds away from the home, and not contributing his or her fair share. Many may simply lack resourcefulness.

Consequently, minority students may have role expectations inadequate to meet the demands of academic life, particularly during the first several years of college.

Intensive recruitment efforts by institutions foster and perpetuate the passive role expectations of these students by insulating them from the mainstream and by directing their progress. A lot of time may be spent in remedial courses and little or none in learning to make the transition from the passive role. Later, when recruitment goals are fulfilled, students are virtually left to fend for themselves. If they somehow get to graduate school, they find that they are ill equipped for the independent, isolated, and assertive role they must assume (Smith et al., 1986).

Programs can pool their efforts through university-wide strategies to offset the paucity of peer and faculty role models and the resultant misperceived role expectations. Compulsory ethnic course offerings are warranted, as are the fostering of informal faculty/student relationships, and clustering (instead of diffusing) of minority students during course advisement to force interactions with other minority students, who can at the least be understanding. The establishment of a meeting place, preferably in the department, where these students can meet and complete assignments has been found to contribute to interactions and increase the time students spend together on campus. These supports are particularly necessary to the "visible" minority students who can feel intimidation and psychological stress in being the "only one" in a class or series of classes. Role models can ease the sense of frustration that often accompanies the isolation that is occasioned by rigorous academic demands, low finances, and disparate role expectations.

TASKS OF PROFESSIONAL SCHOOL PSYCHOLOGY IN RECRUITMENT

Professional school psychologists who advocate more intensive recruitment efforts stress using flexible admissions, financial aid, and scholarships as incentives, along with an aggressive marketing strategy that includes use of special brochures, media advertisement, personal contacts, and current and past student ambassadors (Zins & Halsell, 1986; Novick, 1978).

Though necessary, these approaches have not had the desired impact over the years. More than 5 years after the Novick survey of minority enrollment in U.S. and Canadian school psychology programs was presented at a national convention along with proven suggestions for recruitment, the Zins and Halsell data indicated little increase in minority enrollment patterns for most minority ethnic groups.

Though many external factors, some of which were noted above, conspire to create the minority student enrollment patterns in school psychology, there are forces within the profession that seem to contribute to the current inadequacies in this regard. One is the image school psychologists have as testers. This image — coupled with the finding that "psychologists have not only used psychometric data to serve their own professional interests . . . but more importantly . . . have supported the historical stance of using IQ measures to promote, reinforce, and perpetuate the dominant ideology of the white, upperclass ruling elite" (Sewell, 1981 P. 235) — sends a powerful restraining message to minority students who would consider the profession. The profession sustained considerable notoriety in this regard as a consequence of the publicity occasioned by the recent legal challenges to the profession's use of the IQ tests and other tests considered discriminatory in several states (Bersoff, 1982). Many minority students may be disinclined to pursue a profession that is perceived by many as "legitimatizing" the disabling of minority students (Cummins, 1986).

The profession has recently moved in a positive direction to promote alternative and nondiscriminatory practices throughout its service delivery system through publications such as the present volume appointment of a task force on multicultural issues, selecting minority keynote speakers for its national conventions, and supporting various best practices; however, it has yet to incorporate these efforts by pursuing systematic approaches to assist training programs at a national level in recruitment and retention. Were school psychology to demonstrate that it is a profession that contributes to the empowerment of disadvantaged groups, particularly ethnic minorities, these efforts would do more than a hundred glossy brochures, upscale media "hype," and promises of flexible criteria in attracting and retaining students from these underrepresented groups.

A SUCCESSFUL MODEL FOR MINORITY STUDENT RETENTION — FAMES

School psychology does not stand alone in its need to educate and increase the presence of minorities in its profession. Other professions have had some success in their efforts to meet the challenge through comprehensive efforts at the college level. One such success, developed by the engineering profession, has features that can easily be adapted to meet school psychology's purposes. The FAME (Faculty Advisors for Minority Engineering Students) model highlighted below focuses on an undergraduate population. However, its structural elements can be useful in constructing a viable model for use with graduate students.

Developed and implemented at California State University, Northridge, the FAMES model arose in a program with few minority students, predominantly middle-class white and/or foreign-born faculty who were typically male, older, and technically disposed, rather than people-oriented. In such an atmosphere many faculty were committed to "weeding out the deadwood" and thus disinclined towards "unnecessary coddling" or "spoon feeding" that is often needed to support the success of minority students in higher education. Most faculty members lacked knowledge of minority cultures and had minimal experience in personal interactions with the targeted minority groups. Additional barriers were imposed by the existing distrust of the faculty by the minority students.

In planning the program, leaders chose to utilize the advisement process as the core of their endeavor. In doing so, they recognized that the success of the venture rested upon the extent to which the two disparate groups could grow and interact in a mutually beneficial relationship. In addition to the attitudes, biases, and backgrounds of faculty and students, institutional barriers conspired to pose further obstacles to the success of the program. Among these were pressures upon faculty to publish, low priority attributed to advisement for promotion and career advancement, heavy course loads, and limited office space.

Faculty participants were carefully chosen as a result of interviews, recommendations from department personnel, student evaluations, and volunteers desiring to be involved. Faculty participants were apprised of the crucial need to develop minority engineering talent prior to the program's commencement. The venture began with five faculty members (and later expanded to eight) who early on expressed a desire for training in counseling skills and a need for group discussion among themselves. Subsequent sessions included a combination of informational presentations on cross-cultural issues, counseling issues, and counseling and human relations training. A variety of techniques were used, including lectures, group discussions and encounters, dyad training exercises, videotapes, and critiques of actual counseling sessions.

The program, which was supported by a University grant, evolved over a three year period. One semester of lead time was required prior to program implementation to formulate the various elements. During the initial semester, faculty participants were provided release time and actually devoted 3½ to 4½ hours per week to the training sessions. Two semesters of training sessions were conducted the initial year, and one semester during the second year. By the third year of the FAMES model implementation, it became apparent to the planners that two semesters of training sessions per year were necessary. Consequently, the final model entailed seven training sessions per semester (14 per year). Minimal resource personnel were required including a coordinator, a student assistant, and a consulting psychologist. Students within the intervention were clustered in classes so that supportive peer groups emerged. They received proactive counseling services as well as advisement within the academic mainstream, without having to utilize traditional counseling channels that have not proven effective with many minority students. This procedure avoided pressures to admit that something is wrong with traditional methods (Jackson, 1987). Students were also provided space in the department to meet and associate in an academic environment, consequently enabling them to develop networks, friendships, and supportive resources while spending more time on campus. Students came to value the time that participating faculty spent with them. They felt faculty really listened to them and treated them as individuals, and that the informal meetings with faculty enabled them to approach and talk to faculty more freely.

Evaluation of the model was accomplished by means of pre- and posttraining interviews of faculty, student evaluations, and surveys that revealed significant differences between FAMES participants and non-FAMES students. Quantitative data regarding retention of program participants is not yet available. The success of the FAMES model was suggested by the renewal of the initial grant for an additional two years. Thus, the model was school based in the school of engineering for 5 years altogether. After that period of time, the model was expanded and made available to the entire university community.

There were many benefits to the faculty and, for some, they generalized into greater involvement in initiating or participating in other efforts to benefit minority students at the high school level and in industry. The faculty trainees from the most recent cycle elected to continue the training group on their own time after the "released time" semester. The greatest benefit to faculty was the opportunity to interact with peers in small, supportive, growth-oriented sessions. One faculty member's comments illustrate this perception:

> Being in this training was the only positive strokes I ever got for being honest in my whole professional life. Professors are trained to put on an act with each other, with students, right down the line. . . . It really meant a lot to me, meeting other people . . . talking about our feelings, learning it was okay to talk about our

feelings. . . . I think it will make me a better counselor for all students not just for minority students. (FAMES, 1982, p. 9)

FAMES is unusual among university retention efforts in its emphasis on utilizing the advisement process, in involving faculty and students in growth-oriented experiences, in the degree of administrative and financial support, and in its comprehensiveness. Currently, the model exists in modified form at the university level. It is referred to as The Faculty and Minority Students (FAMS) program. The School of Engineering still has several of its original faculty members who were trained on the FAMES Model and who are now involved in training new faculty and working with minority students within the Minority Engineering Program.

School psychology can borrow elements for use in developing similar models. Because of their background in human relations skills, school psychology faculty would be ahead of engineering faculty in their efforts in one sense. Yet, despite their professional training, the evaluation and critique of cross-cultural interactions with students may uncover delimiting attitudes and behaviors heretofore unscrutinized.

An enlarged pool of qualified minority graduate applicants and motivated, capable graduate minority students who complete their education and enter school psychology, to the improvement of the quality of education for all children, can be the ultimate outcome of comprehensive, substantive, and collaborative efforts on the part of school psychology programs, universities, professional organizations, and governmental agencies.

SUMMARY

Though many minority students attend college, go on to graduate schools, and enter their chosen profession without "special" help, far too many fail to do so despite desire and individual effort. University affirmative action programs are often narrowly conceptualized, fragmented, and variegated, are nonsystematic and lack an empirical foundation. The present chapter has addressed the need to view recruitment and retention of minority students within school psychology as interdependent variables in a broad sociological context that encompasses less salient student characteristics, institutional factors, and issues within the profession that influence the quantity and quality of success. More comprehensive and systematic strategies were advocated. An innovative program within another profession that contained many of the recommended components was described as a model that could be adopted and tailored to school psychology programs.

REFERENCES

Arner, R., & Yates, A. (1979, May). Recruitment of minority graduate students. *Communication, 9,* 1–5.

Axelson, J. A. (1985). *Counseling and development in a multicultural society.* Belmont, CA: Wadsworth.

Bersoff, D. N. (1982). The legal regulation of school psychology. In C. R. Reynolds & T. B. Gutkin (Eds.), *The handbook of school psychology.* New York: Wiley.

Blackwell, J. E. (1983). Strategies for improving the status of Blacks in higher education. *Planning and Change, 14,* 56–73.

Cummins, J. (1986). Psychological assessment of minority students: Out of context, out of focus, out of control? *Journal of Reading, Writing, and Learning Disabilities International, 2,* 9–19.

FAMES Project Faculty and Staff. (1982). *Report of the advisors for minority engineering students.* California State University, Northridge.

Fleming, J. (1984). *Blacks in college.* San Francisco: Jossey-Bass.

Flores, I. (1985, August). *Variables associated with producing greater percentages of minority earned doctorates.* Paper presented at the annual convention of the American Psychological Association, Los Angeles, CA.

Guyette, S., & Heth, C. (1983, April). *American Indian higher education: Needs and projections.* Paper presented at the annual meeting of the American Educational Research Association, Montreal, Quebec.

Hall, M. L., & Allen, W. R. (1982). Race consciousness and achievement: Two issues in the study of Black graduate/professional students. *Integrated Education, 20,* 56–61.

Isaac, P. D. (1986, August). *Recruitment, retention, and graduation of minority graduate students.* Paper presented at the annual convention of the American Psychological Association, Washington, DC.

Jackson, J. (1987). Counseling as a strategy for mainstreaming underprepared students. *Journal of Multicultural Counseling and Development, 15,* 184–190.

Johnson, A. B., & Fiscus, E. (1983, July). *School psychologists' use of techniques for nondiscriminatory assessment.* Paper presented at the Council for Exceptional Children's National Conference on the Exceptional Black Child, Atlanta, GA.

Keeter, L. (1987). Minority students at risk: An interview with Shirley Chisholm. *Journal of Developmental Education, 10,* 18–21.

Lunneborg, P. W., & Lunneborg, C. E. (1985). Student-centered versus university-centered solutions to problems of minority students. *Journal of College Student Personnel, 26,* 224–228.

Mitchell, J. (1982). Reflections of a Black social scientist: Some struggles, some doubts, some hopes. *Harvard Educational Review, 52,* 27–44.

Novick, J. I. (1978). *Survey of minority and bilingual participation in school psychology training.* Unpublished paper, Southern Connecticut State College.

Olson, C. (1988). Recruiting and retaining minority graduate students: A systems perspective. *Journal of Negro Education, 57,* 32–42.

Ponterotto, J. G., Martinez, F. M., & Hayden, D. C. (1986). Student affirmative action programs: A help or hindrance to development of minority graduate students? *Journal of College Student Personnel, 27*(4), 318–325.

Pruitt, A. S. (1983). Does minority graduate education have a future? *Planning and Change, 14,* 14–21.

Richardson, R. C., Jr., Simmons, H., & de los Santos, A. G., Jr. (1987). Graduating minority students. *Change, 19*(3), 20–27.

Scarpaci, J. L., & Fradd, S. H. (1985). Latin Americans at the university level: Implications for instruction. *Journal of Multicultural Counseling and Development, 13,* 183–189.

Schwartz, R. L., & DeSimone, J. (1985). High risks and high returns: College underachievers who excelled in a graduate school program. *Professional Psychologist, 15,* 495–501.

Sewell, T. E. (1981). Shaping the future of school psychology. *School Psychology Review, 10,* 232–242.

Smith, J. H., Simpson-Kirkland, D., Zimmern, J. C., Goldenstein, E., & Prichard, K. (1986). The five most important problems confronting Black students today. *Negro Educational Review, 37,* 52–61.

Smith, W. A., & Allen, W. R. (1984). Modeling Black students academic performance in higher education. *Research in Higher Education, 21,* 210–222.

Witkin, H. A., & Goodenough, D. A. (1981). *Cognitive styles, essence and origins: Field dependence and field independence.* New York: International University Press.

Ysseldyke, J. E., & Task Force Members. (1984). *School psychology: A blueprint for training and practice.* MN: National School Psychology Inservice Training Network.

Zins, J. E., & Halsell, A. (1986). Status of ethnic minority group members in school psychology training programs. *School Psychology Review, 15,* 76–83.

CHAPTER 11

Critical Issues in Training School Psychologists to Serve Minority School Children

Andrés Barona and
Maryann Santos de Barona
Arizona State University

Arthur A. Flores
Texas A & M University

Martha H. Gutierrez
Arizona State University

CHALLENGES FACING SCHOOL PSYCHOLOGY TRAINING

The field of school psychology faces a critical period. The United States is in a state of rapid technological, social, and cultural change. Increasingly, the educational system is being called on to prepare its students for new and more complex roles in a society whose economy is technology-based. At the same time, it is facing problems of unprecedented proportions, among them shrinking financial resources, increasing cultural and linguistic diversity, increasing numbers of economically disadvantaged students, low levels of academic achievement, and high dropout rates.

These circumstances carry a significant impact for school psychologists, who as trained educational specialists are expected to work with students, teachers, and administrators on problems and situations that are clearly related to these phenomena. The many societal changes being experienced dictate that graduates of school psychology training programs be knowledgeable about and prepared to deal with a variety of issues exacerbated by these developments. It will be important to have trained specialists who are familiar with, or who are themselves members of, culturally diverse groups and who are able to bridge the gap between school and community while remaining sensitive to cultural constraints. These professionals should be trained to seek out parental and community support by using the unique social structure of a particular community, and they should be able to design interventions that are culturally appropriate in order to get the best possible results.

The challenges that face school psychology training programs seem clear. First, programs must be concerned with the recruitment and training of both ethnic minority students and culturally and linguistically sensitive nonminority students. Second, the curriculum must be tailored to reflect increasing diversity. While the tasks may be clear, they are complex, both pedagogically and politically. This chapter attempts to address critical factors related to issues of diversity, availability of service providers, the content of training programs, and recruitment and retention in an effort to better meet the educational needs of minority schoolchildren.

Increasing Diversity

The ethnic composition of the United States continues to diversify: Recent figures indicate that 21% of the U.S. population, or about 50 million people, are Black, Hispanic, or Asian (Walton, 1987). Moreover, this percentage is increasing as a result of higher birthrates among these groups. Presently, the nation's Hispanic population totals more than 20 million and is growing at a rate five times as fast as the non-Hispanic population (*U.S. Department of Commerce News,* 1989). Similarly, the Black and Asian-American populations also are rapidly increasing: In only 4 years the number of Blacks increased by more than 2 million over numbers counted in the 1980 census (Reid, 1986), and it is estimated that the Asian-American population may total nearly 10 million by the year 2000, up from 5 million in 1985 ("High achieving," 1985).

Many ethnic minorities have specific needs related to their unique situation in the United States: Many are new arrivals in this country and are unfamiliar with formal U.S. institutions. Nearly 40 million persons of limited English proficiency (LEP) will reside in the United States by the year 2000 (National Advisory Council on Bilingual Education, 1980–1981), with the majority speaking spanish as their primary language. A lack of familiarity with this country and/or linguistic and cultural differences often limit minorities' access to jobs as well as social, medical, and governmental services; these combined factors frequently result in limited access to economic and educational opportunities, which in turn affects the nation's growth and its world economic status.

This increasing cultural and linguistic diversity has a major impact on the U.S. educational system. Ethnic minorities today constitute the majority of school enrollments in 23 of the nation's 25 largest cities (Paige, 1987). Presently, 43.1% of the Hispanic population is "school-age," compared with 34.2% of whites (Fernandez & Guskin, 1981). As mentioned by Halsell Miranda and Santos de Barona in Chapter 7, in the near future nearly 40% of the total school-age population (substantially more than 1 of every 3 students) will be a member of a minority group, many of these from economically disadvantaged backgrounds. The proportion of ethnic minority students in the public schools is expected to increase even further as a result of the higher fertility rates and younger average ages of Black women and Mexican-American women. The average Black and Hispanic is younger than the average white — 25 and 22, respectively, compared with 31 for the average U.S. white. Thus, the typical Hispanic female is just beginning her peak childbearing years and is expected to have more children than the typical white female who is just moving out of this peak period (Astin & Burciaga, 1981; Hodgkinson, 1985; Kaufman, Dolman, & Bowser, 1983). Clearly, these demographic changes have major implications for education in general and specifically for the training of school psychologists.

The U.S. educational system has rarely taken a proactive stance where educational equity for the ethnic minority children is concerned, mostly relying on court decisions such as *Brown v. Board of Education* (1954), *Hobson v. Hansen* (1967), *Parc v. Commonwealth of Pennsylvania* (1972), and the emergence of Public Law 94-142 (Education for All Handicapped Children Act, 1975) to begin remedying inequitable educational policies. Yet, even these mandates have not completely eradicated inequitable practices: Currently, major gaps continue to exist between the guidelines and requirements established by legislative and court mandates and the ability of the educational system to carry out the specified guidelines.

Need for Minority School Psychologists

In stark contrast to the increasing minority population, ethnic minorities historically have been underrepresented as mental health professionals (President's Commission on Mental Health, 1979): The number of enrolled ethnic minorities in school psychology training programs consistently has been under 12% (Brown & Minke, 1984; Zins & Halsell, 1986) and similarly low numbers have been reported in other areas related to mental health (Bernal, Barron, & Leary, 1983). As a result, efforts to provide culturally sensitive and appropriate mental health services have been made difficult. In Chapter 18, Barona and Hernandez point out that unique patterns of responses have been found with different ethnic groups and it has been suggested that ethnic groups may have distinct personality patterns; given these significant ethnic differences, mental health professionals cannot be confident that their clinical interpretations of pathology and health are valid when they are unfamiliar with a particular culture and its unique behaviors and values.

The lack of minority professionals has also been a factor in a low level of mental health services provided to ethnic minorities (Bernal & Padilla, 1982). In Chapter 10, Benson reports that national organizations such as the National Association for School Psychologists (Ysseldyke, 1984) are strongly committed to training minority school psychologists. Indeed, positive efforts in this area are evidenced by the NASP position statement on minority recruitment adopted at the fall 1987 delegate assembly (National Association of School Psychologists, 1989). However, as indicated by the continued low numbers enrolled in programs, recruitment efforts to date have not achieved a widespread measure of success. Benson provides a cogent discussion of the influence of critical institutional components in recruitment; although these factors are extremely important to the process of both recruitment and retention, it also must be recognized that many graduate programs have not been aggressive in their recruiting efforts or in providing incentives to ethnic minority students to enter psychology programs (Barona & Flores, 1984; Bernal & Padilla, 1982). Until more minority health professionals are recruited and trained in mental health services and until the curriculum of training programs adequately prepares *all* its students for work with diverse populations, it is unlikely that minority populations will have adequate access to appropriate mental health services.

Factors Contributing to Low Numbers of Minority School Psychologists

In addition to the aforementioned problems, a number of factors negatively impact upon the ability of graduate and professional programs to recruit, admit, and retain minority students. Central to this problem is the diminishing pool of minority students eligible for admission (Middleton & Mason, 1987), which is occurring despite the increasing numbers of ethnic minorities in the general population. Hispanic and Black students have lower high school completion rates than Anglo students, and the results of a recent study (Brown, 1987) indicated that less than half of all Black and Hispanic students enrolled in academic college preparatory programs while attending high school. For those who continued past high school, some interesting differences were found. Although 21%, 35%, and 38% of Hispanic, Black, and Anglo high school students entered college, over half of the Hispanic students and nearly half of the Black students had not received the bachelor's degree 7 years later, compared to less than one-third of the Anglo students. "Proportionately more Black, Hispanic, and American Indian students delayed entry, stopped out (i.e., dropped out and later returned to college) and dropped out of college than did Asian-American and white students" (Brown, 1987, p. 11). Interestingly, Hispanic students tend to be more heavily concentrated in 2-year institutions, less than one-quarter of these later transferring to a 4-year college or university. Finally, although it is generally accepted that only a small percentage of college graduates continue on to graduate studies, this tendency appears exacerbated for ethnic minorities: only 2% or less of Hispanic and Black high school graduates in 1972 had entered a graduate or professional school by 1979 (Brown, 1987).

Perhaps because of economic conditions, most Black and Hispanic students appear to be choosing fields of study that lead to immediate employment opportunities after completing the undergraduate degree. Unfortunately, most of these minority college graduates enter lower-income occupations and thus may be less financially able to afford the costs of a graduate education at a later date (Nettles, 1987):

> The problem of costs is further complicated by the fact that minority students come disproportionately from families in the lower socioeconomic strata. . . . Those in the higher socioeconomic strata were

five times more likely than those in the lowest strata to attend graduate school (34.6 percent compared with 7.4 percent). . . . Nearly 14 percent of all high school students in the former group, regardless of ability, enter graduate programs, while only 2 percent of graduates from the latter group did so. (p. 1)

It appears that those minority students who do seek advanced degrees rarely do so immediately after completing the undergraduate degree; the average Black, Mexican-American, and Native American taking the Graduate Record Examination (GRE) in 1984 was older than Anglo and Asian-American examinees. Interestingly, research findings have concluded that quantitative GRE scores tend to be systematically reduced in older students (Keller & Sullivan, 1988). In addition, the minorities in the GRE pool were overrepresented in the lowest family income category. These factors may contribute to the fact that in spite of increasing numbers in the general population, there have been decreases in the total numbers of Black and Mexican-American students taking the GRE (Brown, 1987).

Evidence also exists that indicates that ethnic minorities apply to fewer graduate programs (Baird, 1982) and are more likely to accept an initial denial of admissions as final than nonminorities (Grant, 1989). Similarly, minorities are more likely to place greater emphasis on single admissions criteria such as GRE test scores (Powers & Lehman, 1982). Since minorities as a group obtain lower overall scores on this test (Brown, 1987; Duran, 1983; Evans, 1980), it is possible that lower than expected scores may deter minority students from completing the application process if they are unaware that many programs consider the GRE to be only one of several admission criteria and that evidence of leadership, goal orientation, and efforts to correct weaknesses (Grant, 1989) are also strong considerations.

ISSUES IN SCHOOL PSYCHOLOGY TRAINING

The population statistics and research reported here are striking and point to significant problems related to the educational process. Obviously, much more needs to be done to improve the education, training, and preparation of minority students at all levels (Collison, 1988). This chapter addresses three issues related to the training of school psychologists. First, in light of the changing composition of the U.S. population, there is a need to ensure that the content of training programs adequately prepares students to work effectively with all populations. Second, strategies must be developed to successfully increase the number of minority applications and admissions to school psychology training programs. Finally, efforts must be made to increase the completion rates of those minority students who are accepted to and enroll in school psychology training programs. The remainder of this chapter focuses on the areas of training, recruitment, and retention and will examine issues involved in each and provides recommendations for action.

Training Issues

Training school psychologists to serve minority schoolchildren is critical in order to serve the changing population. In the area of assessment, the U.S. Department of Education (USDOE) has emphasized the need for both higher-quality assessment services and for training assessment personnel with specific competencies in nondiscriminatory assessment and evaluation of children with limited English proficiency (LEP) (USDOE, 1983). The rights of bilingual exceptional children and their parents to receive bilingual instruction and support services has been further established in the courts (Baca & Cervantes, 1984). Additionally, professionals must be aware of culturally appropriate ways to interact with children and their parents so that consultation and interventions bring success.

A primary barrier to the delivery of such appropriate educational programs and services has been the lack of trained assessment personnel who are capable of administering and interpreting the results of tests given in the child's primary language (Baca & Cervantes, 1984) and who are both culturally aware and able to intervene in culturally acceptable ways.

Increasing training that specifically addresses diverse populations is critical for a number of reasons. First, although it is widely accepted that specific behaviors are indicative of learning problems, it is less well known that many of these behaviors "can also indicate differences in language and culture when students are in the process of mastering a new language" (Fradd, Barona, & Santos de Barona, 1989, p. 77). As one example, it is often more difficult for students with limited English skills to recall information presented in English or to maintain attention for sustained periods of time (DeBlassie, 1983). Although attention and memory problems often reflect true problems in learning, it is important to understand that many LEP students are unable to automatically translate information. Learning academic subject matter, which is often communicated abstractly and without the benefit of contextual cues, is a laborious and frequently draining process that is difficult to sustain for extended periods. Thus, it is essential that school psychologists become aware of the ways such indicators can influence test results and learning rates and learn to differentiate between problems in learning that are due to disabilities and problems that are influenced by culture or language.

School psychologists also must become aware of how different cultures selectively reinforce different characteristics and behaviors in their children. Without this knowledge, it becomes all too easy to misunderstand a student's behavior and motivation. As an example, Hispanic and Native American children are socialized to cooperate and share rather than to individually achieve; these attitudes directly affect the children's understanding of "shared work" (Charbonneau & John-Steiner, 1988; Delgado-Gaitan & Trueba, 1985). Such differences in socialization may have different implications for school psychologists and other school personnel: Many Native-American children have great difficulty with the direct questioning techniques that are regularly used in teaching and assessment situations. Additionally, Native American parents who participate in meetings with the school are uneasy when controversial or confrontational topics are involved: Strategies utilizing direct questioning "rarely yield answers that truly reflect the thinking or feelings of these parents" (Charbonneau & John-Steiner, 1988, p. 92). It should be noted, however, that while school psychologists are increasing their knowledge of and familiarity with diverse cultures so that behaviors are interpreted correctly, care also must be taken to avoid stereotyping.

Third, cultural information should be acquired through both didactic and experiential approaches so as to enable school psychology students to acquire both a cognitive awareness and understanding of pertinent cultural issues and the practical skills needed to work with minority populations. Although a great deal can be learned through academic coursework, actual interactions are necessary for school psychology students to become familiar and comfortable with individuals of diverse cultures. In this respect, the availability of minority faculty and minority students to sensitize school psychology students from the mainstream culture to differences as well as similarities in cultural values and behaviors is inestimably important. Too often, students possess an understanding of, but have not resolved, these issues either at an emotional or a practical level. Students must become aware of their own feelings and biases on issues such as bilingualism, poverty, and cultural diversity, as well as those of their training supervisors before beginning to function as independent professionals; they must decide, with the guidance of their training supervisors, if they have the ability and skills to work effectively with specific cultural groups.

It must be recognized, however, that modifying a school psychology training program to ensure that its curriculum reflects changing needs assumes that sufficient definitive research information exists to provide to students. In the absence of such research data, the task of preparing students to work with diverse populations is made more difficult. As one example, in the area of personality assessment, although the need to exercise caution when interpreting the responses of Hispanics has been generally accepted, there is very little information available that provides direction on *how* to interpret their responses. Similarly, despite numerous research studies demonstrating the construct validity of the Wechsler Intelligence Scale for Children–Revised (WISC–R) for a variety of populations, most of these studies fail to address issues of language of administration. Such gaps in the research literature suggest an insufficient empirical database to really teach the most appropriate ways to either assess, consult about, or teach minority students. Rather, it is often left to trainers who themselves are either multilingual or multicultural to model techniques and strategies that they have found to be personally effective. This apprentice clinical approach is acceptable and has been an often used training model for many disciplines, but it is imperative that the research base involving diverse populations be increased to a much greater degree.

In light of the dearth of available research, perhaps the first task of school psychology training programs should be to train good researchers who are interested in and willing to investigate the myriad of minority-related issues needed to broaden the educational and psychological fields. Conducting research with minority populations is rarely "clean" research. It is often difficult to design studies that adequately control for factors such as degree of language proficiency or degree of acculturation; at the same time, studies that use samples of convenience are not looked upon favorably when submitted for the publication review process. But minority research needs to be published through mainstream channels in order to reach the appropriate readership. Journal editors must be willing to consider perspectives that conflict with current thinking and that may not be immediately acceptable to or popular with their journal readership.

Along with research skills, training programs must continue to provide a strong program in the basic essentials of school psychology: Graduates must be well grounded in research methods, psychometrics, assessment, diagnosis, and consultation. In addition to ongoing exposure to minority students and to professionals who

are multilingual and/or multicultural, students must attempt to develop or augment their command of languages other than English and must become knowledgeable about pertinent minority-related issues such as the interaction of language with learning, the impact of bilingual education, and ethnic identity. In order to receive adequate exposure to diverse cultures, it will be necessary for interested students to train in locations having high minority concentrations so that they can become involved in both minority research and minority service delivery systems. In this manner, their professional learning and development will reflect the true scientist-practitioner model and will contribute to the production of a badly needed body of literature.

Recruitment

Adequately addressing the cultural and linguistic educational needs of minority children has been hampered by the lack of trained culturally and linguistically similar service providers (Acosta, 1977; Ruiz, 1977). As noted earlier, numerous factors have reduced the total number of ethnic minorities who can be considered as candidates for school psychology training programs. However, such information should not lead to the conclusion that notable increases cannot occur until significant changes are made to improve the progress of minorities through the education pipeline. Rather, it is most important that efforts be made to strengthen all points of the education pipeline to reduce leakage and improve the educational prospects for students at every level. To this end, vigorous efforts must be made in the area of recruitment.

Examining the graduate enrollment patterns of minority students provides some useful information. Clewell (1987) found that many minority students who earned doctorates chose graduate institutions in which they had been previously enrolled; many of these students indicated that their previous attendance at that institution was the most important reason for their selecting the school where they ultimately enrolled and obtained their graduate degrees. This finding suggests that minority students may be less willing to relocate when selecting graduate programs; familiarity with and success at a particular institution may be important factors. This notion is further suggested by the results of studies reporting that minority graduate students often report feeling isolated and alienated in their program of study and experience difficulty establishing relationships with Anglo faculty (Allen, Haddad, & Kirkland, 1984; Carrington & Sedlacek, 1976; Duncan, 1976; Green & McNamara, 1978; as reported in Clewell, 1987). It is also possible that students may be less aware of the existence of programs at other institutions or have not been able to obtain information critical to effective or efficient decision making.

There is some evidence that the graduate program application process may deter minorities from seeking advanced degrees. The process is a complicated one that requires considerable planning, time, and financial resources; additionally, application forms, procedures, requirements, and deadlines vary across institutions. Obtaining information from programs and institutions may be frustrating when, as Barona and Flores (1984) found, institutions sometimes do not respond or provide incorrect or inaccurate information. As noted earlier, ethnic minorities applying to graduate programs tend to be older, have fewer financial resources, do less well on standardized tests, perceive that more emphasis is placed on test scores as an admission criterion, apply to fewer programs, and get accepted to programs less often than do Anglo applicants. These factors clearly contribute to the overall low numbers accepted to and enrolled in school psychology training programs.

The information provided in graduate program application packets may also be related to minority enrollment:

This first communication between applicant and program has recruitment potential to the extent that the program materials inform the student adequately about questions salient to the student's motives for applying to graduate school, encourage the student by describing suitable training, support, and some likelihood of admission, and convey a hospitable view of the learning environment. (Bernal et al., p. 818)

Research involving students' initial inquiries to school psychology training programs produced some interesting results. In one study (Barona & Flores, 1984), a self-identified minority student's request to all APA school psychology doctoral training programs for information on available resources as well as the ethnic composition of faculty and students resulted in only an 83% response rate. The information provided by the responding programs was resolved into six categories: (1) special financial aid, (b) special admissions criteria, (c) minority faculty, (d) minority students, (e) minority training, and (f) minority-related curriculum.[1] A minority recruitment rating (MRR) representing the total number of categories addressed by an institution was computed.

As presented in Table 1, the number of categories addressed by each responding program generally was quite low — 63% of the responding programs addressed only one or two of the information categories and the mean MRR was 1.8. Information regarding the presence of minority students and minority faculty were most frequently reported: Almost 58% of the programs reported minority students enrolled in their departments and approximately 37% reported the presence of minority faculty. Six programs reported using special admissions criteria for minority students, and five programs reported having financial assistance specifically targeted for minorities. Least often provided was information related to minority-related curricula and opportunities for work and training with minority clients: Only three programs (15.8%) reported offering coursework related to the provision of services to minority populations. Generally, programs that offered coursework involving minorities also provided opportunities for directly working with minority populations.

This study also examined the actual enrollment of ethnic minorities in these programs[2] and found the presence of minority faculty to be positively related to a number of recruitment variables, among them the presence of minority students in

TABLE 1
Minority Recruitment Ratings of Accredited School Psychology and Combined Professional-Scientific Psychology Programs

Institution	Special Financial Aid	Special Admissions	Minority Faculty	Minority Students	Opportunity for Minority Training	Minority Courses	Minority Recruitment Rating (MRR)[a]
Arizona State U.			X	X	X	X	4
U. of Arizona							NR
U. of California	X			X			2
U. of Cincinnati	X						1
Florida State U.				X			1
Georgia State U.		X	X	X			3
Indiana State U.		X					1
Indiana U.			X	X			2
U. of Michigan	X						1
U. of Minnesota		X		X			2
U. of Nebraska						X	1
New York U.							NR
U. of North Carolina			X	X	X		3
U. of North Colorado							0
Penn State U.	X	X					2
U. of Rhode Island							WI
Rutgers U.							NR
U. of South Carolina				X			1
Temple U.			X	X			2
U. of Texas		X	X	X			3
U. of Virginia							0
Utah State U.		X					1
Vanderbilt U.	X		X	X	X	X	5
Number of programs providing information	5	6	7	11	3	3	
Percentage of programs providing information	26.3	31.6	36.8	57.8	15.8	15.3	

[a]NR = No response (3 programs); WI = Wrong information (1 program)

a department, the availability of opportunities for training with minority populations, and the composite minority recruitment rating. The reported presence of minority students also was positively related to the composite minority recruitment rating. Interestingly, the schools that provided minority enrollment data in their application materials accounted for more of the total minority student population than the programs that did not.

These results corroborate previous findings that making known the enrollment of minorities of similar ethnicity in a department may be an essential element in the successful recruitment of minority applicants for two reasons. First, it reflects sensitivity to the social and emotional support needs of minority students by conveying the program's commitment to minority enrollment. Second, it indicates to a minority culture applicant that a culturally similar support system is available for the difficult periods of graduate training.

The presence of minority faculty appears to have a significant impact on minority-student enrollment. Results from the Barona and Flores (1984) study suggest that minority students tend to enroll in programs where there are minority faculty. It is likely that knowledge of the presence of minority faculty conveys to the applicant the probability that the formal organization may be sensitive to minority student concerns and that there will be opportunities for training experiences to promote the acquisition of those skills needed to work with minority populations. The presence of a role model who is successfully functioning in the profession may also be an important personal factor for minority applicants.

The presence of minority faculty and minority students additionally may have a more pervasive effect. Both of these variables had strong correlation with the overall minority recruitment rating — that is, programs in which minority faculty and students are already present tend to have higher overall minority recruitment ratings and report information related to special financial aid, flexible admissions criteria, and minority-related curricula. It is possible that these groups may have already succeeded in sensitizing institutions and training programs to the salient issues of minority recruitment and have participated either in the preparation of recruitment materials or in actual recruitment activities such as visits to other campuses or preadmission interviews.

A close look at the admission criteria for programs also may yield useful information. Certain admissions criteria such as standardized test scores have been found to predict Hispanics' achievement less well than for Anglos (Durán, 1983). As a result,

> The college Board and the Educational Testing Service have agreed with the premise that even more caution than usual must be applied to the review and evaluation of U.S. Hispanic test scores, and these organizations are in the process of introducing such cautionary language into the test information related to both test takers and institutions of higher education. (Keller & Sullivan, 1988, p. 12)

Although the use of nontraditional and flexible criteria in the selection of minority applicants frequently has been advocated to increase minority enrollment in professional training programs, Barona and Flores (1984) did not find the use of such criteria to be widely acknowledged: Only 6 of 19 programs (32%) reported having adopted this practice. However, it is possible that

a number of programs actually use special admission criteria but refrain from public acknowledgment of their use except through personal communication. Conversely, it is also possible that special admissions criteria are not used by most schools and that all minority students in these programs have gained entrance on the basis of more traditional admissions criteria. Further comparative examination of minority admissions policies would provide more information related to the means by which minorities enter school psychology training programs.

It is of interest that programs that report flexible admission policies had minority enrollment rates that were substantially lower than programs that do not report such policies: The six schools that publicly acknowledged using special admissions policies accounted for only 19% of the total minority enrollment. While this may initially appear contradictory, it should be noted that only one of these six schools offered financial assistance specifically targeted for minority students. In other words, special financial aid and a flexible admissions policy were not frequently offered by the same training institution, a finding that suggests that comprehensive support for minority students is a rarity.

While the Barona and Flores (1984) study admittedly focused only on one aspect of a multifaceted and complex problem, namely the recruitment potential of information contained in application materials, the findings suggest the contribution of numerous factors in minority enrollment in school psychology training programs. These include minority-related curricula, special financial aid and admissions criteria, and the presence of minority faculty and students. Further in-depth study of the influence of these variables is needed. One avenue by which such study might be accomplished is through surveys of minority students, faculty, and program administrators that would compare the perceptions of each regarding pertinent enrollment factors. Another might be to examine the application materials in all school psychology training programs, doctoral and subdoctoral, to obtain a larger sample and add to the generalizability of this study's results.

Retention

Because research on the factors affecting the retention of graduate minority students has been limited (Clewell, 1987), the perceptions of the present authors regarding retention will be presented and followed by the available research findings.

It is our impression that minority graduate students frequently are assumed, regardless of their actual background and experience, to have been admitted under special conditions with qualifications that are in some way inferior to those of other students. This often inaccurate perception may limit minority students' opportunities. Many minority students do not feel welcome in the general student social milieu and often are not invited to participate in social activities with other students. The types and frequency of interactions therefore are reduced, limiting the communication of helpful information between students regarding available resources and important deadlines. As one example, despite acceptable admission qualifications and progress in program coursework, the authors know of one minority student who had never been involved in any social or professional activities with other students or program faculty. Although enrolled in a graduate program for 2 years, this student was even unaware that a computer workstation was available to students in the department for wordprocessing.

This lack of social interaction often limits access to activities that facilitate professional growth. Minority students' individual strengths may remain unrecognized while those of students who are better integrated into the social network are more visible. When financial or professional opportunities arise, these students often are not considered because their abilities are unknown. Consequently, although it is a well-established fact that most graduate students must supplement any support received through work or loans, it is these authors' impression that many minority students do so in ways that may not contribute to their professional growth.

One study that looked at the characteristics of persisting and nonpersisting Black and Hispanic doctoral students (Clewell, 1987) found that 81% of those who completed their degrees were enrolled full-time in their programs. In this study, there was a tendency for those completing their doctorates to have entered graduate school immediately after completion of the undergraduate degree. Although a majority received support in the form of graduate fellowships, teaching assistantships, research assistantships, or traineeships, many found it necessary to subsidize their education through loans or by working.

In this study, 80% of those obtaining the doctoral degree felt their major advisors had been supportive of their professional development and 68% had participated in professional activities such as publishing or presenting contributions at professional meetings. In addition, many students reported that at least one other person at their graduate institution had been instrumental in their completing their degrees; those frequently mentioned were minority faculty or minority administrators. Thus, it appears that the students who were successful in their efforts to obtain graduate degrees received financial support, were well-integrated into their graduate programs, and had developed a social support network at their institution. Conversely, the students who did not attain the doctorate indicated that external factors related to financial hardship, ineffective advising, lack of support, a hostile environment, and family responsibilities contributed to the decision to leave the program. These students suggested that, in order to increase access and decrease attrition, institutions must increase the availability of financial support, provide more counseling, hire professors who are supportive of minority students as well as minority professors to serve as role models, and provide students' feedback on their progress as well as program requirements.

Clewell (1987), based on the study's findings and a review of the literature, presented a number of policy recommendations aimed at facilitating minorities' fulfillment of the requirements of their graduate programs:

- A supportive major advisor and a support network in graduate school are important aids to retention of minority students. Policies that encourage the formation of a positive relationship with a major advisor and the establishment of a strong support network will help to increase retention.

- The presence of minority faculty and staff in a graduate institution enhances the supportive atmosphere for minority students. Graduate institutions should make every effort to hire minority faculty and staff.

- Minority graduate students are known to experience feelings of alienation and isolation in graduate school. Their participation in professional activities and research projects is one indicator of their integration into departmental life. Policies to encourage such activities at the departmental level would aid retention. (Clewell, 1987, p. 20)

CONCLUSIONS AND RECOMMENDATIONS

The severe underrepresentation of minority students in school psychology training programs is a situation in need of immediate correction if culturally appropriate services are to be provided for minority school children. The most recent corrective measures have been undertaken under the auspices of the federal government (Astin, 1982), with the educational and nongovernmental institutions making few and isolated efforts. In view of recent reductions in federal funding, however, it is imperative that educational institutions and related professional organizations intensify their efforts to improve minority accessibility to professional training programs.

Within the profession of school psychology, consideration of a number of possibilities is needed. First, it is important that the professional school psychology organizations such as NASP and APA improve their dissemination of information that is of specific interest to minority students. Specifically, a nationwide network might be developed to automatically send to minority school psychology applicants information on available external sources of financial support, such as the APA

Minority Fellowship. Such an information network could also disseminate minority enrollment data.

Second, Project 1000 has provided an exceptional working model that simplifies the graduate application process. This project, initially funded by the Carnegie Corporation of New York, is a cooperative effort by the National Hispanic Higher Education Coalition, Educational Testing Services, the College Board, Arizona State University, and several hundred colleges and universities. The project has as its goal the recruitment, admission, and graduation of an additional 1,000 U.S. Hispanic graduate students. Built on a feeder system of over 150 undergraduate institutions and more than 50 graduate schools committed to admitting and graduating larger numbers of Hispanic students (Padilla, 1988), the project serves as a central clearinghouse where students interested in graduate study complete one application that is recognized by all participating institutions. Project staff consult with the applicant regarding graduate program choices, provide information about ways to obtain additional program information, forward the application to up to 10 selected institutions, and, early in the application process, communicate on behalf of the applicants as needed. Project 1000 not only provides a mechanism by which self-identified minority applicants can be matched with appropriate graduate programs but additionally affords a means by which graduate programs can increase their awareness and admission of qualified minority candidates.

Because it provides a way for the burden of achieving equitable minority representation to be shared by educational institutions, all school psychology programs should encourage their institutions' participation in this project. Of course, there are other ways in which the educational institutions can facilitate recruitment. A simple but important step can be to emphasize the need to review and update recruitment materials regularly. It was the impression of the raters in the Barona and Flores study (1984) that application materials rarely were clear about the types of financial assistance available and whether flexible admissions criteria were used.

Therefore it frequently is necessary for the minority applicant who specifically desires and requests this information to track it down independently. This is a task that can result in much lost time and frustration for the applicant.

Third, although an ambitious project, it might be helpful to consider the formulation of flexible admissions standards that could be uniformly and equitably applied by accredited programs in considering minority applicants. Fourth, additional research, by the professional psychology organizations or with their support, in the area of minority recruitment should legitimize this pursuit as well as emphasize the need to strengthen efforts to increase the proportion of ethnic minorities in these professions.

Minority recruitment may be more directly impacted by the participation of minority students and faculty. Such involvement may include assigning a minority faculty and/or student to serve as the personal contact for a minority applicant. The responsibilities of such a contact person could include initially responding to requests with telephone calls or personal letters, guiding the applicant to appropriate offices if a personal visit is made, and maintaining contact and providing additional information, support, and guidance throughout the application process. Finally, a significant effect may also be achieved by directing recruitment efforts toward geographic areas and college campuses with high concentrations of minority students. It is recommended that minority faculty and students be directly involved in the presentation and discussion of information during these recruitment activities.

Once admitted, the student should receive a thorough orientation to the program and the graduate institution and should be made aware of available campus resources. Information to be provided would include the availability of technical support or equipment such as word-processing equipment and data-processing centers; information regarding financial assistance and financial counseling; faculty research interests, ongoing research proj-

ects in the department, and opportunities for involvement; and opportunities for additional social networking. Upon admission, students should immediately be assigned an advisor who provides a clear outline for the proposed sequence of study.

Additionally, efforts should be made to involve the student in ongoing professional activities. Such activities could include participation in faculty research projects, assisting with teaching activities, and becoming involved in field-based settings. Such activities will not only promote the students' professional growth but additionally will facilitate their integration into the program's social milieu.

The recommendations presented here are far from exhaustive. Continued work in the area of training, recruitment, and retention will confirm the utility of these recommendations and generate additional suggestions. The implementation of these and future recommendations will depend on the willingness and commitment of educational and professional institutions to improve on their sense of "response-ability" toward minority applicants.

REFERENCES

Acosta, F. X. (1977). Ethnic variables in psychotherapy: The Mexican-American. In J. L. Martinez (Ed.), *Chicano psychology* (pp. 215–231). New York: Academic.

Allen, W. R., Haddad, A., & Kirkland, M. (1984, November). *Preliminary report: 1982 Graduate Professional Survey, National Study of Black College Students.* Ann Arbor: The University of Michigan Center for Afroamerican and African Studies. Unpublished report.

Astin, A. W. (1982). *Minorities in higher education.* San Francisco: Jossey-Bass.

Astin, H. S., & Burciaga, C. P. (1981). *Chicanos in higher education: Programs and attainment.* Los Angeles: Higher Education Research Institute.

Baca, L. M., & Cervantes, H. T. (1984). *The bilingual special education interface.* Columbus, OH: Merrill.

Baird, L. L. (1982). *An examination of the graduate study application and enrollment decisions of GRE candidates* (ETS RR-82-53). Princeton, NJ: Educational Testing Service.

Barona, A., & Flores, A. A. (1984). *Critical variables in the recruitment of ethnic minorities to APA school psychology doctoral programs.* Unpublished manuscript, Texas A & M University.

Bernal, M. E., Barron, B. M., & Leary, C. (1983). Use of application materials for recruitment of ethnic minority students in psychology. *Professional Psychology: Research and Practice, 14,* 817–829.

Bernal, M. E., & Padilla, A. M. (1982). Status of minority curricula and training in clinical psychology. *American Psychologist, 37,* 780–787.

Brown, D. T., & Minke, K. M. (1984). *Directory of school psychology training programs.* Washington, DC: National Association of School Psychologists.

Brown, S. V. (1987). *Minorities in the graduate education pipeline.* [A research report of the Minority Graduate Education Project, jointly sponsored by the Graduate Record Examinations Board and Educational Testing Service.] Princeton, NJ: Educational Testing Service.

Brown v. Board of Education, 347 U.S. 438 (1954).

Carrington, C. H., & Sedlacek, W. E. (1976). *Attitudes and characteristics of Black graduate students.* College Park, MD: Maryland University, Cultural Study Center. (ERIC Document Reproduction Service No. ED 132 234)

Charbonneau, M. P., & John-Steiner, V. (1988). Patterns of experience and the language of mathematics. In R. R. Cocking & J. P. Mestre (Eds.), *Linguistic and cultural influences on learning mathematics* (pp. 91–100). Hillsdale, NJ: Erlbaum.

Clewell, B. C. (1987). *Retention of Black and Hispanic doctoral students* (ETS RR 87-10). Princeton, NJ: Educational Testing Service.

Collison, M. N. (1988, May 25). Neglect of minorities seen jeopardizing future prosperity. *Chronicles of Higher Education,* pp. 1, 20.

DeBlassie, R. R. (1983). Emotional and behavior disorders in bilingual children. In D. R. Omark & J. G. Erickson (Eds.), *The bilingual exceptional child* (pp. 255–268). Boston: College-Hill.

Delgado-Gaitan, C., & Trueba, H. (1985). Dilemma in the socialization of Mexican-American children: Sharing for cooperation and copying for competition. *Quarterly Newsletter of the laboratory of Comparative Human Cognition, 7,* No. 3.

Duncan, B. L. (1976). Minority students. In J. Katz & R. T. Hartnett (Eds.), *Scholars in the making: The development of graduate and professional students* (pp. 227–241). Cambridge, MA: Ballinger.

Durán, R. (1983). *Hispanics' education and background: Predictors of college achievement.* New York: College Entrance Examination Board.

Education for All Handicapped Children Act of 1975 (PL 94-142). 20 USC Sec. 401 (Supp. 1975).

Evans, F. (1980). *A study of the relationships among speed and power, aptitude test scores and ethnic identity* (College Board Research and Development Report RDR 80-81. No. 2). Princeton, NJ: Educational Testing Service.

Fernandez, R. R., & Guskin, J. T. (1981). Hispanic students and school desegregation. In W. D. Hawley (Ed.), *Effective school desegregation* (pp. 107–140). Beverly Hills, CA: Sage.

Fradd, S. H., Barona, A., & Santos de Barona, A. (1989). Implementing change and monitoring progress. In S. H. Fradd & M. J. Weismantel (Eds.), *Meeting the needs of culturally and linguistically different students: A handbook for educators* (pp. 63–105). Boston: College-Hill.

Grant, B. (1989). Stacking the odds. *Spectrum, 1,* 10–11.

Green, K. C., & McNamara, P. P. (1978). The student experience. *New Directions for Higher Education, 23,* 29–41.

High achieving Asian-Americans are fastest growing minority. (October, 1985). *Population Today,* pp. 2, 8.

Hobson v. Hansen, 269 F. Supp. 401 (D.C. 1967) aff'd sub non., *Smuck v. Hobson,* 408 f.2d 175 (D.C. Cir 1969).

Hodgkinson, H. L. (1985). *All one system.* Washington, DC: Institute for Educational Leadership.

Kaufman, N. S., Dolman, G., Jr., & Bowser, B. P. (1983). *The changing demographics of the Southwest: Data and issues relating to minority representation in postsecondary education in seven southwest states.* Boulder, CO: Western Commission for Higher Education.

Keller, G. D., & Sullivan, M. J. (1988). *Student information booklet: Project 1000.* Tempe, AZ: Project 1000, Arizona State University.

Middleton, E. J., & Mason, E. J. (1987). Introduction. In E. J. Middleton & E. J. Mason (Eds.), *Recruitment and retention of minority students in teacher education: Proceedings of the national invitational conference, March 29–April 1, 1987, Lexington, Kentucky* (pp. 1–12). Dubuque, IA: Kendall/Hunt.

National Association of School Psychologists. (1989). NASP position statement on minority recruitment. *School Psychology Review, 18.*

National Advisory Council on Bilingual Education (1980–1981). *The prospects for bilingual education in the nation* (Fifth annual report of the National Advisory Council for Bilingual Education). Washington, DC: Author.

Nettles, M. (1987). *Financial aid and minority participation in graduate education.* [A research report of the Minority Graduate Education Project, jointly sponsored by the Graduate Record Examinations Board and Educational Testing Service.] Princeton, NJ: Educational Testing Service.

Padilla, R. V. (1988). *Building the foundations: Hispanic Research Center Annual Report 1987–88.* Tempe, AZ: Arizona State University, Hispanic Research Center.

Paige, R. (1987). The recruitment and retention of minorities in teacher education. In E. J. Middleton & E. J. Mason (Eds.), *Recruitment and retention of minority students in teacher education: Proceedings of the national invitational conference, March 29–April 1, 1987, Lexington, Kentucky* (pp. 13–26). Dubuque, IA: Kendall/Hunt.

PARC v. Commonwealth of Pennsylvania, 343 F. Supp. 279 (E.D. Pa 1972).

Powers, D. E., & Lehman, J. (1982). *GRE candidates' perceptions of the importance of graduate admission factors* (GRE No. 81-2). Princeton, NJ: Educational Testing Service.

President's Commission on Mental Health. (1979). *Report to the President from the President's Commission on Mental Health.* Washington, DC: U.S. Government Printing Office.

Reid, J. (1986, February). Immigration and the future U.S. Black population. *Population Today, 14,* 6–8.

Ruiz, R. A. (1977). The delivery of mental health and social change services for Chicanos: Analysis and recommendations. In J. L. Martinez (Ed.), *Chicano psychology* (pp. 233–247). New York: Academic.

U.S. Department of Commerce News. (1989, October 12). [Census Bureau Press release.] Hispanic population surpasses 20 million mark; grows by 39 percent, census bureau reports. (CB 89-58).

U.S. Department of Education. (1983). *To assure the free appropriate public education of all handicapped children: Fifth annual report to Congress on the implementation of Public Law 94-142: The Education for All Handicapped Children Act.* Washington, DC: Author.

Walton, J. (1987). Today's kids, tomorrow's nations. *Communique, 15,* 6–7.

Ysseldyke, J. E., & Task Force Members. (1984). *School psychology: A blueprint for training and practice.* MN: National School Psychology Inservice Training Network.

Zins, J. E., & Halsell, A. (1986). Status of ethnic minority group members in school psychology training programs. *School Psychology Review, 15,* 76–83.

FOOTNOTES

[1] These categories were defined as follows. *Special financial Aid:* Information specifically indicating the availability of financial assistance for ethnic minorities (Blacks, Native Americans, Asian-Americans) in the form of grants, fellowships, and/or loans. *Special admissions criteria:* A statement indicating that minority students were strongly encouraged to apply and/or that additional review procedures might be employed when evaluating minority applicants. *Minority faculty:* Information citing the number of full-time minority faculty teaching in the department in which the school psychology program was housed. *Minority students:* Information citing the number of minority students enrolled in the department in which the school psychology program was housed. *Minority training:* Information announcing the availability of opportunities for work and training with minority clients. This included practica, research, and coursework related to the provision of services to minority populations. *Minority-related curriculum:* Courses with titles containing the word *minority* or reference to a specific minority group.

[2] Enrollment data were provided by the American Psychological Association.

CHAPTER 12

Achieving Equal Educational Outcomes for Black Children

Janice Hale-Benson
Cleveland State University

To be unshackled,
to improve the mind,
to mold the character,
to dream dreams,
to develop the body,
to aspire for greatness,
or to strive for excellence
is the birthright of every child
born into the world . . .
And no society has the right
to smother ambition,
to curb motivation,
and to circumscribe the mind.

Dr. Benjamin E. Mays
Late President-Emeritus,
Morehouse College

The present-day achievement gap between Black and white children that places Black children educationally at risk dictates that the cutting edge of educational reform must be instruction designed to assure to Black children the achievement of equal educational outcomes. Although the achievement gap is most evident among Black lower-income children, it is present in comparisons of Black with white children of middle-income backgrounds as well (Hale-Benson, 1986).

For the past 30 years, desegregation has been a focal point for educational reform that is designed to benefit Black children, but the fact is that in most urban areas there has been a declining pool of white children to integrate with inner-city Black children. In consequence, Black scholars have raised the critical issue of creating schools that educate Black children effectively wherever they are found. Effective response requires that we begin by examining the learning and care-giving settings of early childhood.

Any such examination immediately puts the question of whether we can bring about an improvement in the education of Black children without recognizing their culture. In my opinion, the education of white children is relatively more successful than that of Black children because the schools were designed for white children. As Hakim Rashid (1981) has stated:

> Children from non-European lower socioeconomic status cultural groups are at a disadvantage in the schools because the American educational system has evolved out of a European philosophical, theoretical, and pedagogical context.

W. E. B. DuBois (1903; 1961) described the Black person in the United States as having two warring souls. On one hand, Black people are the product of their African-American heritage and culture. On the other hand, they are shaped by the demands of Euro-American culture. Unfortunately, the Euro-American influence has always been emphasized to the exclusion of the African influence. Said another way, despite the pressure of 400 years in the United States, Blacks have not melted into the pot. Rashid (1981) has pointed out that "the cultural and biological history of African Americans has resulted in an 'essentially African' group of people who must function in 'essentially European' schools" (p. 58).

Failure to perceive Black children in the context of their cultural experience has created the expectation that they are really white children in blackface.

Social scientists engage in a type of chauvinistic ethnocentrism that perpetuates an image of normality in describing white children and an image of pathology in describing Black children. If Johnny cannot read, educators generally suggest that there is an inappropriate match between his level of development and the curriculum or instructional strategies. If Willie cannot read, the appropriateness of instruction is generally not questioned. The explanation offered is that he is either genetically inferior or culturally deprived.

Educational change will not occur until we root the analysis and practice of early childhood education and care-giving of Black children in the context of their culture. We must devise educational strategies that are appropriate for them. Interrelated learning environments must be created in which African-American culture in all of its diversity is integrated comprehensively into the curriculum and the politics of the classroom.

Early childhood education can play an important role in closing the achievement gap between Black and white children in the United States. One explanation for the difficulty Black children experience in school is the fact that they are required to master at least two cultures in order to achieve upward mobility in school and the work place.

It is possible that Black male children may have to master three divergent cultures. I make the point elsewhere (Hale-Benson, 1986) that Black males have a culture that is distinct from white male culture and Black female culture. This culture is not recognized and may even be assaulted at school because it is not understood.

Most elementary school classes are taught by women, which creates a feminine orientation in the classroom. Increasingly we will find, as we enter the twenty-first century, that in most inner-city classrooms the majority of its students will be minority-group children being taught by white female teachers. And invariably white female teachers tend to be more comfortable with and knowledgeable about the behavioral characteristics of white female children and, to a lesser degree, white male children.

Cornbleth and Korth (1980) provided support for this contention in a study of teachers' perceptions and teacher–student interaction in integrated classrooms. The teachers in their study rated white females as having the most desirable personal characteristics and the highest potential for achievement.

There was a trend toward rating white females highest, and rating white males, Black females, and Black males in decreasing order. The white females were highest on *efficiency, organization, reservedness, industriousness,* and *pleasantness* and were lowest on *outspokenness, aggressiveness,* and *outgoingness.* Generally, Black males were mirror reflections of the white females, rating lowest on the former characteristics and highest on the latter; the white males and Black females fall somewhere in between.

These data suggest that there is a cultural configuration in classrooms. It also lends support for the notion that in order to achieve, Black males must acquire behavioral characteristics that are incongruent with the culture they bring to school.

It is important to acknowledge this dual socialization that is required of Black children, because early childhood education can play an important role in fostering biculturalism in Black children, thereby reducing the conflict within children that depletes their energy and clouds their perceptions.

The "intervention" strategies of the 1960s are passé. Recent research by Black scholars (Rashid, 1981; Hale-Benson, 1986) has rejected the notion that Black children are culturally or cognitively deprived. They are seen as members of a culture endowed with specific modes of cognition.

Early childhood education and care-giving must search for cultural continuity — not intervention. Rashid (1981) suggested that

the preschool experience must therefore provide a dynamic blend of African-American culture and that culture which is reflected in the Euro-American educational setting. . . . The African-American child who only sees the Euro-American cultural tradition manifested in the preschool environment can only conclude that the absence of visual representation of his culture connotes his essential worthlessness. (p. 16)

Bruce Hare (1987) has placed the blame for the endangered status of Black youth on the structural inequality of the U.S. educational and occupational systems. He suggested that theories about the biological and cultural inferiority of Black people serve to justify the race, class, and gender inequalities found in the U.S. society. He further posited that

the myth of equal opportunity serves as a smoke screen through which the losers will be led to blame themselves, and be seen by others as getting what they deserve. One might simply ask, for example, how can both inheritance of wealth for some and equal opportunity for all exist in the same social system? (p. 101)

Bowles and Gintis (1976) have pointed out that unequal distribution of wealth, power, and privilege is, and historically has been, the reality of U.S. capitalism, and that such a system *must* produce educational and occupational losers.

Hare (1987) argued that in addition to the inherent intergenerational inequality caused by inheritance, the educational system, through its unequal skill-giving, grading, routing, and credentialing procedures, plays a critical role in fostering structured inequality in the U.S. social system. The occupational structure simply responds to the schools when it slots people into hierarchical positions on the bases of the credentials and skills given by the schools.

The dire statistics on the gamut of problems of Black youths are well known. This chapter will consider how Blacks endowed with equal innate potential in childhood arrive at such a disadvantaged status as youths. I will maintain here that Black children do not enter school disadvantaged: they emerge from school disadvantaged.

There is no question about the fact that the masses of Black children are disproportionately located in families that suffer the turmoil of unemployment, single-parent heads of households, and low-paying occupational positions. This causes them to be at high risk for family instability and deprivation. Hare (1987) pointed out that

in such circumstances, they are also more likely to fall victim to child abuse, inadequate nutrition, poor health care, drugs, crime, and material deprivation. They are more likely to live in below par crowded quarters, with relatives other than their biological parents, and in foster care. Given such possibilities as these, it is a wonder that they survive and thrive as well as they do. Fortunately, indicators are that they are loved and feel loved, but there is no denying that many Black youth must also suffer the consequences of the pressures under which they and their parents live. (p. 104)

The question we will consider in this chapter is how the schools reproduce failure for Black children generation after generation. The experiences provided by the schools will be considered as a central issue because schools are the major socializing institution of the society. Students who drop out or are pushed out of schools are disconnected from the future. The other problems confronting Black youth, such as teen pregnancy, crime, drugs, and unemployment, emanate from school failure.

The activity of the schools is of critical importance to those who design early childcare settings because the current thrust for earlier and earlier entry of children into childcare centers results in an earlier beginning to the generation of their "institutional biographies."

I have pointed out elsewhere (Hale-Benson, 1986) that one explanation for the difficulties Black children experience in school may be their immersion in a culture that is very different from the culture that designed the school. It is essential to lay the foundation for delineating this culture and for identifying those points of mismatch between it and Euro-American culture that may have educational consequences for Black children.

I locate myself clearly among the theorists who trace the genesis of Black culture to the African heritage, while acknowledging that there are other theories.

This has generated a great deal of discussion, because the evidence supporting each theory is inconclusive.

In *Black Children: Their Roots, Culture and Learning Styles,* I also argued for examining this cultural core for Black children in general while acknowledging that lower-income children are most severely affected by the dual socialization that is required to straddle Afro- and Euro-American cultures (Hale-Benson, 1986). In this presentation, I would like to go a step further and consider scholarship that examines the specific interethnic code conflict that transpires between Black children and white teachers and results in failure over time for Black children.

Ray McDermott (1987) offered an interesting analysis in which he defined Black Americans as being a pariah group in U.S. society, defined by Barth (1969) as "actively rejected by the host population because of behavior or characteristics positively condemned" by group standards (p. 31).

McDermott observed that each generation of minority-group children renew their parents' lifestyles, oblivious to the oppression that the host group (in McDermott's terminology) brings down upon them. The structural inequality thesis points out that the host population works actively to defeat the efforts of each and every pariah child to beat the cycle of degradation incurred as a "birthright." Racial markers, low-prestige dialects, school failure, occupational specialties, and lifestyles tag each new generation for low ascribed status.

However, McDermott also set forth the thesis of achieved failure, pointing out that inherited disadvantage as simple tagging is a simplistic explanation. Overt ascription is frowned upon legally and in popular ideologies, yet the pariah boundaries remain firm throughout the society and in school systems. Even without formal institutionalized ascription, pariah status survives into each generation. He suggests that:

> The host population does not simply slot a child on the basis of its parentage and then keep a careful eye out for the child so that he never advances a slot. Rather,

it seems as if the child must learn how to do it himself; he must learn a way of acting normally which the host population will be able to condemn according to the criteria the hosts have learned for evaluating, albeit arbitrarily, their own normal behavior. Pariah status appears almost as achieved as ascribed. (McDermott, 1987, p. 176).

Each new pariah generation affirms the soundness of this classificatory system because they learn and exemplify the behavior essential to the system's maintenance. Rather than regarding themselves as blinded by prejudice, the hosts maintain that they are utilizing standards of evaluation that are used uniformly for all people regardless of race or ethnic identity. The question that McDermott examines is "How is it that what is there for them to see is in fact there?" (p. 176)

His analysis reveals that pariah groups do not enter school disadvantaged; they leave school disadvantaged. Ascription of status does not account for all of this disadvantage; nor do the inherent characteristics of the pariah population account for the disadvantage. Clearly the pariah group regards the host behavior as oppressive; likewise, the host group regards the pariah behavior as inadequate. According to McDermott, the way the two groups find this out about each other is the central problem.

Misunderstandings take place very often in the early grades and the results are disastrous.

> Once a host teacher treats a child as inadequate, the child will find the teacher oppressive. Often, once a child finds a teacher oppressive, the child will start behaving inadequately. After such a point, relations between the child and the teacher regress — the objectionable behavior of each will feed back negatively into the objectionable behavior of the other. (p. 178)

McDermott maintains that a child must *achieve* his pariah status. This status is neither totally ascribed nor naturally acquired by the child. Interethnic code differences cause miscommunication between the teacher and the child. This miscommunication undermines the relations until the affected children begin to form alternatives to the teacher's organization of the classroom. These children construct this new social organization in an attempt to become visible. The attempt results in more condemnation of their behavior and the teacher becomes the administrator *in charge of failure.*

> Teachers do not simply ascribe minority children to failure. Nor do minority children simply drag failure along, either genetically or socially, from the previous generation. Rather, it must be worked out in every classroom, every day, by every teacher and every child in their own peculiar ways. (p. 178)

In McDermott's view, school failure becomes an achievement on the part of pariah children because it is a rational adaptation made to human relations in host schools: Children produce pariah–host statuses in their interactions with each other and their teachers.

Young children are very vulnerable to messages of relationship. I have pointed out elsewhere (Hale-Benson, 1986) that Black children are very adept at nonverbal communication and sensitive to affective cues. In fact, young children upon entering school are more sensitive to relational messages than they are to information transfer.

> School success, an essential ingredient in any child's avoidance of pariah status, is dependent upon high levels of information transfer. In these early stages of school, depending upon how the politics of everyday life are handled, the child defines his relations with his classmates and his teachers. These relations, remember, define the context of whatever information is to be transferred by a communicant. If the wrong messages of relationship are communicated, reading, writing, and arithmetic may take on very different meanings than they do for the child who is more successful in getting good feelings from the politics of the classroom. The wrong messages can result in a learning disability. (McDermott, 1987, p. 181)

In view of the above, it should be apparent that teachers play an important role in establishing the statuses and iden-

tities of children in the classroom, in particular the social organization of status and identity, one example of which is the division of the class into ability groups (McDermott, 1987). This division is made to simplify the administration of the classroom; it determines the level of work engaged in, as well as the people who interact and the kind of feedback received from the teacher.

Now, a child who does not accept his assignment might work harder to catch up with the rest of the class. But McDermott notes that rarely do children reject their assignment — even if assigned to the lowest-status groups. They most often accept their assignment as if it makes sense.

The reason that revolt is rarely attempted in either school, McDermott's analysis holds, is that generally in schools that contain host children, the teacher assigns them to groups on the basis of criteria that the children use in dealing with each other or that their parents and the rest of the community use in dealing with the children. Essentially, the teacher, the children, and the child's community are in agreement. Even if a child is placed in a low-status group, it does not have a deleterious effect if it seems to make sense. "The politics of everyday life in the classroom will be identical to the politics of everyday life outside the classroom and the children's world will be in order" (p. 183).

In contrast, the social organization of minority children by a host group teacher does not proceed as smoothly. There is a reduced likelihood that a host group teacher will organize the classroom into the same ability groups that the minority community might design.

Through ability grouping, children receive messages of relationship from the teacher. Messages of relationship represent the manner in which teachers treat individual children based on the teacher's perceptions or personal feelings about the ability level of that particular child. Host teachers often make mistakes in evaluating the academic abilities of minority children. If these children are erroneously assigned to the lower ability groups, they will reject the messages of relationship conveyed by the teacher. Moreover, a political reorganization of the classroom based on the struggle between peer group and teacher will occur. The peer group will demand that the child defer to the peer group culture which is commonly in opposition to the culture of the teacher.

If the teacher is insensitive to these students' demands, no matter how subtle the insensitivity, for the remainder of the year the children will engage the teacher in small battles over their status and identities. The resolution of these battles will determine whether anything gets done in the classroom. Thus we can see that the politics of daily classroom life determine the amount of information transfer and the development of abilities and disabilities.

In McDermott's theoretical system, the root of pariah–host group divisions originate in small political arenas constituted by dyads and slightly larger groups. Abilities and disabilities arise from the tendency to attend to, think about, and manipulate selected aspects of the environment.

> Just what parts of an environment are attended and mastered depends upon the social meaning of the environment as recorded in the experiences of the developing child. For example, reading materials can or cannot be attended depending upon whether looking at a book is an acceptable activity in a particular social milieu and whether books contain information helpful in operating in a particular social environment. (p. 184)

A chronic educational problem is the high rate of learning disabilities found among Black children. Rates of functional Black illiteracy in the United States are estimated to be around 50% (Thompson, 1966), as compared to 10% for U.S. whites and only 1% for Japanese (Makita, 1968). There have been a number of explanations for this disproportionality that generally suggest some genetic inferiority or cultural deprivation. McDermott suggests that it is caused by selective inattention developed in the politics of everyday life in the classroom.

The work between white teachers and Black children in the areas of status and identity is such a failure that the children mentally tune out and physiologically shut down. The children disattend reading materials and choose to join their peers in a subculture of distraction within the class often resulting in reading disabilities and school failure.

Deprivation theorists generally place the fault on the child or the child's culture. However, achieved failure theorists suggest that achievement has been measured by a biased set of standards. McDermott asserts that achievements take place in a social context: Instead of looking at the skills "stored" in children's bodies, we must look at the social contexts in which the skills are turned into achievements.

Scores on perceptual, intelligence, attitude, language, and even neurological tests are the concrete results of the practical work of persons in a specific situation. Having discernible roots in the social world in which they take place, tests tell us more about the social processes in which a subject is engaged than they reveal about the mental capabilities of any subject.

As McDermott sees it, tests can tell us a great deal about children's thinking about the social acts to be performed during testing. For example, Cazden (1970) has described Black children who do badly on language tests in formal situations and very well in informal situations; the opposite is generally true for white children.

Division of the classroom into two separate worlds, with teachers and children playing different games, results in a social reorganization of the classroom in which the teacher's authority is challenged and information transfer is diminished. Long (1958) proposed the thesis that in the classroom social organization produced by the politics of every day life, reading takes its place as part of the teacher's "ecology of games" (Long, 1958). To read is to buy into the teacher's games and all of the particularities of status and identity that accompany them. Not to read is to buy into the peer group's games and the accompanying statuses and identities. In some sense, reading failure becomes a *social accomplishment* that is supported and rewarded by the peer group.

This phenomenon is not measured by tests. The battle lines that determine whether a child learns to read are drawn by the statuses and identities made available by the teacher and the peer group If the teacher and the children can play the same games, then reading and all other school materials will be easily absorbed (McDermott, 1987, p. 186).

Several researchers (Alitto, 1969; Hostetler & Huntington, 1971; Fishman & Leuders-Salmon, 1972) have noted the success of educational settings established by teachers who are members of the same ethnic and dialect minority as their students. This contrasts with the failure of educational settings directed by outsiders.

A pivotal issue that is related to reading instruction is a struggle for attention. The politics of everyday life, according to McDermott, get inside a child's body and determine what will be perceived; they learn how not to attend to printed information and as a result show high rates of reading disability. The relationship between a high rate of illiteracy and continued pariah status is clear.

In a study of gaze direction, Jackson (1968) found that more than 90% of white children had their eyes fixed on the teacher or reading material at a given time, whereas Deutsch (1963) found that in Harlem elementary schools, the teachers spent more than half their day calling children to attention. Attention patterns seem to be the crux of the struggle in pariah education (Roberts, 1970).

In pariah classrooms, there are teacher games and peer group games. The side one chooses will determine who one pays attention to. To attend to the teacher is to give the teacher a leadership role; to attend to the peer group is to challenge the teacher's authority. McDermott analyzes, "Those who attend learn to read; those who do not attend do not learn how to read" (p. 190).

LANGUAGE CODES

In addition to a shift in perceptual properties, there are subtle but significant changes in use of language among Black children as they move through elementary school. Pariah children code-switch when they change from addressing pariah people to exchange with host people. However, the job of code-switching is difficult, yet teachers regard you as ignorant for using one code and the peer group rejects you for using the other.

William Labov (1964b, p. 91) has delineated the stages in the acquisition of nonstandard English:

Stage 1. (up to age 5): Basic grammatical rules and lexicon are taken from parents.

Stage 2: (age 5–12, the reading years): Peer group vernacular is established.

Stage 3. (adolescence): "The social significance of the dialect characteristics of one's friends becomes gradually apparent."

Stage 4. (high school age): "The child begins to learn how to modify his speech in the direction of the prestige standard in formal situations or even to some extent in casual speech."

Labov & Robins (1969) compared the use of language of (a) Black street gang members, (b) Black children whom the latter regard as "lames," and (c) white lower-income children in the community. The lames are Black children who, although they are in contact with the gangs, accede to participate to some extent in the teacher's ecology of games.

Labov demonstrated a rank-ordering of the three groups' use of language that paralleled their participation in school: The gang showed the most extreme deviance from standard English, the whites deviated least, and the lames fell in between. Labov suggests that the linguistic difference does not *cause* school alienation; rather, that it is an index of the extent to which students have bought out of the games of the school. Adoption of the peer group's linguistic code and alienation from school develop together.

Labov and Robins (1969) have documented the fact that participation in formal peer group organizations and deployment of their linguistic codes correlate very closely with reading scores. None of the 43 gang members they studied were able to achieve a reading score on grade level and most were 2 years behind the national average.

McDermott (1987) reported that a series of sociometric tests administered to sixth-grade Black children in the lowest achievement track consistently placed the nonreaders at the center of all peer group activities. Similar tests that were administered in an all-Black fifth grade that was nontracked showed that the nonreaders were at the center of most peer group activities. His summary observation: "Reading skills do not recommend an actor for leadership. Indeed, the acquisition of such skills can exclude an actor from the peer group ecology of games" (p. 194).

SUMMARY OF ACHIEVED FAILURE PERSPECTIVE

Pariah children in host classrooms learn in a very subtle way to behave in new, peer-culture-sanctioned ways that cause them to acquire pariah status.

The process of learning to behave in a way that builds peer approval in a Black classroom that is administered by a white teacher involves learning to attend to cues produced in the peer group and to disattend cues from the teacher and school, such as demands for attention or the introduction of new tasks such as reading.

McDermott's thesis is that these attention patterns are deeply programmed in the central nervous system. When children attempt to attend to cues that are outside of their normal perceptual patterns, they fail. In this way, when many Black children fail in reading, it appears to be the result of a neurological impairment. These children are not actually impaired at all; they have merely learned over time to attend to different stimuli in a school situation. However, this phenomenon results in their being categorized as disabled and treated as inferior.

COMMUNICATIVE CODE DIFFERENCES

Spindler (1959; 1963) has demonstrated that middle-class teachers attend to middle-class children and label them the most talented and ambitious children in the class. School success follows parallel patterns. Children of lower socioeconomic status

(SES) over time give up trying and amass failing "institutional biographies" (Goffman, 1963) as they move through school, because they are unable to give evidence of their intelligence in terms of the limited code that teachers use for evaluating children.

Black children are particularly at risk for being overlooked because of a nonrecognition of Afro-American culture and the strengths that emerge from that culture. I have pointed out elsewhere (Hale-Benson, 1986) that Western social science overly emphasizes linguistic and logico-mathematical skills in assessing intelligence. Even these skills must be demonstrated in patterns that approximate those used by Anglo-Americans to be recognized by the educational system.

Skills that emerge from Black culture are recognized only when they are extraordinary and are marketable in the capitalist ecosystem, such as the athletic skills of Michael Jordan or the musical skills of Michael Jackson. When these skills are exhibited in early childhood as a part of a pattern that if, with nurturance, could support the self-esteem and achievement of Black children, they are virtually ignored.

Rist (1970) analyzed the effect of dividing a kindergarten classroom into three "ability groups" (the fast, the slow, and the nonlearners at Tables 1, 2, and 3, respectively):

> The organization of the kindergarten classroom according to the expectation of success or failure after the *eighth day of school* [emphasis mine] became the basis for the differential treatment of the children for the remainder of the school year. From the day that the class was assigned permanent seats, the activities in the classroom were perceivably different from previously. The fundamental division of the class into those expected to learn and those expected not to permeated the teacher's orientation to the class. (p. 423)

Teachers' subjective evaluations were shown by Rist to be rooted in their evaluation of the children's physical appearance and interactional and verbal behavior. At Table 1 were children with neater and cleaner clothes, more of them on cold days, and lighter skin. Class leaders and direction-givers were also clustered at Table 1. The children in Tables 2 and 3 spoke less in class, used heavy dialect, and seldom spoke to the teacher.

By the time the children were in the third grade, the ones who started out at the lower tables were still at the lower tables. Once tracked, it is difficult for children to break loose. The lower the table, the less instructional time received. These children are well on the way to amassing institutional biographies that will follow them year to year through the school.

This sorting process continues until each year more and more students are sorted out until a select few reach college. The "select few make it to college on the basis that they are most like their teachers" (McDermott, 1987, p. 198).

In view of Labov's analysis of speech patterns, we can deduce that the children at Table 3 on the whole are not neurologically impaired slow learners. McDermott's theory predicts that by sixth grade, the children at Table 3 will talk the most, be the most popular, and be the best dressers in the class. There is nothing wrong with their native ability; they will just be directing their achievement efforts away from the school.

The reason these children were not selected for achievement in their early years has to do with the communication code conflict between them and their teachers. If they are not able to work out this code conflict in their early years, the children at the lower tables take flight into their own subculture, which becomes oppositional to the classroom culture constructed by the teacher.

A key to the construction of this alternative classroom culture is the fact that culturally similar children are assigned to the lower groups together. Therefore, they are concentrated in larger numbers to construct the revolt and it becomes more powerful. There is a normal development shift away from the teacher and toward the peer group in fourth, fifth, and sixth grades. Therefore the achievement gap between Black and white children becomes most apparent in late elementary school.

The children in the host classroom have three choices (McDermott, 1987). One, they can take the school as a source of identity as do the children at Table 1. Two, they can take the peer group as a source of identity as do the children at Tables 2 and 3. Many of these children are transformed into gangs by late elementary school. The third and worst choice is represented by the children at the lower tables who accept teachers' definitions of them and their abilities and passively fail through school into pariah status.

These children not only fail in school, but also fail in their identity work. Children are better off who dispute the messages of relationship sent by host teachers and cause disruption in the classrooms because they have a better chance of building a solid ego structure appropriate to life in their community that could lead to achievement by an alternative route. The children who passively accept subordinate status do not disrupt the calm classroom status quo, but emerge from the educational experience with a weak ego. "In either response, learning is blocked; in the first case by active selective inattention and misbehavior, in the second case with motivational lag and selective inattention. Neither group learns to read" (McDermott, 1987, p. 199).

McDermott points out that the host group teachers do not create this code difference. Both the children and the teachers bring ethnic group traditions to school. In the early years teachers make the difference because they are not as adaptable as the children. However, in later years, as the peer group gains strength, the children force the distinction between their code and the teacher's code. In *insisting on some expression of their code,* they are learning how to produce pariah status for themselves vis-a-vis the host group.

ETHNIC GROUP IDENTITY AND MOBILITY

Why do Blacks not fare as well as other ethnic groups in working out the politics of the classroom? A possible explanation is found in the work of Robert Havighurst (1976), who suggested a compatibility between the U.S. white Anglo-Saxon Protestant middle-class mainstream and the ethnic cultures of European whites, Jews, Chinese, and Japanese. It seems that Blacks and Hispanics must shed more of the beliefs, values, attitudes, and behavioral styles associated with their ethnicity in order to acquire the somewhat divergent culture of the middle-class mainstream. A dual socialization, or straddling of the two cultures, is required for upward mobility.

I have developed elsewhere (Hale-Benson, 1986) the theory that at the root of Black children's achievement and disciplinary difficulties is the general society's lack of understanding of Afro-American culture and child rearing and its failure to recognize the mismatch between this culture and the Euro-American culture of the schools.

The research of Donald Henderson and Alfonzo Washington (1975) is an example of investigations of Afro-American cultural patterns that may have implications for educational practice. They first affirm a cultural difference between Black children and white children that can be directly attributed to the fact that Black children mature in communities that are culturally different from the communities of the broader society.

> The experience through which the Black child develops his sense of self, his social orientation, and his world view are provided by institutions (such as family, religion) whose characters, structures and functions are very often unique to the Black community. The school, on the other hand, reflects the culture of the wider society and is often unaccommodative to the culturally different Black youngsters.
>
> Indeed, often these differences are defined as deficiencies. These deficiencies are assumed to be significant impediments to "proper" learning in school. Therefore, massive attempts at remediation are undertaken (often, to the detriment of the child). In effect, many school practices are inappropriate for treating the educational needs of Black youngsters. An appropriate treatment of the educational needs of Black youngsters must take into account their unique cultural attributes. (p. 353)

Bruce Hare (1987) noted that as early as preadolescence, Black children tend to have higher peer self-esteem than white children and higher ratings of the importance of being popular and good at sports. His research corroborated that of Bennett and Harris (1982) in noting that Black children do not differ from white children in general self-esteem or in home self-esteem, but tend to have *lower school self-esteem.* This tendency is accompanies by significantly lower standardized reading and mathematics performance.

Given the vulnerability and family turmoil of especially lower-income Black youth, the shift noted by McDermott from the school toward the peer group for positive strokes and affective support is a flight from the failure and ego damage of the school.

Hare defined Black youth culture as a *long-term failure arena.* On a short-term basis, however, Black youths generally exhibit competent, adaptive behavior and achievement in the arenas that are open to them. They usually demonstrate street-wiseness, commonly prevail in playground sports, and frequently excel in domestic and childrearing chores, supplementing family income and taking on other aspects of adult roles at an early age.

Even though this youth culture provides alternative outlets for achievement, it offers little hope of long-term legitimate success. Rather, it carries with it the danger of drafting the youths into the self-destructive worlds of drugs, crime, and sexual promiscuity. This is what my father called "majoring in a minor."

Hare observed that the collectively negative schooling experiences of Black youth produce a generalized antischool sentiment. The accompanying availability of positive peer group experiences and the inability of youths to perceive the long-term consequences of adolescent decisions cause them to make what appears to be a logical decision in shifting loyalties from the school to their peers.

> In the long run, of course, they are disproportionately excluded from the legitimate occupational success possibilities. They are also subsequently blamed as adults for the consequences of school-system-induced self-protection decisions made during adolescence. In this context, the rising crime, drug, and out-of-wedlock

pregnancy rates among Black youth may be seen as a consequence of the interplay of negative schooling experiences as provided by incompetent outsiders, a decline in parental control, and a significant rise in the independence of an attractive peer culture which offers positive strokes and ego-enhancement to a vulnerable population. (Hare, 1987, p. 109–110)

CONNECTING BLACK CHILDREN TO THE FUTURE

The implications of Hare's conclusion in respect to a program for school psychologists are clear. The overriding goal of the helping professions must be to connect Black children to the future. This can be accomplished only after an incisive analysis of the problems they face and an identification of the quicksand and landmines they confront as they move from early childhood through adolescence.

Biculturality: Cultural Translators, Mediators, and Models

A clear goal for Black children and youths is the achievement of biculturality. Success in the undertaking can be determined by the availability of certain types of socializing agents whom Diane De Anda (1984) has identified by their roles as translators, mediators, and models (p. 104).

Translators are members of the minority individual's own ethnic group who have been successful at dual socialization. By sharing their own experiences in negotiating the intricacies of the majority culture and conveying ways to meet the society's demands without compromising ethnic values and norms, they serve as probably the most effective agents of dual socialization.

Mediators are individuals from mainstream culture who can serve as guides for minority persons. These can be formal socializers such as teachers, counselors, and social workers or informal agents of socialization such as peers and mentors. Mediators are not as visible as translators because, not being as familiar with the ethnic culture, they cannot as readily

identify points of convergence or divergence between the two cultures. However, they can offer valuable information that minority persons may not have gained from their own experience.

Models are members of the minority person's ethnic group whose behavior can serve as a pattern to emulate. De Anda suggests that the modeling process can be enhanced by perceived similarity between the model and the individual or the identification of the model as a controller of resources (De Anda, 1984, p. 104).

An important contribution school counselors and school psychologists can make is to devise strategies for providing role models for Black youths who can work with them intimately to assist them in straddling the two divergent cultures in which they participate. There are unique challenges that face Black male and female children. These must be clearly articulated and addressed.

The Black Female

School psychologists must identify and assist in removing critical barriers to achievement for Black female children. For example, the control of fertility is a critical issue in Black female adolescent development. The majority of babies being born in the Black community are to females between the ages of 12 and 20 years.

Apparently, Black middle-class women have concluded that low fertility is key to a middle-class lifestyle, because they have a significantly lower birthrate than white middle-class women: Black professional couples are not reproducing themselves. Given the fact that Black women have the lowest income of any group in the society and the fact that 48% of Black families are headed by women, a low fertility rate makes sense for those who desire some semblance of a middle-class lifestyle. However, there is a major breakdown in communication in transmitting this reality to lower-income Black women.

As a means to counter this situation, some communities have created laudable programs in which a big sister relationship is created between professional Black women and girls in the community who are at risk for having babies out of wedlock.

The Black Male

A key problem in the socialization of Black adolescent males is the fact that the white media impose role models on the Black community. Buffoons like Mr. T or androgynous stars like Michael Jackson and Prince are the overriding images made available to Black boys. Most inner city Black males have virtually no meaningful contact with Black men of achievement or distinction. As Jawanza Kunjufu has stated, "It takes a man to teach a boy how to be a man."

Black males receive very little information about how to transcend their youth peer culture and seek accomplishment in arenas that promise long-term achievement. A worthwhile goal for Black males is to achieve a college education. Robert Staples (1985) has identified the college-educated Black male as a success model. Even though we know that on the average they earn less than a white high school dropout, they still live longer and have a higher quality of life than their less well educated counterparts. Furthermore, 90% of college-educated Black males are married and living with their spouses.

An important issue for school psychologists to address is not only how to increase the numbers of Black males who enroll in college, but also how to increase the numbers who graduate. An important means to that end is for white school psychologists and counselors to become familiar with the success rates of Black colleges. White universities enroll more Black students than Black colleges, but Black colleges produce more graduates than white universities which have more resources and well-endowed facilities.

When white colleges began recruiting Black students in the 1960s, white school counselors began routing Black students away from Black colleges toward the "advantages of integration." Many white school counselors feel that Black colleges are for Black students who cannot gain entrance to white universities.

Jacquelyn Fleming (1985) revealed that Black students grow more intellectually at Black colleges than they do at white colleges and universities. The factors she cited are the likelihood of establishing close mentoring relationships with faculty, more enriched relationships with peers, and more opportunities to provide leadership in co-curricular activities, that is to say activities closely related to the school's curriculum such as debate teams, language clubs, etc. Even though Black colleges in general have very limited resources and many operate under severe financial difficulty, they produce better results for Black students than the more affluent white colleges. In fact, the majority of the well-known leaders in the Black community are products of Black educational institutions. It is important for school psychologists and counselors to be familiar with the benefits to be gained by Black students in these institutions.

Further evidence of the success of Black colleges may be implied in that the enrollments at Howard University and predominantly Black Morehouse College have increased 12% due to transfers of students from predominantly white colleges and universities.

A very promising approach to fostering achievement among Blacks is to complement cultural values and attitudes that are already present in Afro-American culture. Black culture emphasizes sports. Attention should be given to strengthening the role of the *coach* in enhancing Black's achievement. Rather than bemoaning the interest Blacks have in sports, as some leaders do, more study should be given to the success of coaches, like John Thompson of Georgetown, who produce winning teams *and* Black college graduates.

Strengthening the bond between achievement in sports and academic achievement is a reasonable activity, given the fact that in some universities some Black females and almost every Black male enrolled is on an athletic scholarship. While some focus on the exploitation of the male athlete and their disastrous failure rate, it might be more productive to consider the fact that this is the primary avenue that delivers Black males to college. Such a perspective would then cause us to bring more energy to bear on how to more productively utilize this vehicle.

Evaluating the Results of Black Schooling

An important part of the role of school psychologists and counselors in any program designed to connect Black children to the future is to determine whether the curriculum of schools that serve Black children are preparing them to acquire technological skills that will prepare them for employment in the 1990s.

The National Urban Coalition (Bean, 1985) has developed an initiative that is designed to ensure that Black children take courses in the higher math and science sequences beginning with Calculus I and Physics I without which Black children are tracked away from high-paying technological careers. They cite statistics demonstrating that in the 1990s, access by Blacks to 60–80% of career fields will be eliminated because of poor mathematics preparation. In 1982, 62.8% of the jobs offered to college graduates were in the engineering sciences, a field that eminently requires preparation in advanced mathematics. This figure is expected to increase to 80% in the 1990s.

According to the National Urban Coalition, a study in 1980 and 1982 of high school seniors who took math and science courses in Grades 10–12 revealed that 60% of the Asian-American and 30% of the white seniors had taken trigonometry, calculus, and other advanced math courses, whereas only 11% of Black seniors had taken those courses; 27% of the Asian-American and 13% of the white seniors had taken Physics I, whereas only 5.5% of the Black high school seniors had taken first-year physics.

These figures stand in contrast to the findings of a National Assessment of Educational Progress report (1983) that included items designed to assess *student attitudes* towards science. This study revealed that 47% of the 13-year-old white students indicated positive attitudes toward science; 50% of the 13-year-old Black students indicated positive attitudes toward science. Furthermore, the National Urban Coalition indicated that 15% of third-grade Black students expressed an interest in technical occupations.

Study should be made of why these positive attitudes and interests are not translating into achievement in these arenas. A possible explanation offered by the National Urban Coalition is that Black children do not see people who look like them doing math and science in textbooks. There also may be an overemphasis on figures in the civil rights struggle in the creation of heroes in the Black community. In any case, role models in technological careers need to be made more visible to Black children and youth.

Family Life and School Achievement.

Finally, school psychologists can begin to make a contribution to the strengthening of family life in the Black community that can translate into school success for Black children. There is interesting recent scholarship that highlights the relationship between family life and school achievement that is available to all regardless of income level or family composition.

Reginald Clark (1983), in his book *Family Life and School Achievement: Why Poor Black Children Succeed or Fail*, dispels myths about the limitations of family structure or income on children's school achievement. Working mothers, broken homes, poverty, racial or ethnic background, poorly educated parents — these are the usual reasons given for the academic problems of poor urban children. Clark emphasizes the total family life, stating that the most important indicators of academic potential are embedded in family culture.

To support his contentions, Clark conducted 10 intimate case studies of Black families in Chicago. All of these families had incomes at the poverty level, and one-parent and two-parent families were equally represented as were families that had produced either a high- or low-achieving child. Clark made detailed observations on the quality of home life, noting how family habits and interactions affected school success and what characteristics of family life provided children with "school survival skills," a complex of behaviors, attitudes and knowledge that are the essential elements in academic success.

Clark suggested the following success-producing patterns in homes of high achievers that school psychologists can use to help Black parents inculate school survival skills in their children.

1. Frequent school contact initiated by the parent
2. Child has had some stimulating, supportive school teachers
3. Parents psychologically and emotionally calm with child
4. Parents expect to play major role in child's schooling
5. Parents expect child to get postsecondary training
6. Parents have explicit achievement-centered rules and norms
7. Parents establish clear, specific role boundaries and status structures with parents as dominant authority
8. Siblings interact as organized subgroup
9. Conflict between family members is infrequent
10. Parents frequently engage in deliberate achievement-training activities (p. 200).

CONCLUSIONS

A central argument of this chapter is that incisive analysis of the problem of the achievement gap between Black and white students is necessary if we are going to be able to focus our efforts and dwindling resources on the agonizingly slow process of trying to effect meaningful change for Black youths. Presently, we truly risk the loss of an entire generation.

The solution will not be found completely in blaming the victim, nor in blaming the schools. The system that has consistently maintained the position of U.S. Blacks at the bottom of the educational and occupational ladder is extremely complex and has many interlocking components.

It is critical that the schools become more sensitive to ethnic and cultural groups that do not conform to the white upper-income model that the schools are prepared to serve. Only when members of the helping professions are able to demystify Afro-American culture in the diverse ways that it intersects with life at various points on the socioeconomic scale will solutions be found to the question of achieving equal educational outcomes for Black children.

REFERENCES

Allitto, S. (1969). The language issue in communist Chinese education. In C. Hu (Ed.), *Aspects of Chinese education* (pp. 43–59). New York: Teachers College Press.

Barth, F. (1969). Introduction. In F. Barth (Ed.), *Ethnic groups and boundaries* (pp. 9–38). Boston: Little, Brown.

Beane, DeAnna. (1985). *Mathematics and Science: Critical filters for the future.* The Mid-Atlantic Center for Race Equity. The American University, Washington, DC.

Bennett, C., & Harris, J. J. III. (1982). Suspensions and expulsions of male and Black students: A study of the causes of disproportionality. *Urban Education, 16*(4), 339–423.

Bowles, S., & Gintis, H. (1976). *Schooling in capitalist America.* New York: Basic Books.

Cazden, C. (1970). The situation: A neglected source of social class differences in language use. *Journal of Social Issues, 26*(2), 35–60.

Clark, R. M. (1983). *Family life and school achievement: Why poor Black children succeed or fail.* Chicago: The University of Chicago Press.

College Placement Council (CPC) Survey — 1983–1984 Academic Year, Manpower Comments, Professions in Science Technology, Washington, DC.

Cornbleth, C., & Korth, W. (1980). Teacher perceptions and teacher–student interaction in integrated classrooms. *Journal of Experimental Education, 48,* 259–263.

De Anda, D. (1984). Bicultural socialization: Factors affecting the minority experience. *Social Work,* March–April, 29(2), pp. 101–107.

Deutsch, M. (1963). The disadvantaged child and the learning process. In A. Passow (Ed.), *Education in depressed areas.* New York: Teachers College Press.

DuBois, W. E. B. (1903). *The souls of Black folk.* Reprinted 1961. New York: New American Library.

Erikson, E. (1968). *Identity: Youth and crisis.* New York: Norton.

Fishman, J., & Leuders-Salmon, E. (1972). What sociology has to say to the teacher. In C. B. Cazden, V. P. John, & D. Hymes (Eds.), *Functions of language in the classroom* (pp. 67–83). New York: Teachers College Press.

Fleming, J. (1985). *Blacks in college.* San Francisco: Jossey-Bass.

Goffman, E. (1963). *Stigma.* Englewood Cliffs, NJ: Prentice-hall.

Hale-Benson, J. (1986). *Black children: Their roots, culture and learning styles.* Baltimore: Johns Hopkins University Press.

Hare, B. (1987). Structural inequality and the endangered status of Black youth. *Journal of Negro Education, 56*(1), 100–110.

Havighurst, R. J. (1976). The relative importance of social class and ethnicity in human development. *Human Development, 18,* 56–64.

Henderson, D. H., & Washington, A. G. (1975). Cultural differences and the education of Black children: An alternative model for program development. *Journal of Negro Education, 44,* 353–360.

Hostetler, J., & Huntington, G. (1971). *Children in Amish society: Socialization and community education.* New York: Holt, Rinehart and Winston.

Jackson, P. (1968). *Life in the classroom.* New York: Holt, Rinehart and Winston.

Labov, W. (1964a). Phonological correlates of social stratification. *American Anthropologist, 66*(4, part 2), 164–176.

Labov, W. (1964b). Stages in the acquisition of standard English. In R. Shuy (Ed.), *Social dialects and language learning* (pp. 77–104). Champaign, IL: National Council of Teachers of English.

Labov, W. (1969). The logic of nonstandard English, *Florida Foreign Language Reporter, 7*(1), 60–75, p. 169.

Labov, W., & Robins, C. (1969). A note on the relation of reading failure to peer-group status in urban ghettos. *Florida Foreign Language Reporter, 7*(1): 54–57, p. 167.

Long, N. (1958). The local community as an ecology of games. In N. W. Polsby, R. A. Dentler, & P. A. Smith (Eds.), *Politics of social life* (pp. 407–416). Boston: Houghton Mifflin.

Makita, K. (1968). The rarity of reading disability in Japanese children. *American Journal of Orthopsychiatry, 38,* 599–614.

McDermott, R. (1987). Achieving school failure: An anthropological approach to literacy and social stratification. In G. Spindler (Ed.), *Education and cultural process: Anthropological approaches* (2nd ed., pp. 173–204). Prospect Heights, IL: Waveland.

National Assessment of Educational Progress (1983). The Third National Mathematics Assessment: Results, Trends and Issues. Denver, CO: Education Commission of the State.

National Science Foundation. (1984). *Women and minorities in science and engineering.* Washington, DC: National Science Foundation.

Rashid, H. M. (1981). Early childhood education as a cultural transition for African American children. *Educational Research Quarterly, 6,* 55–63.

Rist, R. (1970). Student social class and teacher expectations. *Harvard Educational Review, 40,* 411–451.

Roberts, J. (1970). *Scene of the battle: Group behavior in urban classrooms.* New York: Doubleday.

Spindler, G. (1959–1963). *The transmission of American culture.* Adapted with revision and abridgement. In G. Spindler (Ed.), *Education ad culture.* New York: Holt, Rinehart and Winston, 1963.

Staples, R. (1986). Black male/female relationships. In Hale-Benson, J. (Ed.), *Conference on the Black family: Proceedings,* (pp. 31–35). Cleveland: Olivet Institutional Baptist Church.

Thompson, L. (1966). *Reading disability.* Springfield, IL: Charles C Thomas.

CHAPTER 13

Strategies and Techniques for Establishing Home–School Partnerships with Minority Parents

Patricia A. Edwards
Michigan State University

Parents must make room in their hearts and then in their house and then in their schedule for their children. No poor parent is too poor to do that, and no middle-class parent is too busy.

Jesse Jackson

Parents have involved themselves in the education of children since prehistoric times. The family provided the first informal education for the child through modeling, teaching, and praise or discipline. From the times of early Egyptian, Sumerian, Hebrew, Greek, and Roman days, parents were actively involved in the selection of teachers and the education of their children (Berger, 1987, p. 70). Today, parents are still viewed as their "children's first and most influential teachers," and "what parents do to help their children learn is more important to academic success than how well-off the family is" (U.S. Department of Education, 1986, p. 7). Clark (1983) also believes that "it is not class position that determines a family's ability to support their children's learning, rather it is the quality of life within the home that makes the difference" (p. xiii). He also believes that "the family's main contribution to a child's success in school is made through parents' dispositions and interpersonal relationships with the child in the household. Children receive essential 'survival knowledge' for competent classroom role enactment from their exposure to positive home attitudes and communication encounters" (p. 1). Epps (1983) reiterated Clark's

point, maintaining that "the family is the basic institution through which children learn who they are, where they fit into society, and what kinds of futures they are likely to experience" (p. ix). A strong message was sent to parents by the National Commission on Excellence in Education in its celebrated report *A Nation at Risk.*

You bear a responsibility to participate actively in your child's education. You should encourage more diligent study and discourage satisfaction with mediocrity and the attitude that says "let it slide;" monitor your child's study; encourage good study habits; encourage your child to take more demanding rather than less demanding courses; nurture your child's curiosity, creativity, and confidence; and be an active participant in the work of the schools. (1983, p. 35)

The commissioner's report appeared not to be limited to upper-class and middle-class parents; rather the message seemed to address all parents — irrespective of ethnic groups or whether the parents were single, teenagers, employed, new literates, functionally illiterate, or illiterate. The message clearly said that all parents are wanted and needed, partly because "today's teachers are so overworked writing reports, attending meetings, keeping records, and planning curriculum materials that they feel they hardly have any time to devote to the children they are supposed to be teaching" (Croft, 1979, p. 4). Epstein (1982) expressed a similar view: "Schools cannot always provide individual attention to children who most need extra help on skills, nor can schools always offer a range of activities to enrich the basic educational program" (p. 1). However, it is not surprising that LeGrand (1981) found that the children who need the most help tend to be children from minority groups: "Some children achieve and progress, and others don't; and of the others who don't, more than is conscionable are members of minority groups" (p. 680) and most especially from lower SES backgrounds within these minority groups. Shuck, Ulsh, and Platt (1983) point out that, unfortunately, "lower SES parents appear more reticent about communicating with the school because they often lack confidence, communication skills, and knowledge about learning processes" (p. 524). But Grimmett and McCoy (1980) and other researchers (Bronfenbrenner, 1974; Evans, 1971; Shelton, 1973) have argued that when lower-SES parents (and minority parents) receive assistance from the school system, they become more involved with their children's academic programs. One limitation is that too many school systems have been unsuccessful at attempting to establish home-school partnerships with diverse parent populations. Fortunately, however, a growing number of school systems continually attempt to reach out to these families. Their efforts have been supported by two decades of federal programs and legislation for parent involvement (Head Start, 1965; Head Start Planned Variations, 1967–1971; Follow-Through Programs, 1967; Follow-Through Planned Variations, 1967–1971; Education of All Handicapped Children Act, 1975; Title I, 1981, and its successor, Chapter I, 1974–1975). A major focus in all of these federal initiatives was recognition of parents as those who have principal influence on their children's development and the importance of close cooperation between home and school.

The purpose of this chapter is to discuss issues surrounding why the federal government and state and local agencies have targeted parent involvement as a top priority, barriers that have prevented successful home and school partnerships with certain ethnic groups, and how some school systems have been able to circumvent this situation by developing techniques and strategies to more effectively involve diverse parent populations in the schooling process.

A COMMITMENT TO PARENT EDUCATION

Public education was designed, in theory, to provide an equal opportunity for all children to learn and develop — it was designed to create a chance for upward mobility and achievement regardless of the advantages or disadvantages associated with family circumstances. However, in as much as the United States has faced a serious crisis of poverty and ethnic conflict that has produced social isolation and economic disadvantage for many members of certain ethnic minorities, members of some of these cultures have felt ignored, unknown, unappreciated, and sometimes even oppressed by the dominant groups who controlled important extrafamilial institutions. Salient among these institutions is public education, which to many has appeared unable or unwilling to adapt itself to the special needs of poor and ethnic minority children (Laosa, 1985).

Partly as a result of concern over this situation, the federal government and state and local agencies have made an important step toward disrupting the cycle of poverty experienced by a large sector of the U.S. public. Two ways they have attempted to reverse this situation have been through improving the literacy skills of minority families and increasing the level of their involvement in the schooling process. Although parent education has a long tradition, it has emerged only in the last two decades as a critical issue for the federal government and state and local agencies. Edward Ziegler's remarks at a January 1979 conference of the Education Commission of the States in Denver, provide an excellent rationale for federal, state, and local support of parent involvement.

Although there is controversy today over what the public schools should be trying to accomplish with the limited resources at their disposal, it is difficult to imagine any skill more "basic" than that of being a good parent, or any body of knowledge more crucial than that of knowledge of how to raise a sound family. In fact, as parents and families encounter new stresses and assimilate unfamiliar patterns of behavior at a rate we would have thought impossible several decades ago, more and more people are coming to feel that public schools have responsibility to provide help where it is needed, to offer programs that will assist in the education of Americans for parenthood.

This conclusion — that schools should help people learn to be effective parents — is not a new one, but over the past few years it has been attracting increasing attention from educators, legislators, and the general public. It is part of a larger issue, which is the proper relationship between families and the major supportive institutions of U.S. society, such as schools, social agencies, and health care systems. That the relationship is changing is without doubt. The question facing policy makers is how to foster change in a direction that will strengthen the family and help to build strong communities.

Parent education is not one of the subject areas traditionally included in school curricula. It has, nevertheless, been appearing with greater frequency in recent years, either as an element woven into other subject areas or as a discrete course on its own. The message appears to be that parent education is no passing fad. It is here to stay, and it is challenging public schools to reassess the scope of their educational mission. In view of the growing interest and the profound social values at stake, the time has come for serious consideration of the feasibility of implementing parent education in the public schools. (p. ix)

Once the parent education movement was in motion, however, the following questions arose: Where was it going? Whom would it serve? How would it serve them? At the same 1979 conference of the Education Commission of the States, Ira Gordon emphasized "the need to clarify the goals of parent education before plunging into program development, because different goals will pose different problems in implementation" (Gordon, 1979b, p. xi). In a 1977 article, Gordon had warned that "we should ask ourselves strategic questions [about parent education in public schools]. Why are we doing this? How does it fit into the larger social scheme? What do we hope to accomplish within the narrow confines of a specific program? What else ought to be done? What are our basic assumptions about people — what they need and want, and how they learn and grow, what we desire for them?" (p. 78). While acknowledging that a commitment to parent education was important, Gordon (1979b) felt that it was equally important that the federal government as well as state and local agencies address these questions in a serious manner.

Another important participant in the 1979 Conference of the States Education Commission was a state senator from Minnesota, Jerome M. Hughes. Senator Hughes strongly agreed with the notion that "no matter how well conceived, well financed, and well intended, an education program for children alone that cannot counteract the profound cultural effects of the home will not achieve its goals" (Hughes, 1979, p. 6). But Hughes recognized that the parent education movement was creating yet another function for families in addition to a whole list of other traditional family functions and felt that public schools needed to help parents in meeting and talking with teachers and principals, and with other experts, namely, doctors, social workers, and psychologists. He further stated that "our goal must be to help parents maintain a sense of power, dignity and authority in the rearing of their children . . . if parents have the power to do so, most of them will accept the long-term responsibility of caring for and supporting their children" (p. 9). In order to effectively accomplish this goal, a series of questions, according to Hughes, need to be answered. "How can the parent coordinate the professionals with whom they share the task of raising their children? How does the parent deal with the early childhood expert who is armed with special credentials and sometimes a jargon that most parents cannot understand? How do parents retain responsibility for their children's lives when they rarely have the voice, the authority or the power to make others listen to them?" (p. 8).

There is little doubt that a commitment to parent education exists. But the difficulty of getting results is hardly to be minimized. Francis Roberts (1979) argued that "the process of moving a community to accept serious parent education in the schools can be like the war of the worlds" (p. 10). Roberts then raised a critical question about parent education: "What makes us think the public schools are capable of taking on parent education?" He broached this question with the observation that "lumping of social problems into the box labeled 'need for parent education programs in schools' seems too inclusive. Especially since the schools are in a period when educational goals are being narrowed rather than enlarged, there is reason to be clear about what can be done" (p. 11). Roberts also summarized the comments of Arthur Wise, presented in an article in the *New York University Quarterly*, "The Hyperrationalization of American Education" stated: "In schools and similar organizations, measurable goals crowd out nonmeasurable goals . . . Given a broad array of applications of a proposed policy (in our case parent education) and knowing how hard it is to get any practical application, we will choose those things we think are measurable not because they are most central to the policy but because they do appear measurable" (Roberts, 1979, p. 11).

Perhaps one of the problems facing those supporting parent education has been the notion that policy and decisions should be made on a more centralized basis. It may be that a compulsive tendency of many large and small school systems to operate on the apparently logical but simplistic assumption that there is more wisdom at the center than on the periphery (for example, that the superintendent knows better than the principal what a school needs) has hampered the overall commitment to parent education. The ease with which everybody talks about parent education and the importance of a commitment to it, raises the question: What have school systems across the country done (beyond formal commitment) to make parent education a reality for all parents and especially minority parents?

Beyond the Commitment to Parent Education: What Has Been Accomplished?

Much attention has been given to the possible expansion of parent education in public schools, but more attention needs to be given to the process of organizing programs and to the organizational nature of schools as they relate to parent education. Douglas R. Powell, of the Merrill-Palmer Institute in Detroit, has pointed out (1979) "parent education brings new clients to schools" (p. 14) and that "parent education offers public schools an opportunity to develop a new orientation to children and families, a new sense of what it means to serve a community's educational needs" (p. 17). However, Roberts (1979) appropriately noted that this presents a major challenge for some public schools. More specifically,

In talking about education in the schools, we are apt to easily slide into proposals that deal at surface levels with the deep-seated ways of people. How they work with their own children and how they are prepared for this are matters differing from one subculture to another and, even in these times, from locale to locale. We are dealing with personal meanings, with patterns of culture and ways of people, not with some technical need for information. (pp. 11–12)

NEEDS AND CONCERNS OF MINORITY GROUPS

Recognizing the fact that schools are dealing with people rather than technical information, the National Education Association organized four subcommittees to address the special needs and concerns of ethnic minorities — Blacks, Hispanics, Asians/Pacific Islanders, and Native Americans/Alaska Natives. The findings of the subcommittees as it relates to parents and children are as follows:

Needs and Concerns of U.S. Blacks

The subcommittee reported that lack of access of many Black students to early academic intervention programs more often than not tends to affect their attitudes toward school. Moreover, it was found

(Mack, 1987) that they become "discouraged about school, fail to pass difficult subjects or participate in accelerated programs, and drop out of school at high rates" (p. 8). One of the most alarming findings the subcommittee reported was that "many Black students, although 'energized' and achieving well in lower elementary grades, begin in the upper elementary grades to lose their enthusiasm" (Mack, 1987, p. 8).

Adding to the bleak picture of Black students' survival rates in the educational system is the subcommittee's finding that Black parents "find it difficult to advocate for their children's needs and often are naive about the educational setting and 'special' programs . . . [and] feel uncomfortable visiting their children's schools and participate in school activities only to a limited extent when compared to parents generally" (p. 9). The subcommittee attributed this lack of parental involvement to the time "[school] activities are held, the lack of child care, and the distance between home and school – which many times is increased because of school desegregation" (p. 9). The subcommittee also reported that "schools in the Black community tend not to have outreach programs for parents beyond parent–teacher groups" (p. 9).

Also discouraging in the subcommittee's report was the finding that "some school administrators and teachers continue to perceive Black students as 'poor,' 'unmotivated,' or 'culturally deprived' and consequently unable to learn" (p. 8). As a result, "[The] instructional staff have a tendency to 'dumb down' the curriculum and set lower achievement expectations for Black students" (p. 8). They even track many Black students inappropriately into vocational education or noncollege academic curriculums. Equally as discouraging in the report was the fact that "administrators and teachers, continue to be either uninformed, misinformed, or insensitive about Black culture" (p. 8).

Needs and Concerns of Hispanics

The subcommittee investigating the concerns and needs of Hispanics reported some very depressing findings. For example, "40 percent of Hispanics do not go beyond eighth grade compared to 18 percent of all Americans, [and] the dropout rates for Hispanics in some urban settings are starting at 50 percent and higher" (Wilson, 1987, p. 8).

Because many Hispanic parents cannot help their children with schoolwork because of their own limited English proficiency and lack of education, it does not mean that they are not concerned about their children's school success. They are extremely concerned about "the language assessment instruments used to place Hispanic children in bilingual programs" (p. 9). Justifiably, Hispanic parents feel that the tests "should not be administered by a person other than their child's teacher" (p. 10). They contend that "when teachers have little or no input, [their] children are often misplaced — thus beginning their education in reverse gear" (p. 10). Also troubling to Hispanic parents is that "due to low scores [on] English assessment tests, Hispanic students are often placed in Chapter I classes, where they may receive assistance in reading from a nonbilingual teacher or a teacher not qualified in English-as-a-Second-Language methods" (p. 10).

The subcommittee also revealed that Hispanic parents do not fully trust the schools their children attend. More specifically, "[many] parents feel no one at school cares about Hispanic students [and that] many school personnel expect Hispanic students to perform poorly in schools" (p. 9). They point out that "prejudice, financial considerations, and cultural differences contribute to school system reluctance to consider solutions to the problems faced by Hispanic students" (p. 9).

There is also a great deal of concern and uneasiness in the Hispanic community "about the effects of education reform on Hispanic students, the continued shortages of Hispanic and bilingual teachers and the potential for tracking and the 'pushing out' of Hispanic students" (p. 9). "The Hispanic community expresses much concern about the 'English only' movement throughout the country and the impact of the new immigration reform law on school districts, particularly as it might necessitate changes on the part of the districts that they may be unprepared or unwilling to make" (p. 11).

Needs and Concerns of Asian and Pacific Islanders

The subcommittee reported that "the emotional needs of Asian and Pacific Islander students are not being met" (Chase, 1987, p. 9). In fact, "both foreign and native born, are experiencing identity crises that may lead students to drop out of school or, even more tragically, to commit suicide or, in some cases, homicide" (p. 9). Adding to their emotional stress is the fact that they are "pressured to seek academic excellence or risk losing face" (their credibility or dignity in their family).

The subcommittee also reported that "Asian and Pacific Islander students and staff are isolated within their school settings" (p. 9). Asians and Pacific Islanders also face a number of problems in school: (a) they are not consulted when they are placed in bilingual or limited-English-proficiency programs. (b) They are not given appropriate language proficiency tests. (c) They are mistakenly placed in special education programs while others are denied special education assistance because of language deficiencies (p. 9).

Of concern in the subcommittee's report was the fact that "many districts do not provide adequate bilingual and ESL programs . . . [and that] the failure to provide effective ESL/Bilingual programs has increased the probability of higher school dropout rates among Asian and Pacific Islander students" (p. 10). Also of concern to the subcommittee was that "most school personnel lack an understanding of Asian and Pacific Islander people, their culture, and traditions . . . [and that] because of ignorance or faulty record keeping, many Asian and Pacific Islanders are incorrectly identified" (p. 10).

In these populations parents' experience was found to be similar to that of Hispanic parents. "Language and cultural barriers prevent many Asian and Pacific Islander parents from becoming involved in their children's school activities" (p. 12). Furthermore, "non-English-speaking parents and their English-speaking children are

becoming alienated from one another as children become more and more American-ized" (p. 12). The subcommittee also reported two other important findings: "Asian and Pacific Islander immigrants don't understand how school systems function . . . [and] they lack a political power base in many communities" (p. 11).

It should be noted that even though these parents lack an understanding of how school systems function and oftentimes lack political power in their communities, it does not mean that they lack interest in their children's achievement in school.

Needs and Concerns of Native Americans and Alaska Natives

In the subcommittee's report they stressed the importance of the need for non-Indian people to develop an understanding and respect for Native Americans and Alaska Natives. They also stressed the need to improve the quality of education available to children and adults in these populations. The subcommittee further recommended that "schools should be developed as community centers that are both responsive [to] and reflective of local input and needs [and that the] curriculum should reflect local conditions and locally-developed educational objectives" (Scheife, 1987, p. 21).

Another recommendation by the subcommittee was that "tribal councils, parent advisory committees, Indian boards of education, and other legally-established groups should have maximum authority for making decisions concerning educational policies, financing and expenditures" (p. 21). The subcommittee also suggested that "at the option of local Indian groups, school systems should be coterminous with Indian reservations" (p. 22). Furthermore, "special efforts must be made in training, recruiting, and upgrading Indian teachers, teacher aides, and other persons so they can take over educational responsibilities in schools serving Indian students" (p. 22). Additionally, the subcommittee concluded that "basic instruction in Indian languages should be available at all levels of public schools serving Indian students and for preservice and inservice teachers of Indian students" (p. 22). Finally, "teachers should work with parents and tribal authorities to establish closer home–school relations and to develop approaches that will be more responsive to local conditions and needs" (p. 22).

Common Needs and Concerns of Minority Populations

From the findings of the four NEA subcommittees on minority concerns, it is demonstrable that Blacks, Hispanics, Asian and Pacific Islander populations, and Native Americans and Alaska Natives are deeply concerned with getting an effective and relevant education for their children. They want the educational system to reflect their values and way of life, and they feel they ought to influence and exercise control over ·their children's education. Edwards (1987) has pointed out that "regardless of ethnic background or educational levels, parents want to know specific strategies and approaches that they can be involved in with school personnel, and they want more information about their children's educational programs and progress" (p. 101). If this is indeed true, why haven't more minority parents become more actively involved in the educational achievement of their children? What barriers have precipitated their lack of interest and concern?

BARRIERS TO INVOLVEMENT OF MINORITY PARENTS

One of the interesting barriers to minority parent involvement has been how the minority group itself is viewed by the school system. For example, Asians and Pacific Islanders "are a minority of convenience," noted one of the individuals testifying before the NEA Study Committee (Joe, 1987). In fact, according to the Asians and Pacific Islanders Subcommittee (Chase, 1987), "Asians and Pacific Islanders are often not perceived as minorities" (p. 12), and in many instances, their treatment "borders on neglect" (Tso, 1987): The "good mouthing" of citizens, as well as immigrants, and refugees of Asian and Pacific Islander extraction "has been so effective and so successful today, that after about

25 years of falsely portraying Asians [and Pacific Islanders] as successful members of a so-called 'model minority,' too many people — both white and Black — believe that [they] have no real problems" (Inocencio, 1987). That perspective was emphasized again and again as the committee heard over 50 witnesses and visited 14 schools.

Blacks, Hispanics, and Native Americans/Alaska Natives have not been so positively viewed by public schools. On the contrary, public schools have pinpointed a number of barriers to successfully involving parents from these minority groups — poor literacy skills, language deficits, inability to implement suggestions, cultural distance between school and community, unwillingness or inability to attend meetings, and the inability to recognize their importance to their children's achievement. Unfortunately, teachers and administrators often become angry in these circumstances and complain that the very parents who most need to come fail to become involved, making their job even tougher. Some school personnel, in disgust, even come to the conviction that nothing can be done with these children, since their parents do not support and reinforce their children's school achievement. A statement by White (1975) expressed this view. "The informal education that families provide for their children makes more of an impact on a child's educational development than the formal educational system. If the family does its job well, the professional can provide effective training. If not, there may be little the professional can do to save the child from mediocrity" (p. 4).

Ron Edmonds, a strong advocate in the school effectiveness movement vehemently disagrees with White's position. Ulric Neisser (1986) summarized the remarks Edmonds made at a Cornell conference prior to his death on July 15, 1983. Edmonds argued that:

> minority children's failure to learn can just as easily be seen as the school's failure to teach them. The fact that many poor and minority children fail to master the school curriculum does not reflect deficiencies in the children, but rather inadequacies in the schools themselves. Variability in the

distribution of achievement among school-age children in the United States derives from variability in the nature of the schools to which they go. Achievement is therefore relatively independent of family background, at least if achievement is defined as pupil acquisition of basic schools skills. (p. 6)

While researchers agree that children from different family backgrounds can acquire basic school skills, the general consensus among researchers is that to master these skills children must get some minimal assistance from their families. Families who cannot help their children with their homework, for example, can at least encourage them to do their best in school and support their efforts to do so. Epstein (1986) suggested that teachers can increase the amount of involvement of parents (including minority parents) who have little education. Epstein compared teachers who were active in seeking parental support with those who were not. Differences in these parents' reports of their involvement in learning activities at home from those of more educated parents were significant only in classrooms of teachers who failed to show leadership in parental involvement. Epstein concluded that teachers who got parents involved "mitigated the disadvantages typically associated with race, social class, and level of education" (p. 279).

Schools need to eliminate barriers of race, religion, or economic condition and stereotyped preconceptions about certain minority groups. Hobson (1979) believes that the essence of success in working with parents — no matter where they live or what their circumstances — is a spirit of cooperation with the shared purpose of meeting children's needs (p. 45). She states that there are five essentials of parent involvement. First, school personnel should explore with parents what they want schools to accomplish. Second, they should devise opportunities for parental involvement that they see as practical and meaningful. Third, they should keep reaching out to parents with warmth and sensitivity. Fourth, school personnel should develop an ongoing training program in which parents and staff are both teachers and learners. Fifth, and most important, school personnel should acknowledge that sharing power with parents is not abdication of one's professional leadership role; rather it provides an opportunity to understand parents' interests and goals and to learn ways to help achieve them (pp. 44-45).

In addition to Hobson's five essentials of parent involvement, Rodriguez (1981) has suggested that teachers and administrators assess their school's commitment to a parent involvement effort, and especially to a minority parent involvement effort, by asking themselves such questions as the following: How many parents (and parents from different minority groups) are involved in the school program? How many parents (and minority parents) are involved in each phase of the program: (a) in the classroom, (b) in the decisionmaking, (c) other? How often are parents (and minority parents) making suggestions or asking questions about the educational programs of the district? Is the parental involvement component changing in response to changing needs and skills of parents, community, teachers, and aides? Are parents' attitudes toward schools and teachers changing? Are teachers' attitudes towards parents and and community changing? Are the attitudes of children towards parents, teachers, and the community changing (p. 43)?

It is of critical importance that schools recognize that minority parents can make significant contributions. It is of equal importance that teachers and administrators not prejudge parents and children from certain minority groups. Among the biggest barriers to successful parent involvement are (a) the false labeling of some minority parent groups as not interested in supporting, and as unwilling to support, their children's education (Blacks, Hispanic, Native Americans/Alaska Natives) and (b) communicating to other minority parent groups that it is acceptable if they choose not to become involved in the school because their children have no "real problems" with school (Asians/Pacific Islanders).

Now, more than ever before, some teachers and administrators believe wholeheartedly that certain minority parent groups (Blacks, Hispanics, Native Americans/Alaska Natives) simply don't care and strongly resist being involved in the school's parent involvement efforts. According to McLaughlin and Shields (1987), "what's lacking, in most schools and school districts, are appropriate strategies or structures for involving minority parents" (p. 157). However, Rodriguez (1981) warned that "the failure to involve minority groups' parents in educational policy-making activities of a school represents a tremendous loss in human resources for the parent, the child, the minority group to which he or she belongs, and the school as a whole" (p. 40). How have schools responded to Rodriguez's warning? What strategies and techniques have been developed to involve minority parents? What have been minority parents' responses to these efforts?

DEVELOPMENT OF SCHOOL–PARENT– COMMUNITY INVOLVEMENT MODELS

One way schools have responded to Rodriguez's warning has been through the development of parent involvement models. Ira Gordon (1979a, p. 18) described four models of school–parent–community involvement: the parent impact model, the comprehensive services model, the school impact model, and the community impact model. The parent impact model's goal is to improve family capabilities to provide in the home the type of learning environment that develops readiness for learning. The comprehensive services model's goal is to provide nonacademic services and information to the family that will enable a child to come to school more able to learn. The goal of the school impact model is to make schools more responsive to parents as they are. Finally, the goal of the community impact model is to change all agencies both internally and as they relate to one another.

In the models described by Gordon, parents, including minority parents, have been asked to be partners, collaborators and problem solvers, supporters, advisors and co-decision makers, and sometimes to simply be an interested audience (Henderson, Marburger, & Ooms, 1986). Schools have solicited parent assistance by means

of one-way and two-way communication (Berger, 1987). Forms of one-way communication have included district newsletters, handbooks, happy-grams, newspapers, spontaneous notes, suggestion boxes, yearbooks, and parent questionnaires. Two-way communication has involved August letters, back-to-school nights, breakfast meetings, early-in-the-year contacts, exchanges, fairs, carnivals, suppers, home visits, neighborhood visits, open-door policies, parent–teacher associations, picnics, Saturday morning sessions, school maintenance projects, school programs, telephone calls, and workshops.

France and Meeks (1987) have noted that unfortunately, "functionally illiterate and illiterate parents [mainly minority parents and especially lower-SES minority parents] have been largely ignored by the schools, which go on sending home notices, report cards, homework assignments, information packets, survey forms, and permission slips as though they believe every parent can read and write." (p. 227). Their suggestion: "When there are indications that parents are failing to respond to parent involvement programs because of literacy problems, teachers should take the time to call and arrange conferences during which they can describe some of the ways in which academic success can be fostered outside of direct instruction" (p. 226). Schools should therefore move from simply sending messages home to parents requesting their assistance to organizing programs to improve their skills so that they can provide the requested assistance.

Brady (1977) held that parent involvement is so important that it should be required; but he warned that schools should allow for individual needs, desires, and capabilities. Rich, Van Dien, and Mattox (1979) suggested that "parent participation is most widespread and sustained when parents view their participation as directly linked to the achievement of their children . . . parent/community involvement programs need to include the opportunity for families to supplement and reinforce the development of academic skills with work in the home" (p. 36).

One of the most crucial points addressed to schools by Rich et al. was that "parent–community involvement needs to be viewed as a legitimate activity of the schools and an integral part of its delivery of services, not an add-on" (p. 37). In response to the request of Rich et al., several school systems have developed a variety of strategies for working with minority families. A discussion of these strategies are highlighted below.

Parent Programs in Reading

Programs to help parents help their children in reading have received a great deal of attention (Edwards, 1989; Edwards & Panofsky, 1988; Edwards with Weems, 1988; Spewock, 1988; Lengyel & Baghban, 1980; Raim, 1980; Clegg, 1973; Crosset, 1972; Swift, 1970). Edwards and her colleagues sought to train lower-SES minority parents in how to share books with their young children by modeling for them effective book-reading strategies. The research by Edwards and her colleagues addressed the need to shift from "telling" to "showing" parents how to read to their children. Similarly, Swift (1970) argued that low-income mothers could profit from being trained in how to share books with their preschool children. Spewock (1988) also proposed that parents who have poor attitudes because of their own negative experiences as students could profit from being trained to share books with their preschoolers. The training approaches employed by Edwards and her colleagues, by Swift and by Spewock, all were found to be very successful in improving parent–child reading interactions.

Other successful attempts to involve minority parents in reading have included the following types of approaches. Raim (1980) developed a reading club for low-income Hispanic parents. The purpose of the reading club was to show parents how to construct instructional devices appropriate for their children and to rehearse how to use these devices before using them with their children. Later, under the supervision of the reading teacher, the parents used the materials they had made with their children. Clegg (1973) provided low-income Black parents with individually planned learning games in order to help them increase the

reading achievement of their second-grade children. Crosset (1972) involved low-income Black parents in a PPR (Parent Participation in Reading) Program. The program provided for the parents to observe their children at school in a reading group and then receive personal instruction and materials for home study with their children from a teacher at a "family learning center." Lengyel and Baghban (1980) developed a family reading program and a Sustained Silent Reading (SSR) program. The major objective of this family program was to encourage parents to read to their children for 15 minutes a day, seven days a week, for a period of nine weeks.

Parent Programs in Bilingual Education

A number of programs have been developed to help minority parents support their children's language development (Collazo-Levy & Villegas, 1984; Torres, Young, Goodall, Scorza, & Inman, 1983; Betancourt, 1980; Almeida, 1976; Gunther, 1976; McConnell, 1976). Despite the fact that there is a need for Asian and Pacific Islander parents and students to participate in bilingual or limited English proficiency programs, it appears from an examination of the literature that only one such program has been developed for these parents and students: Torres et al. (1983) described the Chinese Bilingual Education Program that operates at Seward Park and Washington Irving high schools in New York City. The program offers instructional and supportive services to native Chinese speakers of limited English proficiency. Academic and personal counseling was available to students, and family workers made home visits to parents when necessary. In turn, parents were generally responsive, attending program meetings and participating in the voluntary advisory committee.

Most bilingual program efforts have been designed to solicit the participation of Hispanic families, rather than the families of Asian/Pacific Islander and Native American/Alaska Native students. Betancourt (1980) headed a Bilingual Training Institute for parents in San Antonio, Texas, in which parents were trained as tutors and coplanners. Parents were viewed as teachers of their own children, as resources for teachers, and as contributors to curriculum development (by creating and using culturally relevant materials). Almeida (1976) established a program to service the needs of families with working parents, with children whose older siblings had been behind in school achievement, and with serious social and economic problems. The program provided a stimulating preschool learning environment to 63 East Harlem 4-year-olds. In addition, as a result of participation in the bilingual–bicultural class, the pupils were expected to develop a more positive self-image. The results of the program evaluation revealed that pupil achievement levels were above chosen criterion levels and parental involvement in activities was attained almost at proposed criterion levels.

Gunther (1976) involved the families of prekindergarten children in a English-as-a-second language program. The families were selected for the program on the basis of family background and their children's inability to speak English because of recent arrival to the United States. The program activities were based upon the cognitive/affective approach. Growth in social skills, physical abilities, intellectual ability, English fluency, self-image, and parent involvement were assessed. The report concluded that the program was successful in increasing the social skills, physical abilities, and intellectual ability of the 45 pupils. The program was also successful in developing more positive self-image and cultural awareness of the pupils. Parent involvement in school activities was increased. Collazo-Levy and Villegas (1984) described Project Parents, a 3-year program designed to increase parental participation in the educational process. The project focused on parents of Spanish-French/Creole, Greek-, and Italian-speaking primary level students with limited English language skills. Parents participated in classes in ESL and in high school equivalency test preparation. In addition, program staff offered workshops designed to increase parents' understanding of New York City school system operations, and role-playing workshops were designed to

increase parents' self-confidence advocating for their children.

During the 1979–1980 school year, 700 Hispanic students from Grades 1–9 in seven schools in the Bronx participated in the Comprehensive Approach to Bilingual Education Program. The program included an instructional component that emphasized the acquisition of English as a second language, Spanish and English reading skills, cultural awareness, and achievement in social studies. Additional program components included staff development and parent and community participation. Activities planned to involve parents were successful and staff training workshops were satisfactory.

McConnell (1976) designed a bilingual multicultural education program for children of migrant and seasonal farmworkers. The program operates on an interstate and interdistrict basis. Children from south Texas who become interstate migrants are followed from their home community to northern locations. By working cooperatively with the schools, the mobile project staff that follows the children's schooling arranges to work with them on released time from their regular classes, or else after school, providing supplementary education as nearly as possible year-round to a moving population. Parents, as community members, are active in program management decisions involving organization matters, review and input into funding proposals, hiring of teaching staff, deciding how funds raised by parents are used, and participation in program evaluation. Family members participate in the program by acting as teachers or teaching assistants, by assisting with cultural heritage activities, and by providing support services. Of the 169 children served during the 1975–1976 school year, 156 were Mexican-Americans. Overall the program met or exceeded its goals.

Parent Programs to Bridge the Gap Between Home and School

Another approach that has received a moderate amount of attention is programs that seek to bridge the gap between home and school (Brower, 1981; Grimmett & McCoy, 1980; Libarios & Libarios, 1979;

Shelton, 1973). For example, in 1981 Linda Brower organized the Parent Involvement Program, a project that reaches about 50 parents and 325 students enrolled in the LeFlore County (Mississippi) Follow Through Program, most of whom come from Black, low-income families (Brower, 1981). The primary goal of this project is to bridge the gap between home and school by offering support to parents as they become actively involved in their children's education. Developed as part of the local Follow Through Project, the Parent Involvement Program is designed around results of a parent and community survey created to gain information about community interests and needs. Parent workshops play an important role, providing information and curriculum-related activities, health and safety, and community responsibilities. Parents are also encouraged to visit Follow Through classrooms to observe and participate in classroom activities. Home learning aides provide supplemental guidance to parents at home and offer feedback concerning parent–effectiveness.

Grimmett and McCoy (1980) increased lower-SES families in a small midwest community participation in school by communicating with them about their children's reading progress. Specifically, they explained to parents: (a) goals of the reading program; (b) terminology and definitions specific to reading (e.g., accountability and flexible grouping); (c) explanations of the diagnostic-prescriptive cycle; (d) instructional procedures; and (e) student profile components. The results suggested that parent involvement can influence children's reading when parents receive information about the reading program. It was noted that parents need continuous communication with their children's reading teachers in order to increase the quality and the quantity of their involvement in the reading programs.

Libarios and Libarios (1979) designed Project RISE (Resourceful Individuals Seeking Education) at Aiea High School and Leeward Community College on the island of Oahu. This project sought to empower minority students and parents, incorporating them as equal members into the community where they live. The

objectives of the program are to assist all students, especially alienated and culturally different children, in determining their own direction and life goals, to provide a continuum of supportive services for students from culturally different backgrounds, and to enhance and encourage interethnic and intergroup cooperation.

Shelton (1973) sought to determine if economically deprived students' behavior, attendance, and achievement would improve as a result of teacher–parent dialogue and contact through Family Involvement-Communication System (FICS) training. The procedures, developed as FICS training, were based upon the following assumptions: (a) Low-income parents can be trained to teach middle-class teachers to communicate effectively with the parents and children living in low-income neighborhoods, and (b) more open communication and involvement between school and home will enhance the educational growth of youngsters. The results of this investigation indicate that such increased communication and involvement in fact increased children's average daily attendance and achievement.

Parent Programs Addressing Special Concerns

Several programs have been designed to increase minority parent participation in special programs (Brandt, 1986; Gonzales, 1986; Thomas, 1985; Forte & Lee, 1981; Wenn, 1981; Malone, 1977; Champagne & Goldman, 1970; Prentice, 1966). For example, Brandt (1986) reported that the Yale Child Study Center collaborated successfully with the New Haven School System in initiating a school improvement plan that addressed the negative impact of change, social stratification, and conflict and distrust between home and school. Thomas (1985) described a plan to reduce the racial isolation of a Massachusetts school in a predominantly Hispanic neighborhood. Specifically, the school involved different ethnic group parents as advisors and joint decision makers before and after their children arrive at school. To encourage more active participation of language-minority parents, the Oakland (California)

Unified School District initiated a parent leadership institute called OPTIMUM (Gonzalez, 1986). This project helps parents establish cooperative school relationships, understand school organizations, upgrade their own education while helping their children, and capitalize on their linguistic and cultural resources. In the Future Leaders Program in Washington, DC, a much needed enrichment program for minority students, the involvement of the parent is a high priority (Malone, 1977). The idea that practice makes perfect and motivation leads to practice is the premise on which the Future Leaders Program is based. It is the contention of the program that the amount of learning that a normal child can achieve depends upon adults' expectations, acceptance or rejection, and encouragement or discouragement.

Recognizing that rearing children is a difficult task, several programs have sought to help parents do a better job. Forte and Lee (1981) designed the Parent Participation for Basic Skills Improvement Program to help parents help their children in the academic skills. Champagne and Goldman (1970) developed a training program in helping mothers of educationally disadvantaged children use positive reinforcement. Prentice (1966) designed a 3-year project to increase parent participation in the vocational rehabilitation of adolescent and young adult mentally handicapped persons, to develop methods of motivating parents to participate, and to investigate the relationship between parent participation and the retardate's vocational adjustment. Wenn (1981) coordinates Tulane Follow Through, which serves an economically depressed, migrant, bilingual population, has the goal, among others, of providing parents an opportunity to obtain skills and information related to parenting and to encourage parents, many with little previous decision-making experience, to assume roles as leaders and advocates. Parents' involvements include volunteering at the school; tutoring their children at home by using specially developed activities and instructional materials referred to as "Home Secrets" and participating in a Home Learning Center, which is designed to provide learning experiences for children

in neighborhood homes two afternoons a week for 6–8 weeks. Community acceptance is evidenced by the large number of parents who regularly participate in the project. Learning materials are available in Spanish and English to serve a large migrant population in the community.

Programs Involving Parents as Supporters, Advisors, and Interviewers

Programs involving parents as supporters of their children's health and nutrition, and as advisors or interviewers have received a limited amount of attention (Amodeo, Gallegos, & Flores, 1982; Gallegos & Flores, 1982; Tarwater, 1981; Clay, 1967).

Amodeo et al. (1982) suggested that parents of Mexican-American children can provide vital information regarding the education of their gifted children. They can become involved in identifying giftedness once the characteristics are agreed upon. Parents may then request assessment of their children to ascertain whether placement in a special program is appropriate. Once the assessment results are considered in a placement decision, parents are asked to approve the final action. In programming, parents of minority children can help teachers capitalize on the child's cultural background. Parent involvement may be direct (participation in the classroom) or indirect (through communication with the school and with teachers).

Similarly, Gallegos and Flores (1982) reported that parents of gifted minority children need to be involved in their children's education. Since cultural differences and values can present obstacles to communication between parents and the schools, difficulties in assessment and identification of minority gifted students arise over issues related to parents' perceptions of their child's giftedness, their feelings of their responsibility versus the school's in educating their child, the instruments used in assessment, and the prevalent underestimation of the potential of the linguistically or culturally different child. Parents can help in educational programming by providing information about what different cultures value as gifted or talented behaviors. A cultural framework can be applied to specific classroom activities to teach ideological, sociological, attitudinal, and technological–artistic values of the culture. The school can help the parents through direct and indirect contact.

Seeking to increase the effectiveness of parents as teachers of their children, the Home-Based Early Childhood Program sends trained home visitors, through the agency of the Child Health and Development Program located in Huntington, Tennessee, to families to screen for learning problems and to instruct parents in working with their children (Tarwater, 1981). Involved in this project are 175 students and an equal number of parents, about half from low-income families. When children up to 3 years of age are visited at home, their parents receive a Developmental Task List of sequential activities for use with them.

Clay (1967) studied 24 residents of two poverty areas and trained them as nonprofessional parent interviewers of the parents of Head Start children. The purpose of this project was twofold: (a) to obtain parents' attitudes toward the Head Start program attended by their children, and (b) to involve some of the parents in the process of Head Start evaluation and research design. The resulting interviews have been judged to be, on the whole, very satisfactory by the parents and Head Start staff.

Programs Involving Parents as Tutors and Workshops Attendees

Soliciting parental participation in workshops and recruiting them as tutors have been the focus of several programmatic efforts (Rodriguez, 1985; Shuck et al., 1983; Vanden Dries, 1982; Haley, 1981; Kellberg, 1981; Simmons, 1981; Arturo, 1980; High, 1981; Meyers, 1974). In all of the parent involvement efforts cited in this chapter, Native Americans were more often asked to serve as tutors and workshop attendees than in any other capacity. For instance, Simons (1981) involved Native American families (115 parents and 175 children) in a project called the Acoma Partners in Basics. This project develops basic skills (reading, writing, math) through

parental tutoring of young children at home. Locally developed materials reflecting the culture and traditions of the Acoma Pueblo are used to teach or to reinforce these basic skills, which are taught by parents trained to be learning facilitators. In addition, a network of parents and community volunteers provides homework aid and tutoring to students referred by classroom teachers. Bi-monthly workshops focusing on understanding the basic skills areas of reading, writing, and math help parents work with their children in home study situations. Demonstrations, role-plays, and video tapes are used in training, and handouts are given to parents to take home as reminders of important concepts and skills. Vanden Dries (1982) described a program provided by the Indian Education Program of Clark County (Nevada) School District to approximately 45 American Indian students and their parents. The program objectives address tutorial services, career guidance and counseling services, and improving parents' and children's attitudes toward school.

Black parents were the next-largest group requested to serve as tutors and/or participate in workshops. Shuck et al. (1983) encouraged low-SES parents in a large inner-city school district to tutor their children using PEP (Parents Encourage Pupils) calendar books and individualized homework activities tallied by means of a progress chart. The results indicated that the parent tutoring program had a significant impact on the improvement of children's reading scores. Meyers (1974) organized Project SPA (Search for Preventive Approaches), which involved Think Workshops which Harlem parents were trained to experience "fun in thinking" with their children. Significant gains in cognitive skills by both adults and youngsters were realized. Brainstorming as an ego-oriented, rather than a task-oriented, technique helped provide parents, paraprofessionals, and children with ego-strengthening flexibility. Haley's (1981) Home Study Program (Parent/Student Partnership in Learning Programs) located in New Orleans served 38,000 students and their families, who are 85 percent Black and 15 percent white. Four parent workshops were conducted at each of five pilot schools to help parents understand the tutoring process and the use of the Parent Report Form, which provides feedback to parents on their children's progress in basic skills. Specific workshop topics included an overview of the Home Study Program, a discussion of the role of family life in child development, methods of working with children at home, and an introduction to school curriculum. Parents evaluate the workshops and are pre- and post-tested on their knowledge of home study objectives and methodologies. Similarly, High (1981) organized the Home Curriculum Program for 15 middle school students and their parents. The project served a predominantly Black, economically disadvantaged population that also includes Hispanic and Arab-American children. Parents receive services both at school and at home. The Home Curriculum Team receives feedback from parents about particular skills and issues that need to be addressed in workshops. These workshops provide information about such topics as drugs, single parents, the emerging adolescent, parent skills, and the establishment of home learning centers. Under the supervision of a school paraprofessional, parent activity rooms are provided for workshops, individual conferences, and work periods for parents with their children.

A number of programs have encouraged Hispanic families to participate as tutors and workshop attendees. These parents have also been encouraged to serve as volunteers. Arturo (1980) conducted a "Parents Can Be Tutors" Program in Miami, Florida. The families who participated were Hispanic and Haitian-American families whose children (elementary and junior high) had demonstrated difficulty in basic skills acquisition. The program was designed to emphasize the tutoring role of parents in helping their children master minimal basic skills (as defined by the State of Florida) in grades 3, 5, and 8. Parents came to school with their children two nights each week to learn test requirements and how to tutor their children for the test. The Child–Parent Centers project designed to reach educationally deprived students in a large urban school system, including a significant number of minority and bilingual families, provides a highly individual instructional program for preschool children and an at-home program for parents working with them (Kellberg, 1981). Parents are also encouraged to volunteer in the classroom. Auxiliary services including remedial help, speech therapy, and developmental social services are provided. At each center, a parent-resource teacher works with teachers and parents, conducting parenting skills classes, conferences, and sessions to create materials.

Utilizing a workshop format, 10 Hispanic parents of handicapped children were introduced, according to Rodriguez (1985), to techniques in behavior management. The parents (8 females and 2 males, ranging in age from 20 to 45 years) were identified as members of a minority group and as having children in a special education program in the local public schools. Conducted in a lower- to middle-SES area in the southwestern United States, the training program used three cassettes (filmstrips) sequentially presenting the concepts of behavior management. Parents were encouraged to speak and become actively involved in discussions, activities, and practical experiences. Activities and discussions wee conducted in English and/or Spanish to allow parents to communicate in the language most comfortable to them. Parents were individually administered a pre- and a post-test and were given a Parent Feedback Form during the last day of the workshop. Pre- and post-test data revealed that the training program was successful in teaching basic behavior management principles to parents. The feedback form garnered positive comments regarding the workshop as to time, subject, material, and presentations.

CONCLUSIONS

The approaches and strategies highlighted in this chapter demonstrate that when minority parents receive assistance from the school system, they become more involved in their children's educational achievement. The approaches that have tended to be most successful have been programs that involved parents directly in tasks that needed to be done rather than informing them about the tasks. Some examples are programs to help parents help their children in reading and programs to help minority parents support their children's language development. Projects that have definite promise and should be strongly considered as a future trend are those aimed at bridging the gap between home and school, and those involving parents as tutors and workshop attendees. A number of attempts have been made to increase minority parents' participation in special programs, but many of them have not achieved a great deal of success. For example, Champagne and Goldman's (1970) training in the use of positive reinforcement and Prentice's (1966) program for the vocational rehabilitation of mentally handicapped adolescents and young adults were unsuccessful in involving minority parents. Perhaps these efforts failed because of the parents' unwillingness to accept the initial reality of the situation and subsequent circumstances. However, the failure of some programs to involve minority parents should not indicate to school districts that they should curtail their efforts to involve minority parents.

Although there has been a proliferation of attempts to introduce Black and Hispanic families into parent involvement efforts, very few efforts have been made to involve Native Americans/Alaska Natives and even fewer have been made to involve Asians/Pacific Islanders. This trend appears to be consistent with the way public schools view the different minority groups. There is a tendency for schools to have low expectations for Blacks and Hispanics, and to view Native Americans/Alaska Natives in a similar fashion. The fact that Asian/Pacific Islander children are considered to have no real problems with school could account for the low number of attempts to involve their parents. However, we know that Asian/Pacific Islander parents and children could profit immensely from such programmatic efforts.

Schools cannot afford to exclude minority parents as an educational resource. Reaching the family (and especially minority families) is as important as reaching the child (Rich et al., 1979, p. 37). "To touch the child is to touch the parent. To praise the child is to praise the parent. To criticize the child is to hit at the parent. The two are two, but the two are one" (Hymes, 1974, p. 9). Consequently, there is a need to know more about what types or aspects of knowledge are crucial in meeting minority goals. Berger (1987) argued that "the aim for families and schools is not perfection, but adjustment to each other in a close, productive working unit" (p. 3). Kroth (1975, p. 10) made a strong case for parent–child school interaction when he said

> Communicating with parents, particularly minority group parents, requires efforts in searching for ways in which to convey information. Efforts for involving minority group parents should be based on a series of attempts until the right one works. It requires an openness on the part of the teacher to accept the parent, not as a combatant in the battlefield, but rather a useful and reliable resource.

Minority parents can make (and in many instances have made) valuable contributions to home/school partnership, but Rodriguez (1981) warned that there is still a great deal of work to be done in the area of minority group parent involvement. The challenge finally, is to assure each child a rewarding future, which is, of course, the purpose of education.

REFERENCES

Almeida, C. H. (1976). *East Harlem pre-kindergarten center, school year 1975–1976.* Brooklyn, NY: New York City Board of Education, Office of Educational Evaluation. (ERIC Document Reproduction Service No. ED 142 628)

Amodeo, L. B., Gallegos, A. G., & Flores, J. L. (1982, October/November). *Parental involvement in the identification of gifted Mexican-Americans.* Paper presented at the Council for Exceptional Children National Conference for the Exceptional Bilingual Child, Phoenix, Arizona. (ERIC Document Reproduction Service No. ED 228 819)

Annual report of the Texas migrant education program ESEA Title I 1977–1978. (December, 1978). Texas Education Agency, Austin Division of Education. (ERIC Document Reproduction Service No. ED 171 452)

Arturo, R. (1980). Parents Can Be Tutors Program. In D. Safran & O. Moles (Eds.), *Home–school alliances: Approaches to increasing parent involvement in children's learning in upper elementary and junior high schools (grades 4–9)* (pp. 5–6). Washington, DC: National Institute of Education.

Berger, E. H. (1987). *Parents as partners in education: The school and home working together.* Columbus, OH: Merrill.

Betancourt, M. E. (1980). Bilingual Training Institute for Parents. In D. Safran & O. Moles (Eds.), *Home–school alliances: Approaches to increasing parent involvement in children's learning in upper elementary and junior high school (grades 4–9)* (p. 6). Washington, DC: National Institute of Education.

Brady, E. H. (1977). Home–school relations and continuity. *Theory Into Practice, 16,* 41–46.

Brandt, R. S. (1986). On improving achievement of minority children: A conversation with James Comer. *Educational Leadership, 43,* 13–17.

Bronfenbrenner, U. (1974). *A report on longitudinal evaluationls of preschool programs.* (Report No. [OHD] 76-30025). Washington, DC: Department of Health, Education, and Welfare.

Brower, L. (1981). Leflore County, Mississippi Follow Through Parent Involvement Program. In N. Cruz, Jr., N. J. Holland, & M. Garlington (Eds.), *A catalog of parent involvement projects — A collection of quality parent projects for assisting children in the achievement of basic skills* (p. 15). Rosslyn, VA: Inter-America Research Associates.

Burks, G. P. (1981). Project help. In N. Cruz, Jr., N. J. Holland, & M. Garlington (Eds.), *A catalog of parent involvement projects — A collection of quality parent projects for assisting children in the achievement of basic skills* (p. 35). Rosslyn, VA: Inter-American Research Associates.

Champagne, D. W., & Goldman, R. M. (1970, November). *Development of a training program to increase the use of reinforcement in informal teaching by mothers of educationally disadvantaged children.* Paper presented at the Annual Meeting of the American Anthropological Association, San Diego, CA.

Chase, R. F. (Chair). (1987). *Report of the Asian and Pacific Islander Concerns Study Committee.* Washington, DC: National Education Association.

Clark, R. M. (1983). *Family life and school achievement: Why poor Black children succeed or fail.* Chicago: University of Chicago Press.

Clay, S. (1967). *The utilization of non-professional interviewers in the New England and Mississippi samples by the Boston University Head Start evaluation and research program, 1966–1967, Report E-I.* Boston: Boston University. Sponsoring agency: Office of Economic Opportunity, Washington, DC

(ERIC Document Reproduction Service No. ED 022 566)

Clegg, B. E. (1973, March). *The effectiveness of learning games used by economically disadvantaged parents to increase the reading achievement of their children.* Paper presented at the annual meeting of the American Education Research Association, San Francisco.

Collazo-Levy, D., & Villegas, J. (1984). *Project parents: Awareness, education, and involvement.* OEE evaluation report, 1982–1983. Brooklyn: New York City Board of Education, Office of Educational Evaluation. (ERIC Document Reproduction Service No. ED 246 174)

Croft, D. J. (1979). *Parents and teachers: A resource book for home, school and community relations.* Belmont, CA: Wadsworth.

Crosset, R. J., Jr. (1972). *The extent and effect of parents' participating in their children's beginning reading program: An inner-city project.* Doctoral dissertation, University of Cincinnati. (ERIC Document Reproduction Service No. ED 076 946)

Edwards, P. A. (1987). Working with families from diverse backgrounds. In D. S. Strickland & E. J. Cooper (Eds.), *Educating Black children: America's challenge* (pp. 92–104). Washington, DC: Howard University, Bureau of Educational Research, School of Education.

Edwards, P. A. (1989). Supporting lower SES mothers' attempts to provide scaffolding for bookreading. In J. Allen & J. Mason (Eds.), *Risk makers, risk takers, risk breakers: Reducing the risks for young literacy learners* (pp. 222–250). Portsmouth, NH: Heinemann.

Edwards, P. A., & Panofsky, C. (1988, December). *The effect of two training procedures on bookreading interactions of lower SES Headstart mothers and children.* Paper presented at the 38th Annual Meeting of the National Reading Conference, Tucson.

Edwards, P. A., with Weems, N. C. (1988, December), *Lower SES mothers' learning of book reading strategies.* Paper presented at the 38th Annual Meeting of the National Reading Conference, Tucson.

Epps, E. G. (1983). Foreword. In R. M. Clark (Ed.), *Family life and school achievement: Why poor Black children succeed or fail* (p. ix–xiii). Chicago: University of Chicago Press.

Epstein, J. L. (1982). *Student reactions to teacher practices of parent involvement.* Paper presented at the annual meeting of the American Educational Research Association, New York City.

Epstein, J. L. (1986). Parents' reactions to teacher practices of parent involvement. *Elementary School Journal, 86,* 27–94.

Evans, D. (1971). *An instructional program to enhance parent-pupil school interactions.* Arlington, VA. (ERIC Document Reproduction Service No. ED 048 342)

Forte, E. J., & Lee, W. (1981). Parent Partnership Program/Parent Participation for Basic Skills Improvement Project. In N. Cruz, Jr., N. J. Holland, & M. Garlington (Eds.), *A catalog for parent involvement projects — A collection of quality parent projects for assisting children in the achievement of basic skills* (p. 18). Rosslyn, VA: Inter-American Research Associates.

France, M. G., & Meeks, J. W. (1987). Parents who can't read: What the schools can do. *Journal of Reading, 31,* 222–227.

Gallegos, A. Y., & Flores, J. (1982, June). *The role of the family in the identification and education of gifted minority children.* Paper presented at the Gifted Minorities Conference, Tucson. (ERIC Document Reproduction Service No. ED 232 360)

Gonzalez, B. (1986). Schools and the language minority parents: An optimum solution. *Catalyst for Change, 16,* 14–17.

Gordon, I. J. (1977). Parent education and parent involvement: Retrospect and prospect. *Childhood Education, 54,* 71–79.

Gordon, I. J. (1979a). The effects of parent involvement on schooling. In R. S. Brandt (Ed.), *Partners: Parents and schools* (pp. 4–25). Alexandria, VA: Association for Supervision and Curriculum Development.

Gordon, I. J. (1979b). Parent education: A position paper. In W. G. Hill, P. Fox, & C. D. Jones (Eds.), *Families and schools: Implementing parent education* (Report No. 121) (pp. 1–5). Denver, CO: Education Commission of the States.

Grimmet, S. A., & McCoy, M. (1980). Effects of parental communication on reading performance of third grade children. *The Reading Teacher, 34,* 303–308.

Gunther, P. E. (1976). *Basic skills after-school prekindergarten program, 1975–1976.* Brooklyn, NY: New York City Board of Education, Office of Educational Evaluation. (ERIC Document Reproduction Service No. ED 141 476)

Haley, F. M. (1981). Home Study Program (Parent/Student Partnership in Learning Programs). In N. Cruz, Jr., N. J. Holland, & M. Garlington (Eds.), *A catalog of parent involvement projects — A collection of quality parent projects for assisting children in the achievement of basic skills* (p. 13). Rosslyn, VA: Inter-America Research Associates.

Henderson, A., Marburger, C. L., & Ooms, T. (1986). *Beyond the bake sale: An educator's guide to working with parents.* Columbia, MD: National Committee for Citizens in Education.

High, V. (1981). Home Curriculum Program. In N. Cruz, Jr., N. J. Holland, & M. Garlington (Eds.), *A catalog of parent involvement projects — A collection of quality parent projects for assisting children in the achievement of basic skills* (p. 12). Rosslyn, VA: Inter-America Research Associates.

Hobson, P. J. (1979). The partnership with Title I parents. In R. S. Brandt (Ed.), *Partners: Parents and schools* (pp. 41–45). Alexandria, VA: Association for Supervision and Curriculum Development.

Hughes, J. M. (1979). A commitment to parent education. In W. G. Hill, P. Fox, & C. D. Jones (Eds.), *Families and schools: Implementing parent education* (Report No. 121) (pp. 6–9). Denver: Education Commission of the States.

Hymes, J. (1974). *Effective home-school relations.* Sierra Madre, CA: Southern California Association for the Education of Young Children.

Inocencio, E. B. (1987, March 10). Testimony and comments of the Asian American National Network of Information and Employment, presented to the NEA Special Study Committee on Asian and Pacific Islander Concerns, Washington, DC. In R. F. Chase (Chair), *Report of the Asian and Pacific Islander Concerns Study Committee* (p. 9). Washington, DC: National Education Association.

Joe, G. K. (1987, March 17). Testimony and comments of the Council of Asian and American Organizations, presented to the NEA Special Study Committee on Asian and Pacific Islander Concerns, Houston, TX. In R. F. Chase (Chair), *Report of the Asian and Pacific Islander Concerns Study Committee* (p. 9). Washington, DC: National Education Association.

Kellberg, D. (1981). Child-Parent Centers. In N. Cruz, Jr., N. J. Holland, & M. Garlington (Eds.), *A catalog of parent involvement projects — A collection of quality parent projects for assisting children in the achievement of basic skills* (p. 7). Rosslyn, VA: Inter-America Research Associates.

Kroth, R. L. (1975). *Communicating with parents of exceptional children.* Denver: Love Publishing.

Laosa, L. M. (1985). *Indices of the success of Head Start: A critique.* Paper presented at the conference "Research Directions for Minority Scholars Involved With Head Start Programs," at Howard University, Washington, DC, sponsored by the U.S. Administration for Children, Youth, and Families.

LeGrand, K. R. (1981). Perspective on minority education: An interview with anthropologist John Ogbu. *Journal of Reading, 24,* 680–686.

Lengyel, J. & Baghban, M. (1980). *The effects of a family reading program and SSR on reading achievement and attitudes.* (ERIC Document Reproduction Service No. ED 211 925)

Libarios, E., & Libarios, S. (1979). Project R.I.S.E. and community education. *Educational Perspectives, 18,* 38–42.

Mack, P. (Chair, Report of the Black Concerns Study Committee). (1987). Washington, DC: National Education Association.

Malone, F. M. (1977). The future leaders programs in Washington, DC. *Social Education, 41,* 656–658.

McConnell, B. (1976). *Bilingual mini-school tutoring project. A state of Washington URRD (Urban, Rural, Racial, Disadvantaged) Program. Final Evaluation, 1975-76 Program Year.* Olympia, WA: Washington Office of the State Superintendent of Public Instruction. (ERIC Document Reproduction Service No. 135 508)

McLaughlin, M. W., & Shields, P. M. (1987). Involving low-income parents in the schools: A role for policy? *Phi Delta Kappan, 69,* 156–160.

Meyers, E. O. (1974). Doing your own think: Transmission of cognitive skills to inner city children. *American Journal of Orthopsychiatry, 44,* 596–603.

National Commission on Excellence in Education (1983). *A Nation at Risk: The Imperative For Educational Reform.* Washington, DC: U.S. Department of Education.

Neisser, U. (1986). New answers to an old question. In U. Neisser (Ed.), *The school achievement of minority children: New perspectives* (pp. 1–17). Hillsdale, NJ: Erlbaum.

Powell, D. R. (1979). Organizational problems in institutionalizing parent education in the public schools. In W. G. Hill, P. Fox, & C. D. Jones (Eds.), *Families and schools: Implementing parent education* (Report No. 121) (pp. 14–18). Denver, CO: Education Commission of the States.

Prentice, G. R. (1966). *Increasing parental contribution to work adjustment for the retarded.* Final Report. Milwaukee, WI: United Association for Retarded Children. (ERIC Document Reproduction Service No. ED 015 559)

Raim, J. (1980). Who learns when parents teach their children? *The Reading Teacher, 34,* 152–155.

Rich, D., Van Dien, J., & Mattox, B. (1979). Families as educators of their own children. In R. S. Brandt (Ed.), *Partners: Parents and schools* (pp. 26–40). Alexandria, VA: Association for Supervision and Curriculum Development.

Roberts, F. (1979). Education for parenthood: Alternative strategies for the public schools. In W. G. Hill, P. Fox, & C. D. Jones (Eds.), *Families and schools: Implementing parent education* (Report No. 121) (pp. 10–13). Denver, CO: Education Commission of the States.

Rodriguez, R. F. (1981). The involvement of minority group parents in school. *Teacher Education and Special Education, 4,* 40–44.

Rodriguez, R. F. (1985). *A behavior management training model for parents of minority group handicapped children.* (ERIC Document Reproduction Service No. ED 254 390)

Schleife, R. (Chair). *Report of the American Indian/ Alaska Native Concerns* (1987). Washington, DC: National Education Association.

Shelton, J. (1973). *An analysis of a family involvement communication system in a Title I elementary school: Final report.* Arlington, VA. (ERIC Document Reproduction Service No. ED 082 091)

Shuck, A., Ulsh, F., & Platt, J. S. (1983). Parents Encourage Pupils (PEP): An inner-city parent involvement reading project. *The Reading Teacher, 36,* 524–529.

Simons, S. (1981). Acoma Partners in Basics. In N. Cruz, Jr., N. J. Holland, & M. Garlington (Ed.), *A catalog of parent involvement projects — A collection of quality parent projects for assisting children in the achievement for basic skills* (p. 4). Rosslyn, VA: Inter-America Research Associates.

Spewock, T. S. (1988). Training parents to teach their preschoolers through literature. *The Reading Teacher, 41,* 648–652.

Swift, M. S. (1970). Training poverty mothers in communication skills. *The Reading Teacher, 23,* 360–367.

Tarwater, S. (1981). Home-Based Early Childhood Program. In N. Cruz, Jr., N. J. Holland, & M. Garlington (Eds.), *A catalog of parent involvement projects — A collection of parent involvement projects for assisting children in the achievement of basic skills* (p. 42). Rosslyn, VA: Inter-America Research Associates.

Thomas, K. M. (1985). Parent involvement and Springfield's Chestnut Street Junior High School. *Equity and Choice, 1,* 44–46.

Torres, J. A., Young, J., Goodall, K., Scorza, M. A., & Inman, D. L. (1983). *Seward Park High School. Washington Irving High School. Chinese bilingual education program, 1981–1982* (OEE Evaluation Report). Brooklyn, NJ: New York City Board of Education Office of Educational Evaluation. (ERIC Document Reproduction Service No. ED 234 130)

Tso, J. C. (1987, March 9). Testimony and comments of the organization of Chinese Americans, Inc., presented to the NEA Special Study Committee on Asian and Pacific Islander Concerns, Washington, DC. In R. F. Chase (Chair), *Report of the Asian and Pacific Islander Concerns Study Committee* (p. 9). Washington, DC: National Education Association.

U.S. Department of Education (1986). *What works: Research about teaching and learning*. Washington, DC: U.S. Department of Education.

Vanden Dries, A. (1982). *Indian education comprehensive program. End of year report, fiscal year 1982*. Las Vegas, NV: Clark County School District. (ERIC Document Reproduction Service No. ED 226 922)

Wenn, M. (1981). Tulare Follow Through. In N. Cruz, Jr., N. J. Holland, & M. Garlington (Eds.), *A catalog of parent involvement projects — A collection of quality parent projects for assisting children in the achievement of basic skills* (p. 25). Rosslyn, VA: Inter-America Research Associates.

White, B. L. (1975). *The first three years of life*. Englewood Cliffs, NJ: Prentice-Hall.

Wilson, J. (Chair). *Report of the Hispanic Concerns Study Committee* (1987). Washington, DC: National Education Association.

Ziegler, E. (1979). Introduction. In W. G. Hill, P. Fox, & C. D. Jones (Eds.), *Families and schools: Implementing parent education* (Report No. 121) (pp. ix–xiii). Denver, CO: Education Commission of the States.

CHAPTER 14

Insuring Equity in Education: Preparing School Personnel for Culturally and Linguistically Divergent At-Risk Handicapped Students

Sandra H. Fradd,
M. Jeanne Weismantel,
Vivian I. Correa
University of Florida
Bob Algozzine
University of North Carolina, Charlotte

Students in schools across the nation are at risk of educational, social, and eventually economic failure. The short-term impact of the failure of this growing group of students affects the teachers and other students, as well as the citizens and the local community. The long-term impact is on the nation, its social and economic systems, its government, and democratic way of life. While the proportion of population at risk has grown rapidly over the past decades, school personnel have not been prepared to effectively address the needs of these students. Our views in regard to the specific group of at-risk students who are linguistically and culturally different, and who are handicapped or appear handicapped because of their prior experiences, suggests analysis by topics: (a) description of a target population and the factors that increase the risk of educational failure for these students; (b) a review of programs designed to meet these students' needs, both as to provision of services and preparation of personnel; (c) evaluation of one specific program of personnel preparation; (d) discussion of factors beyond programmatic concerns that must be considered in organizing school systems to meet the needs of these at-risk students.

IDENTIFYING THE TARGET POPULATIONS AND THE FACTORS THAT INCREASE THE RISK OF EDUCATIONAL FAILURE

During the decade of the 1980s, educators and personnel who determine educational policy at the state and national levels have initiated legislation and policy changes aimed at reforming and restructuring schools. Generally, school reform has focused on raising achievement standards (Hodgkinson, 1988). The push to compete in an information-based economy driven by an expanding system of electronic technology has heightened the need for a highly educated work force. This push has shifted the instructional emphasis of many school systems toward academic outcomes that can be measured by standardized tests (Howe, 1983; Yeakey, 1982). At the same time, there has been a corresponding lessening of interest in long-range social results that characterized the previous decades, an era when previously disenfranchised populations began to enter educational systems across the nation (Clark, Astuto, & Rooney, 1983). During the 1960s and early 1970s, the disadvantaged, the racial, linguistic, and ethnic minorities, and the physically and intellectually impaired students began to exercise their political rights in obtaining access to the mainstream.

The economic situation today presents a strong contrast to the period of relative national prosperity when resources were available for new social programs (Fradd, 1987). The 1980s has been a period of economic restructuring, a time punctuated by periods of both high and low inflation, unemployment, and financial regrouping in real estate, banking, manufacturing, and agriculture. Financial restructuring has resulted in reductions in the funds available for many programs that require specialized services. At the same time the numbers of students requiring these services have been increasing (Moran, 1984).

Population Variables

Educationally disadvantaged at-risk students are those who are most likely to achieve only minimal success in school systems as the systems are currently organized. These students come from socioeconomic, cultural, and linguistic backgrounds that are different from those of the mainstream population (Levin, 1985).

People in the mainstream, dominant culture are, for the most part, white, non-Hispanic, and middle-class. In respect to educational attainment, most mainstream adults have completed high school and some level of college training. Their income covers basic needs and allows some spending options. Family housing provides space for privacy and study (Levin, 1985). Because this group predominates, most people from this group understand the established and implied rules for successful achievement and participation in the social and economic systems. They also know how to access and utilize community resources and networks that increase possibilities for success.

In contrast, educationally disadvantaged students come, more often, from families with limited income and little formal education. Frequently students from this group do not have access to the home and community resources that encourage educational success. A large portion of the families of these students are immigrants. Many of these families, approximately 17%

of the total student population, are of non-English-language backgrounds (NELB) (Waggoner, 1984). While not all NELB students encounter major difficulties in achieving academic success, many do. Disadvantaged, at-risk students tend to have lower test scores than their peers and frequently drop out before completing high school (Levin, 1985). Low achievers and students who drop out of school generally fail to contribute to the economic growth of the nation. When unsuccessful students represented only a small percentage of the total student population, the long-term effects were felt mainly by individuals and their immediate families. As the numbers increase, the impact is felt across the nation.

In the 1980s, schools are enrolling increasing proportions of students living in poverty. The number and percentage of children below the poverty level increased from 1970 to 1986 (U.S. Department of Commerce, 1988). The educationally disadvantaged student population is increasing at a far more rapid rate than that of the mainstream population. Between one-third and one-half of the school population in many states is educationally disadvantaged and at risk of educational failure (Hodgkinson, 1988). Between 1976 and 1984, the numbers of white and Black students declined, while the number of culturally and linguistically diverse student populations increased. For example, the number of school-age Asian students increased by more than 85% and the number of Hispanic students by 28% (Chandler & Stein, 1987). The major factors in the substantial increase of certain groups are sustained high birth rates and high levels of immigration. The number of students who are of limited English proficiency (LEP) is not known because there is no uniform measure for determining English proficiency or reporting the data (Fradd, 1987; U.S. General Accounting Office, 1987). Estimates of the numbers of LEP students run as high as 5 million, or approximately one-eighth of the school population (Plisko, 1984).

Another growing group of students who have received little attention, but who also contribute to the population of students at risk, are those who are mildly handicapped. An estimated 10% of the total school-age population receives special education services. The number of students identified as learning-disabled has nearly doubled during the period from 1977 to 1981 (U.S. General Accounting Office, 1981). Approximately 80% of incarcerated young persons are illiterate (Hodgkinson, 1988). It is suspected that many of these people are mildly handicapped and NELB.

School Factors

School systems continue to reflect the perceptions and interests of the mainstream population. To date the effects of reform have been most clearly observed in efforts to increase academic attainment, by such means as implementing competency standards for promotion and graduation, lengthening the school day, and increasing the reading level of standard course texts. Efforts have also been directed at increasing the level of faculty competence through a number of means, such as general teacher tests, subject-specific certification examinations, lengthening of preservice training programs from 4 years to 5 years, and increasing the number of in-service training programs (Carnegie Foundation for the Advancement of Teaching, 1988).

For students who are not academically successful, raising educational demands can have the effect of increasing dropout rates. Unless students perceive that educational endeavors have a significant reward for them, unless they feel themselves to be a part of the educational system, and unless they find instructional personnel who make the educational process meaningful, educational reform will have a negative economic impact. If efforts at educational reform are to have a substantial long-term impact on the capacity of the nation to sustain and increase economic growth, reform must address the needs of all students. At a national level, some efforts have been made to call attention to the needs of the educationally disadvantaged, students who are at risk of educational failure (National Coalition of Advocates for Students, 1985; 1988). To date, these efforts have made little impact in terms of policy change or program implementation. Re-

cently state and national policy makers have initiated research activities to study the issues.

At the state and district levels there are several reasons why education reforms have failed to address the learning needs of linguistically and culturally different students. These reasons are somewhat tautological and include (a) the reality that these difficulties have not been well understood or conceptualized by policy makers and those at the forefront of the reform movement; (b) the fact that trained personnel and appropriate programs have not been available; and (c) the fact that training has not been widely available to assist personnel in conceptualizing issues and preparing them to meet students' needs. Policy makers and educators alike have persisted in pedagogical debates such as the need for bilingual education versus teaching English to speakers of other languages (ESOL) instead of defining students' needs and developing appropriate responses (Braden & Fradd, 1987; Fernandez-Zayas, 1988).

In earlier times, employment requiring primarily manual labor was a ready alternative to the completion of high school (Fernandez-Zayas, 1988), but in an increasingly technological society, positions requiring manual labor have decreased substantially. School personnel face a large group of students who differ in some way from the mainstream population in the 1980s. Without successful interventions, there will be damaging long-term social and economic consequences for the nation, including increased costs for social services, welfare, and medical assistance, increased delinquency and crime, and the growth of a large underclass that cannot sustain itself or contribute to national economic productivity.

Educational Responsibilities

Before school districts can begin to address the needs of handicapped, culturally and linguistically divergent students, or provide appropriate special education services for these students, the needs of the larger group of students who can effectively participate in regular educational programs must be satisfied. During the 1960s and 1970s, legal issues of *compliance* in enrolling students were at the forefront of educational concerns. During the 1980s the focus has shifted from compliance to *achievement*. The courts have held the expectation that all students should have instruction that is meaningful and appropriate to their needs. A three-pronged test of educational appropriateness for LEP students has been established by courts at the federal district level (Fradd & Vega, 1987); it defines the following indicators of educational appropriateness: instructional programs that (a) reflect sound pedagogy and research-based theory; (b) are well implemented and contain sufficient resources, trained personnel, and facilities to insure success; and (c) include procedures for monitoring student progress and achievement, and ensure success.

Assessment. In spite of the requirement that in order to receive federal support all states must give assurances that students are being assessed in their native language or mode of communication, few training programs provide personnel with bilingual assessment skills (Salend & Fradd, 1985; 1986). If personnel are not prepared to provide native-language assessment in languages other than English, how is it possible that states that have been flooded with linguistically and culturally different students have been able to provide assurances of native-language assessment? Evaluations of state statistics reveal both overrepresentation and underrepresentation of culturally and linguistically divergent students within specific categories of special education (Heller, Holtzman, & Messick, 1982; Ortiz, 1984) and in the percentage of LEP students receiving special education services in general (Fradd, Weismantel, Correa, & Algozzine, 1988). Determining the educational needs of LEP students who are experiencing problems can be difficult. Whether the problems are those encountered in the process of acquiring proficiency in English or are additional difficulties experienced by students with learning handicaps, the issues related to assessment and instruction are complex. Assessing students' learning and

behavioral problems fairly, and providing appropriate instruction when the languages the students use are different from the language of examiners or teachers requires that a number of trained persons become involved in the assessment and instruction process.

Instruction. To provide appropriate educational programs, it is also necessary to understand the impact of culture, the development of language, and the relationship between language and cognition. Culturally knowledgeable and sensitive personnel can, for example, develop strategies for determining whether erratic behavior is due to behavior disorders or to adjustment in new living conditions (Castaneda, Herald, & Ramirez, 1974). Instructional personnel can develop skill in providing meaningful communication and in monitoring students' progress, whether the students are handicapped or limited in English proficiency, or both.

Curriculum and program development. Improving the assessment and instruction process to include the use of the native language and information about the culture of the students is not enough. Placing immigrant students in special education has been called "in-school deportation" and regarded as the means by which regular programs rid themselves of students who do not conform (National Coalition of Advocates for Students, 1988). Unless the resources of regular and special education programs and services are harnessed into a concerted effort at conceptualizing and implementing appropriate programs, the fragmentation that currently is observed in many school districts will continue to grow into the 1990s and on into the twenty-first century.

Few research-based, pedagogically sound programs for handicapped LEP and NELB students currently exist. Few programs with fully trained personnel, appropriate curricula, and adequate resources and facilities have been implemented. Little attention has been directed to the consequences of placing LEP and NELB students in either mainstreamed or special education programs (Martinez, 1987). If school systems are serious about meeting the needs of all students, not just those who are capable of high academic achievement, strategies for training personnel and providing adequate resources and services must be given high priority.

PROGRAM MODELS

Because school systems have encountered difficulties in locating and funding the trained personnel to implement effective instructional programs for handicapped LEP students, a variety of service and instruction models have evolved (Ortiz, 1984). Each of these models has its particular set of strengths and weaknesses.

The Bilingual Support Model

In the bilingual support model, bilingual paraprofessionals work with monolingual special education teachers to provide instruction. Special education personnel depend on the assistance of the bilingual paraprofessionals to communicate effectively with students whose primary expressive language is not English. Paraprofessionals are also able to assist instructional and support personnel in communicating with parents and the ethnic community although these paraprofessionals are a valuable asset, their presence can introduce an unsettling element into the instructional process. Personnel who have not been trained in the use of interpreters and cultural informants often feel threatened by the presence of these people or the use of non-English languages in the school. Furthermore, paraprofessionals sometimes express the notion that they are not really a part of the instructional process or that their efforts are misunderstood and unappreciated (Ortiz, 1984).

The Coordinated Services Model

In the coordinated services model, a team composed of special education and bilingual education personnel work together to develop and implement programs for handicapped LEP students. Strong coordination efforts are also required from the administration, as well as instructional and support personnel, such as guidance

counselors, speech and language specialists, and the school psychologist. Since at least two teachers with specialized training are required to implement this model, it is often not as cost-effective as other models. Additional problems include the fact that few personnel trained in one field are aware of the skills and resources, or the pedagogical orientation, of team colleagues trained in other fields. As a result, both sets of professionals often feel threatened and intimidated (Baca & Cervantes, 1982; Hudson & Fradd, 1987). Training in the process of conceptualizing and coordinating programs is required for these teams to be successful.

The Integrated Bilingual Special Education Model

The integrated bilingual special education model is based on the development of a group of personnel who not only are trained in special education, but are also bilingual in the languages of the students and the school. When available, such personnel can provide a linguistic and cultural bridge between the classroom and the home, and between the special education program and regular education. This model works most effectively if there is only one language other than English used by the students. The major difference between this model and the standard special education program is that personnel speak the languages of their students and understand their culture; but special education personnel who are bilingual still require specialized training in assessment, language development, and crosscultural communication as well as many other sills needed to implement successful programs (Baca, 1984).

Obstacles to Successful Implementation of Current Models

In the implementation of any of these three models major difficulties arise in developing effective programs for LEP and NELB handicapped and at-risk students. These difficulties center around the lack of integrating pedagogically sound programs, the scarcity of materials and resources, and the need for collaboration and interaction between specialized and regular programs.

Lack of appropriate curricula. There is no curriculum designed specifically for students who are both handicapped and LEP. Commercial enterprises have been reluctant to initiate materials development in this area because of the limited number of students who would be consumers of their products and the number of languages in which materials might be required. In large school districts, as many as 15–18 languages are found in a single classroom. As a result of this linguistic diversity, instructional personnel must develop their own curricula and adapt materials and instructional frameworks from sources designed for regular and special education for monolingual students. Little time, facilities, or resources are allocated to the process of curriculum development. Much of the curriculum development and materials adaptations is done on the instructors' own time, after school. Community volunteers may be the only source of assistance for handicapped students from infrequently spoken languages.

Lack of integration and support. Instructional and paraprofessional personnel employed in specialized programs are frequently not perceived as an integral part of the total school effort. Their services are often rendered in the auditorium, at the back of the cafeteria, under the stairs, and in small storage closets. They are not seen and do not see themselves, as contributing substantially to the benefit of the school. If the students they teach misbehave in other settings, these personnel are sometimes made to feel as if, in some way, they are personally responsible. Furthermore, when these personnel have no one in the school with whom they can share the triumphs and difficulties of their students, they may feel marginalized.

As handicapped LEP students acclimate to their educational surrounding, they begin to share their daily concerns with their teachers. Instructional personnel who work with these students and who provide the cultural, linguistic, and educational link between these students and the mainstream are often the only ones in the school or district who understand and can articulate their students' needs at a programmatic level. Frequently the burden for integrating the special service programs with the regular programs is placed primarily on them; they must interface with personnel from a number of different fields in order for their students to receive services and to become a part of the school.

In response to these limitations, a fourth model of specialized services has been developed, a model that empowers the special service personnel and the regular service personnel alike and enables everyone to become responsible for and responsive to the needs of at-risk students.

Developing a Comprehensive Training and Service Delivery Model

There will never be sufficient bilingual personnel to meet the instructional needs of all the at-risk culturally and linguistically different students in school districts across the nation. The debate between bilingual and ESOL education has led educators to realize that the language of instruction, while an important concern, is secondary to the question of providing programs that can lead students to academic success (Fernandez-Zayas, 1988). The issue of meeting the needs of all students must be seen as a school and a school district responsibility, rather than the special concern of a few people within the community or the school. From that perspective, all school personnel must be trained to work with these students and to interact with specialized personnel whose primary responsibility it is to instruct the students. The emphasis is on the development of English language proficiency, along with social and academic skills that enable students to participate effectively in the mainstream. This does not preclude the use of non-English languages in assessment and instruction; it does preclude viewing the personnel who provide non-English language support and instruction as the only ones responsible for instructional outcomes.

Few institutions of higher education are prepared to train personnel to work with at-risk culturally and linguistically different students. Even fewer have been trained to meet the needs of the subset of these students who are handicapped. Therefore, a new personnel preparation model, as well as a comprehensive instruction and support model, must be conceptualized and implemented. This comprehensive training effort must be initiated, funded, and supported at all three levels of government: local, state, and federal.

Federal commitment. At the federal level there have been several tentative efforts at collaboration between the two offices within the U.S. Department of Education that are responsible for conceptualizing and funding programs in the areas of bilingual and special education: the Office of Bilingual Education and Minority Languages Affairs (OBEMLA) and the Office of Special Education and Rehabilitative Services (OSERS). Principally, these collaborative efforts have taken the form of meetings held to set up task forces to identify common goals and resources. Unfortunately, to date little substantive, long-term gain has resulted from these meetings. The task forces were short-lived (Baca & Cervantes, 1984).

Of a more practical nature, both OBEMLA and OSERS, having identified personnel preparation for meeting the needs of linguistically and culturally different at-risk and handicapped students as a major need, have funded a number of personnel preparation programs through both offices. However, in some cases there have been overlaps between the two funding sources; in other cases gaps remain. Neither office has developed a comprehensive plan for funding the programs needed for personnel working with handicaped LEP and NLB students.

State involvement. Several states have begun to develop broad personnel competencies and comprehensive training that interrelate bilingual/ESOL and special education. Other states have identified the need for such training, but have not yet set into place the mechanisms that insure that educational personnel will have such training. Some states have effective personnel preparation programs, but have not yet implemented the requirement that all preservice participants receive the training.

One state requires that all personnel seeking certification in ESOL take at least one course in special education (Fradd, Gard, & Weismantel, 1988).

Local efforts. The primary responsibility for implementing effective educational programs falls on local educational agencies (LEAs). Personnel working in bilingual, special education, and bilingual special education programs have identified a number of competencies as essential in meeting the needs of LEP at-risk and handicapped students (Fradd, Algozzine, & Salend, 1988). Some of the most highly ranked instructional skills are the following abilities: (a) to effectively develop students' English language proficiency; (b) to adapt materials and resources appropriate to students' needs; (c) to assess students, develop appropriate instructional interventions, and monitor students' progress; (d) to effectively communicate with culturally and linguistically different families; and (e) to serve as a resource to other school personnel in meeting the needs of at-risk and handicapped students.

From this list it can be seen that personnel must be genuinely interested in ensuring that culturally and linguistically different students do develop effective interpersonal and academic language skills in English, that the needs of these students are assessed and met through the development of appropriate curricula and materials, and that through effective communication and interactions with parents and other school personnel the students are integrated into the school program as a whole.

Responses to Identified
Training Needs

The development of programs that adequately prepare personnel to meet the needs of culturally and linguistically different at-risk and handicapped students is a major task that requires coordination and cooperation of a number of different elements (Bermudez, Fradd, & Haulman, 1988). A review of existing bilingual and multicultural special education projects found four types of programs: (a) traditional special education programs with bilingual students; (b) traditional special education programs with infused bilingual, multicultural content; (c) training designed to specifically prepare personnel to work in the field of bilingual special education; and (d) integrated training (Baca, 1984; Valero-Figuiera, 1986).

The traditional model with bilingual students. In this model an institution of higher education (IHE) recruits for training in the field of special education majors who are fluent in the target languages of the region it serves. No special accommodation is made for these students; they receive the same training as all the other students. Training institutions have reported that this model graduates the most students, at both the graduate and undergraduate levels (Baca, 1984). Since no specific accommodation is made with regard to specialized topics or information, the expectation is that the students use their own experiences to convey course information in bilingual, multicultural contexts. Teachers so trained, in effect, must add their own instructional component derived from personal experience rather than empirical research. The level of bilingual language proficiency and extent of the multicultural experience of these trainers are not established by all IHEs. While this may be a popular method for training personnel, it may also be the least effective in regard to the specific content and appropriate competencies needed in the field (Baca, 1984).

The traditional special education model with infused bilingual, multicultural content. A second model offers traditional special education coursework with bilingual, multicultural information infused into it. Lectures on topics relevant to meeting the needs of handicapped LEP students are offered for each course. Although this training does not comprehensively address the training needs of personnel working with LEP handicapped students, it does serve the purpose of sensitizing a larger group of students and faculty to the needs of LEP children than does the traditional model. A further advantage, of course, is that both bilingual and monolingual students can participate in the training.

Specifically designed bilingual/ESOL special education training. In this model students participate in training specifically designed to prepare them to address the needs of handicapped linguistically diverse populations. Although this is currently the most prevalent type of training, at the time that the survey was conducted few personnel had been graduated, because this model of specialized training has been recently inaugurated. If this model is to be generally implemented, more qualified personnel must become available to conduct the training than currently exist.

Integrated training. The integrated model requires specialized lectures and the infusion of special content into traditional special education courses. In addition, the personnel teach a course on cultural pluralism that treats issues such as ethnicity, litigation, and legislation that all program participants must take. This model has a three-level structure. On the first level, students take general courses in special education; at the second level, program students take specially adapted sections of established specialized coursework, such as language assessment; at the third level, additional courses have been developed that are specific to the needs of the target students. Throughout the educational process, participants engage in practicums relevant to their interests and the particular needs of linguistically and culturally diverse populations.

This model does contain some problems. Difficulties arise in the infusion process because course syllabi are already full. Information offered during guest lectures is too frequently viewed as peripheral to the instructional focus of the course; consequently, there is a persistent risk that the infusion process will become person-specific, the director being essential for program maintenance. Additionally, there are problems in implementing a relevant training program in locales in which the public schools have a multiplicity of languages, only a few of which are represented in the training.

Difficulties in Implementing Training

The above review of current program models presents some program-specific difficulties. The following review focuses on difficulties germane to most or all of the programs. Initially, there are few skilled personnel specifically qualified to conduct training designed to meet the needs of at-risk handicapped linguistically diverse populations. This lack again is self-perpetuating. The lack of qualified personnel makes program implementation difficult and without effective, qualified trainers, the development of a cadre of personnel at the national, state, and local levels, including IHEs, is nearly impossible.

In order to overcome the lack of qualified personnel, some IHEs have sought to combine the strengths of several persons in the area of bilingual/ESOL and special education. An informal review of training projects reveals that this effort is not always successful either in respect to conceptualizing the needs or organizing the adequate responses. Efforts to develop interdisciplinary curricula can also promote the tendency toward fragmentation and controversy over ownership (Bermudez, Fradd, & Haulman, 1988). Frequently the program requirements for graduation and credentialing in special education preclude students' participation in more than two electives at the master's level. This limitation means that interested students must take additional coursework that is not required of other students, or that special training must be completed in a minimal amount of time. Although all 50 states offer certification in special education, only one currently offers credentialing in the area of bilingual special education (Salend & Fradd, 1985; 1986).

Clearly, not all training needs can be satisfied with a preservice focus; once personnel gain experience in the field, their perceptions of the need and value of additional training changes. Therefore, preservice efforts must be combined with in-service training and credentialing (Fradd, Algozzine, & Salend, 1988).

Lack of appropriate instructional resources is another difficulty in implementing effective programs. There are few appropriate texts or other instructional materials that can be used for specialized course development. Since the demand for these materials is limited, few publishers have been interested in meeting this need commercially.

Little research has been conducted in the field. Not enough is known about the acquisition of English language proficiency by students who are handicapped or about students with only oral language traditions. Since research in the field of bilingual education is currently at the descriptive level, a great deal of investigative effort is still required in order to develop the knowledge base required to train personnel in sound pedagogical practices that meet the needs of at-risk and handicapped linguistically diverse students.

A review of programs seeking to implement such training found that project directors had identified the following needs and priorities (Baca, 1984): (a) institutionalization; (b) recruitment; (c) institutional cooperation and support; (d) cooperation with local educational agencies; (e) curricula development, program planning, and content infusion; (f) in-service training; and (g) research. Although this study was conducted in 1982, informal data collection confirm that the areas listed above continue to be of major concern. The following case study describes a project that combines strengths of the previously discussed training models in an effort to provide comprehensive training opportunities in the state of Florida

INFUSION: A COMPREHENSIVE TRAINING MODEL

In the fall of 1986 the University of Florida received a grant to implement training in bilingual special education, entitled Bilingual/ESOL Special Education INFUSION and Teacher Training, known as INFUSION, for short. Funded by OBEMLA within the U.S. Department of Education, this project has as its major goal the preparation of personnel to meet the needs of handicapped and at-risk LEP students in the state. This goal is being met through the achievement of four specific objectives:

- Recruitment of personnel who are interested in expanding their knowledge and competencies in meeting the needs of at-risk and handicapped LEP students; training is provided through academic year programs and summer institutes.

- Infusion of bilingual, multicultural content into the graduate level core curriculum in special education.

- Development of a network of personnel within the national, state, and local agencies who will work collaboratively to meet the needs of LEP handicapped and at-risk students.

- Development of a personnel preparation model that can be replicated in other IHEs and in other states to meet similar training needs.

In order to achieve these objectives, the faculty and staff of the Department of Special Education have developed a comprehensive model of school personnel training. The development of this model has been facilitated by the foundation laid by two earlier projects, Consortium and BEST Practices.

Consortium and BEST Practices

The first two projects in bilingual/ESOL special education carried out at the University of Florida responded to identified training needs. The state of Florida has the fourth-largest LEP and NELB populations in the nation (Oxford-Carpenter et al., 1984). In 1985 Florida public schools enrolled 161,660 identified NELB students. Of these, 34,326 received English language instruction as LEP students. During the 1985 school year only 3% of the LEP students were reported to receive any type of special education services. Speech and language services accounted for 50% of the services these LEP students were receiving. Only 1.5% of LEP students received any special education services other than speech and language development. This includes services to the severe and profoundly handicapped, physically and sensorally impaired, behavior-disordered, and the mildly handicapped.

Using federal guidelines that indicate that approximately 10–12% of the school-age populations receive special education services, approximately 3,500–4,200 students would have been expected to have been identified, at least seven times the number actually identified. These figures indicate that the LEP population has been underidentified and underserved, and illustrates the need for well-trained, competent personnel who can both assess and instruct these students.

A major reason for the difficulties in identification is that there has been little training available in Florida to provide personnel with the skills necessary to meet this growing need. The shortage of trained personnel has been identified in Florida's Comprehensive System of Personnel Development as being critical since 1983 (Bureau of Education for Exceptional Students, 1983).

Consortium. In 1984 a large Central Florida school district contacted the University of Florida because bilingual school psychologists there had identified more than 50 handicapped LEP students and the district wanted to implement a program that would meet the students' needs. A training proposal was developed and submitted to OSERS, U.S. Department of Education, and funding to carry out a two-year project was received beginning in the fall of 1985. The project has been referred to as "Consortium" because it involved not only the school district making the request, but also two other adjoining districts with similar students. Faculty and consultants traveled to the central Florida training sites to observe participants at work and to provide training and follow-up. A major outcome of this project has been the implementation of a well-conceptualized program that responds to the needs of Hispanic handicapped LEP students (Fradd, Algozzine, Hallman, & Doherty, 1987).

BEST Practices. During the same year, 1985, the University of Florida received a second grant, BEST Practices in Bilingual Special Education, from OBEMLA, U.S. Department of Education. In this project, Florida school districts were invited to nominate personnel who had been observed to be effective in working with handicapped and at-risk LEP students. These applications were reviewed and a cross section of participants were selected to come to the University of Florida once a month from February through May, to share their ideas, and to receive training in meeting the needs of at-risk and handicapped LEP students. This one-year training project culminated with a two-week workshop in the summer of 1986 in which participants presented projects and extended the previous training they had received. A major outcome of this project was articulation between the project personnel and the participants, both at the participants' work sites and during the training at the university. From this experience, the participants realized that they were not working alone, and they developed confidence in their own abilities to provide appropriate services to their students. Project personnel identified important training needs and resources for effectively implementing training (Fradd & Halsall, 1986).

Foundation of the inservice model beginnings. At the completion of these two projects, a consensus was reached that although these projects were successful beginnings, a major training need remained. Personnel, on their own, had intuitively developed appropriate responses to their students' needs. However, these responses were neither comprehensive nor adequate. Personnel needed a theoretical research base from which to make educational decisions, and they needed specific information in such areas as language assessment and development. Important additional needs were identified by the participants and staff. The need to remain connected and collaborative and the need to create a comprehensive approach to addressing the requirements of school personnel working with LEP at-risk students within the state became apparent. Apparent also was the need to integrate this information into an already established framework. The completion of these projects enabled faculty and staff to construct a strong resource base from which to launch a comprehensive training effort within the state. This comprehensive base consisted of three types of resources: people, materials, and curricula. The INFUSION effort had begun long before funding was received in 1986. This foundation is depicted in Figure 1, an ever-expanding network, a fishing cast net.

INFUSION as a Set of Outcomes

Persons. As participants in the previous training programs have become articulate in discussing the needs of LEP students, they have been invited to use their skills to provide training and present their research findings for school districts and professional organizations in the state and region, as well as at the national and international levels. These people began the INFUSION network; they continue to assist in its expansion. Many have returned to participate on the advisory council. Others return to continue their studies. Still others work within their school districts to provide INFUSION with reports on the progress of their students and on new ideas and resources that they are developing. Throughout the implementation of the project, many of these people have exerted leadership roles in increasing the project's effectiveness.

In addition to maintaining contact with previous participants, INFUSION invites personnel from other countries and other cultures to participate. Some serve in the capacity of consultants, others as graduate students, and others as advisors and informants. These people provide a rich resource of ideas, information, and support to the project.

Materials. Because of the lack of materials when training began, materials acquisition and development have been given a high priority. Some of the most relevant materials have been developed by training participants themselves. Others have been developed by the faculty, staff, and consultants. The project participants render an important service in reviewing these materials and providing input as to their adequacy and appropriateness. The

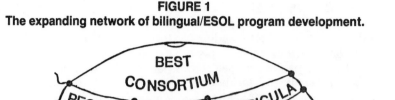

FIGURE 1
The expanding network of bilingual/ESOL program development.

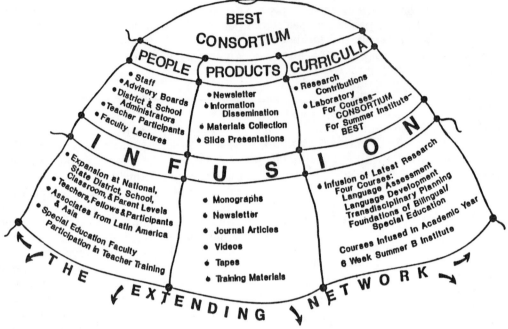

development of materials and the development of curricula move in tandem.

Curricula. In response to an identified training need, four courses have been developed as part of the INFUSION project.

- Language assessment of LEP handicapped and at-risk students.

- Language development for LEP handicapped and at-risk students.

- Foundations of bilingual special education.

- Working in a multicultural system.

These courses form the core of the Summer Institute and are also taught during the academic year. Syllabi for these courses have been developed, and the material and content of the courses have been tested. Participants provide valuable feedback on the appropriateness and relevance of the training. Based on this feedback and on

observed training needs, course content and materials continue to be developed, modified, and upgraded.

INFUSION as a Process

The INFUSION model is a broad-based program of integrating all the successful elements of previously established bilingual special education programs, building on strengths while also addressing areas of need. The project objectives, the process, and the products of the model constitute a very comprehensive project.

The recruitment process. The INFUSION program recruits as its primary focus bilingual NELB personnel. Priority is given to the participation of these persons who are also referred to in the federal regulations as minority-language personnel. However, INFUSION also actively encourages monolingual English speakers. The academic year training is available at the master's, specialist, and doctoral level. A summer institute is available to personnel seeking advanced degrees, but it is primarily targeted to practitioners in the field who want to extend their expertise.

The INFUSION model recruits not only students to participate in the training, but also staff and consultants to assist in providing training. A major criterion for participation with the group, either as a consultant or training participant, is an interest in working with NELB and LEP persons. In addition to enlisting the assistance of paid personnel, the project enlists the aid of many unpaid helpers who provide ideas and support the work of the infusion process.

The infusion process. The project is diversified, rather than person-specific. During the first year personnel initiated the infusion of bilingual, multicultural content into the core curriculum. During the second year, while the project personnel provided further infusion of content, the other faculty and students became actively involved in the process of infusion. A major part of the project's goal will be fulfilled during the third year a a result of the efforts made during the second year. Individual faculty members have become actively engaged in introducing their own courses into monographs and course lectures specifically designed to address the needs of LEP students. Class quizzes and course requirements have included mastery of this information. In addition, professors' knowledge has grown as they have responded to students' inquiries, supervised students' field experiences, collaborated in publishing papers, made state and national presentations, and overseen students' research projects. One of the best ways to promote the infusion process is by encouraging faculty to provide input into the specialized courses that were developed for the project. By providing guest lectures in these courses, faculty became familiar with the context and focus of the intended training. They realized that these issues were not necessarily as they had been conceptualized and that as faculty, they could make substantial contributions to meeting the needs of linguistically and culturally divergent populations.

The impact of the infusion process described above has touched every aspect of department life. The needs of LEP students are no longer seen as separate from the special education paradigm. Department members, whether they are bilingual or monolingual, realize that issues of language and culture are important topics of consideration in assessment and instruction. More importantly, professors have been actively engaged in using information relevant to the needs of LEP students in the courses they teach. They share information with INFUSION staff and participants. The most important part of the infusion process is accomplished as topics of daily conversations include issues of native language assessment and instruction. The sense that these topics are an appropriate part of daily exchanges, rather than specialized topics or concerns, exemplifies the level of infusion achieved.

The network development process. Developing a network is an essential part of the INFUSION process. Networks are important for several reasons. Enfranchisement and effective participation can occur only when persons and systems are actively linked through understanding and the sharing of knowledge, which occur only among persons who have confidence in each other. Networking begins at a personal level: Only after personal trust and confidence have been established can institutions effectively share information.

Making personal linkages has been the first step in network development. Maintaining and building networks has become the second step. This process requires a commitment of time and resources both to formally sharing information through letters, reports, and newsletters, and to informally sharing information at professional meetings, presentations, and gatherings. INFUSION personnel have actively sought out ways to make formal linkages and to unify groups of persons with common interests. They have also sought out opportunities to articulate project goals in the context of the overall mission to meet the needs of LEP students.

The results have been significant as project participants have continued to share information and to assist in recruiting additional participants. INFUSION personnel have been requested to make presentations throughout the state and region. Maintaining the focus of the network on the development of collaborative efforts toward meeting students' needs minimizes considerations of personal gain that many networking efforts appear to promote, and places the emphasis on a cause that transcends individualgoals and gains.

The model development process. As the INFUSION project completes its third and final year of funding, the model continues to unfold. The development of a model for personnel preparation is a natural outgrowth of the INFUSION process. It is a model that values diversity and seeks to train personnel to cooperate and collaborate, not only because such collaboration serves to conserve scarce resources, but also because it inspires creativity and promotes greater productivity and more positive results than any one person or group could realize alone. Implementation of the model in other IHEs and other states will require site-specific modifications, but the process of determining needs and available resources, recruiting dedicated students and faculty, and articulating common concerns remains the same.

The INFUSION process, as a positive force for collaboration, is depicted by the logo presented in Figure 2. What at first is seen as the letter "i," representing the word "infusion," can also be perceived as a little girl standing inside a rectangle and a circle. It can also be seen as a dynamic triangle moving upward to merge with the circle. At the concrete level associated with the figure of the little girl, this symbol can be interpreted as the protective covering of language and culture with which each student enters the educational process. It can also be seen as protective encirclement, which teachers and parents can provide to their children. At an abstract level, it can be seen as the conceptualization of the INFUSION process. The triangle with a tail

represents the body of knowledge contained in the area of bilingual, multicultural studies; the circle represents special education. Currently these two bodies are not well integrated; each represents separate constituencies as well as separate professional paradigms. Considerable effort is still required to develop a comprehensive approach to personnel preparation that unifies the resources, skills, and information that reside in each profession. A third interpretation of this symbol is that the circle represents the current school system, in which a large portion of the students, represented in the darker shade, are still unsuccessful. The triangle with the extended tail represents that large and growing body of students who are still entering into the system. The dark portion of the rectangle represents the unmet needs of newly arrived students. School personnel still require training in the area of the dark portion in order to promote educational success for the students they teach.

As those brought into the INFUSION process also begin to share their interests, enthusiasm, and resources, the process becomes collaborative. The participants realize that their interests overlap not only in a few discrete areas, but in many broad, comprehensive ways. They develop strategies for sharing, project development, networking, and, above all, pressing for positive mutual benefit. Collaboration is seen as a *natural* and *necessary* outgrowth of INFUSION. The collaborative process is depicted in Figure 3. In this figure three hands are superimposed over a cube that is poised above a map of the state of Florida. The hands can be interpreted as a number of different groups, such as the state, the university, and the local educational agency working together to develop effective programs. They can also be seen as the collaboration of bilingual, ESOL, and special education, or parents, teachers, and students. The cube is a multifaceted geometric shape in which the material for developing effective programs resides. The hands provide the vehicle through which the material is developed, expanded, and shared.

FIGURE 2
The INFUSION symbol.

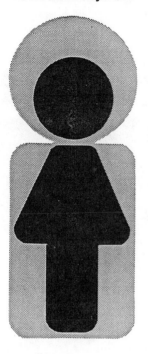

**An Extension of the INFUSION
Model: Collaboration and Reform**

The need for training and training materials continues. As needs have continued to be identified, faculty and staff have responded. In 1987 OBEMLA funded the Collaboration and Reform Project to extend the INFUSION model throughout the College of Education and the University of Florida system in order to provide information and materials to concerned students and faculty interested in at-risk and handicapped LEP and NELB students. Materials are organized into five training modules:

1. The Foundatons of Bilingual/ESOL Special Education: Meeting the Neds of Minority Language Students

2. Bilingual Language Assessment

3. Language Development and English-as-a-Second-Language Instruction in Bilingual Special Education

4. Working with the Parents and the Community

5. Transdisciplinary Teaming

The modules are being developed to respond to three different levels of interest and practice and to appeal to a variety of audiences. The modules are depicted as a cube divided by levels of interest and audiences, as presented in Figure 4.

FIGURE 3
The collaboration symbol.

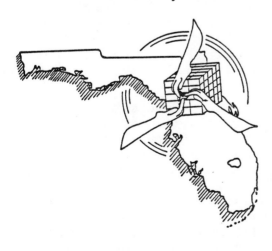

ISSUES AFFECTING LONG-TERM PERSONNEL PREPARATION OUTCOMES

Although substantial progress has been made toward reaching the project's goals, not all aspects of the process of developing effective programs for preparing personnel to work with handicapped and at-risk LEP students are positive. Like the difficulties encountered by many similar projects, there are many factors beyond the scope or the control of the project that impact substantially on the results of long-term training.

To date efforts to meet the educational needs of LEP at-risk and handicapped students have been made primarily at the

FIGURE 4
The collaboration cube showing contents, audiences, and levels of material preparation in the University of Florida bilingual special education INFUSION project's collaboration and reform model.

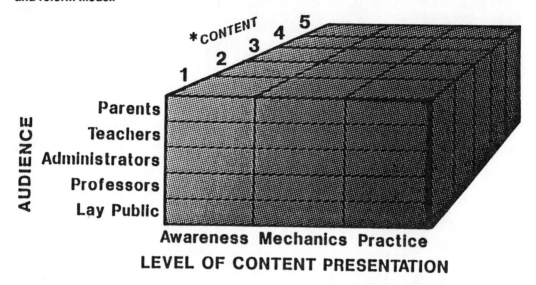

*content
1. Foundatons of Bilingual/ESOL Special Education: Meeting the Needs of Minority Language Students
2, Bilingual Language Assessment
3. Language Development and English as a Second Language Instruction in Bilingual Special Education
4. Working with te Parents and the Community
5. Transdisciplinary Teaming

local level. Several school districts in Florida have implemented effective programs that serve as models for other districts with similar needs. The federal government, through OBEMLA and OSERS, has supported local efforts by funding 3-year transitional bilingual and special populations programs to develop bilingual/ESOL special education. The university continues to work with concerned school districts and with the state to disseminate information, to provide training, and to implement additional training programs as needs are identified. However, there are a number of limitations to effective development of a concerted effort toward program development involving local, state, and university personnel.

Impediments to Program Continuation

There are a number of impediments to the continuation of training and materials development in the area of bilingual/ESOL special education. These include (a) lack of institutionalization; (b) lack of designated personnel who are responsible for program supervision; and (c) lack of awareness of the needs of LEP and NELB students. While these limitations are rooted in the particular circumstances of the state of Florida, they are representative of similar constraints in many other states (Salend & Fradd, 1985; 1986).

Lack of institutionalization. Training programs in bilingual/ESOL special education are federally funded. The educational process is a constantly changing and renewing cycle of new personnel and students. Although the INFUSION process ensures that current personnel, both faculty and staff, have become concerned about the educational needs of LEP students, what will happen when funding stops and no permanent position is funded to continue the training? Will new faculty and staff employed after the project is completed also become concerned? Will the new personnel have the information from which to prepare lectures and course materials to share with their students? Will the new students who have never been exposed to children with special needs raise serious questions and participate in research as they did during the period when the projects were funded?

Federal funding is provided for short-term program development, usually in response to a funding cycle of 3 years. Once federal funding stops, state and local agencies are expected to continue the programs initiated through federal funds. The bilingual/ESOL special education programs available in Florida, as in many other states, are federally funded. The course content, the materials, and modules will remain after federal funds stop. But because the programs have not been institutionalized, there is nothing to indicate that the training efforts provided through federal funds will be continued or that the materials developed through these projects will even be used. Concerted efforts are required if the present training is to continue.

Lack of designated personnel. There is a lack of designated, trained state and district personnel who are responsible for implementing and supervising programs to meet the needs of students who are both handicapped and limited in English proficiency. At the state level, a position has been designated within the Bureau of Exceptional Education, but the person who fills that position has been charged with the responsibility for carrying out many other projects, many of which have a higher priority. Other personnel within the Florida State Education Agency (SEA) are also concerned about the high dropout rates of NELB and LEP students and are seeking solutions to this serious problem. However, the absence of any definition of the problem and of personnel responsible for effectuating solutions inhibits interdepartmental collaboration.

Within LEAs there are few administrators who have received training or are aware of the issues facing at-risk and handicapped LEP and NELB students. Long-term training is still required in order to develop a cadre of administrative personnel in bilingual/ESOL and special education who are knowledgeable about the problems that NELB and LEP students face in entering the mainstream culture and economy. In school districts where such personnel are present, effective programs are being implemented; and the numbers of LEP students receiving special educational services more closely resemble state and national statistics in these districts than in districts where no personnel have been designated or trained. In districts with trained administrators, effective accommodations for NELB students are also implemented. In fact, parents specifically seek out school districts providing specialized services.

Because of the limited number of trained administrative personnel currently responsible for supervising programs in bilingual/ESOL special education, the number of students identified as needing services continues to remain depressed. However, since the 1985 statistics were released, the unofficial number of LEP students in the state receiving special education services has more than tripled as a result of effective assessment procedures implemented by model school districts.

Lack of awareness. A lack of awareness of the needs of at-risk LEP and NELB students is prevalent throughout the state and nation. The "Let them learn English" movements continue to gain visibility. While no thoughtful person wants any students not to learn English, a great deal of time and effort is required in the learning process in order to acquire a new language. Slow learners and mildly handicapped students have a difficult time making rapid transitions and successful assimilation into the English-speaking world. The INFUSION philosophy is that it is not only desirable, but essential, that students become proficient in English and develop appropriate academic and social skills to enable them to be successful, contributing members of society. However, the fact remains that in many cases, the use of non-

English languages has produced in a few minutes to a few weeks what had not occurred with handicapped students in several years of English-only instruction. Collaboration in the use of both English and non-English languages for both academic skill development and social interaction can be a powerful resource in meeting students' needs.

A lack of awareness of the power and benefit of using other languages exists not only with LEAs, but also at the SEA and IHE levels. Evidence of this limitation can be seen in the lack of commitment to programs that are making a difference and which, with support, can continue to contribute to the responsiveness of the educational system to the needs of minority language students.

Continued Needs Require Increased Awareness and Commitment

There has been a grass roots movement toward improving educational responsiveness and for the development of meaningful educational programs (Association for Supervision and Curriculum Development, 1988). Evidence of this movement can be found in the numbers of school personnel who are seeking additional training, such as that provided by INFUSION, even when it does not provide a credential or an economic advantage. One of the reasons for this movement is that school personnel on the front lines of education, those who interact with students on a daily basis, are aware of the harsh consequences of educational failure. They want students to succeed. This grassroots effort has been articulated in the development of policy statements and special interest groups within a number of national professional organizations. Groups such as the Association for Supervision and Curriculum Development (ASCD), the Council for Exceptional Children (CEC), the National Association of Bilingual Education (NABE), the National Association of School Psychologists (NASP), the National Council of Teachers of English (NCTE), and Teachers of English to Speakers of Other Languages (TESOL) have all taken active

positions advocating for responsive programs.

The *importance* of and *urgency* for developing responsive programs put the issue of English-only instruction versus the use of English in combination with other languages in a new context. Discussion moves from the political arena of bilingual education versus English-only instruction into the area of pedagogical responsibility. The need is not for more language instruction, but for a comprehensive restructuring of the way in which students are assessed and instruction is delivered. Restructuring requires a systematic realization of the shared responsibility for defining students' needs and managing their successes. The effort moves away from integrating students and content into an already established framework and seeks to restructure the framework to promote collaboration and sharing of responsibility.

Is the process of infusion, collaboration, and responsibility-sharing possible, if there are no personnel preparation programs that question the current system? Can the restructuring process be possible if there are no institutions that provide a visionary look at what is and what can be; that ask the hard questions about how the system determines students' needs and provides them with appropriate and meaningful programs; and that promote the erasing of artificial barriers such as regular and special education and the joining of forces in a comprehensive effort to empower both educational personnel and the students who look to them for success? The answer lies not in the perpetuation of federally funded programs, but in the resolutions of personnel within each state to make the hard decisions needed to develop effective responses. The students, the future wage earners or welfare recipients of the nation, will not go away; their numbers continue to increase. The eventual outcomes of decisions to educate of ignore students will determine the economic and social status of the nation for decades into the future. The decisions about how to educate these students and how to prepare personnel to respond to their needs will shape the nation's future in ways that have not yet been considered. INFUSION and

Collaboration have begun a educational process that can serve as a model for future training, if those who currently determine and implement educational policy are willing to invest the resources to meet the need.

REFERENCES

Association for Supervision and Curriculum Development. (January, 1988). Restructured schools: Frequently invoked, rarely defined. *ASCD Update* (pp. 1, 6-7).

Baca, L. (1984). Teacher education programs. In P. C. Chinn (Ed.), *Educational of culturally and linguistically different exceptional children* (pp. 101-123). Reston, VA: Council for Exceptional Children.

Baca, L., & Cervantes, H. (1984). *The bilingual special education interface.* Columbus, OH: Merrill.

Bermudez, A., Fradd, S. H., & Haulman, A. (1988). *Examining the process of coordination in preparing personnel to work with limited English proficient students.* Unpublished manuscript. Gainesville: University of Florida.

Braden, J. P., & Fradd, S. H. (1987). Proactive school organization: Identifying and meeting special population needs. In S. H. Fradd & W. J. Tikunoff (Eds.), *Bilingual education and bilingual special education: A guide for administrators* (pp. 211-230). Boston: Little, Brown.

Bureau of Education for Exceptional Students. (1983). *Florida's comprehensive system of personnel development.* Tallahassee: Department of Education.

Carnegie Foundation for the Advancement of Teaching. (1988). An imperiled generation: Serving urban schools. *Education of the Disadvantaged, 21*(6), 47-49.

Castaneda, A., Herold, P. L., & Ramirez, M. (1974). *New approaches to bilingual bicultural education.* Austin, TX: Dissemination and Assessment Center for Bilingual Education.

Chandler, M. O., & Stein, J. D. (Eds.). (1987). *The condition of education.* Statistical report. Washington, DC: U.S. Department of Education, Center for Educational Statistics.

Clark, D. L., Astuto, T. A., & Rooney, D. M. (1983). The changing nature of federal education policy in the 1980s. *Phi Delta Kappan, 65,* 188-193.

Fernandez-Zayas, M. (1988). Los desertores escolares: Tragedia nacional hispana. *Replica, 19,* 8-10.

Fradd, S. H. (1987). Accommodating the needs of limited English proficient students in regular classrooms. In S. H. Fradd & W. J. Tikunoff (Eds.), *Bilingual education and bilingual special education: A guide for administrators* (pp. 137-182). Boston: Little, Brown.

Fradd, S. H., Algozzine, B., Hallman, C. L., & Doherty, E. (1987). *University of Florida bilingual/ESOL special education training project (Consortium). Final evaluation report.* (Special projects G008530250). Gainesville: University of Florida, Department of Special Education.

Fradd, S. H., Algozzine, B., & Salend, S. J. (1988). A survey of training needs in bilingual special education. *Journal of Educational Issues of Language Minority Students, 2,* 5-16.

Fradd, S. H., Gard, R., & Weismantel, M. J. (1988, September). *Meeting the needs of handicapped limited English proficient students in ESOL classrooms: A review of state certification requirements.* Paper presented at the Southeast Regional TESOL Conference, Orlando, Florida.

Fradd, S. H., & Halsall, S. W. (1986). *BEST practices in bilingual special education evaluation report.* (Special projects G008525164). Gainesville: University of Florida, Department of Special Education.

Fradd, S. H., Weismantel, M., Correa, V. I., & Algozzine, B. (1988). Developing a personnel training model for meeting the needs of handicapped and at risk language minority students. *Teacher Education and Special Education, 11*(1), 30-38.

Heller, K. A., Holtzman, W. H., & Messick, S. (1982). *Placing children in special education: A strategy for equity.* Washington, DC: National Academy Press.

Hodgkinson, H. (1988). The right schools for the right kids. *Educational Leadership, 45,* 10-14.

Howe, H. (1983). Education moves to the center stage: An awareness of recent studies. *Phi Delta Kappan, 65,* 107-173.

Hudson, P. J., & Fradd, S. H. (1987). Learning strategy instruction: Modifications to meet the educational needs of limited English proficient learning disabled students. *Journal of Reading, Writing and Learning Disabilities International, 3,* 195-212.

Levin, H. M. (1985). *The educational disadvantaged: A national crisis.* Philadelphia: Public/Private Ventures.

Martinez, M. G. (1985). Creating artificial handicaps for handicapped and limited English proficient children. *Congressional Records Proceedings & Debates of the 100th Congress, 1st session, 133*(131).

Moran, M. R. (1984). Excellence at the cost of instructional equity: The potential impact of recommended reforms upon law achieving students. *Focus on Exceptional Children, 16,* 1-12.

National Coalition of Advocates for Students. (1985). *Barriers to excellence: Our children at risk.* Boston: Author.

National coalition of Advocates for Students. (1988). *New voices: Immigrant students in U.S. public schools.* Boston: Author.

Ortiz, A. (1984). Language and curriculum development for exceptional bilingual children. In P. Chinn (Ed.), *Education of culturally and linguistically different children* (pp. 77–100). Reston, VA: Council for Exceptional Children.

Oxford-Carpenter, R., Pol, L., Lopez, D., Stupp, P., Gendell, U., & Peng, S. (1984). *Demographic projections of non-English language background and limited English proficient persons in the United States to the year 2000 by state, age, and language.* Rosslyn, VA: National Clearinghouse for Bilingual Education.

Plisko, V. W. (Ed.). (1984). *The condition of education.* Washington, DC: U.S. Department of Education, National Center for Education Statistics.

Salend, S. J., & Fradd, S. (1985). Certification and training program requirements for bilingual special education. *Teacher Education and Special Education, 8,* 198–202.

Salend, S. J., & Fradd, S. (1986). Nationwide availability of services for limited English proficient handicapped students. *Journal of Special Education, 20,* 127–135.

U.S. Department of Commerce. (1988). *Statistical Abstract of the United States.* Washington, DC: Bureau of the Census.

U.S. General Accounting Office. (1981). *Disparities still exist in who gets special education.* Washington, DC: Author.

U.S. General Accounting Office. (1987). *Bilingual education information on limited English proficient students.* Washington, DC: Author.

Valero-Figuiera, E. (1986). Bilingual special education personnel preparation: An integrated model. *Teacher Education and Special Education, 9*(2), 82–88.

Waggoner, D. (1984). The need for bilingual education: Estimates from the 1980 census. *Journal of the National Association for Bilingual Education, 8,* 1–14.

Yeakey, C. C. (1982). Block grants and public schools: Implications for educational policy and decision making. *Educational Horizons, 61,* 18–25.

Part IV:
Assessment

Preschool Screening of Ethnic Minority Children and Children of Poverty: Issues for Practice and Research

Robert C. Pianta and
Ronald E. Reeve
University of Virginia

INTRODUCTION

Clearly there is a need to develop efficient means of identifying children at risk for early school failure. Far too many children become casualties in our present system. More than 10% of the primary grade population is labeled with an identified handicap through the special education system (Hallahan & Kauffman, 1982; U.S. Office of Education, 1987). Retention rates, another indication of failure, ranged from 1.1% to 15.3% of first graders in a 13-state study (Rose, Medway, Cantrell, & Manus, 1983), and a large percentage of children are identified for services through federal Chapter 1 programs as well as locally based remedial efforts (Ysseldyke & Algozzine, 1982). These figures do *not* include those children who attain marginal success in the primary grades, only to become identified failures (e.g., dropouts) in later years, when developmental stress is higher and increased demands are placed upon them. Nor do they include children who are unsuccessful in the primary grades for primarily social or behavioral reasons. These data suggest that between 20% and 40% of schoolchildren nationwide (and nearly 100% in some areas or within certain groups) face a high likelihood of some form of failure in the primary grades. Children of poverty and ethnic minority children are consistently overrepresented in failure populations.

As attention is now being turned to reducing the rate of failure in the primary grades, an increased emphasis has been placed upon prevention and early intervention efforts in the public schools (National Commission on Excellence in Education, 1983). Most authors agree that identifying children, prior to school placement, who are likely to fail is a necessary first step in prevention and early intervention efforts (e.g., Keogh, Wilcoxen, & Bernheimer, 1986).

The overrepresentation of ethnic minorities and children of poverty in the population of children showing early school failure has been well documented. These groups make up a disproportionate percentage of the children referred for special education (Gartner & Lipsky, 1987), speech and language services, and retention (Pianta & Reeve, manuscript in preparation). The data clearly point to a crisis in the education of ethnic minority children and children of poverty, at the same time that the demands on the educational system to produce highly skilled workers are increasing. This situation creates pressure, on both the educational system and the children served by that system, that has exacerbated the vulnerability of minority and children of poverty educated within the mainstream culture. The task of early intervention and prevention, of which screening programs are a part, is to find a way to ameliorate this vulnerability, and to accommodate these students' needs in a pluralistic context. For that reason, it is critical that any consideration of preschool screening with ethnic minority children and children of poverty recognize the complex interplay between assessment issues for these two groups *and* the equally troublesome assessment issues associated with any screening procedures involving children so young. The resulting combination of these issues represents a significant challenge to school psychologists and other educational professionals.

Interest in prevention and early intervention programs in the public schools has been kindled by several related forces, including research data that demonstrate the positive effects of early intervention programs (Lazar & Darlington, 1982; Ramey, Bryant, Sparling, & Wasik, 1985), dissatisfaction with the outcomes and procedures of special education programs (Gartner & Lipsky, 1987), and increased awareness of the impact of factors such as divorce, poverty, and child maltreatment (Garbarino, 1982). Most important, however, is the fact that although the public schools face increasing numbers of children failing to meet academic, social, or behavioral standards, *schools conduct little or no systematic assessment of children's competencies and weaknesses prior to school entry* (Bursaw & Ysseldyke, 1986; Lehr, Ysseldyke, & Thurlow, 1986). For the most part, schools have operated under a remedial or corrective approach, using assessment only *after a problem has surfaced*. This pattern of practice, along with the lack of validated screening measures, is a significant impediment to offering preventive services and has a substantial negative impact on the school success of those children who are in greatest need of services. The wait-and-see attitude adopted by many school systems with regard to early intervention and prevention for any other than the most severely handicapped students is a policy that increases the risk for subsequent failure for these students.

ISSUES IN IDENTIFICATION OF RISK FOR EARLY SCHOOL FAILURE

Most current screening programs are inappropriate for several reasons. These include a lack of longitudinal research on the processes underlying school failure, the controversy over developmental versus readiness approaches to screening, techni-cal adequacy issues, and the predominance of simplistic prediction models.

The Need for Longitudinal Research

Data regarding the relationship between multiple risk factors and educational outcomes, which could form the basis for developing screening programs sensitive to the needs of young ethnic minority or children of poverty, are scarce. One factor affecting this problem has been the lack of descriptive research on comprehensive educational results for *all* students in the primary grades. Researchers and educators have focused almost exclusively on academic skills learning and acquired factual knowledge as the primary outcome variables in which they are interested. Unfortunately, this focus excludes many of the social and affective outcomes that, in young children, form part of their foundation for later skill learning and academic success (Entwistle & Hayduk, 1981; Pallas, Entwistle, Alexander, & Cadigan, 1987).

The predictive data that do exist tend to be the product of elaborate, expensive assessments conducted solely within a research context (Ramey, Bryant, Sparling, & Wasik, 1985). Although these data have been extremely informative about the processes underlying change and stability in development in risk populations, the measures used as predictors of later development tend to be resource-intensive and thus beyond the capacity of schools to implement on a wide scale. Therefore, although these research projects have been informative about the factors underlying school success and failure, as well as the processes of intervention, a need exists for longitudinal research using instruments that are suited to implementation in school systems.

Developmental versus Readiness Approaches

A wide variety of screening instruments have been used to identify preschool children in need of services (Bursaw & Ysseldyke, 1986; Lehr, Ysseldyke, & Thurlow, 1986; Meisels, 1987), and there is considerable disagreement in practice as to which measures are best suited for the task. These instruments are designed for decision-making. That is, the utility of an instrument is based on its ability to enhance the identification of children who are most likely to have difficulty succeeding in school. Both the instruments chosen and the decision-making context have implications for use with ethnic minority children and children of poverty.

The most popular type of instrument used in preschool screening is a *readiness* test, which takes as its objective the documentation of a child's level of mastery of tasks and skills to be further developed in the upcoming curriculum (Meisels, 1987). Another type of measure, termed *developmental* by Meisels, assesses the abilities that underlie mastery of curricular tasks and skills (Shipman, 1987). Readiness and developmental instruments differ vastly on the content of the assessment and on data utilization.

Examination of current practice suggests that readiness assessment is more widely used than developmental assessment for identification of preschool children who may be in need of intervention services (Meisels, 1987), under the logically faulty assumption that those children who do not show mastery on tasks that they have not been taught are likely to fail. Readiness and skill-based assessments also fail to acknowledge that prediction of later levels of competencies does not depend on measurement of preceding levels of precisely equivalent competencies (Sroufe & Rutter, 1984). Rather, outcome behaviors and skills (the things schools are interested in predicting) are built upon simpler and more fundamental patterns of behavioral organization that have critical periods for development at earlier points in the children's lives.

Thus a skill-based approach to identification of preschoolers at risk for early school failure is likely to focus on superficial behaviors or skills that may well be more the results of environmental influences (teaching) and are therefore more likely to fail to predict the outcome of instruction; by focusing on superficial behavioral patterns, skill-based approaches will fail to assess the less differentiated yet fundamen-

tal, global patterns of behavioral organization that underlie later competency (Shipman, 1987).

For ethnic minority and children of poverty, readiness or skill-based assessment instruments, used as the sole measure for screening decisions, can result in overrepresentation among risk populations. For ethnic minority children, whose developmental context has been different from mainstream culture, and for children of poverty, who also have a different cultural background as well as possible deprivation, there is often a mismatch between the instructional and cultural context of the preschool years and the established curriculum of the school. In this case, it may be very important to choose screening instruments that are *not* heavily weighted with items from the school curriculum but instead reflect underlying learning and/or developmental processes.

Technical Adequacy

Among the technical adequacy problems with a skill-based approach is the fact that they are by nature criterion-referenced. Therefore, although they are suitable for making decisions about placing an individual child in a curriculum sequence, they are invalid with respect to normative or comparative decisions designed to identify individuals or subpopulations for services (Salvia & Ysseldyke, 1982).

At this time, there are many assessment instruments that are used to determine the placement needs of preschool children, most of which have received negative reviews (Meisels, 1987; Shipman, 1987). In fact, Meisel's (1987) recent review of screening instruments recommends very few of the many tests available. Citing a survey of 177 school districts in the state of New York in which it was found that 155 different tests or procedures were being used for screening (Joiner, 1977), Meisels (1987) noted that only 16 of the tests could be considered even marginally appropriate. In the absence of tests that satisfy criteria for reliability and validity, children in need of special services are overlooked, some children who are not at risk are being identified as at risk, parents are alarmed, teachers and administrators are upset, and resources are squandered (Meisels, 1987; Shepard, 1987).

Development and implementation of an acceptable screening battery requires study of the predictive validity of the instrument(s) in order to describe and improve accuracy. This would include systematic collection of follow-up data on outcomes of interest, a procedure that is rarely followed (Ysseldyke et al., 1986). For example, in several states, the percentage of districts that evaluate the adequacy and accuracy of their screening decisions has been found to be less than 10% (Meisels, 1987). Therefore, as noted earlier, even though there are considerable flaws in the actual content of the screening data collected, there is *even poorer utilization of whatever information is collected.* The result is a system of decision making that is at best tentative and most likely indefensible, is not data-based, and has unknown utility.

In addition, many potentially valid predictors of early school adjustment, such as measures of parent–child interaction (Pianta, Erickson, Wagner, Kreutzer, & Egeland submitted for publication), are unused because of their genesis in research projects (Lidz, 1987). Again, current practice results in decisions about individual children, programs and policies that are ill-informed at best and at worst are not defensible. It is of critical importance to develop screening batteries for which predictive validity has been examined. In the case of ethnic minority children and children of poverty, this involves establishment of differential validity as well.

Overall, the problems associated with readiness or skill-based assessments make them suspect for use as the primary screening instrument for preschool children. By and large, the inferences drawn from such instruments are not likely to be as reliable as the inferences drawn from measures of underlying ability.

Single and Multiple Domain Models

Recently several prospective, longitudinal (long-term and short-term) studies have greatly contributed to our understanding of the factors underlying competent and incompetent development and the shifts that take place between them over time (Egeland & Sroufe, 1983; Ramey et al., 1985; Werner & Smith, 1982). The results of these studies have significant implications for policy and program development in respect to children at risk for early school failure, since they directly address the problem of identifying the multiple early predictors of problem and of positive outcomes. In particular they clearly suggest several major domains in which screening in the preschool years is very likely to improve informed and defensible (valid) identification of children at risk for later academic, social, and behavioral incompetence. These domains include family functioning, demographic and contextual factors, social competence, parent–child interaction patterns and relationships, cognitive and language functioning, and certain health and physiological factors. It can be argued on the strength of these studies that each one of these areas reflects a major pathway/process underlying children's competence at all stages of development. Therefore, knowledge of a child's status in these domains at one point in time will be predictive of patterns of competence at later points (Sroufe & Rutter, 1984; Waters & Sroufe, 1983).

These studies argue for a multiple domain approach to screening. Just as in assessment of intelligence, in which diverse abilities are tapped by a range of items, application of the entire set of items increasing prediction over what would be obtained with only one type of item, so with a multiple domain screening battery information from a variety of areas increases predictive validity. For ethnic minority children and children of poverty, multiple domain approaches also have the advantage of not constraining performance to one area in which a child may be weak simply on the basis of past experience or learning history. When developmental measures of underlying ability are combined with readiness assessment and measures that assess other important aspects of development, such as parental social support or family stress, the resulting multiple domain battery is more likely to produce enhanced predictive validity for differentiated outcomes than is a single domain approach using either readiness or developmental measures alone.

Utilizing Screening and Outcome Data: Interactive Models

Despite the proliferation of screening measures, the models used to predict outcomes are not very sophisticated (Meisels, 1987; Ysseldyke, et al., 1986). Statistical models used to predict results for children in applied settings have not kept pace with models currently used in basic research. By and large a *main effects* model is used in practice to predict outcome; almost *all* commercially available screening measures use a main effects model (Meisels, 1987). That is, only the main effects of the measure are used to predict; the interactive effects of *combinations* of variables are overlooked despite research from the developmental and educational literatures that suggest that these combinations are critical in helping to understand, and to statistically account for, the outcomes children achieve (Garmezy, Masten, & Tellegen, 1984; Maccoby & Martin, 1983).

AN EXAMPLE OF MULTIPLE DOMAIN SCREENING: PROJECT PATS

The authors are cooperating with a local school district to develop and implement a screening program, assess its predictive validity for a range of educational outcomes, and assess the impact of ethnic and economic background on screening and identification decisions. The project involves a comprehensive multiple domain screening battery administered upon entry in kindergarten, and a series of follow-up assessments, twice in kindergarten and once in the first grade. The measures and procedures are described in detail in the following sections, along with the background literature that provides the rationale for their use.

Factors Included in Multiple Domain Screening to Predict Early School Outcomes

In this section we briefly survey the literature on some of the factors affecting school success that may be important for inclusion in multiple domain batteries.

Demographic and family contextual factors. A great number of studies have confirmed the risk to a child's development that are present in deficient family and community environments (Garbarino, 1982). Ramey, Stedman, Borders-Patterson, and Mengel (1978) linked broad demographic indicators to academic failure in first grade, retention in first grade, and conduct problems. Parental age, income, education, and occupation, as well as the number of persons living in the home, repeatedly have been shown to predict the nature of academic and behavioral adjustment in the primary grades (Ramey et al., 1985). Although the causal links between these demographic factors and educational outcomes have been the source of great debate and controversy, they remain clear choices for inclusion in batteries of measures intended to screen for early school competence. In our screening, a Parent Interview contains questions on number and age of persons living in the household, their relationships to each other and the child, and educational level and occupation of persons in the household.

Parents' experiences of social support have been linked to family and child competence across a range of demographic levels and types of risk (Belle, 1982; Crnic, Greenberg, Ragozin, & Basham, 1983; Pianta, Egeland, & Sroufe, in press). For example, social support, both for caregivers and children under stress, has been identified as a central factor leading to competence in high-risk samples (Crockenberg & McCluskey, 1986). Information regarding the amount and quality of support experienced by parents is not obtained routinely in public school screening procedures (Meisels, 1987; Ysseldyke, et al., 1986); the result is a loss of information that could be highly useful for predicting children's competence as well as for identifying families and parents in need of intervention.

One reason these data are not collected may be a feeling that such information is "private" or would be intrusive to parents; but it also can be argued that obtaining and using this type of information in a sensitive manner might be a first step toward establishing positive school–family relationships (Garbarino, 1982). This information can be collected in screening procedures using semistructured interview techniques (Egeland & Sroufe, 1983). In our project, data are obtained from each child's parent on the amount of instrumental and emotional support they (the caregiver) has experienced within the past 6 months. Each parent/caregiver is asked questions, with examples, about who provides them with instrumental or social support *and* how frequently they see this person. In our collection of these data, parents have responded positively and openly; in fact many parents used the data collection process as an opportunity to inform school personnel of recent family changes that they felt might have an impact on their child. They expressed positive feelings about having the opportunity to talk with school staff regarding these matters.

Behavior problems and competencies. For some preschool children, behavior problems already exist that have been manifested with peers or adults outside of the context of the parent–child relationship. Children who, at school entry, are seen as aggressive or withdrawn, or who exhibit low-frequency behaviors such as bizarre reactions to events or people, are at high risk for failing to establish appropriate social relationships with peers and adults in school and for not adapting to academic demands (Rutter, 1975). On the basis of the relationship between parents' report of behavior problems in the preschool years and behavior problems in the primary grades, many school systems include such reports in their screening programs in some form (Ysseldyke et al., 1986).

Currently, however, there are few or no parent report measures both of behavior problems *and* of competencies that can be used for *screening* purposes and that have been validated for samples of 4- to 5-year-olds. Existing instruments, for example, the Child Behavior Checklist (Achenbach, 1980), are either too solely pathology-oriented or too long for use in screening. A focus on only problem behaviors, as is common on these instruments, does not allow for identification of resilient children with strengths that may compensate for risks in other domains. In our research we have developed a 46-item scale to assess both problem behaviors and areas of competence. This scale has shown internal consistency reliability and has three subscales validated through factor analysis (Competence, Acting Out, Anxiety). Each of these subscales and the total scale score correlate with teacher ratings of classroom behavior and add incremental validity when combined with predictors such as IQ and fine motor ability.

In addition to the behavior rating scale completed by the parent, other behavior ratings are obtained by the examiners during the screening sessions. Immediately after the administration of cognitive measures, the examiner rates the child on Anxiety and Task Orientation, two 5-point scales representing important aspects of the quality of the child's adaptation to the task. In a pilot investigation, interrater agreement during training sessions was calculated at .85, and children who were rated a 4 or 5 on anxiety or 1 or 2 on task orientation had a very high likelihood (.80) of being recommended for retention.

Cognitive and language functioning. Children who are functioning poorly with regard to cognitive and language tasks in the preschool period have a high probability of difficulties in adapting to the task demands of school (Elkind, 1987; Ramey et al., 1982; Shipman, 1987). Performance on intelligence tests has long been recognized as a strong predictor of academic competence and achievement in school. It also has been recognized with increasing frequency that language competence (receptive, expressive, pragmatic) represents a major, if not fundamental, set of abilities which determine the degree of ease or difficulty a child will have with demands of school (Elkind, 1987; Shipman, 1987). It is widely accepted that screening procedures need to sample functioning in these areas (Meisels, 1987). The measure of cognitive development we have used is a two-subtest short form of the Stanford-Binet Intelligence Scale–Revised, Fourth Edition (Thorndike, Hagen, & Sattler, 1986). This instrument provides the most recent and comprehensive normative data for the assessment of intelligence in the preschool years. The two subtests chosen for this screening, Vocabulary and Bead Memory, are highly correlated with the general intelligence factor at this age, and they tap different major types of cognitive processing (verbal and spatial). Each child's language development is screened with the Fluharty Preschool Speech and Language Screening Test (FPSLST) (Fluharty, 1978). This instrument yields four subtest scores, one each in the areas of Identification, Articulation, Comprehension, and Production. Our data indicate that both of these domains, cognitive and speech/language, contribute to prediction of behavioral and academic adjustment in kindergarten.

Health factors. Screening for the biological and health factors underlying developmental competence is necessary in order to provide the type of broad scope screen intended to "catch" as many children at risk as possible. Even though most children with moderate to severe biological risk are known to service providers prior to the preschool years (Keogh et al., 1986), there is increasing evidence that mild biological risk (prenatal and perinatal conditions, birth trauma, and head injuries) is often unseen prior to school entry and is later detected through academic failure, and that in some SES strata or under certain cultural/demographic conditions even moderate and severe biological risk can go undetected or unreported (Birch & Gussow, 1980; Keogh et al., 1986). We assess this area with a standard vision and hearing screen as well as an interview with the parents regarding the children's health history. The vision and hearing screen has identified low-incidence problems that greatly interfere with school adaptation. The interview procedures on health history have revealed children with significant medical, health, or injury-related conditions. Treating these conditions as risk factors has improved our

predictions of competence, especially in the academic area. The interviews require very little time, and the information obtained has proven quite useful.

Motor development. Children's gross and fine motor development in the preschool years is viewed as a domain underlying similar competencies in later years as well as significantly contributing to competence in academic and social areas (Shipman, 1987). Motor abilities have been declared to be the developmental precursors to academic success or failure, although the predictive validity of most of these claims has gone unevaluated (Salvia & Ysseldyke, 1982). Our data strongly supports the predictive validity of fine motor assessment. Five subtests making up the Motor scale of the McCarthy Scales of Children's Abilities (McCarthy, 1972) are administered to each child. Gross and fine motor skills are assessed by the Leg Coordination, Arm Coordination, Imitative Action, Draw-a-Design, and Draw-a-Child subtests. The sum of these subtests is used to determine the Motor scale standard score. The reliability of this scale within the 4- to 5-year age range is .84. Our initial results strongly suggest that the two subtests assessing fine motor skills, Draw-a-Design and Draw-a-Child, are especially good predictors of early school success.

Outcome or Follow-up Assessment

Selecting the outcomes that will define success in the early school years, during which there is interest in prevention, is of major importance, since these outcomes form the foundation for later success or failure (Pianta, in press). By and large, educational systems have focused almost exclusively on academic success or failure as the primary means by which they describe and intervene with students. What has emerged from recent research on the reasons why children fail, are retained, or are referred for special education is the finding that social, emotional, and behavioral factors play very important roles as dimensions of "school adaptation" and in turn as predictors of later success or failure

(Hightower et al., 1986; Ysseldyke, Christenson, Pianta, & Algozzine, 1983).

It is especially important to identify the differentiated outcomes attained by ethnic minority and children of poverty. Despite the elevated risk status of these *groups* it is quite clear that many *individuals* within these groups are quite successful in school, work, and play. Therefore, we need to learn about what influences are associated with success for students within risk groups and then translate these findings into early intervention and prevention programs. Clearly, programs of multiple domain screening *and* assessment of differentiated outcomes are important components of the risk reduction process.

It is essential, therefore, to describe patterns of school functioning across *multiple outcome domains*, in addition to the academic area, in order to obtain an accurate assessment of the need for prevention and intervention. Description of these patterns also facilitates the identification of resilient children who have differential strengths and weaknesses. Therefore, in our program, we use several outcome measures: teacher ratings of behavior problems, work habits, and social competence; standardized achievement tests; criterion-referenced academic skills measures; assessment of teacher–child relationships; and for selected children, observation of classroom behavior and interaction with their teachers.

Two areas with important implications for prevention are teacher–child relationships and home–school contact (Pianta, 1988; Power & Bartholomew, 1987). Given the strong influence of child–parent relationships on adaptation to preschool (Egeland & Sroufe, 1983), and given the data on the buffering role that child–teacher relationships have in promoting resilience (Garmezy, 1984; Werner & Smith, 1982), it is reasonable to expect the quality of relationships with teachers to serve as a major marker of the transition to school and of the quality of adaptation to school. In our current research we have piloted, with 75 children and 25 teachers, a questionnaire designed to assess a teacher's perception of the degree to which individual children feel secure in using the teacher as an emotional

and instrumental resource (Pianta, 1988). We will begin using this scale with all children and teachers at all follow-up assessments and, in selected cases, observing child–teacher interaction in a laboratory task.

Finally, we track the type and frequency of home–school contacts to assess the quality of the family–school relationship. That the strength of this relationship has significance for a child's development has been strongly supported (Garbarino, 1982). We use systematic data on the frequency and nature of home–school contacts to assess the extent to which they serve as moderators of the risk–outcome relation and in turn are important predictors of future success.

Implementation

We use a formative strategy through which, over the course of 3–5 years, a district has the opportunity (a) to develop and implement a defined screening procedure with clear rules for identification of at-risk children that match local constraints/desires, (b) to implement an intervention program, (c) to collect follow-up measures on the entire population to assess the outcomes which were targeted for prediction and intervention, (d) to assess the hit rate for the identification procedures and the degree of success of the intervention, (d) to refine identification and intervention procedures accordingly, and (f) to reevaluate.

This formative data utilization strategy, based on locally and nationally normed screening procedures, can result in identification decisions that are based on solid information and can be evaluated with regard to any number of criteria. This type of system would be a vast improvement over existing practices.

CONCLUSIONS

Identifying children at risk for academic and social failure is a necessary first step prior to implementing prevention and early intervention programs. While preschool screening programs are commonplace, they typically are inadequate because of their utilization of readiness (as opposed to developmental) approaches, their overuse of technically poor and conceptually invalid instruments, and their reliance on simplistic, main-effects models for prediction of risk. This unfortunate situation has occurred because of the scarcity of longitudinal research and because the research that has been done is not well known to practitioners.

At this time we advocate the use of multiple domain screening programs such as the one described in this chapter, and we urge that these programs be linked to ongoing follow-up research of the type we have described so that the screening can be constantly revalidated for the purposes for which the school wishes to use it.

REFERENCES

Achenbach, T. (1980). *The Child Behavior Checklist — Parent Report Form*. University of Vermont: Child Psychiatry Associates.

Belle, D. (1982). The stress of caring: Women as providers of social support. In L. Goldberger & S. Breznitz (Eds.), *Handbook of stress*. New York: Free Press.

Birch, H., & Gussow, J. (1970). *Disadvantaged children*. New York: Grune & Stratton.

Bursaw, R. A., & Ysseldyke, J. E. (1986). *Preschool screening referral rates in Minnesota school districts across two years*. Minneapolis: University of Minnesota, Early Childhood Assessment Project.

Crnic, K., Greenberg, M., Ragozin, A., Robinson, N., & Basham, R. (1983). Effects of stress and social support on mothers and premature and full term infants. *Child Development, 54,* 209–217.

Crockenberg, S., & McCluskey, K. (1986). Change in maternal behavior during the baby's first year of life. *Child Development, 57,* 746–753.

Egeland, B., & Sroufe, L. A. (1983). *Early Maladaptation: A Prospective-Transactional Study: Final Report*. Washington, DC: Maternal and Child Health and Crippled Children's Services Research Grants Program.

Elkind, D. (1987). *Readiness for what?* Paper presented at the Symposium Assessment of Readiness for School: Implications for a Statistical Program. Washington, DC: Center for Education Statistics.

Entwistle, D., & Hayduk, L. (1981). Academic expectations and the school attainment of young children. *Sociology of Education, 54,* 34–50.

Fluharty, N. (1978). *Fluharty Preschool Speech and Language Screening Test*. Boston: Teaching Resources.

Garbarino, J. (1982). *Children and families in the social environment*. New York: Aldine.

Garmezy, N. (1984). Stress-resistant children: The search for protective factors. In J. E. Stevenson (Ed.), *Aspects of current child psychiatry research*. Oxford: Pergamon.

Garmezy, N., Masten, A., & Tellegen, A. (1984). The study of stress and competence in children: A building block for developmental psychopathology. *Child Development, 55,* 97–111.

Gartner, A., & Lipsky, D. K. (1987). Beyond special education: Toward a quality system for all students. *Harvard Educational Review, 57,* 367–395.

Hallahan, D. P., & Kaufman, J. M. (1982). *Exceptional children*. Englewood Cliffs, NJ: Prentice-Hall.

Hightower, A. D., Work, W. C., Cowen, E. L., Lotyczewski, B. S., Spinell, A. P., Guare, J. C., & Rohrbeck, C. A. (1986). The Teacher–Child Rating Scale: A brief objective measure of elementary children's school problem behaviors and competences. *School Psychology Review, 15,* 393–409.

Joiner, L. M. (1977). A technical analysis of the variation in screening instruments and programs in New York State. New York City University of New York, Center for Advanced Study in Education.

Keogh, B. K., Wilcoxen, A. G., & Bernheimer, L. (1986). Prevention services for at risk children: Evidence for policy and practice. In D. Farran & J. McKinney (Eds.), *Risk in intellectual and psychosocial development* (pp. 287–316). New York: Academic.

Lehr, C. A., Ysseldyke, J. E., & Thurlow, M. L. (1986). *Assessment practices in model early childhood educational programs*. Minneapolis: University of Minnesota, Early Childhood Assessment Project.

Lidz, C. S. (1987). *Dynamic assessment*. New York: Guilford.

Maccoby, E., & Martin, J. (1983). Socialization in the context of the family: Parent–child interaction. In P. Mussen (Ed.), *Handbook of child psychology: Vol. 4*. M. Hetherington (Ed.), *Socialization, personality, and social development* (pp. 1–102.). New York: Wiley.

McCarthy, D. (1972). Manual for McCarthy Scales of Children's Abilities. New York: Psychological Corporation.

Meisels, S. J. (1987). Uses and abuses of developmental screening and school readiness testing. *Young Children, 42,* 4–9.

National Commission on Excellence in Education. (1983). *A nation at risk: The imperative for educational reform.* Washington, DC: U.S. Government Printing Office.

Pallas, A. M., Entwistle, D. R., Alexander, K. L., & Cadigan, D. (1987). Children who do exceptionally well in first grade. *Sociology of Education, 60,* 257–271.

Pianta, R. (in press). Widening the debate on educational reform: Prevention as a viable alternative. *Exceptional Children.*

Pianta, R. (1988). The Teacher–Child Relationship Scale. Charlottesville, VA: University of Virginia.

Pianta, R., & Reeve, R. E. (in preparation). The multiple predictors of retention in kindergarten. Manuscript in preparation.

Pianta, R., Egeland, B., & Sroufe, L. A. (in press). A prospective, longitudinal investigation of competence and maladaptation in middle childhood. In J. Rolf, A. Masten, D. Cicchetti, K. Nuechterlein, & S. Weintraub (Eds.), *Risk and protective factors in the development of psychopathology.* New York: Cambridge University Press.

Pianta, R., & Reeve, R. E. (1987). The Preschool Behavior Rating Scale. Charlottesville, VA: University of Virginia, Project PATS.

Pianta, R., Erickson, M. F., Wagner, N., Kreutzer, T., & Egeland, B. (submitted for publication). The relationship of parent–child interaction measures to referral for help in the primary grades. *School Psychology Review.*

Power, T. J., & Bartholomew, K. L. (1987). Family-school relationship patterns: An ecological assessment. *School Psychology Review, 16,* 498–512.

Ramey, C. T., Bryant, D. M., Sparling, J. J., & Wasik, B. H. (1985). Project CARE: A Comparison of two early intervention strategies to prevent retarded development. *Topics in Early Childhood Special Education, 5*(2), 12–25.

Ramey, C. T., MacPhee, D., & Yates, K. O. (1982). Preventing developmental retardation: A general systems model. In L. A. Bond & J. M. Joffe (Eds.), *Facilitating infant and early childhood development* (pp. 343–401). Hanover, NH: University Press of New England.

Ramey, C. T., Stedman, D. S., Borders-Patterson, A., & Mengel, W. (1978). Predicting school failure from information available at birth. *American Journal of Mental Deficiency,* Vol. 82, 525–534.

Rose, J. S., Medway, F. J., Cantrell, V. L., & Marus, S. H. (1983). A fresh look at the retention–promotion controversy. *Journal of School Psychology, 31,* 201–211.

Rutter, M. (1975). *Helping troubled children.* London: Penguin.

Salvia, J., & Ysseldyke, J. E. (1982). *Assessment in special and remedial education.* Boston: Houghton-Mifflin.

Shepard, L. (1987). *The assessment of readiness for school: Psychometric and other considerations.* Paper presented at the Symposium Assessment of Readiness for School: Implications for a Statistical Program. Washington, DC: Center for Education Statistics.

Shipman, V. (1987). Basic abilities needed as a precondition for school. Paper presented at the Symposium Assessment of Readiness for School: Implications for a Statistical Program. Washington, DC: Center for Education Statistics.

Sroufe, L. A., & Rutter, M. (1984). The domain of developmental psychopathology. *Child Development, 55,* 17–29.

Thorndike, R. L., Hagen, E. P., & Sattler, J. M. (1986). *Guide for administering and scoring the Stanford-Binet Intelligence Scale: Fourth Edition.* Chicago: Riverside.

U.S. Office of Education. (1987). *Ninth Annual Report to Congress on the Implementation of the Education of the Handicapped Act.* Washington, DC: U.S. Government Printing Office.

Waters, E., & Sroufe, L. A. (1983). Social competence as a developmental construct. *Developmental Review, 3,* 79–97.

Werner, E. E., & Smith, R. S. (1982). *Vulnerable but invincible: A longitudinal study of resilient children and youth.* New York: McGraw-Hill.

Ysseldyke, J. E., & Algozzine, B. (1982). *Critical issues in remedial and special education.* Boston: Houghton-Mifflin.

Ysseldyke, J., Christenson, S., Pianta, R., & Algozzine, B. (1983). An analysis of teachers reasons and desired outcomes for students referred for psychoeducational assessment. *Journal of Psychoeducational Assessment, 1,* 73–83.

Ysseldyke, J. E., Thurlow, M. L., O'Sullivan, P. J., Weiss, J. A., Nania, P. A., & Lehr, C. A. (1986). *Policy analysis of screening and referral for early childhood special education programs.* Minneapolis: University of Minnesota, Early Childhood Assessment Project.

CHAPTER 16

Step-by-Step Procedure for the Assessment of Language Minority Children

Linda C. Caterino
Western Behavioral Professionals

Psychoeducational assessment is one of the primary responsibilities of the school psychologist. It can be an extremely significant event in a student's school career, since important placement decisions are based on the results of the evaluation procedure. The procedure is even more critical when it is used with non-English-speaking (NEP) children, or students who have limited English language proficiency (LEP) (Barona & Santos de Barona, 1987). Here the match between the child and the educational environment is less exact, since there are so few bilingual psychologists and most of the typical evaluation procedures are designed for the majority Anglo culture. Thus, the assessment process must be executed with extreme care when the psychologist is working with the LEP or NEP student. Although much of the debate about eliminating standardized test instruments completely for these children is over, and most psychologists agree that there may be a need for standardized assessment at times, typical testing procedures still need to be adapted for the LEP or NEP child. Let us review the steps of the evaluation procedure for these children.

THE EVALUATION PROCEDURE

The Referral Process

Usually the LEP child is referred to the school psychologist through the standard school referral process. Typically the student is not mastering basic academic concepts or is exhibiting unacceptable or unusual behavior at school. The first step

for the school psychologist is to exercise her or his skills as a consultant (DeBlassie & Franco, 1983) just as one would with a native English speaker.

Record Review

Prior to convening an interdisciplinary meeting the psychologist should review whatever school records are available in order to gather more information about the referred child. The child's attendance record should be checked in order to determine if the child has attended school for an adequate amount of time to have benefited from school instruction. This is particularly important with bilingual or LEP children, since they may not have been exposed to the routine educational curriculum. They may have recently immigrated to the United States and may not have attended school regularly, if at all in their native land. Their schooling may have been interrupted, particularly if their parents are involved in migrant farm work or if they frequently return to their homeland. In addition, undocumented aliens may not always enroll their children in school for fear of deportation.

The record review process will also tell school staff what kind of special assistance, if any, the children under consideration have had if they have been previously enrolled in schools. For example, they may have attended a bilingual program in which they were taught exclusively in their first language and have now moved to a new school before the transition to English was completed. In these cases, even children who have been instructed in a U.S. school may have learned to read in their primary language and not in English.

It is also important to determine if children who might be LEP or NEP have attended a preschool program such as Headstart or if kindergarten brought their first exposure to English. The psychologist should determine if they have received any ESL (English as a second language) assistance or if they have been enrolled in any special education programs, such as speech and language, learning disabilities, or mentally or emotionally handicapped. The children's records should also be checked for evidence of any grade retentions. Any informal interventions should also be noted. Children's cumulative records should provide information concerning their scores on standardized tests as well as the level of mastery of district objectives. School records can and should be requested from foreign countries in order to determine if the students were experiencing academic difficulties prior to leaving their homeland. Medical records, including vision and hearing test results, should also be reviewed.

Interdisciplinary Team Meeting

The psychologist should then convene an interdisciplinary team meeting consisting of the school administrator, classroom and special education teachers, the speech pathologist, and whatever special area teachers as may be necessary. At such meetings, referral agents should share their concerns about the student. They should be encouraged to bring samples of the student's work as well as records of test scores and other information concerning homework and classroom habits. All concerned teachers should discuss their contacts with the referred students. The psychologist can share such information as can be gleaned from school records in cases in which there is no personal direct contact with the child. The psychologist should attempt to assist the referral agent, usually the classroom teacher, in specifically defining the referral problems, and in forming goals for the student. The team

should then attempt to devise appropriate interventions.

The team may determine that it does not yet have adequate information about a given child, and the teacher or psychologist may be directed to obtain more information about the student, including gathering baseline data for specific behaviors or testing specific academic skills through normative or criterion-referenced techniques. On the other hand, the team may feel that it is ready to implement a specific intervention procedure with the student. In either case, the next step should be an in-depth observation of the child by the psychologist. Usually the psychologist may wish to wait until after the first interdisciplinary meeting so as to focus on the teacher's specific concerns and observe the reported problematic behaviors.

Behavioral Observations

Several observation periods are recommended for sampling a variety of classroom activities so as to gain a complete profile of the student. For example, it can be valuable to observe bilingual children in their regular classroom and in an ESL/LEP class to determine if there are any changes in their behavior when they are able to use their primary language (as they typically are in bilingual resource classes). The evaluation should include formal record-keeping procedures (such as time sampling) as well as informal anecdotes. An observation of a same-sexed and same-age peer from the same culture, and if possible with an immigration history similar to that of each target child, can also provide valuable information.

Parent Interviews

Even though a child's parents have been previously notified of the intervention procedures and may have even been part of a home-based program, they need to be contacted again. Formal written permission, after a discussion of parental rights, must be obtained. In addition, an in-depth parent interview should be conducted by the school psychologist, with the aid of an interpreter, if necessary. A home visit which will usually provide the psychologist with invaluable information should always be made. Unfortunately most home visits are made during the day while the child is in school. It is preferable to schedule these visits near the end of the school day, so that some private time with parents is possible prior to the child's arrival from school, following which the child's inter-actions with family members can be assessed. These visits can be quite inform-ative: children who are shy at school may be found to be quite dominant at home and may even help interpret for their parents. A child's social and play opportunities should also be observed. For example, does the child have the opportunity to play with same-age English-speaking children? What language is used at home with parents, peers, and siblings? Are there extended family members living in the household? The psychologist should observe parent–child interactions as well as the presence of material items such as running water, heat, electricity, and television. If television and/or radio are present, what language is listened to and are educational shows available to the child? Does the home contain books, magazines, newspapers, educational games, and so on? Does the child have a quiet place to do homework? What are the child's household chores and/or work requirements? Finally, what is the parents' attitude toward the school and toward education in general?

The actual interview should review the child's developmental history, health problems, and educational history as well as any social or developmental concerns. If any health records or medications are available, they should be examined. Paren-tal concerns about the child's behavior should also be addressed since this may be one of the few opportunities the psychol-ogist will have to meet privately with the parent. And finally, what are the parents' expectations for the student?

Initial Intervention

After meeting with the parents and gathering all necessary information, the interdisciplinary team should determine the most effective intervention for each child.

Specific intervention procedures can take the form of a referral to a formal program such as speech, ESL or LEP, or they can be individually designed programs such as behavior modification techniques, preci-sion teaching, peer tutoring, individual or group counseling, or social skills training. An interesting technique to aid in social adaptation may be to pair a referred child with another student from the same cultural background and language group for an interim period in order to aid the child's initial adjustment. Any proposed interven-tions should be shared with the children's parents and parental permission should be secured.

After 2–3 weeks of the intervention period, the interdisciplinary team needs to reconvene to determine if the interventions have been successful and should be con-tinued, or if alternative intervention strat-egies should be developed. Information concerning the observation periods should be shared at this time. Parents should be notified about any progress made during the intervention period. Another interven-tion may be tried for a further 2–3 weeks. If after that time little or no improvement is noted, the team will probably come to the decision that a formal evaluation should be conducted by the school psychologist. Messick (1984) stated that, in order to lessen the risk of stigma and misclassification, formal assessment procedures should not be implemented until any deficiencies in a child's academic environment have been ruled out and it can be documented that the child has failed to learn under reason-able alternative approaches. Thus, formal evaluation should proceed only when all other interventions have been unsuccessful or if the child's problems appear to be extremely severe.

Psychologists must be certain to clarify the goals of the evaluation procedure with school staff and to inform them of the limitations of psychoeducational assess-ment with bilingual students. They should impress upon the staff that standardized tests are low in predictive validity when used with students who are culturally or linguistically different, but that they may yield important diagnostic information; hopefully this will assist the staff in developing realistic expectations of the evaluation. Once all the information has been compiled and the goals of the referral agent have been clarified, the psychologist is ready to administer the standardized assessment instruments.

THE ASSESSMENT BATTERY

Language Dominance Assessment

First, the language dominance measures should be administered. These may be given by a speech and language pathologist or a school psychologist — someone fluent in the child's primary language. The language dominance testing procedure is not a language preference measure, but rather an assessment of the children's relative strengths in their first language (L_1) and English (L_2). As such it should be broad-based. The child's receptive (listening and reading) and expressive (speaking and writing) skills should be measured, as well as mastery of linguistic skills, including phonology, semantics, and syntax (Mattes & Omark, 1984; McLaughlin & Lewis, 1986). In addition, language samples should be taken to ascertain the subjects' communication skills in informal situations (Erickson, 1981; Prutting, 1983).

Unfortunately many language dominance measures have not been well developed, particularly in reference to their technical excellence, and most have been published without reliability and validity data (Silverman, Noa, & Russell, 1976). Of the 27 language dominance measures reviewed by Oakland, De Luna, and Morgan in 1977, only 9 reported any kind of reliability data. Willig (1986) reported that "tests of language proficiency have low reliability and low convergent validity." Furthermore, Omark (1981) reported that most of these measures were standardized on predominantly Anglo samples.

Most of the language dominance tests assess only one or two aspects of language. For example, the James Language Dominance Test (James, 1974) and the Dos Amigos Verbal Language Scales (Critchlow, 1974) purport to determine language dominance at the vocabulary level only. The Bilingual Syntax Measure (Burt, Dulay,

& Hernandez-Chavez, 1975), the Basic Inventory of Natural Language (Herbert, Moesser, & Sancho, 1974), and the Mat-Sea-Cal Instruments for Assessing Language Proficiency (Matluck & Mace-Matluck, 1974) all attempt to establish dominance through the mastery of grammatical features. The Language Assessment Scales I and II (DeAvila & Duncan, 1981) assess auditory discrimination, articulation, receptive syntax, expressive vocabulary, and oral production, but they include only a small sample of each behavior (Ramirez, 1985). Much depends on the authors' conception of language (e.g., whether language is a global function or many separate proficiencies).

Not surprisingly, since the language dominance measures may assess different components of language, they may yield different dominance scores for the same child. A child who is dominant in the vocabulary of one language may be dominant in the syntax of another (Rodriguez-Brown & Elias-Olivares, 1982; Ulibarri, Spencer, & Rivas, 1981). In addition, language dominance measures, aside from not correlating too well with each other, may not correlate well with independent language samples (Gerken, 1978b).

Often the results of language dominance measures will reveal that a child speaks a combination of languages (DeAvila & Havassy, 1974); however, the language dominance measures may not indicate a high level of fluency in either language. Even if the dominance measure indicates fluency in English, the psychologist should be aware of the distinction made by Cummins and his colleagues (1979, 1980, 1981, 1984; Cummins & McNeely, 1987) between basic interpersonal communication skills (BICS) and cognitive/academic language proficiency (CALP): Typically an immigrant child may establish the first skill (BICS) within 2 years, yet the second (CALP) may take as long as 5–7 years after exposure to L_2. It has not really been established what level of language is assessed by each language dominance measure. However, by using the best language dominance measure for each child based on his/her age and circumstance (see Appendix I for a list of measures), as well as a language sample in both languages, and home language information, language dominance can be established with some level of certainty.

The use of translations. At this point it is important to note that the translation of a standardized test into a child's primary language is not enough to assure that the test is unbiased. Translation will not guarantee that the content of the test is appropriate for a particular group, since translation of tests commonly used in U.S. schools still reflects the concepts of the dominant U.S. culture (Mercer, 1979). Moreover, it is difficult to provide a translation that would be appropriate for all dialects of a single language group. For example, the Spanish of Puerto Ricans in Florida is different from the Spanish of Mexican-Americans in California (Lynch & Lewis, 1982). Furthermore, direct translation does not yield technically equivalent forms owing to changes in the level of difficulty and the fact that for some concepts there may be no direct conceptual equivalent in the second language (Olmedo, 1981; DeAvila & Havassy, 1974). In order to be considered unbiased, a test must be specifically designed to sample appropriate concepts in the culture and must have been normed on the group in question. For example, norming in Mexico City does not guarantee that a test is appropriate for a Mexican-American group in Phoenix, Arizona.

Use of spontaneous translation provided by interpreters is also fraught with problems. The interpreter may not be perfectly fluent in both languages and if fluent, may still be a poor translator since translation requires other skills such as good short-term memory, as well as just language skill. In addition, the interpreter may not be properly trained in test administration procedures and may overidentify with the children to be tested, and subconsciously prompt them. Also knowledge of the child's primary language does not ensure that the interpreter can relate to them or their culture and provide the proper amount of encouragement and support. Nuttal, Landurand, and Goldman (1984) stated that interpreters should be avoided if possible, but Plata (1982), while aware of many of the problems involved with using interpreters, held that "using interpreters to try to compromise the effect of the examiner's language on test results is better than no attempt at all" (p. 4). In some cases, if a child speaks a relatively rare language, interpreters may be the only solution.

The environment of children who were born in the United States or have lived here for an extended period of time is most probably a combination of the native and the U.S. culture, and their language may well be a combination of their L_1 and English. These children cannot be properly evaluated by using either an English language test or a test in their L_1. A combination of assessment measures should be employed.

Cognitive Assessment

After the child's language dominance has been determined, the next step is the assessment of cognitive abilities. The psychologist must then select the most appropriate measure.

The best procedure for evaluating children who have recently immigrated is to use a test developed and normed in their own country and administered in their L_1. The Bateria Kaufman de Evaluación para Niños (Kaufman & Kaufman, in preparation) was intended to be a test that would be appropriate for natives of Latin American countries and recent immigrants; however, recent word from the publisher (AGS) indicates that plans for such a project are "now on hold". The Escala de Inteligencia Wechsler para Niños–Revisada (Wechsler, 1982) is a Spanish translation of the WISC-R developed in Puerto Rico, but it is still essentially designed for the majority Anglo population and does not provide separate norms. The Bateria Woodcock Psico-Educativa en Español (Woodcock, 1982) is also available in Spanish, but like the English version, it needs much more research to determine its predictive validity (Cummins & Mascato, 1984).

Locally devised tests that have been normed in their own environment are theoretically more appropriate for children of distinct cultural groups, if these tests can demonstrate technical adequacy and appropriate reliability and validity. Usually, however, this is too great a task for an individual community to undertake. In addition, critics (DeBlassie & Franco, 1983) state that specific regional–ethnic norms may lead to reduced expectations for certain ethnic groups. Furthermore, there are just too many ethnic minorities to provide appropriate local norms for each one.

Another alternative assessment measure that has been advocated for use with culturally different students is the System of Multicultural Pluralistic Assessment (SOMPA) (Mercer & Lewis, 1978). The SOMPA uses the English version of the WISC-R but employs pluralistic norms to determine an estimated learning potential (ELP). Although the SOMPA appears to have been well-intentioned, there have been numerous criticisms of the procedure. For example, the test was normed on only California students and has not been found to generalize well to other areas of the country. Oakland (1983) found the predictive validity of the SOMPA to be quite low. He stated that the WISC-R IQs correlated in the .70s with reading and math achievement, but that ELPs correlated in only the middle to high .40s: "The concurrent prediction of reading and math achievement clearly are made more accurately with the IQ data" (p. 59). The SOMPA has been found to keep many children who would previously have been placed in special education in regular education, but it may also deny some children needed services.

Another option designed for the cognitive assessment of LEP students is the use of nonverbal assessment techniques such as the Culture Fair Intelligence Tests (CFIT) (Cattell & Cattell, 1977), the Leiter International Performance Scale (Leiter, 1979), the Raven Progressive Matrices (Raven, 1986), the Columbia Mental Maturity Scales (Burgemeister, Hollander, Blum, & Lorge, 1972), and the Test of Non-Verbal Intelligence (TONI) (Brown, Sherbenou, & Dollar, 1982). The Performance scales of the Wechsler series and, more recently, the Nonverbal scale of the Kaufman Assessment Battery for Children (Kaufman & Kaufman, 1983) have been used.

Several researchers have found that bilingual children score higher on nonverbal measures than on verbal scales (Christiansen & Livermore, 1970; Gerken, 1978a; Altus, 1953). Kaufman (1979) states that while the Verbal IQ is the best predictor of school achievement for U.S. Anglos, it may not be best for Spanish-speaking youngsters in the primary grades.

Wilen and Sweeting (1986) recommended the use of the Leiter and Columbia in the assessment of LEP students. The Columbia measures general reasoning ability and perceptual discrimination. The test does have Spanish directions, but its psychometric properties have not been well established (Sattler, 1974). The Raven also measures figural reasoning. It was originally standardized in England, but recently it has been restandardized for U.S. youngsters. The Cattell Culture-Fair series is available for children from age 4 to adult. The test measures such perceptual tasks as completing a series and classifying and solving incomplete designs, and it includes directions in Spanish. But again, its predictive validity with LEP students is not well documented.

The Test of Non-Verbal Intelligence appears to be a potentially useful measure. The directions can be given by pantomime and the subject responds by pointing to one of several possible answers. It, too, measures figural reasoning. Its standardization procedure sampled the United States in terms of ethnicity, geography, sex, race, and urban vs. rural. Its internal consistency and alternate form reliability are adequate. It also demonstrates appropriate validity with other nonverbal measures; however, it, too, requires more data to support its use with bilingual students.

There have been several criticisms of nonverbal, culture-fair measures. The foremost has been advanced by Anastasi (1976), who stated that "no single test can be universally applicable or equally fair to more than one cultural group, especially if the cultures are quite dissimilar" (p. 345).

Oakland and Matusek (1977) supported this statement and posited that if a test is to be universally appropriate it will not be able to assess important psychological characteristics. Finally, Cummins

(1984) held that culture-free would be tantamount to experience-free.

Aside from the theoretical arguments, another criticism of culture-fair tests is that many have weak technical data and several (e.g., Leiter) were not normed on bilingual U.S. populations. Oakland and Matusek (1977) reported that culture-fair measures do not yield similar means and standard deviations for different racial groups and social classes. Another criticism is the nonpredictability of the nonverbal measures for academic performance (Mercer, 1979b).

Oller (1981) presented an interesting criticism of nonverbal tests, particularly the Raven: "Solutions require utilization of deep grammatical structures including subject–predicate relations, negative conjunctions and abstract lexicon capable of differentiating abstract concepts and relationships." In other words, solutions to these nonverbal tasks require language mediation. But there is no reason why students cannot use their L_1 or even both languages to solve these problems; hence, knowledge of two languages can be a benefit in that if a solution is not readily apparent through mediation in one language, the second can be tried (Peal & Lambert, 1962).

According to Nuttal (1987) the WISC-R Performance scale is commonly used with bilingual children, and Esquivel (1985) reported that the Block Design subtest was found to have the most crosscultural validity and to correlate significantly with classroom math performance. However, the psychologist must always bear in mind that although the WISC-R was standardized on 2,200 individuals, the exact percentage of specific minorities represented is at best difficult to ascertain. For example, only 25 children tested were members of Indian, Oriental, or other minority groups (approximately 1%), and we do not know how many of these students came from bilingual households. In addition, "Puerto Ricans and Chicanos were categorized as white or nonwhite in accordance with visible physical characteristics" (Wechsler, 1974).

The K-ABC nonverbal scale probably represents one of the most attractive nonverbal alternatives, pending further data gathering on the TONI. The test can be given in pantomime and only motor responses are required; however, an important criticism of the K-ABC is that it overrepresents middle socioeconomic class subjects and higher educational levels in its Mexican-American norm group. A further concern is its failure to sample an adequate number of skills. For example, many critics maintain that it does not assess complex cognitive skills.

Another point to mention in respect to nonverbal testing is that a level of test-taking sophistication is required even for these tests. Children who have never been exposed to puzzles and educational games or who do not understand how to function in a competitive situation or how to comply with time limits will have great difficulty on these tests. The behavior of the examiner even on nonverbal tests is also important. Thomas, Hertzig, Drym, and Fernandez (1971) found that bilingual children will perform better when tested by examiners who encourage children to participate, verbalize, and persevere. In addition, it may be necessary for psychologists to alter the pace of their testing. For example, Brandt (1984) reported that Native Americans may wait up to 11–12 seconds before beginning speech, whereas Anglo English speakers usually pause only 1–2 seconds.

Another alternative to traditional testing is the Cartoon Conservation Scales (DeAvila & Havassy, 1974). Here the child is exposed to eight Piagetian tasks (conservation of number, length, substance, distance, horizontality and volume, as well as perspective and probability), using a cartoon-like format. The examinee can respond to either spoken or written language (English or Spanish). DeAvila found that the performance of Mexican-American and Anglo-American samples were both within expected limits of cognitive development for their chronological age and no significant differences between groups were rated.

A further possibility is the use of the Learning Potential Assessment Device (LPAD) (Feuerstein, 1979). This test represents an innovative test–teach–test approach. Feuerstein believes that children learn through their interaction with adults in mediated learning experiments. Cultural deprivation, then, is the result of inadequate mediated learning. While using the LPAD, the tester assumes the role of teacher and attempts to provide the student with mediated learning. For example, the student may first perform a reasoning task, such as the Raven matrices without examiner assistance. The examiner then teaches the appropriate strategy to the student, who then takes the test again without coaching. The examiner attempts to assess the student's cognitive modifiability or ability to learn rather than a current "static" intellectual state. The primary disadvantage of the LPAD is that it is not normed and requires a great deal of time to administer. Moreover, the predictive validity with academic achievement is still to be determined. Again, more data are necessary in order to wholeheartedly accept the LPAD assessment as the instrument of choice for bilingual students.

While we are able to obtain a general estimate of children's intellectual potential by using nonverbal measures, we are not able to obtain information on their verbal abilities. We can also look at the full battery of the K-ABC or the Verbal scale of the WISC-R in a diagnostic manner in order to obtain more information on the students' capabilities. However, all school staff must be made aware of the limitations of the Verbal scale of the WISC-R and cautioned to look at the subtest pattern of strengths and weaknesses rather than focusing on the IQ figures, if these measures are to be used competently. Receptive vocabulary in English may be assessed with the Peabody Picture Vocabulary Test–Revised (PPVT–R) and may be compared to the Test de Vocabulario en Imagenes Peabody (TVIP) (Dunn, Lugo, Padilla, & Dunn, 1986). The TVIP uses Spanish words to measure receptive vocabulary skills. It is not an exact translation of the PPVT-R; instead all words from both forms of the PPVT-R were translated into Spanish and critiqued for their appropriateness to Spanish culture. Following field testing and item analysis, the test was shortened and separately standardized on Spanish-speaking children in Puerto Rico and Mexico. A drawback, however, is that norms are not available for

children from Spanish-speaking cultures within the United States.

DeBlassie and Franco (1983) write:

> We stress that the use of test and nontest data with culturally different Mexican-American and other minority group youth should place emphasis on description and prescription rather than on selection and prediction. In short, the predictive validity of most standardized test scores is poor, while the diagnostic validity is excellent, if they are used in conjunction with other data such as nontest data and demographic information. (p. 65)

Psychologists who become aware of the typical test profile of bilingual children can use these data in the analysis of individual youngsters. For example, the bilingual child will typically exhibit depressed scores on the Information, Vocabulary, Comprehension, and Similarities subtests of the WISC-R. Usually the Digit Span and Arithmetic subtest scores are the LEP student's highest verbal scores (Cummins, 1984). Upon observing that a student's lowest scores were on the Digit Span and Arithmetic subtests, that low scores were also found on the K-ABC Number Recall and Word Order subtests, and that similar behavior was exhibited in classroom observations, a school psychologist might well hypothesize that the child is experiencing an auditory memory or attentional problem. Moreover, the child's auditory memory skills could also be assessed in both L_1 and L_2 to determine if any between-language differences are evidenced. Baca and Cervantes (1984) and Cleary, Humphreys, Kendricks, and Wesman (1975) have proposed that tests in both languages should be used, since either learning score, standing alone, is undoubtedly an underestimate of the bilingual child's current repertoire because abilities in the two languages cannot overlap completely.

Thus, it would appear that recent immigrants whose primary language is not English should be evaluated in their native language. If tests in their native language are not available, they should be evaluated by nonverbal techniques, or DeAvila's Cartoon Conservation Scales or Feuerstein's LPAD. Children who show equivalent ability in English and their L₁ should be evaluated with a nonverbal measure supplemented with additional diagnostic information from verbal measures in both their L_1 and L_2. Children who demonstrate dominance in English and have been in this country more than 5 years can be evaluated by traditional methods.

Academic Assessment

Evaluation of academic skills can be performed through samples of classroom work as well as normative and criterion-referenced techniques. Cummins (1984) stated that after 2 years in the host country the children's academic skills should be assessed in the language of instruction.

Precision teaching techniques using local norms can also be quite useful; for example, the evaluator can examine the slope of a child's learning curves for different skills and compare them with those of other LEP and/or educationally handicapped children in the classroom. A comparison between the child's mastery of a skill in L_1 and L_2 can also be useful. An exceptionally long time to reach criterion may indicate the presence of learning problems.

A few academic tests in Spanish are available for use with newly arrived immigrants from Spanish-speaking countries or for children educated in bilingual classes in the United States. Of particular interest are the Prueba de Lectura y Lenguaje Escrito (PLLE) (Hammill, Larsen, Wiederholt, & Fountain-Chambers, 1982) and the Bateria Woodcock Psico-Educativa en Español (Woodcock, 1982). The PLLE test measures reading vocabulary, reading comprehension, writing skills, and spelling. It can be used with students in grades 3–10 and can be group-administered or individually administered. The test was normed on Spanish-speaking children in Mexico and Puerto Rico. The Woodcock also measures reading, math, and writing skills.

Social, Emotional, and Behavioral Assessment

The evaluation of bilingual children's social, emotional, and behavioral skills can also be quite difficult. At times it is difficult to discriminate problems stemming from language difference from problems resulting from behavior. For example, attentional difficulties can be found to be a function of poor receptive language skills in English rather than a symptom of anxiety or misbehavior. Esquivel (1985) and Wilen and Sweeting (1986) have written of the emotional and behavioral difficulties that can arise when children migrate to a completely new environment. They noted that these children may have had to leave behind family members or may have escaped from their homeland with a great deal of trauma.

In addition, the school situation can be quite different for these children. For example, Condon, Peters, and Sueiro-Ross (1979), as cited in Wilen and Sweeting (1986), stated that Mexican schools can be very authoritarian and some Mexican children may find it difficult to adjust to the new freedom they encounter in U.S. schools. Frequently, too, immigrant children may have to live in a state of poverty until their parents can find appropriate jobs, and the stress of poverty can trigger emotional reactions in the family.

It is important for school psychologists to become aware of acceptable cultural behaviors for the minority group of which their students are members. This can be done by employing cultural consultants who are members of the children's cultural group. In addition, Bernal (1977) has stressed the importance of parental and ethnic group involvement. The behaviors that are acceptable in the children's cultural community must be determined so that culturally different behaviors are not misdiagnosed as pathological or erroneously explained away as a mere cultural difference. For example, certain behaviors (e.g., lack of direct eye contact with Native American students) may not be directly attributable to shyness, but may be part of a politeness phenomenon or dominance-subordination procedures appropriate to their culture (Brandt, 1984).

Barona and Santos de Barona (1987) state that, in evaluating emotional and behavioral areas, "It is helpful to use a combination of assessment strategies that include, but are not limited to, clinical interviews, self-monitoring forms, behavioral observations, standardized testing, self-report forms and ratings from significant others" (p. 207).

Costantino and his colleagues (Costantino, 1982; cited in Esquivel, 1985) have designed an instrument, Tell-Me-A-Story (TEMAS), for use with Spanish-speaking students. The TEMAS is similar in format to the Thematic Apperception Test (Murray, 1971) but consists of minority and nonminority stimulus cards. The minority cards display predominantly Hispanic and Blacks in urban areas, and the nonminority cards show the same interaction with mostly nonminority figures. TEMAS also offers an objective scoring system with age-referenced norms. These are separate norms for sex and racial–ethnic groups. Reliability coefficients for the TEMAS range from the .40s to the .90s for specific scales.

Few other social–emotional measures have been specifically designed for bilingual children, although translations of such tests as the Early School Personality Questionnaire (ESPQ), the Children's Personality Questionnaire (CPQ), the High School Personality Questionnaire (HSPQ), the Children's Apperception Test (CAT), the Minnesota Multiphasic Personality Inventory (MMPI), and the Psychological Screening Inventory (PSI) are available. Inadequate research has been conducted to determine if these personality tests are applicable to bilingual children. Argulewicz, Abel, and Shuster (1985) suggested that the Children's Anxiety Scale (CAS) could be used with Mexican-American students. They found similar reliability across ethnic and gender groups when they administered these tests to kindergartners in Phoenix. However, they did not provide any predictive validity data in their study. Behavior rating scales have also been used with LEP students. Brown and Hammill (1982) have developed a rating scale in Spanish, the Perfil de Evaluación del Comportamiento (PEC), which is analogous to their Behavior Rating Profile (1978) in English. The PEC was normed on students in the United States and Mexico.

It provides teacher, parent, and student rating forms for an ecological approach.

Adaptive behavior measures can be used with children who are experiencing emotional problems as well as those suspected of mental deficiency. Two of these tests are available in Spanish: the Vineland (Sparrow, Balla, & Cicchetti, 1984) and the Adaptive Behavior Inventory for Children (ABIC) (Mercer & Lewis, 1978).

Critics have voiced concerns about the ABIC similar to their reservations about the rest of the SOMPA — specifically the lack of national norms. Another concern is the "no opportunity" category by which children are given one point even if they have not been allowed to complete a particular activity. The revised Vineland Adaptive Behavior Scales samples behavior from the following domains: communication, daily living skills, motor skills, and socialization, including interpersonal relationships, play and leisure time, and coping skills. The Vineland was standardized on a representative national sample, with no separate norms given for specific ethnic groups. Any test results should of course also be validated by observations and clinical interviews in the child's dominant language. In addition, the psychologist should determine if pathological behavior patterns are observed in different settings and not only in the classroom — that is, the behavior patterns should be noted by parents at home and be observed in social as well as academic environments.

FORMULATING THE PLACEMENT DECISION

After an evaluation is completed and all necessary data gathered, the interdisciplinary team should reconvene. All members need to be updated on the progress of the interventions in effect as well as the results of the psychological tests. The parents of children under examination need to be present at such meetings in order to participate in making the appropriate placement decisions for their children. If parents are unable or unwilling to come to the school, the psychologist may coordinate meetings at their home with the parents' approval. Role playing and other preparations may assist anxious parents in becoming more comfortable when meeting with school staff.

Legally, of course, parents need to be apprised of their placement rights in their primary language — whether or not the team decision is to place a child in a special education program. If a child is to be so placed, the parents also need to participate in formulating the child's individual education plan.

If it is determined that an LEP child needs special education assistance, the committee should not neglect the child's English language needs. In the past, federal regulations prohibited placement in both special education and ESL programs. This prohibition was detrimental to such LEP students as may have needed remediation in both academic and language areas.

Federal regulations require that special education students be reevaluated every 3 years. However, owing to the possibility that LEP students' needs may change more rapidly as their language improves, they should be reevaluated more frequently, if possible on an annual basis.

SUMMARY

While school psychologists can never be truly certain about the best course of action for an individual child and particularly for an LEP child, by checking at each point for biases in their procedure they can be certain that they have conducted the assessment in the most comprehensive manner possible (Tucker, 1980). They need to use reliable test instruments that have demonstrated appropriate validity for LEP students. They should be flexible enough to adapt their typical evaluation procedures to accommodate the needs of the LEP students. They may need to use more informal measures in their test battery and rely more heavily on parents and community consultants. They should, of course, be sure that they have not attempted the evaluation prematurely, but only after all other interventions have been tried with little or no success.

Another point for psychologists to keep in mind is Cummins' (1984) opinion that

special education may be a way to justify the lack of success with a child that has resulted from the inappropriateness of the educational system's regular program. Blaming the child serves to take the emphasis off of the educational system, thus preventing needed changes (Cummins & McNeely, 1987). The role of the psychologist is to determine the most appropriate educational programming for all children, including NEP and LEP students. If curriculum changes need to be made in order to improve the remediation of LEP students, the psychologist must then become involved in district curriculum planning, rather than merely selecting children for special education programming.

Finally, program evaluation of district special education and ESL programs should be made in order to determine what progress is being made by students in these programs, with particular attention being paid to the progress of LEP students. Information from the district program evaluation should be used to make needed curriculum changes, in order to improve programming for NEP and LEP special education students.

REFERENCES

Altus, G. J. (1953). WISC patterns of a selected sample of bilingual school children. *Journal of Genetic Psychology, 83,* 241–248.

Anastasi, A. (1976). *Psychological testing* (4th ed.). New York: MacMillan.

Argulewicz, E. N., Abel, R. R., & Shuster, S. A. (1985). Reliability and content validity of the Children's Anxiety Scale for Anglo-American and Mexican-American Kindergarten Children. *School Psychology Review, 14*(2), 236–238.

Baca, L. M., & Cervantes, H. T. (1984). *The bilingual special education interface.* St. Louis: Times-Mirror/ Mosby.

Barona, A., & Santos de Barona, M. (1987). A model for assessment of limited English proficiency students referred for special education services. In S. H. Fradd & W. J. Tikunoff (Eds.), *Bilingual education and bilingual special education* (pp. 183–209). San Diego, CA: College Hill Press.

Bernal, E. M. (1977). Introduction: Perspectives or non-discriminatory assessment. In T. Oakland (Ed.), *Educational assessment of minority children*. New York: Brunner/Mazel.

Brandt, E. A. (1984). The cognitive function of American Indian children. A critique of McShane and Plas. *School Psychology Review, 13*(1), 74–82.

Brown, L., & Hammill, D. (1978). *Behavior Rating Profile*. Austin, TX: Pro-Ed.

Brown, L., & Hammill, D. (1982). *Perfil de Evaluación del Comportamiento*. Austin, TX: Pro-Ed.

Brown, L., Sherbenou, R. J., & Dollar, S. F. (1982). *Test of Nonverbal Intelligence*. Austin, TX: Pro-Ed.

Burgemeister, B., Hollander Blum, L., & Lorge, I. (1972). *Columbia Mental Maturity Scale*. New York: Psychological Corporation.

Burt, M. K., Dulay, H., & Hernandez-Chavez, E. (1975). *Bilingual Syntax Measure*. New York: Psychological Corporation.

Cattell, R. B., & Cattell, A. K. S. (1977). *The Culture Fair Series*. Champaign, IL: Institute for Personality and Ability Testing.

Christiansen, T., & Livermore, G. A. (1970). A comparison of Anglo American and Spanish American children on the WISC. *Journal of Social Psychology, 81*, 9–14.

Cleary, A., Humphreys, L. G., Kendricks, S. A., & Wesman, A. (1975). Educational uses of tests with disadvantaged students. *American Psychology, 30*, 15–41.

Condon, E. C., Peters, J. J., & Suerro-Ross, C. (1979). Special education and the Hispanic child: Culture perspectives (Contract #300-78-0326). Philadelphia: Temple University, Mid-Atlantic Teacher Corps Network; U.S. Office of Education, Department of HEW. Cited in Wilen, D. K., & Sweeting, C. V. M. (1986). Assessment of Hispanic students. *School Psychology Review, 15*, 59–75.

Costantino, G. (1982). Temas: A new technique for personality assessment and psycho-therapy for Hispanic children. *Research Bulletin,* Hispanic Research Center Fordham University, 5 3–6. Cited in Esquivel, G. (1985). Assessment of limited English proficient and bilingual children. In A. Thomas & J. Grimes (Eds.), *Best practices in school psychology* (pp. 113–123). Kent, OH: National Association of School Psychology.

Critchlow, D. (1974). *Dos Amigos Verbal Language Scale*. San Rafale, CA: Academic Therapy Publishers.

Cummins, J. A. (1979). Linguistic interdependence and the educational development of bilingual children. *Review of Educational Research, 49*, 222–251.

Cummins, J. A. (1980). Psychological assessment of immigrant children: Logic of intuition. *Journal of Multilingual and Multicultural Development, 1*(2), 97–111.

Cummins, J. A. (1981). Age on arrival and immigrant second language learning in Canada: A reassessment. *Applied Linguistics, 2*, 132–149.

Cummins, J. A. (1984). *Bilingualism and special education: Issues in assessment and pedagogy*. San Diego, CA: College Hill.

Cummins, J. A., & McNeely, S. N. (1987). Language development, academic learning and empowering minority students. In S. H. Fradd & W. J. Tikunoff (Eds.), *Bilingual education and bilingual special education: A guide for administrators*. San Diego: College Hill.

Cummins, J. A., & Moscato, E. A. (1984). Research on the Woodcock-Johnson Psycho-educational Battery: Implication for practice and future investigations. *School Psychology Review, 13*(1), 33–40.

DeAvila, E. A., & Duncan, S. E. (1981). *Language Assessment Scales*. Corte Madera, CA: Linguametrics Group.

DeAvila, E. A., & Havassy, B. (1974). The testing of minority children: A new Piagetian approach. *Today's Education, 63*, 72–75.

DeAvila, E. A., & Havassy, B. (1975). *Cartoon Conservation Scales*. Corte Madera, CA: Linguametrics Group.

DeBlassie, R. R., & Franco, J. N. (1983). Psychological and educational assessment of bilingual children. In D. R. Omark & J. G. Erickson (Eds.), *The bilingual exceptional child* (pp. 55–68). San Diego, CA: College Hill.

Dunn, L. M., Lugo, D. E., Padilla, E. R., & Dunn, L. M. (1986). *Test de Vocabulario Imagenes Peabody*. Circle Pines, MN: American Guidance Service.

Erickson, J. G. (1981). Communication assessment of the bilingual bicultural child: An overview. In J. G. Erickson & D. R. Omark (Eds.), *Communication assessment of the bilingual bicultural child: Issues and guidelines* (pp. 1–24). Baltimore, MD: University Park Press.

Esquivel, G. B. (1985). Best practices in the assessment of limited English proficiency and bilingual children. In A. Thomas & J. Grimes (Eds.), *Best practices in school psychology* (pp. 113–123). Kent, OH: National Association of School Psychologists.

Feuerstein, R. (1979). *The dynamic assessment of retarded performers: The Learning Potential Assessment Device. Theory, instruments and techniques*. Baltimore, MD: University Park.

Gerken, K. (1978a). Performance of Mexican American children on intelligence tests. *Exceptional Children, 44*, 438–443.

Gerken, K. (1978b). Language dominance: A comparison of measures. *Language Speech and Hearing Services in Schools, 9*, 187–196.

Hammill, D., Larsen, S., Wiederholt, J., & Fountain-Chambers, J. (1982). *Prueba deLectura y Lenguaje Escrito: A test of reading and writing in Spanish.* Austin, TX: Pro-Ed.

Herbert, C. H., Moesser, A. I., & Sancho, A. R. (1974). *Basic Inventory of Natural Language.* San Bernardino, CA: CHEC Point Systems.

James, P. (1974). *James Language Dominance Test.* Austin, TX: Learning Concepts.

Kaufman, A. S. (1979). *Intelligence testing with the WISC-R.* New York: Wiley.

Kaufman, A., & Kaufman, N. (1983). Kaufman Assessment Battery for Children. Circle Pines, MN: American Guidance Service.

Kaufman, A., & Kaufman, N. (in preparation). *Bateria Kaufman de Evaluación para Niños.* Circle Pines, MN: American Guidance Service.

Leiter, R. G. (1979). *Leiter International Performance Scale.* Chicago: Stoelting.

Lynch, E. W., & Lewis, R. B. (1982). Multicultural considerations in assessment and treatment of learning disabilities. *Learning Disabilities, 1*, 93–103.

Matluck, J. H., & Mace-Matluck, B. (1974). *Mat-Sea-Cal.* Arlington, VA: Center for Applied Linguistics.

Mattes, L. J., & Omark, D. R. (1984). *Speech and language assessment of the bilingual handicapped.* San Diego, CA: College Hill.

McLaughlin, J. A., & Lewis, R. B. (1986). *Assessing special students.* Columbus, OH: Merrill.

Mercer, J. R. (1979a). *Technical manual, System of Multicultural Pluralistic Assessment.* Cleveland: Psychological Corporation.

Mercer, J. R. (1979b). In defense of radically and culturally nondiscriminatory assessment. *School Psychology Digest, 8*, 89–115.

Mercer, J. R., & Lewis, J. F. (1978). *System of Multicultural Pluralistic Assessment.* New York: Psychological Corporation.

Messick, S. (1984). Assessment in context: Appraising student performance in relation to instruction quality. *Educational Researcher, 13*(3), 3–8.

Murray, M. A. (1971). *Thematic Apperception Test.* Cambridge, MA: Harvard University Press.

Nuttal, E. (1987). Survey of current practices in the psychological assessment of limited-English-proficiency handicapped children. *Journal of School Psychology, 25*, 53–61.

Nuttal, E. V., Landurand, P. M., & Goldman, P. (1984). A critical look at testing and evaluation from a cross-cultural perspective. In P. C. Chin (Ed.), *Education of culturally and linguistically different exceptional children.* Reston, VA: Council for Exceptional Children.

Oakland, T. (1983). Concurrent predictive validity estimates for the WISC-R and ELPs by racial–ethnic and SES groups. *School Psychology Review, 12*(1), 57–61.

Oakland, T., & Matusek, P. (1977). Using tests in nondiscriminatory assessment. In T. Oakland (Ed.), *Psychological and educational assessment of minority children* (pp. 52–69). New York: Brunner/Mazel.

Oakland, T., DeLuna, C., & Morgan, C. (1977). Annotated bibliography of language dominance measures. In T. Oakland (Ed.), *Psychological and educational assessment of minority children* (pp. 196–232). New York: Brunner/Mazel.

Oller, J. W., Jr. (1981). Language as intelligence. *Language Learning, 31*, 465–492.

Olmedo, E. L. (1981). Testing linguistic minorities. *American Psychologist, 36*(10), 1078–1085.

Omark, D. R. (1981). Conceptualization of bilingual children: testing the norm. In J. G. Erickson & D. R. Omark (Eds.), *Communication assessment of the bilingual bicultural child* (pp. 99–114). Baltimore: University Park Press.

Peal, E., & Lambert, W. (1962). The relation of bilingualism to intelligence. *Psychological Monographs, 76*(546), 1–23.

Plata, M. (1982). *Assessment, placement and programming of bilingual exceptional pupils: A practical approach.* Reston, VA: ERIC Clearinghouse on Handicapped and Gifted Children, Council for Exceptional Children.

Prutting, D. A. (1983). Assessing communication behavior using a language sample. In D. R. Omark & J. G. Erickson (Eds.), *The bilingual exceptional child* (pp. 89–99). San Diego, CA: College Hill.

Ramirez, A. G. (1985). *Bilingualism through schooling: Cross-cultural education for minority and majority students.* Albany: State University of New York Press.

Raven, J. C. (1986). *Raven Progressive Matrices.* New York: Psychological Corporation.

Rodriguez-Brown, F., & Elias-Olivares, L. (1982). A search for congruency in language proficiency testing: What the tests measure, what the child does. *Bilingual Education Paper Series*, Vol. 5, No. 7. Los Angeles: Evaluation, Dissemination and Assessment Center.

Sattler, J. (1974). *Assessment of children's intelligence.* Philadelphia: Saunders.

Sattler, J. (1982). *Assessment of children's intelligence and special abilities* (2nd ed.). Boston: Allyn & Bacon.

Silverman, R. J., Noa, J. K., & Russell, R. H. (1976). *Oral language tests for bilingual students: An evaluation of language dominance and proficiency instruments.* Portland, OR: North West Regional Education Laboratory.

Sparrow, S. S., Balla, D. A., & Cicchetti, D. V. (1985). *Vineland Adaptive Behavior Scales.* Circle Pines, MN: American Guidance Service.

Thomas, A., Hertzig, M. E., Drym, I., & Fernandez, P. (1971). Examiner effect in IQ testing of Puerto Rican working class children. *American Journal of Orthopsychiatry, 41,* 809–821.

Tucker, J. A. (1980). *Nineteen steps for assuring nonbiased placement of students in special education.* Reston, VA: Council for Exceptional Children.

Ulibarri, D. M., Spencer, M. L., & Rivas, G. A. (1981). Language proficiency and academic achievement: A study of language proficiency tests and their relationship to school ratings as predictors of academic achievement. *NABE Journal, 3,* 47–80.

Wechsler, D. (1974). *Wechsler Intelligence Scale for Children-Revised.* New York: Psychological Corporation.

Wechsler, D. (1982). *Escala de Inteligencia Wechsler para Niños-Revisada.* New York: Psychological Corporation.

Wilen, D. K., & Sweeting, C. V. M. (1986). Assessment of limited English proficient Hispanic students. *School Psychology Review, 15*(1), 59–75.

Willig, A. C. (1986). Special education and the culturally and linguistically different child: An overview of issues and challenges. *Reading, Writing, and Learning Disabilities, 2,* 161–173.

Woodcock, R. (1982). *Bateria Woodcock Psico-Educativa en español.* Hingham, MA: Teaching Resources.

APPENDIX I

Language Dominance Measures

Basic Inventory of Natural Language (BINL). (Herbert, Moesser, & Sancho, 11979).

Ber-Sil Spanish Test. (Beringer, 1972–1977).

Bilingual Syntax Measure. (Burt, Dulay, & Hernandez-Chavez, 1975).

Del Rio Language Screening Test. (Toronto, Leverman, Hanna, Rosenzweigt, & Maldonado, 1975).

Dos Amigos Verbal Language Scale (Critchlow, 1975).

Flexibility Language Dominance Tests, Spanish/English. (Keller, 1982).

Home Bilingual Usage Estimate. (Skoczylas, 1971).

James Language Dominance Test. (James, 1975).

Language Assessment Scales (LAS). (DeAvila & Duncan, 1981).

Mat-Sea-Cal Instruments for Assessing Language Proficiency. (Matluck & Mace-Matluck, 1974).

Primary Acquisition of Language (PAL). (Apodaca & Enriquez, 1975).

Prueba del Desarrollo Inicial del Lenguaje. (Hresko, Reid, & Hamill, 1982).

Test for Auditory Comprehension of Language, English/Spanish. (Carrow, 1973).

Woodcock Language Proficiency Battery, English/Spanish. (Woodcock, 1980–1981).

CHAPTER 17

Identifying the Culturally Diverse Gifted Child

Cheryll A. Pearson
Scott County School District

Stephen T. DeMers
University of Kentucky

For nearly two decades, litigation and debate have focused on the overrepresentation of culturally diverse children in special education programs. Overrepresentation has been directly linked to measurement issues. For example, it has been argued that intelligence tests are biased against culturally different children, that it is inappropriate to administer tests requiring facility in English to non-English speaking children, and that comprehensive assessment techniques have not been used as a basis for making decisions about educational placements. Central to this contention is the belief that faulty assessment practices have led to overidentification of culturally different children for special education programs that have been viewed as substandard and dead end.

Unfortunately, in our preoccupation with the issues of overrepresentation, a converse but equally critical problem has been overlooked: namely, the underidentification of culturally different children for gifted and talented programs. Owing to measurement problems affecting identification/selection decisions, gifted children from culturally diverse backgrounds present the greatest risk: "of being unrecognized and not being provided adequate or appropriate educational services" (Jacob K. Javits Gifted and Talented Children and Youth Education Act of 1987, Section 2).

Measurement issues are common focal points in both the over and underidentification of culturally different children for special programs. Court cases involving the placement of ethnic minority children in special education classes have challenged the adequacy of commonly used measures and evaluation procedures. Given such controversy, it is surprising that tests and practices criticized as being biased against culturally different groups are commonly used to identify giftedness in these populations.

Fortunately, litigation addressing the overrepresentation of culturally different children has prompted more careful examination and modification of identification procedures for special education programs. In order to adequately identify giftedness in culturally different populations, the same scrutiny and modification of procedures seems warranted.

The purpose of this chapter is to examine the adequacy of various methods for identifying giftedness in culturally diverse children. Initially, however, we examine the concepts of giftedness and cultural diversity. Following this, the strengths and weaknesses of commonly used identification methods are discussed. Also, recommendations are made regarding the utility of these methods for identifying giftedness in children from culturally different backgrounds. Finally, assessment systems designed to identify culturally different gifted children are described.

CONCEPTS OF GIFTEDNESS

Like other complex psychological constructs, giftedness eludes precise definition. Definitions commonly refer to single abilities such as intelligence (Fox 1981), potential for high academic achievement (Whitmore, 1980), or creativity (Torrance, 1984). Some definitions include a combination of characteristics. For instance, Baldwin (1978) focused on the presence of high ability, task commitment, and problem-solving ability in cognitive, psychosocial, psychomotor, and creative areas.

Fortunately, the current federal definition, which states and school systems with gifted programs commonly ascribe to, is comprehensive and includes a broad spectrum of abilities. Specifically, Public Law 91-230 defines gifted and talented children as those identified at the preschool, elementary, or secondary level who possess "demonstrated or potential abilities that give evidence of high performance capability in areas such as intellectual, creative, specific academic, or leadership ability, or in the performing and visual arts" (Gifted and Talented Children's Education Act of 1978, Section 902). On this basis of such broad definitions, it has been estimated that approximately 3–5% of the school-age population is gifted (Harrington, 1982).

Although definitions of giftedness focus on a variety of abilities, children identified as gifted generally fall within a narrower category. It appears that children most readily identified as gifted are those who fill the societal needs as defined at a given time (Fischman, 1985). The current ideal seems to favor the highly achieving, highly motivated students (Fischman, 1985) who demonstrate an aptitude for school work (Gallagher, 1966). In fact, Grinter (1975) estimated that about 95% of children identified as gifted possess high intellectual (i.e., IQs ≥ 130) or academic capability. Therefore, the identification process usually focuses on children's performance on intelligence tests (Renzulli, 1975) and on academic superiority (Fischman, 1985), to the exclusion of the existence of the broader spectrum of valuable characteristics (Renzulli, 1975).

Another limiting factor in selection procedures is the requirement that both intellectual and academic superiority be demonstrated. Often, youngsters who function at or above the 98th percentile in academic achievement are not considered for gifted programs unless their IQs are commensurate with their achievement (Fischman, 1985). Unfortunately, identification practices that emphasize high achievement and high IQ almost inevitably identify children with a background of high socioeconomic status (SES) and exclude culturally and linguistically different children (Fischman, 1985). Essentially school districts tend to seek and find white, middle-class academic achievers (Richert, 1985). Culturally different children, on the other hand, are typically overlooked. In Terman and Oden's (1947) classic investigation, Italian, Portuguese, Mexican, and black children were least frequently identified as gifted.

CULTURALLY DIFFERENT POPULATIONS

The dominant national culture shared by most individuals in this country is known as *macroculture* (Gollnick & Chinn, 1986). Within the U.S. macroculture, numerous subcultures based on national or ethnic origin, socioeconomic status, and primary language also exist. Members of these subcultures usually share certain cultural patterns that are not common to the U.S. macroculture (Gollnick & Chinn, 1986). Also, individuals may be members of one or several subcultures. For instance, a Mexican-American child, whose primary language is Spanish, may also be from a low-SES background. Thus, this child is a member of three subcultures based on ethnic, linguistic, and socioeconomic identity.

It is often assumed that children who are members of minority subcultures are educationally, environmentally, or economically deprived. Consequently, such children are automatically, and sometimes inappropriately, labeled "disadvantaged." Not only does this label have negative connotations, but it also may be misleading. For instance, an ethnically different child from an affluent background who is afforded the same educational and environmental advantages of children from the majority culture should not be regarded as disadvantaged.

On the other hand, membership in various ethnic, linguistic or socioeconomic groups does imply that the group members share some cultural patterns that set them apart from the macroculture. Thus, children who are members of various subcultures can be viewed as culturally diverse. Other writers have used this label to describe children who are members of subcultures. For example Clark (1983) used the label *culturally diverse* to describe children who are reared in a culture that has values and attitudes that differ significantly from those of the macroculture. Similarly, Baldwin (1978) defined culturally different children as those who grow up in conditions of geographic isolation or socioeconomic deprivation or who are racially, ethnically, or linguistically different.

The present authors have chosen to use the less pejorative and perhaps more accurate labels *culturally different* or *culturally diverse* to describe children who are members of subcultures. In this chapter, the focus will be on gifted children who are ethnically or linguistically different from the majority culture and those who are from low SES backgrounds.

CHARACTERISTICS OF GIFTED CHILDREN FROM CULTURALLY DIVERSE BACKGROUNDS

Renzulli (1975) observed that culturally diverse children are the nation's largest untapped source of human intelligence and creativity. Recent census data indicate that nearly 18% of the U.S. population is non-Anglo and that incomes of 12.4% of the U.S. population are below poverty level (U.S. Census Bureau, 1987). Thus, millions of individuals fit into the *culturally different* category.

Although there is much diversity within this group, some characteristics associated with giftedness in culturally diverse children have been identified. Personal, school, and social characteristics of culturally different gifted children that can serve as behavioral guides to identification have been described by Baldwin (1973), Farrell (1973), McMillin, (1975), and Torrance (1964) (see Clark, 1983). In respect to personal characteristics, culturally diverse gifted children tend to be more alert, curious, independent, resourceful, and wil-

ling to take initiative. Also, they are eager to try new things, imaginative in their thinking, fluent in nonverbal communication, able to learn through experience, and they possess varied interests.

In the schools, culturally different gifted children often exhibit high mathematical ability and a more flexible approach to problem solving, are able to retain and use information, show a desire to learn, and respond well to visual media. Additionally, they are able to recognize relationships between seemingly unrelated ideas, they use language that is rich in imagery, and they are imaginative story tellers. Socially, these children may demonstrate leadership ability within their cultural peer group, as well as responsible social behavior, a mature sense of humor, and entrepreneurial ability.

Other characteristics associated with cultural diversity may obscure giftedness and prevent identification. Clark (1983) described a number of culturally determined traits that run counter to stereotypic views of giftedness. For instance, Asian children tend to be quiet, are less likely to join in group discussions, have had little experience with independent thinking, value conformity, and tend to be self-critical. Jewish culture tends to value achievement; consequently, some Jewish children exhibit competitive and perfectionistic attitudes that cause tension and frustration in learning new material (Clark, 1983).

Mexican-American children may be less familiar with the English language and thus may be less verbal in a classroom in which English is the dominant language. Also, Mexican-American children tend to be less competitive than Anglos and their families often place more emphasis on the family than on achievement and individual development. In addition, they may place little value on education after high school (Clark, 1983).

Black children often have limited experience with extended language patterns; therefore they may not be as verbally fluent as other gifted children (Clark, 1983). Similarly, some Native Americans have had little exposure to the English language and tend to be quiet in the classroom. Also, they tend to learn through listening, rather than active questioning, and value humbleness and patience over achievement and quick success in school (Utah Indian Education Newsletter, 1976).

The academic performance of gifted minority children may be depressed by cultural expectations and peer pressure. Lindstrom and Van Sant (1986) observed that expectations for achievement have traditionally been low for minority students. Disadvantaged peers may pressure gifted students to conform to group norms by eschewing the values of the majority culture (e.g., achievement in school) (Lindstrom & Van Sant, 1986). Additionally, minority children who are successful in school may have to contend with negative social consequences. For example, minority students often are pressured into staying in their cultural peer group by denying methods used by the majority culture to gain success (again, academic achievement is a prime example) (Colangelo & Zaffran, 1979). Peers may even ostracize gifted students who strive to achieve good grades (Lindstrom & Van Sant, 1986).

It also has been suggested that many culturally different children are ill prepared for the task demands of school (Davis & Rimm, 1985) and that they suffer from inferior schooling (Gay, 1978). As a result of their less adequate school experience, culturally diverse gifted children may not develop basic academic skills that are prerequisite to performance of higher cognitive tasks (Davis & Rimm, 1985). This contention is supported by the finding that the academic performance of children from low-SES backgrounds tends to be below that of middle-class children (Coleman et al., 1966). Therefore, giftedness in culturally different children may be obscured by academic underachievement.

The affects on development that derive from a history of cultural disadvantage have been compared to those of emotional disturbance (Gowan, 1968). Gowan suggested that motivational, nutritional, developmental, social, and cultural factors associated with cultural disadvantage tend to flatten out a child's peak performance, making it inconsistent and keeping it below test potential. Furthermore, it was suggested that the effectiveness of disadvantaged gifted children is undermined by alienation, which results in hostility or resentment toward authority that blocks creative performance (Gowan, 1968).

In summary, culturally different gifted children exhibit different strengths than majority culture gifted children. For instance, they may be fluent in nonverbal, rather than in verbal, communication. They may be imaginative story tellers rather than prolific writers. Also, the culturally different gifted child may be a leader in her or his own peer group rather than president of the student council. Unfortunately, teachers generally are not trained to look for such characteristics in nominating children for gifted and talented programs. To further complicate matters, culturally different gifted children may exhibit behaviors that are antithetical to views of giftedness. For example, because linguistically different children have had less experience with the English language, they may be uncommunicative in class. Additionally, because of differences in cultural values, some gifted children may be noncompetitive and may place little value on academic achievement. Because culturally different gifted children exhibit such behaviors and because identification practices often emphasize high academic achievement and high scores on IQ tests, the culturally and/or linguistically different child is often excluded in the search for giftedness.

RATIONALE FOR IDENTIFYING CULTURALLY DIVERSE GIFTED CHILDREN

Identifying culturally different children for gifted programs is important for several reasons. First, gifted and talented programs provide an opportunity for children to adequately develop their special abilities and skills. Second, gifted and talented programs provide the opportunity for those enrolled to associate with children who have similar abilities, concerns, sensibilities, and interests (Fischman, 1985). Third, the Jacob & Javits Gifted and Talented Children and Youth Education Act of 1987 recently passed in Congress, specifies that services for the gifted must be extended to children from disadvantaged backgrounds in recognition of the fact that such children are "a national resource vital to the future of the Nation and its security and well-being." Finally, failing to identify culturally different gifted children for special programs is a tragic waste of a vital resource (Torrance, 1977).

OVERVIEW OF PROBLEMS WITH COMMONLY USED IDENTIFICATION METHODS

Although identifying culturally different gifted children is a pressing demand, there are numerous problems with current methods. For instance, many commonly used tests are inadequate: Fischman (1985) has even claimed that there are no acceptable psychometric means to identify giftedness in culturally different children. In any case, there are several problems associated with using tests to identify giftedness in culturally diverse populations.

First, identification usually places too much emphasis on IQ tests (Minner & Prater, n.d.). In fact, individual IQ tests and achievement tests tend to be the most frequently used methods to identify giftedness (Jenkins, 1979; Martinson, 1973). Overreliance on one type of test score ignores the existence and worth of a broader spectrum of highly valuable human characteristics (Gallagher, 1975). Second, minority children often lack an orientation to testing (Rosenfield, 1983), and their test performance may not adequately reflect their capability. For example, Sullivan (1973) pointed out that the use of achievement tests may actually impede the identification of gifted black children because of their less than optimal performance, which is characterized by guessing, skipping items, and lack of effort.

Third, minorities often are inadequately represented in norming samples of many commonly used instruments (Bernal, 1979). Consequently, such tests may not be appropriate for culturally different children, and generally there is no means to compare their performance to that of children from similar backgrounds. Furthermore, Renzulli (1973) suggested

that standardized measures are often heavily culturally loaded and thus discriminate against children who are culturally different. Similarly, Harrington (1982) argued that IQ tests may be culturally biased against minorities in terms of item selection, subtest construction, and standardization. In light of such views, tests may tend to identify highly acculturated gifted children (Rosenfield, 1983) rather than those who identify with a minority culture.

Another problem in obtaining valid test results for culturally different children is related to test administration. For instance, in a review of the literature on experimenter effects in bicultural testing, Sattler (1970) concluded that examiner characterists play a critical role in cognitive performance. Specifically, the race of the tester has been shown to affect the test results of black students (Katz, Robinson, Epps, & Wally, 1964; Katz, Roberts, & Robinson, 1965). The latter investigators concluded that the "white environment" may be stressful and threatening to black children and that testing in such settings may undermine the accuracy of scores. Specific examiner variables such as bilingualism, ethnicity, and style of test administration also have been shown to affect the test performance of Spanish-speaking children (Bordie, 1970; Palomares & Johnson, 1966; Thomas, Hertzig, Dryman, & Fernandez, 1971). Therefore, the test performance of culturally diverse gifted children may be less than optimal owing to the influence of environmental and examiner characteristics.

The problems associated with using norm-referenced, standardized measures to identify giftedness in culturally different populations has led to the development and use of alternative methods such as checklists, rating scales, and inventories. These methods usually rely on parent, teacher, and peer observations and are useful in identifying gifted youngsters who may be overlooked by traditional psychometric measures (Fischman, 1985). Although nominations have been shown to have predictive value, fear of subjectivity often leads to their exclusion in efforts to identify giftedness (Alvino, McDonnell, & Richert, 1981). Also, such methods have been criticized as being arbitrary and crude (Gear, 1976).

In summary, problems associated with commonly used methods to identify giftedness complicate the identification of culturally different children. In the following sections, specific identification procedures are evaluated and recommendations are made for improving their utility for identifying gifted children from culturally different backgrounds.

STRENGTHS AND WEAKNESSES OF SPECIFIC IDENTIFICATION METHODS

IQ Tests

Individual IQ tests are the most preferred (Martinson, 1973) and most frequently used method for identifying giftedness (Rosenfield, 1983). The popularity of IQ tests for this purpose seems to be justifiable, given that about 95% of those identified as gifted possess high intellectual ability or academic ability (Grinter, 1975). IQ tests are probably the best single method for identifying children who fall into this category of giftedness because they measure intellectual ability and are also one of the best predictors of academic achievement and success (Kaufman & Harrison, 1986).

IQ tests have a number of strengths that support the view that they are the best method available for the identification of children with superior cognitive ability (Berdine & Blackhurst, 1986; Martinson, 1973). First, IQ tests have the best psychometric properties of all individual tests used with gifted children (Kaufman & Harrison, 1986). Therefore, scores provide a more valid and accurate assessment of a child's cognitive ability.

Second, some IQ tests (e.g., the WISC-R and K-ABC) provide information on functioning and abilities in a variety of areas (Kaufman & Harrison, 1986). For instance, Verbal and Performance IQ scores and subtest analysis of the WISC-R may be useful in identifying specific strengths. Additionally, the Performance scales of the WISC-R reportedly provide a fairer assessment of the abilities of culturally different

children (Kaufman & Harrison, 1986). In fact, Kaufman (1979) suggested that higher Performance scores, in comparison with verbal scores, may be of use in determining the true intellectual ability or "potential" of culturally diverse children.

Third, because individual tests are less dependent on classroom skills, such as reading and following written directions, they are more likely to identify gifted children who are atypical. This is particularly relevant in the identification of culturally diverse gifted children, who may be underachieving in the classroom because of peer pressure (Lindstrom & Van Sant, 1986) or inadequate academic and classroom survival skills (Davis & Rimm, 1985).

Fourth, during the administration of individual IQ tests, examiners can obtain observational data (Kaufman & Harrison, 1986) that is valuable in evaluating emotional, motivational, or other factors that might affect test performance. Observational data can be particularly important in determining whether a child lacks an orientation toward testing or has been affected by examiner or environmental characteristics that have been shown to affect the performance of culturally diverse children (Katz et al., 1964; Katz, et al., 1965; Sattler, 1970).

However, there are also disadvantages associated with the use of individual IQ tests. First, identification can be both expensive and time-consuming. Specifically, these tests require trained personnel for administration and interpretation (Berdine & Blackhurst, 1986). Also, it is especially time-consuming to administer IQ tests to bright children (Killian & Hughes, 1978), who may not meet discontinuance criteria until reaching advanced items. Second, studies have shown that culturally diverse children, in comparison with children from the majority culture, tend to perform poorly on most measures of intelligence (Torrance, 1971). Their depressed performance may be the result of problems discussed in the previous section — a lack of orientation to testing (Rosenfield, 1983), examiner characteristics (Bordie, 1970) and environmental variables (Katz et al., 1964; Katz et al., 1965; Palomares & Johnson, 1966; Sattler, 1970;

Thomas et al., 1971) and the possibility that tests may be culturally loaded (Renzulli, 1973).

In spite of their weaknesses, IQ tests are more accurate and useful in the identification process than either group aptitude tests, teacher nominations (Whitmore, 1980), or parent nominations (Kaufman, 1976). When used properly, they can contribute valuable information in the identification of giftedness. In using IQ tests to identify giftedness in culturally diverse children, the following recommendations may be helpful. First, IQ test scores should not be the only criterion used to determine giftedness (Kaufman & Harrison, 1986), specifically because they do not assess creativity, specific academic ability, leadership ability, or ability in the performance and visual arts, all of which are characteristics that are indicative of giftedness according to PL 91-230. IQ test data can be supplemented with inventories, information from peers, interviews, case studies, performance evaluations, and culture-fair tests; all of these supplementary instruments are viewed as promising means for identifying giftedness in poor, minority, and bilingual populations (Richert, 1985).

Second, Harrington (1982) cautioned against applying arbitrary cutoff scores in identifying giftedness. Use of strict cutoffs negates the natural fluctuation of IQ scores that can be caused by environmental and examiner variables. This is especially relevant in evaluating culturally diverse children because such variables have been shown to influence their test performance differentially (Katz et al., 1964; Katz et al., 1965; Sattler, 1970). Rather than applying cutoff scores, Kaufman and Harrison (1986) suggested that the standard error of measure be considered in the identification process.

Third, to mitigate the effect of cultural bias inherent in some IQ tests, Tunney (1973 cited in Rubenzer, 1979), recommended that the children scoring in the top 5% of the group being tested be identified as gifted and talented. Finally, examiners should use IQ tests that have been recommended for the identification of gifted children from culturally diverse backgrounds. A list of such tests was generated

from research commissioned by the U.S. Department of Education to determine more equitable practices for the identification of giftedness. Recommended tests include the Kaufman Assessment Battery for Children, the Columbia Mental Maturity Scale, the Lattel Culture Fair Intelligence Series, and the Raven's Progressive Matrices. For a complete listing of recommended tests, the reader is referred to Richert (1985).

Achievement Tests

According to PL 91-230, high performance capability in specific academic areas is viewed as one aspect of giftedness (Gifted and Talented Children's Education Act of 1978, Section 902). Also, it had previously been established that the majority of children identified as gifted possess high intellectual or academic capability (Grinter, 1975). Therefore, it is not surprising that achievement tests are commonly used in the identification process. In fact, the results of a survey conducted by Jenkins (1979) indicated that achievement tests were one of the most frequently used instruments to identify giftedness at the preschool and primary level.

Achievement tests are useful in identifying academic giftedness because they are the best predictors of outstanding academic capability (Rosenfield, 1983) and indicate aptitude in specific academic areas (Berdine & Blackhurst, 1986). Also, standardized achievement tests tend to be well developed psychometrically, in terms of their ability to assess general academic functioning in reading, language, and math (Rosenfield, 1983). An appealing aspect of using achievement tests to identify giftedness is that they are generally more economical and less time consuming to administer than individual IQ tests. In fact, achievement test information is often readily available in children's cumulative scholastic records (Berdine & Blackhurst, 1986). Furthermore, no special training is required to administer many achievement tests.

There also are disadvantages associated with using achievement tests to determine giftedness. First, achievement

tests are likely to fail to identify intellectually gifted children who are underachievers, especially children from culturally
different backgrounds (Berdine & Blackhurst, 1986). Second, performance on such
tests is limited by the curriculum structure
in particular grades. Therefore, children's
scores may vary as a function of the school
they attend (Hagan, 1980). These first two
limitations seem particularly relevant, given
that culturally different children are not
afforded adequate schooling (Gay, 1978)
and therefore do not develop basic academic skills that are prerequisite to successful performance on achievement tests
(Davis & Rimm, 1985). Also, Evans de
Bernard (1985) observed that Hispanic
bilingual children in the United States have
demonstrated a lower rate of achievement
than Anglos on standardized tests of reading
achievement. Scores from these tests are
often used as major criteria for class
placement and advancement in school. As
a result, Hispanic children have been
virtually excluded from programs for the
gifted and talented (Evans de Bernard,
1985). A third weakness of achievement
tests is that they focus on school skills and
do not measure the ability to learn in
nonschool settings (Hall, 1983). This renders
problematic the identification of culturally
different children, who often exhibit their
talents only outside of the schools.

Given the limitations of achievement
tests in identifying gifted children from
culturally diverse backgrounds, the following points are recommended. Since, like IQ
tests, achievement tests tap only one aspect
of giftedness, they should be only one part
of a multifaceted evaluation in identifying
giftedness in culturally diverse populations.
To counter the criticism that achievement
test scores may vary as a function of the
school a child attends, local norms should
be developed so that children can more
fairly be compared to their peers. Children
falling within the upper percentile ranks of
local norms can then be considered for
gifted programs. Finally, because achievement tests do not measure nonschool
learning, test scores should be considered
in conjunction with information from peers
and parents who are familiar with the child's
behavior in other settings.

Nominations

Nominations are another popular
method of choosing, or identifying children
who are gifted. A nationwide survey that
included teachers of the gifted, university
professors, and state consultants revealed
that nominations were the second most
frequently used method for identifying
giftedness (Alvino, McDonnell, & Richert,
1981). In a similar study, Marland (1972)
found that 93% of those surveyed used
nominations to identify giftedness and that
75% of those surveyed recommended the
practice.

The nomination process takes place in
one of two ways. Teachers, parents, or
students may simply be asked to choose
a child or children they believe to be gifted,
or they may be required to complete a
checklist or rating scale, for example, the
Scale for Rating Behavior Characteristics
of Superior Students (Renzulli & Hartman,
1971). Nominations may be used as the only
criteria for giftedness, but more often than
not they are considered in conjunction with
data from tests. In contrast to IQ and
achievement tests, nominations are generally indirect (the child is generally not
involved in the process), subjective (decisions are based on the nominators' views
about candidates), and usually unstandard-
ized (each nominator may go about the
nomination process in a different way and
may attach different meanings to the term
giftedness).

Teachers are frequently involved in the
nominating process and are felt to be crucial
because they are in an excellent position
to observe students (Frasier, 1980). Research findings, however, cast doubt on the
accuracy of teacher nominations. Skager
and Fitz-Gibbon (1972) found that 4 of 9
gifted students were not nominated by
teachers. Similarly, Gear (1976) found that
teachers were about 50% inaccurate in
identifying gifted students. The inaccuracy
of teacher nominations in identifying
giftedness may be attributed to teachers'
lack of information about characteristics of
gifted children who do not conform to
stereotypes (Gear, 1976). In essence,
teachers tend to be impressed by, and thus

overrate, dutiful and hard-working children (Gallagher, 1975).

Whitmore (1980) indicated that teachers are inclined to nominate as gifted those students who are striving, conforming, high achievers — discounting the possibility that those who do not exhibit good student behavior may be gifted. In support of this, Hall (1983) found evidence to support that teachers tended to rate students who exhibited the characteristics of gifted underachievers as average or below average. The results indicate that few teachers are willing to nominate students as gifted if they exhibit patterns of underachievement (e.g., problem behavior and low self-concept). Ziv (1977) also observed that the discrepancy between potential and classroom achievement, as measured in grades and teachers' assessments, reflected such factors as neatness, good behavior, motivation, attitude, and so forth. Thus, the use of teacher nominations, without consideration of test scores, may result in the exclusion of gifted underachievers.

In brief, a major problem with using teacher nominations is that gifted children who are atypical may not be identified. Thus, teacher nominations are more likely to underidentify giftedness in culturally different children, who frequently do not exhibit appropriate classroom skills and who do not value school achievement. Furthermore, Hect (1975) suggested that teachers tended to rate as more desirable and successful those students who are most similar to themselves in social, racial, and economic background. This tendency is clearly problematic when middle-class, white teachers are asked to nominate children from culturally different backgrounds.

Parents, peers, and potentially eligible children themselves also may be involved in the nomination process. Peer and parent nominations are particularly useful because they provide information that may not be readily observed by school personnel (Frasier, 1980). Interesting enough, Jacobs (1971) concluded that parent referrals tended to be more conservative and accurate than teacher nominations. Renzulli and Smith (1977) found that peer nominations were accurate in identifying gifted

children from minority backgrounds. Self-nominations also may be of value in identifying giftedness: Alexander (1985) found that gifted students tended to rate their own intelligence accurately.

Although a great deal of controversy surrounds the use of nominations in identifying giftedness, a panel of researchers (commissioned by the U.S. Department of Education to develop recommendations for the identification of gifted and talented youth) suggested that nominations by a teacher, a parent, peer, and self are a promising means of identifying giftedness in children from poor, culturally different, and bilingual backgrounds (Richert, 1985). Nominations contribute unique information that supplements test data because they take into account the opinions of people who interact with the potentially gifted child on a daily basis and in a variety of settings.

Those wishing to use nominations should consider the following recommendations. First, the items of nominations should reflect the goals of the program for which children are being selected (Richert, 1985). Second, when possible, checklists and rating scales should be research-based (Richert, 1985). The National Report on Identification, Assessment, and Recommendations for Comprehensive Identification of Gifted and Talented Youth (Richert, Alvino, McDonnel, 1982) furnishes examples of research-based lists. Third, owing to their limitations, nominations should supplement, rather than replace, objective test data (Skager & Fitz-Gibbon, 1972). However, nominations should complement, rather than confirm test data (Richert, 1985). Fourth, nominations should be sought from a variety of sources (Frasier, 1980). Fifth, when rating scales or nomination forms are used, it is important to assess respondents' understanding of the items (Frasier, 1980). Ideally, however, those using checklists and rating scales should be trained to observe the characteristics of giftedness, but should also be especially sensitive to the negative behaviors that might obscure giftedness (Richert, 1985). Finally, when scales or forms are used, respondents should have had the opportunity to observe each of the behaviors listed (Frasier, 1980).

Systems of Identification

Several systems have been designed specifically to identify gifted children from culturally diverse backgrounds. Gay (1978) proposed a multifaceted evaluation plan for identifying black gifted children. As a first step, Gay suggested getting a commitment to the plan from the school personnel. Following this, the entire student population is screened with ability or achievement tests, to identify the top 10% of each class. In addition, teachers' ratings are obtained, the assumption being made that the teachers have previously received in-service training on the rating system. Student case studies are then assembled, parental involvement is secured, and students are individually tested and interviewed. Candidates then perform a group task so that leadership ability and supportive behavior can be assessed. Weighted scores are then assigned for performance in each area. Finally, candidates are rated and the identification committee makes a final selection.

Gay's system has both strengths and weaknesses. Although the plan is comprehensive, it is also time-consuming and expensive. It is apparent that the school would indeed need to be committed to the identification task. A major strength of this system, however, is that culturally diverse children would be compared with their peers. For instance, screening entails selecting the children who score in the top 10% in each class. Thus, children's performance is compared with that of their cultural peers rather than against test norms that may be based primarily on performance by majority culture children.

Dabney's (1981) model also focused on the identification of black youths and was based on an adapted version of the Baldwin Identification Matrix (Baldwin, 1978). The adapted version of Baldwin's Matrix gives weight to the clinical judgment of the examiner, summarizes a variety of data, and provides estimates of learning potential that are, in part, referenced to local norms. In her system, weighted scores represent a child's ability in reading, math, social studies, writing, leadership, creativity, and motivation. After matrix scores are calculated, cutoff scores are established and the final selection is made by a committee.

A strength of Dabney's (1981) system is that a variety of information is included. In addition to academic variables, motivation, leadership, creativity, and the examiner's observations are considered. Another strength is that local norms are used so that culturally different children are more fairly compared with their peers. A problem with Dabney's very comprehensive system, however, is that, as with Gay's system, identification becomes both time-consuming and expensive.

Whitmore (1980) also has suggested a multimethod approach. This includes obtaining parent and/or teacher referrals, based on guided reports of children's behavior (e.g., a rating scale or behavior checklist). Next, individual or group screening tests are administered (e.g., the PPVT, WRAT, California Test of Mental Maturity). An individual IQ test such as the WISC-R or Stanford-Binet is then administered. Finally, each child's nonintellectual characteristics are assessed.

Whitmore's model is based on more commonly used methods of identification and seems to focus on an intellectual/academic view of giftedness. Because the first step of her plan focuses on teacher nomination, atypical gifted children (e.g., disadvantaged, minority, and underachieving children) may be underidentified, in view of the limitations of teacher nominations (Gear, 1976; Skager & Fitz-Gibbon, 1972). The second step of the process would also tend to eliminate underachieving children who are intellectually or creatively gifted. A major strength of her model, however, is that several sources of information are considered. Specifically, information from teachers and parents and nonintellectual characteristics are considered in addition to test scores.

Torrance (1984) also established principles for the identification of giftedness. He suggested that several talents be considered in the search for giftedness. Also, he suggested that creativity should be one of the criteria used in the identification process. Torrance (1984) also recommended that the examiner select test procedures that permit a child to respond in the best possible modality, so that those who do not have adequate academic ability will not be discriminated against. Finally, in assessing culturally diverse children, he suggested that the tasks used should tap the kinds of excellence valued by the child's culture.

Although Torrance's guidelines are relevant to the identification of giftedness in culturally diverse children, there are several limitations in respect to the time and expense of adhering to these principles. First, it could be time-consuming for examiners to determine the most effective mode of expression for each child under consideration. Furthermore, it may prove difficult to adapt or to find a test that evaluates the child through the preferred modality once it is identified. Also, unless the examiner is of the same culture as the child, it may be difficult to determine and to measure the kind of excellence valued by the child's culture.

In summary, though each system described has strengths and weaknesses, they represent an attempt at improving current practices. Clearly, more research is needed in this area to determine the most effective and efficient way to identify these children.

CONCLUSIONS

Some generalizations can be drawn from the literature on the identification of gifted children from culturally diverse backgrounds. First, information from several different sources should be considered (Dabney, 1981; Gay, 1978; Whitmore, 1980). Specifically, intellectual ability and academic achievement should be considered jointly with information from nominations, rather than in isolation. Also, it should be remembered that giftedness may be exhibited in many areas. Rather than being academically gifted, culturally diverse students may be creatively gifted, or may possess leadership ability or ability in the performing arts. Thus, nominations and other alternatives should be considered because IQ and achievement tests are not

designed to provide information about every facet of giftedness.

Second, in using tests to identify giftedness in culturally diverse populations, the effects of environmental variables and examiner characteristics on test performance should be considered (Katz et al., 1964; Katz et al., 1965; Sattler, 1970). The use of strict cutoff scores to identify children for programs should be avoided. Instead, identification criteria should include a range of scores, based on the standard error of measure. This practice accounts for possible score fluctuation due to environmental or examiner characteristics (Kaufman & Harrison, 1986).

Third, because of the possible cultural bias of many tests, examiners may want to rely on local norms or may want to consider children to be gifted who obtain the highest scores in the population being considered (Dabney, 1981; Tunney, 1972 cited in Rubenzer, 1979). In this manner, culturally different children will be compared with their cultural peers, rather than with children of the majority culture. Also, tests recommended for use with culturally different children should be used when possible (Richert, 1985). Fourth, though achievement test information is usually more readily available, IQ tests and nominations seem to be more promising for identifying gifted children from culturally different backgrounds.

Ultimately, however, the design of the identification plan must reflect the program with which it is associated. Specifically, the design of the identification system should be guided by the goals of the program and the type of children who will be served. Assessment should measure behaviors that are similar to those which are the focus of the program. Also, the identification process should be validated. In other words, those identified by the process should experience success in the program (Feldhusen, Asher, & Hoover, 1984)

In short, identifying culturally diverse gifted children is a complex and challenging process. However, weighing the strengths and weaknesses of the various methods and systems of identification can provide a basis for decision making or, at least, for further exploration into the identification of gifted children from culturally diverse backgrounds.

REFERENCES

Alexander, P. A. (1985). Gifted and nongifted students' perceptions of intelligence. *Gifted Child Quarterly, 29*(3), 137–143.

Alvino, J., McDonnell, R. C., & Richert, S. (1981) National survey of identification practices in gifted and talented. *Exceptional Children, 48*, 124–132.

Baldwin, A. (1973, March). *Identifying the disadvantaged.* Paper presented at the First National Conference on the Disadvantaged Gifted, Ventura, CA.

Baldwin, A. (1978). The Baldwin Identification Matrix. In A. Baldwin, G. Gear, & L. Lucito (Eds.), *Educational planning for the gifted.* Reston, VA: Council for Exceptional Children.

Baldwin, A. Y. (1978). *Educational planning for the gifted: Overcoming cultural, geographic and socioeconomic barriers.* Reston, VA: Council for Exceptional Children. (ERIC Document Reproduction Service No. Ed 161 173)

Berdine, B., & Blackhurst, E. (1986). *Introduction to special education* (2nd ed.). New York: Little, Brown.

Bernal, E. (1979). The education of the culturally different gifted. In A. H. Passow (Ed.), *The gifted and the talented: Their education and development.* Chicago: University of Chicago Press.

Bordie, J. (1970). Language tests and linguistically different learners: The sad state of the art. *Elementary English, 47*, 814–828.

Clark, B. (1983). *Growing up gifted.* Columbus, OH: Merrill.

Colangelo, N., & Zaffran, R. T. (1979). Special issues in counseling the gifted. *Counseling and Human Development, 11*(5), 1–12.

Coleman, J. S., Campbell, E. Q., Hobson, C. J., McPhartland, J., Mood, A. M., Weinfield, F. D., & York, R. L. (1966). *Equality of educational opportunity.* Catalogue Num FS 5.238-38001. Washington, DC: Government Printing Office.

Dabney, M. G. (1981, February). *An identification curriculum and evaluation model for gifted Black adolescents: Part I.* Paper presented at the Council for Exceptional Children Conference on the Exceptional Black Child, New Orleans.

Davis, G. A., & Rimm, S. B. (1985). *Education of the gifted and talented.* Englewood Cliffs, NJ: Prentice-Hall.

Evans de Bernard, A. (1985). Why José can't get in the gifted class: The bilingual child and standardized reading tests. *Roeper Review, 8*(2), 80–82.

Farrell, P. (1973, March). *Teacher involvement in identification.* Paper presented at the First National Conference on the Disadvantaged Gifted, Ventura, CA.

Feldhusen, J. F., Asher, J. W., & Hoover, S. M. (1984). Problems in the identification of giftedness, talent, or ability. *Gifted Child Quarterly, 28*(4), 149–151.

Fischman, R. (1985). Best practices in the evaluation of gifted children. In A. Thomas & J. Grimes (Eds.), *Best practices in school psychology* (pp. 143–155). Kent, OH: National Association of School Psychologists.

Fox, L. H. (1981). Identification of the academically gifted. *American Psychologist, 36*(10), 1103–1111.

Frasier, M. M. (1980). Screening and identification of gifted students. In J. B. Jordan & J. A. Gross (Eds.), *An administrator's handbook on designing programs for the gifted and talented* (pp. 48–55). Reston, VA: Council for Exceptional Children and Association for the Gifted.

Gallagher, J. J. (1966). *Research summary on gifted child education.* Springfield, IL: Department of Public Instruction.

Gallagher, J. J. (1975). *Teaching the gifted child* (2nd ed.). Boston: Allyn and Bacon.

Gay, J. E. (1978). A proposed plan for identifying black gifted children. *Gifted Child Quarterly, 22*(3), 353–360.

Gear, G. H. (1976). Accuracy of teacher judgment in identifying intellectually gifted children: A review of the literature. *Gifted Child Quarterly, 20*(4), 478–490.

Gifted and Talented Children's Education Act of 1978. § 902, 20 U.S.C. § 2701 (1978).

Gollnick, D. M., & Chinn, P. C. (1986). *Multicultural education in a pluralistic society* (2nd ed.). Columbus, OH: Merrill.

Gowan, J. C. (1986). Issues in the education of disadvantaged gifted children. *Gifted Child Quarterly, 12*, 115–119.

Grinter, R. (1975, February). *Identification processes.* Presentation to Wisconsin Council for Gifted and Talented.

Hagan, E. (1980). *Identification of the gifted.* New York: Teachers College Press.

Hall, E. G. (1983). Recognizing gifted underachievers. *Roeper Review, 5*(4), 23–25.

Harrington, R. G. (1982). Caution: Standardized testing may be hazardous to the educational programs of intellectually gifted children. *Education, 2*(103), 112–117.

Hect, K. A. (1975). Teacher ratings of potential dropouts and academically gifted children. Are they related? *Journal of Teacher Education, 26,* 172–175.

Jacobs, J. (1971). Effectiveness of teacher and parent identification of gifted children as a function of school level. *Psychology in the Schools, 8,* 140–142.

Jacob, K. Javits Gifted and Talented Children and Youth Education Act of 1987. H. R. 543 § 303IS (1988).

Jenkins, R. (1979). *A resource guide to preschool and primary programs for the gifted and talented.* Mansfield Center, CT: Creative Learning Press.

Katz, I., Roberts, S., & Robinson, J. (1965). Effects of difficulty, race of administrator and instructions on Negro digit-symbol performance. *Journal of Personality and Social Psychology, 70,* 53–59.

Katz, I., Robinson, J., Epps, E., & Wally, P. (1964). Effects of race of experimenter and test vs. neutral instructions on expression of hostility in Negro boys. *Journal of Social Issues, 20,* 54–59.

Kaufman, A. S. (1979). *Intelligent testing with the WISC-R.* New York: Wiley.

Kaufman, A. S., & Harrison, P. L. (1986). Intelligence tests and gifted assessment: What are the positives? *Roeper Review, 8*(3), 154–159.

Kaufman, F. (1976). *Your gifted child and you.* Reston, VA: Council for Exceptional Children.

Killian, J. B., & Hughes, L. C. (1978). Comparison of short forms of the Wechsler Intelligence Scales for Children-Revised in the screening of gifted children. *Gifted Child Quarterly, 22,* 111-115.

Lindstrom, R. R., & Van Sant, S. (1986). Special issues in working with gifted minority adolescents. *Journal of Counseling and Development, 64,* 583–586.

Marland, S. P. (1972). *Education of the gifted and talented.* Washington, DC: U.S. Office of Education.

Martinson, R. A. (1973). Children with superior cognitive abilities. In L. Dunn (Ed.), *Exceptional children in the schools.* New York: Holt, Rinehart & Winston.

McMillin, D. (1975, May). *Separate criteria: An alternative for the identification of disadvantaged gifted.* Paper presented at the National Teacher Institute on Disadvantaged Gifted. Los Angeles.

Minner, S., & Prater, G. (no date provided). *Identification of gifted minority, handicapped, and disadvantaged children: A review.* Unpublished manuscript. Murray State University, Department of Special Education, Murray, Kentucky.

Palomores, U., & Johnson, L. (1966). Evaluation of Mexican American pupils for EMR classes. *California Education, 3*(8), 27–29.

Philosophical basis for a culturally responsive education process. (1976, December). *Utah Indian Education Newsletter.*

Renzulli, J. (1973). Talent potential in minority group students. *Exceptional Children, 39,* 437–444.

Renzulli, J. (1975). Identifying key features in programs for the gifted. In W. Barbe & J. Renzulli (Eds.), *Psychology and education of the gifted.* New York: Irvington.

Renzulli, J., & Hartman, R. (1971). Scale for rating behavioral characteristics of superior students. *Exceptional Children, 38*(3), 243–248.

Renzulli, J., & Smith, L. H. (1977, May). Two approaches to identification of gifted students. *Exceptional Children, 43*(8), 512–518.

Richert, E. S. (1985). Identification of gifted students: An update. *Roeper Review, 8*(2), 68–72.

Richert, E. S., Alvino, J. J., & McDonnel, R. C. (1982). *National report on identification: Assessment and recommendations for comprehensive identification of gifted and talented youth.* Washington, DC: Educational Resource Center.

Rosenfield, S. (1983). Assessment of the gifted child. In T. R. Kratochwill (Ed.), *Advances in school psychology* (Vol. 3). Hillsdale, NJ: Erlbaum.

Rubenzer, R. (1979). Identification and evaluation procedures for gifted and talented programs. *Gifted Child Quarterly, 23*(2), 304–316.

Sattler, J. (1970). Racial "experimenter effects" in experimentation, testing, interviewing, and psychotherapy. *Psychological Bulletin, 73*(2), 137–160.

Skager, R., & Fitz-Gibbon, C. (1972). *Mentally gifted disadvantaged students: An investigation of methods of identification, including the use of "culture fair" tests, at the eighth grade level.* Los Angeles, CA: University of California, National Center for Educational Research and Development. (ERIC Document Service No. ED 080 583)

Sullivan, A. R. (1973). The identification of gifted and academically talented Black students: A hidden exceptionality. *Journal of Special Education, 7*(4), 373–379.

Terman, L., & Oden, M. (1947). *Genetic studies of genius: Vol. 4. The gifted child grows up.* Stanford, CA: Stanford University Press.

Thomas, A., Hertzig, M. E., Dryman, I., & Fernandez, P. (1971). Examiner effect in IQ testing of Puerto Rican working-class children. *The American Journal of Orthopsychiatry, 41*(5), 809–821.

Torrance, E. P. (1964). Identifying the creatively gifted among economically and culturally disadvantaged children. *Gifted Child Quarterly, 8*(4), 171–176.

Torrance, E. P. (1971). Are the Torrance Tests of Creative Thinking biased against or in favor of "disadvantaged" groups? *Gifted Child Quarterly, 15,* 75–80.

Torrance, E. P. (1977). *Discovery and nurturance of giftedness in the culturally different.* Reston, VA: Council for Exceptional Children.

Torrance, E. P. (1984). The role of creativity in identification of the gifted and talented. *Gifted Child Quarterly, 28*(4), 153–156.

U.S. Bureau of the Census, Statistical abstract of the United States: 1988 (108th edition) Washington, DC, 1987.

Whitmore, J. R. (1980). *Giftedness, conflict, and underachievement.* Boston, Allyn and Bacon.

Ziv, A. (1977). *Counseling the intellectually gifted child.* Toronto, Ontario: University of Toronto Governing Council.

CHAPTER 18

Use of Projective Techniques in the Assessment of Hispanic School Children

Andrés Barona
Arizona State University

Arthur E. Hernandez
University of Texas at San Antonio

Considerable attention has been focused on the need for accurate assessment of minority children so that the incidence of misdiagnosis and inappropriate placement into special educational settings might be minimized. Much controversy has arisen over the fact that children of diverse ethnic backgrounds perform differentially on standardized tests of intelligence, and efforts have been made by individual parents, minority group organizations, and civil rights groups to reduce the cultural bias effects of many of these measures through various avenues (Barona, 1982; Reynolds, Plake, & Harding, 1983). In recent years, there has been general agreement that, for the purposes of special class placement, the whole child must be examined: This examination should include a review of data related to the child's intellectual, sociocultural, physical, and emotional functioning. Since minority children as a group tend to perform poorly on intelligence tests, the use of sociocultural and emotional data has been promoted to avoid the inappropriate placement of disproportionate numbers of these children in special education classes (Scott, 1981).

Using a multidimensional perspective to study children's functioning initially appears to be an inherently sound approach. It has good potential for minimizing the differential and often negative effects found for many minority groups on standardized measures. However, such an approach contains several major assumptions: (a) It is assumed that evaluators participating in the child's examination are aware of and sensitive to the child's sociocultural background, (b) it is assumed that evaluators understand how unique background characteristics may affect performance on many standardized instruments, (c) it is assumed that sociocultural factors are taken into account during the interpretation of test results, and (d) it is assumed that any additional measures used to evaluate the effects of either sociocultural background or personality functioning are themselves valid and reliable measures for the purposes for which they are used.

There is some question, however, as to whether these assumptions are met consistently. For example, it would be expected that if emotional and/or sociocultural data were taken into account regularly in interpreting test data, the prevalence of psychological disorders would be comparable for different ethnic groups. Epidemiological surveys (Baskin, Bluestone, & Nelson, 1981; Gross, Knatterud, & Donner, 1969), however, have indicated that the rates of psychological disorders are substantially higher among ethnic minority populations than among nonminority populations. Such disparity has been attributed to bias that "intrudes in clinical judgment and decision making when nonminority clinicians, along with their armory of standardized tests, lack sensitivity to the values, behavioral norms, and linguistic variability" of individuals of diverse culture (Malgady, Rogler, & Costantino, 1987, p. 229).

Similarly, the instruments and procedures used to evaluate personality functioning in both minority and nonminority populations have been criticized (Gittelman Klein, 1986; Kline, 1976; Malgady, Rogler, & Costantino, 1987; Martin, 1983; Padilla & Ruiz, 1973; Rogler, Cooney, Costantino, Earley, Grossman, Gurak, Malgady, & Rodriguez, 1983). Projective testing seems to be the technique of choice in the personality evaluation of school-age children (Obrzut, 1982), and the use of projective techniques by practitioners appears to be both extensive and growing in popularity (Howes, 1981; Pruitt, Smith, Thelen, & Lubin, 1985). However, research involving the use of projective techniques, while never prolific, has declined in recent years (Pruitt et al., 1985), and significant questions regarding the reliability and validity of projective instruments and procedures remain unanswered.

For example, empirical research indicates that it has not been determined if projective testing adds to what is already known about the child (Gittelman Klein, 1986). In addition, it currently is not known if accurate conclusions can be drawn from projective testing in children: Tests such as the Draw-A-Person (DAP) and the Thematic Apperception Test (TAT) have not demonstrated satisfactory validity (Gittelman Klein, 1986), and a longitudinal study of normal children between 8 and 16 years who were tested numerous times with the Rorschach failed to find consistency in scores over time (Exner, Thomas, & Mason, 1985). Finally, professional opinions about projective techniques such as the Rorschach, TAT, and Sentence Completion have grown more negative (Pruitt et al., 1985). These findings have led to the recommendation that, since projectives do not provide adequate information to diagnose behavioral or emotional disorders, they should not be used to make important decisions about children (Gittelman Klein, 1986; Kline, 1976).

Projective testing, which has its roots in psychoanalytic theory, assumes that similar psychological processes account for all aspects of human behavior (Gittelman Klein, 1986). However, there is "Little evidence to document the belief that children's personality characteristics are well estimated by projective testing" (Gittelman Klein, 1986, p. 379). Moreover, little attention has been paid to the possibility of ethnic differences in areas other than intelligence testing, although some work exists that involves objective personality measures (Reynolds, 1981). In particular, the issue of differential responses on projective tests has not been investigated in any detail. Projective tests frequently are used for personality assessments (Lachar & LaCombe, 1983; Vukovich, 1983), especially by school psychologists (Goh & Fuller, 1983). In the special education referral process, they historically have been directed toward the classification of children by determining a pupil's emotional status (Peterson & Batsche, 1983). Additionally, responses to projective techniques in some instances have been used as indirect evidence to support or refute performance on measures of intelligence. Although the determination of emotional status relies heavily on clinical interpretation of responses, clinicians and evaluators have been trained to view certain types of responses as indicators of pathology or health. These indicators rarely have been challenged on the basis of ethnic differences. It has been documented that Hispanic and Spanish language-dominant children are administered more projective tests than their English-language dominant Anglo and Black peers (Vukovich, 1983). Clearly, if ethnic differences are found with projective assessment techniques, it will be necessary to reexamine the assumptions regarding the generalizability of these previously widely accepted symbols.

Some evidence exists to indicate that individuals of different ethnic backgrounds respond differently on personality tests such as the Minnesota Multiphasic Personality Inventory (MMPI) (Dolan, Roberts, Penk, Robinowitz, & Atkins, 1983; Fuller & Maloney, 1984; Holland, 1979; McCreary & Padilla, 1977; McGill, 1980; Orozco & Montgomery, 1982; Page & Bozlee, 1982; Plemons, 1977), and caution has been recommended to its use with ethnic minority groups (Dana, 1988). These studies generally have dealt with adult populations: very little investigation has been conducted in the area of projective tests that require a more clinical interpretation, particularly as it pertains to Hispanic children and adults. Indeed, a review of the literature from 1965 to the present resulted in the identification of only a handful of articles related either directly or indirectly to Hispanics' performance on projective personality measures (Costantino, Malgady, & Vasquez, 1981; Costantino & Malgady, 1983; Diaz-Guerrero, 1981; Fabrega, Swartz, & Wallace, 1968; Fuller & Maloney, 1984; Gonzales, 1982; Holtzman, Diaz-Guerrero, & Swartz, 1975; Johnson & Sikes, 1965; Kagan & Knight, 1981; Moseley, 1967; Tamm, 1967). Moreover, a review of almost 14,000 articles dealing with personality assessment between 1938 and 1970 (Padilla & Ruiz, 1977) uncovered only six additional articles involving the personality assessment of Hispanic Americans. Of these, only three utilized projective tests to evaluate emotional status (Kaplan, 1955; Kaplan, Rickers-Ovsiankina, & Joseph, 1956; Johnson & Sikes, 1965).

It is hoped this review of the current available literature pertaining to the use of projective assessment techniques with Hispanics will encourage caution in the general application of these techniques with Hispanics as well as point out directions for future research in this area.

Three areas of research are reviewed: first, the available literature involving general differences among ethnic groups on projective techniques; then a description of projective response differences that occur and are due to the language of response; and finally, the issue of the degree of acculturation and its effect on responses to projective techniques.

ETHNIC GROUP DIFFERENCES

In a longitudinal project begun in 1964 and conducted in Austin, Texas and Mexico City, careful matching was made of Mexican and U.S. children in the first, fourth, and seventh grades on the variables of sex, age, and father's education and occupation (Holtzman, Diaz-Guerrero, & Swartz, 1975). The Holtzman Inkblot Technique was the instrument of comparison, and it was found that the children from the two cultures were differentiated on the basis of reaction time, use of color, and ability to integrate and ascribe more definite form to parts of the inkblot. Additionally, the responses of the U.S. children showed a greater degree of anxious and hostile content and more deviant thinking than did those of the Mexican children.

Similar results were found in another study (Tamm, 1967), in which bilingual children of both Mexican and U.S. descent residing in Mexico City and attending the same school were examined by the Holtzman Inkblot Technique. Mexican and U.S. children were found to be distinctly different at all age levels studied, and it was suggested that fundamental cultural differences existed that were unaffected by the experiences provided through formal schooling.

Significant differences were found between ethnic groups in one study in which the Draw-A-Person test was administered to over 3,000 Mexican-American, Pueblo Indian, Navajo Indian, Black, and Anglo elementary school children between the ages of 5 and 9 years (Gonzales, 1982). Using the Koppitz scoring procedure, which consists of grouping items by percentage of occurrence into Expected, Common, Not Unusual, or Exceptional categories, a comparison of drawings for the five ethnic groups indicated that a significant number of items changed between those scoring categories (i.e., Expected, Exceptional) that affected IQ estimates. As a result, both the final score interpretation of the Draw-A-Person and the determination of IQ were affected. Significant differences also were noted in the percentage of items drawn by the groups. Because of the differential performance by the ethnic groups on this type of projective technique, caution was recommended in interpreting the test results of minority group members.

Similarly, the responses on the Rorschach and the Thematic Apperception Test were examined for 25 psychiatric subjects from three racial/ethnic groups (Johnson

& Sikes, 1965). Although numerous statistically significant differences appeared between the groups, the major point of interest for this review is the finding that Mexican-American patients displayed a unique pattern of responses on both projective measures. On the Rorschach, Mexican-Americans saw much latent hostility in the world; on the TAT, family was consistently viewed as united, the father being seen as absolutely supreme and the mother as self-sacrificing. Neither the Black nor the Anglo comparison groups held these views.

In another study, two judges attempted to determine if Rorschach responses could be categorized on the basis of ethnicity (Kaplan, Rickers-Ovsiankina, & Joseph, 1956). One judge, familiar with the ethnic categories included in the study, was quite successful in sorting the Rorschach responses, whereas the second judge, unfamiliar with the categories, was unable to sort the records in any meaningful way. These results were interpreted by the authors as providing support for the notion that ethnic groups have a distinct "modal personality" pattern, and the authors suggest that persons unfamiliar with a minority culture might interpret test results in an entirely different way than those who are aware of cultural differences. The results of this study have been received with hesitance by some researchers (Padilla & Ruiz, 1975), who suggested that the judges' ability to differentiate among different ethnicities may have been affected by motivational factors.

Another study that involved an attempt to differentiate ethnic groups by their responses on projective techniques (i.e., the Holtzman Inkblot Technique) successfully avoided the issues of motivational problems and bias in judgment by using a computer scoring procedure. The responses of college students from seven cultures (Argentina, Mexico, Panama, Venezuela, the United States, and two groups in Colombia: Bogotá and Cartagena) were compared by multivariate techniques (Moseley, 1967). No South American student was misclassified as being either Central or North American, and only one Central American was misclassified as South American. There was some error, however, in the classification of North and Central Americans: 21% of U.S. subjects were misclassified as Mexican, and 17% and 24% of Mexicans were misclassified as U.S. and Panamanian, respectively. These results suggest that the degree of similarity in personality patterns between cultures as measured by the Holtzman Inkblot Technique parallels the degree of cultural exchange between those cultures (Rabin, 1981).

Distinct social motives were found in a study in which Mexican-American and Anglo schoolchildren in the fourth through the sixth grades were studied (Kagan & Knight, 1981). Although projective techniques were only tangentially involved, the results of this study serve to highlight the issue of both the differential influences of ethnicity and qualitative differences in performance when projective stimuli are used with Hispanic children.

Traditionally, most studies involving ethnic group differences compare a minority culture with the Anglo core culture in the United States. In a departure from this methodology, a group of Mexican mothers were examined against a group of urban Mexican-American mothers by means of the Holtzman Inkblot Technique (Diaz-Guerrero, 1981). The Mexican-American mothers obtained higher movement, integration, and human response scores than their Mexican counterparts. Additionally, differences in perception and cognition were noted. The discrepancies were attributed to unique cultural aspects of each group. These results clearly emphasize the fact that the Mexican-American group is a separate entity and should not be unilaterally compared by either Mexican or Anglo standards. Rather, it appears that separate norms are needed that specifically involve the Mexican-American.

LANGUAGE OF RESPONSE

The Murray Thematic Apperception Test (TAT) was compared with a similar test designed for urban Hispanic children called the Tell-Me-A-Story Test (TEMAS) (Costantino, Malgady, & Vasquez, 1981) in a sample of 76 Hispanic fourth and fifth graders. The TEMAS, which has demonstrated promising evidence of reliability and criterion-related validity (Malgady, Costantino, & Rogler, 1984), differs from the TAT in that its stimulus cards depict ethnic minority figures, cultural themes, and urban backgrounds. A tendency to be more elaborative and to respond in Spanish was found with the TEMAS pictures. Interestingly, English was used more often when the TAT cards were administered, whereas there was a tendency to shift to Spanish when the TEMAS cards were presented. Although the children were functionally fluent in English, it appears that the more relevant themes of the TEMAS were culturally best elaborated on and described in Spanish. Culture and language appears to have had a direct effect on the outcome of this test.

In a similar study, the verbal fluency of Hispanic, Black, and white elementary school children were compared on the TAT and two versions of the TEMAS (Costantino & Malgady, 1983). As with the earlier study, Hispanics were more verbally fluent on the TEMAS than on the TAT. Additionally, there was a trend, although not significant, for ethnic minorities to be more expressive on the minority TEMAS while whites were more fluent on the nonminority TEMAS. The authors concluded that the inclusion of cultural symbols and familiar environmental scenes increased verbal elaboration.

Finally, the clinical implications of bilingualism were stressed by Peck (1974), who reported that fluency in a second language frequently was diminished in stressful situations, such as psychiatric interviews.

DEGREE OF ACCULTURATION

Some evidence indicates that the degree of acculturation may affect the generalizability of traditional projective indicators. When acculturation was measured by a well-developed acculturation scale (Cuellar, Harris, & Jasso, 1980), more acculturated Mexican-American males obtained lower scores on several clinical scales than did less acculturated Mexican-American males (Orozco & Montgomery, 1982). In another study, minority group

members were subdivided on the basis of prior military service (Kaplan, 1955), the assumption being made that veterans were more acculturated than nonveterans. Both groups were evaluated by the Rorschach. It was found that veterans perceived "human movement" with greater frequency and relied more on color than their nonveteran counterparts, and it was suggested that greater acculturation had a definite influence on Rorschach performance. It should be noted, however, that at least one critic of this study has suggested certain questions arise in that the intent of this study was to use the Rorschach to detect cultural differences:

> The problem comes in interpretation. If and when differences appear, there may be some difficulty in determining whether they are due to individual personality, culture-group membership, personal experiences with the majority group, some other extraneous group variable, or the interaction of all these factors. (Padilla & Ruiz, 1977, p. 104)

Acculturation was also seen as a factor in a study in which Anglo-American, Mexican-American, and Black hospitalized schizophrenic patients were compared on the short version of the Holtzman Inkblot Technique (Fabrega, Swartz, & Wallace, 1968). No appreciable differences were found between the three ethnic groups and it was suggested that the Mexican-Americans in the sample "may have been sufficiently acculturated to Anglo patterns and values to no longer show the projective responses typical of Mexicans" (p. 232).

SUMMARY

Over the years, there has been considerable controversy over both the value and adequacy of the methods used in the assessment of personality (Goh & Fuller, 1983). The poor predictive validity of projective techniques has been a criticism (Little, 1959; Suinn & Oskamp, 1969), as has been the lack of adequate norm referencing of many of the instruments (Edelbrock, 1983). The ability of these measures to provide information that can be used to develop interventions that yield positive results for the student has been suggested as a criterion to evaluate the instrument's usefulness (Peterson & Batsche, 1983). At the present time, however, there is no evidence to indicate whether this recommendation has been implemented.

Despite the issues surrounding the use of projective measures in the assessment of children's personality, the use of projective instruments appears to be flourishing. Techniques are "in various stages of development and with varying degrees of established validity and reliability" (Obrzut & Zucker, 1983, p. 85). Training institutions are spending less time teaching projective techniques (Shemberg & Keeley, 1970; Thelen, Varble, & Johnson, 1968; Pruitt et al., 1985), and professionals are familiarizing themselves with projective instruments primarily through self-study (Vukovich, 1983). Nonetheless, over half of the school psychologists in one survey reported using projectives in the majority of their evaluations (Prout, 1983), even though they felt inadequately trained. Additionally, Hispanics are administered projective tests more frequently than their Anglo and Black counterparts (Vukovich, 1983).

The use of projective measures has been criticized (Peterson & Batsche, 1983). When viewed against a backdrop of inadequate predictive validity and poorly trained professionals, the use of projective techniques certainly calls for caution. Although limited by the scarcity of research on performance by Hispanics on traditional projective techniques, the studies that have been reviewed create uncertainty as to whether the longstanding assumption that their responses on projective measures are nondistinct from those of Anglos is valid. Cultural differences appear to be evident when personality is assessed by a variety of projective techniques. These differences have been strikingly demonstrated by the Austin–Mexico City studies as well as by the results of the social motivation study. Unique response patterns appear for the Hispanic on traditional projective techniques, and variations in verbal fluency have been noted for the Hispanic on more recently developed instruments. Whether these differences are due to variations in

cognitive style, perception, social motivation, or language differences has not yet been ascertained, although recent findings suggest that each of these variables is involved (Ardila-Espinel, 1982; Kagan, 1981).

It has commonly been accepted that quantitative differences exist in the test performance of the two groups. The Hispanic also appears to differ in a number of qualitative ways from the Anglo. At present, the lack of research involving the assessment of emotional status of Hispanics prevents a definitive statement regarding any possible qualitative differences that might exist. Regardless of the cause of these differences, it is evident that action must be taken to avert the negative consequences of having professionals unfamiliar with response variations attributable to cultural diversity administer and interpret instruments that they may already feel inadequately prepared to use.

Research must continue on those measures that are frequently used with Hispanics and Spanish-language-dominant children to document cultural variations in responses. Instruments that are more conducive to verbal expressiveness in the culturally different child must be developed that demonstrate satisfactory levels of reliability and validity. Professionals must be familiarized both with these instruments and with cultural differences to avoid misinterpretation of responses. Clearly, until such time as these steps are taken, extreme caution should be exercised in both evaluating and interpreting the performance of Hispanics on projective measures.

REFERENCES

Ardila-Espinel, N. (1982). Criterios y valores de la cultura anglo-saxo-americana y de la cultura latina: Sus implicaciones para la psicologia transcultural. *Revista Latinoamericana de Psicologia, 141*, 63–79.

Barona, A. (1982). *The utility of sociocultural variables and WISC-R factors of intelligence as predictors of special education eligibility: Multiple regression analyses.* Doctoral dissertation. The University of Texas at Austin.

Baskin, D., Bluestone, H., & Nelson, M. (1981). Ethnicity and psychiatric diagnosis. *Journal of Clinical Psychology, 37*, 529–537.

Costantino, G., & Malgady, R. G. (1983). Verbal fluency of hispanic, black, and white children on TAT and TEMAS, a new thematic apperception test. *Hispanic Journal of Behavioral Sciences, 5,* 199–206.

Costantino, G., Malgady, R. G., & Vasquez, C. (1981). A comparison of the Murray TAT and a new Thematic Apperception Test for urban Hispanic children. *Hispanic Journal of Behavioral Sciences, 3,* 291–300.

Cuellar, I., Harris, L. C., & Jasso, R. (1980). A acculturation scale for Mexican American normal and clinical populations. *Hispanic Journal of Behavioral Sciences, 2,* 199–217.

Dana, R. H. (1988). Culturally diverse groups and MMPI interpretation. *Professional Psychology: Research and Practice, 19,* 490–495.

Diaz-Guerrero, R. (1981). El enfoque cultura-contracultural de desarollo humano y social: El caso de las madres en cuatro subculturas mexicanas. *Revista de la Association Latinoamericana de Psicologia Social, 1,* 75–92.

Dolan, M. P., Roberts, W. R., Penk, W. E., Robinowitz, R., & Atkins, H. G. (1983). Personality differences among Black, white, and Hispanic-American male heroin addicts on MMPI content scales. *Journal of Clinical Psychology, 39,* 807–813.

Edelbrock, C. (1983). Problems and issues in using rating scales to assess child personality and psychopathology. *School Psychology Review, 12,* 293–299.

Exner, J. E., Thomas, E. A., & Mason, B. (1985). Children's Rorschachs: Description and prediction. *Journal of Personality Assessment, 49,* 13–20.

Fabrega, H., Swartz, J. D., & Wallace, C. A. (1968). Ethnic differences in psychopathology. II. Specific differences with emphasis on a Mexican-American group. *Psychiatric Research, 6,* 221–235.

Fuller, C. G., & Maloney, N. H. (1984). A comparison of English and Spanish (Nunez) translations of the MMPI. *Journal of Personality Assessment, 48,* 130–131.

Gittelman Klein, R. (1986). Questioning the usefulness of projective psychological tests for children. *Developmental and Behavioral Pediatrics, 7,* 378–382.

Goh, D. S., & Fuller, G. B. (1983). Current practices in the assessment of personality and behavior by school psychologists. *School Psychology Review, 12,* 240–243.

Gonzales, E. (1982). A cross-cultural comparison of the developmental items of five ethnic groups in the southwest. *Journal of Personality Assessment, 46,* 26–31.

Gross, H., Knatterud, G., & Donner, L. (1969). The effect of race and sex on the variation of diagnosis and disposition in the psychiatric emergency room. *Journal of Nervous and Mental Diseases, 148,* 638–642.

Holland, T. R. (1979). Ethnic group differences in MMPI profile patterns and factorial structure among adult offenders. *Journal of Personality Assessment, 43,* 72–77.

Holtzman, W. H., Diaz-Guerrero, R., & Swartz, J. D. (1975). *Personality development in two cultures: A Cross-cultural longitudinal study of school children in Mexico and the United States.* Austin, Texas: University of Texas Press.

Howes, R. J. (1981). The Rorschach: Does it have a future? *Journal of Personality Assessment, 45,* 339–351.

Johnson, D. L., & Sikes, M. P. (1965). Rorschach and TAT responses of Negro, Mexican-American, and Anglo psychiatric patients. *Journal of Projective Techniques, 29,* 183–188.

Kagan, S. (1981). Ecology and the acculturation of cognitive and social styles among Mexican-American children. *Hispanic Journal of Behavioral Sciences, 3,* 111–114.

Kagan, S., & Knight, G. P. (1981). Social motives among Anglo-American and Mexican-American children: Experimental and projective measures. *Journal of Research in Personality, 15*(1), 93–106.

Kaplan, B. (1955). Reflections of the acculturation process in the Rorschach test. *Journal of Projective Techniques, 19,* 30–35.

Kaplan, B., Rickers-Ovsiankina, M. A., & Joseph, A. (1956). An attempt to sort Rorschach records from four cultures. *Journal of Projective Techniques, 20,* 172–180.

Kline, P. (1976). *Psychological testing.* London: Malaby.

Lachar, D., & LaCombe, J. A. (1983). Objective personality assessment: The Personality Inventory for Children and its applications in the school setting. *School Psychology Review, 12,* 399–406.

Little, K. B. (1959). Problems in the validation of projective techniques. *Journal of Projective Techniques, 23,* 287–290.

Malgady, R. G., Costantino, G., & Rogler, L. (1984). Development of a thematic apperception test (TEMAS) for urban Hispanic children. *Journal of Consulting and Clinical Psychology, 52,* 986–996.

Malgady, R. G., Rogler, L. H., & Costantino, G. (1987). Ethnocultural and linguistic bias in mental health evaluation of hispanics. *American Psychologist, 42,* 228–234.

Martin, R. P. (1983). The ethical issues in the use and interpretation of the Draw-A-Person Test and other similar projective techniques. *School Psychologist, 38*(6), 8.

McCreary, C., & Padilla, E. (1977). MMPI differences among Black, Mexican-American and White male offenders. *Journal of Clinical Psychology, 33,* 171–177.

McGill, J. C. (1980). MMPI score differences among Anglo, Black, and Mexican-American welfare recipients. *Journal of Clinical Psychology, 36,* 147–151.

Moseley, E. J. (1967). Multivariate comparison of seven cultures: Argentina, Colombia (Bogotá), Colombia (Cartagena), Mexico, Panama, United States, and Venezuela. In C. F. Hereford & L. Natalicio (Eds.), *Aportaciones de la Psicologia a la Investigacion Transcultural* (pp. 291–304). Mexico City: F. Trillas.

Obrzut, J. E. (1982, August). *Review of projective personality assessment techniques.* Paper presented at the 90th Convention of the American Psychological Association, Washington, DC.

Obrzut, J. E., & Zucker, S. (1983). Projective personality assessment techniques. In G. W. Hynd (Ed.), *The school psychologist* (pp. 195–229). New York: Syracuse University Press.

Orozco, S., & Montgomery, G. (1982). *Mexican American's performance on the MMPI as a function of level of acculturation.* Paper presented at the meeting of the Southwestern Psychological Association, Dallas.

Padilla, A. M., & Ruiz, R. A. (1973). *Latino mental health: A review of the literature* (DHEW Publication No. HSM 73-9143). Washington, DC: U.S. Government Printing Office.

Padilla, A. M., & Ruiz, R. A. (1977). Personality assessment and test interpretation of Mexican-Americans: A critique. *Journal of Consulting and Clinical Psychology, 45,* 149–150.

Page, R. D., & Bozlee, S. (1982). A cross-cultural MMPI comparison of alcoholics. *Psychological Reports, 50,* 639–646.

Peck, E. (1974). The relationship of disease and other stress to second language. *International Journal of Social Psychiatry, 20,* 128–133.

Peterson, D. W., & Batsche, G. M. (1983). School psychology and projective assessment: A growing incompatibility. *School Psychology Review, 12,* 440–445.

Plemons, G. (1977). A comparison of MMPI scores of Anglo and Mexican-American psychiatrist patients. *Journal of Consulting and Clinical Psychology, 45,* 149–150.

Prout, H. T. (1983). School psychologists and social-emotional assessment techniques: Patterns in training and use. *School Psychology Review, 12,* 377–384.

Pruitt, J. A., Smith, M. C., Thelen, M. H., & Lubin, B. (1985). Attitudes of academic clinical psychologists toward projective techniques: 1968-1983. *Professional Psychology: Research and Practice, 16,* 781–788.

Rabin, A. I. (1981). *Assessment with projective techniques.* New York: Springer.

Reynolds, C. R. (1981, August). *Test bias: In God we trust, all others must have data.* Invited address to the annual meeting of the American Psychological Association, Los Angeles.

Reynolds, C. R., Plake, B. S., & Harding, R. E. (1983). Item bias in the assessment of children's anxiety: Race and sex interaction on items of the Revised Children's Manifest Anxiety Scale. *Journal of Psychoeducational Assessment, 1,* 17–24.

Rogler, L., Cooney, R., Costantino, G., Earley, B., Grossman, B., Gurak, D., Malgady, R., & Rodriguez, O. (1983). *A conceptual framework for mental health research on Hispanic populations* (Monograph No. 10). Bronx, NY: Fordham University, Hispanic Research Center.

Scott, R. (1981). FM: Clinically meaningful Rorschach index with minority children. *Psychology in the Schools, 18,* 429–433.

Shemberg, K., & Keeley, S. (1970). Psychodiagnostic training in the academic setting: Past and present. *Journal of Consulting and Clinical Psychology, 38,* 205–211.

Suinn, R. M., & Oskamp, S. (1969). *The predictive validity of projective measures.* Springfield, IL: Thomas.

Tamm, M. (1967). Resultadores preliminares de un estudio transcultural y desarollo de la personalidad de ninos mexicanos y norteamericanos. In C. F. Hereford & L. Natalicio (Eds.), *Aportaciones de la Psicologia a la Investigacion Transcultural* (pp. 159–164). Mexico City: F. Trillas.

Thelen, M. H., Varble, D. L., & Johnson, J. (1968). Attitudes of academic clinical psychologists toward projective techniques. *American Psychologist, 23,* 517–521.

Vukovich, D. H. (1983). The use of projective assessment by school psychologists. *School Psychology Review, 12,* 358–364.

CHAPTER 19

Perspectives on Language Proficiency Assessment

Arnulfo G. Ramirez
State University of New York at Albany

INTRODUCTION

The measurement of language proficiency is influenced by conceptions regarding language itself, developments in language testing theory, and educational issues (e.g., identification of pupils of "limited" English-speaking proficiency and assignment of students to different educational programs on the basis of language proficiency levels). Individual bilingualism is usually evaluated in terms of the person's relative knowledge of the two languages, including knowledge of different aspects of language (grammar, vocabulary, pronunciation), language skills (listening, speaking, reading, and writing), and the sociolinguistic dimensions of language (style, language varieties, functions). The depiction of bilingual proficiency from a behavioral–structural model of language tends to be associated with discrete-point testing, involving specific linguistic items scored on the basis of grammatical accuracy. The assessment of bilingual competence from a communicative perspective focuses on an "integrated" global ability, involving the functional use of language in a given sociolinguistic situation. Testing of competence in communication is an active field in language research, but most assessment instruments used in educational programs serving ethnolinguistic minority children focus on grammatical skills. The choice of a particular language test can influence educational decisions regarding the entry/exit criteria used in bilingual programs for language-minority school-children in the United States.

The purpose of this chapter is to review the assessment of language proficiency with respect to (a) certain aspects of linguistic competence (vocabulary, grammar, and language skills), (b) types of linguistic competence tests, (c) notions of communicative competence, (d) components of communicative competence, and (e) issues in language testing.

ASPECTS OF LINGUISTIC COMPETENCE

Linguistic competence usually refers to the ability to produce (and recognize) structures that are grammatically correct. Davies (1978, p. 149) described this ability as an "analytically discrete" skill reflected in the speaker's mastery of the formal grammar of the language. Palmer (1979, p. 170) viewed this competence as a "compartmentalized control" of language.

Studies of bilingual proficiency focusing on "discrete" elements of language have examined various linguistic dimensions. In the area of vocabulary, Cohen (1975) asked Spanish–English bilingual pupils to name objects found in settings associated with the domains of home, education, religion, and neighborhood. These domains were based on the findings of Greenfield and Fishman (1971), who investigated language use patterns among members of a Puerto Rican community in Jersey City. Cohen selected the settings of kitchen, school, church, and street and asked each child to name as many objects as possible for each location within a period of 45 seconds. The task was given in both English and Spanish, thus yielding the relative size of the child's active vocabulary in each language in the four contexts.

Along the same lines, Ramirez and Politzer (1975) developed a vocabulary-by-domain test that consisted of four sections (home, neighborhood, church, and school), each with eight items, and required the pupil to match one of three sentences with a picture. A "balance" score for each domain could be derived by contrasting the correct number of items obtained for English and Spanish. Figure 1 illustrates graphically the notion of vocabulary-by-domain for these four areas as well as for subject matter vocabulary associated with math and art.

Hinofotis (1977) explored the notion of lexical dominance in Greek and English by using a picture vocabulary test and word association tasks. The picture vocabulary test consisted of two sets of 60 pictures, each depicting simple objects to be named by the pupil in each language. A language dominance score was determined for each subject by calculating the difference in seconds between the mean times for the two sets of pictures in Greek and English. The word association task involved two procedures — first, naming in each language as many words as possible associated with nine stimulus objects (e.g., a doll, phonograph record, spoon, towel, pencil, apple, stuffed animal); second, requiring each subject to name words in each language associated with seven word classes (toys, furniture, animals, fruits, clothes, sweets, and kitchen). Each task yielded a mean number of words by language and by category, thus indicating the subject's relative control of each language.

The assessment of relative bilingual proficiency by grammatical categories has been characterized from different perspectives. Carrow (1971) compared preschoolers' comprehension of English and Spanish structures, including such components as nouns, pronouns, plurals, negatives, tense markers, and noun phrases with adjective modifiers. Peña (1967) measured among first graders the productive use of six basic sentence patterns and five basic transformations (e.g., negation, questions, passives) for both English and Spanish based on *The Grammatical Structures of English and Spanish* by Stockwell, Bowen, and Martin (1965). Ramirez and Politzer (1975) assessed bilingual proficiency by asking pupils in grades 1, 3, 5, and 7 to perform linguistic operations requiring (a) change from singular to plural, (b) change from plural to singular, (c) change from present to past, (d) change from affirmative to negative, (e) indication of location, (f) conversion of indirect to direct question, (g) conversion of indirect to direct command, (h) conversion of direct to indirect question, (i) conversion of direct to indirect

FIGURE 1.

Vocabulary-by-Domain Test. Reproduced from Ramirez (1979a, p. 161).

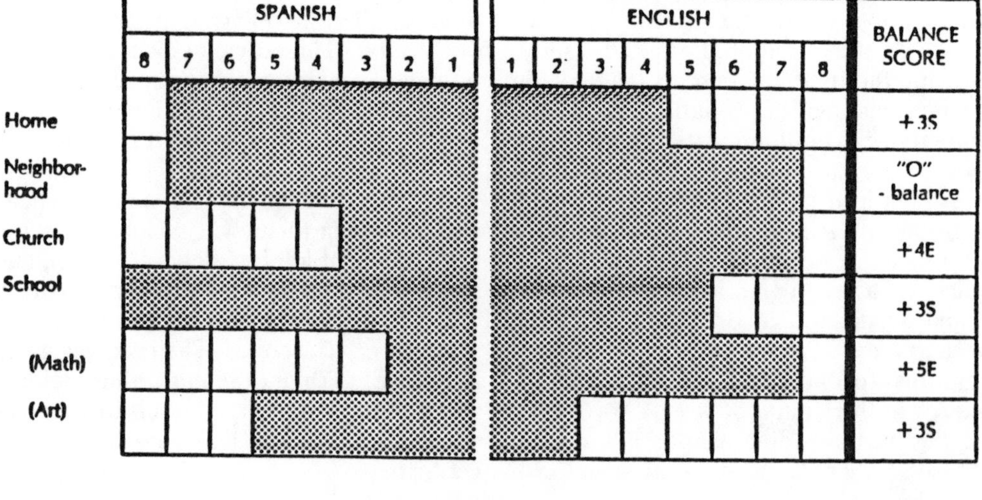

Domain	SPANISH (8 7 6 5 4 3 2 1) — ENGLISH (1 2 3 4 5 6 7 8)	BALANCE SCORE
Home		+3S
Neighborhood		"O" - balance
Church		+4E
School		+3S
(Math)		+5E
(Art)		+3S

command, and (j) change from positive to comparative in adjectives and adverbs. Two items were included in each category and each item was accompanied by two related pictures — one described in a sentence by the test administrator and one completed by the student.

Relative bilingual proficiency can be depicted in relation to a pupil's control of specific grammatical categories in the two languages. Table 1 illustrates the performance of a student exhibiting a greater mastery of Spanish grammar (total score = 15) than English grammar scored by a parallel English test (total score = 9). Another method for indicating relative proficiency involves the use of performance levels. Performance on the two parallel tests, each with 2 items, could be expressed in terms of five levels, each level including four correct/acceptable responses. Figure 2 represents the performance of four pupils. Student A (S_5 E_5) has a higher degree of "balance" than student D (S_3 E_3), and student B (S_4 E_2) is more dominant in Spanish while student C (S_2 E_4) is the opposite.

Some individuals could be classified as passive bilinguals (oral proficiency in one language, receptive language skills — listening comprehension — in the other), others as productive bilinguals (oral abilities in both languages; mastery of formal and informal varieties in one language, informal/colloquial variety in the other language), and some as biliterate bilinguals (oral and written competence in both languages; mastery of formal and informal varieties in both languages, literary variety in one language). Table 2 presents possible types of bilinguals according to language skills. Student A, who comprehends and speaks both languages, can be described as a productive bilingual. Student D is both bilingual and biliterate, whereas student B is literate only in L_1, and student C is able to read and write in L_2. Student E has a passive knowledge (oral comprehension) of L_2.

Studies of English and Spanish bilingualism in terms of language skills have been conducted with test development efforts in various states. Brown and Zirkel (1977) reported on some of the results with

New York City's Language Assessment Battery, and Agrawal (1979) described the construction of Chicago Board of Education's Short Tests of Linguistic Skills. Language skills in French and English have been assessed in Canadian "immersion" bilingual projects (Swain & Lapkin, 1982). Cohen (1975) investigated the development of English and Spanish language skills among pupils in a bilingual program in California. These same pupils were tested by Chun and Politzer (1975) and Merino (1982) with measures to determine comprehension and production of various grammatical features. Merino included items from seven categories (number, gender, past tense, word order, Spanish subjunctive/English equivalents, relatives, and conditions). Chun and Politzer (1975) examined 14 categories (e.g., singular/plural, present/past, mass/-count noun, subject pronouns, active/passive sentences with agent/object reversals). The 14 categories for both the comprehension and production tasks were translated into French and were used to assess language development among pupils attending a French/English bilingual school in grades K, 2, 3, and 5 in San Francisco.

LINGUISTIC COMPETENCE TESTS

Many of the assessment instruments available and currently used in bilingual education programs have been described by Silverman et al. (1976) and Pletcher et al. (1978). The majority of the instruments focus on linguistic competence and concentrate on the oral channel of communication, testing pupils' speaking ability. Most of the instruments can be classified in one of three categories:

1. Those that determine the language dominance or bilinguals at the level of vocabulary (e.g., Crane Oral Dominance Test, James Language Dominance Test, Dos Amigos Verbal Language Scales).

2. Those that establish the language dominance of bilinguals through the mastery of grammatical features/syntactic structures or sentence complexity (e.g., Bilingual Syntax Measure and Basic Inventory of Natural Language).

TABLE 1.

Relative bilingual proficiency in grammatical categories

Category	Item	English		Spanish	
I	1, 2	+	–	+	+
II	3, 4	+	–	✓	+
III	5, 6	✓	✓	+	+
IV	7, 8	+	+	–	+
V	9, 10	+	✓	+	+
VI	11, 12	–	–	–	–
VII	13, 14	–	–	✓	–
VIII	15, 16	–	–	+	+
IX	17, 18	–	–	–	✓
X	19, 20	–	–	+	✓
Total		5 + 3 = 8 correct		11 + 4 = 15 correct	

Symbols: +, correct response;
　　　　 ✓, acceptable response;
　　　　 –, incorrect response;

FIGURE 2.

Relative bilingual proficiency in terms of performance levels

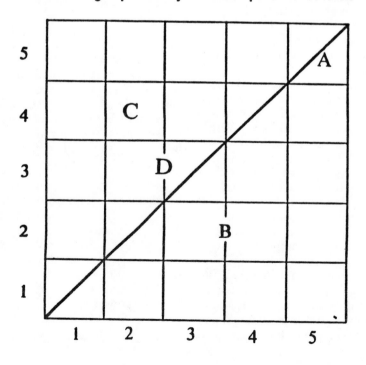

TABLE 2.

Bilingual proficiency according to four language skills for five students (A-E)

Language skill	A		B		C		D		E	
	L_1	L_2	L_1	L_2	L_1	L_2	L_1	L_2	L_1	L_2
Listening	+	+	+	+	+	+	+	+	+	+
Speaking	+	+	+	+	+	+	+	+	+	+
Reading	−	−	+	−	−	+	+	+	+	−
Writing	−	−	+	−	−	+	+	+	+	−

3. Those that determine establishment of dominance according to the four language skills — listening, speaking, reading, and writing (e.g., Language Assessment Battery, Marysville Test of Language Dominance).

A few tests, such as the Language Assessment Scales (LAS I and II), include various linguistic components: (a) Phonology (phonemic distinctions); (b) Lexicon (word identification through pictures); Syntax (associating a picture with a sentence and recalling a story); (d) Pragmatic use of language (teacher rates the child's ability to complete tasks requiring language — playing with peers, shopping at the store). The fourth dimension is not included in the scoring calculations, but may be used as a comparison with the pupil's final proficiency level.

NOTIONS OF COMMUNICATIVE COMPETENCE

The notion of *competence* was initially used to characterize a speaker's underlying knowledge of the system of a language, which includes the rules for generating grammatical sentences (Chomsky, 1965). Competence was viewed as the native speaker's internalized grammar, consisting of a complex system of rules, operating at different levels — syntactic, lexical, phonological, sémantic — to determine the organization of grammatical forms for various communicative purposes. This type of competence cannot be directly observed and is likened to an idealized speaker-hearer who does not display imperfect "performance" errors that can arise from such factors as memory limitations, distractions, shifts of attention, and hesitation phenomena (repeats, false starts, pauses, omissions, and additions).

The term *communicative competence* has been used by a number of observers since the 1970s to depict a range of ability wider than that associated with a grammatical knowledge of language (Hymes, 1985). This broader linguistic competence involves such aspects as social and functional rules of language use and the skills to negotiate meanings interpersonally within specific sociocultural situations (Hymes, 1972). Paulston (1974), for example, distinguished between *linguistic* and *communicative* competence to underscore the essential difference between the knowledge about language rules and structures and knowledge that enables a person to communicate effectively in face-to-face interactions.

Other terms associated with a broader view of grammatical competence have been proposed. Scholars concerned with verbal art conceive of *rhetorical* competence (Steinmann, 1982) and *narrative* competence (McLendon, 1977). Those concerned with the interpersonal uses of language identify *conversational* competence (Kennan, 1974), *interactional* competence (Erickson & Schultz, 1981), *social* competence (Cicourel, 1981), and *sociolinguistic* competence (Troike, 1970). These kinds of competence suggest that a multitude of abilities or skills constitute knowledge and command of a language.

Components of Communicative Competence

The depiction of linguistic abilities according to a behavioral–structural model of language tends to segment language into discrete, independently measurable components. Hernández-Chávez, Burt, and Dulay (1978) characterized language in terms of a three-dimensional matrix constructed with 64 possible separate proficiencies. One of the dimensions consists of the aspects of language — vocabulary, grammatical structures, pronunciation, and semantics. A second includes the oral and written modalities of language, with comprehension and production abilities related to the oral channel and reading and writing abilities associated with the written mode. The third component incorporates sociolinguistic performance with respect to usage considerations (speech styles and communicative functions of language) and language varieties (standard and nonstandard dialects and sociolinguistic domains such as home, school, work, neighborhood, and church).

Oller (1978, 1979), on the other hand, argued that "there exists a global language proficiency factor which accounts for the bulk of the reliable variance in a wide variety of language proficiency measures" (1978, p. 413). This single-concept expression of proficiency, described as *expectancy grammar*, is strongly related to cognitive variables and academic achievement measures and appears to exist across all four language skills (listening, speaking, reading, and writing). This global ability is attributed to the fact that "in the meaningful use of language, some sort of pragmatic expectancy grammar must function in all cases" (1979, p. 25), and this perceptual ability is "a psychologically real system that sequentially orders linguistic elements in time and in relation to extra-linguistic elements in meaningful ways" (1979, p. 25). This position emphasizes the central role that expectation and prediction play across language tasks and the fact that language itself cannot be meaningfully segmented into separate, discrete components.

A twofold approach for characterizing language proficiency has been proposed by Cummins (1980, 1983). Initially, he distinguished between basic interpersonal communicative skills (BICS) and cognitive/academic language proficiency (CALP). The BICS dimension of proficiency is the communicative capacity of language that all children acquire in order to be able to function in daily face-to-face exchanges. CALP involves the ability to manipulate or reflect upon the features of language (reading a text, writing an essay), independently of extralinguistic supports (e.g., gestures, situational cues). The BICS–CALP distinction was later modified to include a developmental perspective for describing relationships between academic performance and language proficiency. Thus, the framework conceptualized language proficiency along two continua. The horizontal continuum distinguishes between *context-embedded* versus *context-reduced* communication (see Figure 3).

In context-embedded communication (BICS) the participants can negotiate meaning through the use of gestures and feedback to indicate that the message has not been understood, and the language is supported by a wide range of situational cues. Context-reduced communication (CALP), in contrast, relies primarily on linguistic cues to establish meaning and in some cases this may involve suspending knowledge of the "real" world so as to interpret or manipulate the logic of communication correctly. A good amount of classroom language is context-reduced, requiring linguistic messages to be elaborated precisely and explicitly so that misunderstanding is minimized, as in writing a letter, answering an essay question, or reading an article. Context-embedded communication, on the other hand, is more typical of interactive situations outside the classroom. This form of communication derives part of its meaning from interpersonal involvement in a shared reality, which makes it unnecessary to elaborate explicitly the linguistic message.

The vertical continuum addresses the developmental aspect of communicative proficiency in relation to the degree of active cognitive involvement in the task or activity. Cognitively demanding tasks such as persuading another person or writing a composition to explain a complicated process require the individual to process a considerable amount of information simultaneously or in close succession in order to complete the activity. Cognitively unde-

FIGURE 3.

Range of contextual support and degree of cognitive involvement in communicative activities. From Cummins (1981, p. 12).

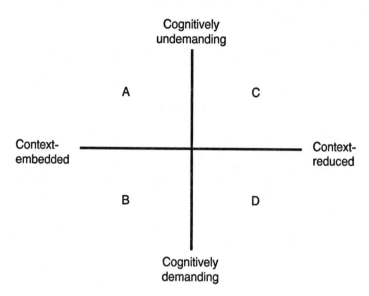

manding tasks, at the other end of the vertical continuum, consist of communicative activities that require little cognitive involvement, and the linguistic requirements have become automatized as in greetings, asking for permission, filling out a form with personal information, or locating the title of a story/chapter.

A fourfold concept of communicative competence has been advanced by Canale (1983) that is based on a framework by Canale and Swain (1980) and specifies three interacting factors. According to Canale (1984), linguistic communication can be characterized in terms of various systems of knowledge and skills noted in four areas:

1. Grammatical competence: mastery of the language code (verbal or nonverbal), thus concerned with such features as lexical items and rules of sentence formation, pronunciation, and literal meaning.
2. Sociolinguistic competence: mastery of appropriate language use in different sociolinguistic contexts, with emphasis on appropriateness of meanings (e.g., attitudes, speech acts, and propositions) and appropriateness of forms (e.g., register, nonverbal expression, and intonation).

3. Discourse competence: mastery of how to combine and interpret forms and meanings to achieve a unified spoken or written text in different genres by using (a) cohesion devices to relate utterance forms (e.g., pronouns, transition words, and parallel structures) and (b) coherence rules to organize meanings (e.g., repetition, progression, consistency, and relevance of ideas).
4. Strategic competence: mastery of verbal and nonverbal strategies (a) to compensate for breakdowns in communication due to insufficient competence or to performance limitations (e.g., strategies such as use of dictionaries, paraphrase, and gestures) and (b) to enhance the effectiveness of communication (e.g., deliberately slow and soft speech for rhetorical effect). (Canale, 1984, p. 112)

It is important to note that communicative competence here is used to refer to both "knowledge" and "skill" in using language. Actual communication involves the realization of various underlying systems of knowledge (e.g., linguistic and nonlinguistic — "knowledge" of the world) and skills (e.g., using the sociolinguistic conventions of a given language) under limiting psychological and environmental conditions such as memory and perceptual constraints, fatigue, and nervousness (Canale, 1983, p. 5). This framework of four subsystems does not describe how these factors interact with one another and how they develop among learners/users.

Attempts to validate Canale and Swain's (1980) hypothesized components of communicative competence by Bachman and Palmer (1982) resulted in the identification of three distinct traits: linguistic competence, pragmatic competence, and sociolinguistic competence. Grammatical competence includes morphology and syntax, both of which can vary in range and accuracy. Phonology and graphology are excluded, since they are viewed as channels rather than components of communication. Pragmatic competence is associated with the ability to express and comprehend messages and includes as subtraits vocabulary, cohesion, and organization (coherence). Sociolinguistic competence incorporates the ability to distinguish registers, nativeness, and control of nonliteral, figurative language and relevant cultural allusions. This framework appears to have the status of a model in that it establishes through confirmatory factor analysis the independence of the various components or traits. Yet Cummins and Swain (1986, p. 208) noted that Bachman and Palmer were unable to distinguish grammatical competence from pragmatic competence among the ESL students at the university level. Similarly, among sixth-grade French language immersion students, the results of the factor analysis failed to show the validity of three postulated traits — grammatical, sociolinguistic, and discourse competence. Only grammar and discourse competence emerged as distinct traits among this group of language learners, but only when they are considered in the wider context of immersion students along with native speakers of French.

Other frameworks for depicting communicative competence have been proposed more recently. Faerch, Haestrup, and Phillipson (1984) argued that communicative competence consists of phonology/orthography, grammar, vocabulary, pragmatics, discourse, communication strate-

gies, and fluency. Bachman's (1987) model incorporates aspects from Canale and Swain in a different formulation. Language competence includes two major components — organizational competence, consisting of grammatical competence, and textual competence along with various subskills. Pragmatic competence, another aspect of language competence, involves the functional uses of language (illocutionary competence) along with sociolinguistic competence. Strategic competence is a set of general abilities that utilize all of the elements of language competence in addition to psychomotor skills in the process of negotiating meaning (see Figure 4).

Conceptions of communicative competence have important implications for how language is tested and how language is taught within a communication perspective. Determining the construct validity of the various components that make up the different models noted above may be a difficult stage in the search for an absolute model of communicative competence. Cummins and Swain (1986, p. 208) suggested the need to test how the various components or traits of communicative competence become differentiated from each other for particular groups of students in specific learning situations.

COMMUNICATIVE COMPETENCE TESTING

A number of studies have examined various dimensions of communicative competence in relation to linguistic competence (grammatical knowledge). Communicative competence as a concept has been operationalized in various ways. Overall (1978) determined the extent to which discrete-point English grammar tests relate to communicative competence as measured by sociolinguistic situations involving role-playing tasks with puppets used to represent different participants (teacher, pupil, principal) while performing various speech acts (requesting, explaining, asking for permission). The correlational analysis among the two linguistic competence (grammar) tests and the communicative measure revealed a strong linear

FIGURE 4.

**A framework for describing communicative language proficiency.
From Bachman (1987).**

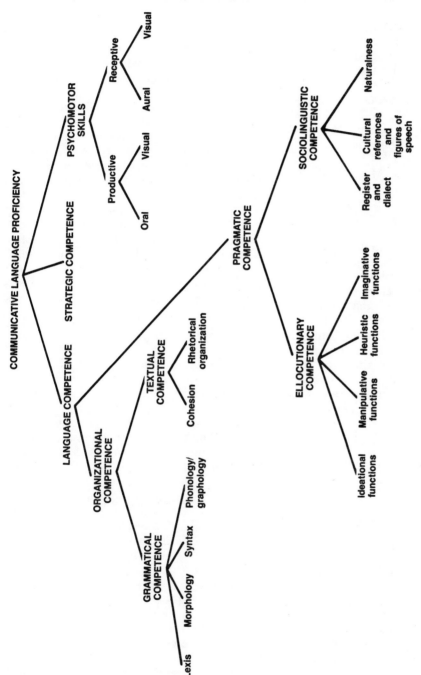

relationship. However, a closer examination of the results through the use of scatter-grams indicated a curvilinear relationship between the two types of proficiency. Separate correlations for the students' scores on the lower and upper ends of the curve tended to be much lower than the overall correlations, suggesting that discrete-point grammatical tests may not be an accurate indication of students' communicative abilities at beginning or advanced levels of second-language proficiency, especially in the case of Spanish-speaking students enrolled in a bilingual program at the elementary grades.

Along these lines, McGroarty (1981) investigated the relationship between linguistic competence (mastery of simple grammatical categories) and communicative competence (ability to convey information) in English among high school Spanish-speaking students in an effort to determine if these two competencies constitute different sets of skills and the extent to which they overlap. The initial results appeared to indicate that linguistic competence predicted communicative competence. However, a scatterplot analysis indicated greater variation in communicative competence at all levels. In addition, the two measures were found to correlate only moderately. The students' performance in small-group discussion, particularly with respect to "total information statements" and "range of informative categories," related strongly to linguistic competence assessed orally. Both types of proficiencies were positively associated with school achievement as measured by the number of "competencies" passed on a graduation competency test. It was also noted that the ability to transmit information effectively generally increases with age/grade level.

Politzer and Ramirez (1981) contrasted the linguistic and communicative competence in both English and Spanish among high school students enrolled in a bilingual program. Linguistic competence was measured through a commercially available grammar test, communicative competence was operationalized as the ability to analyze and convey information effectively both in the receptive and productive modes, and sociolinguistic competence was defined as the ability to recognize and interpret direct and indirect speech acts. Some of the major findings of the study indicate the following conclusions:

1. Communicative competence as defined in this study was found to be distinct from linguistic competence, which is only one of the components of communicative competence.

2. Linguistic competence in English, as well as communicative competence both receptive and productive in English and Spanish, were related (a) to cognitive/academic performance, defined in terms of the number of competencies passed on the graduation "competency" test, and (b) to a field-independent learning style.

3. Sociolinguistic competence was associated with linguistic competence in both English and Spanish, but it correlated negatively across languages. However, as an ability it appeared to have been mastered by many of these students.

Ramirez (1984) utilized the same instruments and procedures as in the previous study by Politzer and Ramirez (1981) to examine the relationship between communicative competence and linguistic competence in both English and Spanish among Spanish/English bilingual pupils in three elementary schools and one high school. The significant relationships from the language test results of students in the two bilingual elementary schools and the bilingual high school can be summarized as follows: (a) linguistic competence in English and Spanish were negatively related; (b) productive communicative competence in English and Spanish were moderately related for the high school group but for only one of the elementary school groups; (c) receptive communicative competence across the two languages was unrelated in two of the schools and moderately related in one school; (d) sociolinguistic competence (recognition of direct and indirect speech acts) correlated highly within each language and across the two languages in the two elementary schools; (e) sociolinguistic competence and receptive communicative competence were related across languages in three of the schools; and (f) productive communicative competence and sociolinguistic competence were moderately related within each language for the high school group and one of the bilingual elementary schools. Thus, communicative competence appeared to be influenced by school and by age differences among the pupils.

The measurement of sociolinguistic competence through the use of a discrete-point, multiple-choice format differed from the linguistic demands required in the transmission of information mode used in the productive communication task. With respect to achievement measures, English linguistic competence and productive/receptive communicative competence related to academic/cognitive performance as measured by the number of "competencies" passed by the high school group on the graduation competency test and to scores on both the CTBS (Comprehensive Test of Basic Skills) and CAT (California Achievement Test) attained by pupils in the elementary schools. English sociolinguistic competence was related to achievement in English language skills and mathematics computation and concepts in all three elementary schools. Productive communicative competence in Spanish was related to English cognitive/academic achievement for the high school group, and receptive communication competence in Spanish was associated with English language and mathematics skills among the pupils in the three elementary schools.

It was noted that the different relationship patterns between the language measures and achievement tests were partly due to the age and grade factors and the home language use situations as well as with the students' self-concepts and learning styles. High school students who were field-dependent did not perform well on other linguistic or communicative language measures. In addition, a positive self-concept was associated with higher scores on communicative proficiency measures in both languages. Thus, performances of communicative competence measures may be influenced by nonlinguistic factors such as affective variables and the cognitive dimensions of the task.

The concept of communicative competence with respect to the several components proposed by Canale and Swain (1980) and Canale (1983) has been investigated in several Canadian studies. Swain (1985) examined the traits of grammatical, discourse, and sociolinguistic competence by using oral and literacy-based methods. Each trait was assessed through parallel methods (oral production tasks, multiple-choice test formats, and a written production task). The trait of grammatical competence was operationalized by criteria involving rules of morphology and syntax with a major focus on verb and preposition usage. Discourse competence was defined as the ability to produce and recognize coherent and cohesive devices in texts. Sociolinguistic competence was judged by the ability to produce and recognize socially appropriate language in a given sociocultural context.

Intercorrelations in terms of the three traits and the three methods make it difficult to offer even a simple explanation. Some pairs of tests that shared neither trait nor method correlated more highly than those that had the same trait or method. Thus, grammatical competency as measured by a multiple-choice test correlated highly with discourse competence as reflected through written production. The distinct traits of grammatical and discourse competence, previously noted when immersion students along with native French speakers were included, did not emerge as separate components with this group of sixth-grade French immersion students. The homogeneity of the immersion sample may not have enabled factor analysis procedures to reveal a distinction; in addition, using correlational approaches to test components of communicative competence is problematic.

Cummins and Swain (1986) reported significant differences between native French speakers and English speakers receiving immersion education with respect to grammatical, sociolinguistic, and discourse indices as opposed to distinct components. For example, immersion students differ significantly from native speakers on most grammatical measures and on discourse and sociolinguistic measures which require grammatical knowledge to produce the correct linguistic forms. On the other hand, differences were minimal on those discourse and sociolinguistic indices for which grammatical accuracy plays a minor role in the production of correct linguistic forms. These findings suggest that when sociolinguistic and discourse competences are defined to exclude the mastery of correct (grammatical) linguistic forms, they can be acquired by second language learning in French immersion programs at levels similar to those of native speakers, whereas grammatical competence (mastery of the linguistic code especially in the areas of morphology and syntax) remains distinctly different from that of native French speakers.

Placing these findings within Cummins' (1983) model of context-embedded and context-reduced modes of communication and the role of cognitive or personal attributes, various explanations are offered by Cummins and Swain (1986) to provide a theoretical synthesis for research data from majority and minority/immigrant second language learners in Canada. They note, for example, that context-embedded grammatical skills in a second language develop primarily as a function of exposure to and use of the L_2 in the environment, whereas context-reduced academic skills are relatively more dependent on the cognitive attributes of the individual. French immersion students tend not to develop native-like proficiency in the area of grammatical accuracy in both written and oral modalities because of limited interaction with native French speakers. On the other hand, the degree of native-like proficiency achieved by immersion students in discourse and reading skills is largely determined by the cognitive attributes of the learner, at least to the same extent as they are influenced by exposure and use of the language in the environment.

Immigrant students do acquire grammatical skills in the second language, at least in the oral modality, within a relatively short period because of their contact with native speakers and use of the second language beyond the classroom. Their attainment of age-appropriate academic skills through the second language tends to take 5–7 years of exposure; this pace is similar to that of French immersion students but it varies more with the cognitive and personality attributes of the learner. Thus, in the case of Japanese students learning English in Toronto, Cummins et al. (1984) found that levels of cognitive/academic proficiency in both English and Japanese among these middle-class "temporary residents" were interdependent and that indices of students' background and personal attributes were strongly related to English academic proficiency and interactional style. The opposite was true for grammatical proficiency, which was more influenced by indices of students' exposure to and use of English. Overall, the determinants of academic proficiency are based on cognitive variables, and those associated with interaction are influenced by personality attributes.

These findings are used to propose a model of attribute-based proficiency that places the components of communicative competence in a different structure. The interrelationships of the specific components can vary according to attributes of the learner and the type of learning environment. Cummins and Swain (1986, p. 212) offer the following conclusion:

> L_2 grammatical proficiency in both context-embedded and context-reduced modes is strongly dependent on the amount and type of input received by the individual. Development of context-reduced L_2 grammatical proficiency also depends significantly on attributes of the individual whereas this is not the case, to the same extent, for L_2 context-embedded grammatical proficiency. Discourse and sociolinguistic proficiency, on the other hand, appear less dependent on exposure to the L_2 in the environment and, in the context-reduced mode, are attribute-based in that strong cross-lingual and cognitive relationships are observed.

The framework proposed by Cummins and Swain (1986) for examining the different components of language proficiency can be used to interpret the findings of some studies conducted in the United States. For example, Saville-Troike (1984) studied a group of ESL learners to determine "what really matters in second language learning for academic achievement." She found that aspects of grammatical competence (morphology and syntax) did not correlate with academic achievement as measured by the reading subtest of the CTBS. In addition, there was a low correlation between academic achievement and interaction with peers and adults in English. Students' exposure to and use of English did relate with measures of grammatical knowledge. Academic achievement in the content areas as measured by English tests was associated with knowledge of concepts taught in the native language, suggesting some cross-lingual transfer. Some of the lowest academic achievers were those who were most successful at interpersonal communication (oral discourse competence), especially in peer situations. Hayes-Brown (1984) found in her research that both linguistic and communicative competence measures provided various types of information that significantly improved the prediction of English achievement as measured by the CTBS Total Reading and Language scores. The communicative skills measure, involving both storytelling and role-playing tasks (oral discourse and strategic competence), was the best predictor of academic achievement (written discourse and grammatical sensitivity). The communicative competence measure also correlated with the other linguistic competence measures, one focusing on vocabulary knowledge and the other one on grammatical competence. Thus, communicative competence as defined here involved vocabulary (concepts) knowledge as well as grammatical competence. At the same time, the discourse aspect of storytelling and role playing explained at least 52% of variance on English achievement. Thus, for this group of third-grade bilingual students in Santa Clara County, California, the interactions among the different components of proficiency — grammatical, discourse, and sociolinguistic — in both context-reduced and context-embedded situations resulted in a particular set of relationships.

ISSUES IN LANGUAGE TESTING

The term *communicative competence* may involve a multitude of abilities or skills associated with knowing and using a language. Communicative proficiency has been characterized as involving anywhere from one global, underlying language ability to as many as 64 separate components. The uniqueness of each component or trait may vary as a result of the type of learner (age, linguistic background, cultural background) and the learning context (second/foreign language situation, compensatory bilingual program, immersion education for majority pupils). The components of language proficiency (grammatical, discourse, and sociolinguistic) may interact in particular ways, given context-embedded and context-reduced modes as well as the cognitive dimensions of the tasks.

Communicative competence is often characterized as an "integrated control" (Palmer, 1979, p. 170) of language that is reflected in the speaker's ability to understand and use language appropriately to communicate in various situations. The testing of communicative competence tends to be based on the concept of global ability (integrating the different elements of language — grammar, vocabulary, etc.) involved in communicative acts (giving directions, requesting permission, apologizing, etc.). In most instances, specific situations requiring communication are described by the examiner and rating scales are used to evaluate how effectively the examinee has performed the particular communicative act.

One of the characteristics of communicative testing is the strong emphasis on actual use of language in real-life settings, usually based on the communicative needs of the learners. As a result, language tests are a collection of tasks at different levels (beginning, intermediate, and advanced) with respect to different language abilities (listening, speaking, reading, and writing) rather than one overall test of language proficiency. Communicative tests are necessarily integrative tests, since the learner has to "bring together" the various elements of language involved in performing different communicative acts. Quantitative assessment procedures (right/wrong; yes/no) may be unsuitable in many cases, because the performance of certain tasks/ functions (e.g., giving directions orally, requesting information in a letter, reading a map or timetable) may be best evaluated by such criteria as accuracy, appropriateness, and flexibility. This requires the use of rating scales to assess relative proficiency on various dimensions, which constitute collectively an overall/global ability with respect to the performance of a specific language task.

The discrete-item approach tends to focus on a specific aspect of language (phonology, morphology, syntax, and vocabulary), and this usually means that the emphasis is on a single one of the parts that makeup the total situation. One may wonder what the contribution of a particular aspect or level of language is to the global communicative task. Canale and Swain (1980) pointed out that the discrete-point tests may be more appropriate for assessing communicative competence, but integrative ones might be more suitable for assessing actual communicative performance. The distinction of competence (receptive/interpretative knowledge of language) versus performance (productive/integrative use of language) may be meaningful in deciding the proportion of language tasks that can be assessed through pencil-and-paper tests and those that can be tested through actual performance of simulated communicative tasks (e.g., telephoning, ordering meals, applying for a job).

In the case of language-minority pupils in the United States, no single language proficiency measure can account for all the linguistic abilities that a student possesses. Tests of grammatical competence may not indicate the degree to which students can interact with peers or teachers or perform on cognitive and academic tasks.

There is a lack of comparability in the level designations among the major language tests that are commercially available. Hayes-Brown (1984) found that approximately 30% of the students in her sample were inconsistently classified by means of any two instruments designed to measure linguistic or communicative competence. Ulibarri, Spencer, and Rivas (1981) reported important differences in the degree of agreement in the classification of FES (fluent English speakers), NES (non-English-speaking) and LES (limited-English speakers). Degree of agreement varies by grade as well as by test pairs. Agreement among Grade 1 pupils ranges between 40% and 45% for the three pairs of tests: LAS (Language Assessment Scales), BSM (Bilingual Syntax Measure), and BINL (Basic Inventory of Natural Language). At the third-grade level agreement is highest (61%) between BINL and LAS and the lowest (30%) between BSM and LAS. At the fifth-grade level the results are somewhat similar, with 65% agreement for BINL and LAS, 27% for BSM and LAS, and 39% for BINL and BSM. Spearman's correlations between test raw scores show different results, indicating, for example, many more crossovers in comparisons involving the BINL. Levels of language proficiency that are provided by the test authors should not be accepted as valid indicators of linguistic abilities. Local grade levels may need to be developed and used as criteria for cutoff scores.

Differences in performance on linguistic or communicative competence measures may be due to differences in format or scoring procedures rather than specific components of language proficiency. Language items may involve discrete-point scoring or global assessment by rating scales that require interrater agreement. Some items may require convergent answers, while others may elicit divergent replies with many possible answers. Some items may be single sentences or phrases that are unrelated to one another, and others may demand sequential naturalistic discourse along the scheme proposed by Omaggio (1983) and illustrated in Figure 5.

Traditional items on a grammar test would fall in Quadrant A in Figure 5 since they usually focus on isolated sentences or phrases and are scored with a right/wrong criterion. A cloze passage, an example of a reading task, calls for discrete-point semantic–grammatical choices and requires students to "fill" gaps in a text. Such a technique has an integrative format that can be scored objectively (Quadrant C). Slash sentences, sometimes called "dehydrated" sentences (John/home — John went home/ John likes his home/John lives in a comfortable home), require students to create full, grammatical sentences. This activity is

FIGURE 5.

Locating test items according to convergent/divergent answers and single sentences/sequential discourse. (Reproduced from Omaggio, 1983, p. 10).

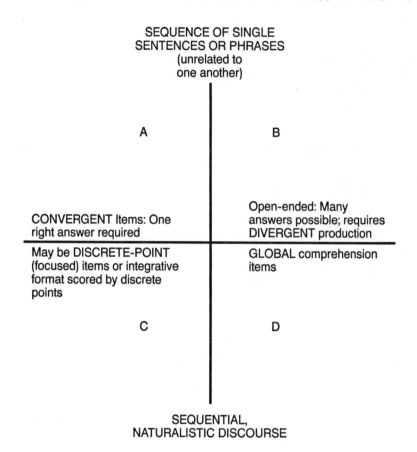

essentially open-ended, allowing a number of divergent answers (Quadrant B). Items in Quadrant D can include actual performance tasks (e.g., ordering a meal, playing the role of a buyer or seller, filling out a form or report of an accident) as well as global/specific understanding of spoken or written texts (e.g., answering comprehension questions, writing a summary, recording specific information to fill an incomplete chart, schedule, table, or special form). This scheme, when superimposed over Cummins' (1983) framework, which incorporates the range of contextual support and degree of cognitive involvement, provides additional considerations for language proficiency assessment.

Finally, the issue of which aspects of language proficiency should be used for placement (entry) and reclassification (exit) among pupils of non-English-language background. Cummins (1981) favors the use of CALP-type measures (context-reduced, cognitive/academic language proficiency) rather than BICS-type measures (context-embedded, basic interpersonal communication skills). At present, tests presenting grammatical, sociolinguistic discourse, and strategic language tasks that could be incorporated into this framework are unavailable for wide-scale use. Canale (1984) reported on some of the studies undertaken at the Ontario Institute for Studies in Education to prepare communicative assessment instruments both in English and French to serve the needs of Franco-Ontarian educators. The project follows the fourfold concept of communicative proficiency and acknowledges the role that other systems of knowledge and skills play in what is viewed as language proficiency. The individual is seen to bring to the test situation a "knowledge" of the world and certain perceptual strategies, personality characteristics, and motivational factors. Troike (1984) emphasized the importance of "input" variables such as socioeconomic status and sociocultural factors that ultimately affect students' opportunities for gaining "knowledge of the world" and their sociolinguistic styles, which in turn may interact in unique ways with different aspects of communicative competence, particularly among ethnolinguistic-minority groups.

Another example from Canada (Cummins & Swain, 1986) is the development of a large-scale communicative language testing program for French immersion students. Four basic principles have guided the development of this project, starting with a 12-page student booklet titled *A vous la parole* ("the floor is yours"), (a) concentrating on the book contents, (b) generating specific communicative tasks, (c) eliciting the learners' best performance, and (d) working for "washback" — teacher involvement in test development, administration, and scoring.

Communicative competence testing in the United States in recent years has tended to follow an ethnographic/sociolinguistic approach. Researchers following this tradition have been able to demonstrate, for example, that the range of linguistic and interactional skills among young children obtainable through structured interviews, observation, or "naturalistic" interactional situations cannot be adequately tapped by any single test, since communicative intent can only be evaluated in terms of the participants' mutual definition in given interactional contexts (Bennett & Slaughter, 1983). Questioning strategies among bilingual pupils with different levels of proficiency in English and Spanish can be influenced by the classroom structure (e.g., students working in small groups; students

communicating with the teacher's aide), type of setting (home, neighborhood, classroom), and lesson event (Rodriguez-Brown & Elias-Olivares, 1983). Teachers in a study conducted in Tucson were trained to observe students' linguistic behavior in different situations and with various participants in order to appreciate the students' varied repertoires in functional language use (Phillips, 1983). The limitations of an ethnographic/sociolinguistic approach to language proficiency assessment were found to be set by such factors as (a) the working relationship between teachers and administrators, (b) the time required to become familiar with the procedures, (c) teachers' educational backgrounds, and (d) the characteristics of the approach itself, which required systematic observation by a participant (teacher) observer of students' actual language use in naturally occurring communication situations in different contexts (Simich-Dudgeon & Rivera, 1983). These procedures, however, may be very important for providing descriptive data on how students use language in different contexts when interacting with different participants. Time limitations and financial considerations may make this approach impractical for assessing all students for placement (entry) purposes. Saville-Troike (1983) noted that this approach may be particularly useful at least when making program exit decisions: Will the student be able to participate effectively in an English-only classroom?

Language enters the classroom both as a system of communication and as a means of learning. It can be both process and product. Talking, listening, reading, and writing are four modalities of language that are interrelated in the process of teaching. The specific components of communicative competence that come into play when students make oral reports, tell stories, answer questions, and take standardized tests may indeed go beyond knowing and using a language. What kind of language proficiency do language minority students need in order to function effectively in an all English classroom? The answer may come only after a detailed analysis of what demands are made on students' language resources and what linguistic resources students have to meet these curricular demands (Ramirez, 1982). Answers to the questions related to language proficiency and classroom demands may surpass psychometric considerations in test construction and the appropriateness of ethnographic/sociolinguistic approaches to proficiency assessment. The issues here involve considerations beyond language proficiency and include such factors as school language policies (i.e., how language is used in teaching and learning) and the function of educational institutions in society.

REFERENCES

Agrawal, K. C. (1979). The "Short Tests of Linguistic Skills" and their calibration. *TESOL Quarterly, 13,* 185–208.

Bachman, L. (1987). *Fundamental considerations in language testing.* Reading, MA: Addison-Wesley.

Bachman, L., & Palmer, A. (1982). The construct validation of some components of communicative proficiency. *TESOL Quarterly, 16,* 449–465.

Bennett, A., & Slaughter, H. (1983). A sociolinguistic/discourse approach to the description of the communicative competence of linguistic minority children. In C. Rivera (Ed.), *An ethnographic/sociolinguistic approach to language proficiency assessment* (pp. 2–26). Avon, England: Multilingual Matters.

Brown, M. E., & Zirkel, P. A. (1977). *Imerging instrumentation for assessing language dominance.* In Occasional Papers on Linguistics, No. 1, pp. 202–225. Carbondale, IL: Southern Illinois University, Department of Linguistics.

Canale, M. (1983). From communicative competence to communicative language pedagogy. In. J. Richards & R. Schmidt (Eds.), *Language and communication* (pp. 2–25). New York: Longman.

Canale, M. (1984). A communicative approach to language proficiency assessment in a minority setting. In C. Rivera (Ed.), *Communicative competence approaches to language proficiency assessment: Research and application* (pp. 107–122). Avon, England: Multilingual Matters.

Canale, M., & Swain, M. (1980). Theoretical bases of communicative approaches to second language teaching and testing. *Applied Linguistics, 1*(1), 1–47.

Carrow, E. (1971). Comprehension of English and Spanish by preschool Mexican-American children. *Modern Language Journal, 50,* 299–306.

Chomsky, N. (1965). *Aspects of the theory of syntax.* Cambridge, MA: MIT Press.

Chun, J. A., & Politzer, R. L. (1975). *A study of language acquisition in two bilingual schools.* Stanford University, School of Education.

Cicourel, A. (1981). Notes on the integration of micro- and macrolevels of analysis. In K. Knorr-Cetina & A. V. Cicourel (Eds.), *Advances in social theory and methodology* (pp. 51–80). London: Routledge and Kegan Paul.

Cohen, A. D. (1975). *A sociolinguistic approach to bilingual education.* Rowley, MA: Newbury House.

Cummins, J. (1980). The cross-lingual dimensions of language proficiency: Implications for bilingual education and the optimal age issue. *TESOL Quarterly, 14,* 175–187.

Cummins, J. (1981). The role of primary language development in promoting educational success for language minority students. In California State Department of Education, *Schooling and language minority students: A theoretical framework* (pp. 3–49). Los Angeles: California State University.

Cummins, J. (1983). Language proficiency and academic achievement. In J. W. Oller, Jr. (Ed.), *Issues in language testing research* (pp. 108–126). Rowley, MA: Newbury House.

Cummins, J., & Swain, M. (1986). *Bilingualism in education.* New York: Longman.

Cummins, J., Swain, M., Nakajima, K., Handscombe, J., Green, D., & Tran, C. (1984). Linguistic interdependence among Japanese and Vietnamese immigrant students. In C. Rivera (Ed.), *Communicative competence approaches to language proficiency assessment: Research and application* (pp. 60–81). Avon, England: Multilingual Matters.

Davies, A. (1978). Language testing. *Language Teaching and Linguistics Abstracts, 11,* 145–159, 215–231.

Erickson, F., & Schultz, J. (1981). When is a context? Some issues and methods in the analysis of social competence. In J. Green & C. Wallat (Eds.), *Ethnography and language in educational settings: Vol. 5. Advances in discourse processes* (pp. 147–160). Norwood, NJ: Ablex.

Faerch, C., Haastrup, K., & Phillipson, R. (1984). *Learner language and language learning.* Copenhagen: Gyldendals Sprogbibliotek.

Greenfield, L., & Fishman, J. A. (1971). Situational measures of normative language views of person, place and topic among Puerto Rican bilinguals. In J. A. Fishman, R. L. Cooper, R. Ma, et al. (Eds.), *Bilingualism in the Barrio* (Indiana University Publications, Language Science Monograph #7, pp. 233–351). The Hague: Mouton.

Hayes-Brown, Z. A. (1984). Linguistic and communicative assessment of bilingual children. In C. Rivera (Ed.), *Placement procedures in bilingual education: Education and policy issues* (pp. 40–105). Avon, England: Multilingual Matters.

Hernández-Chávez, E., Burt, M. K., & Dulay, H. C. (1978). Language dominance and proficiency testing: Some general considerations. *National Association of Bilingual Education Journal, 3*, 41–54.

Hinofotis, F. B. (1977). Lexical dominance: A case study of English and Greek. In *Occasional papers on linguistics*, No. 1, pp. 241–245. Carbondale, IL: Southern University Department of Linguistics.

Hymes, D. (1972). On communicative competence. In J. B. Pride & J. Holmes (Eds.), *Sociolinguistics* (pp. 269–293). London: Penguin.

Hymes, D. H. (1985). Toward linguistic competence. *Revue de l'Aila, 2*, 9–23.

Kennan, E. O. (1974). Conversational competence in children. *Journal of Child Language, 1*, 163–185.

McGroarty, M. E. (1981). *English language tests, school language use, and achievement in Spanish-speaking high school students.* Unpublished doctoral dissertation, Stanford University, California.

McLendon, S. (1977). Cultural presupposition and discourse analysis: Patterns of presupposition and assertion of information in Eastern Pomo and Russian narrative. In M. Saville-Troike (Ed.), *Linguistics and anthropology* (pp. 153–189). Washington, DC: Georgetown University, Round Table on Languages and Linguistics.

Merino, B. J. (1982). Order and pace in the syntactic development of bilingual children. In J. A. Fishman & G. D. Keller (Eds.), *Bilingual education for Hispanic students in the United States* (pp. 446–464). New York: Columbia University, Teacher College.

Oller, J. W., Jr. (1978). The language factor in the evaluation of bilingual education. In J. E. Alatis (Ed.), *Georgetown University Round Table on Languages and Linguistics* (pp. 410–422). Washington, DC: Georgetown University Press.

Oller, J. W., Jr. (1979). *Language tests at school: A pragmatic approach.* New York: Longman.

Omaggio, A. (1983). *Proficiency-oriented classroom testing.* Washington, DC: Center for Applied Linguistics.

Overall, P. M. (1978). *Assessment of the communicative competence in English of Spanish-speaking children in the fourth and sixth grades.* Unpublished doctoral dissertation, Stanford University, California.

Palmer, A. (1979). Compartmentalized and integrated control: An assessment of some evidence for two kinds of competence and implications for the classroom. *Language Learning, 29*(1), 169–180.

Paulston, C. B. (1974). Linguistics and communicative competence. *TESOL Quarterly, 8*, 347–362.

Peña, A. A. (1967). *A comparative study of selected syntactical structures of the oral language status in Spanish and English of disadvantaged first-grade Spanish Speaking children.* Unpublished doctoral dissertation, University of Texas at Austin.

Phillips, S. U. (1983). An ethnographic approach to bilingual language proficiency assessment. In C. Rivera (Ed.), *An ethnographic/sociolinguistic approach to language proficiency assessment* (pp. 88–106). Avon, England: Multilingual Matters.

Pletcher, B., Locks, N., Reynolds, D., & Sisson, B. (1978). *A guide to assessment instruments for limited English speaking students.* New York: Santillana.

Politzer, R. L., & Ramirez, A. G. (1981). Linguistic and communicative competence of students in a Spanish/English bilingual high school program. *National Association of Bilingual Education Journal, 5*(3), 81–104.

Ramirez, A. G. (1982). Language. In D. G. Wallace (Ed.), *Developing basic skills programs in secondary schools* (pp. 20–30). Alexandria, VA: Association for Supervision and Curriculum Development.

Ramirez, A. G. (1984). Pupil characteristics and performance on linguistics and communicative language measures. In C. Rivera (Ed.), *Communicative competence approaches to language proficiency assessment: Research and application* (pp. 82–106). Avon, England: Multilingual Matters.

Ramirez, A. G., & Politzer, R. L. (1975). The development of Spanish/English bilingualism in a dominant Spanish-speaking environment. *ATIBOS: Journal of Chicano Research,* Summer, pp. 31–51.

Rodriguez-Brown, F., & Elias-Olivares, L. (1983). Linguistic repertoires, communicative competence and the Hispanic child. In C. Rivera (Ed.), *An ethnographic/sociolinguistic approach to language proficiency assessment* (pp. 27–41). Avon, England: Multilingual Matters.

Saville-Troike, M. (1983). An anthropological linguistic perspective on uses of ethnography in bilingual language proficiency assessment. In C. Rivera (Ed.), *An ethnographic sociolinguistic approach to language proficiency assessment* (pp. 131–136). Avon, England: Multilingual Matters.

Saville-Troike, M. (1984). What *really* matters in second language learning for academic achievement? *TESOL Quarterly, 18*(2), 199–219.

Silverman, R. J., Noa, J. K., Russell, R. H., & Molina, J. C. (1976). *Oral language tests for bilingual students.* Portland, OR: North West Regional Laboratory.

Simich-Dudgeon, C., & Rivera, C. (1983). Teacher training and ethnographic/sociolinguistic issues in the assessment of bilingual students' language proficiency. In C. Rivera (Ed.), *An ethnographic/sociolinguistic approach to language proficiency assessment* (pp. 107–130). Avon, England: Multilingual Matters.

Steinmann, M. (1982). Speech-act theory and writing. In M. Nystrand (Ed.), *What writers know. The language, process and structure of written discourse* (pp. 291–324). New York: Academic Press.

Stockwell, R. P., Bowen, J. D., & Martin, J. W. (1965). *The grammatical structures of English and Spanish.* Chicago: University of Chicago Press.

Swain, M. (1985). Communicative competence: Some roles of comprehensible input and comprehensible output in its development. In S. Gass & C. Madden (Ed.), *Input in second language acquisition* (pp. 235–253). Rowley, MA: Newbury House.

Swain, M. K., & Lapkin, S. (1982). *Evaluating bilingual education: A Canadian case study.* Avon, England: Multilingual Matters.

Troike, R. C. (1970). Receptive competence, productive competence, and performance. In J. Alatis (Ed.), *Linguistics and the teaching of standard English to speakers of other languages and dialects* (pp. 63–74). Washington, DC: Georgetown University, Round Table on Languages and Linguistics.

Troike, R. C. (1984). SCALP: Social and cultural aspects of language proficiency. In C. Rivera (Ed.), *Language proficiency and academic achievement* (pp. 44–54). Avon, England: Multilingual Matters.

Ulibarri, D. M., Spencer, M. L., & Rivas, G. A. (1981). Language proficiency and academic achievement: A study of language proficiency tests and their relationships to school ratings as predictors of academic achievement. *National Association of Bilingual Education Journal, 5*(3), 47–80.

CHAPTER 20

Use of Achievement Tests with Non-Native English-Speaking Language Minority Students

Daniel M. Ulibarri
NuLearning Technology[1]
Antioch, California

Concern over the inappropriate use of tests with non-native-English-speaking (NNES) students came to the educational forefront in a May 24, 1971, memorandum written by the director of the U.S. Office for Civil Rights. The director warned against the use of testing instruments and placement procedures that "essentially measure or evaluate English language skills" (De Avila, Cervantes, & Duncan, 1978).

Since then, attempts have been made to address the misuse of standardized achievement tests with NNES students. Nevertheless, the problems and conditions that existed in the sixties prevail in U.S. public schools. Rather than limiting the use of tests or being more cautious in their use, schools continue to use and rely on tests to make decisions about minority students and NNES students (Center for the Study of Evaluation [CSE], 1983; Ulibarri, Eshgh, & Wong-Fillmore, 1985).

WHO ARE NNES STUDENTS?

NNES students are, in practice, the same as language-minority students, that is, students who themselves speak or whose parents speak a non-English language, or who come from a home where a language other than English is spoken. Because language proficiency definitions and the methods for assessing language proficiency vary tremendously (Ulibarri, Spencer, & Rivas, 1981; Ulibarri, 1986), children labeled NNES encompass the full range of English proficiency from "no English" to "near native proficiency." Although many

of these students possess functional oral skills in English, they often lack the specific academic language skills necessary to successfully perform on standardized tests and in mainstream U.S. classrooms.

Similarly, students who are classified as NNES by federal and state laws encompass a wide range of proficiency in their native language. Thus, it cannot be assumed that NNES students fall primarily within the "near native" proficiency range in their non-English native language, or that they will necessarily be "dominant" in their non-English language.

There are two primary reasons why NNES students are not necessarily dominant in their native language. First, the federal definition of native language with respect to persons of limited-English-proficiency (LEP) includes "the language normally used by such individuals, or in the case of a child, the language normally used by the parents of the child" (U.S. PL 98-511–Oct. 19, 20 USC 3223, 703(a)(2)). Second, most U.S. student's literacy education is in English and not in their native language. Thus, not only do they not have literacy skills in their native language; they are better at taking tests in English than they are in their native language.

NNES students can also be classified as LEP even though English is their "dominant" language. This is because the standard definition for limited English proficiency is that provided for in the Bilingual Education Act (PL 98-511, cited above). It includes individuals who because of a non-native-English-language background "have sufficient difficulty speaking, reading, writing, or understanding the English language to deny such individuals the opportunity to learn successfully in classrooms where the language of instruction is English or to participate fully in our society." This definition does not require that the student speak a non-English language, or be dominant in a non-English language — only that, because of a non-native-language background, the student is having difficulty in school.

There are two important things to be remembered about this definition that are important to the issue of achievement testing. First, proficiency in a non-English language is not required. Second, English language proficiency is defined within the context of the school classroom.

Too many people overlook both of these facts. Yet both are critical in making decisions about appropriate instructional strategies for students and in assessing language proficiency and student achievement. For example, educators and policymakers are often too quick to assume that because a student is not clearly dominant in a non-English language, they do not need to be concerned about the effect of language on instruction or testing. Yet it is clear from the definition of who is in need of language services that English language proficiency is still a concern even for students whose dominant language is not their native language.

There is an ongoing disagreement over the appropriate method for assessing English language proficiency. The argument centers on whether language proficiency is seen as a unitary construct or trait or whether it is viewed as a combination of various language skills. Some researchers have discussed the issue in terms of measurement (i.e., discrete point vs. continuous methods of assessment), and some in terms of communicative versus linguistic competence. However, the disagreement is moot, since it is clear that language proficiency, as defined by "law," refers to the ability to function in the English-speaking classroom. As such, language proficiency must include an achievement component; this requirement suggests that (a) the intent for defining language proficiency was to include more than one component; (b) linguistic skills related to achievement were to be included in the definition; and (c) English language proficiency affects student achievement.

LANGUAGE ISSUES IN ASSESSMENT

The question of English language proficiency is not generally considered as central to the discussion of testing issues with NNES students who are neither classified as LEP, nor clearly dominant in a non-English language. However, it is precisely because of the variability in English language proficiency, and the failure to recognize that language still impacts on NNES students' achievement, that language proficiency is an extremely important factor.

Language proficiency and content familiarity as well as cultural factors can greatly affect NNES students' performance in school and on standardized tests, regardless of whether they are LEP or English-dominant. Because of this, their educational futures are severely restricted when these tests are used as diagnostic tools to place and stream these students into various educational tracts in the schools (DeBlassie, 1980).

Test publishers do not always include provisions for screening NNES students or take into account English language proficiency for students who are not LEP. Decisions concerning the use of a test are left up to school districts. Unfair use of achievement tests occurs when the test measures something other than the content area skills it is designed to assess, e.g. language proficiency. This results in the placement or tracking of NNES students according to what often amounts to relative attainment of English language skills rather than content skills.

Confounding the problem is that standardized achievement tests are not diagnostic, but are being used for tracking within classrooms in which students are either separated according to "ability" levels and "pace" of learning or separated completely in terms of distinct content and course requirements. Though one can usually make a distinction between ability groupings and tracking, school personnel in practice have difficulty separating the two (Aspira, 1980).

In either case tracking determines the type, quantity, and quality of instruction that students receive (DeBlassie, 1980). Since NNES students generally perform poorly on achievement tests, ey are tracked into nonacademic or no -college-bound tracts co sisting of remedial or watered-down c rriculum strands. The result of this kind of tracking is that the students are den ed access ot only to opportunities to develop advanced knowledge and skills, but also to higher education opportunities that more severely affect life ambitions.

Several states and school districts are currently using standardized tests as part of their classification criteria to determine limited English proficiency for NNES students. This can lead to two problems. One problem is that students are not being transferred from language related programs into mainstream classes, since test scores reflect both language proficiency and other low-achievement factors common to minorities in general (California State Department of Education Symposium on Language Proficiency, 1983). An even more serious problem that is overlooked is that students who are mainstreamed still score at the lower end of the standardized test distribution, since most exit criteria are set around the 30th percentile (e.g., De Avila et al., 1978; Ulibarri, 1983). With these scores, students exiting from language-related programs are mainstreamed into lower educational tracts based on language proficiency rather than on academic ability, even though the students are not "classified" as LEP.

Most alarming is that the influence of standardized tests, particularly with NNES and other minorities, has increased rather than decreased. Even though school personnel report an increased dependency on teacher-made tests and minimum competency tests, it has been documented that this occurs primarily in schools serving populations of high socioeconomic status (SES). Teachers and principals in low-SES schools continue to use the results of standardized tests for making decisions

about placement and tracking of their students more than do their counterparts at high-SES schools (Center for the Study of Evaluation, 1983). The implications for NNES students are clear. Since NNES students tend to be from low-SES backgrounds and are known to do poorly on standardized tests, their academic futures can be negatively influenced by the administrative emphasis placed on these test results.

Thus, the greater reliance on standardized achievement testing and the trend toward tracking many NNES students into nonacademic and remedial tracts appear to be taking place as the minority population in U.S. schools increases. Moreover, this practice begins when NNES students first enter school — leading to a relatively poor prognosis for most NNES students. While some high achievers among this group will be able to advance to high levels of academic and career success, most will be designated to fill increasingly marginal positions.

The purpose of this chapter is to illustrate that there indeed exists a need to examine and rethink how standardized tests are used with NNES students. It should be emphasized that this problem is not restricted to students with a Spanish-language background. Asian students are experiencing similar difficulties. Changes in the Asian population residing in the United States have brought corresponding changes in their performance as an NNES group on achievement tests. Recent studies show that 50–80% of NNES Asian students were "overrepresented in the lower three stanines (23rd percentile)," compared to published national norms in total reading, total language, and total math (Mace-Matluck, Hoover, & Dominguez, 1983).

The material that follows provides an overview of four major concerns, for which practical solutions and recommendations are offered for future direction at the federal, state, and local levels. The four concerns are (a) federal influence on the use of standardized tests; (b) the consequences of achievement testing on NNES students; (c) the influence of language on standardized achievement and measures;

(d) the technical issues surrounding test bias and fair test use.

The goal is to demonstrate the need to examine standardized testing of NNES students more carefully. One contention is that the NNES population deserves or requires this extra consideration to obviate not only their personal loss from lack of educational advancement, but also the negative impact that this loss has on society.

If the educational system is deficient in any single aspect of its task to educate all segments of the population, then it is lacking overall. This effort is in keeping with the current movement of education excellence. The strength of a nation rests in the quality and effectiveness of its education system and the development of its greatest resources — its children.

INFLUENCE OF FEDERAL AND STATE POLICY

Federal and state policies on standardized testing are affecting the education of NNES students in U.S. public schools. While these effects are usually indirect, they are nonetheless significant. The federal government does not mandate school policy, but does include programs under which state and local use of the federal funds is prescribed.

Most significant is the requirement of some form of standardized tests for evaluating the impact of programs funded under various state and federal laws. While program evaluation is necessary, it is precisely the "mandated" use of tests that allows for group comparisons that is at the heart of the problem.

Four federal laws enacted between 1963 and 1975 set the pattern for federal and state policy on major educational programs: Vocational Education Act of 1963; the Elementary and Secondary Education Act (ESEA) of 1965–1968 (including Title 1, Chapter 1, Bilingual Education Act, Migrant Education Act); the Indian Education Act of 1972; and the Special Education Act (Public Law 94-142) of 1975.

Most of these federal laws contain explicit requirements for objective test-score data as a major determinant of the

success or failure of a given program. Consider the following examples:

Chapter 1 (ESEA of 1965) requires states to "evaluate in quantitative terms the effectiveness of each formally organized program or project supported by federal, state, or local funds." (Code of Federal Regulations, Title 34, Part 400.402, 1983, 32–33).

The Bilingual Education Act of 1984 and the revised act of 1987 require that applicants for grants evaluate the achievement levels of their LEP students by comparing with standardized achievement tests norms (Code of Federal Regulations, Title 34, Part 500.5 and 500.52, 1987, 58).

The Indian Education Act provides that in order to receive entitlement grants a local district must present an evaluation plan that includes "an objective quantifiable method including an appropriate measurement of educational achievement to determine if the project meets each of its objectives" (Code of Federal Regulations, Title 34, Part 251.33, 1983, 592).

Immediately after the enactment of these laws, there began a series of federal- and state-sponsored reform movements, which had a major impact on education at the district level. These were the minimum competency testing movement which started up in the 1970s, and the Excellence in Education movement, which began in the 1980s. This section will examine these laws and movements as they have come to affect the use of standardized achievement testing in states with the largest numbers of NNES students and will discuss how district-level practices have been influenced by policy.

Competency Testing

The minimum competency testing movement reached its apex in the late 1970s and early 1980s. About 40 states instituted minimum competency tests in an effort to ensure that elementary and secondary students would be able to achieve a certain level of competency in content subjects. Some states exempted NNES students from taking the tests; others mandated the tests for all students. In both cases, questions arose as to the fairness for NNES students

(Quezada, 1979). In other words, students were penalized whether they were tested or exempted from testing.

In states such as Connecticut, which exempted NNES students, there was evidence that certain formal and informal practices hampered these students' academic achievement.

1. The exempted students may have lost out on classroom instruction time because teachers devoted extra time to those students who did take the test.

2. These students may have received a certificate of attendance rather than a high school diploma. This certificate is valued far less than a diploma among colleges and potential employers.

3. These students may have been denied remedial services in states where services were prescribed on the basis of test scores.

4. They may have encountered a greater chance of grade retention in cases in which promotion was partially based on test scores.

In other states, such as California, in which NNES students take these tests alongside their native English-speaking counterparts, other problems have hampered NNES students' achievement. Among them are the increased likelihood of (a) being unfairly relegated to learning-disabled (LD) or educably mentally retarded (EMR) classes solely or largely on the basis of test scores; (b) being tested over material they never covered as a result of losing instruction time in content subjects when they were pulled out to attend classes in English as a second language (ESL); (c) being unfairly tracked into vocational or general education tracts when they were capable of learning subject matter in the college preparatory tract (Quezada, 1979).

NNES students are often impeded in their educational progress by standardized achievement tests that operate under an assumption that "English is the only language of teaching and assessment" (Gold, 1985, p. 3). However, students in bilingual education classes are already of limited English proficiency and should, in Gold's view, be tested in their native languages in the content subjects.

Excellence in Education

In April 1983, the National Commission on Excellence in Education released its report, *A Nation at Risk: The Imperative for Educational Reform*. This report called on state and local educational agencies to respond to the crisis in education by promoting an agenda of excellence. Even before the report was issued, states had begun giving standardized achievement tests to graduating secondary students, as a result of the competency testing movement. States began giving similar standardized achievement tests to all secondary-level students and subsequently to elementary students as well. As a result of the Commission's report, this trend intensified. It was particularly noticeable in states with large concentrations of NNES students.

For example, the U.S. Department of Education reported the following developments. (a) Florida approved a state wide testing program, Standards of Excellence; (b) New York added more subjects to its statewide proficiency examination and directed local boards of education to identify and improve schools after low-performing students had been identified by standardized tests; (c) California expanded its testing program, making testing mandatory for students in Grades 8 and 10; (d) Texas required its Texas Assessment of Basic Skills test to be taken in third, fifth, and ninth grades; (e) Arizona developed a third-grade test and required junior and senior high students to be tested (National Commission on Excellence in Education, 1983).

Practical Consequences of Federal and State Policies

A number of research projects have investigated the interaction between federal and state policy and actual practices in school districts as these affect achievement testing for NNES students. A recent investigation sponsored by the National Institute of Education examined projects funded by the Vocational Education Act (Lukas, 1981). The investigators studied the 15 states with the largest student populations, including a significant NNES population, and found a pattern of reluctance to offer major vocational programs to NNES students. In some states, state officials were sometimes resistant to serving the NNES population, believing in some cases that the numbers were too high and that most were illegal aliens. Several officials stated that students should learn English before being accepted into the program and often the primary determinant of entry into the program was performance on standardized achievement tests.

The National Commission on Secondary Education for Hispanics (1984) found that relative to the large proportion of Hispanics in vocational education tracts, few attended state-of-the-art training programs that equipped them for the job market. Hispanics who failed the standardized achievement tests being implemented in the eighth grade never received services to upgrade their performance and thus were often relegated to low-level vocational programs (Hispanic Office of Planning and Evaluation, 1984). Most Hispanic youths are not being trained in high technology skills that are in demand. Instead they are placed in less important job training courses, which usually prepare them for dead-end, low-paying service jobs.

When standardized tests are used for placement purposes without regard for the influence of English language skills, NNES students are unfairly assessed in terms of their English language proficiency. The influence of language on test scores is a primary factor in test bias and unfair test use, which will be discussed in a later section.

IMPACT OF ACHIEVEMENT TESTS ON NNES STUDENTS

Tracking of NNES Students

The increased reliance on standardized testing that flows both from the mandates of federal laws and from the response to educational reform movements has led to an increase in tracking NNES students into nonacademic programs. Such a consequence of federal and state policy was illustrated by a national survey of Hispanic high school students conducted by the National Commission on Secondary Education for Hispanics (1984). The commission found that 75% of Hispanics were in vocational and general education tracts even though many were capable of doing well in academic subjects. The National Council of La Raza (1985) has found that now, as in the past, Hispanics are generally being steered toward general education and vocational courses by educators whose low expectations cause them to routinely track Hispanics in this manner.

A review of the literature on tracking revealed general agreement that achievement tests are often used to track minority children and that these children are overrepresented in nonacademic tracts:

> Despite the call in several of the recent studies for an end to tracking, a number of factors are pushing school districts and legislatures in the opposite direction. It seems fair to assume that the immediate future is likely to bring greater ethnic and socioeconomic segregation through tracking than that presently existing . . . failure by poor and minority children to pass "gate" tests will frequently be accompanied by their reference to a "remedial" track. . . . History warns us that these "remedial" tracks often end up as leveled programs that merely set a lower standard for participants rather than remediating their needs with the end of returning them to a fully competitive position. (Roos, 1984, pp. 75–76)

A report on Hispanic students in Boston (Hispanic Office of Planning and Evaluation, 1984, p. v) reached similar conclusions. Results from the Boston study indicated that efforts to introduce competency-based testing and promotion policies in the Boston Public Schools did not favor Hispanic students because they lacked the support services to help students meet the standards.

Once tracked, it is hard to change classification (Oakes, 1983). Rosenbaum (1980) reported that in the selection of career tracts (i.e., college-bound or vocational-education-bound) students are often misled into believing that they may switch tracts at any time. However, the only pattern Rosenbaum discovered was a downward movement. Movement upward into academic tracts required prerequisite courses that NNES students often lacked. When students applied for college admission, they were penalized again by institutional weighing of grades according to academic tract.

The results of several studies show that NNES students are disproportionately tracked into remedial educational programs, and inadequate vocational education programs and are excluded from advanced and normal educational curriculums. According to Carter and Segura (1979)

> "Mexican Americans were more likely to be found in low ability tracks in schools with more Anglos." (p. 161) These groups become stable in junior high school and continue into senior high school where it is almost impossible to move out of a curricular track.

Interpretation of Achievement Test Scores

The use of achievement tests has contributed to a bleak educational future for many NNES students. When students enter school, it is likely that they will be tested; these test scores, if not used for actual placement, will be used to explain the students' poor performance, when in fact their performance could be due to other social and linguistic characteristics. If these test scores had been properly addressed, a significantly different outcome could have resulted. A national report on the use of tests in schools quotes one teacher as follows:

> They give me each kid's standardized-test score on my class roster. If one stands out, I usually check with the counselor to be sure the kid should really be assigned to geometry. (CSE, 1983, p. 141)

A continuing problem posed by the use of tests with NNES students is the interpretation made from test scores. Test scores are intended as measures of current knowledge or level of skill development. However, with NNES students you cannot make this interpretation without taking into account the cultural and linguistic specificity of the test. Yet test scores are often interpreted as if they were measures of ability or academic potential (DeBlassie, 1980). In these cases, students are rather capriciously labeled and not provided with the opportunity to learn.

Use of standardized tests for eligibility or student classification purposes creates a potential for misclassification and misplacement. Several states use standardized tests as part of the requirement for identifying and reclassifying students as LEP and for entering and exiting students from English language programs. Their use as part of an exit criterion can result in placement of newly mainstreamed students in remedial classes or classes with low academic expectations. Since most exit criteria are set at the 30th percentile (De Avila et al., 1978; Ulibarri, 1983), students placed out of language programs are mainstreamed into lower educational tracts on the basis of language proficiency rather than academic ability.

In addition, the CSE report concluded that federal and state standardized testing or minimum competency testing requirements contribute to making "test scores especially salient in the very schools where more students more often have difficulty doing well on formal tests" (p. 142). This result is alarming, since it indicates that tests are being more frequently used, and are having a greater influence on NNES and other minority students' education — rather than less, as one might have supposed, given all the publicity and controversy of the sixties and seventies. Moreover, in response to the question "Are standardized test batteries and minimum competency scores consulted in student placement?" (p. 131), the results from the CSE study on the use of tests found that

> they are most often consulted as part of an automatic or cursory gate-keeping procedure. Law or policy guidelines direct that students with scores below a certain cut-off point be placed in a compensatory program or remedial class. (p. 131)

When used for evaluation of special programs, standardized tests can indicate that a program is not effective when in fact it is both effective and needed by NNES students. This occurs because of the mismatch between the students' linguistic background, the program's curricular objective, and what the test actually measures. This happens because school districts often have only one test available to them and they are not trained or equipped to take on the responsibility for determining the appropriate use of the test in different situations.

Increased Influence of Achievement Tests with NNES Students

According to principals' reports, the results of formal tests carry more weight and have greater consequences in schools serving low socioeconomic status (SES) neighborhoods, where NNES students are usually found, than in those serving high-SES communities (CSE, 1983, p. 141). The CSE report also stated that formal standardized achievement testing plays a role in the placement of NNES and LEP students (many of whom come from lower-SES families) in bilingual programs.

Apparently state and federal policy, together with recent educational trends such as back-to-basics and educational-excellence programs, have swept NNES students into their network of activities without regard to the impact of tests and other decision-making procedures. These activities lead to an overdependence, either directly or indirectly, on the results of standardized test performance. They have had the effect of imposing standardized tests on the "psyche" of teachers and principals such that they tend to overemphasize and rely on the results of these tests when making decisions regarding low-SES and NNES students. Although one might speculate that the effect is indirect, since it occurs coincidentally with legislative and policy requirements for the use of standardized tests, the CSE report on the use of tests commented that

> these findings suggest that external test results become more important to teachers only when something or someone impels or induces teachers to treat them as more important. (CSE, 1983, p. 30)

Impact on Higher Education and Career Opportunities

In the midst of these developments, a larger interrelated societal trend affecting NNES students' academic progress is becoming visible. This trend is characterized by the simultaneous decline in minority student enrollment in four-year colleges and elite institutions. The greater reliance on standardized achievement testing and the trend toward tracking many NNES students into nonacademic tracts appear to be taking place as universities become more elite and minority participation declines.

These practices combine to establish a relatively poor prognosis for most NNES students. Some high achievers among this group will be able to advance to high levels of academic and career success, but most will be destined to fill marginal positions.

Educators, policy makers, and all who are concerned with public education and minority advancement need to examine future policy considerations in light of these developments. They must deal with the question raised by an expert on tracking practices: "Are students' rights to equal protection of the laws and due process being violated by the processes and effects of ability grouping and tracking?" (Oakes, 1983, p. 816).

LANGUAGE PROFICIENCY AND ACHIEVEMENT TESTS

Language Proficiency Demands of Achievement Tests[1]

The single most critical issue regarding the use of standardized tests with NNES students is the confounding of language competence with academic competencies that achievement tests are supposed to assess. Some language-testing researchers feel that achievement tests are, in many respects, nothing more than measures of English-language proficiency, even for those who speak English as their native language (Oller & Perkins, 1978). The basis for this position is that performance on achievement tests is highly correlated with performance on tests designed specifically to assess language proficiency. Students who may be otherwise equally competent can show considerable differences in how proficient they are in English, and their achievement test scores often reflect this variation. Research (e.g., De Avila, 1973; De Avila, Duncan, Ulibarri, & Flemming, 1983; Ulibarri et al., 1981; Ulibarri et al., 1985) indicates that language is the single most critical factor in predicting NNES students' performance on academic achievement tests.

Should this be surprising? It stands to reason that student's language proficiency in a particular language will correlate with their achievement on a test that is administered in that language. Similarly, one could argue that language proficiency tests are measures of school achievement. Either of these positions could be true depending on whether the students taking the tests are homogeneous with respect to language or to achievement.

To interpret achievement test scores as a true measure of achievement, it must be assumed that students are more or less of the same level of "basic" language proficiency. With respect to NNES students such an assumption cannot be made without taking specifically into account their English-language proficiency.

In the following, specific examples of how language proficiency comes into play on achievement tests is demonstrated. The examples are organized according to three main categories of confounding language factors on achievement test performance:

1. The content of achievement tests is similar to that of language proficiency tests (e.g., "verbal" and "nonverbal" subscales, vocabulary, language arts, and language usage subscales).
2. Content analysis of items, including arithmetic computation problems, indicates a language requirement.
3. Verbal standardized instructions in English are required to administer the tests.

Similarity of Content

Language proficiency becomes apparent in achievement tests from a review of the content similarity of test subscales and test items on achievement, IQ, language

proficiency, and personality tests. In fact, achievement tests are made up of subtests specifically designed to measure language ability. Thus, there are "verbal" and "nonverbal" subscales, vocabulary, language arts, and language usage subscales.

Achievement tests, for example, the California Achievement Test (CAT), and the IOWA Test of Basic Skills (ITBS), divide language into two categories, "reading" and "language." From the example items reproduced below it would be a challenging task to determine which items are taken from an intelligence test, an achievement test, a personality test, a language test, or none of the above.

1. Accomplished means
   a. said   b. completed   c. written
   d. overlooked   e. forgotten

2. Explain why this sentence is not correct: The judge said to the prisoner, "You're to be hanged and I hope it will be a warning to you."

3. Countless means:
   a. few   b. innumerable   c. crazy
   d. royalty   e. foreign

4. Vanish-fade; appear-?
   Which of these words should you use to complete the second pair?
   a. vision   b. materialize
   c. incarnate   d. flesh   e. embody

5. Hollow means the same as:
   a. empty   b. light   c. hungry

6. Which of these words belongs together: hat, room, ribbon, basket, dress?

7. Inefficient means:
   a. avoidable   b. able
   c. incompetent   d. ruly

8. Why is it good to hold elections by secret ballot?

9. Define the following words:
   a. pity   b. curiosity   c. grief
   d. surprise

10. Are your folks reasonable to you when they demand obedience? (Gunnarsson, 1978, p. 21)

Item 1 comes from an achievement test, items 5 and 10 come from a personality test, and the rest come from either IQ or mental abilities tests, which are also similar to achievement tests. None of the items come from language proficiency tests.

The following items taken from several well-known tests exemplify the points made here. The tests from which these examples have been drawn are Comprehensive Tests of Basic Skills, Level 1, Form T, McGraw-Hill, 1975, hereafter "CTBS1-T"; Cooperative Primary Tests, ETS, 1967, hereafter "CPT" 1 and the California Achievement Tests, Level 2, Form A, McGraw-Hill, 1970, hereafter "CAT2-a."

Sections of achievement tests that are most obviously like language proficiency tests are those dealing, naturally enough, with language arts and reading. Both the CTBS1-T and the CAT2-A have reading vocabulary sections in which the student reads a phrase, and then selects from a list the word that is closest in meaning to a designated word in the phrase. For example:

From the CAT2-A:	From the CTBS1-T:
swift *trip*	finish a *chore*
jet	design
journey	jingle
tractor	job
trot	problem

Such items are used in language tests to assess lexical knowledge and familiarity with the phraseological patterns of the language. They assess more than word recognition. In order to decide which of the list of words is similar in meaning to the designated word, the student not only has to be able to read the words, but must also know what they mean and how they are used by speakers of the language.

In the language arts sections of the achievement tests, students are more likely to be tested on their ability to make phonemic discriminations much as in language proficiency tests whose objective is to assess the extent to which the test-taker has mastered the sound system of the language being tested.

Achievement test sections that assess matters of usage are also very much like proficiency tests in that they are directly concerned with knowledge of the language. Achievement tests are more concerned with "correct" or prescriptive usages, than with actual usage as are proficiency tests. Hence,

the "correct" answer to a question about language usage may or may not be what people would actually say, and the test-taker who is not altogether familiar with "prescribed" usages will be likely to select the wrong answer. For example, in the CAT2-A, we find items of the following sort:

Lisa and ____ are going to the school play.
___ them ___ they

Toni and ____ like to camp.
___ her ___ his
___ him ___ she

According to the rules of English that are taught in school, the correct pronoun choices for the conjunctions in these two items are "they" and "she." In real life it is extremely rare for English speakers to conjoin a pronoun to another nominal (except for the first person singular). It is much more common for someone to say "Toni and Jane like to camp," or "Lisa and her friends" or "Lisa and her sisters."

Thus, questions that ask students to select the "correct" form of such a conjunction require sensitivity to classroom doctrines about proper English rather than exposure to English in use. It would seem that questions of language usage, whether or not they are based on aspects of language that are taught in school, depend on the test-taker's familiarity with the language itself.

Sections of tests that assess reading or listening comprehension are also very much like proficiency tests in which the object is to assess the extent to which the test-taker has mastered the forms and structures of the language and can apply them in interpreting texts. Their purpose in reading or in listening tests is to assess reading ability or the ability to listen, recall, and draw inferences from texts. The assumption is that students know the language, and can therefore draw upon that knowledge to interpret the materials they are reading or hearing. For example, in the following item from the CPT students are asked to listen to the text and then answer some questions that require that they envision the objects and situations that are being described:

When the children got to the airport the next day, a guide met them and took them to the top of the building. There they watched planes landing and taking off. Next they went inside a hangar where the planes are kept. The guide explained the main parts of an airplane to the class. He told them about the cockpit where the pilot and co-pilot sit. He showed them the instrument panel that looks like the dashboard of a car but has more gauges on it. He also explained about propellers, jet engines and many other things. After they left the hangar, they went to the cafeteria inside the terminal building and ate lunch. The children were so excited they could hardly wait for the special surprise the guide had arranged for them.

The questions asked of the students are these:

1. Where did the guide take the children first?
2. Which of these is an instrument panel?
3. What do you think the surprise was?

It should be realized that language-minority students are not likely to have had the kind of first-hand experience with airports that might aid them in guessing at what they do not understand in this passage, and they are not likely to have had any reason to become familiar with such words as *hangar, cockpit, instrument panel, dashboard,* and *gauge.* In short, a child with absolutely no deficit in the powers of envisionment and memory assessed by this item could perform poorly for irrelevant reasons.

Linguistic Requirements of Test Items

It would be difficult to find any aspect of standardized tests that does not depend on the test-taker's familiarity with, and proficiency in the language in which the test is given. The examples that have been described as being like the materials used in language proficiency tests are the most obvious. But there is much in these tests that depends on more subtle aspects of linguistic knowledge.

Some questions can be answered readily only if the academic history of a student happens, by accident, to include

drill on a particular point; in consequence they are not reliable measures of achievement, ability, or linguistic competence. A sample from the Reading Comprehension section of the CAT2-A is shown on the following page.

Asked whether "The Pet Parade" is to be found in pages 18 through 22 or 18 through 23, students first have to know a special meaning of the preposition "through." But they would also have to know whether a new topic in a book is always introduced on a new page. A student who is unsure of this might examine the test booklet itself — which occasionally introduces a new segment in the middle of a page — and would come up with the "wrong" answer.

Items that depend on knowledge apparently based solely on materials covered in the curriculum, but that in fact depend on highly specialized linguistic conventions and usages encountered primarily in tests can easily be found in tests like the CTBS1-T or the CAT2-A. Certain questions are almost always confusing to students who have not been trained in the special area of test-writing. This is especially true of "Best Title" questions, where a passage that lacks a point, a theme, or a plot is paired with four choices of "titles," none of which could actually be a title of the piece, but one of which is supposed to be seen as less inappropriate than the others. The following item from CAT2-A is a good example:

> Once there was a little girl named Bess. She visited her grandfather who lived near a circus. There were many elephants, monkeys, and lions in the circus. She liked the monkeys best.

> Which of these is the best title for this story?

> ___ "The Circus"
> ___ "The Elephant"
> ___ "The Lion"
> ___ "The Monkey"

The linguistic demands of test items can be further compounded by cultural expectations. For example, questions concerning "story continuations" may depend on culture-specific knowledge of

TABLE OF CONTENTS

Page 25 tells about	The story of "The Pet Parade" is found on pages:	"Tom and His Neighbors" begins on page
apples	18 through 2	8
the clown	18 through 23	12
the fox	23 through 27	18
Tom	28 through 35	28

genre: Oftentimes the genre in question, one especially nurtured in children's reading passages, is that of accounts of children behaving virtuously. We find in the CAT2-A a "story" in which children learn what it takes to make paste:

> The children in Mrs. Kim's room were talking about how to make scrapbooks. Eva said, "I will bring some pictures." "I will bring some scissors," Monty said. Marie said, "And I will bring some paper." The children decided they would need more paste than they had. To make paste they would need water, flour, and salt. Eva said, "I will bring a pan to mix them in."

Among the questions the test-taker must answer: "Which of the following sentences finishes the story correctly?" The "correct" answer is "The children decided to make their own paste." One of the alternatives is "The children decided to use glue instead." In order to answer this question correctly, the reader would have to infer from Eva's statement, "I will bring a pan to mix them in" that the class actually had on hand all of the ingredients that were needed for making paste, and that the class was actually going to undertake the messy enterprise of mixing some up. Children who understand and choose the more rational answer over the "correct" answer may not have assimilated into the proper mood of the classroom, in which self-reliance, cooperation, and resourcefulness are admirable qualities, but at the same time, neither

are they displaying a genuine deficit in academic achievement.

Whenever a test item presupposes linguistic knowledge or knowledge of cultural practices unique to the English-speaking world, a bias is introduced, especially if the item is deliberately provided with distractions that compound the problem. In the CTBS1-T, a story is told of a new boy in school who keeps nervously tending his (red) hair and who blushes easily. The question is why the boy is called Red, and the choices include he blushed easily and that was the color of his hair. A student who does not know of the custom of using Red as a nickname for red-headed individuals (for example, a student from a community in which there were no redheads) would have to guess the reason, and the "blushing" guess would be just as good as the answer recognized as correct.

Finally, we come to examples of ways in which arithmetic problems also suffer from language interference. The following examples show the language requirements of two arithmetic problems:

1. Tony bought a second-hand bicycle for $28. He paid two-thirds of what the bicycle cost new. How much did it cost new?

2. A jacket that usually sells for $32 was on sale for one-fourth less. When no one bought it, the store-owner reduced the sale price by one-half. How much

it cost after the second price reduction? (Gunnarsson, 1978, p. 26)

Obviously these arithmetic problems include a language component because they are the well-known and dreaded "word problems." Perhaps not so obvious is the subtle logical requirements of the problems that are dependent on linguistic and cultural understanding. For example, in the first question you must know what "second-hand" means. Although it is relevant to the context and therefore to understanding the problems, it is not really relevant to the arithmetic skills being measured.

Another example of linguistic interference is in the following:

Which of the following rules should be used to find the formula for a triangle?

1. Divide area by length
2. Divide the sum of the upper and lower sides by 2
3. Multiply length by width by height
4. Multiply ½ base by altitude

According to Gunnarsson, the "student must verbalize a concept that may not be very clear in his mind. He must convert a mental picture of a mathematical operation into words. What is required seems to be a kind of mental essay" (p. 31). Wong-Fillmore, Ammon, McLaughlin, and Ammon (1985) commented that Asian students often overcome the linguistic problem in mathematical word problems by ignoring the English language context of the item and focusing instead in the numeric values provided. In this way they are often able to overcome the linguistic demands of the task.

Language Demands of Test Instructions

Instructions for taking standardized tests are almost always given in the language in which the test is administered, and they are usually read to the test-takers. At times, this poses a problem for NNES students, since a relatively high level of proficiency in English is required for comprehending the instructions. Consider, for example, the following instructions, which are provided for a section on "capitalization" in the

CAT2-A Language subtest:

Look at the first sentence next to the A. Now look at the group of five numerals and the N next to the sentence. For each item decide which word in the sentence needs to be capitalized. Capitalization means using a big letter at the beginning of a word. Count from the beginning of each line to find out the number of the word that needs capitalization. Then fill in the space which shows that number. If no words needs to be capitalized, fill in the space which shows the N for "None."

The difficulty of the instruction far outweighs the difficulty of the principle being tested here. Unfortunately, a child may know perfectly well what the capitalization rules are for English but nevertheless have a hard time dealing with this part of the test because of the instructions.

Finally, De Avila et al. (1978) have provided an example of how administering tests to NNES students assumes that they come to the testing situation as well-prepared as mainstream students and as familiar with the fundamental knowledge required to take the test. The following example demonstrates how language and cultural values can influence test-taking skills:

One can understand a Latin American child's reluctance to attempt an answer to a test question when he or she has been reared within a tradition which disapproves of this type of hablando sin saber (speaking without knowing). (De Avila et al., 1978, p. 12)

Empirical Support for the Influence of Language on Tests

In support of the content analysis described in the previous section are studies that have examined the commonalities of various tests or that have looked at the effect of language on NNES students' test performance. For example, several studies reviewed by Oller and Perkins (1978) show that achievement, IQ, and language proficiency tests are highly correlated. In examinations of the underlying factor common to these tests, Oller and Perkins (1978) reported that language proficiency as opposed to a more general factor of intelligence is the primary element common to test performance.

> At present the accumulating research evidence seems to suggest that a vast array of education tests that go by many different names may be measures of language proficiency more than anything else. (p. 14)

Ulibarri et al. (1981), De Avila et al. (1983), De Avila and Havassy (1974), and De Blassie (1980) as well as others documented in this chapter, have shown the importance of language proficiency in academic achievement test scores. Ulibarri et al. (1981) reported that NNES students classified according to level of English language proficiency consistently showed differences in academic achievement tests scores in both reading and math. De Avila (1973) showed that when language and cultural factors were taken into account, there were no significant differences between NNES students' scores and those of native-English-speaking students. In addition, using neo-Piagetian assessment instruments that controlled for language in their administration, De Avila and Havassy (1974), found no significant differences in the cognitive development of NNES students. However, significant differences in the level of achievement of the two groups were found. De Avila and Havassy (1974) concluded that although the NNES students were equivalent with respect to cognitive development, they were not equal in academic achievement. Thus while NNES students had the ability, they were not achieving.

De Blassie (1980) reviewed several studies and concluded that virtually all of the observed group differences between NNES and native-English-speaking students can be accounted for by language and other cultural variables. Several studies have shown a consistent pattern of NNES students scoring higher on nonverbal, arithmetic computation, and performance measures than on verbal tests (DeBlassie, 1980; Cordasco, 1978; Coleman et al., 1966).

Dallabetta (1980) examined the effects of language on standardized testing of Anglo and Mexican-American children and reported that language is a critical factor in achievement testing and that English-speaking minority-language children and LEP children experience a disadvantage in the administration of standardized testing. This research and the research of De Avila et al. (1978, 1983) showed that increased ability to function in the English language correlated with the degree to which children produced higher scores on achievement tests administered in English.

Other researchers have suggested that structural and idiomatic differences between the English and Spanish languages and an underdeveloped perception of English phonology have a detrimental effect on the test performance of NNES students (Matluck & Mace, 1973). These authors pointed out that the problems involve auditory discrimination and therefore are not an indication of intellectual deficit.

Attempts to Control for Language Proficiency Differences of NNES

Sufficient reason exists to be concerned by the influence of language factors on achievement test scores. One might suppose that the issue could be addressed by addressing language differences in the test administration process or by screening students for English language proficiency. The problem is that there is not agreement on what constitutes an appropriate cutoff level of performance to determine language proficiency. Several studies (e.g., Ulibarri et al., 1981) have shown that differences in the language proficiency classifications of students result when they are assessed by different tests. The same students administered dissimilar tests and evaluated against variant cutoff scores will be classified differently with respect to language proficiency depending on the district language proficiency requirements.

In actual practice, English language proficiency is determined by local criteria, even though the definition is provided in federal legislation. Hence, there are many NNES students who are considered proficient in English by one criterion but would not be so classified by another.

In addition, many school districts do not have formal language proficiency assessment procedures and use achievement test scores to determine language proficiency.

There are several measures that test makers and researchers have taken to compensate for students who are known to have a language problem. These include use of translated tests and translated test administration procedures; provisions for pretraining and prescreening of language proficiency; development of ethnically specific norms; and finally, opting not to test NNES students at all. In general, these procedures have not proven to be adequate to deal with the language problem.

De Avila et al. (1978) have pointed out that it is virtually impossible to use a single translation because of geographic and dialect variations in the native language. In addition, direct translations do not result in equal item difficulties across languages. Ultimately, direct translations suffer from the same problem that is inherent in English language achievement tests: They assume students come to the test situation with similar background experience in their native language. As pointed out in the introduction to this chapter, NNES students are generally not literate in their native language.

McArthur (1981) administered tests to NNES students in English and in their native language to examine the students' performance comparatively. The results on the Comprehensive Test of Basic Skills (CTBS) English language version and Spanish language version differed significantly. This supports the contention that direct translation from English to Spanish for bilingual vocabulary testing may not be adequate for the needs of Hispanic students, even when the Spanish version is a rather faithful translation of the English version.

Cabello (1981) conducted a study to compare the content, concepts, and vocabulary presented in bilingual curricula with those in monolingual curricula. She administered the English and Spanish versions of the CTBS to 1,259 elementary students in 81 schools in five California school districts. The results indicated three possible sources of bias: (a) problems inherent in translation; (b) incongruence in match between curriculum, instructional material, and test content; and (c) intervening cultural values.

Finally, it is often found that NNES students perform better on achievement tests in English than on tests in their native language. The reason for this is that many language-minority students in the United States have never received a formal education in their native language and thus are not experienced in the literacy or testing context of their native language. However, the better performance on achievement tests in English does not mean that they are more proficient in English. In neither language is one likely to obtain a true indication of what the student knows. Moreover, use of the native language on achievement tests taken in English, even if only for test administration purposes, violates the rigid requirements imposed by the standardization process. Deviations from the publishers recommended procedures devaluates interpretation of scores based on normative data.

The claim that standardized achievement tests are overly influenced by English language proficiency is well supported by several empirical studies. That the tests measure only language, in general, is probably an extreme view, but one that cannot be dismissed for NNES students.

In the following section, problems inherent in the development and validation of tests are discussed. Information on this process is critical to understanding the issues that have been discussed and in particular to understanding the technical problems of test bias and test validity.

TECHNICAL ISSUES

Test Bias and Test Validity

The validity of standardized tests has been a major concern of educators and others interested in the performance of minority students in the United States. When standardized tests are administered to NNES students, validity becomes a concern because these tests may be measuring factors other than those that were designed to measure in the native-English-speaking population. Unfortunately, this concern is traditionally translated into claims that the tests are biased against minority and NNES student populations. This designation is unfortunate because research has not supported the claim that the tests are biased. To the contrary, studies designed to examine charges of test bias indicate that bias against minorities does not exist, or that where bias does exist, it is in favor of minority students (e.g., see Jensen, 1980).

The reason that test bias is often not found is that standard definitions for test bias typically are couched in terms of consistent over- or underestimates of test scores, rather than a determination of whether tests are measuring the same thing for minority students as they are for mainstream students. Thus, the issue of whether the tests are validly measuring what they are supposed to measure with certain minority groups is often not addressed. Therefore, the claim should not be that the tests are biased, but that in many cases they are not valid for the population they are being used to assess.

It is surprising and difficult to understand why technical differences in definitions have been allowed to obscure the issue. Thorndike pinpointed the problem in the early 1970s (Thorndike, 1971), yet it wasn't until 1975 that psychometricians recognized that the issue was one of validity (McNemar, 1975; Anastasi, 1976). Nevertheless, investigation has not been refocused on test validity per se. Instead the focus has shifted from test bias to concern over the fair use of tests.

Psychometric definitions and semantics aside, the use of tests that are not equally valid measures for particular groups will lead to an unfair outcome. Whether it is labeled test bias or unfair use is unimportant to the lives of children. For the purposes of the present investigation, a test that measures something other than what it purports to measure is held to be burdened by "test bias," whether or not the test itself is biased. This perspective will stand as the point of departure for the following discussion of the role the validity problem has played in the controversy over achievement testing with NNES students.

Causes of Test Bias

It is well established that student backgrounds significantly effect both academic achievement test scores and success in school. When these factors are controlled, group differences in test performance are significantly reduced (DeBlassie, 1980; Mercer, 1975). Many researchers have concluded that test content, method of communication in responding to test items, and other aspects of the test administration process are dependent on cultural context and language.

Most, if not all, tests assume a particular sociocultural and linguistic background orientation. Students' scores reflect such factors as socioeconomic status and familiarity with the language and cultural frame of reference of the test designers and the norming populaton. Furthermore, the test situation itself is one that requires special experience. It is all too often assumed that NNES and other minority group students have the special skills and background required for dealing with the test-taking situation and that their scores reflect a lack of whatever it is the tests are assessing, rather than a lack of familiarity with such tests.

Finally, a significant factor in the test-taking repertoire of NNES students is the degree of difficulty presented by the test items. Sabatino (1973) found that "successful test-taking (in English) depended on central information processing variables which required a knowledge of linguistic rules in English not necessarily possessed by bilingual speakers." (pp. 565) This finding was supported by a study that showed that even nonverbal test items present difficulties in the degree of difficulty for minority students (Ulibarri, 1983). The results indicated that presenting a problem in an unfamiliar context increases the amount of information that needs to be processed and results in greater item difficulty.

Nevertheless, just as academic achievement tests reflect a specific cultural orientation, so do the schools and classrooms NNES students attend. If students do not know the specific culture or the context in which the test items are presented, they will have difficulty succeeding in the classroom that also requires knowledge of the mainstream culture.

Researchers acknowledge that test scores reflect a student's exposure to and assimilation of the mainstream or dominant culture that is reflected in the schools. Since these factors also impact on school success, they argue that certain students come to school differentially prepared to deal with the experiences of schooling. For this reason, neither group differences alone, nor the findings that the differences can be reduced by controlling for background factors, are sufficient to conclude that tests are bias measures (Cleary, Humphreys, Kendrick, & Wesman, 1975).

Because tests have predictive validity — i.e., they correlate with school grades and predict later academic achievement — they are interpreted by teachers to be measures of learning ability and academic potential as well as current level of knowledge (DeBlassie, 1980). This interpretation, however, presupposes that minority students will not be able to acquire this knowledge, or that appropriate intervention strategies either will not be provided or will not make any difference in potential achievement.

The real rub, though, is that tests with predictive validity are used to track students, and thus place them in educational programs and curriculums that are remedial, slow-learner-oriented, or watered down academically. It follows, then, that these students will continue to perform poorly on academic achievement tests when compared with mainstream students. Thus, the tests' so-called predictive validity is "self-fulfilling," as are teachers' expectations.

The argument that tests merely reflect differences that already exist, but not true potential is an issue because it leads to the continued misuse of tests. What is missing rrom all of this, and what leads to tracking in the first place, is the original issue — whether tests are measuring what the student actually knows in a particular content or subject matter area. In other words, does failure on a particular item mean that the student does not have the particular skill or knowledge being as-

sessed? How would the student perform if the test item were presented in a different context, or a context that was not dependent upon a specific set of "background" requirements? This is the main issue in using standardized achievement tests with minority students, and it is best answered in a statement by Cole and Bruner (1971, p. 874): "Cultural differences reside more in the differences in the situation in which different cultural groups apply their skills than to difference in the skills possessed by the groups."

Whether tests have predictive validity or merely reflect the heterogeneity of society is not the issue. The issue is that certain background factors affect test performance. The main background variable that distinguishes NNES students from mainstream and other minority students is language background. Given that the main technical issue is validity, our examination of the fair use of tests with NNES students focuses on language and its effect on the validity of standardized tests with respect to this NNES population.

Built-in Bias in the Test Construction Process

Several researchers have questioned the use of standardized tests with minority students in general because of the way the tests are developed, standardized, and validated (McClelland, 1973; Williams, Mosby, & Hinson, 1978). With regard to standardization, minorities are not usually included in the standardization norming sample. More important to this issue, however, is the charge of circular validity in both the test development and validation process. Indeed, it is this aspect of the test construction process that in effect supercedes all others.

In the following, we discuss the process of test item selection and validation to describe the circular validity process that, it is claimed, produces a built-in bias. Moreover, because of this process, many of the attempts to empirically find bias in tests or to conduct other research to identify the problems of testing with NNES students and other minorities is obscured.

Item Development and Selection

To be sure, the process of selecting items for inclusion in standardized achievement tests is a careful and professional process. It is not the point here to call into question this process other than to point out that the accepted technical approaches to validating the selection of these items can lead to problems.

First of all, test items are selected from a rather large pool of items that "experts" have judged to be representative of particular content areas. These items are also subjectively examined for cultural content and for linguistic or other possible bias, including whether they adequately reflect curriculum objectives. One would think that given this screening, potential biases would be reduced to a minimum. However, Jensen (1980) has shown that attempts to subjectively identify test bias by visual inspection of items virtually never works. In fact, he reported that most items so identified usually show smaller ethnic group differences than other items. Thus, the possibility that item bias is eliminated is still open to question.

The main concern for potential bias comes in the technical aspects of item selection. The process is based on the logical argument that a "good" item is one that discriminate between preselected criterion groups of students who are "known" to have or not have the characteristic that the test is trying to measure, and therefore should prove successful or not successful, respectively, on the item. Conversely, a bad item does not show this type of discrimination or shows the opposite of what is expected. It is in this process, specifically the selection of criterion groups, that the problem occurs.

After an initial set of trial items have been selected for inclusion in a test they are statistically examined to identify positive and negative discriminating test items — that is, items that can discriminate between individuals known to be members of preselected criterion groups (e.g., students with good grades vs. students with low grades). Positive discriminating test items are those that students with high grades pass and students with low grades fail. Conversely, negative discriminating items are those which students with high grades fail and students with low grades pass. Desired items, of course, are those that positively discriminate between the preselected or "known" criterion groups.

Since any items on which students on the supposed low-grade criterion group have passed are eliminated, the differences between the two groups becomes even greater and further emphasizes any social differences between the groups that constituted the initial group membership. It is here where bias can enter into the process. In what McClelland (1973) calls the circular validity process, minorities and low-SES students are already excluded from the "high scorers" group by virtue of preexisting inequities in society. Any characteristics of test taking peculiar to minorities are not included in the test-taking process; items that reflect such characteristics are in fact eliminated.

Items that correlate with each other, or otherwise cohere in this psychometric process are then combined to form the basis for a test. The degree of correlation of the test items is called the construct validity of the test. Once this process is completed, the test must be validated against some criterion.

A second type of validity, predictive validity, is established by determining whether the test can discriminate between "known" achievers and nonachievers (generally identified by school grades or teachers' recommendations). Again, any preexisting social biases in the nomination or criterion group selection process are automatically built into the system. The problem is that since minority students are already excluded by the socialization process and thus are not represented in the high-grades criterion group, social characteristics that distinguish the two groups are automatically built into the item selection process.

In short, the apparent predictive validity is likely to be due in some part or completely to characteristics common to the criterion group. Such a test has the effect of selecting individuals most like the criterion group, in terms of race, SES, sex, and language (McClelland, 1973; Eells, Davis, Havighurst, Herrick, & Tyler, 1951).

The overall result of item selection and test validation produces a false sense of confidence in the testing process.

While this is a brief and rather simple description of the test development process, it does illustrate the potential for false confidence in the tests and the arguments that have been made in the process. It is true that there are new techniques for item selection based on the Item Response Theory, which purports to avoid problems of building in group differences. However, most of the tests now used in the schools are based, more or less, on the above process.

Furthermore, not all researchers are concerned about this potential problem. Some researchers feel that tests simply mirror society and that it is society that must change, not the tests. Presumably when society changes, the tests will also change (e.g., Anastasi, 1976). On the other hand, tests may simply serve to maintain the present inequities. Misdiagnosis, and misplacement of students, have a cumulative and deleterious effect from which most of today's minority students can never recover. In any case, the movement from consideration of test bias to fair-test use is premature at best.

CONCLUSIONS

This chapter is the result of an extensive screening of more than 500 documents as well as discussions with experts in the field. The results document a series of continuing problems associated with the use of standardized achievement tests with non-native-English-speaking (NNES) students. The review included state and federal policy related to the use of standardized tests, technical problems involved in their development and use, and the technical issues of test bias and fair test use. Research evidence supports the conclusion that standardized tests do not assess NNES students fairly and accurately and that these students are thereby subject to exclusion from the educational opportunities offered by the U.S. educational system.

Such exclusion results primarily from the use of standardized test results as a criterion for placing students — both as a group and individually — in nonacademic (non-college-bound) and remedial tracts. Since NNES students tend to score lower on achievement tests, they are more likely to be placed in nonacademic tracts, thereby denying the students exposure to an instructional program that can effectively lead to a change in performance.

The general problem, that standardized tests often do not reflect the curriculum or instructional program of test takers, is further aggravated for NNES students who not only fail to receive a generally equivalent instructional program, but receive one that is specifically less likely to cover the content assessed by a standardized achievement test. Thus, when the students are retested, there is a continuing and predictable pattern of low scores. It is predictable precisely because the students have not been provided with an instructional program that would lead to an expectation for a change in performance.

The sad and perhaps alarming fact is that the negative impact of standardized achievement tests on NNES students has been pointed out for the last 20–30 years with no apparent change in the situation. Generally, schools are concerned primarily with the policy issues associated with program placement (e.g., bilingual or special ed) and eligibility criteria. This concern is then reinforced by federal and state policies that require the use of standardized achievement tests. As a result, little attention is given to the obvious background differences NNES students bring to the testing situation. These conditions continue to exist with no apparent effort to change the way tests affect these students.

The primary conclusion is that there is indeed a serious problem in the use of standardized tests with NNES students. Oftentimes, standardized tests are used more and have more of an impact on NNES students than on native-English-speaking students. Moreover, the negative impact of testing on NNES students' education goes unnoticed in the schools.

In the following discussion, the main conclusions of this chapter are summarized in the context of the key technical and practical issues that have been identified.

The chapter concludes by offering potential solutions to the key problems in particular and to the use of tests with NNES students in general, and by making recommendations as to what steps might be taken to effect these solutions. Several technical issues are associated with standardized tests and with the present conditions that contribute to the continued deleterious impact that standardized testing has on NNES students. The discussion that follows touches on the most important issues found in the literature.

Role of Federal and State Policy

A review of the literature on test use, relevant legislation, and state mandates indicates that, more often than not, legislative mandates require the use of standardized tests or other means for group comparisons. The CSE review of test use in U.S. schools (CSE, 1983) reported that the interpretation of tests scores varies according to the socioeconomic status of the school. It was found that in making decisions about a student's ability as well as the instructional content the student would receive, low-SES schools place a greater emphasis on test scores than higher-SES schools.

It is apparent that state and federal policy, together with recent educational trends such as back-to-basics and educational-excellence programs have led, either directly or indirectly, to an overdependence among teachers and principals on the standardized test performance of students. The back-to-basics and educational-excellence trends have made improved student performance their goal, and the most common way of assessing such progress has invariably led to the use of standardized tests. While one might speculate that the resulting overdependence on tests is an indirect effect, since it coincides with legislative and policy requirements, the CSE report suggested that external influences can directly influence teachers to place greater reliance on test results and to have more faith in their use and validity with low-SES and language-minority students.

Use and Interpretation of Standardized Tests

The major finding of this chapter is that NNES students are overwhelmingly at a disadvantage when standardized achievement tests are used to make decisions concerning the students' education. Such tests are used to assess NNES students' academic potential in specific curriculum strands, and consequently for placement, tracking, program eligibility, and judgments on learning abilities or disabilities.

Standardized achievement tests are also used for decisions on program effectiveness, student certification, graduation, and promotion. In many states, and even in some research studies, standardized test items or similar types of test items are being employed as measures of English language proficiency.

Since standardized test scores are often used to assess the academic potential of NNES students without regard to the skewing effects of the students' cultural background and English proficiency, NNES students are often judged to have lesser abilities or academic potential than they in fact possess. Thus labeled, the students have fewer opportunities to receive a challenging curriculum. If standardized tests are not used for actual placement, the lower results are often used to explain the students' poor performance in class. Consequently, schools do not address the social and linguistic factors that are actually the cause of the low scores.

Several states use standardized test scores as part of the entry-exit criteria for NNES students in bilingual programs or for identifying and reclassifying them as limited-English-proficiency (LEP) students. The confounding of language proficiency skills and achievement skills does not preclude the tests' use for such purposes; however, using the test as part of an exit criterion can result in the placement of newly mainstreamed students in remedial classes or classes with low academic expectations.

When used for evaluation of special programs, the misleadingly low standardized test scores of NNES students can lead school officials to judge a program as ineffective, when in fact the previously mentioned skewing of test results is the problem. A mismatch between what has been taught and what the test actually covers can also lead to faulty assessment of program quality.

While one can blame the schools for the use of a test in this way, it should be noted that school districts often do not have the qualified personnel to avoid the problem. School districts that do not have the personnel are certainly not in a position to select different tests for all the different programs. To maintain cost effectiveness, school districts have the restriction of using one test for intradistrict as well as interdistrict evaluations.

Role of English Language Proficiency

Considerable evidence has been presented that points to the problem of language in test performance. Many NNES students who are not classified as LEP, and who are thus considered to be students in the mainstream or part of special educational programs directed toward "disadvantaged" students, are still limited or only functionally proficient in English. There are two reasons for this. First, definitions of LEP differ to such an extent that students can easily be classified as LEP by one criterion and not by another. Some definitions are based only on oral proficiency, whereas others include literacy skills in addition to oral proficiency. The variation is so great that it occurs not only from school district to school district, but even from school to school. Second, many students have simply been reclassified as non-LEP because eligibility for services ends after a set time period (e.g., 3 years) or simply because no program is in place to meet the students' special language needs.

Sufficient evidence has come to light to cause concern about the influence of language in the testing even of students who are not LEP. Much of the research cited in this chapter deals with this issue for language-minority students who speak English. For NNES students the problem is only compounded. Conceptions of the influence of language range from the extreme claims that achievement tests are

no more than language proficiency tests to examples that clearly indicate that language is most certainly an intervening factor that could invalidate a test. Language becomes a factor in the content and context of items, in the administration of the tests, in responding to the test, and finally, in the interpretation of test results from norms that include a particular standard of English proficiency.

While English proficiency is a critical goal for NNES students, it should not be the factor that limits their academic progress while they acquire English and other skills that allow them to function in the mainstream curriculum. NNES students will have to, and should be able to, succeed in the mainstream; thus, they should be able to cope with these tests. However, the tests are not intended to measure children's knowledge of the English language, but rather what they know and how well they can apply their knowledge. As it is now, language proficiency intervenes in the process. The result, as documented here, is devastating at first and becomes more destructive over the years.

Test Construction and Validation

Current methods of item development and selection, test construction, and validation can easily incorporate built-in discrimination into tests. This contributes not only to erroneous test results, but also to a false security regarding the test's validity and lack of bias.

Methods of test development and validation incorporate a *circular validity*. Circular validity occurs when the ability of test items to discriminate between achiever and nonachiever criterion groups is based on comparisons of responses obtained from groups that are traditionally perceived as achievers and nonachievers. *Traditionally perceived* means groups that are nominated as achievers and nonachievers by some external criteria. The problem is that external criteria and hence the criterion groups embody the same biases — the results of years of poverty, poor education, and discrimination — that characterize the groups to be evaluated. In short, external characteristics that distinguish between the achieving and nonachieving groups (e.g., race, socioeconomic status or language) are also reflected in the content of the test that is designed to distinguish between and therefore reliably predict achievers and nonachievers.

The statistical and psychometric properties of tests also contribute to technical difficulties in the use of tests with NNES students. The reliability of standardized achievement tests are highest around the middle range of scores and lowest at the upper or lower bounds — precisely where most decisions are made. Since language-minority students generally score at the lower levels, their scores are subject to the most error in interpretation.

Test Bias and the Fair Use of Tests

The issue of test bias concerns whether test scores represent a valid assessment of language-minority students' abilities. The main concern with the use of tests with NNES and other minority students is that the scores do not reflect actual achievement, since extraneous factors are also being measured. Considerable empirical evidence exists to show that other factors, specifically language, are indeed involved.

Unfortunately, criticisms of tests on these grounds have mistakenly used the term *test bias*, when in fact this particular term has a specific and different meaning in the field of psychometrics. The criticism should be that the tests are not valid measures and that, because of this, comparisons with norm or mainstream students lead to biased interpretations. In short, a purely statistical or psychometric response to the criticism that tests are biased does not address the pertinent issue. Statistical definitions of test bias refer to specific properties and outcomes associated with consistent over- or underpredictions, not whether a test is a valid measure for a particular group.

Because studies based on statistical definitions point to an absence of bias, criticism of the testing process has shifted from test bias to "fair test use." But an emphasis on the fair use of tests assumes that tests are valid measures, and has removed the burden from test publishers,

placing it instead on unsophisticated test users. Test users are neither equipped nor professionally trained to absorb this responsibility without more direction. The one group that perhaps uses tests most frequently – teachers — are reported to lack the skills and knowledge of test construction and measurement concepts (CSE, 1983).

Placing the burden for the correct use of tests, and of sensitivity to test bias and test validity, on the users has had other side effects. For example, it has produced an unwarranted faith in tests, owing primarily to the ready availability of the tests and the endorsement of tests by "authorities," which lead the users to believe that test deficiencies have already been addressed. Thus, even though there is widespread knowledge of the dangers of the administration of standardized tests with specific populations, their use continues to have a detrimental and deleterious impact on the education of NNES students. This is indicated by the fact that teachers use achievement tests, and rely on their results more extensively with precisely those students whom the tests are most likely to adversely affect.

Test Validity

The single most consistent criticism of standardized tests is that they fail to provide valid assessments of NNES students' repertoires of skills and knowledge. According to some, a biased test is one that measures different things for different groups. This chapter has argued that this definition is the most appropriate, since it is consistent with the way most people think of and define test bias.

Several empirical studies have been cited in this report that indicate an obvious linguistic and cultural bias in standardized tests. These studies show that by taking into account environmental and background factors or by controlling for them through various paradigms, language-minority students' test scores are improved. However, many psychologists and psychometricians argue that group differences alone (due to socioeconomic, language, and cultural factors) are not sufficient to infer test bias, unless it is assumed a priori that no group differences should exist. In response, one can only ask what evidence there is, other than test results themselves, that would lead one not to make this assumption. Indeed, this review indicates that the steps involved in developing, constructing, and validating standardized tests can lead to biases along socioeconomic, linguistic, and cultural lines. Finally, the fact that group differences do not exist alone, but occur in conjunction with evidence of the influence of language and other factors, leads to the conclusion that test use under these circumstances is biased.

Potential Solutions

Criterion-referenced tests. Criterion-referenced tests depend upon an absolute standard. Many of the state-mandated minimum competency tests are purported criterion-referenced tests, yet many problems arise when they are used for tracking students or assigning students to special curricula. NNES students who score poorly on such tests can be unjustly labeled as low achievers and then relegated to an inferior remedial curriculum. These tests can also suffer from the inclusion of language factors and have most certainly not undergone rigorous study as to their validity beyond simple content validity or inspection.

Learning potential assessment devices. The learning potential assessment approach (e.g., Feuerstein, 1979; Merz, 1978, p. 69) is based on a student's ability to profit from problem-relevant instruction (Williams et al., 1978). It involves engaging students in the opportunity to receive instruction or coaching in the underlying skills and entails three steps: pretesting, coaching or training, and posttesting. According to Williams et al. (1978), "the learning potential paradigm minimized the effects of cultural differences by providing all subjects with appropriate experiences relevant to dealing with the task at hand" (p. 70). Successful results for Blacks and NNES students was demonstrated by Ulibarri (1983). Using a test that is considered to be relatively "culture-free" and employing this paradigm, Ulibarri reported significant gains on the Raven Progressive Matrices Test for minor-

ity students while little or nonsignificant gains occurred for Anglo students.

Neo-Piagetian cognitive developmental. De Avila, Havassy, and Pascual-Leone (1976) used a neo-Piagetian assessment approach consisting of paper and pencil Piagetian conservation tasks. This approach includes two things relevant to the present discussion: (a) experimental repertoire control, and (b) nonstandardized use of language. De Avila (1973) described experimental repertoire control as a process in which subject differences are removed through pretraining procedures. Nonstandardized assessment procedures focus on communication of the testing instructions during the total assessment process. Test administrators are allowed to use various languages or other means to communicate the task instructions. In each step of the assessment process an attempt is made to ensure that the student understands the task at hand. These two characteristics of the neo-Piagetian approach are similar in rationale to the approach used in the learning potential assessment device method. In both cases an attempt is made to control or otherwise rule out competing sources of test score differences that are unrelated to what is to be assessed.

Culture-specific approaches. Several attempts have been made to develop culture-specific tests, but they have not been successful (Williams et al., 1978). According to Williams et al. (1978): "Culture specific tests have had the advantage of dealing with content material that is familiar to the minority student. This means that the student already has stored away mental images of the material so that he does not have to deal with the foreign or unfamiliar aspects of these materials." (p. 71) With a combination of dialect-specific and culture-specific tests one would have a better chance of measuring what the minority child knows.

This approach has several problems not the least of which is the development costs associated with such a task on a national level. More important, however, for NNES students, it assumes one-dialect and one-cultural experience. Several researchers cited in this report have described the problems in such an assumption. Certainly we could not have several different tests, but who would decide which test a child would take? The main importance of culture-specific tests is to show that minority students can perform certain tasks when they are presented in a context in which they are familiar

RECOMMENDATIONS

It is extremely difficult to offer recommendations or solutions to the problems associated with the use of standardized achievement tests with NNES students. Information reported in this chapter has illustrated the enormous extent and complexity of the problem. Nevertheless, there are some common threads that run throughout the controversy, as well as empirical evidence to lead to the recommendations made below. These recommendations certainly will not answer or address all the problems, but they do point in directions in which improvement can be made without placing undue costs and burdens on school districts. Also, these recommendations are made with the understanding and acceptance that the use of achievement tests is so ingrained in U.S. educational practice that their application will continue. In short, the goal is improvement, not only of test scores, but also in the education that NNES students receive.

1. Federal policy (or state policy) should prohibit or restrict the requirement of the use of standardized achievement testing of individual students in evaluation and eligibility requirements. This can be accomplished for program evaluation requirements by allowing testing of students according to a "matrix" sampling approach. This means that only randomly selected students are tested on randomly selected items on subtests. The obtained data can be used for group evaluation without the need for individual student data. Also, it would be less expensive and time-consuming, leaving more time and resources for direct instruction. For selection, eligibility, and reclassification requirements, multiple sources of information should be used. This information should take into account language and background

factors and should show convergent validity — that is, the criteria should not contradict each other, but show consistency as well as constancy.

2. Individual student achievement data for NNES students should not be placed in students' "cumulative records" or school folders. They should be kept in a separate program evaluation file or on computer tapes for group analysis only. That is, they should not be readily accessible to teachers or counselors. This will alarm some educators who think that surely counselors must have access to test data to make decisions about students, but it is precisely this belief that is at the heart of the problem. Put simply, this review indicates that test data are of little utility for teachers and other school personnel except in certain instances and that they are more likely to have a negative than a positive impact.

3. Test publishers should include warnings or other caveats concerning the application of tests; they simply cannot leave the responsibility to users. Users are not equipped to direct, nor do they have access to persons who can direct, the correct use of the results of these tests. This review indicates that leaving the responsibility to the user does not work.

4. Test publishers should list ways in which tests can be used more fairly in respect to administration, interpretation, and avoidance of possible sources of invalidating variations in test conditions such as language, background, and so forth. They should give examples of how tests should not be used and interpreted and for whom. Current warnings are not strong enough.

5. Federal, state, and local policy should encourage in-service training for professionals who use tests in the schools. Currently, federal program laws require this training, but they rarely enforce or monitor such training.

6. Schools and test publishers should encourage the development of test-taking strategies and language skills prior to assessment. And these should certainly be required before remedial education pro-

grams are recommended. Similarly, test publishers or districts should establish language requirements for testing even for NNES students who are not LEP.

7. Regarding the fair use of tests, an expanded definition of fairness as related to NNES students would designate tests that produce a score such that performance or variation cannot be explained by English language proficiency: That is, *a test is fair if level of language proficiency within NNES populations no longer predicts degree of academic achievement.*

REFERENCES

Anastasi, A. (1976). *Psychological testing* (4th ed.). New York: Macmillan.

Aspira, Inc. (1980). *Trends in segregation of Hispanic students in major school districts having a large Hispanic enrollment. Desegregation and the Hispano in America: An overview*, Vol. 1 (Final Report). New York: Aspira, Inc. (ERIC Document Reproduction Service No. ED 190 270)

Cabello, B. (1981). *Potential sources of bias in dual language achievement tests.* Los Angeles: University of California, Center for the Study of Evaluation. (ERIC Document Reproduction Service No. ED 218 320)

California State Department of Education Symposium on Language Proficiency. (1983). Sacramento, CA: California State Department of Education, Language Policy Review Committee, Bilingual Bicultural Office.

Carter, T. P., & Segura, R. D. (1979). *Mexican Americans in the school: A decade of change.* New York: College Entrance Examination Board.

Center for the Study of Evaluation (CSE). (1983). *Use of achievement tests in the United States* (Report prepared for the U.S. Congress). Washington, DC: Office of Technology Assessment.

Cleary, A., Humphreys, L., Kendrick, S., & Wesman, A. (1975). Educational use of tests with disadvantaged students. *American Psychologist, 30,* 15–41.

Cole, M., & Bruner, J. S. (1971). Cultural differences and inferences about psychological processes. *American Psychologist, 26*(10), 867–876.

Coleman, J. S., Campbell, E. Q., Hobsen, C. J., McPartland, J., Mood, A., Weinfeld, F. D., & York, R. L. (1966). *Equality of educational opportunity.* Washington, DC: U.S. Government Printing Office.

Cordasco, F. (1978). Bilingual education dramatizes hopes of millions. *NJEA Review, 51*(7), 16–17.

Dallabetta, P. M. (1980). A study of standardized testing of first grade children in Hogales, Arizona by language dominance (Doctoral dissertation, Northern Arizona University, 1980). *Dissertation Abstracts International, 41,* 864A.

De Avila, E. (1973). *The influence of language on test performance.* Paper presented at the annual meeting of the American Educational Research Association (AERA), Chicago.

De Avila, E., Cervantes, R., & Duncan, S. E. (1978). Bilingual program exit criteria. *CABE Research Journal, 1*(2), 19–23.

De Avila, E., Duncan, S., Ulibarri, D., & Flemming, J. (1983). Predicting the academic success of language minority students from developmental, cognitive style, linguistic and teacher perception measures. In E. E. Garcia (Ed.), *The Mexican-American child: Language, cognition, and social development* (pp. 59–106). Tempe, AZ: Arizona State University.

De Avila, E., & Havassy, B. (1974). The testing of minority children: A neo-Piagetian approach. *Today's Education, 63*(4), 72–75.

De Avila, E., Havassy, B., & Pascual-Leone, J. (1976). *Mexican-American children: A neo-Piagetian analysis.* Washington, DC: Georgetown University Press.

DeBlassie, R. R. (1980). *Testing Mexican-American youth: A nondiscriminatory approach.* Boston: Teaching Resources Corp.

Eells, K., Davis, A., Havighurst, R. J., Herrick, V. E., & Tyler, R. (1951). *Intelligence and cultural differences: A study of cultural learning and problem-solving.* Chicago: University of Chicago Press.

Feuerstein, R. (1979). *The dynamic assessment of retarded performers: The learning potential assessment device, theory, instruments, and techniques.* Baltimore: University Park Press.

Gold, N. C. (1985). Competency testing for limited-English proficient students. In *English Language Development. Proceedings of a conference on issues in English language development for minority language education* (pp. 57–62). Arlington, VA: National Clearinghouse for Bilingual Education. (ERIC Document Reproduction Service No. ED 273 151)

Gunnarsson, B. (1978). A look at the content similarities between intelligence, achievement, personality, and language tests. In J. W. Oller, & K. Perkins (Eds.), *Language in education: Testing the tests* (pp. 17–35). Rowley, MA: Newbury House.

Hispanic Office of Planning and Evaluation Report. (1984). Boston: Boston Public School Administration.

Jensen, A. (1980). *Bias in mental testing.* New York: Free Press; Macmillan.

Lukas, C. V. (1981). *Special needs populations in vocational education.* Washington, DC: National Institute of Education, Educational Policy and Organization Program. (ERIC Document Reproduction Service No. ED 211 731)

Mace-Matluck, B. J., Hoover, W. A., & Dominguez, D. (1983). *Language and literacy learning in bilingual instruction: A case study of practices and outcomes.* Austin, TX: Southwest Educational Development Lab, Division of Language and Literacy. (ERIC Document Reproduction Service No. ED 245 574)

Matluck, J. H., & Mace, B. J. (1973). Language characteristics of Mexican-American children: Implications for assessment. In T. Oakland & B. N. Phillips (Eds.), *Assessing minority group children* (pp. 365–386). New York: Behavioral Publications.

McArthur, D. L. (1981). *Performance patterns of bilingual children tested in both languages.* Los Angeles: University of California, Center for the Study of Evaluation. (ERIC Document Reproduction Service No. ED 218 321)

McClelland, D. C. (1973). Testing for competence rather than for "intelligence." *American Psychologist, 28*(1), 1–14.

McNemar, Q. (1975). On so-called test bias. *American Psychologist, 30,* 848–851.

Mercer, J. R. (1975). *Labeling the mentally retarded.* Berkeley, CA: University of California Press.

Merz, W. R. (1978). Test fairness and test bias: A review of procedures. In M. J. Wargo & D. R. Green (Eds.), *Achievement testing of disadvantaged and minority students for educational program evaluation* (pp. 129–151). New York: CTB McGraw-Hill.

National Commission on Excellence in Education. (1983). *A nation at risk: The imperative for educational reform.* Washington, DC: U.S. Government Printing Office.

National Commission on Secondary Education for Hispanics. (1984). *Make something happen. Hispanics and urban high school reform,* Vols. 1 and 2. (Report of the National Commission on Secondary Education for Hispanics.) New York: Hispanic Policy Development Project. (ERIC Document Reproduction Service No. ED 253 598 and ED 253 599)

National Council of LaRaza. (1985). *Testimony presented to the House Postsecondary Education Subcommittee on the reauthorization of Title I of the Higher Education Act.* Washington, DC: NCLR. (ERIC Document Reproduction Service No. ED 262 125)

Oakes, J. (1983). Tracking and ability grouping in American schools: Some constitutional questions. *Teachers College Record, 84*(4), 801–819.

Oller, J. W., & Perkins, K. (1978). *Language in education: Testing the tests.* Rowley, MA: Newbury House.

Quezada, R. (1979). Desegregation: Future issues & trends. *Planning and Changing, 10*(2), 118–120.

Roos, P. D. (1984). *The handicapped, limited English proficient student: A school district's obligation.* Miami, FL: National Origin Desegregation Assistance Center. (ERIC Document Reproduction Service No. ED 257 923)

Rosenbaum, J. (1980). Making inequality: Track misconceptions and frustrated college plans: An analysis of the effect of tracks and track perceptions in the national longitudinal survey. *Sociology of Education, 53,* 74–88.

Sabatino, D. A. (1973). Special education and the culturally different child: Implications for assessment and intervention. *Exceptional Children, 39*(7), 563–567.

Thorndike, R. L. (1971). Concepts of culture-fairness. *Journal of Educational Measurement, 8,* 63–70.

Ulibarri, D. (1982). Cognitive processing theory and culture-loading: A neo-Piagetian approach to test bias (Doctoral dissertation, University of California–Berkeley, 1981). *Dissertation Abstracts International, 43,* 2586A.

Ulibarri, D. (1983). Documenting language assessment. In *The Evaluation, Dissemination, and Assessment Center Guide to bilingual program evaluation.* Dallas, TX: EDAC–Dallas.

Ulibarri, D. (1986). *Review of national estimates of the number of limited English proficient students in the U.S.* Washington, DC: Congressional Record, Committee on Labor and Education.

Ulibarri, D., Eshgh, R., & Wong-Fillmore, L. (1985). *Standardized achievement testing of non-native English speaking students in the U.S.* (Final report to U.S. Congress.) Washington, DC: Office of Technology Assessment.

Ulibarri, D., Spencer, M., & Rivas, G. (1981). Language proficiency and academic achievement: A study of language proficiency tests and their relationship to school ratings as predictors of academic achievement. *NABE Journal, 5*(3), 47–80.

Williams, R. L., Mosby, D., & Hinson, V. (1978). Critical issues in achievement testing of children from diverse ethnic backgrounds. In M. J. Wargo & D. R. Green (Eds.), *Achievement testing of disadvantaged and minority students for educational program evaluation* (pp. 41–72). New York: CTB McGraw-Hill.

Wong-Fillmore, L., Ammon, P., McLaughlin, B., & Ammon, M. (1985). *Learning English through bilingual instruction* (Final Report). Washington, DC: National Institute of Education. (ERIC Document Reproduction Service No. ED 259 579)

FOOTNOTES

[1]Currently Supervisor of Human Resources and Research, Pacific Gas and Electric Company.

[2]The linguistic analysis of test items in this section was contributed by Dr. Lilly Wong-Fillmore as a consultant to the original study.